Summary of Interest Factors and Other Useful Formulas

Flow Type	Factor Notation	Goal	Formula	Equivalent Cash Flow Diagrams
Single payment	Future worth $(F/P, i, N)$	Find: F Given: P	$F = P(1 + i)^N$	
	Present worth $(P/F, i, N)$	Find: P Given: F	$P = F(1 + i)^{-N}$	
Equal payment series	Future worth $(F/A, i, N)$	Find: F Given: A	$F = \left[\dfrac{(1 + i)^N - 1}{i} \right]$	
	Sinking fund $(A/F, i, N)$	Find: A Given: F	$A = \left[\dfrac{i}{(1 + i)^N - 1} \right]$	
	Present worth $(P/A, i, N)$	Find: P Given: A	$P = \left[\dfrac{(1 + i)^N - 1}{i(1 + i)^N} \right]$	
	Capital recovery $(A/P, i, N)$	Find: A Given: P	$A = \left[\dfrac{i(1 + i)^N}{(1 + i)^N - 1} \right]$	
Linear gradient series	Present worth $(P/G, i, N)$	Find: P Given: G	$P = G\left[\dfrac{(1 + i)^N - iN - 1}{i^2(1 + i)^N} \right]$	
	Equal payment $(A/G, i, N)$	Find: A Given: G	$A = G\left[\dfrac{(1 + i)^N - iN - 1}{i(1 + i)^N - i} \right]$	
Geometric gradient series	Present worth $(P/A_1, g, i, N)$	Find: P Given: g	$P = \left[A_1\left[\dfrac{1 - (1 + g)^N(1 + i)^{-N}}{i - g} \right] \\ A_1\left(\dfrac{N}{1 + i} \right), \text{ if } i = g \right]$	

	Discrete Case	**Continuous Case**
Effective interest rate per payment period	$i = \left(1 + \dfrac{r}{CK} \right)^C - 1$	$i = e^{r/K} - 1$
Market interest rate	$i = i' + \bar{f} + i'\bar{f}$	$i = i' + \bar{f}$
Net present worth	$\text{PW}(i) = \displaystyle\sum_{n=0}^{N} A_n(1 + i)^{-n}$	
Capitalized equivalent worth	$\text{CE}(i) = \dfrac{A}{i}$	
Capital recovery with return	$\text{CR}(i) = (I - S)(A/P, i, N) + iS$	

	Discrete Case	**Continuous Case**
Internal rate of return	$$PW(i^*) = \dfrac{A_0}{(1 + i^*)} + \dfrac{A_1}{(1 + i^*)} + \cdots + \dfrac{A_N}{(1 + i^*)} = 0$$	
Benefit–cost ratio	$$BC(i) = \dfrac{B}{I + C'}$$	
Profitability index	$$PI(i) = \dfrac{B - C'}{I}$$	

Summary of Project Analysis Methods

Analysis Method	Description	Single Project Evaluation	Mutually Exclusive Projects	
			Revenue Projects	**Service Projects**
Payback period PP	A method for determining the length of time required to recover the cost of an investment. Management sets the benchmark PP°.	$PP < PP^\circ$	Select the one with shortest PP	
Discounted payback period $PP(i)$	A variation of payback period when factors in the time value of money. Management sets the benchmark $PP^\bullet$.	$PP(i) < PP^\bullet$	Select the one with shortest $PP(i)$	
Present worth $PW(i)$	A method that translates a project's cash flows into an equivalent net present value.	$PW(i) > 0$	Select the one with the largest PW	Select the one with the least negative PW
Future worth $FW(i)$	A variation of the PW: A project's cash flows are translated into an equivalent net future value.	$FW(i) > 0$	Select the one with the largest FW	Select the one with the least negative FW
Capitalized equivalent $CE(i)$	A variation of the PW: A perpetual or very long-lived project that generates a constant stream of annual net cash flow.	$CE(i) > 0$	Select the one with the largest CE	Select the one with the least negative CE
Annual equivalence $AE(i)$	A variation of the PW: A project's cash flows are translated into an annual equivalent sum.	$AE(i) > 0$	Select the one with the largest AE	Select the one with the least negative AE
Internal rate of return IRR	A relative percentage method that measures the yield as a percentage of investment over the life of a project: The IRR must exceed the minimum required rate of return (MARR).	$IRR > MARR$	Incremental analysis: If $IRR_{A2\text{-}A1} > MARR$, select the higher cost investment project, A2.	
Benefit–cost ratio $BC(i)$	A relative measure to evaluate public projects by finding the ratio of the equivalent benefits over the equivalent costs.	$BC(i) > 1$	Incremental analysis: If $BC(i)_{A2\text{-}A1} > 1$, select the higher cost investment project, A2.	
Profitability index $PI(i)$	A relative measure to evaluate projects by calculating the ratio of the equivalent net benefits over the equivalent net investment.	$PI(i) > 1$	Incremental analysis: If $PI(i)_{A2\text{-}A1} > 1$, select the higher cost investment project, A2.	

To my mentors: James R. Buck (late),
Gerald J. Thuesen, and
Vernon E. Unger

PREFACE

Why Fundamentals of Engineering Economics?

Engineering economics is one of the most practical subject matters in the engineering curriculum, but it is an always challenging, ever-changing discipline. *Contemporary Engineering Economics* (*CEE*), now in its fifth edition, was first published in 1993, and since then, we have tried to reflect changes in the business world in each new edition along with the latest innovations in education and publishing. These changes have resulted in a better, more complete textbook, but one that is much longer than it was originally intended. This may present a problem: Today, covering the textbook in a single term is increasingly difficult. Therefore, we decided to create *Fundamentals of Engineering Economics* (*FEE*) for those who like *contemporary* but think a smaller, more concise textbook would better serve their needs.

Goals of the Text

This text aims not only to provide sound and comprehensive coverage of the concepts of engineering economics but also to address the practical concerns of engineering economics. More specifically, this text has the following goals:

1. To build a thorough understanding of the theoretical and conceptual basis upon which the practice of financial project analysis is built.

2. To satisfy the very practical needs of the engineer toward making informed financial decisions when acting as a team member or project manager for an engineering project.

3. To incorporate all critical decision-making tools—including the most contemporary, computer-oriented ones that engineers bring to the task of making informed financial decisions.

4. To appeal to the full range of engineering disciplines for which this course is often required: industrial, civil, mechanical, electrical, computer, aerospace, chemical, and manufacturing engineering as well as engineering technology.

Intended Market and Use

This text is intended for use in introductory engineering economics courses. Unlike the larger textbook (*CEE*), it is possible to cover *FEE* in a single term and perhaps even to supplement it with a few outside readings or case studies. Although the chapters in *FEE* are arranged logically, they are written in a flexible, modular format, allowing instructors to cover the material in a different sequence.

New to This Edition

Much of the content has been streamlined to provide materials in depth and to reflect the challenges in contemporary engineering economics. Some of the highlighted changes are as follows:

- All chapter opening vignettes—a trademark of *Fundamentals of Engineering Economics*—have been revised or completely replaced with more current and thought-provoking examples from both service and manufacturing sectors.

Chapters	Chapter Opening Vignettes	Company	Sector	Industry
1	• Social networking	Facebook	Technology services	Internet software/Services
2	• Powerball lottery	Personal	Consumer	Gaming
3	• Credit cards	Personal	Financial	Banking
4	• Dallas Cowboys	Dallas Cowboys	Entertainment	Sports
5	• LCD glass manufacturing	Corning Glass	Manufacturing	Electronic components
6	• Owning a corporate jet	Hawker Beechcraft Corporation	Electronic technology	Aerospace/ Defense
7	• What's a degree really worth?	Personal	Consumer	Education
8	• High-speed Internet	Australian Government	Public	Computer communication
9	• Obama to propose tax write-off for business	U.S. Government	Public	Taxation
10	• Coke leveraging its investment in plant-based packaging	Coca Cola	Consumer nondurables	Beverages/ Packaging
11	• Japanese oil company looks to the rising sun	Solar Frontier KK's	Energy	Integrated oil
12	• Finding a fix for the Tappan Zee Bridge	State of New York	Public	Construction
13	• Warren Buffett	Berkshire Hathaway	Finance	Property/ Insurance

- **Self-Test Questions** have been added at the end of each chapter (131 problems in total), and worked-out solutions to the questions are provided in Appendix A. These questions are formatted in a style suitable for Fundamentals Engineering Exam review and were created to help students prepare for a typical class exam common to introductory engineering economic courses.

- The Benefit–Cost Analysis section has been moved to Chapter 8 as a part of measure of investment chapters. The profitability index is included in this chapter.
- Most of the end-of-chapter problems are revised to reflect the changes in the main text. There are 708 problems, including 131 self-test questions, 43% of which are new or updated.
- Various Excel® spreadsheet modeling techniques are introduced throughout the chapters, and the original Excel files are provided online at the Companion Website. Most worksheets have been redesigned with graphical outputs.
- Some other specific content changes made in the third edition are as follows:
  - In Chapter 1, a cost reduction (Apple's iPad®) project is introduced.
  - In Chapter 2, a new retirement planning example is introduced.
  - In Chapter 4, all CPI- and inflation-related data have been updated.
  - In Chapter 5, an example of comparing mutually exclusive revenue projects is provided.
  - In Chapter 6, a section on capital cost has been expanded with an automobile ownership example.
  - In Chapter 8, benefit–cost contents have been streamlined, and a new section on the profitability index has been created.
  - In Chapter 11, the section on risk-adjusted discount rate approach is expanded in which the risk element is incorporated through the cost of capital.
  - In Chapter 13, all financial statements for Lam Research Corporation have been updated, and a new set of financial ratio analysis is provided. Investment strategies have been added as a part of managing personal financial asset under uncertainty.

Features of the Book

FEE is significantly different from *CEE*, but most of the chapters will be familiar to users of *CEE*. Although we pruned some material and clarified, updated, and otherwise improved all of the chapters, *FEE* should still be considered an alternative and streamlined version of *CEE*.

We did retain all of the pedagogical elements and supporting materials that helped make *CEE* so successful. For example:

- Each chapter opens with a real economic vignette describing how an individual decision maker or actual corporation has wrestled with the issues discussed in the chapter. These opening cases heighten students' interest by pointing out the real-world relevance and applicability of what might otherwise seem to be dry technical material.

- In working out each individual chapters example problems, students are encouraged to highlight the critical data provided by each question, isolate the question being asked, and outline the correct approach in the solution under the headings **Given**, **Find**, **Approach**, and **Comments**, respectively. This convention is employed throughout the text. This guidance is intended to stimulate student curiosity to look beyond the mechanics of problem solving to explore "what-if" issues, alternative solution methods, and the interpretation of the solutions.

- There are a large number of end-of-chapter problems and exam-type questions varying in level of difficulty; these problems thoroughly cover the book's various topics.

- Most chapters contain a section titled "Short Case Studies with Excel," enabling students to use Excel to answer a set of questions. These problems reinforce the concepts covered in the chapter and provide students an opportunity to become more proficient with the use of an electronic spreadsheet.
- All Excel spreadsheets now contain easy-to-follow call-out formulas. The integration of Excel is another important feature of *FEE*. Students have increased access to and familiarity with Excel, and instructors have more inclination either to treat these topics explicitly in the course or to encourage students to experiment independently. One could argue that the use of Excel will undermine true understanding of course concepts. This text does not promote the trivial or mindless use of Excel as a replacement for genuine understanding of and skill in applying traditional solution methods. Rather, it focuses on Excel's productivity-enhancing benefits for complex project cash flow development and analysis.

Instructor may access additional teaching support from Pearson's website. Some of these are password protected and instructor using the book can obtain a password by registering at the Pearson website.

You can access the material at www.pearsoned.co.in/ChanSPark

Acknowledgments

This book reflects the efforts of a great many individuals over a number of years. In particular, I would like to recognize the following individuals whose reviews and comments for the previous editions have contributed to this edition. Once again, I would like to thank each of them:

- Roland K. Arter, *Summit College—University of Akron*
- Kandace Ballard, *Quorum Business Solutions, Inc.*
- John L. Evans, *Auburn University*
- Dolores Gooding, *University of South Florida*
- Bruce Hartsough, *University of California at Davis*
- Kyongsun Kim, *Republic of Korea Army*
- Hwansik Lee, *Republic of Korea Army*
- Matthew Marshall, *Rochester Institute of Technology*
- Bruce McCann, *University of Texas at Austin*
- Michael Park, *Mckinsey & Company*
- Richard V. Petitt, *United States Military Academy*
- Linda Ann Riley, *Roger Williams University*
- Iris V. Rivero, *Texas Tech University*
- Bhaba R. Sarker, *Louisiana State University*
- James R. Smith, *Tennessee Technological University*
- Donald R. Smith, *Texas A&M University*
- Stan Uryasev, *University of Florida*

I also wish to thank the following individuals for their additional input to the new edition: Kandace Ballard, John Evans, Linda Ann Riley, and Bhaba Sarker who offered numerous comments to improve the presentation of the materials. Thanks also go to Edward Park who read the entire manuscript from a student's point of view and made many constructive comments; Daphne Ku, Seungbae Park, and Wonsuk Kang who helped me develop the Instructor's Manual; Orhan Dengiz who helped me develop the book Website; Holly Stark, my editor, and Scott Disanno, senior managing editor, both at Prentice Hall, who assumed responsibility for the overall project; and Maheswari PonSaravanan at Jouve, India, the project manager, who oversaw the entire book production.

CHAN S. PARK
AUBURN, ALABAMA

CONTENTS

Preface 5

PART I UNDERSTANDING MONEY AND ITS MANAGEMENT 19

Chapter 1   Engineering Economic Decisions 20

1.1	The Rational Decision-Making Process	22
	1.1.1 How Do We Make Typical Personal Decisions?	22
	1.1.2 How Do We Approach an Engineering Design Problem?	25
	1.1.3 What Makes Economic Decisions Different from Other Design Decisions?	27
1.2	The Engineer's Role in Business	28
	1.2.1 Making Capital-Expenditure Decisions	28
	1.2.2 Large-Scale Engineering Economic Decisions	28
	1.2.3 Impact of Engineering Projects on Financial Statements	30
1.3	Types of Strategic Engineering Economic Decisions	31
	1.3.1 New Products or Product Expansion	32
	1.3.2 Equipment and Process Selection	32
	1.3.3 Cost Reduction	33
	1.3.4 Equipment Replacement	34
	1.3.5 Service or Quality Improvement	34
1.4	Fundamental Principles in Engineering Economics	35
	Summary	36
	Self-Test Questions	37
	Problems	37

Chapter 2   Time Value of Money 38

2.1	Interest: The Cost of Money	40
	2.1.1 The Time Value of Money	40
	2.1.2 Elements of Transactions Involving Interest	42
	2.1.3 Methods of Calculating Interest	44
2.2	Economic Equivalence	46
	2.2.1 Definition and Simple Calculations	47
	2.2.2 Equivalence Calculations Require a Common Time Basis for Comparison	50
2.3	Interest Formulas for Single Cash Flows	51
	2.3.1 Compound-Amount Factor	51
	2.3.2 Present-Worth Factor	53
	2.3.3 Solving for Time and Interest Rates	56

2.4   Uneven-Payment Series   58

2.5   Equal-Payment Series   60
     2.5.1   Compound-Amount Factor: Find F, Given A, i, and N 60
     2.5.2   Sinking-Fund Factor: Find A, Given F, i, and N 64
     2.5.3   Capital-Recovery Factor (Annuity Factor): Find A, Given P, i, and N 66
     2.5.4   Present-Worth Factor: Find P, Given A, i, and N 69
     2.5.5   Present Value of Perpetuities   74

2.6   Dealing with Gradient Series   76
     2.6.1   Handling Linear Gradient Series   76
     2.6.2   Handling Geometric Gradient Series   82

2.7   More on Equivalence Calculations   86
     Summary   92
     Self-Test Questions   93
     Problems   97

Chapter 3   Understanding Money Management   112

3.1   Market Interest Rates   114
     3.1.1   Nominal Interest Rates   114
     3.1.2   Annual Effective Yields   115

3.2   Calculating Effective Interest Rates Based on Payment Periods   118
     3.2.1   Discrete Compounding   118
     3.2.2   Continuous Compounding   119

3.3   Equivalence Calculations with Effective Interest Rates   121
     3.3.1   Compounding Period Equal to Payment Period   121
     3.3.2   Compounding Occurs at a Different Rate than That at Which Payments Are Made   124

3.4   Debt Management   128
     3.4.1   Borrowing with Credit Cards   128
     3.4.2   Commercial Loans—Calculating Principal and Interest Payments   131
     3.4.3   Comparing Different Financing Options   134
     Summary   139
     Self-Test Questions   141
     Problems   144

Chapter 4   Equivalence Calculations under Inflation   158

4.1   Measure of Inflation   159
     4.1.1   Consumer Price Index   160
     4.1.2   Producer Price Index   161
     4.1.3   Average Inflation Rate   163
     4.1.4   General Inflation Rate $(\bar{f})$ versus Specific Inflation Rate (f_j) 164

4.2   Actual Versus Constant Dollars   166
          4.2.1   Conversion from Constant to Actual Dollars   167
          4.2.2   Conversion from Actual to Constant Dollars   168
4.3   Equivalence Calculations under Inflation   172
          4.3.1   Market and Inflation-Free Interest Rates   173
          4.3.2   Constant-Dollar Analysis   173
          4.3.3   Actual-Dollar Analysis   174
          4.3.4   Mixed-Dollar Analysis   178
          Summary   181
          Self-Test Questions   182
          Problems   184

PART 2 EVALUATING BUSINESS AND ENGINEERING ASSETS 191

Chapter 5   Present-Worth Analysis 192

5.1   Loan versus Project Cash Flows   194
5.2   Initial Project Screening Methods   195
          5.2.1   Benefits and Flaws of Payback Screening   197
          5.2.2   Discounted-Payback Period   198
5.3   Present-Worth Analysis   200
          5.3.1   Net-Present-Worth Criterion   200
          5.3.2   Guidelines for Selecting a MARR   205
          5.3.3   Meaning of Net Present Worth   206
          5.3.4   Net Future Worth and Project Balance Diagram   210
          5.3.5   Capitalized-Equivalent Method   211
5.4   Methods to Compare Mutually Exclusive Alternatives   213
          5.4.1   Doing Nothing Is a Decision Option   214
          5.4.2   Service Projects versus Revenue Projects   214
          5.4.3   Analysis Period Equals Project Lives   215
          5.4.4   Analysis Period Differs from Project Lives   219
          Summary   225
          Self-Test Questions   225
          Problems   228

Chapter 6   Annual Equivalence Analysis 248

6.1   Annual-Equivalent Worth Criterion   250
          6.1.1   Benefits of AE Analysis   254
          6.1.2   Capital (Ownership) Costs versus Operating Costs   254
6.2   Applying Annual-Worth Analysis   259
          6.2.1   Unit-Profit or Unit-Cost Calculation   259
          6.2.2   Make-or-Buy Decision   263

6.3   Comparing Mutually Exclusive Projects   266
      6.3.1   Analysis Period Equals Project Lives   266
      6.3.2   Analysis Period Differs from Project Lives   271
      Summary   274
      Self-Test Questions   274
      Problems   277

Chapter 7   Rate-of-Return Analysis   294

7.1   Rate of Return   296
      7.1.1   Return on Investment   296
      7.1.2   Return on Invested Capital   297
7.2   Methods for Finding Rate of Return   298
      7.2.1   Simple versus Nonsimple Investments   298
      7.2.2   Computational Methods   300
7.3   Internal-Rate-of-Return Criterion   307
      7.3.1   Relationship to the PW Analysis   307
      7.3.2   Decision Rule for Simple Investments   307
      7.3.3   Decision Rule for Nonsimple Investments   311
7.4   Incremental Analysis for Comparing Mutually Exclusive Alternatives   313
      7.4.1   Flaws in Project Ranking by IRR   313
      7.4.2   Incremental-Investment Analysis   314
      7.4.3   Handling Unequal Service Lives   320
      Summary   322
      Self-Test Questions   322
      Problems   326

Chapter 7A   Resolution of Multiple Rates of Return   342

7A-1   Net-Investment Test   342
7A-2   The Need for an External Interest Rate   344
7A-3   Calculation of Return on Invested Capital for Mixed Investments   345

Chapter 8   Benefit–Cost Analysis   350

8.1   Evaluation of Public Projects   352
      8.1.1   Valuation of Benefits and Costs   353
      8.1.2   Users' Benefits   353
      8.1.3   Sponsor's Costs   353
      8.1.4   Social Discount Rate   354
8.2   Benefit–Cost Analysis   355
      8.2.1   Definition of Benefit–Cost Ratio   355
      8.2.2   Incremental B/C-Ratio Analysis   358

8.3 Profitability Index 362
    8.3.1 Definition of Profitability Index 362
    8.3.2 Incremental PI Ratio Analysis for Mutually Exclusive Alternatives 364
8.4 Highway Benefit–Cost Analysis 366
    8.4.1 Define the Base Case and the Proposed Alternatives 366
    8.4.2 Highway User Benefits 367
    8.4.3 Sponsors' Costs 367
    8.4.4 Illustrating Case Example 368
    Summary 372
    Self-Test Questions 372
    Problems 375

PART 3 DEVELOPMENT OF PROJECT CASH FLOWS 383

Chapter 9   Accounting for Depreciation and Income Taxes 384

9.1 Accounting Depreciation 386
    9.1.1 Depreciable Property 386
    9.1.2 Cost Basis 387
    9.1.3 Useful Life and Salvage Value 388
    9.1.4 Depreciation Methods: Book and Tax Depreciation 388
9.2 Book Depreciation Methods 390
    9.2.1 Straight-Line Method 390
    9.2.2 Declining-Balance Method 392
    9.2.3 Units-of-Production Method 396
9.3 Tax Depreciation Methods 397
    9.3.1 MACRS Recovery Periods 397
    9.3.2 MACRS Depreciation: Personal Property 398
    9.3.3 MACRS Depreciation: Real Property 401
9.4 Corporate Taxes 403
    9.4.1 How to Determine "Accounting Profit" 403
    9.4.2 U.S. Corporate Income Tax Rates 405
    9.4.3 Gain Taxes on Asset Disposals 407
    Summary 411
    Self-Test Questions 412
    Problems 414

Chapter 10   Project Cash-Flow Analysis 426

10.1 Understanding Project Cost Elements 428
    10.1.1 Classifying Costs for Manufacturing Environments 428
    10.1.2 Classifying Costs for Financial Statements 430
    10.1.3 Classifying Costs for Predicting Cost Behavior 431
10.2 Why Do We Need to Use Cash Flows in Economic Analysis? 435

10.3	Income-Tax Rate to Be Used in Project Evaluation	436
10.4	Incremental Cash Flows from Undertaking a Project	439
	10.4.1 Operating Activities	439
	10.4.2 Investing Activities	442
	10.4.3 Financing Activities	443
10.5	Developing Project Cash Flow Statements	443
	10.5.1 When Projects Require Only Operating and Investing Activities	443
	10.5.2 When Projects Are Financed with Borrowed Funds	447
10.6	Effects of Inflation on Project Cash Flows	449
	10.6.1 Depreciation Allowance under Inflation	449
	10.6.2 Handling Multiple Inflation Rates	453
	Summary	455
	Self-Test Questions	456
	Problems	459

Chapter 11   Handling Project Uncertainty   480

11.1	Origins of Project Risk	483
11.2	Methods of Describing Project Risk	483
	11.2.1 Sensitivity Analysis	483
	11.2.2 Sensitivity Analysis for Mutually Exclusive Alternatives	488
	11.2.3 Break-Even Analysis	491
	11.2.4 Scenario Analysis	492
11.3	Probabilistic Cash Flow Analysis	495
	11.3.1 Including Risk in Investment Evaluation	496
	11.3.2 Aggregating Risk over Time	497
	11.3.3 Estimating Risky Cash Flows	500
11.4	Considering the Project Risk by Discount Rate	504
	11.4.1 Determining the Company Cost of Capital	504
	11.4.2 Project Cost of Capital: Risk-Adjusted Discount Rate Approach	509
	Summary	511
	Self-Test Questions	512
	Problems	514

PART 4 SPECIAL TOPICS IN ENGINEERING ECONOMICS   529

Chapter 12   Replacement Decisions   530

12.1	Replacement-Analysis Fundamentals	532
	12.1.1 Basic Concepts and Terminology	533
	12.1.2 Approaches for Comparing Defender and Challenger	535
12.2	Economic Service Life	539

12.3   Replacement Analysis When the Required Service Period Is Long   545
    12.3.1 Required Assumptions and Decision Frameworks   545
    12.3.2 Handling Unequal Service Life Problems
          in Replacement Analysis   546
    12.3.3 Replacement Strategies under the Infinite Planning Horizon   546
12.4   Replacement Analysis with Tax Considerations   552
    Summary   559
    Self-Test Questions   560
    Problems   561

Chapter 13   Understanding Financial Statements   574

13.1   Accounting: The Basis of Decision Making   576
13.2   Financial Status for Businesses   577
    13.2.1 The Balance Sheet   579
    13.2.2 The Income Statement   584
    13.2.3 The Cash-Flow Statement   586
13.3   Using Ratios to Make Business Decisions   592
    13.3.1 Debt Management Analysis   592
    13.3.2 Liquidity Analysis   595
    13.3.3 Asset Management Analysis   596
    13.3.4 Profitability Analysis   597
    13.3.5 Market-Value Analysis   599
    13.3.6 Limitations of Financial Ratios in Business Decisions   601
    13.3.7 Where We Get the Most Up-to-Date Financial Information   603
13.4   Principle of Investing in Financial Assets   603
    13.4.1 Trade-Off between Risk and Reward   603
    13.4.2 Broader Diversification Reduces Risk   603
    13.4.3 Broader Diversification Increases Expected Return   605
    Summary   607
    Self-Test Questions   608
    Problems   612

Appendix A   Answers to the Self-Test Questions   621

Appendix B   Interest Factors for Discrete Compounding   649

Appendix C   How to Read the Cumulative Standardized Normal Distribution Function   679

Index   683

Understanding Money and Its Management

CHAPTER ONE

Engineering Economic Decisions

Facebook: From College Startup to Online Trailblazer In February 2004, college student Mark Zuckerberg launched Facebook, a social networking site. With presently 800 million individual users, what started as a networking site for Harvard students quickly grew in scope and functionality and evolved into a must-have form of communication for people and businesses around the world. It has consistently out performed its competitors and has fast become the pre-eminent social networking site in country after country.

Through content sharing, recommendations and reviews, Facebook puts emphasis on online personal and professional relationships, not on abstract data, database driven metrics, or the algorithmic use of search terms. With users able to "like" something within the framework of Facebook itself, Facebook has propagated itself across other websites. It is thus blazing new territory in terms of Internet advertising, sales, and the notion of consumer privacy.

This has the potential to put Facebook in direct competition with Google, with recommendations within the Facebook environment potentially having more impact on personal choice than algorithm-based search results conventionally secured through Google.

Moreover, Facebook only continues to grow, in users and in value. Early in 2011, the value of Facebook was raised to nearly $50 billion owing to investments from Goldman Sachs and an unnamed Russian investor. And with rumors circulating that the company will be going public in the near future, there's no telling how that value may increase in the coming months—posing a threat to the impersonal search-based results Internet mogul Google has to offer.

Of course, Google can't afford to sit idle and watch Facebook make inroads into their key business model, i.e., making money from pay per click on advertising banners. To overcome its past miscues in the social networking space, Google came up with its own social networking site named Google+. In July 2011, Google+ launched and already had more than 60 million subscribers within only a half year of inception. If this trend continues, some analysts expect to see nearly 400 million users by 2013. Who know what will happen? Although, there are still plenty of questions left about the fate and future of Google+, Zuckerberg has to watch Google+ closely, which could yet prove to be a sizable alternative to Facebook for the technology and advertising industries alike.

The story of how a college student was motivated to invent a social network and eventually transform his invention into a multibillion-dollar business is not an uncommon one in today's market. Companies like Google™, Dell®, Microsoft®, and Yahoo!® produce computer-related products and have market values of several billion dollars. These companies were all founded by highly motivated young college students just like Mr. Zuckerberg. Also common among these successful businesses is their capable and imaginative engineers who constantly generate sound ideas for capital investment, execute them well, and obtain good results. You might wonder what role these engineers play in making such business decisions: What specific tasks are assigned to these engineers, and what tools and techniques are available to them for making such capital-investment decisions? In this book, we will consider many investment situations, personal as well as business. The focus will be to evaluate engineering projects based on the merits of economic desirability and the respective firm's investment climate.

1.1 The Rational Decision-Making Process

We, as individuals or business-persons, constantly make decisions in our daily lives. Most are made automatically without realizing that we are actually following some sort of logical decision flowchart. Rational decision making is often a complex process that includes a number of essential elements. This chapter will provide examples of how two engineering students approached their financial and engineering design problems using flexible, rational decision making. By reviewing these examples, we will be able to identify some essential elements common to any rational decision-making process. The first example illustrates how a student named Jane narrowed down her choice between two competing alternatives when leasing an automobile. The second example illustrates how a typical class project idea evolves and how a student named Sonya approached the design problem by following a logical method of analysis.

1.1.1 How Do We Make Typical Personal Decisions?

For Jane Williams, a senior at the University of Arizona, the future holds a new car. Her 2002 Saturn has clocked almost 150,000 miles, and she wants to replace it soon. But how to do it—should she buy or lease? In either case, "Car payments would be difficult," said the engineering major, who works as a part-time cashier at a local supermarket. "I have never leased before, but I am leaning toward it this time to save on the down payment. I also don't want to worry about major repairs." For Jane, leasing would provide the warranty protection she wants, along with a new car every three years. On the other hand, she would be limited to driving only a specified number of miles, about 12,000 per year, after which she would have to pay 20 cents or more per mile. Jane is well aware that choosing the right vehicle and the best possible financing are important decision. Yet, at this point, Jane is unsure of the implications of buying versus leasing.

Establishing the Goal or Objective

Jane decided to research the local papers and the Internet for the latest lease programs, including factory-subsidized "sweetheart" deals and special incentive packages. Of the cars that were within her budget, the 2011 Ford Focus and the 2011 Honda Civic Coupe DX appeared to be equally attractive in terms of style, price, and options. Jane decided to visit the dealers' lots to see how both models looked and to take them for a test drive. Both cars gave her very satisfactory driving experiences. Jane thought that it would be prudent to thoroughly examine the many technical and safety features of both vehicles. After her examination, it seemed that both models were virtually identical in terms of reliability, safety features, and quality.

Evaluation of Feasible Alternatives

Jane estimated that her 2002 Saturn could be traded in for around $2,200. This amount would be just enough to make any down payment required for leasing the new automobile. Through her research, Jane learned that there are two types of leases: open-end and closed-end. The most popular by far was closed-end because open-end leases potentially expose the consumer to higher payments at the end of the lease if the car depreciates faster than expected. If Jane were to take a closed-end lease, she could just return the vehicle at the end of the lease and "walk away" to lease or buy another vehicle; however, she would still have to pay for extra mileage or excess wear or damage. She thought that since she would not be a "pedal-to-the-metal driver," closed-end charges would not be a problem for her.

To get the best financial deal, Jane obtained some financial facts from both dealers on their best offers. With each offer, she added up all the costs of leasing from the down payment to the disposition fee due at the end of the lease. This sum would determine the total cost of leasing that vehicle, not counting routine items such as oil changes and other maintenance. (See Table 1.1 for a comparison of the costs of both offers.)

It appeared that by leasing the Ford Focus, Jane could save about $1,010 in total payments [(47 × $60 monthly lease payment savings less $1,810 total due at signing (including the first month's payment savings)] over the Honda Civic. But, she has to pay $250 on the disposition fee (which leasing the Honda did not require), for a total savings of $760.[2] However, if she were to drive any additional miles over the limit,

TABLE 1.1 **Financial Data for Auto Leasing: Focus versus Honda**

Auto Leasing	Focus	Honda	Difference Focus vs. Honda
1. Manufacturer's suggested retail price (MSRP)	$16,640	$16,155	+$485
2. Lease length (months)	48	48	
3. Allowed mileage (miles)	48,000	48,000	
4. Monthly lease payment	$215	$275	−$60
5. Mileage surcharge over 48,000 miles	$0.20	$0.15	+ $0.05
6. Disposition fee at lease end	$250	$0	+$250
7. Total due at signing:			
• First month's lease payment	$215	$275	−$60
• Down payment	$1,500	$0	+$1,500
• Administrative fee	$495	$0	+$495
• Refundable security deposit	$200	$325	−$125
Total	$2,410	$600	+ $1,810

- Models compared: The 2011 Focus and the 2011 Honda Civic Coupe DX, both with automatic transmission and A/C.
- Disposition fee: This is a paperwork charge for getting the vehicle ready for resale after the lease ends.

[2] If Jane considered the time value of money in her comparison, the amount of actual savings would be less than $760, which we demonstrate in Chapter 2.

her savings would be reduced by 5 cents (the difference between the two cars' mileage surcharges) for each additional mile. Jane would need to drive about 15,200 extra miles over the limit in order to lose all the savings. Because she could not anticipate her exact driving needs after graduation and it was difficult to come up with $2,410 due at lease signing, she decided to lease the Honda Civic DX. Certainly, any monetary savings would be important, but she preferred having some flexibility in her future driving needs.

Knowing Other Opportunities

If Jane had been interested in buying the car, it would have been even more challenging to determine precisely whether she would be better off buying than leasing. To make a comparison of leasing versus buying, Jane could have considered what she likely would pay for the same vehicle under both scenarios. If she would own the car for as long as she would lease it, she could sell the car and use the proceeds to pay off any outstanding loan. If finances were her only consideration, her choice would depend on the specifics of the deal. But beyond finances, she would need to consider the positives and negatives of her personal preferences. By leasing, she would never experience the joy of the final payment—but she would have a new car every three years.

Review of Jane's Decision-Making Process

Now let us revisit the decision-making process in a more structured way. The analysis can be thought of as including the six steps summarized in Figure 1.1.

These six steps are known as the *rational decision-making process*. Certainly, we do not follow all six steps in every decision problem. Some decision problems may not require much time and effort. Quite often, we base our decisions solely on emotional reasons. However, for any complex economic decision problem, a structured framework proves to be worthwhile.

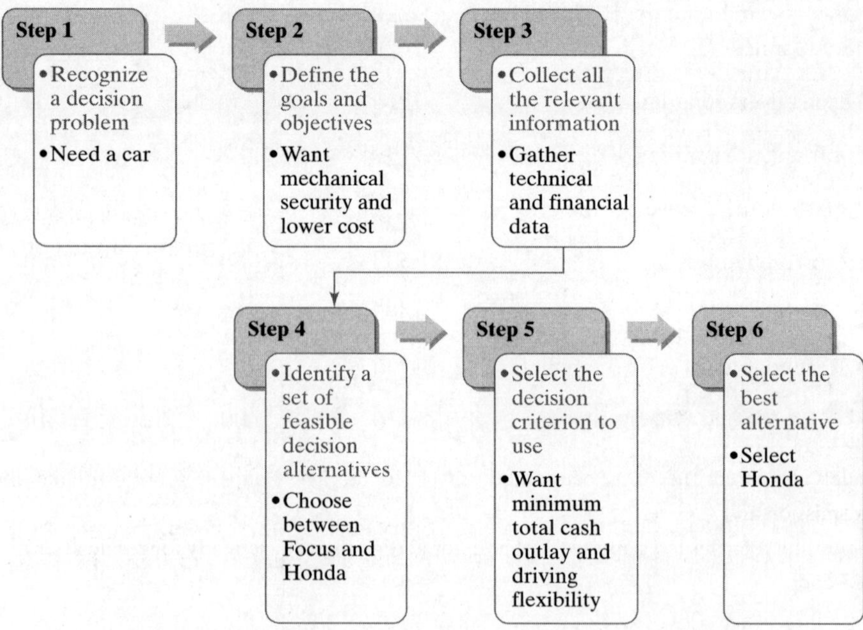

Figure I.I   Logical steps to follow in a car-leasing decision

1.1.2 How Do We Approach an Engineering Design Problem?

The idea of design and development is what most distinguishes engineering from science, the latter being concerned principally with understanding the world as it is. Decisions made during the engineering design phase of a product's development determine the majority of the costs for manufacturing that product. As design and manufacturing processes become more complex, the engineer will increasingly be called upon to make decisions that involve cost. In this section, we provide an example of how engineers move from "concept" to "product." The story of how an electrical engineering student approached her design problem and exercised her judgment has much to teach us about some of the fundamental characteristics of the human endeavor known as *engineering decision making.*[3]

Getting an Idea: Necessity Is the Mother of Invention

Throughout history, necessity has proven to be the mother of invention. Most people abhor lukewarm beverages, especially during the hot days of summer. So, several years ago, Sonya Talton, an electrical engineering student at Johns Hopkins University, had a revolutionary idea—a self-chilling soda can!

Picture this: It is one of those sweltering, muggy August afternoons. Your friends have finally gotten their acts together for a picnic at the lake. Together, you pull out the items you brought with you: blankets, sunscreen, sandwiches, chips, and soda. You wipe the sweat from your neck, reach for a soda, and realize that it is about the same temperature as the 90°F afternoon. Great start! And, of course, no one wants to go back to the store for more ice! Why does someone not come up with a soda container that can chill itself?

Setting Design Goals and Objectives

So as the term project in her engineering graphics and design course, Sonya decided to devise a self-chilling soda can. The professor stressed innovative thinking and urged students to consider practical, but novel, concepts. The first thing Sonya needed to do was to establish some goals for the project:

- Get the soda as cold as possible in the shortest possible time.
- Keep the container design simple.
- Keep the size and weight of the newly designed container similar to that of the traditional soda can. (This factor would allow beverage companies to use existing vending machines and storage equipment.)
- Keep the production costs low.
- Make the product environmentally safe.

Evaluating Design Alternatives

With these goals in mind, Sonya had to think of a practical, yet innovative, way of chilling the can. Ice was the obvious choice—practical, but not innovative. Sonya had a great idea: What about a chemical ice pack? Sonya asked herself what would go inside such an ice pack. The answer she came up with was ammonium nitrate (NH_4NO_3) and

---

[3] The original ideas for self-chilling soda can were introduced in *1991 Annual Report,* GWC Whiting School of Engineering, Johns Hopkins University.

Figure 1.2 Conceptual design for self-chilling soda can

a water pouch. When pressure is applied to the chemical ice pack, the water pouch breaks and mixes with the NH_4NO_3, creating an endothermic reaction (the absorption of heat). The NH_4NO_3 draws the heat out of the soda, causing it to chill (see Figure 1.2). How much water should go in the water pouch? After several trials involving different amounts of water, Sonya found that she could chill the soda can from 80°F to 48°F in a three-minute period using 115 mL of water. Next, she needed to determine how cold a refrigerated soda gets as a basis for comparison. She put a can in the fridge for two days and found that it chilled to 41°F. Sonya's idea was definitely feasible. But was it economically marketable?

Gauging Product Cost and Price

In Sonya's engineering graphics and design course, the professor emphasized the importance of marketing surveys and benefit–cost analyses as ways to gauge a product's potential and economic feasibility. To determine the marketability of her self-chilling soda can, Sonya surveyed approximately 80 people. She asked them only two questions: (1) How old were they? and (2) How much would they be willing to pay for a self-chilling can of soda? The under-21 group was willing to pay the most, 84 cents, on average. The 40-plus bunch wanted to pay only 68 cents, on average. Overall, members of the entire surveyed group would be willing to spend 75 cents for a self-chilling soda can. (This poll was hardly a scientific market survey, but it did give Sonya a feel for what would be a reasonable price for her product.)

The next hurdle was to determine the existing production cost of one traditional can of soda. Also, how much more would it cost to produce the self-chiller? Would it be profitable? She went to the library, and there she found the bulk cost of the chemicals and materials she would need. Then she calculated how much money would be required for production of one unit of soda. She could not believe it! It would cost only 12 cents to manufacture (and transport) one can of soda. The self-chiller would cost 2 or 3 cents more. That was not bad, considering that the average consumer was willing to pay up to 25 cents more for the self-chilling can than for the traditional one that typically costs 50 cents.

Considering Green Engineering

The only two constraints left to consider were possible chemical contamination of the soda and recyclability. Theoretically, it should be possible to build a machine that would drain the solution from the can and recrystallize it. The ammonium nitrate could then be reused in future soda cans; in addition, the plastic outer can could be recycled. Chemical contamination of the soda, however, was a big concern. Unfortunately, there was absolutely no way to ensure that the chemical and the soda would never come in contact with one another inside the cans. To ease consumer fears, Sonya decided that a color or odor indicator could be added to alert the consumer to contamination if it occurred.

What Is the Next Step?

What is Sonya's conclusion? The self-chilling beverage container (can) would be a wonderful technological advancement. The product would be convenient for the beach, picnics, sporting events, and barbecues. Its design would incorporate consumer convenience while addressing environmental concerns. It would be innovative, yet inexpensive, and it would have an economic as well as a social impact on society. Sonya would explore the possibility of patent application of her idea.[4] In the meantime, she would shop for any business venture capitalist who would be interested in investing money to develop the product.

1.1.3 What Makes Economic Decisions Different from Other Design Decisions?

Economic decisions are fundamentally different from the types of decisions typically encountered in engineering design. In a design situation, the engineer uses known physical properties, the principles of chemistry and physics, engineering design correlations, and engineering judgment to arrive at a workable and optimal design. If the judgment is sound, the calculations are done correctly, and we ignore potential technological advances, the design is time invariant. In other words, if the engineering design to meet a particular need is done today, next year, or in five years' time, the final design will not need to change significantly.

In considering economic decisions, the measurement of investment attractiveness, which is the subject of this book, is relatively straightforward. However, information required in such evaluations always involves predicting, or forecasting, product sales,

---

[4]As of this printing, Sonya's invention has not yet made to consumer market.

product selling price, and various costs over some future time frame—5 years, 10 years, even 25 years.

All such forecasts have two things in common. First, they are never completely accurate when compared with the actual values realized at future times. Second, a prediction or forecast made today is likely to be different than one made at some point in the future. It is this ever-changing view of the future that can make it necessary to revisit and even alter previous economic decisions. Thus, unlike engineering design outcomes, the conclusions reached through economic evaluation are not necessarily time invariant. Economic decisions have to be based on the best information available at the time of the decision and a thorough understanding of the uncertainties in the forecasted data.

1.2 The Engineer's Role in Business

What role do engineers play within a firm? What specific tasks are assigned to the engineering staff, and what tools and techniques are available to it to improve a firm's profits? Engineers are called upon to participate in a variety of decision-making processes ranging from manufacturing and marketing to finances. We will restrict our focus here to various economic decisions related to engineering projects. We refer to these decisions as **engineering economic decisions**.

1.2.1 Making Capital-Expenditure Decisions

In manufacturing, engineering is involved in every detail of producing goods, from conceptual design to shipping. In fact, engineering decisions account for the majority (some say 85%) of product costs. Engineers must consider the effective use of fixed capital assets such as buildings and machinery. One of the engineer's primary tasks is to plan for the acquisition of equipment (**capital expenditure**) that will enable the firm to design and manufacture products economically (see Figure 1.3).

With the purchase of any fixed asset—equipment, for example—we need to estimate the profits (more precisely, the cash flows) that the asset will generate during its service period. In other words, we have to make capital-expenditure decisions based on predictions about the future. Suppose, for example, that you are considering the purchase of a deburring machine to meet the anticipated demand for hubs and sleeves used in the production of gear couplings. You expect the machine to last 10 years. This purchase decision thus involves an implicit 10-year sales forecast for the gear couplings, which means that a long waiting period will be required before you will know whether the purchase was justified.

An inaccurate estimate of asset needs can have serious consequences. If you invest too much in assets, you incur unnecessarily heavy expenses. Spending too little on fixed assets is also harmful, because your firm's equipment may be too obsolete to make products competitively; without an adequate capacity, you may lose a portion of your market share to rival firms. Regaining lost customers involves heavy marketing expenses and may even require price reductions or product improvements, both of which are costly.

1.2.2 Large-Scale Engineering Economic Decisions

The economic decisions that engineers make in business differ very little from those made by Sonya in designing the self-chilling soda can, except for the scale of the concern. Let us consider a real-world engineering decision problem on a much larger

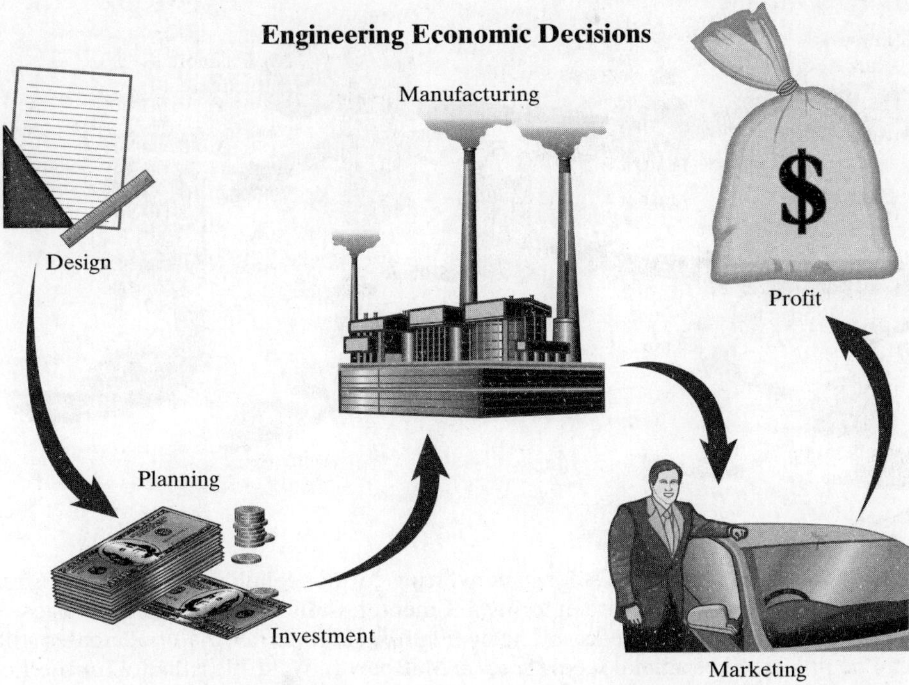

Figure 1.3 One of the primary functions of engineers: Making capital-budgeting decisions

scale: As the United States continues to move away from its dependency on foreign oil, the need to commercialize cellulosic ethanol is apparent.

One of the first commercial-scale, cellulosic ethanol plants, which is scheduled to begin operations in Iowa early in 2012, will produce 25 million gallons of ethanol per year from corncobs, leaves, and husks provided by farmers in the area around Emmetsburg, Iowa.[5] This project is a part of ethanol expansion plans announced in 2006 by Voyager Ethanol to construct a $200 million commercial-scale biorefinery plant with a production capacity of 125 million gallons per year.[6] The design calls for advanced corn fractionation and lignocellulosic conversion technologies to produce ethanol from corn fiber and corn stover. Once constructed, the plant will reportedly turn 11% more ethanol from one bushel of corn and 27% more ethanol from an acre of corn while using 83% less energy than a traditional corn-to-ethanol plant. The conceptual process of producing cellulosic ethanol similar to Voyager Ethanol's is shown in Figure 1.4.

Deriving ethanol from cellulose—found in the cornstalks and the straw of grains and grasses—consumes far less fossil fuel than deriving ethanol from corn kernels. But technically, it is challenging to coax the natural enzymes needed for conversion to multiply and work inside the large bioreactors required for volume production.

Although the management of Voyager has already decided to build the ethanol plant, the engineers involved in making the engineering economic decision are still

[5] Project LIBERTY—Cellulosic Ethanol by POET for America, May 30, 2011 (www.poet.com/innovation/cellulosic/projectliberty/index.asp).
[6] "$200 M Cellulose-to-Ethanol Production Facility Planned in Iowa," November 22, 2006. Broin Companies will convert a dry mill ethanol plant into bio-refinery by 2009, at www.RenewableEnergyAccess.com.

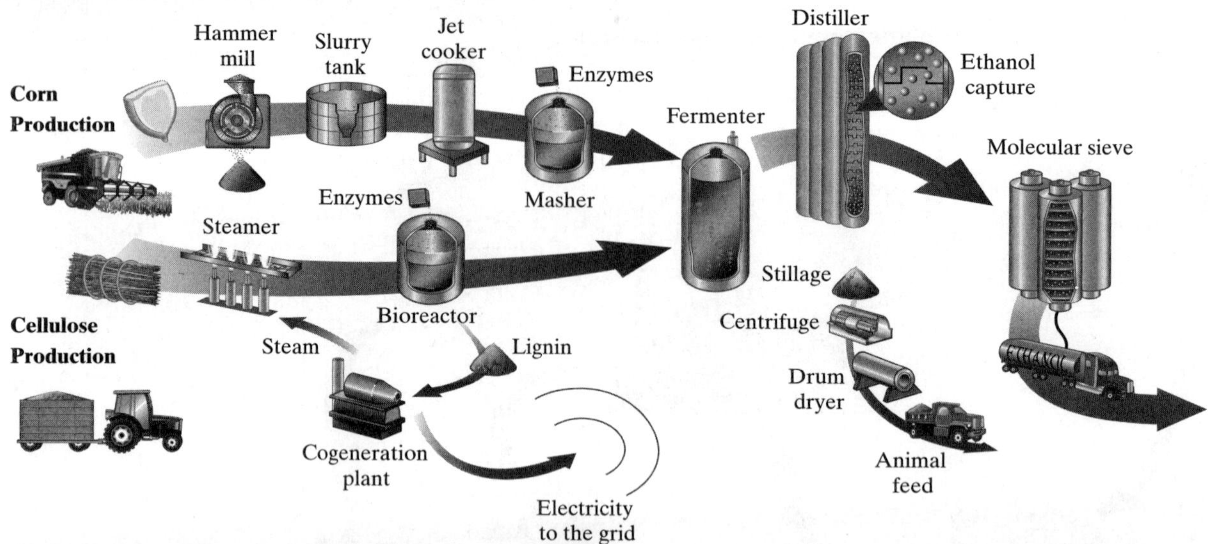

Figure 1.4 Ethanol from kernels or stalks. The initial steps in converting corn or cellulose into ethanol differ significantly. Corn is ground, cooked, and mashed before entering a fomenter. Cellulose is steamed to expose fibers that enzymes then convert into sugars in a bioreactor. The distillation of either raw material creates stillage, a valuable by-product that can be processed as animal feed. (*Source:* Matthew L. Wald, "Is Ethanol for the Long Haul?," *Scientific American,* 296 (1), January 2007, pp. 42–49. Printed with permission from Scientific American, www.sciam.com)

debating about whether the cost of producing ethanol would be sufficiently competitive with gasoline to justify its production.

Obviously, an engineering economic decision at this level is more complex and more significant to the company than a decision about purchasing a new lathe. Projects of this nature involve large sums of money invested over long periods of time, and it is difficult to predict their market demand accurately. An erroneous forecast of product demand can have serious consequences: With any overexpansion, having to pay for unused raw materials and finished products causes unnecessary expenses. In the case of Voyager Ethanol, if the cellulose ethanol technology does not work in a commercial-scale operation, or if the ethanol is too costly to produce to be competitive in the marketplace, the financial risk would be too great to ignore.

1.2.3 Impact of Engineering Projects on Financial Statements

Engineers must also understand the business environment in which a company's major business decisions are made. It is important for an engineering project to generate profits, but the project also must strengthen the firm's overall financial position. How do we measure Voyager's success in the ethanol project? Will enough ethanol be produced, for example, to generate sufficient profits? While the ethanol project will provide a substitute for foreign oil, the bottom-line concern is its financial performance over the long run.

Regardless of the form of a business, each company has to produce basic financial statements at the end of each operating cycle (typically, a year). These financial statements provide the basis for future investment analysis. In practice, we seldom make investment decisions based solely on an estimate of a project's profitability because we must also consider the project's overall impact on the financial strength and position of

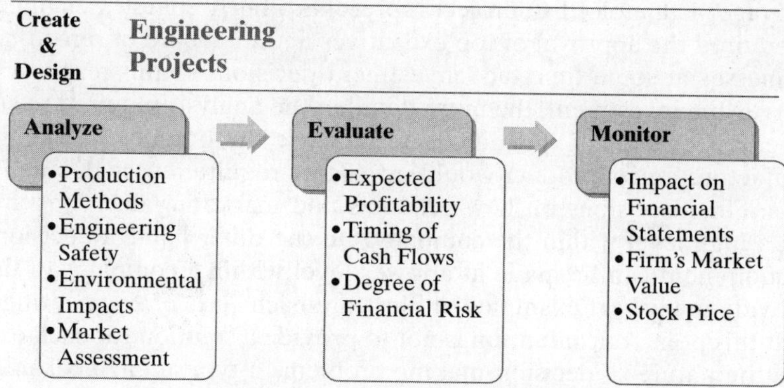

Figure 1.5   How a successful engineering project affects a firm's market value

the company. For example, some companies with low cash flow may be unable to bear the risk of a large project like ethanol even if it might be profitable (see Figure 1.5).

Suppose that you are the president of Voyager Ethanol, LLC. Also suppose that you hold some shares in the company, which makes you one of the company's many owners. What objectives would you set for the company? One of your objectives should be to increase the company's value to its owners (including yourself) as much as possible. While all firms operate to generate profit, what determines the market value of a company are not profits, per se, but rather, cash flows. It is, after all, the available cash that determines the future investments and growth of the firm. The market price of your company's stock to some extent represents the value of your company. Multiple factors affect your company's market value: present and expected future earnings, the timing and duration of these earnings, and the risks associated with the earnings. Certainly, any successful investment decision will increase a company's market value. Stock price can be a good indicator of your company's financial health and may also reflect the market's attitude about how well your company is managed for the benefit of its owners.

If investors like the ethanol project, the result will be an increased demand for the company's stock. This increased demand, in turn, will cause stock prices, and hence, shareholder wealth, to increase. Any successful investment decision on ethanol's scale will tend to increase a firm's stock prices in the marketplace and promote long-term success. Thus, in making a large-scale engineering project decision, we must consider the project's possible effect on the firm's market value. (We will consider this important issue in Chapter 13.)

1.3 Types of Strategic Engineering Economic Decisions

A project idea such as constructing an ethanol plant can originate from many different levels in an organization. Since some ideas are good, while others are not, it is necessary to establish procedures for screening projects. Many large companies have a specialized project analysis division that actively searches for new ideas, projects, and ventures. Once project ideas are identified, they are typically classified as (1) new products or product expansion, (2) equipment and process selection, (3) cost reduction, (4) equipment replacement, or (5) service or quality improvement. This classification scheme allows management to address key questions such as the following: Can the existing plant be used to achieve the new production levels? Does the firm have the capital to undertake this new investment? Does the new proposal warrant the recruitment of new technical personnel? The answers to these questions help firms screen out proposals that arc not feasible.

The Voyager Ethanol, LLC, project represents a fairly complex engineering decision that required the approval of top executives and the board of directors. Virtually all big businesses at some time face investment decisions of this magnitude. In general, the larger the investment, the more detailed the analysis required to support the expenditure. For example, expenditures to increase the output of existing products or to manufacture a new product would invariably require a very detailed economic justification. Final decisions on new products and marketing decisions are generally made at a high level within the company. On the other hand, a decision to repair damaged equipment can be made at a lower level within a company. In this section, we will provide many real examples to illustrate each class of engineering economic decision. At this point, our intention is not to provide a solution for each example but to describe the nature of decision-making problems a typical engineer might face in the real world.

1.3.1 New Products or Product Expansion

Investments in this category are those that increase the revenues of a company if output is increased. There are two common types of expansion decision problems. The first type includes decisions about expenditures to increase the output of existing production or distribution facilities. In these situations, we are basically asking, "Shall we build or otherwise acquire a new facility?" The expected future cash inflows in this investment category are the revenues from the goods and services produced in the new facility.

The second type of decision problem includes the consideration of expenditures necessary to produce a new product or to expand into a new geographic area. These projects normally require large sums of money over long periods. For example, Apple Computer's investment in iPad®'s A4 chip is estimated to be $1 billion. The cost for Apple to build the $500 base model iPad is estimated to be $229.35. Figure 1.6 illustrates the estimated manufacturing costs for iPads with different design features.

Clearly, the profit margin for the iPad varies with the different design features—the high-end product being more profitable. At the time of its introduction, the main question was, "Will there be enough demand for the iPad so that Apple could recoup the investment and be the market leader in the table PC market?" Now, the question after iPad is in the market is, "Will the iPad repeat iPhone® history so that it becomes Apple's most successful product ever?"[7]

1.3.2 Equipment and Process Selection

This class of engineering decision problem involves selecting the best course of action when there are several ways to meet a project's requirements. Which of several proposed items of equipment shall we purchase for a given purpose? The choice often hinges on which item is expected to generate the largest savings (or return on the investment). The choice of material will dictate the manufacturing process involved. (See Figure 1.7 on making a 0.5 liter polyethylene terephthalate (PET) barrier beer bottle.) Many factors will affect the ultimate choice of the material, and engineers should consider all major cost elements, such as machinery and equipment, tooling, labor, and material. Other factors may include press and assembly, production and engineered scrap, the number of dies and tools, and the cycle times for various processes.

---

[7] In fact, the iPad turned out to be a smashing success and contributed to sending Apple's stock to an all-time high. Consequently, Apple introduced an improved version, iPad 2, in April 2011.

	16GB		32GB		64GB	
	Without 3G	With 3G	Without 3G	With 3G	Without 3G	With 3G
Core Components						
Display and Touchscreen	$80.00	$80.00	$80.00	$80.00	$80.00	$80.00
Electromechanical and Mechanical	$35.30	$35.30	$35.30	$35.30	$35.30	$35.30
Battery (1)	$17.50	$17.50	$17.50	$17.50	$17.50	$17.50
MPU and Memory	$28.90	$28.90	$28.90	$28.90	$28.90	$28.90
A4 Processor (2)	$17.00	$17.00	$17.00	$17.00	$17.00	$17.00
Supporting DRAM (3)	$11.90	$11.90	$11.90	$11.90	$11.90	$11.90
WLAN n + BT + FM (4)	$8.05	$8.05	$8.05	$8.05	$8.05	$8.05
User Interface Components (5)	$10.20	$10.20	$10.20	$10.20	$10.20	$10.20
Other Power Management Components	$2.40	$2.40	$2.40	$2.40	$2.40	$2.40
Configuration-Dependent Components						
NAND Flash	$29.50	$29.50	$59.00	$59.00	$118.00	$118.00
Wireless (6)		$24.50		$24.50		$24.50
GPS		$2.60		$2.60		$2.60
Other Costs						
Box Contents	$7.50	$7.50	$7.50	$7.50	$7.50	$7.50
Totals						
Total Materials Cost	**$219.35**	**$246.45**	**$248.85**	**$275.95**	**$307.85**	**$334.95**
Total Manufacturing Cost	**$10.00**	**$11.20**	**$10.00**	**$11.20**	**$10.00**	**$11.20**
Grand Total	*$229.35*	*$257.65*	*$258.85*	*$287.15*	*$317.85*	*$346.15*
Retail Price	**$499.00**	**$629.00**	**$599.00**	**$729.00**	**$699.00**	**$829.00**

Source: IHS iSuppli Corporation February 2010. "Apple iPad Components Cost At Least $259." Bloomberg Businessweek, April 07, 2010 (http://www.businessweek.com/technology/content/apr2010/tc2010046_788280.htm)

Figure 1.6   Launching iPad® and estimated manufacturing costs for iPad with different design features (IHS iSuppli estimates that the iPad 2 with 32 gigabytes of flash memory costs Apple $323.35 for the wireless versions. The device sells for $729.)

1.3.3 Cost Reduction

A cost-reduction project attempts to lower a firm's operating costs. Typically, we need to consider whether a company should buy equipment to perform an operation now done manually or in some other way spend money now in order to save more money later. The expected future cash inflows from this investment are savings resulting from lower operating costs. Or perhaps the firm needs to decide whether to produce a part

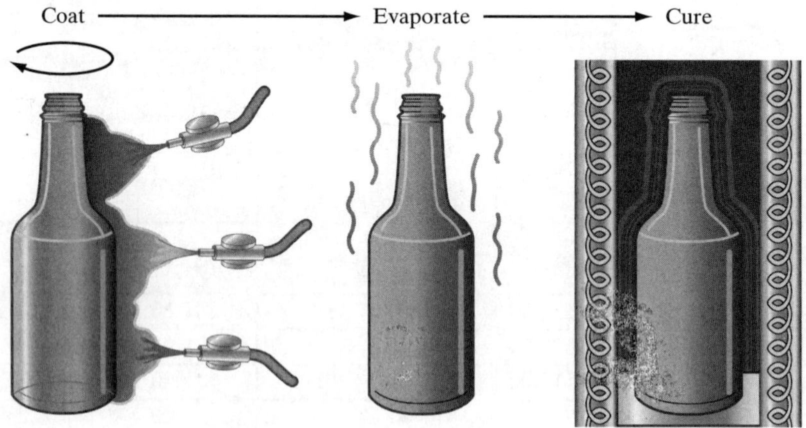

	Five-Layer Bottle	Three-Layer with External Coating
• Capacity	20,000 bottles/hour	20,000 bottles/hour
• Capital investment	$10.8 million	$7.5 million
• Direct manufacturing cost	$59.35/1,000 bottles	$66.57/1,000 bottles

Figure 1.7 Making plastic beer bottles by two different manufacturing processes

for a product in-house or to buy it from a supplier to reduce the total production cost. This is commonly known as a *make-or-buy* (or *outsourcing*) *analysis*.

1.3.4 Equipment Replacement

This category of investment decision involves considering the expenditure necessary to replace worn-out or obsolete equipment. For example, a company may purchase 10 large presses with the expectation that it will produce stamped metal parts for 10 years. After five years, however, it may become necessary to produce the parts in plastic, which would require retiring the presses early and purchasing plastic-molding machines. Similarly, a company may find that, for competitive reasons, larger and more accurate parts are required, which will make the purchased machines obsolete earlier than expected.

1.3.5 Service or Quality Improvement

The service sector of the U.S. economy dominates both gross domestic product (GDP) and total employment. It is also the fastest growing part of the economy and the one offering the most fertile opportunities for productivity improvement. For example, service activities now approach 80% of U.S. employment, far outstripping sectors such as manufacturing (14%) and agriculture (2%). New service activities are continually emerging throughout the economy as forces such as globalization, e-commerce, and

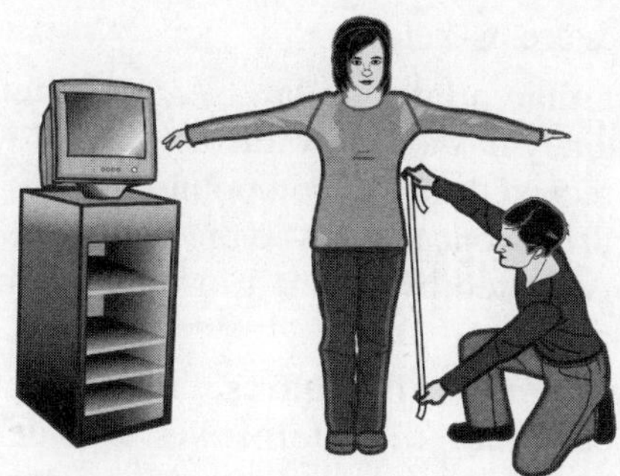

A sales clerk measures the customer, using instructions from a computer as an aid.

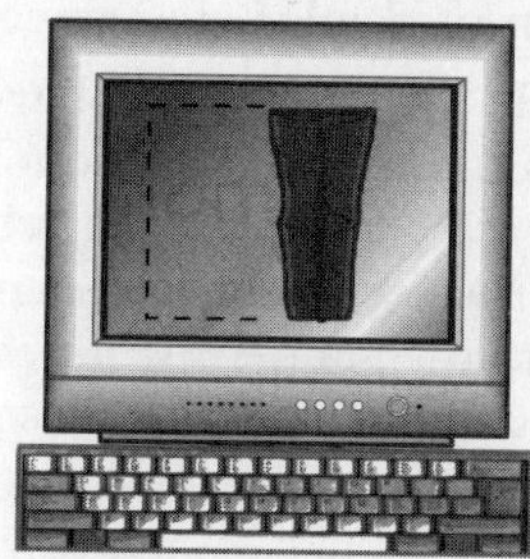

The clerk enters the measurements and adjusts the data, according to the customer's reaction to the samples.

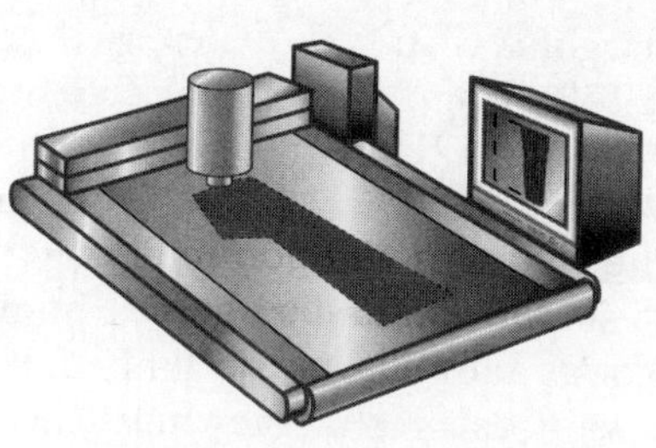

The final measurements are relayed to a computerized fabric cutting machine at the factory.

Bar codes are attached to the clothing to track it as it is assembled, washed, and prepared for shipment.

Figure 1.8   To make customized blue jeans for women, a new computerized system is being installed at some retail stores, allowing women to place customized orders

environmental reuse concerns create the need by businesses for ever more decentralization and outsourcing of operations and processes.

Investments in this category include any activities to support the improvement of productivity, quality, and customer satisfaction in the service sector, such as in the financial, healthcare, and retail industries. See Figure 1.8 for an example of a service improvement in retail where a blue jeans manufacturer is considering installing robotic tailors. The manufacturer's main problem is to determine how much demand the women's line would generate: How many more jeans would the manufacturer need to sell to justify the cost of additional tailors? This analysis should involve a comparison of the cost of operating additional robotic tailors with additional revenues generated by increased jeans sales.

1.4 Fundamental Principles in Engineering Economics

This book focuses on the principles and procedures for making sound engineering economic decisions. To the first-time student of engineering economics, anything related to money matters may seem quite strange compared with other engineering subjects. However, the decision logic involved in problem solving is quite similar to any other engineering subject matter; there are basic fundamental principles to follow in any engineering economic decision. These principles unite to form the concepts and techniques presented in the text, thereby allowing us to focus on the logic underlying the practice of engineering economics.

The four principles of engineering economics are as follows:

- **Principle 1: An earlier dollar is worth more than a later dollar.** A fundamental concept in engineering economics is that money has a time value associated with it. Because we can earn interest on money received today (compound interest), it is better to receive money earlier than later. This concept will be the basic foundation for all engineering project evaluation. As noted by Albert Einstein, the most powerful force in the universe is compound interest.

- **Principle 2: All that counts is the differences among alternatives.** An economic decision should be based on the differences among the alternatives considered. All that is common is irrelevant to the decision. Certainly, any economic decision is no better than any one of the alternatives being considered. Therefore, an economic decision should be based on the objective of making the best use of limited resources. Whenever a choice is made, something is given up. The *opportunity cost* of a choice is the value of the best alternative given up.

- **Principle 3: Marginal revenue must exceed marginal cost.** Any increased economic activity must be justified based on the following fundamental economic principle: Marginal revenue must exceed marginal cost. Here, the marginal revenue is the additional revenue made possible by increasing the activity by one unit (or a small unit). Similarly, marginal cost is the additional cost incurred by the same increase in activity. Productive resources, such as natural resources, human resources, and capital goods available to make goods and services, are limited. People cannot have all the goods and services they want; as a result, they must choose resources that produce with the best economy.

- **Principle 4: Additional risk is not taken without expected additional return.** For delaying consumption, investors demand a minimum return that must be greater than the anticipated rate of inflation or than any perceived risk. If they do not see themselves receiving enough to compensate for anticipated inflation and perceived investment risk, investors may purchase whatever goods they desire ahead of time or invest in assets that would provide a sufficient return to compensate for any loss from inflation or potential risk.

These four principles are as much statements of common sense as they are theoretical principles. They provide the logic behind what follows in this book. We build on the principles and attempt to draw out their implications for decision making. As we continue, try to keep in mind that while the topics being treated may change from chapter to chapter, the logic driving our treatment of them is constant and rooted in these four fundamental principles.

SUMMARY

- This chapter provides an overview of a variety of engineering economic problems that commonly are found in the business world. We examined the place of engineers in a firm, and we saw that engineers play an increasingly important role in companies, as evidenced in Voyager Ethanol's development of a commercial-scale biorefinery plant. Commonly, engineers participate in a variety of strategic business decisions ranging from product design to marketing.

- The term *engineering economic decision* refers to all investment decisions relating to an engineering project. The most interesting facet of an economic decision, from an engineer's point of view, is the evaluation of costs and benefits associated with making a capital investment.

■ The five main types of engineering economic decisions are (1) new products or product expansion, (2) equipment and process selection, (3) cost reduction, (4) equipment replacement, and (5) service or quality improvement,

■ The factors of time and uncertainty are the defining aspects of any investment project.

SELF-TEST QUESTIONS

1s.1 Which of the following statements is incorrect?
(a) Economic decisions are time invariant.
(b) Time and risk are the most important factors in any investment evaluation.
(c) For a large-scale engineering project, engineers must consider the impact of the project on the company's financial statements.
(d) One of the primary roles of engineers is to make capital expenditure decisions.

1s.2 When evaluating a large-scale engineering project, which of the following items is important?
(a) Expected profitability
(b) Timing of cash flows
(c) Degree of financial risk
(d) All of the above

1s.3 Which of the following statements defines the discipline of engineering economics most closely?
(a) Economic decisions made by engineers.
(b) Economic decisions related to financial assets.
(c) Economic decisions primarily for real assets and services from engineering projects.
(d) Any economic decision related to the time value of money.

1s.4 Which of the following statements is not one of the four fundamental principles of engineering economics?
(a) Receiving a dollar today is worth more than a dollar received in the future.
(b) To expect a higher return on investment, you need to take a higher risk.
(c) Marginal revenue must exceed marginal cost to justify any production.
(d) When you are comparing different alternatives, you must not focus only differences in alternatives.

PROBLEMS

1.1 Read the *Wall Street Journal* over a one-week period and identify the business investment news using one of the categories—(1) new products or product expansion, (2) equipment and process selection, (3) cost reduction, (4) equipment replacement, or (5) service or quality improvement.

1.2 By reading any business publication give examples that illustrate one of the four fundamental principles of engineering economics.

CHAPTER TWO

Time Value of Money

Winner of $25.6 Million Powerball Jackpot Claims Prize[1] Jimmy Freeman, a retired U.S. Navy civilian worker from Fall River, Massachusetts, came forward to claim his jackpot just several hours after learning he won the $25.6 million prize in the June 8th Powerball drawing. His winning numbers, 14-37-44-45-53, PB 29, were selected by Quic Pic. Freeman said he plays a few dollars every-day around town, mostly Quic Pics, and he has always prayed and dreamed that he would someday win a big jackpot—today his dream came true.

Powerball®[2] is a combined large jackpot game and a cash game. Every Wednesday and Saturday night at 10:59 p.m. Eastern Time, we draw five white balls out of a drum with 59 balls and one red ball [in green here] out of a drum with 39 red balls [in green here].

Match	Prize	Odds
● ● ● ● ● + ●	Grand Prize	1 in 195,249,054.00
● ● ● ● ●	$200,000	1 in 5,138,133.00
● ● ● ● + ●	$10,000	1 in 723, 144.64
● ● ● ●	$100	1 in 19,030.12
● ● ● + ●	$100	1 in 13,644.24
● ● ●	$7	1 in 359.06
● ● + ●	$7	1 in 787.17
● + ●	$4	1 in 123.48
●	$3	1 in 61.74

The overall odds of winning a prize are 1 in 35.11.
The odds presented here are based on a $1 play (rounded to two decimal places).

Players win by matching one of the 9 Ways to Win. The jackpot (won by matching all five white balls in any order and the red [in green here] Powerball) is either an annuitized prize paid out over 29 years

[1] "Jimmy Freeman—Winner of $25.6 Million Powerball Jackpot Claims Prize," Powerball Press Release, June 8, 2011.
[2] *Source:* www.powerball.com.

(30 payments) or a lump sum payment. Each ticket costs $1.[3] If the winner chooses the annuity, the annual payment will be increased each year by the percentage set out in the Powerball game rules. Freeman opted to take the one-time, lump sum payment[4] of $13.5 million ($13,493,470.86 before taxes, to be exact). It will take approximately two weeks to process the multistate prize payment.

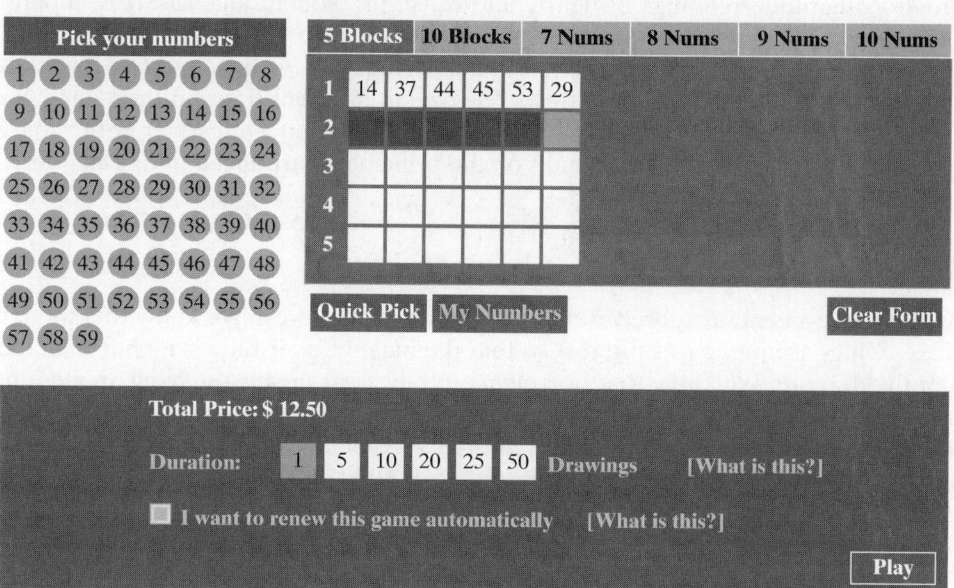

If you were the winner of the aforementioned jackpot, you might well wonder why the value of the single-sum payment—$13.5 million paid immediately—is so much lower than the total value of the annuity payments—$25.6 million paid in 30 installments over 29 years (the first installment is paid immediately). Isn't receiving $25.6 million overall a lot better than receiving just $13.5 million now? The answer to your question involves the principles we will discuss in this chapter, namely, the operation of interest and the time value of money.

---

[3] The price of a Powerball ticket will double in 2012 when the multistate lottery marks its 20th anniversary. The jackpots also will increase.

[4] In Powerball history between 2003 and 2011, only three out of 115 winners opted for annuity options.

The question we just posed provides a good starting point for this chapter. If it is better to receive a dollar today than it is to receive a dollar in 10 years, how do we quantify the difference? Our lottery example is complex. Instead of a choice between two single payments, the lottery winners were faced with a decision between a single payment now and a series of future payments. First, most people familiar with investments would tell you that receiving $13.5 million today is likely to prove a better deal than taking $853,333 a year for 29 years. In fact, based on the principles you will learn in this chapter, the real present value of the 29-year payment series—the value that you could receive today in the financial marketplace for the promise of $853,333 a year for the next 29 years—can be shown to be considerably less than $13.5 million. And that is even before we consider the effects of inflation! The reason for this surprising result is the **time value of money**; the earlier a sum of money is received, the more it is worth because over time money can earn more money via interest.

In engineering economic analysis, the principles discussed in this chapter are regarded as the underpinnings of nearly all project investment analysis. It is imperative to understand these principles because we always need to account for the effect of interest operating on sums of cash over time. Fortunately, we have interest formulas that allow us to place different cash flows received at different times in the same time frame to make comparisons possible. As will become apparent, almost our entire study of engineering economic analysis is built on the principles introduced in this chapter.

2.1 Interest: The Cost of Money

Most of us have a general appreciation of the concept of interest. We know that money left in a savings account earns interest so that the balance over time is higher than the sum of the deposits. We know that borrowing to buy a car means repaying an amount over time, including the interest, and thus the amount paid is more than the amount borrowed. However, what may be unfamiliar to us is that, in the financial world, money itself is a commodity, and like other goods that are bought and sold, money costs money.

The cost of money is established and measured by an **interest rate**, a percentage that is periodically applied and added to an amount (or to varying amounts) of money over a specified length of time. When money is borrowed, the interest paid is the charge to the borrower for the use of the lender's property. When money is loaned or invested, the interest earned is the lender's gain for providing a good to another person. **Interest**, then, may be defined as the cost of having money available for use. In this section, we examine how interest operates in a free-market economy and establish a basis for understanding the more complex interest relationships that are presented later in the chapter.

2.1.1 The Time Value of Money

The time value of money seems like a sophisticated concept, yet it is one that you encounter every day. Should you buy something today or buy it later? Here is a simple example of how your buying behavior can have varying results: Pretend you have $100 and you want to buy a $100 refrigerator for your dorm room. (Assume that you are currently sharing a large refrigerator with your roommates in a common area.)

- If you buy it now, you end up broke. But if you invest your money at 6% annual interest, then in a year you can still buy the refrigerator, and you will have $6 left

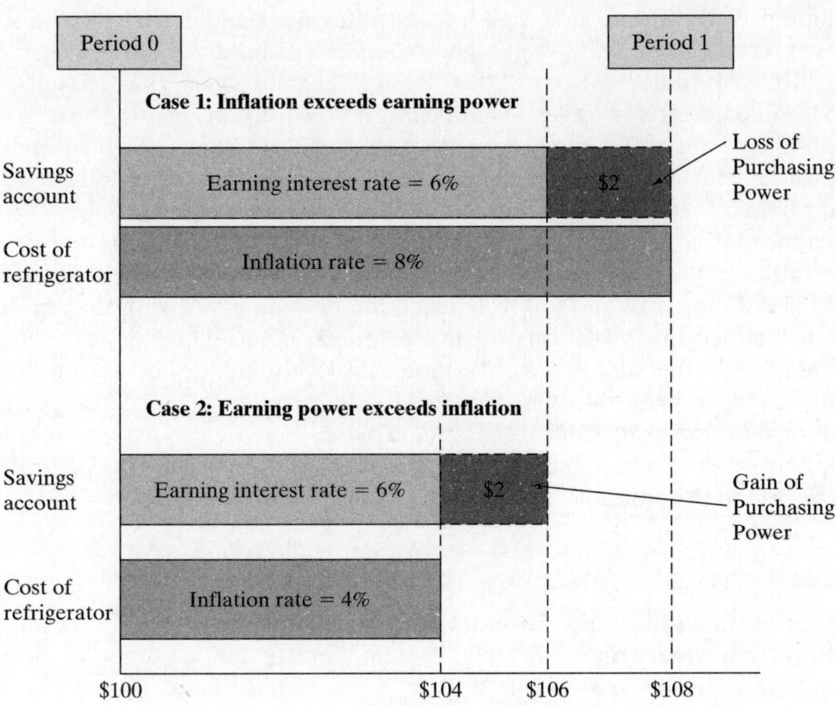

Figure 2.1   Gains achieved or losses incurred by delaying consumption

over. Clearly, you need to ask yourself whether the inconvenience of not having the refrigerator in your own room for a year can be compensated by the financial gain in the amount of $6.

- If the price of the refrigerator increases at an annual rate of 8% due to inflation, then you will not have enough money (you will be $2 short) to buy the refrigerator a year from now (Case 1 in Figure 2.1). In that case, you probably are better off buying the refrigerator now. If the inflation rate is running at only 4%, then you will have $2 left over if you buy the refrigerator a year from now (Case 2 in Figure 2.1).

Clearly, the rate at which you earn interest should be higher than the inflation rate in order to make any economic sense of the delayed purchase. In other words, in an inflationary economy, your purchasing power will continue to decrease as you further delay the purchase of the refrigerator. In order to make up for this future loss in purchasing power, the rate at which you earn interest must be sufficiently higher than the anticipated inflation rate. After all, time, like money, is a finite resource. There are only 24 hours in a day, so time has to be budgeted, too. What this example illustrates is that we must connect *earning power* and *purchasing power* to the concept of time.

The way interest operates reflects the fact that money has a time value. This is why amounts of interest depend on lengths of time; interest rates, for example, are typically given in terms of a percentage per year. We may define the principle of the time value of money as follows: The economic value of a sum depends on when the sum is received. Because money has both **earning power** and **purchasing power** over time (i.e., it can be put to work, earning more money for its owner), a dollar received today has a higher value than a dollar received at some future time. When we deal with large amounts of money, long periods of time, and high interest rates, a change in the value of a sum of money over time becomes extremely significant. For example, at a current annual interest rate of 10%, $1 million will earn $100,000 in interest in a year; thus, to wait a year to receive $1 million clearly involves a significant sacrifice. When deciding among alternative proposals, we must take into account the operation of interest and the time value of money in order to make valid comparisons of different amounts at various times.

When financial institutions quote lending or borrowing interest rates in the marketplace, those interest rates reflect the desired earning rate as well as any protection from loss in the future purchasing power of money because of inflation. Interest rates, adjusted for inflation, rise and fall to balance the amount saved with the amount borrowed, which affects the allocation of scarce resources between present and future uses.

Unless stated otherwise, we will assume that the interest rates used in this book reflect the **market interest rate**, which considers the earning power of money as well as the effect of inflation perceived in the marketplace. We will also assume that all cash flow transactions are given in terms of **actual dollars**, for which the effect of inflation, if any, is reflected in the amount.

2.1.2 Elements of Transactions Involving Interest

Many types of transactions involve interest (e.g., borrowing money, investing money, or purchasing machinery on credit), and certain elements are common to all of these types of transactions. These elements are:

1. The initial amount of money invested or borrowed in a transaction is called the **principal** (P).
2. The **interest rate** (i) measures the cost or price of money and is expressed as a percentage per period of time.
3. A period of time called the **interest period** (n) determines how frequently interest is calculated. (Note that, even though the length of time of an interest period can vary, interest rates are frequently quoted in terms of an annual percentage rate. We will discuss this potentially confusing aspect of interest in Chapter 3.)
4. A specified length of time marks the duration of the transaction and thereby establishes a certain **number of interest periods** (N).
5. **A plan for receipts or disbursements** (A_n) yields a particular cash flow pattern over a specified length of time. (For example, we might have a series of equal monthly payments that repay a loan.)
6. A **future amount of money** (F) results from the cumulative effects of the interest rate over a number of interest periods.

Example of an Interest Transaction

As an example of how the elements we have just defined are used in a particular situation, let us suppose that you apply for an education loan in the amount of $30,000 from a bank at a 9% annual interest rate. In addition, you pay a $300 loan origination fee[5] when

---

[5] The loan origination fee covers the administrative costs of processing the loan. It is often expressed in points. One point is 1% of the loan amount. In our example, the $30,000 loan with a loan origination fee of one point would mean the borrower pays a $300 fee. This is equivalent to financing $29,700, but the payments are based on a $30,000 loan. Both payment plans are based on a rate of 9% interest.

TABLE 2.1 **Repayment Plans Offered by the Lender**

End of Year	Receipts	Payments	
		Plan 1	Plan 2
Year 0	$30,000	$300.00	$300.00
Year 1		$7,712.77	0
Year 2		$7,712.77	0
Year 3		$7,712.77	0
Year 4		$7,712.77	0
Year 5		$7,712.77	$46,158.72

the loan commences. The bank offers two repayment plans, one with equal payments made at the end of every year for the next five years (installment plan) and the other with a single payment made after the loan period of five years (deferment plan). These payment plans are summarized in Table 2.1.

- In Plan 1, the principal amount, P, is $30,000 and the interest rate, i, is 9%. The interest period, n, is one year, and the duration of the transaction is five years, which means that there are five interest periods ($N = 5$). It bears repeating that while one year is a common interest period, interest is frequently calculated at other intervals as well—monthly, quarterly, or semiannually, for instance. For this reason, we used the term **period** rather than **year** when we defined the preceding list of variables. The receipts and disbursements planned over the duration of this transaction yield a cash flow pattern of five equal payments, A, of $7,712.77 each, paid at year-end during years 1 through 5.
- Plan 2 has most of the elements of Plan 1 except that instead of five equal repayments, we have a grace period followed by a single future repayment (lump sum), F, of $46,158.72.

Cash Flow Diagrams

Problems involving the time value of money can be conveniently represented in graphic form with a **cash flow diagram** (Figure 2.2). Cash flow diagrams represent time by a horizontal line marked off with the number of interest periods specified. Arrows represent the cash flows over time at relevant periods. Upward arrows represent positive flows (receipts), and downward arrows represent negative flows (expenditures). Note, too, that the arrows actually represent **net cash flows**; two or more receipts or disbursements made at the same time are summed and shown as a single arrow. For example, $30,000 received during the same period as a $300 payment is being made would be recorded as an upward arrow of $29,700. The lengths of the arrows can also suggest the relative values of particular cash flows.

Cash flow diagrams function in a manner similar to free-body diagrams or circuit diagrams, which most engineers frequently use. Cash flow diagrams give a convenient summary of all the important elements of a problem and serve as a reference point for determining whether the elements of a problem have been converted into their

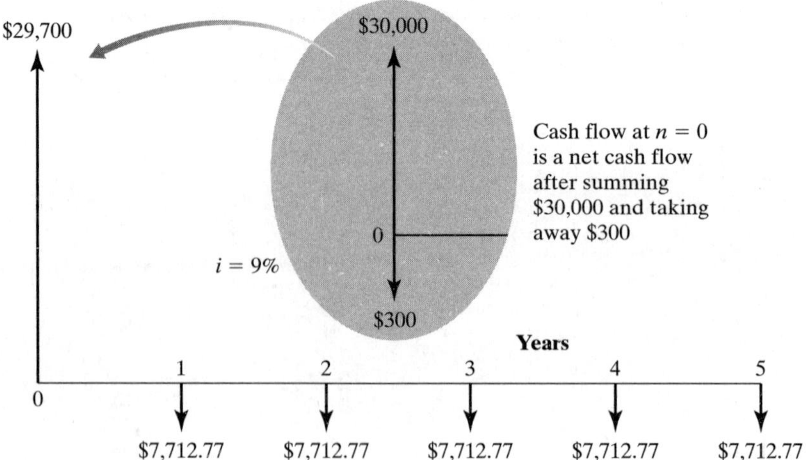

Figure 2.2 A cash flow diagram for Plan 1 of the loan repayment example

appropriate parameters. This book frequently employs this graphic tool, and you are strongly encouraged to develop the habit of using well-labeled cash flow diagrams as a means to identify and summarize pertinent information in a cash flow problem. Similarly, a table such as Table 2.1 can help you organize information in another summary format.

End-of-Period Convention

In practice, cash flows can occur at the *beginning* or in the *middle* of an interest period or at practically any point in time. One of the simplifying assumptions we make in engineering economic analysis is the **end-of-period convention**, which is the practice of placing all cash flow transactions at the *end* of an interest period. This assumption relieves us of the responsibility of dealing with the effects of interest within an interest period, which would greatly complicate our calculations. Like many of the simplifying assumptions and estimates we make in modeling engineering economic problems, the end-of-period convention inevitably leads to some discrepancies between our model and real-world results.

Suppose, for example, that $100,000 is deposited during the first month of the year in an account with an interest period of one year and an interest rate of 10% per year. In such a case, if the deposit is withdrawn one month before the end of the year, the investor would experience a loss of $10,000—all of it interest! This results because, under the end-of-period convention, the $100,000 deposit made during the interest period is viewed as if it were made at the end of the year, as opposed to 11 months earlier. This example gives you a sense of why financial institutions choose interest periods that are less than one year, even though they usually quote their rate in terms of *annual percentage*. Armed with an understanding of the basic elements involved in interest problems, we can now begin to look at the details of calculating interest.

2.1.3 Methods of Calculating Interest

Money can be loaned and repaid in many ways, and similarly, money can earn interest in many different ways. Usually, however, at the end of each interest period, the interest earned on the principal amount is calculated according to a specified interest rate. There are two computational schemes for calculating this earned interest yield: **simple interest** and **compound interest**.

Simple Interest

The first scheme considers interest earned on only the principal amount during each interest period. In other words, the interest earned during each interest period does not earn additional interest in the remaining periods, *even if you do not withdraw the earned interest.*

In general, for a deposit of P dollars at a simple interest rate of i for N periods, the total earned interest I would be

$$I = (iP)N. \tag{2.1}$$

The total amount available at the end of N periods, F, thus would be

$$F = P + I = P(1 + iN). \tag{2.2}$$

Simple interest is commonly used with add-on loans or bonds.

Compound Interest

Under a compound interest scheme, the interest earned in each period is calculated based on the total amount at the end of the previous period. This total amount includes the original principal plus the accumulated interest that has been left in the account. In this case, you are, in effect, increasing the deposit amount by the amount of interest earned. In general, if you deposited (invested) P dollars at an interest rate i, you would have $P + iP = P(1 + i)$ dollars at the end of one interest period. If the entire amount (principal and interest) were reinvested at the same rate i for another period, you would have at the end of the second period

$$P(1 + i) + i[P(1 + i)] = P(1 + i)(1 + i)$$
$$= P(1 + i)^2.$$

Continuing, we see that the balance after period three is

$$P(1 + i)^2 + i[P(1 + i)^2] = P(1 + i)^3.$$

This interest-earning process repeats, and after N periods, the total accumulated value (balance) F will grow to

$$F = P(1 + i)^N. \tag{2.3}$$

Engineering economic analysis uses the compound interest scheme exclusively, as it is most frequently practiced in the real world.

EXAMPLE 2.1 Simple versus Compound Interest

Suppose you deposit $1,000 in a bank savings account that pays interest at a rate of 8% per year. Assume that you do not withdraw the interest earned at the end of each period (year) but instead let it accumulate. (1) How much would you have at the end of year 3 with simple interest? (2) How much would you have at the end of year 3 with compound interest?

DISSECTING THE PROBLEM

Given: $P = \$1,000, N = 3$ years, and $i = 8\%$ per year.
Find: F.

METHODOLOGY

Use Eqs. (2.2) and (2.3) to calculate the total amount accumulated under each computational scheme.

SOLUTION

(a) Simple interest: Using Eq. (2.2) we calculate F as

$$F = \$1,000 \left[1 + (0.08)3 \right] = \$1,240.$$

Year by year, the interest accrues as shown:

End of Year	Beginning Balance	Interest Earned	Ending Balance
1	$1,000	$80	$1,080
2	$1,080	$80	$1,160
3	$1,160	$80	$1,240

(b) Compound interest: Applying Eq. (2.3) to our three-year, 8% case, we obtain

$$F = \$1,000 \, (1 + 0.08)^3 = \$1,259.71.$$

The total interest earned is \$259.71, which is \$19.71 more than accumulated under the simple-interest method. We can keep track of the interest-accruing process more precisely as follows:

End of Year	Beginning Balance	Interest Earned	Ending Balance
1	$1,000.00	$80.00	1,080.00
2	$1,080.00	$86.40	1,166.40
3	$1,166.40	$93.31	1,259.71

COMMENTS: At the end of the first year, you would have a total of \$1,080—\$1,000 plus \$80 in interest. In effect, at the beginning of the second year, you would be depositing \$1,080, rather than \$1,000. Thus, at the end of the second year, the interest earned would be 0.08(\$1,080) = \$86.40 and the balance would be \$1,080 + \$86.40 = \$1,166.40. This is the equivalent amount you would be depositing at the beginning of the third year, and the interest earned for that period would be 0.08(\$1,166.40) = \$93.31. With a beginning principal amount of \$1,166.40 plus the \$93.31 interest, the total balance would be \$1,259.71 at the end of year 3.

2.2 Economic Equivalence

The observation that money has a time value leads us to an important question: If receiving \$100 today is not the same as receiving \$100 at any future point, how do we measure and compare various cash flows? How do we know, for example, whether we

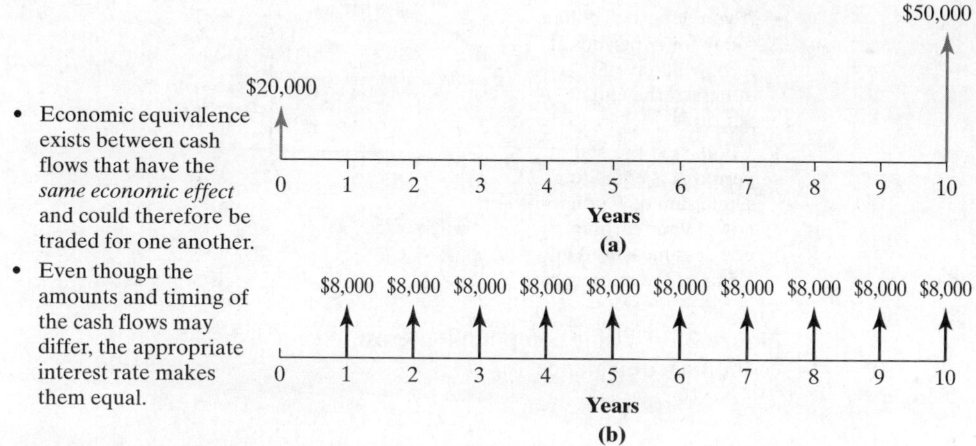

- Economic equivalence exists between cash flows that have the *same economic effect* and could therefore be traded for one another.
- Even though the amounts and timing of the cash flows may differ, the appropriate interest rate makes them equal.

Figure 2.3   Which option would you prefer? (a) Two payments ($20,000 now and $50,000 at the end of 10 years) or (b) 10 equal annual receipts in the amount of $8,000 each

should prefer to have $20,000 today and $50,000 in 10 years from now, or $8,000 each year for the next 10 years? (See Figure 2.3.) In this section, we will describe the basic analytical techniques for making these comparisons. Then in Section 2.3, we will use these techniques to develop a series of formulas that can greatly simplify our calculations.

2.2.1 Definition and Simple Calculations

The central factor in deciding among alternative cash flows involves comparing their economic worth. This would be a simple matter if, in the comparison, we did not need to consider the time value of money. We could simply add up the individual payments within a cash flow, treating receipts as positive cash flows and payments (disbursements) as negative cash flows. The fact that money has a time value makes our calculations more complicated. Calculations for determining the economic effects of one or more cash flows are based on the concept of economic equivalence.

Economic equivalence exists between cash flows that have the same economic effect and could therefore be traded for one another in the financial marketplace (which we assume to exist). Economic equivalence refers to the fact that any cash flow—whether a single payment or a series of payments—can be converted to an *equivalent* cash flow at any point in time. The critical thinking on the present value of future cash flows is that the present sum is equivalent in value to the future cash flows because, if you had the present value today, you could transform it into the future cash flows simply by investing it at the interest rate, also referred to as the **discount rate**. This process is shown in Figure 2.4.

The strict concept of equivalence may be extended to include the comparison of alternatives. For instance, we could compare the values of two proposals by finding the equivalent values of each at any common point in time. If financial proposals that appear to be quite different could turn out to have the same monetary value, then we can be *economically indifferent* in choosing between them. Likewise, in terms of economic effect, one would be an even exchange for the other, so there is no reason to prefer one over the other.

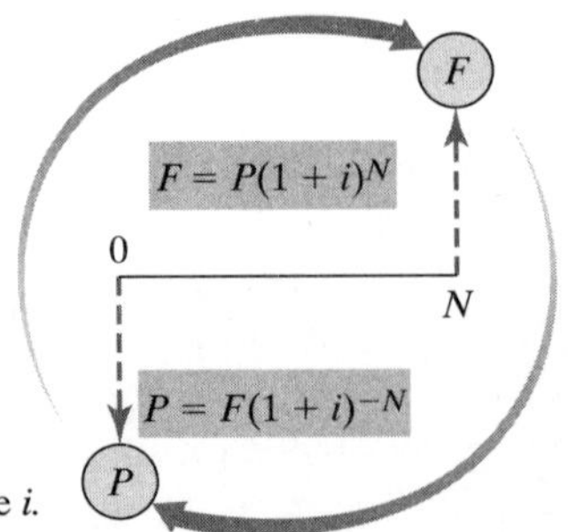

Figure 2.4   Using compound interest to establish economic equivalence

A way to see the concepts of equivalence and economic indifference at work in the real world is to note the variety of payment plans offered by lending institutions for consumer loans. Recall Table 2.1, where we showed two different repayment plans for a loan of $30,000 for five years at an annual interest rate of 9%. You will notice that the two plans require significantly different repayment patterns and different total amounts of repayment. However, because of the time value of money, these plans are equivalent—economically, the bank is indifferent to the consumer's choice of plan. We will now discuss how such equivalence relationships are established.

Equivalence Calculations: A Simple Example

Equivalence calculations can be viewed as an application of the compound-interest relationships we learned in Section 2.1. Suppose, for example, that we invest $1,000 at 12% annual interest for five years. The formula developed for calculating compound interest, $F = P(1 + i)^N$ [Eq. (2.3)], expresses the equivalence between some present amount P and a future amount F for a given interest rate i and a number of interest periods, N. Therefore, at the end of the investment period, our sums grow to

$$\$1,000(1 + 0.12)^5 = \$1,762.34.$$

Thus, we can say that at 12% interest, $1,000 received now is equivalent to $1,762.34 received in five years, and we could trade $1,000 now for the promise of receiving $1,762.34 in five years. Example 2.2 further demonstrates the application of this basic technique.

EXAMPLE 2.2 Equivalence

Suppose you are offered the alternative of receiving either $2,007 at the end of five years or $1,500 today. There is no question that the $2,007 will be paid in full (i.e., there's no risk of nonreceipt). Assuming that the money will not be needed in the next five years, you would deposit the $1,500 in an account that pays $i\%$ interest. What value of i would make you indifferent to your choice between $1,500 today and the promise of $2,007 at the end of five years?

DISSECTING THE PROBLEM

Our job is to determine the present amount that is economically equivalent to $2,007 in five years, given the investment potential of $i\%$ per year. Note that the statement of the problem assumes that you would exercise the option of using the earning power of your money by depositing it. The "indifference" ascribed to you refers to economic indifference; that is, within a marketplace where $i\%$ is the applicable interest rate, you could trade one cash flow for the other.

Given: $F = \$2,007, N = 5\,\text{years}, P = \$1,500$. See Figure 2.5a.
Find: i.

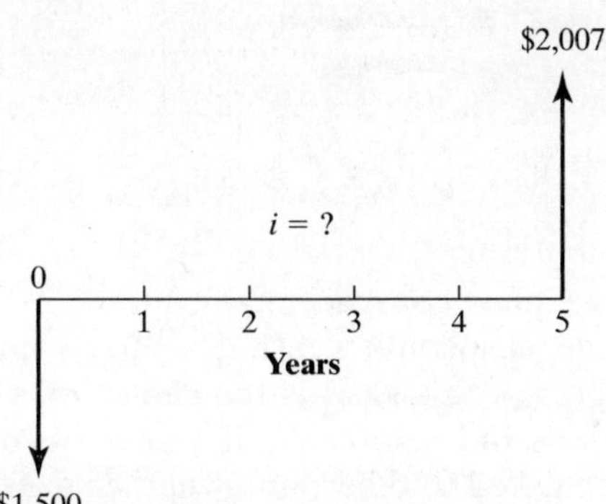

Figure 2.5a Cash flow diagram

METHODOLOGY

Use Eq. (2.3), $F = P(1 + i)^N$ and solve for i.

SOLUTION

Using the expression of Eq. (2.3) we obtain

$$\$2,007 = \$1,500(1 + i)^5$$

Solving for i yields:

$$i = \left(\frac{F}{P}\right)^{1/N} - 1 = \left(\frac{2,007}{1,500}\right)^{1/5} - 1$$

$$= 0.06 \ (\text{or } 6\%).$$

We can summarize the problem graphically as in Figure 2.5b.

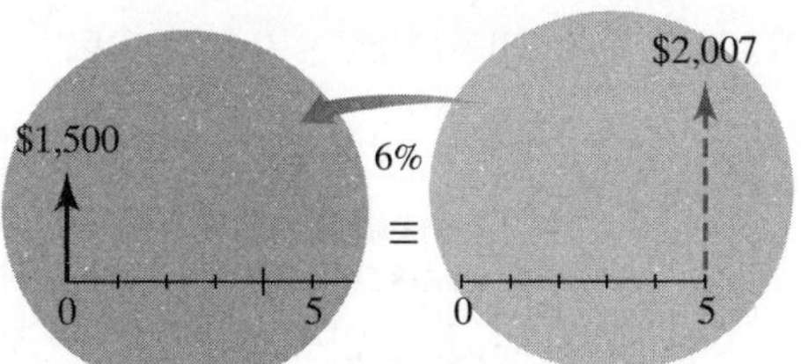

- Step 1: Determine the base period, say, year 0.
- Step 2: Identify the interest rate to use.
- Step 3: Calculate equivalent value at the base period.

$i = 3\%, P = \$2,007(1 + 0.03)^{-5} = \$1,731$
$i = 6\%, P = \$2,007(1 + 0.06)^{-5} = \$1,500$
$i = 9\%, P = \$2,007(1 + 0.09)^{-5} = \$1,304$

Figure 2.5b Equivalence calculations at varying interest rate

COMMENTS: In this example, it is clear that if i is anything less than 6%, you would prefer the promise of $2,007 in five years to $1,500 today; if i is more than 6%, you would prefer $1,500 now. As you may have already guessed, at a lower interest rate, P must be higher in order to be equivalent to the future amount. For example, at $i = 4\%, P = \$1,650$.

2.2.2 Equivalence Calculations Require a Common Time Basis for Comparison

Just as we must convert fractions to common denominators in order to add them together, we must convert cash flows to a common basis in order to compare their values. One aspect of this basis is the choice of a single point in time at which to make our calculations. In Example 2.2, if we had been given the magnitude of each cash flow and had been asked to determine whether the two were equivalent, we could have chosen any reference point and used the compound-interest formula to find the value of each cash flow at that point. As you can readily see, the choice of $n = 0$ or $n = 5$ would make our problem simpler, because we would need to make only one set of calculations: At 6% interest, either convert $1,500 at time 0 to its equivalent value at time 5, or convert $2,007 at time 5 to its equivalent value at time 0.

When selecting a point in time at which to compare the values of alternative cash flows, we commonly use either the present time, which yields what is called the **present worth** of the cash flows, or some point in the future, which yields their **future worth**. The choice of the point in time to use often depends on the circumstances surrounding a particular decision, or the choice may be made for convenience. For instance, if the present worth is known for the first two of three alternatives, simply calculating the present worth of the third will allow us to compare all three. For an illustration, consider Example 2.3.

EXAMPLE 2.3 Equivalence Calculations

Consider the cash flow series given in Figure 2.6. Compute the equivalent lump-sum amount at $n = 3$ at 10% annual interest.

DISSECTING THE PROBLEM

Given: The cash flows given in Figure 2.6, and $i = 10\%$ per year.
Find: V_3 (or equivalent worth at $n = 3$).

METHODOLOGY

We find the equivalent worth at $n = 3$ in two steps. First, we find the future worth of each cash flow at $n = 3$ for all cash flows that occur before $n = 3$. Second, we find the present worth of each cash flow at $n = 3$ for all cash flows that occur after $n = 3$.

SOLUTION

- **Step 1:** Find the equivalent lump-sum payment of the first four payments at $n = 3$:

$$\$100(1 + 0.10)^3 + \$80(1 + 0.10)^2$$
$$+ \$120(1 + 0.10)^1 + \$150 = \$511.90.$$

- **Step 2:** Find the equivalent lump-sum payment of the remaining two payments at $n = 3$:

$$\$200(1 + 0.10)^{-1} + \$100(1 + 0.10)^{-2} = \$264.46.$$

- **Step 3:** Find V_3, the total equivalent value:

$$V_3 = \$511.90 + \$264.46 = \$776.36.$$

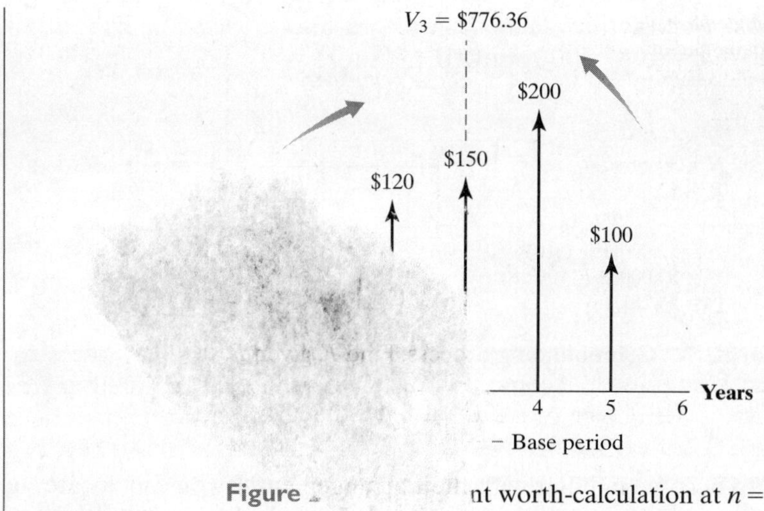

Figure _ _ nt worth-calculation at $n = 3$

2.3 Interest Formulas for Single Cash Flows

We begin our coverage of interest formulas by considering the simplest of cash flows:
single cash flows.

2.3.1 Compound-Amount Factor

Given a present sum P invested for N interest periods at interest rate i, what sum will
have accumulated at the end of the N periods? You probably noticed right away that
this description matches the case we first encountered in describing compound interest. To solve for F (the future sum), we use Eq. (2.3):

$$F = P(1 + i)^N.$$

Because of its origin in the compound-interest calculation, the factor $(1 + i)^N$ is
known as the **compound-amount factor**. Like the concept of equivalence, this factor
is one of the foundations of engineering economic analysis. Given this factor, all other
important interest formulas can be derived.

The process of finding F is often called the **compounding process**. The cash flow
transaction is illustrated in Figure 2.7. (Note the time-scale convention: The first period
begins at $n = 0$ and ends at $n = 1$.) If a calculator is handy, it is easy enough to calculate $(1 + i)^N$ directly.

Interest Tables

Interest formulas such as the one developed in Eq. (2.3), $F = P(1 + i)^N$, allow us to
substitute known values from a particular situation into the equation and solve for
the unknown. Before the calculator was developed, solving these equations was very
tedious. Imagine needing to solve by hand an equation with a large value of N, such as
$F = \$20,000(1 + 0.12)^{15}$. More complex formulas required even more involved calcu-
lations. To simplify the process, tables of compound-interest factors were developed.
These tables allow us to find the appropriate factor for a given interest rate and the
number of interest periods. Even though calculators are now readily available, it is still
often convenient to use these tables, which are included in this text in Appendix B.

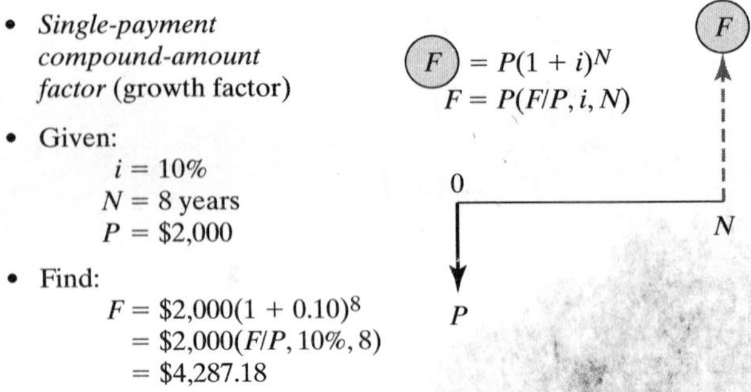

Figure 2.7   Compounding process: Find F, given P, i, and N

Take some time now to become familiar with their arrangement. If you can, locate the compound-interest factor for the example just presented, in which we know P and, to find F, we need to know the factor by which to multiply \$20,000 when the interest rate i is 12% and the number of periods is 15:

$$F = \$20,000 \underbrace{(1 + 0.12)^{15}}_{5.4736} = \$109,472.$$

Factor Notation

As we continue to develop interest formulas in the rest of this chapter, we will express the resulting compound-interest factors in a conventional notation that can be substituted into a formula to indicate precisely which table factor to use in solving an equation. In the preceding example, for instance, the formula derived as Eq. (2.3) is $F = P(1 + i)^N$. To specify how the interest tables are to be used, we may also express that factor in a functional notation as $(F/P, i, N)$, which is read as "Find F, given P, i, and N." This factor is known as the **single-payment compound-amount factor**. When we incorporate the table factor into the formula, the formula is expressed as follows:

$$F = P(1 + i)^N = P(F/P, i, N).$$

Thus, in the preceding example, where we had $F = \$20,000(1.12)^{15}$, we can now write $F = \$20,000(F/P, 12\%, 15)$. The table factor tells us to use the 12% interest table and find the factor in the F/P column for $N = 15$. Because using the interest tables is often the easiest way to solve an equation, this factor notation is included for each of the formulas derived in the upcoming sections.

EXAMPLE 2.4 Single Amounts: Find *F*, Given *P*, *i*, and *N*

If you had \$1,000 now and invested it at 7% interest compounded annually, how much would it be worth in eight years (Figure 2.8)?

DISSECTING THE PROBLEM	
	Given: $P = \$1,000$, $i = 7\%$ per year, and $N = 8$ years. **Find:** F.

METHODOLOGY	SOLUTION
Method 1: Using a Calculator You can simply use a calculator to evaluate the $(1 + i)^N$ term (financial calculators are preprogrammed to solve most future-value problems).	$$F = \$1,000(1 + 0.07)^8$$ $$= \$1,718.19.$$
Method 2: Using Compound-Interest Tables The interest tables can be used to locate the compound-amount factor for $i = 7\%$ and $N = 8$. The number you get can be substituted into the equation. Compound-interest tables are included in Appendix B of this book.	Using this method, we obtain $$F = \$1,000(F/P,7\%,8) = \$1,000(1.7182) = \$1,718.20.$$ This amount is essentially identical to the value obtained by direct evaluation of the single cash flow compound-amount factor. The slight deviation is due to rounding differences.
Method 3: Using a Computer Many financial software programs for solving compound-interest problems are available for use with personal computers. As summarized in the back cover, many spreadsheet programs such as Excel also provide financial functions to evaluate various interest formulas.	With Excel, the future-worth calculation looks like the following: $$= FV(7\%,8,0,-1000,0)$$ $$= \$1,718.20.$$ 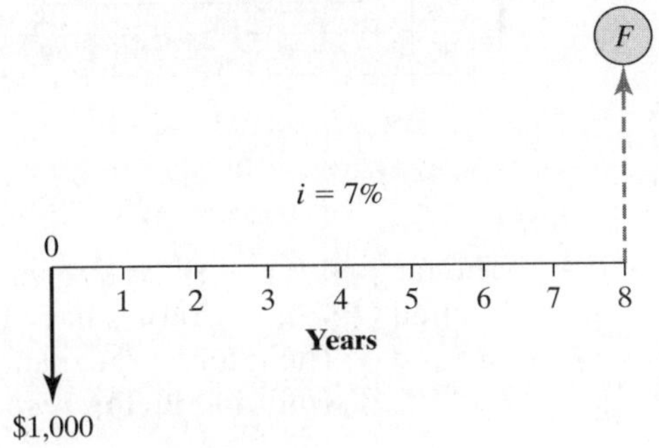

Figure 2.8   Cash flow diagram

COMMENTS: A better way to take advantage of the powerful features of Excel is to develop a worksheet as shown in Table 2.2. Here, we are not calculating just the future worth of the single payment today. Instead, we can show in both tabular and graphical form how the deposit balances change over time. For example, the $1,000 deposit today will grow to $1,500.73 in six years. If you want to see how the cash balances change over time at a higher interest rate, say, 10%, you just change the interest rate in cell C6 and press the "ENTER" button.

2.3.2 Present-Worth Factor

Finding the present worth of a future sum is simply the reverse of compounding and is known as the **discounting process**. (See Figure 2.9.) In Eq. (2.3), we can see that if we need to find a present sum P, given a future sum F, we simply solve for P:

$$P = F\left[\frac{1}{(1 + i)^N}\right] = F(P/F,i,N). \tag{2.4}$$

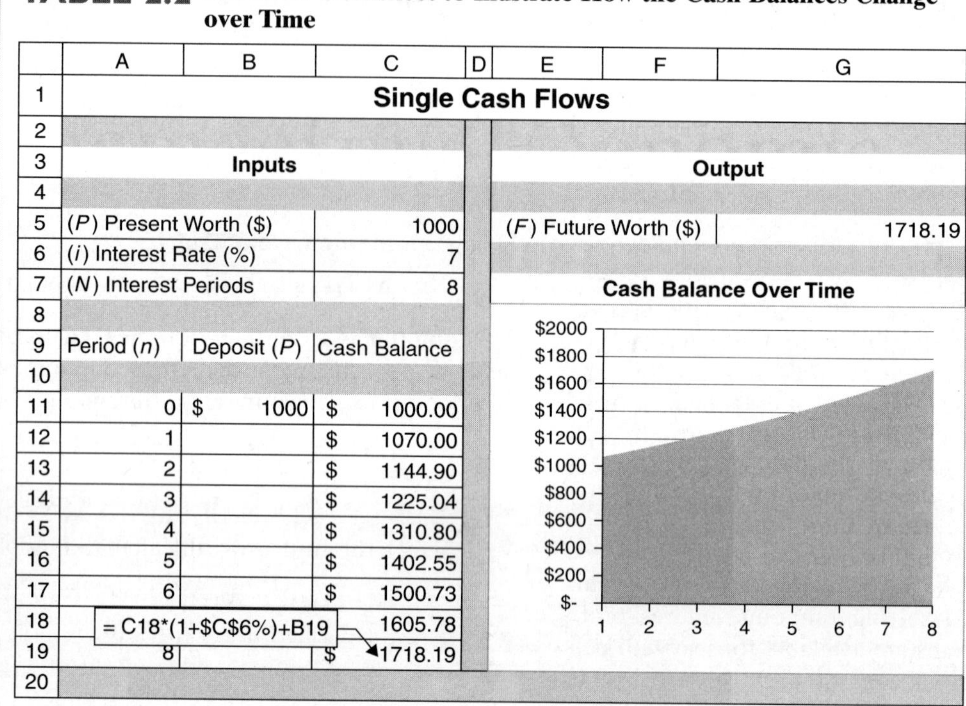

TABLE 2.2 An Excel Worksheet to Illustrate How the Cash Balances Change over Time

	A	B	C	D	E	F	G
1	**Single Cash Flows**						
2							
3	**Inputs**				**Output**		
4							
5	(*P*) Present Worth ($)		1000		(*F*) Future Worth ($)		1718.19
6	(*i*) Interest Rate (%)		7				
7	(*N*) Interest Periods		8		**Cash Balance Over Time**		
8							
9	Period (*n*)	Deposit (*P*)	Cash Balance				
10							
11	0	$ 1000	$ 1000.00				
12	1		$ 1070.00				
13	2		$ 1144.90				
14	3		$ 1225.04				
15	4		$ 1310.80				
16	5		$ 1402.55				
17	6		$ 1500.73				
18	= C18*(1+$C$6%)+B19		1605.78				
19	8		$ 1718.19				
20							

The factor $1/(1 + i)^N$ is known as the **single-payment present-worth factor** and is designated $(P/F, i, N)$. Tables have been constructed for P/F factors and for various values of i and N. The interest rate i and the P/F factor are also referred to as the **discount rate** and the **discounting factor**, respectively.

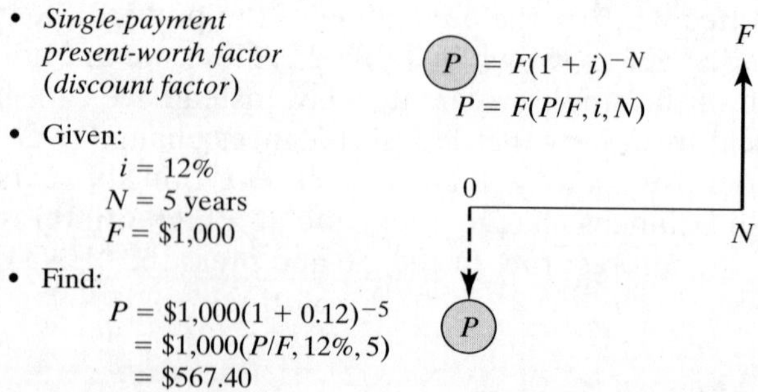

Figure 2.9 Discounting process: Find P, given F, i, and N

EXAMPLE 2.5 Single Amounts: Find *P*, Given *F*, *i*, and *N*

A zero-coupon bond[6] is a popular variation on the bond theme for some investors. What should be the price of an eight-year zero-coupon bond with a face value of $1,000 if similar, nonzero-coupon bonds are yielding 6% annual interest?

DISSECTING THE PROBLEM

As an investor of a zero-coupon bond, you do not receive any interest payments until the bond reaches maturity. When the bond matures, you will receive $1,000 (the face value). In lieu of getting interest payments, you can buy the bond at a discount. The question is, "What should the price of the bond be in order to realize a 6% return on your investment?" (See Figure 2.10.)

METHODOLOGY

Using a calculator may be the best way to make this simple calculation. It is equivalent to finding the present value of the $1,000 face value at 6% interest.

Given: $F = \$1,000, i = 6\%$ per year, and $N = 8$ years.
Find: P.

SOLUTION

Using a calculator, we obtain

$$P = \$1,000(1 + 0.06)^{-8} = \$1,000(0.6274) = \$627.40.$$

We can also use the interest tables to find that

$$P = \$1,000(\overset{(0.6274)}{P/F, 6\%, 8}) = \$627.40.$$

Again, you could also use a financial calculator or computer to find the present worth. With Excel, the present-value calculation looks like the following:

$$= \text{PV}(6\%,8,0,1000,0)$$
$$= -\$627.40.$$

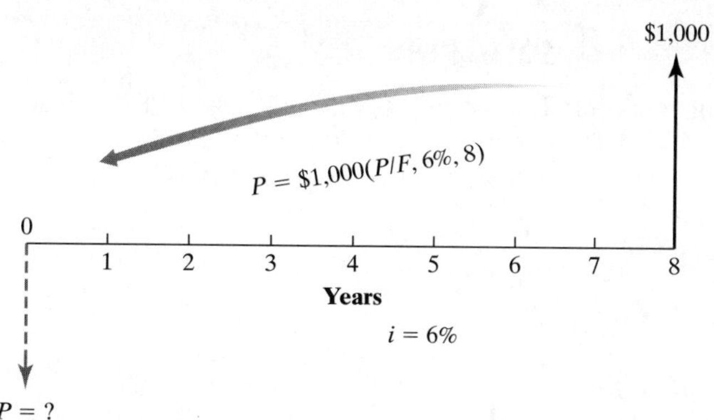

Figure 2.10 Cash flow diagram

[6] Bonds are loans that investors make to corporations and governments. In Example 2.5, the $1,000 of principal is the **face value** of the bond, the yearly interest payment is its **coupon**, and the length of the loan is the bond's **maturity**.

2.3.3 Solving for Time and Interest Rates

At this point, you should realize that the compounding and discounting processes are reciprocals of one another and that we have been dealing with one equation in two forms:

$$\text{Future-value form: } F = P(1 + i)^N$$

and

$$\text{Present-value form: } P = F(1 + i)^{-N}.$$

There are four variables in these equations: P, F, N, and i. If you know the values of any three, you can find the value of the fourth. Thus far, we have always given you the interest rate (i) and the number of years (N), plus either P or F. In many situations, though, you will need to solve for i or N, as we discuss next.

EXAMPLE 2.6 Solving for i

Suppose you buy a share of stock for $10 and sell it for $20; your profit is thus $10. If that happens within a year, your rate of return is an impressive 100% ($10/$10 = 1). If it takes five years, what would be the rate of return on your investment? (See Figure 2.11.)

DISSECTING THE PROBLEM

Here, we know P, F, and N, but we do not know i, the interest rate you will earn on your investment. This type of rate of return calculation is straightforward, since you make only a one-time lump-sum investment.

Given: $P = \$10$, $F = \$20$, and $N = 5$ years.
Find: i.

METHODOLOGY

We start with the following relationship:

$$F = P(1 + i)^N.$$

We then substitute in the given values:

$$\$20 = \$10(1 + i)^5.$$

Next, we solve for i by one of two methods.

Method 1: Trial and Error
Go through a trial-and-error process in which you insert different values of i into the equation until you find a value that "works," in the sense that the right-hand side of the equation equals $20.

SOLUTION

The solution value is $i = 14.87\%$. The trial-and-error procedure is extremely tedious and inefficient for most problems, so it is not widely practiced in the real world.

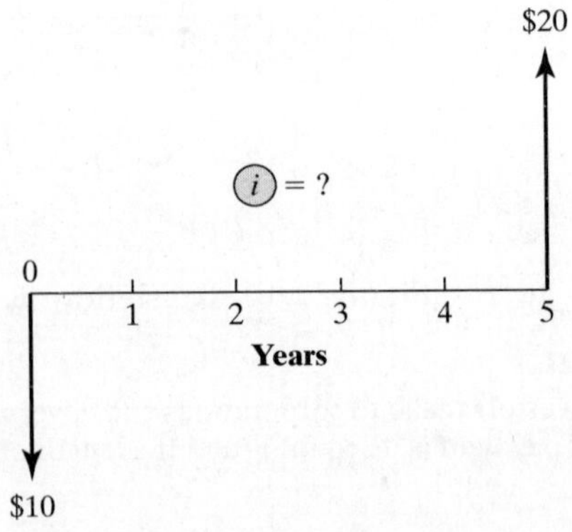

Figure 2.11 Cash flow diagram

METHODOLOGY	**SOLUTION**
Method 2: Interest Tables You can solve the problem by using the interest tables in Appendix B.	Start with the equation $$\$20 = \$10(1 + i)^5,$$ which is equivalent to $$2 = (1 + i)^5 = (F/P, i, 5).$$ Now look across the $N = 5$ row under the $(F/P, i, 5)$ column until you can locate the value of 2. This value is approximated in the 15% interest table at $(F/P, 15\%, 5) = 2.0114$, so the interest rate at which \$10 grows to \$20 over five years is very close to 15%. This procedure will be very tedious for fractional interest rates or when N is not a whole number, as you may have to approximate the solution by linear interpolation.
Method 3: Practical Approach The most practical approach is to use either a financial calculator or an electronic spreadsheet such as Excel. A financial function such as RATE(N, 0, P, F) allows us to calculate an unknown interest rate.	The precise command statement would be as follows: $$= \text{RATE}(5,0,-10,20) = 14.87\%.$$ Note that we enter the present value (P) as a negative number in order to indicate a cash outflow in Excel.

EXAMPLE 2.7 Single Amounts: Find **N**, Given **P**, **F**, and **i**

You have just purchased 200 shares of General Electric stock at \$15 per share. You will sell the stock when its market price doubles. If you expect the stock price to increase 12% per year, how long do you expect to wait before selling the stock? (See Figure 2.12.)

DISSECTING THE PROBLEM	
	Given: $P = \$3,000$, $F = \$6,000$, and $i = 12\%$ per year. **Find:** N (years).

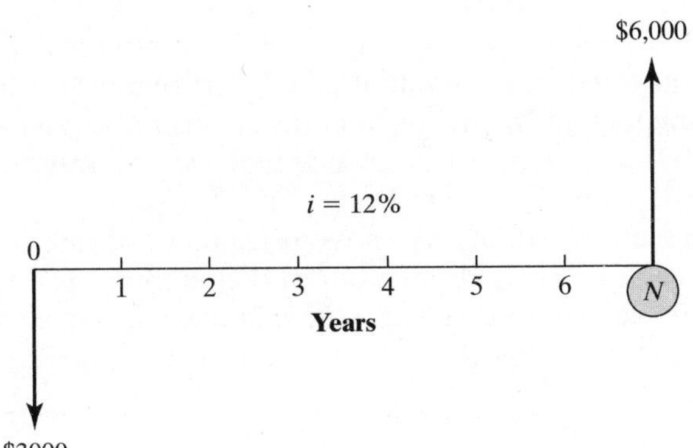

Figure 2.12 Cash flow diagram

METHODOLOGY	**SOLUTION**
Method 1: Using a Calculator Using the single-payment compound-amount factor, we write $$F = P(1 + i)^N = P(F/P, i, N),$$ which in this case is $$\$6,000 = \$3,000(1 + 0.12)^N$$ $$= \$3,000(F/P, 12\%, N),$$ or $$2 = (1.12)^N = (F/P, 12\%, N).$$	We start with $$\log 2 = N \log 1.12.$$ Solving for N gives $$N = \frac{\log 2}{\log 1.12}$$ $$= 6.12 \approx 6 \text{ years.}$$
Method 2: Using a Spreadsheet Program Again, we could use a computer spreadsheet program to find N.	Within Excel, the financial function NPER(i, 0, P, F) computes the number of compounding periods it will take an investment P to grow to a future value F, earning a fixed interest rate i per compounding period. In our example, the Excel command would look like this: $$= \text{NPER}(12\%, 0, -3000, 6000).$$ The calculated result is 6.1163 years.

COMMENTS: A very handy rule called the *Rule of 72* can determine approximately how long it will take for a sum of money to double. The rule states that to find the time it takes for the present sum of money to grow by a factor of two, we divide 72 by the interest rate. For our example, the interest rate is 12%. Therefore, the Rule of 72 indicates that it will take $\frac{72}{12} = 6$ years for a sum to double. This result is, in fact, relatively close to our exact solution.

2.4 Uneven-Payment Series

A common cash flow transaction involves a series of disbursements or receipts. Familiar examples of series payments are payment of installments on car loans and home mortgage payments, which typically involve identical sums to be paid at regular intervals. When there is no clear pattern over the series, we call the transaction an *uneven cash flow series*.

We can find the present worth of any uneven stream of payments by calculating the present worth of each individual payment and summing the results. Once the present worth is found, we can make other equivalence calculations. (For instance, future worth can be calculated by the interest factors developed in the previous section.)

EXAMPLE 2.8 Tuition Prepayment Option

The Tuition Prepayment Option (TPO) offered by many colleges provides savings by eliminating future tuition increases. When you enroll in the plan, you prepay all remaining undergraduate tuition and required fees at the rate in effect when you enter the plan. Tuition and fees (not including room and board) for the 2011–2012 academic year are $37,489 at Harvard University. Total undergraduate tuition for an entering freshman at this rate is $149,956. Tuition, fees, room, and board normally increase each year, but it is difficult to predict by how much, since costs depend on future economic trends and institutional priorities. The following chart lists the tuition and required fee rates since 2007:

Academic Year	Tuition and Fees	Required Prepayment
2007–2008	$31,665	$126,660
2008–2009	$32,882	$131,528
2009–2010	$33,983	$135,932
2010–2011	$36,143	$144,572
2011–2012	$37,489	$149,956

Suppose that you enrolled in the TPO for the academic year 2008–2009. In 2012, looking back four years from the time of enrollment, knowing now exactly what the actual tuitions were, do you think your decision was justified in an economic sense to prepay "when money saved or invested was earning" at an interest rate of 6%?

DISSECTING THE PROBLEM

This problem is equivalent to asking what value of P would make you indifferent in your choice between P dollars today and the future expense stream of ($32,882, $33,983, $36,143, $37,489).

Given: Uneven cash flow in Figure 2.13; $i = 6\%$ per year.
Find: P.

METHODOLOGY

One way to deal with an uneven series of cash flows is to calculate the equivalent present value of each single cash flow and then sum the present values to find P. In other words, the cash flow is broken into four parts, as shown in Figure 2.13.

SOLUTION

Assuming that the tuition payment occurs at the beginning of each academic year, we sum the individual present values as follows:

$$P = \$32{,}882 + \$33{,}983(P/F, 6\%, 1) + \$36{,}143(P/F, 6\%, 2)$$
$$+ \$37{,}489(P/F, 6\%, 3)$$
$$= \$128{,}585 < \$131{,}528.$$

Since the equivalent present worth amount of the future tuition payments is less than the required prepayment amount at the beginning of the 2008–2009 academic year, you would be better off paying tuition on a yearly basis.

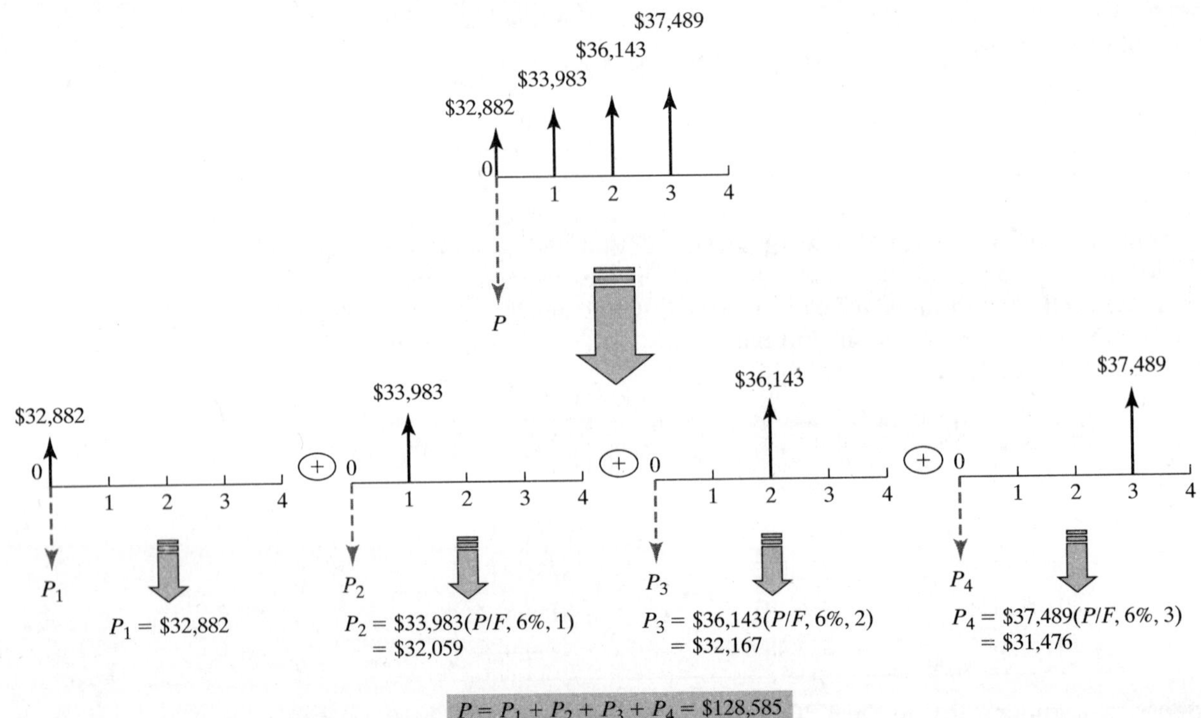

Figure 2.13 Decomposition of uneven cash flow series

COMMENTS: Of course, you do not know in advance how much the future tuition would increase, so the difference between $128,585 and $131,528 (or $2,943) may be viewed as the risk premium you may choose to pay to lock in the future tuition at your freshman year amount.

2.5 Equal-Payment Series

As we learned in Example 2.8, we can always find the present worth of a stream of future cash flows by summing the present worth of each individual cash flow. However, if cash flow regularities are present within the stream, the use of shortcuts, such as finding the present worth of an equal-payment (or a uniform) series, may be possible. We often encounter transactions in which a uniform series of payments exists. Rental payments, bond interest payments, and commercial installment plans are based on uniform payment series. Our concern is to find the equivalent present worth (P) or future worth (F) of such a series, as illustrated in Figure 2.14.

2.5.1 Compound-Amount Factor: Find F, Given A, i, and N

Suppose we are interested in the future amount F of a fund to which we contribute A dollars each period and on which we earn interest at a rate of i per period. The contributions are made at the end of each of the N periods. These transactions are graphically illustrated in Figure 2.15. Looking at this diagram, we see that if an amount A is invested at the end of each period for N periods, the total amount F that can be withdrawn at the end of N periods will be the sum of the compound amounts of the individual deposits.

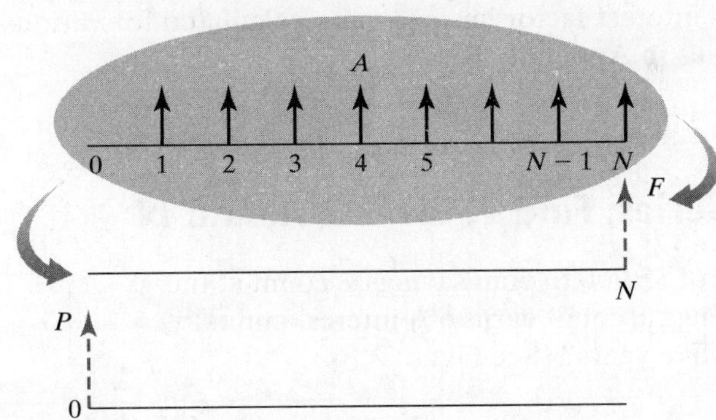

Figure 2.14   Equal-payment series: Find equivalent P or F

As shown in Figure 2.15, the A dollars we put into the fund at the end of the first period will be worth $A(1 + i)^{N-1}$ at the end of N periods. The A dollars we put into the fund at the end of the second period will be worth $A(1 + i)^{N-2}$, and so forth. Finally, the last A dollars that we contribute at the end of the Nth period will be worth exactly A dollars at that time. This means we have a series in the form

$$F = A(1 + i)^{N-1} + A(1 + i)^{N-2} + \cdots + A(1 + i) + A,$$

or, expressed alternatively,

$$F = A + A(1 + i) + A(1 + i)^2 + \cdots + A(1 + i)^{N-1}. \tag{2.5}$$

Multiplying Eq. (2.5) by $(1 + i)$ results in

$$(1 + i)F = A(1 + i) + A(1 + i)^2 + \cdots + A(1 + i)^N. \tag{2.6}$$

Subtracting Eq. (2.5) from Eq. (2.6) to eliminate common terms gives us

$$F(1 + i) - F = -A + A(1 + i)^N.$$

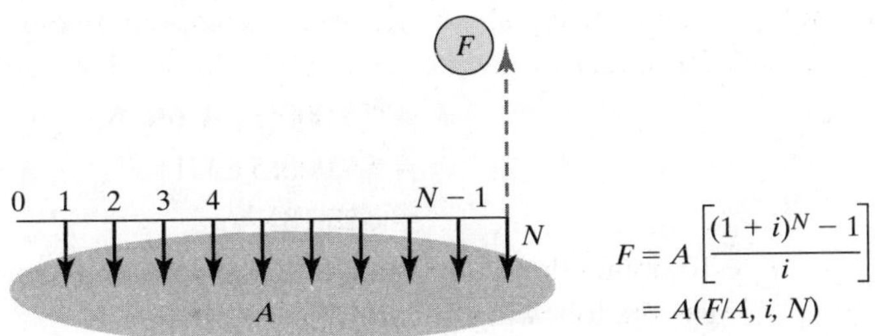

$$F = A\left[\frac{(1 + i)^N - 1}{i}\right]$$

$$= A(F/A, i, N)$$

Figure 2.15   Cash flow diagram of the relationship between A and F

Solving for F yields

$$F = A\left[\frac{(1 + i)^N - 1}{i}\right] = A(F/A, i, N). \tag{2.7}$$

The bracketed term in Eq. (2.7) is called the **equal-payment-series compound-amount factor** (also known as the **uniform-series compound-amount factor**); its factor notation is $(F/A, i, N)$. This interest factor has been also calculated for various combinations of i and N in the tables in Appendix B.

EXAMPLE 2.9 Equal-Payment Series: Find *F*, Given *i*, *A*, and *N*

Suppose you make an annual contribution of $5,000 to your savings account at the end of each year for five years. If your savings account earns 6% interest annually, how much can be withdrawn at the end of five years? (See Figure 2.16.)

DISSECTING THE PROBLEM

Given: $A = \$5,000, N = 5$ years, and $i = 6\%$ per year.

Find: F.

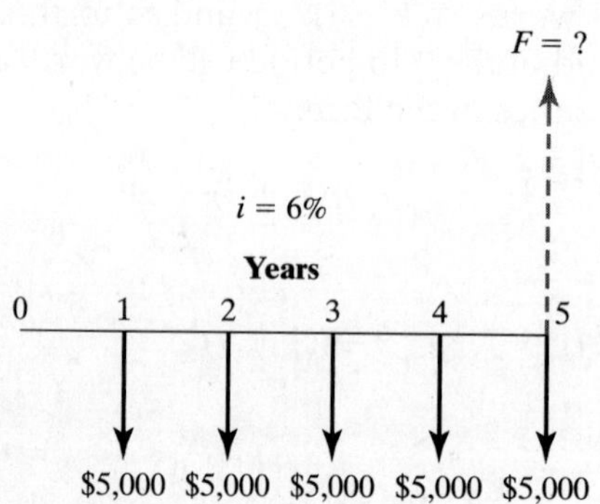

Figure 2.16 Cash flow diagram

METHODOLOGY

Use the equal-payment-series compound-amount factor and Excel.

SOLUTION

Using the equal-payment-series compound-amount factor, we obtain

$$F = \$5,000(F/A, 6\%, 5)$$
$$= \$5,000(5.6371)$$
$$= \$28,185.46.$$

To obtain the future value of the annuity in Excel, we may use the following financial function:

$$= FV(6\%, 5, -5000, 0).$$

COMMENTS: We may be able to keep track of how the periodic balances grow in the savings account as follows:

Year	1	2	3	4	5
Beginning Balance	0	$5,000.00	$10,300.00	$15,918.00	$21,873.08
Interest Earned (6%)	0	300.00	618.00	955.08	1,312.38
Deposit Made	5,000.00	5,000.00	5,000.00	5,000.00	5,000.00
Ending Balance	**$5,000.00**	**$10,300.00**	**$15,918.00**	**$21,873.08**	**$28,185.46**

As shown in Table 2.3, an Excel worksheet can be easily created to determine the periodic cash balance over time.

TABLE 2.3 **An Excel Worksheet to Illustrate How the Cash Balance Changes over Time**

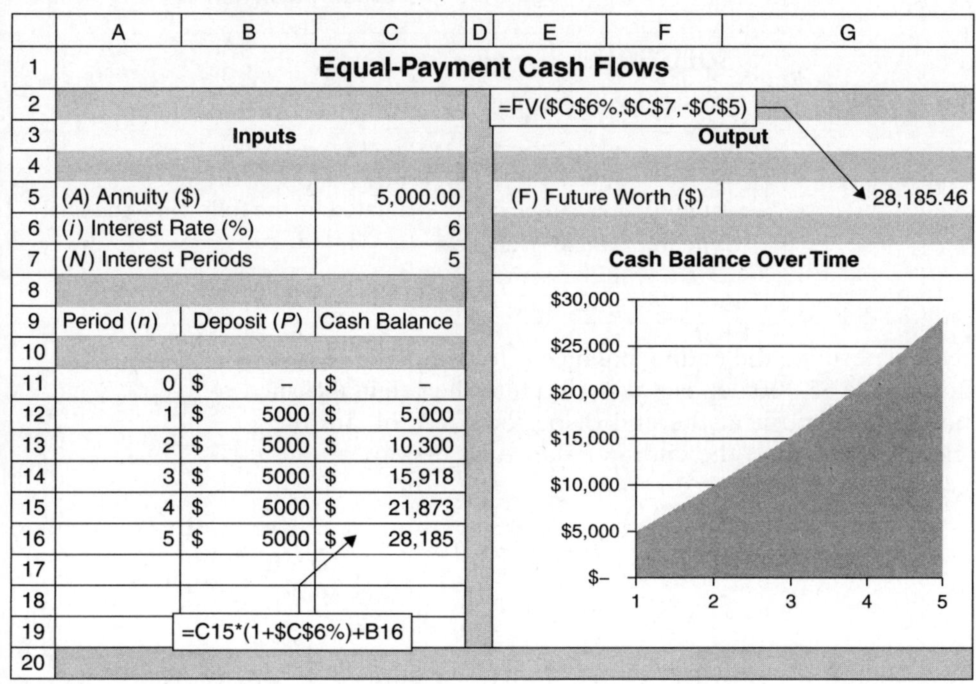

EXAMPLE 2.10 Handling Time Shifts in an Equal-Payment Series

In Example 2.9, all five deposits were made at the *end* of each period—the first deposit being made at the end of the first period. Suppose that all deposits were made at the *beginning* of each period instead or commonly known as "**annuity due.**" How would you compute the balance at the end of period 5?

DISSECTING THE PROBLEM

Compare Figure 2.17 with Figure 2.16. Each payment in Figure 2.17 has been shifted one year earlier; thus, each payment is compounded for one extra year. Note that with the end-of-year deposit, the ending balance F was $28,185.46. With the beginning-of-year deposit, the same balance accumulates by the end of period 4. This balance can earn interest for one additional year.

Given: Cash flow diagram in Figure 2.17; $i = 6\%$ per year.

Find: F.

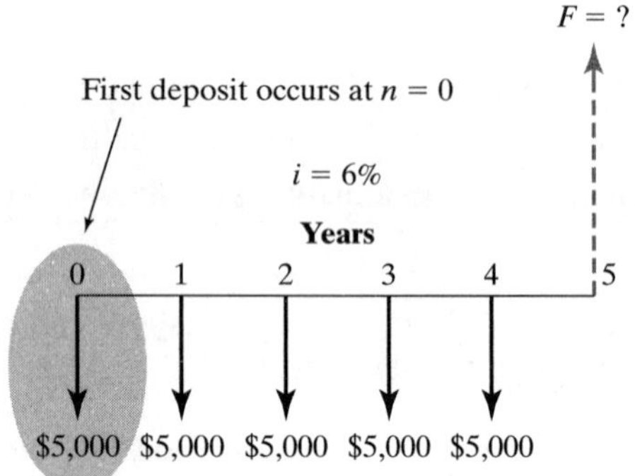

Figure 2.17   Cash flow diagram

METHODOLOGY

Use the future value (FV) command in Excel.

SOLUTION

We can easily calculate the resulting balance as

$$F = \$28{,}185.46(1.06) = \$29{,}876.59.$$

Annuity due can be easily evaluated by the following financial function available in Excel:

$$= \text{FV}(6\%, 5, -5{,}000, 1)$$

COMMENTS: Another way to determine the ending balance is to compare the two cash flow patterns. By adding the $5,000 deposit at period 0 to the original cash flow and subtracting the $5,000 deposit at the end of period 5, we obtain the second cash flow. Therefore, we can find the ending balance by making an adjustment to the $28,185.46:

$$F = \$28{,}185.46 + \$5{,}000(F/P, 6\%, 5) - \$5{,}000 = \$29{,}876.59.$$

2.5.2 Sinking-Fund Factor: Find A, Given F, i, and N

If we solve Eq. (2.7) for A, we obtain

$$A = F\left[\frac{i}{(1 + i)^N - 1}\right] = F(A/F, i, N). \tag{2.8}$$

The term within the brackets is called the **equal-payment-series sinking-fund factor**, or just **sinking-fund factor**, and is referred to with the notation $(A/F, i, N)$. A sinking fund is an interest-bearing account into which a fixed sum is deposited each interest period; it is commonly established for the purpose of replacing fixed assets.

EXAMPLE 2.11 College Savings Plan: Find *A*, Given *F, N,* and *i*

You want to set up a college savings plan for your daughter. She is currently 10 years old and will go to college at age 18. You assume that when she starts college, she will need at least $100,000 in the bank. How much do you need to save each year in order to have the necessary funds if the current rate of interest is 7%? Assume that end-of-year deposits are made.

DISSECTING THE PROBLEM	
	Given: Cash flow diagram in Figure 2.18; $i = 7\%$ per year, and $N = 8$ years. **Find:** *A*.

METHODOLOGY	SOLUTION
Method 1: Sinking-Fund Factor	Using the sinking-fund factors, we obtain $$A = \$100{,}000(A/F, 7\%, 8)$$ $$= \$9{,}746.78.$$

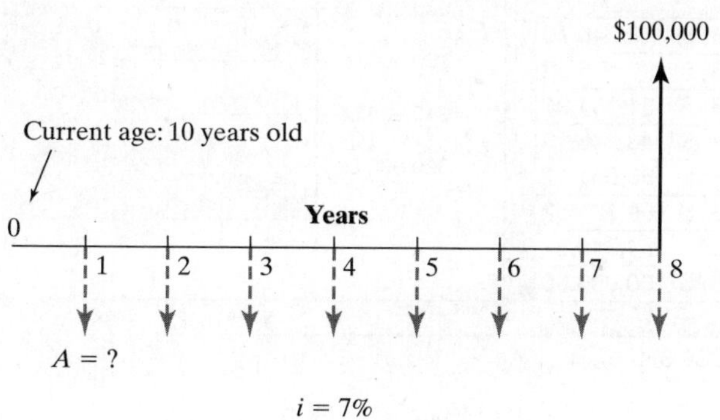

Figure 2.18   Cash flow diagram

Method 2: Excel's PMT Function	Or, using the Excel's built-in financial function, we get the same result: $$= \text{PMT}(7\%, 8, 0, 100000)$$ $$= -\$9{,}746.78.$$

COMMENTS: With Excel, we can easily confirm the process of accumulating $100,000 at the end of 8 years. As shown in Table 2.4, the cash balance at the end of year 1 will be just $9,746.78, as the first deposit has no time to earn any interest. At the end of year 2, the cash balance consists of two contributions: The deposit made at the end of year 1 will grow to $9,746.78(1 + 0.07) = $10,429.05, and the second deposit, made at the end of year 2, will yield $9,746.78, resulting in a total of $20,175.83. If the process continues for the remaining deposit periods, the final balance will be exactly $100,000.

TABLE 2.4   An Excel Worksheet to Illustrate the Cash Balances over Time

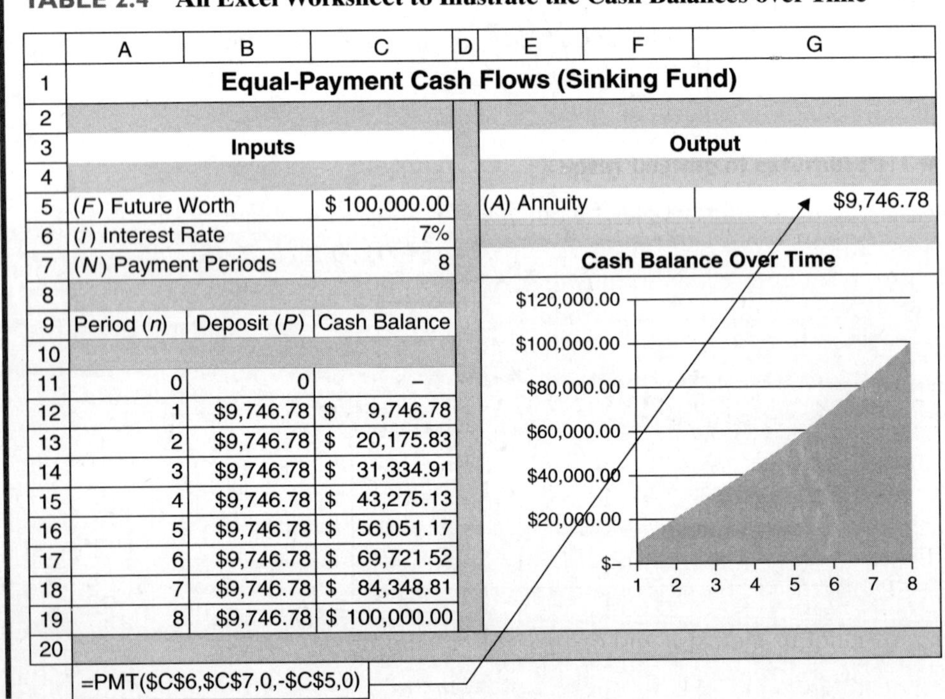

2.5.3 Capital-Recovery Factor (Annuity Factor): Find A, Given P, i, and N

We can determine the amount of a periodic payment, A, if we know P, i, and N. Figure 2.19 illustrates this situation. To relate P to A, recall the relationship between P and F in Eq. (2.3): $F = P(1 + i)^N$. By replacing F in Eq. (2.8) by $P(1 + i)^N$, we get

$$A = P(1 + i)^N \left[\frac{i}{(1 + i)^N - 1} \right],$$

or

$$A = P \left[\frac{i(1 + i)^N}{(1 + i)^N - 1} \right] = P(A/P, i, N). \tag{2.9}$$

Now we have an equation for determining the value of the series of end-of-period payments, A, when the present sum P is known. The portion within the brackets is called the **capital-recovery factor**, which is designated $(A/P, i, N)$. In finance, this A/P factor

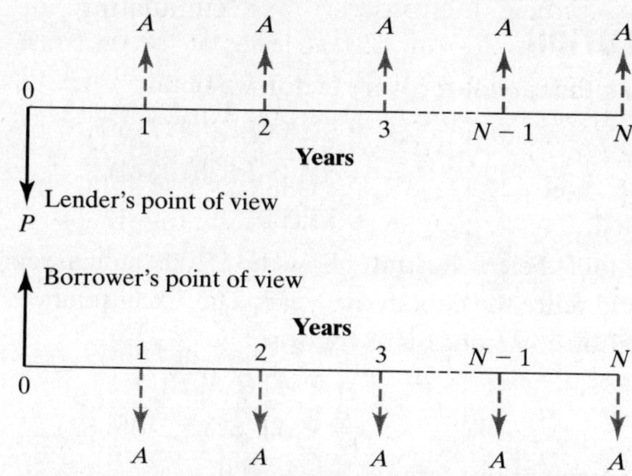

Figure 2.19 Cash flow diagram of the relationship between P and A

is referred to as the **annuity factor**. The annuity factor indicates a series of payments of a fixed, or constant, amount for a specified number of periods.

EXAMPLE 2.12 Paying Off an Educational Loan: Find *A*, Given *P, i,* and *N*

You borrowed $21,061.82 to finance the educational expenses for your senior year of college. The loan will be paid off over five years. The loan carries an interest rate of 6% per year and is to be repaid in equal annual installments over the next five years. Assume that the money was borrowed at the beginning of your senior year and that the first installment will be due a year later. Compute the amount of the annual installments (Figure 2.20).

DISSECTING THE PROBLEM

Given: $P = \$21,061.82, i = 6\%$ per year, and $N = 5$ years.

Find: A.

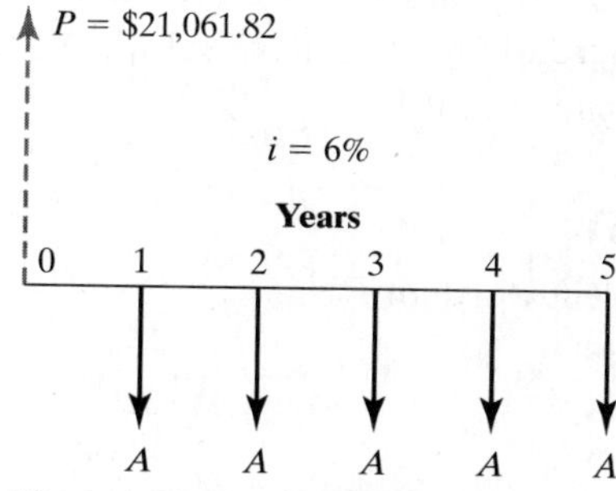

Figure 2.20 Cash flow diagram

METHODOLOGY

Use the capital-recovery factor.

SOLUTION

Using the capital-recovery factor, we obtain

$$A = \$21{,}061.82(A/P, 6\%, 5)$$
$$= \$21{,}061.82(0.2374)$$
$$= \$5{,}000.$$

The table below illustrates how the $5,000 annual repayment plan would retire the debt in five years. The Excel solution, with annuity function commands, is as follows:

$$= \text{PMT}(i, N, P)$$
$$= \text{PMT}(6\%, 5, 21061.82).$$

The result of this formula is $-$5,000.

Year	1	2	3	4	5
Beginning Balance	$21,061.82	$17,325.53	$13,365.06	$9,166.96	$4,716.98
Interest Charged (6%)	1,263.71	1,039.53	801.90	550.02	283.02
Payment Made	−5,000.00	−5,000.00	−5,000.00	−5,000.00	−5,000.00
Ending Balance	$17,325.53	$13,365.06	$9,166.96	$4,716.98	$0.00

EXAMPLE 2.13 Deferred Loan Repayments

Suppose, in Example 2.12, that you want to negotiate with the bank to defer the first loan installment until the end of year 2. (But you still desire to make five equal installments at 6% interest.) If the bank wishes to earn the same profit, what should be the new annual installment? (See Figure 2.21.)

DISSECTING THE PROBLEM

In deferring one year, the bank will add the interest accrued during the first year to the principal. In other words, we need to find the equivalent worth of $21,061.82 at the end of year 1, P'.

Given: $P = \$21{,}061.82$, $i = 6\%$ per year, and $N = 5$ years, but the first payment occurs at the end of year 2.

Find: A.

METHODOLOGY

Calculate equivalent worth of P'.

SOLUTION

$$P' = \$21{,}061.82(F/P, 6\%, 1)$$
$$= \$22{,}325.53.$$

Thus, you are borrowing $22,325.53 for five years. For the loan to be retired with five equal installments, the deferred equal annual payment, A', will be

$$A' = \$22,325.53(A/P, 6\%, 5)$$
$$= \$5,300.$$

By deferring the first payment for one year, you need to make an additional $300 in payments each year.

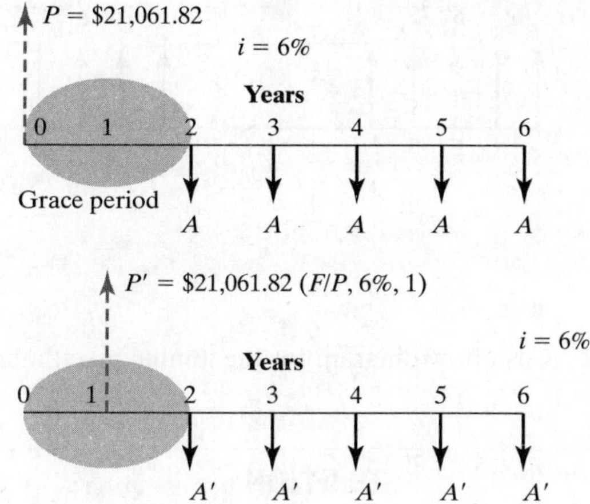

Figure 2.21 A deferred-loan cash flow diagram

2.5.4 Present-Worth Factor: Find P, Given A, i, and N

What would you have to invest now in order to withdraw A dollars at the end of each of the next N periods? We now face just the opposite of the equal-payment capital-recovery factor situation: A is known, but P has to be determined. With the capital-recovery factor given in Eq. (2.9), solving for P gives us

$$P = A\left[\frac{(1 + i)^N - 1}{i(1 + i)^N}\right] = A(P/A, i, N). \tag{2.10}$$

The bracketed term is referred to as the **equal-payment-series present-worth factor** and is designated $(P/A, i, N)$.

EXAMPLE 2.14 Equal-Payment Series: Find P, Given A, i, and N

A truck driver from Georgia won Powerball, a multistate lottery game similar to the one introduced in the chapter opening story. The winner could choose between a single lump sum of $116.5 million or a total of $195 million paid out over 20 annual installments (or $9.75 million per year and the first installment being paid out immediately). The truck driver opted for the lump sum. From a strictly economic standpoint, did he make the more lucrative choice?

DISSECTING THE PROBLEM

If the winner could invest his money at 8% annual interest, what is the lump-sum amount that would make him indifferent to each payment plan? (See Figure 2.22.)

Given: $i = 8\%$ per year, $A = \$9.75$ million, and $N = 19$ years.

Find: P.

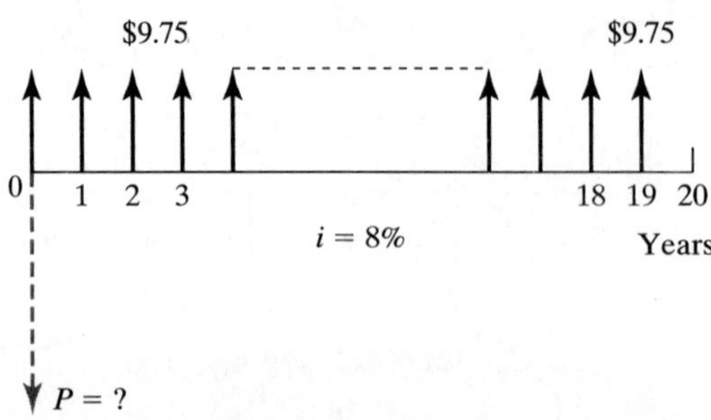

Figure 2.22 Cash flow diagram for the annual installment option

METHODOLOGY

Method 1: Interest Factor Solution

Method 2: Excel Solution

SOLUTION

$P = \$9.75 + \$9.75(P/A, 8\%, 19) = \$9.75 + \$93.64$

$\quad = \$103.39 \text{ million.}$

$\quad = PV(8\%, 20, 9.75,, 1) = -\$103.39 \text{ million.}$

COMMENTS: Clearly, we can tell the winner that giving up $9.75 million a year for 20 years to receive $116.5 million today is a winning proposition if he can earn an 8% return on its investment. At this point, we may be interested in knowing the minimum rate of return at which accepting the $116.5 million lump sum would make sense. Since we know that $P = \$116.5$ million, $N = 19$ and $A = \$9.75$ million, we solve for i.

$$\$116.5 = \$9.75 + \$9.75(P/A, i, 19)$$

$$(P/A, i, 19) = \frac{\$116.5 - \$9.75}{\$9.75} = 10.9487.$$

If you know the cash flows and the present value (or future value) of a cash flow stream, you can determine the interest rate. In this case, we are looking for the interest rate that causes the *P/A* factor to equal $(P/A, i, 19) = 10.9487$. Since we are dealing with an annuity due, we could proceed as follows:

- With a financial calculator, enter $N = 19, P = -106.75$, and $A = 9.75$, and then press the *i* key to find that $i = 6.2436\%$. For a typical financial calculator, the symbols such as PV, PMT, and FV are commonly adopted on its keypad. These symbols correspond to PV $= P$, PMT $= A$, and FV $= F$, respectively. Note that, just as with Excel, either P or A must be entered as a negative number to evaluate i correctly.

- If you want to use the compound-interest tables, look up the values of $(P/A, i, 19)$ that are closest to 10.9487. In the P/A column with $N = 19$ in Appendix B (page 631), you will find that $(P/A, 6\%, 19) = 11.1581$ and $(P/A, 7\%, 19) = 10.3356$. Then, we may approximate i by a linear **interpolation** as shown in Table 2.5:

$$i \cong 7\% - (1\%)\frac{10.9487 - 10.3356}{11.1581 - 10.3356} = 7\% - (1\%)\frac{0.6131}{0.8225}$$

$$= 6.2546\%.$$

- In Excel, simply apply the following command to solve the unknown-interest-rate problem for an annuity:

$$= \text{RATE}(N,A,P,F,type,guess)$$

$$= \text{RATE}(19, 9.75, -106.75, 0, 0, 5\%)$$

$$= 6.2436\%.$$

As long as the lottery winner can find a financial investment that provides a rate of return higher than 6.2436%, his decision to go with the lump-sum payment option appears to be a sound one. Table 2.6 illustrates why the lump-sum amount (calculated at \$116.5 million) deposited at an interest rate of 6.2436% is equivalent to receiving 20 installments of \$9.75 million. In other words, if you deposit the lump-sum amount today in a bank account that pays 6.2436% annual interest, you will be able to withdraw \$9.75 million annually over 19 years. At the end of that time, your bank account will show a zero balance.

TABLE 2.5 **Finding Unknown i by a Linear Interpolation**

	K	L	M	N	O	P
14						
15	**Interest Rate**	**$(P/A, i, 19)$**				
16						
17	6%	11.1581				
18						
19	i	10.9487				
20						
21	7%	10.3356				
22						
23	a	$7\% - i$				
24	b	0.6131				
25	c	1%				
26	d	0.8225				
27						
28	i	6.2546%				
29						

TABLE 2.6 **An Excel Worksheet to Illustrate the Process of Deleting $104 Million Initial Cash Balance over Time**

	A	B	C	D	E	F	G	H
1	Equal-Payment Cash Flows (Present Worth)							
2								
3	Inputs					Output		
4								
5	(A) Annuity			$ 9.75		(P) Present Worth		$116.50
6	(i) Interest Rate			6.2436%				
7	(N) Payment Period			19		Cash Balance Over Time		
8								
9	Period (n)	Deposit	Withdrawal	Cash Balance				
10								
11	0	$116.50	($9.75)	$106.75				
12	1		($9.75)	$103.67				
13	2		($9.75)	$100.39				
14	3		($9.75)	$96.91				
15	4		($9.75)	$93.21				
16	5		($9.75)	$89.28				
17	6		($9.75)	$85.10				
18	7		($9.75)	$80.66				
19	8		($9.75)	$75.95				
20	9		($9.75)	$70.94				
21	10		($9.75)	$65.62				
22	11		($9.75)	$59.97				
23	12		($9.75)	$53.96				
24	13		($9.75)	$47.58				
25	14		($9.75)	$40.80				
26	15		($9.75)	$33.60				
27	16		($9.75)	$25.95				
28	17		($9.75)	$17.82				
29	18		($9.75)	$9.18				
30	19		($9.75)	$0.00				
31								

`=PV($D$6,$D$7,-$D$5,0,0)+$D$5`

EXAMPLE 2.15 Start Saving Money as Soon as Possible: Composite Series That Requires Both (F/P, i, N) and (F/A, i, N) Factors

Consider the following two savings plans that you think about starting at the age of 21:

- Option 1: Save $2,000 a year for 10 years. At the end of 10 years, make no further investments, but invest the amount accumulated at the end of every 10 years until you reach the age of 65. (Assume that the first deposit will be made when you are 22.)

- Option 2: Do nothing for the first 10 years. Start saving $2,000 a year every year thereafter until you reach the age of 65. (Assume that the first deposit will be made when you turn 32.)

If you were able to invest your money at 8% over the planning horizon, which plan would result in more money saved by the time you are 65? (See Figure 2.23.)

DISSECTING THE PROBLEM	
	Given: $i = 8\%$ per year, deposit scenarios shown in Figure 2.23. **Find:** F when you are 65.
METHODOLOGY **SOLUTION**	
Method 1: Computing the Final Balance in Two Steps for Early Savings Plan	First, compute the accumulated balance at the end of 10 years (when you are 31). Call this amount F_{31}. $$F_{31} = \$2,000(F/A, 8\%, 10) = \$28,973.$$ Then use this amount to compute the result of reinvesting the entire balance for another 34 years. Call this final result F_{65}. $$F_{65} = \$28,973(F/P, 8\%, 34) = \$396,646.$$
Method 2: Deferred Savings Plan	Since you have only 34 years to invest, the resulting balance will be $$F_{65} = \$2,000(F/A, 8\%, 34) = \$317,253.$$ With the early savings plan, you will be able to save \$79,393 more.

COMMENTS: In this example, the assumed interest rate is 8%. Certainly, we would be interested in knowing at what interest rate these two options would be equivalent. We can use Excel's **Goal Seek**[7] function to answer this question. As shown in Table 2.7, we enter the amount of deposits over 44 years in the second and third columns. Cells F10 and F12, respectively, display the future value of each option. Cell F14 contains the difference between the future values of the two options, or $= F10 - F12$. To begin using the Goal Seek function, first define Cell F14 as your *set cell*. Specify *set value* as 0, and set the *By changing cell* to be F8. Use the Goal Seek function to change the interest rate in Cell F8 incrementally until the value in Cell F14 equals 0. The break-even interest rate is 6.538%.

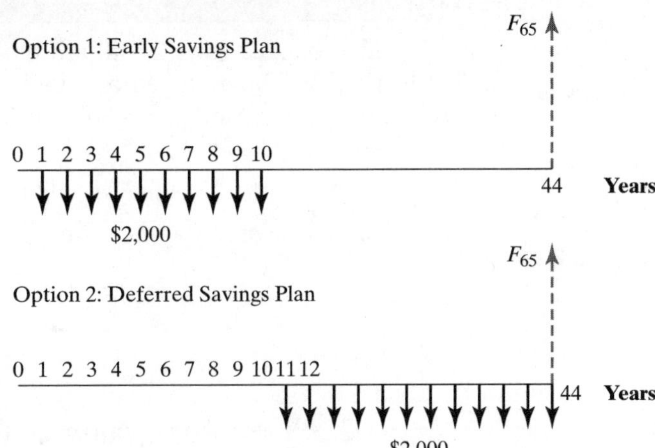

Figure 2.23 Cash flow diagram's for two different savings plans

---

[7] Goal Seek is part of a suite of commands sometimes called *what-if analysis* tools in Microsoft Excel. When you know the desired result of a single *formula* but not the input value the formula needs to determine the result, you can use the Goal Seek feature by clicking **Goal Seek** on the **Tools** menu. When you are *goal seeking,* Excel varies the value in one specific cell until a formula that is dependent on that cell returns the result you want.

TABLE 2.7 Using the Goal Seek to Find the Break-Even Interest Rate to Make Two Options Equivalent

	A	B	C	D	E	F	G	H
1								
2	Year	Option 1	Option 2		Goal Seek Function Parameters			
3								
4	0							
5	1	-$2,000						
6	2	-$2,000			=FV(F8,10,-2000)*(1+F8)^(34)			
7	3	-$2,000						
8	4	-$2,000			Interest rate (%)	8%	By changing cell	
9	5	-$2,000						
10	6	-$2,000			FV of Option 1	$ 396,645.95		
11	7	-$2,000						
12	8	-$2,000			FV of Option 2	$317,253.34		
13	9	-$2,000						
14	10	-$2,000			Difference	$ 79,392.61	Set cell	
15	11		-$2,000					
16	12		-$2,000					
17	13		-$2,000		=FV(F8,34,-2000)	=$F$10-$F$12		
18	14		-$2,000					
19	15		-$2,000					
20	16		-$2,000					
21	17		-$2,000					
22	18		-$2,000					
23	19		-$2,000					
41	37		-$2,000					
42	38		-$2,000					
43	39		-$2,000					
44	40		-$2,000					
45	41		-$2,000					
46	42		-$2,000					
47	43		-$2,000					
48	44		-$2,000					
49								

Note that in Table 2.7, rows 24–40 are hidden from display to reduce the size of the table. Clearly, it will be quite tedious if we resort on an analytical method. To do so, we may select the base period at $n = 10$ and find the equivalent value of a stream of payments at that base period:

$$\$2,000(F/A, i, 10) = \$2,000(P/A, i, 34)$$

and solve for unknown i by a linear interpolation method as shown in Table 2.5.

2.5.5 Present Value of Perpetuities

A perpetuity is a stream of cash flows that continues forever. A good example is a share of preferred stock that pays a fixed cash dividend each period (usually a quarter of a year) and never matures. An interesting feature of any perpetual annuity is that you cannot compute the future value of its cash flows because it is infinite. However, it has a well-defined present value. It appears counterintuitive that a series of cash flows that lasts forever can have a finite value today.

So what is the value of a perpetuity? We know how to calculate the present value for an equal-payment series with the finite stream as shown in Eq. (2.10). If we take a limit on this equation by letting $N \rightarrow \infty$, we can find the closed-form solution as follows:

$$P = \frac{A}{i}. \tag{2.11}$$

To illustrate, consider Example 2.16.

EXAMPLE 2.16 Present Value of Perpetuities: Find *P*, Given *A*, *i*, and *N*

Consider a perpetual stream of $1,000 per year, as depicted in Figure 2.24. If the interest rate is 10% per year, how much is this perpetuity worth today?

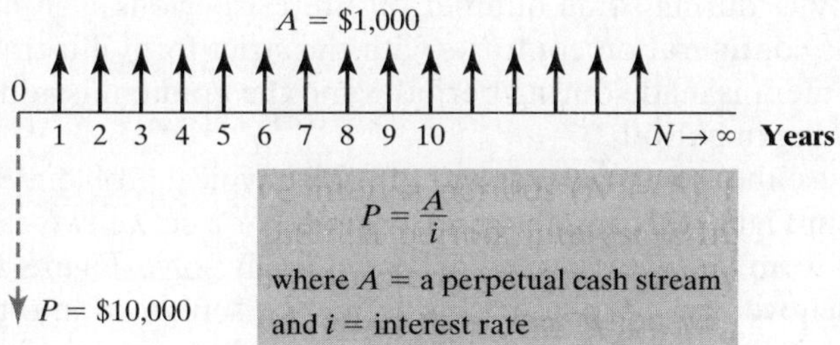

Figure 2.24 Present value of perpetual cash streams

DISSECTING THE PROBLEM

The question is basically: "How much do you need to deposit now in an account that pays 10% interest such that you will be able to withdraw $1,000 a year forever?" (See Figure 2.24.)

Given: $i = 10\%$ per year, $A = \$1,000$, and $N = \infty$ years.

Find: P.

METHODOLOGY

SOLUTION

$$P = \frac{A}{i} = \frac{\$1,000}{0.10}$$

$$= \$10,000$$

$$= \text{PV}(8\%, 20, 9.75,, 1) = -\$103.39 \text{ million}.$$

COMMENTS: If you put in $10,000, then at the end of the first year, you would have $11,000 in the account. You take out $1,000, leaving $10,000 for the next year. Clearly, if the interest rate stays at 10% per year, you will not eat into the principal, so you could continue to take out $1,000 every year forever.

2.6 Dealing with Gradient Series

Engineers frequently encounter situations involving periodic payments that increase or decrease by a constant amount G or constant percentage (growth rate) from period to period. We can easily develop a series of interest formulas for this situation, but Excel will be a more practical tool to calculate equivalent values for these types of cash flows.

2.6.1 Handling Linear Gradient Series

Sometimes, cash flows will increase or decrease by a set amount, G, the gradient amount. This type of series is known as a **strict gradient series**, as seen in Figure 2.25. Note that each payment is $A_n = (n - 1)G$. Note also that the series begins with a zero cash flow at the end of period 1. If $G > 0$, the series is referred to as an *increasing* gradient series. If $G < 0$, it is referred to as a *decreasing* gradient series.

Linear Gradient Series as Composite Series

Unfortunately, the strict form of the increasing or decreasing gradient series does not correspond to the form that most engineering economic problems take. A typical problem involving a linear gradient series includes an initial payment during period 1 that increases by G during some number of interest periods, a situation illustrated in Figure 2.26. This configuration contrasts with the strict form illustrated in Figure 2.25, in which no payment is made during period 1 and the gradient is added to the previous payment beginning in period 2.

In order to use the strict gradient series to solve typical problems, we must view cash flows as shown in Figure 2.26 as a **composite series**, or a set of two cash flows, each corresponding to a form that we can recognize and easily solve. Figure 2.26 illustrates that the form in which we find a typical cash flow can be separated into two components: a uniform series of N payments of amount A_1 and a gradient series of increments of a constant amount G. The need to view cash flows that involve linear gradient series as composites of two series is very important for the solution of problems, as we shall now see.

Present-Worth Factor: Linear Gradient: Find P, Given G, N, and i

How much would you have to deposit now in order to withdraw the gradient amounts specified in Figure 2.27?

To find an expression for the present amount P, we apply the single-payment present-worth factor to each term of the series, obtaining

$$P = 0 + \frac{G}{(1 + i)^2} + \frac{2G}{(1 + i)^3} + \cdots + \frac{(N - 1)G}{(1 + i)^N},$$

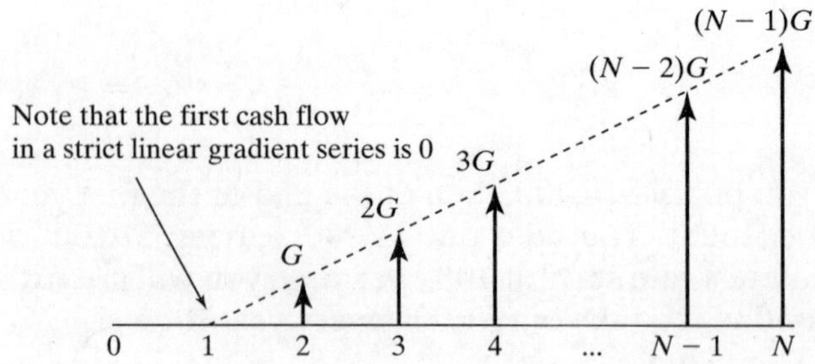

Figure 2.25   Cash flow diagram of a strict gradient series

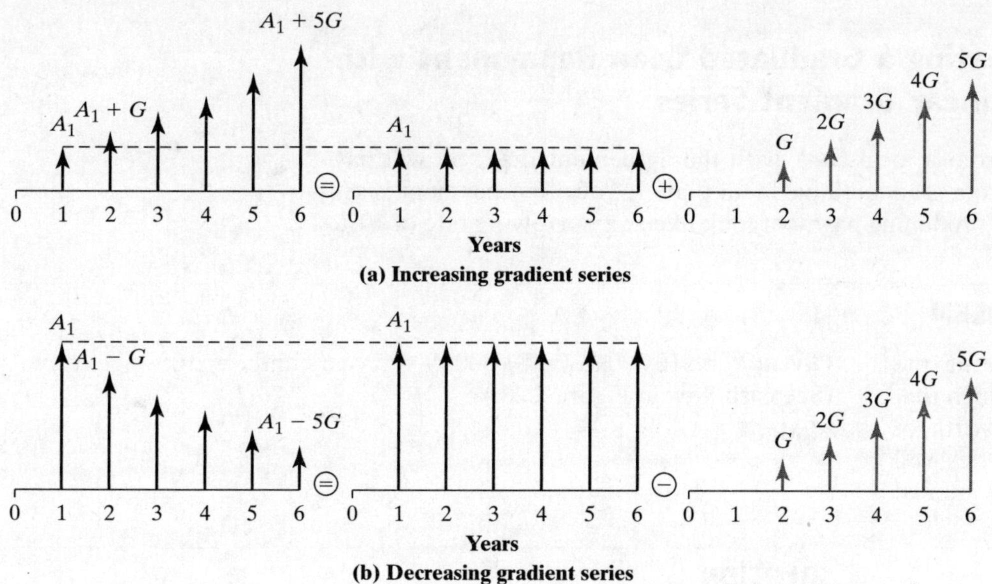

(a) Increasing gradient series

(b) Decreasing gradient series

Figure 2.26   Two types of linear gradient series as composites of a uniform series of N payments of A_1 and a gradient series of increments of a constant amount G

or

$$P = \sum_{n=1}^{N} (n - 1)G(1 + i)^{-n}. \tag{2.12}$$

After some algebraic operations, we obtain

$$P = G\left[\frac{(1 + i)^N - iN - 1}{i^2(1 + i)^N}\right] = G(P/G, i, N). \tag{2.13}$$

The resulting factor in brackets is called the **gradient-series present-worth factor**[8] and is designated by the notation $(P/G, i, N)$.

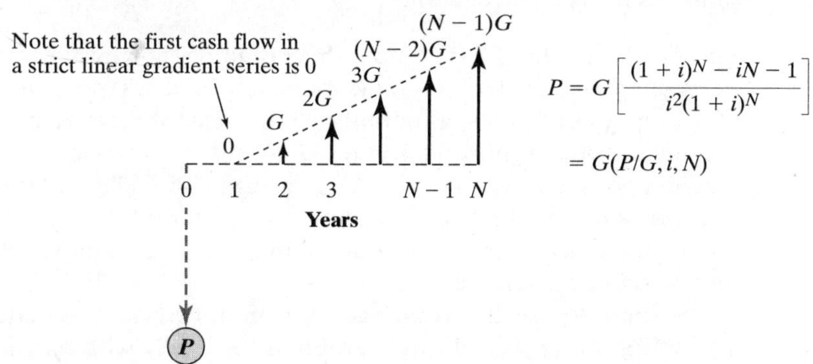

Figure 2.27   Cash flow diagram of a strict gradient series

[8] We can obtain an equal-payment series equivalent to the gradient series by multiplying Eq. (2.13) by Eq. (2.9). The resulting factor is referred to as the **gradient-to-equal payment series conversion factor** with designation of $(A/G, i, N)$, or $A = G\left[\dfrac{(1 + i)^N - iN - 1}{i[(1 + i)^N - 1]}\right]$.

EXAMPLE 2.17 Creating a Graduated Loan Repayment with a Linear Gradient Series

You borrowed $10,000 from a local bank with the agreement that you will pay back the loan according to a graduated payment plan. If your first payment is set at $1,500, what would the remaining payment look like at a borrowing rate of 10% over five years?

DISSECTING THE PROBLEM

Basically, we are calculating the amount of gradient (G) such that the equivalent present worth of the gradient payment series will be exactly $10,000 at an interest rate of 10%.

Given: $P = \$10,000, A_1 = \$1,500, N = 5$ years, and $i = 10\%$ per year. (See cash flow in Figure 2.28.)

Find: G.

METHODOLOGY

Method 1: Calculate Present Value

SOLUTION

Since the loan payment series consists of two parts—(1) a $1,500 equal-payment series and (2) a strict gradient series (unknown, yet to be determined)—we can calculate the present value of each series and equate them with $10,000:

$$\$10,000 = \$1,500(P/A, 10\%, 5) + G(P/G, 10\%, 5)$$

$$= \$5,686.18 + 6.8618G$$

$$6.8618G = \$4,313.82$$

$$G = \$628.67.$$

Method 2: Use Excel's Goal Seek

Using the **Goal Seek** function in Excel, we could reproduce the same result, as in Table 2.8.

First, we designate cells B4 (interest rate) and B5 (borrowing amount) as input cells and cells E4 (gradient amount) and E5 (present worth of the repayment series) as output cells. In terms of repayment series, the equal-payment portion is entered in cells B12 through B16. The gradient portion is listed in cells C12 through C16. Cells D12 through D16 contain the repayment amount in each period over the life of the loan. Finally, cells E12 through E16 display the equivalent present worth of the loan repayment.

Second, to use the **Goal Seek** function, we will designate cell E4 as "By changing cell" and cell E5 as "Set cell" with its value at 10,000. The gradient amounts shown in cells C12 through C16 are obtained by varying the initial gradient amount in cell E4. The correct gradient amount (G) is determined at $628.67, which will cause the set cell value to be exactly $10,000.

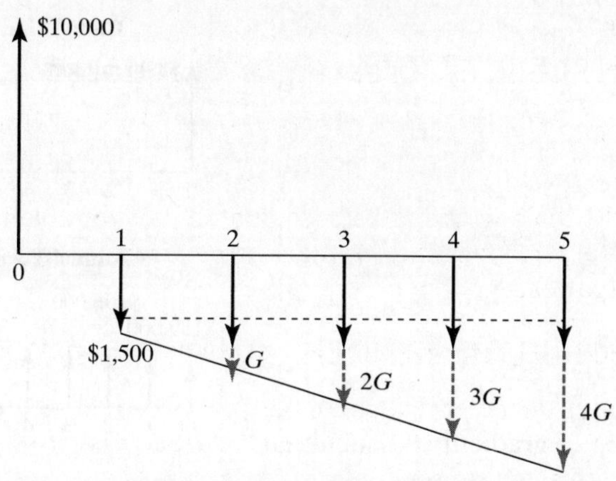

Figure 2.28 Cash flow diagram representing a graduated payment plan

TABLE 2.8 **An Excel Worksheet to Determine the Size of the Gradient Amount (Example 2.17**

	A	B	C	D	E	F	G	H	I
1	Example 2.16								
2									
3	Input:			Output:					
4	Interest Rate (%)	10		Gradient (G)	$628.67	By changing cell			
5	Borrowing (B)	$10,000		Present Worth (P)	$10,000.00	Set cell			
6									
7									
8	Period		Repayment Series		Present Worth	=SUM(E12:E16)			
9	(n)	A1	G	Total					
10									
11	0								
12	1	$1,500.00	$0.00	$1,500.00	$1,363.64				
13	2	$1,500.00	$628.67	$2,128.67	$1,759.23	=D13*(1+$B$4)^(-A13)			
14	3	$1,500.00	$1,257.34	$2,757.34	$2,071.63				
15	4	$1,500.00	$1,886.01	$3,386.01	$2,312.69				
16	5	$1,500.00	$2,514.69	$4,014.69	$2,492.80				
17									
18									
19		=$E$4*(A16-1)		=B16+C16					
20									
21									

EXAMPLE 2.18 Equivalent Cash Value

So, what could be better than winning a SuperLotto Plus jackpot? Choosing how to receive your winnings! Before playing a SuperLotto Plus jackpot, you have a choice between getting the entire jackpot in 26 annual graduated payments or receiving one lump sum that will be less than the announced jackpot. (See Figure 2.29.) What would these choices come out to for an announced jackpot of $7 million?

- **Lump-sum cash-value option:** The winner would receive the present cash value of the announced jackpot in one lump sum. In this case, the winner would receive about 49.43%, or $3.46 million, in one lump sum (less tax withholdings).

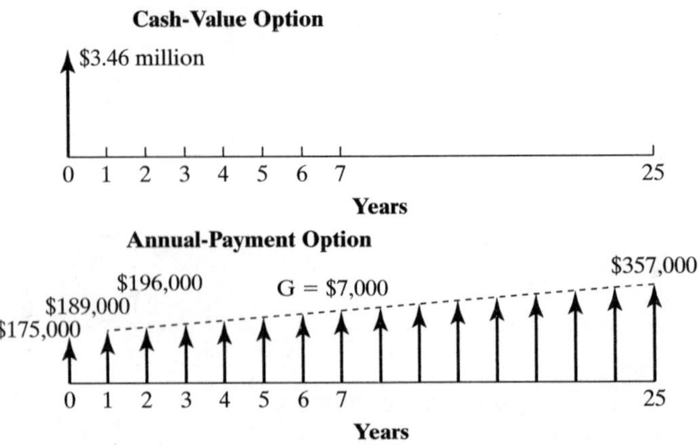

Figure 2.29 Cash flow diagram

This cash value is based on average market costs determined by U.S. Treasury zero-coupon bonds with 5.3383% annual yield.

- **Annual-payments option:** The winner would receive the jackpot in 26 graduated annual payments. In this case, the winner would receive $175,000 as the first payment (2.5% of the total jackpot amount) immediately. The second payment would be $189,000. Over the course of the next 25 years, these payments would gradually increase each year by $7,000 to a final payment of $357,000.

If the U.S. Treasury zero-coupon rate is reduced to 4.5% (instead of 5.338%) at the time of winning, what would be the equivalent cash value of the lottery?

DISSECTING THE PROBLEM

This problem is identical to asking what the equivalent present worth for this annual-payment series is at 4.5% interest.

Given: $A_0 = \$175,000, A_1 = \$189,000, G = \$7,000$ (from payment periods 2 to 25), $i = 4.5\%$ per year, and $N = 25$ years, as shown in Figure 2.29.

Find: P.

METHODOLOGY

Method 1: Compute the Equivalent Cash Value
Note that the annual payment series consists of a single payment at $n = 0$ and a linear gradient series.

SOLUTION

This method yields the following:

$$P = \$175,000 + 189,000(P/A, 4.5\%, 25)$$
$$+ \$7,000(P/G, 4.5\%, 25)$$
$$= \$3,990,189.$$

The cash value now has increased from $3.46 million to $3.99 million. In other words, if you check the "Cash Value" box on your lottery ticket and you win, you will receive the present cash value of the announced jackpot in one lump sum in the amount of $3.99 million.

Method 2: Excel Spreadsheet
Using Excel, we could reproduce the same result, as in Table 2.9.

In obtaining column C of the spreadsheet in Table 2.9, we could get the annual cash flow amount in each year by adding $7,000 to the amount in the previous period. For example, Cell C14 is obtained by = C13 + $C$7. Then Cell C15 is obtained by = C14 + $C$7 and so on.

TABLE 2.9 **An Excel Worksheet to Calculate Equivalent Cash Value**

	A	B	C	D	E
1	**Example 2.18: Cash Value Calculation**				
2					
3					
4		Winning Jackpot	$ 7,000,000		
5		Interest Rate (%)	4.50%		
6		Base Amount	$ 189,000		
7		Gradient Amount	$ 7,000		
8					
9	**Payment**	**Payment Schedule**	**Annual Payment**	**Discounting**	**Present**
10	**Period**	**as % of Jackpot**	**before Taxes**	**Factor (4.5%)**	**Cash Value**
11					
12	0	2.50%	$ 175,000	1.00000	$ 175,000
13	1	2.70%	$ 189,000	0.95694	$ 180,861
14	2	2.80%	$ 196,000	0.91573	$ 179,483
15	3	2.90%	$ 203,000	0.87630	$ 177,888
16	4	3.00%	$ 210,000	0.83856	$ 176,098
17	5	3.10%	$ 217,000	0.80245	$ 174,132
18	6	3.20%	$ 224,000	0.76790	$ 172,009
19	7	3.30%	$ 231,000	0.73483	$ 169,745
20	8	3.40%	$ 238,000	0.70319	$ 167,358
21	9	3.50%	$ 245,000	0.67290	$ 164,862
22	10	3.60%	$ 252,000	0.64393	$ 162,270
23	11	3.70%	$ 259,000	0.61620	$ 159,595
24	12	3.80%	$ 266,000	0.58966	$ 156,851
25	13	3.90%	$ 273,000	0.56427	$ 154,046
26	14	4.00%	$ 280,000	0.53997	$ 151,192
27	15	4.10%	$ 287,000	0.51672	$ 148,299
28	16	4.20%	$ 294,000	0.49447	$ 145,374
29	17	4.30%	$ 301,000	0.47318	$ 142,426
30	18	4.40%	$ 308,000	0.45280	$ 139,463
31	19	4.50%	$ 315,000	0.43330	$ 136,490
32	20	4.60%	$ 322,000	0.41464	$ 133,515
33	21	4.70%	$ 329,000	0.39679	$ 130,543
34	22	4.80%	$ 336,000	0.37970	$ 127,579
35	23	4.90%	$ 343,000	0.36335	$ 124,629
36	24	5.00%	$ 350,000	0.34770	$ 121,696
37	25	5.10%	$ 357,000	0.33273	$ 118,785
38					
39	**Total**		$ 7,000,000		$ 3,990,189
40					
41					
42		=B36+0.001		=(1+$C$5)^(-A37)	
43			=$C$4*B37		=SUM(E12:E37)
44					
45				=C37*D37	
46					

2.6.2 Handling Geometric Gradient Series

Another kind of gradient series is formed when the series in a cash flow is determined, not by some fixed amount like $500 but by some *fixed rate* expressed as a percentage. Many engineering economic problems, particularly those relating to construction costs or maintenance costs, involve cash flows that increase or decrease over time by a constant percentage (**geometric**), a process that is called **compound growth**. Price changes caused by inflation are a good example of such a geometric series.

If we use g to designate the percentage change in a payment from one period to the next, the magnitude of the nth payment A_n is related to the first payment A_1 as follows:

$$A_n = A_1(1 + g)^{n-1}, n = 1, 2, \ldots, N. \tag{2.14}$$

The g can take either a positive or a negative sign, depending on the type of cash flow. If $g > 0$, the series will increase; if $g < 0$, the series will decrease. Figure 2.30 illustrates the cash flow diagram for this situation.

Present-Worth Factor: Find P, Given $A_1, g, i,$ and N

Notice that the present worth P_n of any cash flow A_n at an interest rate i is

$$P_n = A_n(1 + i)^{-n} = A_1(1 + g)^{n-1}(1 + i)^{-n}. \tag{2.15}$$

To find an expression for the present amount for the entire series, P, we apply the **single-payment present-worth factor** to each term of the series:

$$P = \sum_{n=1}^{N} A_1(1 + g)^{n-1}(1 + i)^{-n}.$$

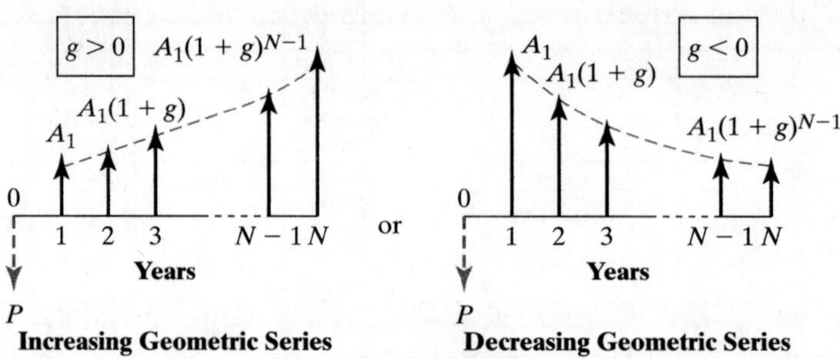

$$P = \begin{cases} A_1\left[\dfrac{1 - (1 + g)^N (1 + i)^{-N}}{i - g}\right], & \text{if } i \neq g; \\[2ex] A_1\dfrac{N}{(1 + i)}, & \text{if } i = g \end{cases}$$

Figure 2.30 A geometrically increasing or decreasing gradient series

The expression in Eq. (2.15) has the following closed expression:

$$P = \begin{cases} A_1\left[\dfrac{1 - (1 + g)^N(1 + i)^{-N}}{i - g}\right] & \text{if } i \neq g, \\[2em] A_1\left(\dfrac{N}{1 + i}\right) & \text{if } i = g. \end{cases} \qquad (2.16)$$

Or we can write

$$P = A_1(P/A_1,g,i,N).$$

The factor within brackets is called the **geometric-gradient-series present-worth factor** and is designated $(P/A_1, g, i, N)$. In the special case where $i = g$, Eq. (2.16) becomes $P = [A_1/(1 + i)]N$.

There is an alternative way to derive the geometric-gradient-series present-worth factor. Bringing the constant term $A_1(1 + g)^{-1}$ in Eq. (2.15) outside the summation yields

$$P = \frac{A_1}{(1 + g)}\sum_{n=1}^{N}\left[\frac{1 + g}{1 + i}\right]^n = \frac{A_1}{(1 + g)}\sum_{n=1}^{N}\frac{1}{\left[1 + \dfrac{i - g}{1 + g}\right]^n}. \qquad (2.17)$$

If we define

$$g' = \frac{i - g}{1 + g},$$

then we can rewrite P as follows:

$$P = \frac{A_1}{(1 + g)}\sum_{n=1}^{N}(1 + g')^{-n} = \frac{A_1}{(1 + g)}(P/A,g',N). \qquad (2.18)$$

We do not need another interest-factor table for this **geometric-gradient-series present-worth factor** as we can evaluate the factor with $(P/A,g',N)$. In the special case where $i = g$, Eq. (2.18) becomes $P = [A_1/(1 + i)]N$, as $g' = 0$.

EXAMPLE 2.19 Required Cost-of-Living Adjustment Calculation

Suppose that your retirement benefits during your first year of retirement are $50,000. Assume that this amount is just enough to meet your cost of living during the first year. However, your cost of living is expected to increase at an annual rate of 5% due to inflation. Suppose you do not expect to receive any cost-of-living adjustment in your retirement pension. Then, some of your future cost of living has to come from savings other than retirement pension. If your savings account earns 7% interest a year, how much should you set aside in order to meet this future increase in the cost of living over 25 years?

DISSECTING THE PROBLEM

Given: $A_1 = \$50,000, g = 5\%, i = 7\%$ per year, and $N = 25$ years, as shown in Figure 2.31.

Find: P.

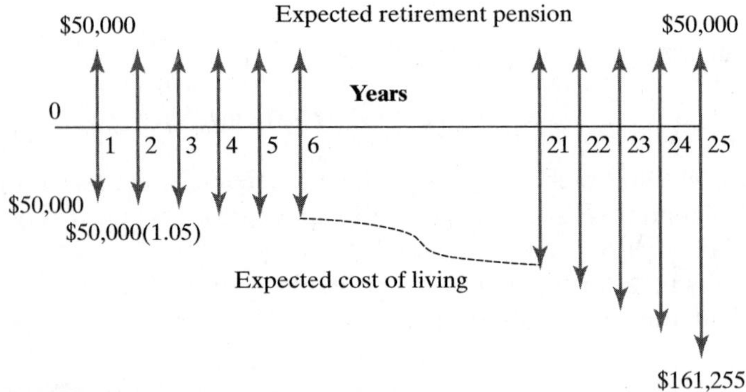

Figure 2.31   Cash flow diagram

METHODOLOGY

Method 1: Calculate Present Worth

SOLUTION

- Find the equivalent amount of total benefits paid over 25 years:

$$P = \$50,000(P/A, 7\%, 25)$$
$$= \$582,679.$$

- Find the equivalent amount of total cost of living with inflation. Using Eq. (2.16), the equivalent present worth of the cost of living is

$$P = \$50,000(P/A_1, 5\%, 7\%, 25)$$
$$= \$50,000\left[\frac{1 - (1 + 0.05)^{25}(1 + 0.07)^{-25}}{0.07 - 0.05}\right]$$
$$= \$50,000(18.8033)$$
$$= \$940,167.22.$$

Alternatively, to use Eq. (2.18), we need to find the value of g':

$$g' = \frac{0.07 - 0.05}{1 + 0.05} = 0.019048.$$

Then, using Eq. (2.18), we find P to be

$$P = \frac{50,000}{1 + 0.05}(P/A, 1.9048\%, 25)$$
$$= \$940,167.$$

Method 2: Excel Worksheet

Or you can confirm the P value through an Excel worksheet as shown in Table 2.10. The required additional savings to meet the future increase in cost of living will be

$$\Delta P = \$940{,}167 - \$582{,}679$$
$$= \$357{,}488.$$

TABLE 2.10 **An Excel Worksheet to Illustrate the Process of Calculating the Savings Required for Retirement**

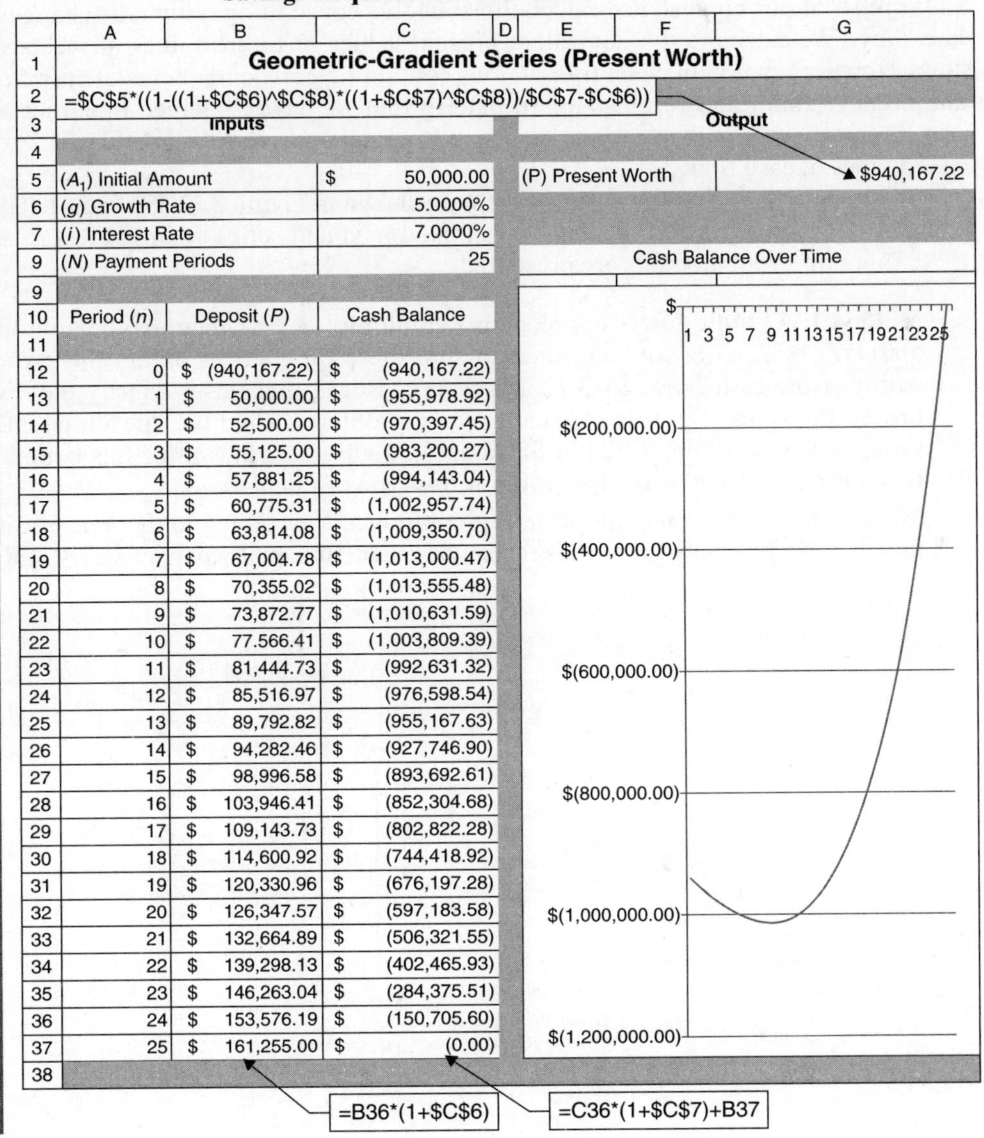

	A	B	C	D E F	G
1		**Geometric-Gradient Series (Present Worth)**			
2	=$C$5*((1-((1+$C$6)^$C$8)*((1+$C$7)^$C$8))/$C$7-$C$6))				
3		Inputs			Output
4					
5	(A_1) Initial Amount	$	50,000.00	(P) Present Worth	$940,167.22
6	(g) Growth Rate		5.0000%		
7	(i) Interest Rate		7.0000%		
9	(N) Payment Periods		25	Cash Balance Over Time	
9					
10	Period (n)	Deposit (P)	Cash Balance		
11					
12	0	$ (940,167.22)	$ (940,167.22)		
13	1	$ 50,000.00	$ (955,978.92)		
14	2	$ 52,500.00	$ (970,397.45)		
15	3	$ 55,125.00	$ (983,200.27)		
16	4	$ 57,881.25	$ (994,143.04)		
17	5	$ 60,775.31	$ (1,002,957.74)		
18	6	$ 63,814.08	$ (1,009,350.70)		
19	7	$ 67,004.78	$ (1,013,000.47)		
20	8	$ 70,355.02	$ (1,013,555.48)		
21	9	$ 73,872.77	$ (1,010,631.59)		
22	10	$ 77.566.41	$ (1,003,809.39)		
23	11	$ 81,444.73	$ (992,631.32)		
24	12	$ 85,516.97	$ (976,598.54)		
25	13	$ 89,792.82	$ (955,167.63)		
26	14	$ 94,282.46	$ (927,746.90)		
27	15	$ 98,996.58	$ (893,692.61)		
28	16	$ 103,946.41	$ (852,304.68)		
29	17	$ 109,143.73	$ (802,822.28)		
30	18	$ 114,600.92	$ (744,418.92)		
31	19	$ 120,330.96	$ (676,197.28)		
32	20	$ 126,347.57	$ (597,183.58)		
33	21	$ 132,664.89	$ (506,321.55)		
34	22	$ 139,298.13	$ (402,465.93)		
35	23	$ 146,263.04	$ (284,375.51)		
36	24	$ 153,576.19	$ (150,705.60)		
37	25	$ 161,255.00	$ (0.00)		
38					

=B36*(1+$C$6)   =C36*(1+$C$7)+B37

Table 2.11 summarizes the interest formulas developed in this section and the cash flow situations in which they should be used. Recall that all the interest formulas developed in this section are applicable to situations only *where the interest (compounding) period is the same as the payment period* (e.g., annual compounding with annual payment). We also present some of Excel's useful financial commands in this table.

2.7 More on Equivalence Calculations

So far most of our equivalence calculations involve constant or systematic changes in cash flows. We calculate the equivalent present values or future values of these cash flows. However, many financial transactions contain several components of cash flows that do not exhibit an overall standard pattern that we have examined in earlier section. Consequently, it is necessary to expand our analysis to handle situations with mixed types of cash flows.

To illustrate, consider the cash flow stream shown in Figure 2.32. We want to compute the equivalent present worth for this mixed-payment series at an interest rate of 15%. Three different methods are presented.

Method 1: A "brute-force" approach is to multiply each payment by the appropriate $(P/F, 10\%, n)$ factors and then to sum these products to obtain the present worth of the cash flows, $543.72 in this case. Recall that this is exactly the same procedure we used to solve the category of problems called the uneven-payment series, which were described in Section 2.4. Figure 2.32 illustrates this computational method. Excel is the best tool for this type of calculation.

Method 2: We may group the cash flow components according to the type of cash flow pattern that they fit, such as the single payment, equal-payment series, and so

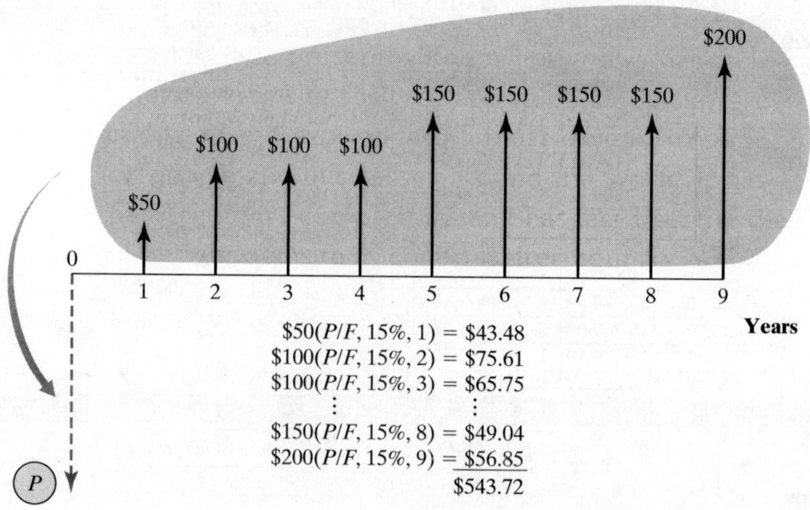

Figure 2.32 Method 1: A "brute-force" approach using P/F factors

TABLE 2.11 Summary of Compound-Interest Formulas

Flow Type	Factor Notation	Formula	Excel Command	Cash Flow Diagram
SINGLE	Compound Amount $(F/P, i, N)$	$F = P(1 + i)^N$	$= \text{FV}(i\%, N, 0, P)$	
	Present Worth $(P/F, i, N)$	$P = F(1 + i)^{-N}$	$= \text{PV}(i\%, N, 0, F)$	
EQUAL PAYMENT SERIES	Compound Amount $(F/A, i, N)$	$F = A\left[\dfrac{(1 + i)^N - 1}{i}\right]$	$= \text{FV}(i\%, N, A)$	
	Sinking Fund $(A/F, i, N)$	$A = F\left[\dfrac{i}{(1 + i)^N - 1}\right]$	$= \text{PMT}(i\%, N, 0, F)$	
	Present Worth $(P/A, i, N)$	$P = A\left[\dfrac{(1 + i)^N - 1}{i(1 + i)^N}\right]$	$= \text{PV}(i\%, N, A)$	
	Capital Recovery $(A/P, i, N)$	$A = P\left[\dfrac{i(1 + i)^N}{(1 + i)^N - 1}\right]$	$= \text{PMT}(i\%, N, P)$	
GRADIENT SERIES	Linear Gradient Present Worth $(P/G, i, N)$	$P = G\left[\dfrac{(1 + i)^N - iN - 1}{i^2(1 + i)^N}\right]$		
	Equal-Payment Conversion Factor $(A/G, i, N)$	$A = G\left[\dfrac{(1 + i)^N - iN - 1}{i(1 + i)^N - i}\right]$		
SERIES	Geometric-Gradient Present Worth $(P/A_1, g, i, N)$	$P = \left[\begin{array}{c} A_1\left[\dfrac{1 - (1 + g)^N(1 + i)^{-N}}{i - g}\right] \\[2ex] A_1\left(\dfrac{N}{1 + i}\right), (\text{if } i = g) \end{array}\right]$		

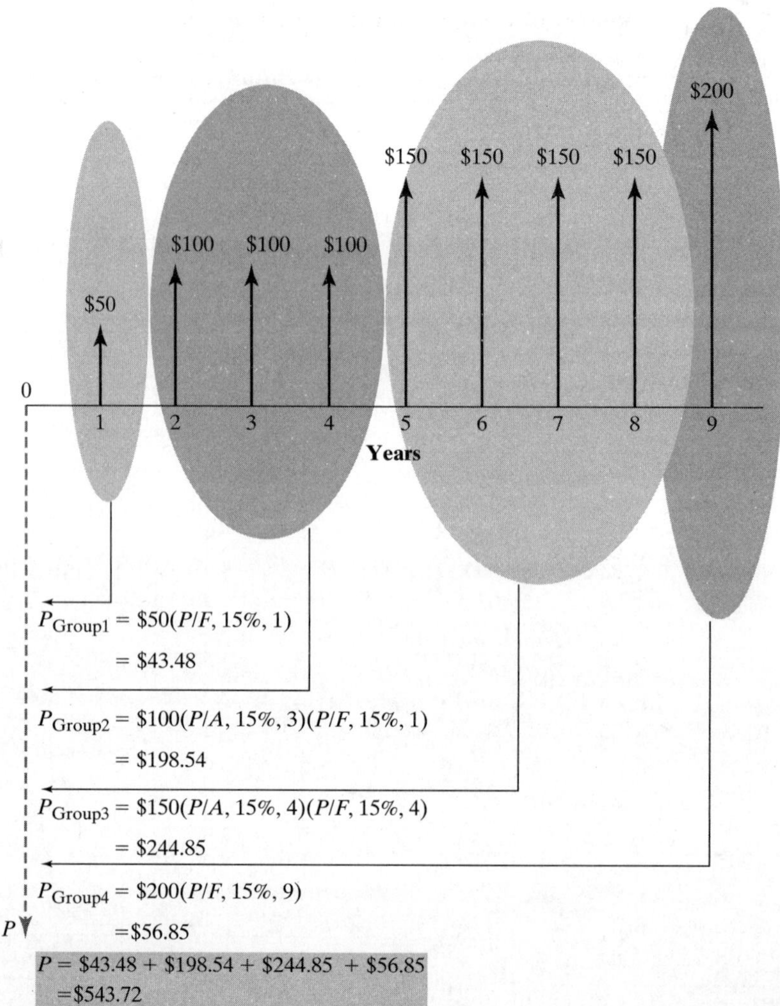

Figure 2.33 Method 2: Grouping approach using P/F and P/A factors

forth as shown in Figure 2.33. Then the solution procedure involves the following steps:

- Group 1: Find the present worth of $50 due in year 1:

$$\$50(P/F, 15\%, 1) = \$43.48.$$

- Group 2: Find the equivalent worth of a $100 equal-payment series at year 1 (V_1), and then bring in this equivalent worth at year 0:

$$\underbrace{\$100(P/A, 15\%, 3)}_{V_1}(P/F, 15\%, 1) = \$198.54.$$

- Group 3: Find the equivalent worth of a $150 equal-payment series at year 4 (V_4), and then bring in this equivalent worth at year 0.

$$\underbrace{\$150(P/A,15\%,4)}_{V_4}(P/F,15\%,4) = \$244.85.$$

- Group 4: Find the equivalent present worth of the $200 due in year 9:

$$\$200(P/F,15\%,9) = \$56.85.$$

- For the group total, sum the components:

$$P = \$43.48 + \$198.54 + \$244.85 + \$56.85$$
$$= \$543.72.$$

A pictorial view of this computational process is also given in Figure 2.33. Either the brute-force method in Figure 2.32 or the method using both the (P/A, i, n) and (P/F, i, n) factors in Figure 2.33 can be used to solve problems of this type. Method 2 is much easier if the annuity component runs for many years, however. For example, this solution would be clearly superior for finding the equivalent present worth of a payment stream consisting of $50 in year 1, $200 in years 2 through 19, and $500 in year 20.

TABLE 2.12 **Method 3: Using Excel to Compute the Present Worth**

	A	B	C	D
1	**Composite Cash Flows**			
2				
3	**Input:**			
4	Interest Rate (%)	15%		=NPV($B$4,B12:B20)
5	**Output:**			
6	Present Worth (P)	$543.72		
7				
8	Period	Cash	Present	
9	(n)	Flow	Worth	
10				
11	0			
12	1	$50.00	$43.48	←=B12*(1+$B$4)^(-A12)
13	2	$100.00	$75.61	←=B13*(1+$B$4)^(-A13)
14	3	$100.00	$65.75	←=B14*(1+$B$4)^(-A14)
15	4	$100.00	$57.18	←=B15*(1+$B$4)^(-A15)
16	5	$150.00	$74.58	←=B16*(1+$B$4)^(-A16)
17	6	$150.00	$64.85	←=B17*(1+$B$4)^(-A17)
18	7	$150.00	$56.39	←=B18*(1+$B$4)^(-A18)
19	8	$150.00	$49.04	←=B19*(1+$B$4)^(-A19)
20	9	$200.00	$56.85	←=B20*(1+$B$4)^(-A20)
21				
22			$543.72	
23				=SUM(C12:C20)
24				
25				

Method 3: With Excel, we may create a worksheet as shown in Table 2.12. In computing the present worth of the entire series, we may compute the equivalent present worth for each cash flow and sum them up. Or we could use the NPV function with the parameters, $= \text{NPV}(\$B\$4, B12\!:\!B20)$, which will calculate the present worth of the entire series.

EXAMPLE 2.20 Retirement Planning: Composite Series That Requires Multiple Interest Factors

You want to supplement your retirement income through IRA contributions. You have 15 years left until retirement and you are going to make 15 equal annual deposits into your IRA until you retire with the first deposit being made at the end of year 1. You need to save enough so that you can make 10 annual withdrawals that will begin at the end of year 16. The first withdrawal will be $10,000, and each subsequent withdrawal will increase at a rate of 4% over the previous year's withdrawal in line with expected increase in cost-of-living. Your last withdrawal will be at the end of year 25. What is the amount of the equal annual deposit amount (C) for the first 15 years? Assume the interest rate is 8% compounded annually before and after you retire.

DISSECTING THE PROBLEM

Given: $i = 8\%$ per year, deposit and withdrawal series shown in Figure 2.34a.

Find: A

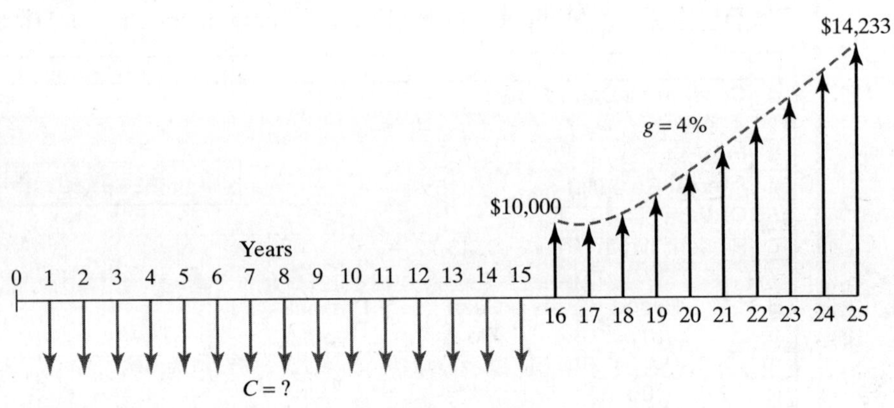

Figure 2.34a Establishing a retirement fund (Example 2.20).

METHODOLOGY

Method 1: Establish the Economic Equivalence at Period 0

SOLUTION

First, compute the equivalent worth of the total deposit series at $n = 0$.

$$P_{\text{deposit}} = C(P/A, 8\%, 15) = 8.5595C.$$

Find the equivalent single lump-sum withdrawal now in two steps by finding the equivalent amount at $n = 15$ and then bring this value back to $n = 0$:

$$P_{\text{withdrawal}} = \$10,000 \underbrace{(P/A_1, 4\%, 8\%, 10)}_{7.8590} \underbrace{(P/F, 8\%, 15)}_{0.3152}$$

where the underbrace over $(P/A_1, 4\%, 8\%, 10)$ is labeled V_{15} and the underbrace over $(P/F, 8\%, 15)$ is labeled Discounting factor.

Since the two amounts are equivalent, by equating, we obtain C.

$$8.5595C = \$24{,}771.60$$
$$C = \$2{,}894.$$

Method 2: Establish the Economic Equivalence at $n = 15$.

First, compute the accumulated balance at the end of 15 years. Call this amount F_{15}.

$$F_{15} = C(F/A, 8\%, 15) = \$27.1521C.$$

Then find the equivalent lump-sum withdrawal at the end of retirement contribution, $n = 15$. Call this $V15$:

$$V_{15} = \$10{,}000(P/A_1, 4\%, 8\%, 15) = \$78{,}590.$$

Since the two amounts must be the same, $F_{15} = V_{15}$, we obtain

$$27.1521C = \$78{,}590$$
$$C = \$2{,}894.$$

The computational steps are illustrated in Figure 2.34b.

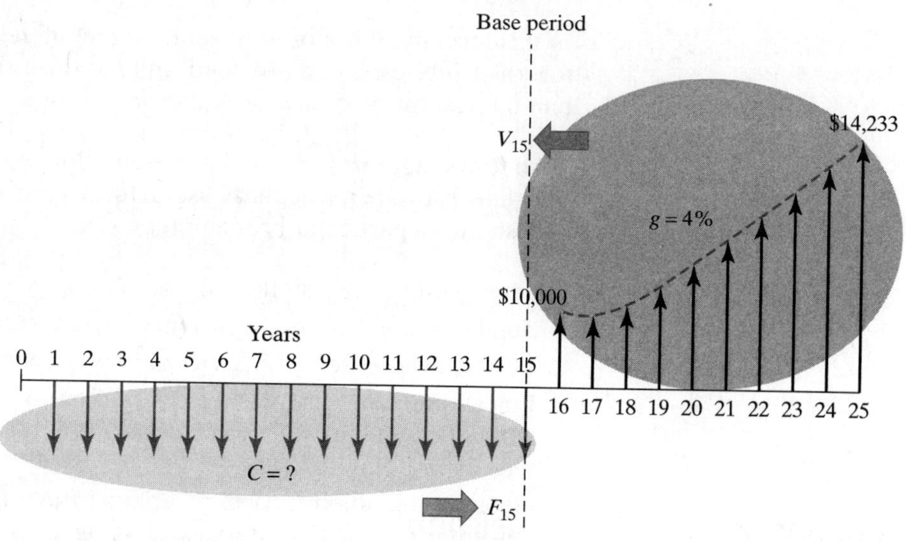

Figure 2.34b Establishing economic equivalence by selecting the base period at $n = 15$.

COMMENTS: In general, Method 2 is the more efficient way to obtain an equivalence solution to this type of decision problem as it requires fewer interest factors.

SUMMARY

- Money has a time value because it can earn more money over time. A number of terms involving the time value of money were introduced in this chapter:

  Interest *is the cost of money. More specifically, it is a cost to the borrower and an earning to the lender above and beyond the initial sum borrowed or loaned.*

  Interest rate *is a percentage periodically applied to a sum of money to determine the amount of interest to be added to that sum.*

  Simple interest *is the practice of charging an interest rate only to an initial sum.*

  Compound interest *is the practice of charging an interest rate to an initial sum and to any previously accumulated interest that has not been withdrawn from the initial sum. Compound interest is by far the most commonly used system in the real world.*

  Economic equivalence *exists between individual cash flows or between patterns of cash flows that have the same value. Even though the amounts and timing of the cash flows may differ, the appropriate interest rate makes them equal.*

- The following compound-interest formula is perhaps the single most important equation in this text:

$$F = P(1 + i)^N.$$

  In this formula, P is a present sum, i is the interest rate, N is the number of periods for which interest is compounded, and F is the resulting future sum. All other important interest formulas are derived from this one.

- **Cash flow diagrams** are visual representations of cash inflows and outflows along a time line. They are particularly useful for helping us detect which of the five patterns of cash flow a particular problem represents.

- The five patterns of cash flow are as follows:

  1. Single payment: A single present or future cash flow.
  2. Equal-payment series: A series of flows of equal amounts at regular intervals.
  3. Linear gradient series: A series of flows increasing or decreasing by a fixed amount at regular intervals. Excel is one of the most convenient tools to solve this type of cash flow series.
  4. Geometric-gradient series: A series of flows increasing or decreasing by a fixed percentage at regular intervals. Once again, this type of cash flow series is a good candidate for solution by using Excel.
  5. Uneven series: A series of flows exhibiting no overall pattern. However, patterns might be detected for portions of the series.

- **Cash flow patterns** are significant because they allow us to develop **interest formulas**, which streamline the solution of equivalence problems. Table 2.11 summarizes the important interest formulas that form the foundation for all other analyses you will conduct in engineering economic analysis.

SELF-TEST QUESTIONS

2s.1 You wish to have $20,000 in an account 8 years from now. How much money must be deposited in the account now in order to have this amount if the account pays 12% compounded annually?

(a) $8,490

(b) $8,871

(c) $7,632

(d) $8,078

2s.2 Assume that $1,000 is deposited today, two years from now, four years from now, six years from now, and eight years from now. At 8% interest compounded annually, determine the future value at the end of year 9.

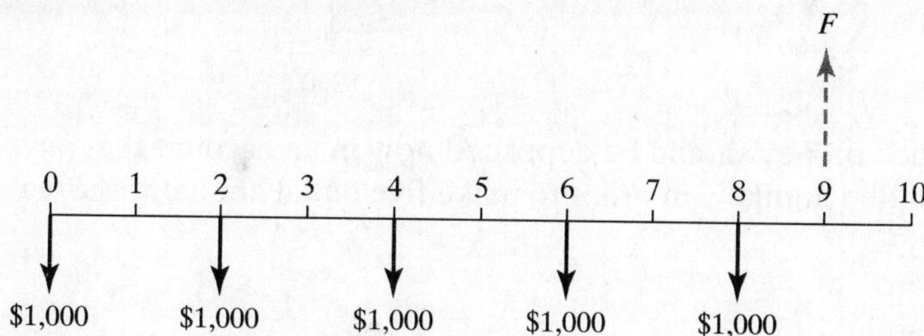

(a) $4,174

(b) $7,521

(c) $2,085

(d) $1,895

2s.3 What single payment at the end of year 5 is equivalent to an equal annual series of payments of $600 beginning at the end of year 3 and ending at the end of year 12? The interest rate is 10% compounded annually.

(a) $4,907

(b) $6,260

(c) $6,762

(d) $6,883

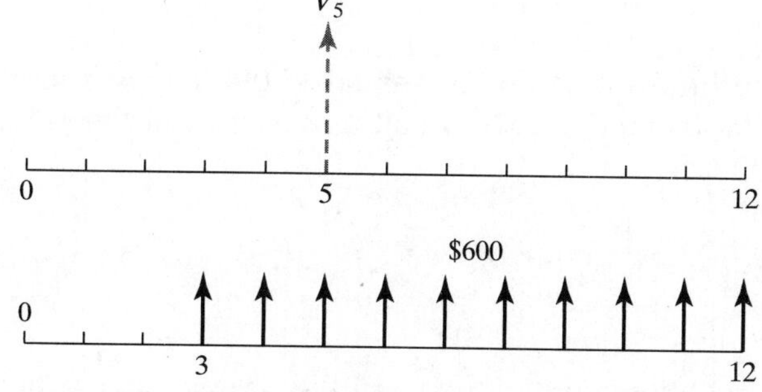

2s.4 Four years ago, you opened a mutual fund account and made three deposits ($100 four years ago, $X three years ago, and $200 a year ago) where you earned varying interest rates, according to the diagram that follows. Today your balance shows $800. Determine the amount of the deposit made three years ago (X). See the following figure.

(a) −$115.3

(b) −$100.7

(c) −$103.2

(d) −$105.4

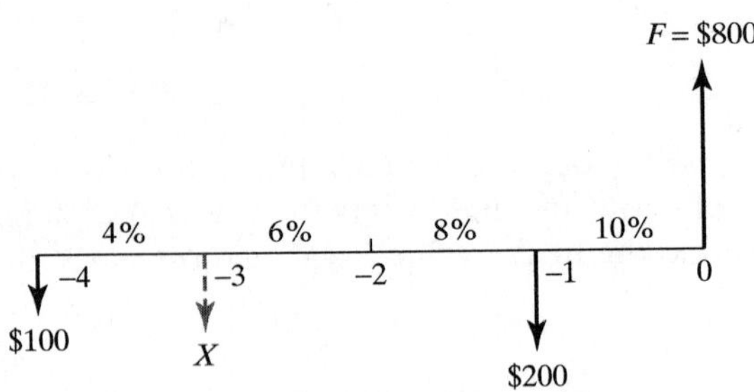

2s.5 How much money should be deposited now in an account that pays 12% interest compounded annually in order to make five equal annual withdrawals of $8,000?

(a) $8,052

(b) $9,050

(c) $16,761

(d) $28,839

2s.6 State the value of C that makes the following two cash flow transactions economically equivalent at an interest rate of 12%

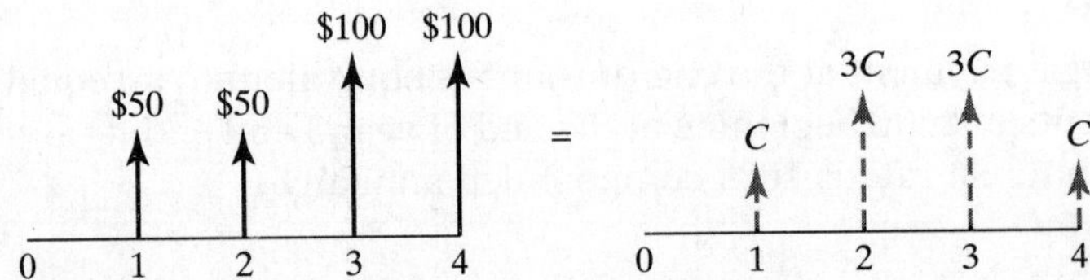

(a) $29.365

(b) $33.598

(c) $47.433

(d) $43.796

2s.7 Calculate the future worth of 20 annual $3,000 deposits in a savings account that earns 8% (compounded annually). Assume all deposits are made at the *beginning* of each year.

(a) $126,005

(b) $111,529

(c) $148,268

(d) $192,037

2s.8 You have borrowed $28,000 at an interest rate of 12% compounded annually. Equal payments will be made over a four-year period, with each payment made at the end of the corresponding year? What is the interest payment for the second year?

(a) $1,800

(b) $2,251

(c) $1,089

(d) $2,657

2s.9   The following two cash flows are said to be economically equivalent at 8% interest. Determine the value of X for the second cash flow series.

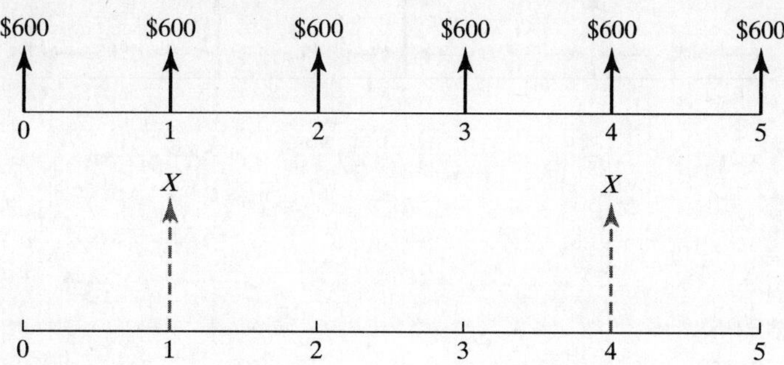

(a) $X = $1,505

(b) $X = $1,726

(c) $X = $1,197

(d) $X = $1,192

2s.10   What is the amount of ten equal annual deposits that can provide five annual withdrawals, where a first withdrawal of $2,000 is made at the end of year 11 and subsequent withdrawals increase at the rate of 5% per year over the previous year's if the interest rate is 7% compounded annually?

(a) $745

(b) $652

(c) $1,000

(d) $1,563

2s.11   You borrowed $5,000 to finance your educational expenses at the beginning of your junior year of college at an interest rate of 10% compounded annually. You are required to pay off the loan with five equal annual installments, but the first payment will be deferred until your graduation. Determine the value of C, the amount of annual payments.

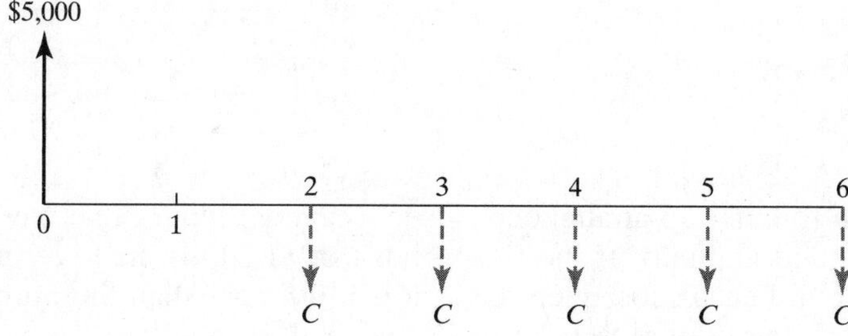

(a) $C = $891

(b) $C = $1,082

(c) $C = $1,407

(d) $C = $1,222

2s.12 Consider the accompanying cash flow series at varying interest rates. What is the equivalent present worth of the cash flow series?

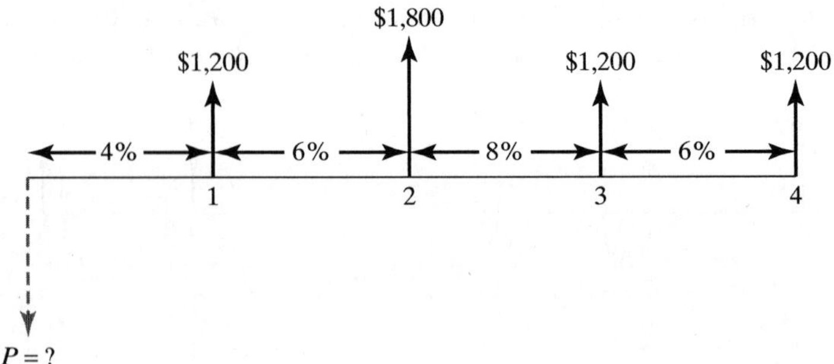

(a) $P = \$5,068$
(b) $P = \$4,442$
(c) $P = \$4,745$
(d) $P = \$3,833$

2s.13 At what annual interest rate will $1,200 invested today be worth $2,500 in 12 years?
(a) 6.5%
(b) 7.2%
(c) 9.02%
(d) 5.8%

2s.14 If you borrow $25,000 at an interest rate of 6%, compounded annually, with the repayment schedule as shown, what is the amount A? (Note that there is a missing payment in year 5.)

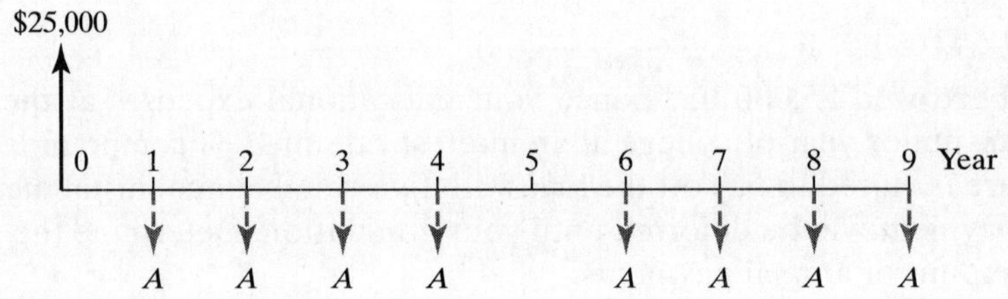

(a) $A = \$4,129$
(b) $A = \$4,793$
(c) $A = \$3,193$
(d) $A = \$3,593$

2s.15 You plan to make 15 annual deposits in a saving account that pays 6% interest compounded annually. If the first deposit of $1,200 is made at the end of the first year and each subsequent deposit is $400 more than the previous one, the value of the account at the end of 15 years will be nearly:
(a) $87,021
(b) $92,242
(c) $97,777
(d) $83,104

2s.16 How long would it take an investment to *triple* if the interest rate is 6% compounded annually?
(a) 9.90 years
(b) 12.23 years
(c) 14.65 years
(d) 18.85 years

2s.17 If you borrow $20,000 at an interest rate of 8%, compounded annually with the following repayment schedule, what is the required amount A?

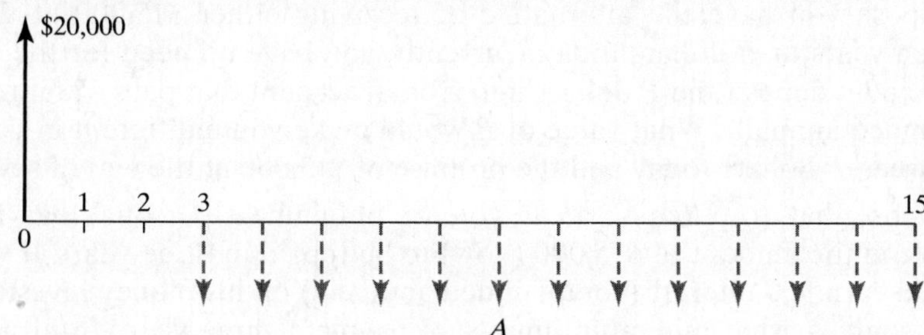

(a) $A = $2,951
(b) $A = $3,967
(c) $A = $3,101
(d) $A = $2,324

2s.18 If $1,500 is deposited in a savings account at the beginning of each year for 20 years (a total number of deposits = 20) and the account draws interest at 8% compounded annually, the value of the account at the end of 20 years will be nearly:
(a) $71,400
(b) $74,936
(c) $74,996
(d) $74,144

PROBLEMS

Methods of Calculating Interest

2.1 What is the amount of interest earned on $5,000 for three years at 8% simple interest per year?

2.2 You deposit $5,000 in a savings account that earns 6% simple interest per year. How many years will it take to double your balance? If, instead, you deposit the $5,000 in another savings account that earns 5% interest compounded yearly, how many years will it take to double your balance?

2.3 Compare the interest earned on $8,000 for 15 years at 8% simple interest with the amount of interest earned if interest were compounded annually.

2.4 Bank A pays 8% simple interest on its savings account balances. Bank B pays 7% interest compounded annually. If you made a $5,000 deposit in each bank, which bank provides you with more money at the end of 10 years?

2.5 You are considering investing $4,000 at an interest rate of 5% compounded annually for five years, or investing the $4,000 at 6% per year simple interest for seven years. Which option is better?

2.6 You are about to borrow $8,000 from a bank at an interest rate of 8% compounded annually. You are required to make five equal annual repayments in the amount of $2,004 per year, with the first repayment occurring at the end of year one. For each year, show the interest payment and principal payment.

The Concept of Equivalence

2.7 Suppose you have the alternative of receiving either $15,000 at the end of seven years or P dollars today. Currently, you have no need for the money, so you could deposit the P dollars into a bank account that pays 6% interest compounded annually. What value of P would make you indifferent in your choice between P dollars today and the promise of $15,000 at the end of seven years?

2.8 Suppose that, to purchase a car, you are obtaining a personal loan from your uncle in the amount of $75,000 (now) to be repaid in three years. If your uncle could earn 9% interest (compounded annually) on his money invested in various sources, what minimum lump-sum payment three years from now would make your uncle happy economically?

2.9 Which of the following alternatives would you choose, assuming an interest rate of 9% compounded annually?
Alternative 1: Receive $150 today;
Alternative 2: Receive $200 two years from now.
Alternative 3: Receive $250 five years from now.

Single Payments (Use of *F/P* or *P/F* Factors)

2.10 Today you deposited $10,000 in a savings account paying 7% annual interest. How much should you have at the end of five years?

2.11 If the interest rate is 6%, what is the present value of $800 paid at the end of year 10?

2.12 If the interest rate is 9%, what is the two-year discount rate?

2.13 State the amount accumulated by each of the following present investments:
(a) $5,000 in 6 years at 7% compounded annually.
(b) $1,3000 in 8years at 6% compounded annually.
(c) $16,000 in 25 years at 10% compounded annually.
(d) $10,000 in 10 years at 5% compounded annually.

2.14 State the present worth of the following future payments:
(a) $8,000 five years from now at 8% compounded annually.
(b) $10,000 six years from now at 10% compounded annually.
(c) $12,000 eight years from now at 7% compounded annually.
(d) $18,000 ten years from now at 9% compounded annually.

2.15 Assuming an interest rate of 10% compounded annually, answer the following questions:
(a) How much money can be loaned now if $20,000 is to be repaid at the end of five years?
(b) How much money will be required in five years in order to repay a $15,000 loan borrowed now?

2.16 How many years will it take an investment to quadruple if the interest rate is 9% compounded annually?

2.17 How many years will it take to triple your investment of $8,000 if it has an interest rate of 7% compounded annually?

2.18 You bought 100 shares of GE stock for $25,000 on October 23, 2011. Your intention is to keep the stock until it doubles in value. If you expect 12% annual growth for GE stock, how many years do you expect to hold onto the stock? Compare your answer with the solution obtained by the Rule of 72 (discussed in Example 2.7).

2.19 In 1739, Nader Shah sold the Kohinoor diamond to Queen Victoria for $34. If he saved just $5 from the proceeds in a bank account that paid an 6% annual interest, how much would his descendents have in 2020?

2.20 If you want to withdraw $20,000 at the end of two years and $55,000 at the end of four years, how much should you deposit now into an account that pays 12% interest compounded annually? See the accompanying cash flow diagram.

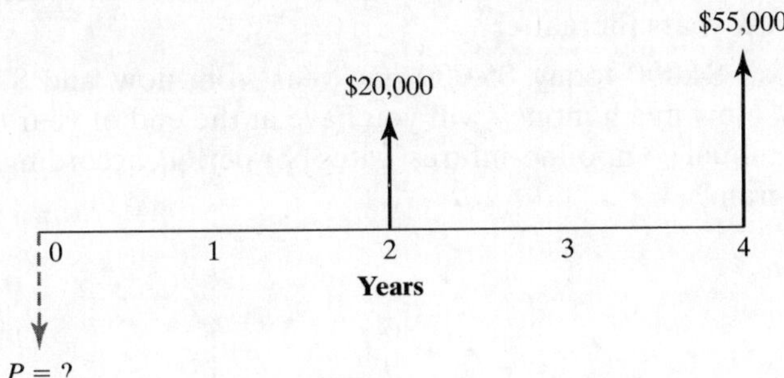

2.21 You are interested in buying a piece of real estate property that could be worth $450,000 in five years. If your earning interest rate is 5%, how much would you be willing to pay for this property now?

2.22 John and Susan just opened savings accounts at two different banks. Each deposited $1,000. John's bank pays simple interest at an annual rate of 10%, whereas Susan's bank pays compound interest at an annual rate of 9.5%. No principal or interest will be taken out of the accounts for a period of five years. At the end of five years, whose balance will be higher and by how much (to the nearest dollar)?

Uneven-Payment Series

2.23 A project is expected to generate a cash flow of $8000 in year 1, $2000 in year 2, and $5000 in year 3. At an interest rate of 8%, what is the maximum amount that you could invest in the project at year 0?

2.24 If you desire to withdraw the given amounts over the next five years from a savings account that earns 7% interest compounded annually, how much do you need to deposit now?

Year	Amount
2	$5,000
3	$6,000
4	$8,200
5	$4,500

2.25 If \$4,000 is invested now, \$7,000 two years from now, and \$5,000 four years from now at an interest rate of 9% compounded annually, what will be the total amount in 8 years?

2.26 A local newspaper headline blared, "Bo Smith Signs for \$30 Million." The article revealed that Bo Smith, the former record-breaking running back from Football University, signed a \$30 million package with the Nebraska Lions. The terms of the contract were \$3 million immediately, \$2.4 million per year for the first five years (with the first payment after one year), and \$3 million per year for the next five years (with the first payment at the end of year 6). If the interest rate is 8% compounded annually, what is Bo's contract worth at the time of contract signing?

2.27 How much invested now at an interest rate of 10% compounded annually would be just sufficient to provide three payments as follows: the first payment in the amount of \$5,000 occurring two years from now, the second payment in the amount of \$7,000 four years thereafter, and the third payment in the amount of \$9,000 six years thereafter?

2.28 You deposit \$4,000 today, \$5,000 one year from now, and \$7,000 three years from now. How much money will you have at the end of year three if there are different annual compound-interest rates per period, according to the accompanying diagram?

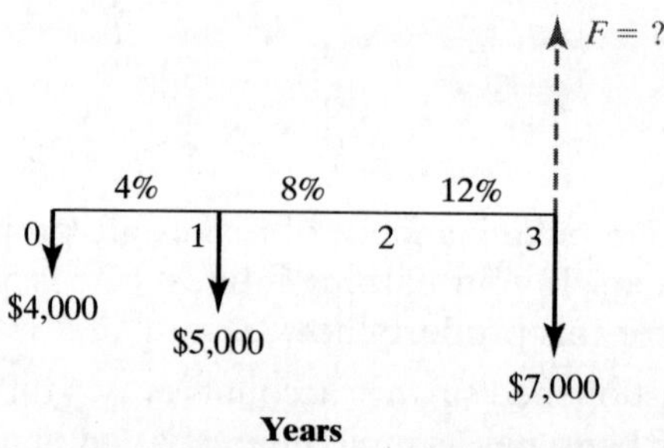

2.29 A company borrowed \$200,000 at an interest rate of 8% compounded annually over six years. The loan will be repaid in installments at the end of each year, according to the accompanying repayment schedule. What will be the size of the last payment (X) that will pay off the loan?

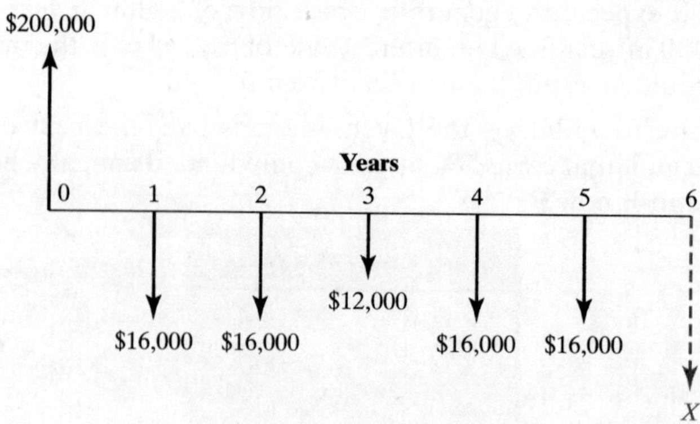

2.30 You are preparing to buy a vacation home five years from now. The home will cost $100,000 at that time. You plan on saving three deposits at an interest rate of 10%:

Deposit 1: Deposit $12,000 today.

Deposit 2: Deposit $15,000 two years from now.

Deposit 3: Deposit $ X three years from now.

How much do you need to invest in year three to ensure that you have the necessary funds to buy the vacation home at the end of year five?

2.31 The accompanying diagram shows the anticipated cash dividends for Delta Electronics over the next four years. John is interested in buying some shares of this stock for a total of $1000 and will hold them for four years. If John's interest rate is known to be 12% compounded annually, what would be the desired (minimum) total selling price for the set of shares at the end of the fourth year?

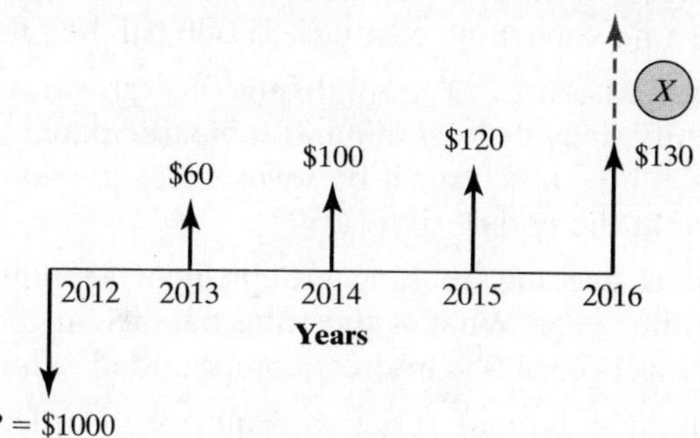

2.32 You are considering a machine that is expected to produce the following cash flows: $50,000 in year 1, $65,000 in year 2, $55,000 in year 3, $46,000 in year 4, and $39,000 in year 5. If your interest rate is 10%, what would be your maximum offer (purchase price) on this machine?

Equal-Payment Series

2.33 You are planning to contribute $8,000 a year into a mutual fund that earns an average of 8% per year. If you continue to contribute for the next 10 years, how much would you have in your account?

2.34 What is the future worth of a series of equal yearly deposits of $6,000 for 6 years in a savings account that earns 5% annual compound interest if
(a) all deposits are made at the *end* of each year?
(b) all deposits are made at the *beginning* of each year?

2.35 What is the future worth of each given series of payments?
(a) $8,000 at the end of each year for five years at 7% compounded annually.
(b) $10,000 at the end of each year for eight years at 8% compounded annually.
(c) $18,000 at the end of each year for 20 years at 10% compounded annually.
(d) $7,000 at the end of each year for 12 years at 12% compounded annually.

2.36 What equal annual series of payments must be paid into a sinking fund in order to accumulate each of the following given amounts?
(a) $28,000 in 12 years at 6% compounded annually.
(b) $21,000 in 10 years at 8% compounded annually.

     (c) $10,000 in 20 years at 7% compounded annually.

     (d) $15,000 in 11 years at 9% compounded annually.

2.37 Your company wants to set aside a fixed amount every year to a sinking fund to replace a piece of industrial equipment costing $375,000 at the end of eight years from now. The sinking fund is expected to earn 7% interest. How much must your company deposit each year to meet this goal?

2.38 You want to save the down payment required to purchase a vacation home at the end of four years. If the required down payment is $75,000 and you can earn 6% a year on your savings account, how much do you need to set aside at the end of each year for the next four years?

2.39 Part of the income that a machine generates is put into a sinking fund to pay for replacement of the machine when it wears out. If $5,000 is deposited every year at 7% interest compounded annually, how many years must the machine be kept before a new machine costing $55,000 can be purchased?

2.40 A no-load (commission-free) mutual fund has grown at a rate of 10% compounded annually since its beginning. If it is anticipated that it will continue to grow at this rate, how much must be invested every year so that $120,000 will be accumulated at the end of six years?

2.41 You open a bank account, making a deposit of $10000 now and deposits of $5,000 every other year. What is the total balance at the end of 8 years from now if your deposits earn 5% interest compounded annually?

2.42 What equal-annual-payment series is required in order to repay each given present amount?

     (a) $28,000 in four years at 7% interest compounded annually.

     (b) $4,800 in five years at 8% interest compounded annually.

     (c) $9,000 in six years at 5% interest compounded annually.

     (d) $33,000 in 15 years at 7% interest compounded annually.

2.43 You have borrowed $28,000 at an interest rate of 12% compounded annually. Equal payments will be made over a four-year period, with each payment made at the end of the corresponding year. What is the amount of the annual payment? What is the interest payment for the second year?

2.44 What is the present worth of each given series of payments?

     (a) $12,000 at the end of each year for five years at 5% compounded annually.

     (b) $18,000 at the end of each year for 12 years at 8% compounded annually.

     (c) $10,500 at the end of each year for seven years at 12% compounded annually.

     (d) $8,000 at the end of each year for 40 years at 6% compounded annually.

2.45 From the interest tables in Appendix B, determine the value of the following factors by interpolation, and compare the results with those obtained from evaluating the *A/P* and *P/A* interest formulas:

     (a) The capital-recovery factor for 36 periods at 6.25% compound interest.

     (b) The equal-payment-series present-worth factor for 125 periods at 9.25% compound interest.

2.46 If $800 is deposited in a savings account at the *beginning* of each year for 12 years and the account earns 8% interest compounded annually, what will be the balance on the account the end of the 15 years (F)?

2.47 If you borrow $9,000 and agree to repay the loan in six equal annual payments at an interest rate of 10%, what will the annual payment be? What if you make the first payment on the loan at the end of second year?

2.48 A company is considering replacing an old piece of industrial equipment to reduce operating and maintenance cost. A new equipment is quoted at $215,000. After 12 years, the machine would have no value, but it would save as much as $35,000 in operating and maintenance cost. If the firm's interest rate is 9%, is it worth buying the new equipment?

2.49 An investment costs $4,500 and pays $300 in perpetuity. What is the interest earned on this investment?

2.50 At an interest rate of 12%, what is the present value of an asset that produces $800 a year in perpetuity?

Linear Gradient Series

2.51 Kim deposits her annual bonus into a savings account that pays 7% interest compounded annually. The size of her bonus increases by $3,000 each year, and the initial bonus amount is $10,000. Determine how much will be in the account immediately after the fifth deposit.

2.52 Five annual deposits in the amounts of $15,000, $14,000, $13,000, $12,000, and $11,000 are made into a fund that pays interest at a rate of 7% compounded annually. Determine the amount in the fund immediately after the fifth deposit.

2.53 Compute the value of P for the accompanying cash flow diagram. Assume $i = 6\%$ per year.

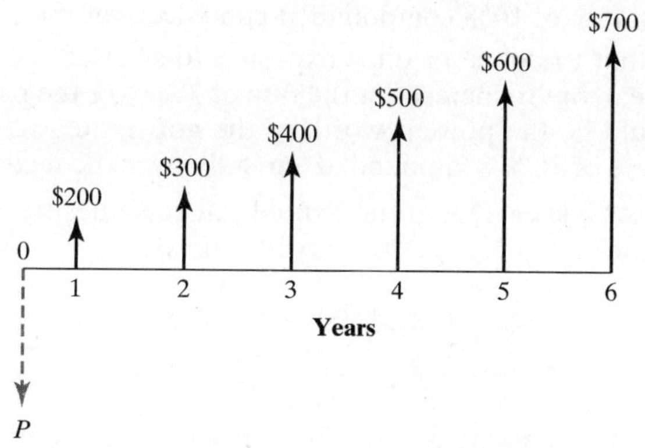

2.54 What is the equal-payment series for 10 years that is equivalent to a payment series starting with $10,000 at the end of the first year and decreasing by $1,000 each year over 10 years? Interest is 7% compounded annually.

2.55 The maintenance expense on a machine is expected to be $5,000 during the first year and to increase $500 each year for the following ten years. What present sum of money should be set aside now to pay for the required maintenance expenses over the ten-year period? (Assume 8% compound interest per year.)

2.56 Consider the cash flow series given in the accompanying table. What value of C makes the deposit series equivalent to the withdrawal series at an interest rate of 6% compounded annually?

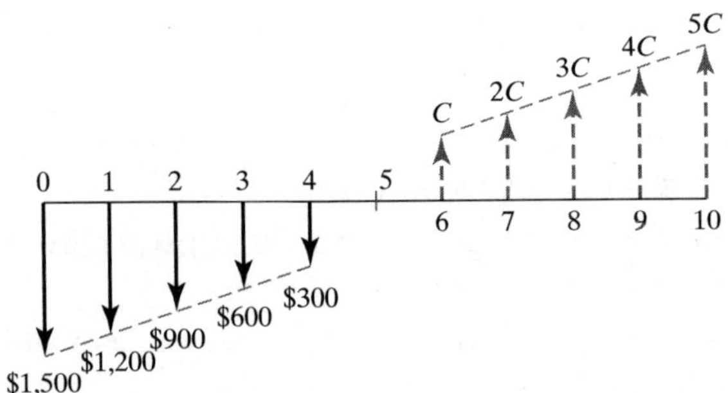

Geometric-Gradient Series

2.57 Matt Christopher is a 30-year-old mechanical engineer, and his salary next year will be $80,000. Matt expects that his salary will increase at a steady rate of 6% per year until his retirement at age 60. If he saves 10% of his salary each year and invest these savings at an interest rate of 8%, how much will he have at his retirement?

2.58 Suppose that an oil well is expected to produce 12, 00,000 barrels of oil during its first production year. However, its subsequent production (yield) is expected to decrease by 9% over the previous year's production. The oil well has a proven reserve of 10,500,000 barrels.

(a) Suppose that the price of oil is expected to be $120 per barrel for the next six years. What would be the present worth of the anticipated revenue trim at an interest rate of 10% compounded annually over the next six years?

(b) Suppose that the price of oil is expected to start at $120 per barrel during the first year, but to increase at the rate of 3% over the previous year's price. What would be the present worth of the anticipated revenue stream at an interest rate of 10% compounded annually over the next seven years?

2.59 A city engineer has estimated the annual toll revenues from a proposed highway construction project over 20 years as follows:

$$A_n = (\$2,000,000)(n)(1.06)^{n-1}$$
$$n = 1, 2, \ldots, 20.$$

To determine the amount of debt financing through bonds, the engineer was asked to present the estimated total present value of toll revenue at an interest rate of 6%. Assuming annual compounding, find the present value of the estimated toll revenue.

2.60 What is the amount of 10 equal annual deposits that can provide five annual withdrawals, when a first withdrawal of $3,000 is made at the end of year 11 and subsequent withdrawals increase at the rate of 6% per year over the previous year's rate if

(a) the interest rate is 8% compounded annually?

(b) the interest rate is 6% compounded annually?

2.61 You are planning to save $1 million for retirement over the next 30 years.

(a) If you are earning interest at the rate of 6% and you live 20 years after retirement, what annual level of living expenses will those savings support?

(b) Suppose your retirement living expenses will increase at an annual rate of 3% due to inflation. Determine the annual spending plan in line with your inflation.

Equivalence Calculations

2.62 What value of C makes the two cash flows equal? Assume $i = 12\%$.

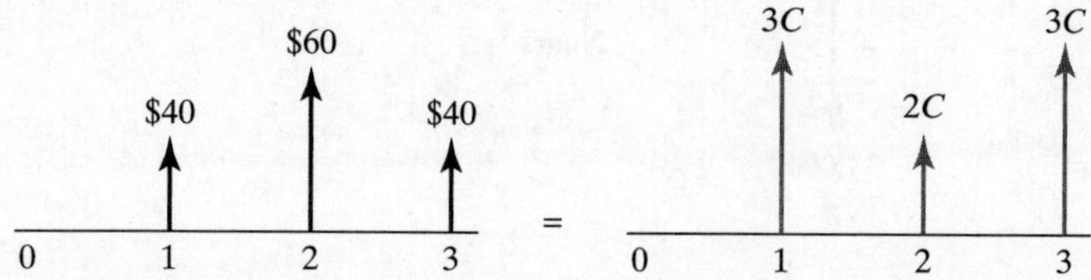

2.63 Find the present worth of the cash receipts in the accompanying diagram if $i = 8\%$ compounded annually, with only *four interest factors*.

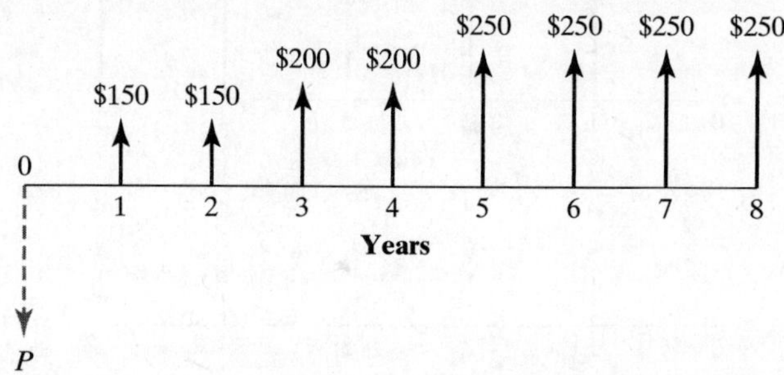

2.64 In computing the equivalent present worth of each given cash flow series at period zero, which of the following expressions is *incorrect*?

(a) $P = \$500(P/A, i, 4)(P/F, i, 4)$.

(b) $P = \$500(F/A, i, 4)(P/F, i, 7)$.

(c) $P = \$500(P/A, i, 7) - \$100(P/A, i, 3)$.

(d) $P = \$500[(P/F, i, 4) + (P/F, i, 5) + (P/F, i, 6) + (P/F, i, 7)]$.

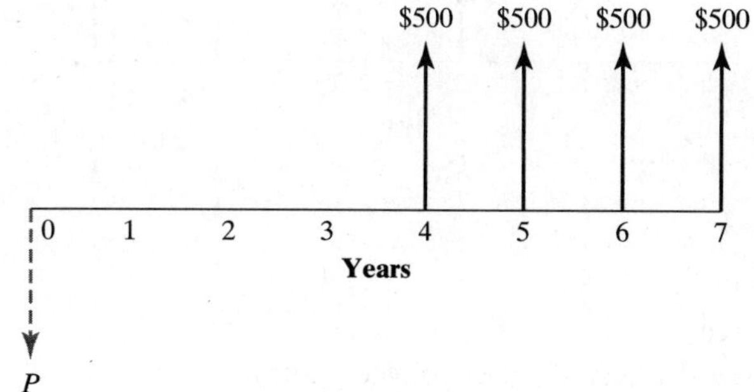

2.65 Find the equivalent present worth of the cash receipts in the accompanying diagram, where $i = 8\%$ compounded annually. In other words, how much do you have to deposit now (with the second deposit in the amount of $600 at the end of the first year) so that you will be able to withdraw $300 at the end of the second year through the fourth year, and $800 at the end of the fifth year, where the bank pays you 8% annual interest on your balance?

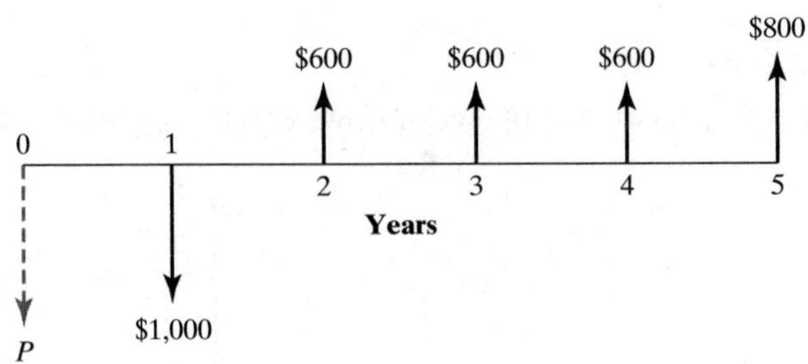

2.66 What value of A makes the two annual cash flows shown in the following diagram equivalent at 12% interest compounded annually?

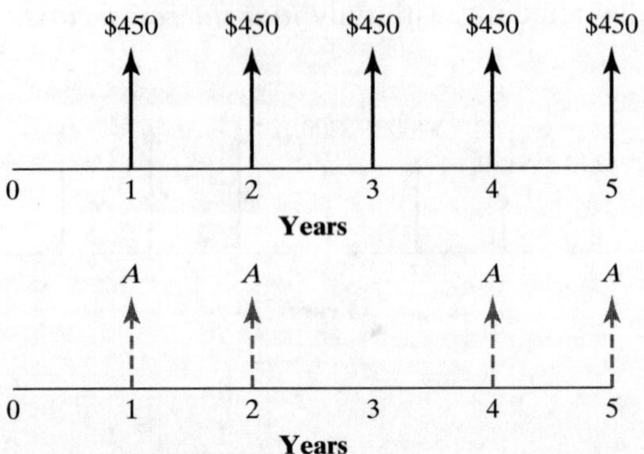

2.67 The two cash flow transactions shown in the accompanying cash flow diagram are said to be equivalent at 8% interest compounded annually. Find the unknown X value that satisfies the equivalence.

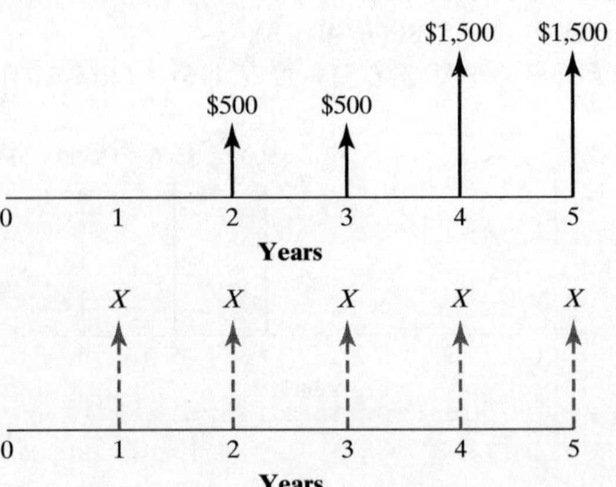

2.68 State the value of C that makes the following two cash flow transactions economically equivalent at an interest rate of 12%:

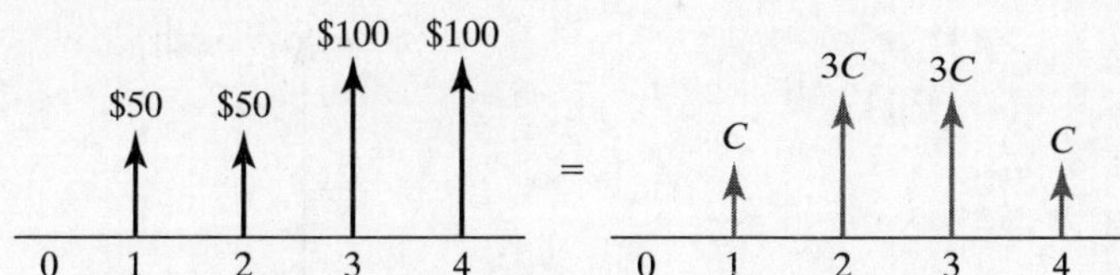

2.69 From the following cash flow diagram, find the value of C that will establish economic equivalence between the deposit series and the withdrawal series at an interest rate of 8% compounded annually.

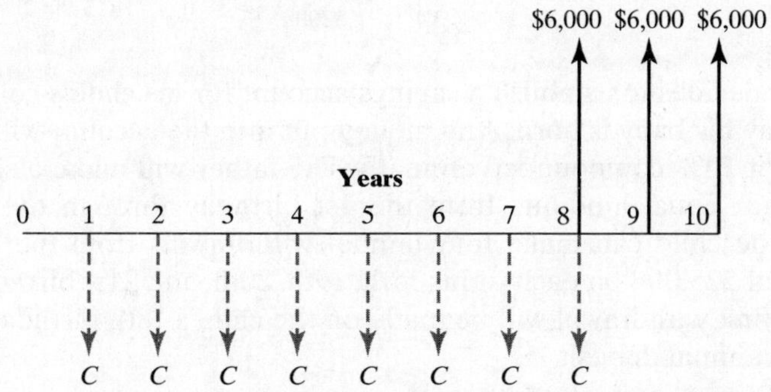

2.70 The following equation describes the conversion of a cash flow into an equivalent equal-payment series with $N = 10$:

$$A = [1000 + 20(A/G, 8\%, 7)]$$
$$\times (P/A, 8\%, 7)(A/P, 6\%, 10)$$
$$+ [300(F/A, 8\%, 3) - 1500] \, (A/F, 8\%, 10).$$

Given the equation, reconstruct the original cash flow diagram.

2.71 Consider the following cash flow diagram. What value of C makes the inflow series equivalent to the outflow series at an interest rate of 10% compounded annually?

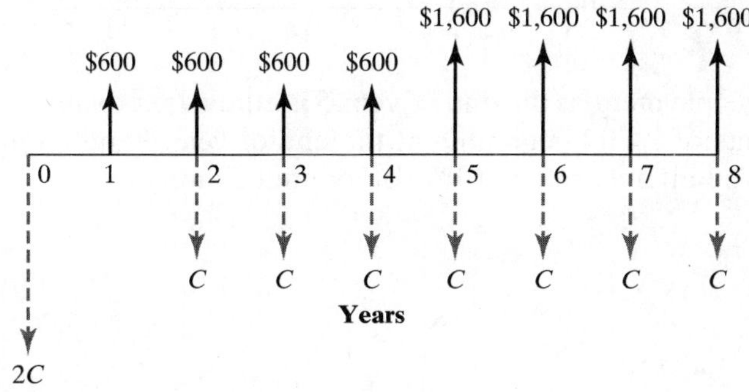

2.72 Four years ago, you opened a mutual fund account and made three deposits ($100 four years ago, X three years ago, and $200 a year ago) where you earned varying interest rates, according to the diagram that follows. Today your balance shows $800. Determine the amount of the deposit made three years ago (X).

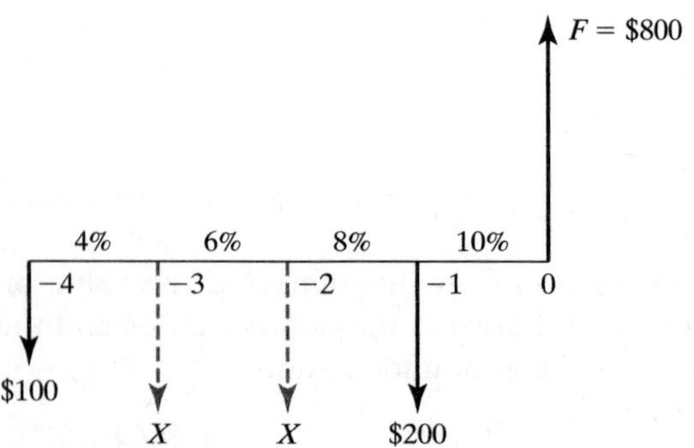

2.73 A father decides to establish a savings account for his child's college education on the day his baby is born. Any money put into the account will earn an interest rate of 10% compounded annually. The father will make a series of annual deposits in equal amounts from the 1st birthday through the 18th birthday so that the child can make four annual withdrawals from the account in the amount of $25,000 on each of his 18th, 19th, 20th, and 21st birthdays. Assuming that the first withdrawal will be made on the child's 18th birthday, calculate the required annual deposit A.

2.74 Find the value of X such that the two cash flow transactions are economically equivalent at 12% compounded annually.

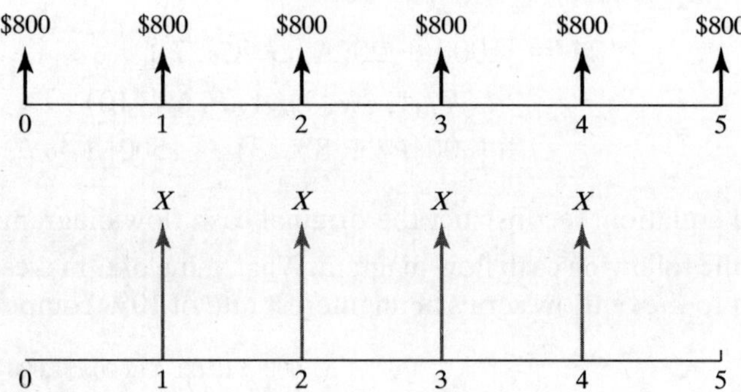

2.75 What single payment at the end of year 5 is equivalent to an equal annual series of payments of $1200 beginning at the end of year 3 and ending at the end of year 12? The interest rate is 10% compounded annually.

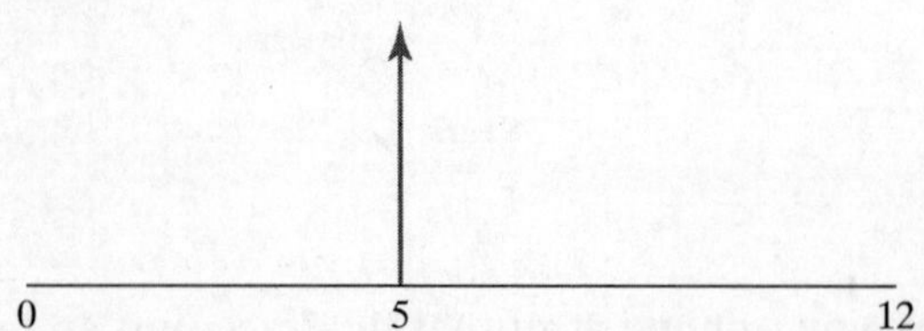

2.76 You borrowed $5,000 to finance your educational expenses at the beginning of your junior year of college at an interest rate of 8% compounded annually. You are required to pay off the loan with five equal annual installments, but the first payment will be deferred until your graduation. Determine the value of C, the amount of annual payments.

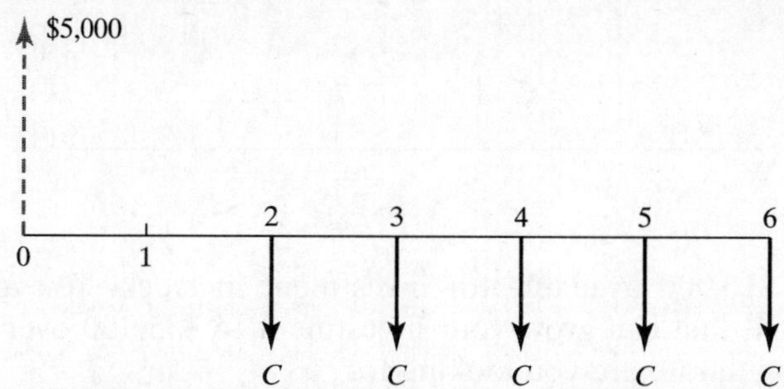

2.77 Consider the accompanying cash flow series at varying interest rates. What is the equivalent present worth of the cash flow series?

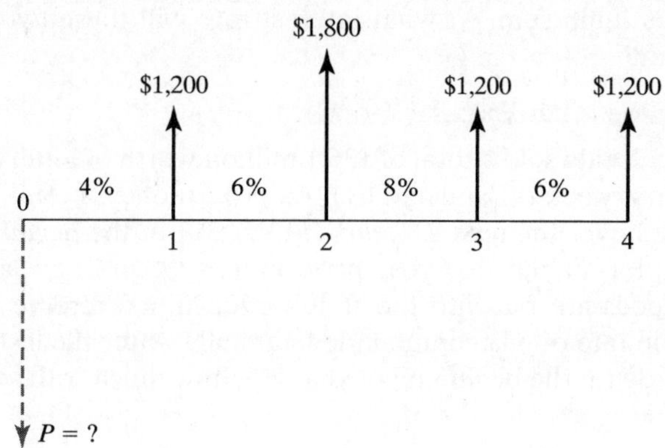

Solving for an Unknown Interest Rate

2.78 It is said that a lump-sum amount of $50,000 at the end of five years is equivalent to an equal-payment series of $5,000 per year for 10 years, where the first payment occurs at the end of year 1. What earning interest is assumed in this calculation?

2.79 At what rate of interest compounded annually will an investment double in five years? Find the answers by using (1) the exact formula and (2) the Rule of 72.

2.80 Determine the interest rate i that makes the pairs of cash flows shown in the following diagrams economically equivalent.

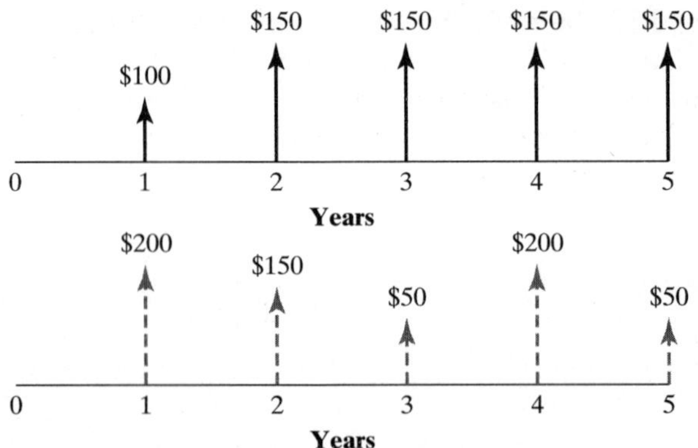

2.81 You have $10,000 available for investment in stock. You are looking for a growth stock that can grow your investment to $35,000 over five years. What kind of growth rate are you looking for?

2.82 Recently, a suburban Chicago couple won Powerball, a multistate lottery game. The game had rolled over for several weeks, so a huge jackpot was at stake. Ticket buyers had the choice between a single lump sum of $104 million or a total of $198 million paid out over 25 years (or $7.92 million per year and the payment is made immediately) should they win the game. The winning couple opted for the lump sum. At what interest rate will these two payment options be equivalent?

Short Case Studies with Excel

2.83 The state of Florida sold a total of $36.1 million worth of lottery tickets at $1 each during the first week of January 2011. As prize money, a total of $41 million will be distributed over the next 21 years ($1,952,381 at the *beginning* of each year). The distribution of the first-year prize money occurs now, and the remaining lottery proceeds are put into the state's educational reserve funds, which earn interest at the rate of 6% compounded annually. After the last prize distribution has been made (at the beginning of year 21), how much will be left in the reserve account?

2.84 A newspaper headline reads, "Millionaire Babies: How to Save Our Social Security System." It sounds a little wild, but the concept expressed in the title of this newspaper headline probably refers to an economic plan proposed by a member of Congress. Senator Bob Kerrey (D-Nebraska) has proposed giving every newborn baby a $1,000 government savings account at birth, followed by five annual contributions of $500 each. (Kerrey offered this idea in a speech devoted to tackling Social Security reform.) If the funds are left untouched in an investment account, Kerrey says, then by the time each baby reaches age 65, his or her $3,500 contribution will have grown to $600,000 over the years, even at medium returns for a thrift-savings plan. At about 9.4% compounded annually, the balance would grow to be $1,005,132. (How would you calculate this number?) Since about 4 million babies are born each year, the proposal would cost the federal government $4 billion annually. About 90% of the total annual Social Security tax collections of more than $300 billion is used to pay current beneficiaries, making Social Security one of the largest federal programs in dollar expenditure. The remaining 10% is invested in interest-bearing government bonds that finance the day-to-day expenses of the federal government. Discuss the economics of Senator Bob Kerrey's Social Security savings plan.

2.85   In 2011, Kevin Jones, Texas Tigers quarterback, agreed to an eight-year, $50 million contract that at the time made him the highest-paid player in professional football history. The contract included a signing bonus of $11 million and called for annual salaries of $2.5 million in 2011, $1.75 million in 2012, $4.15 million in 2013, $4.90 million in 2014, $5.25 million in 2015, $6.2 million in 2016, $6.75 million in 2017, and $7.5 million in 2018. The $11 million signing bonus was prorated over the course of the contract so that an additional $1.375 million was paid each year over the eight-year contract period. With the salary paid at the beginning of each season, what is the worth of his contract at an interest rate of 6%?

CHAPTER THREE

Understanding Money Management

How Do You Manage Your Credit Card Debt? Most college students carry at least one or two credit cards so that they may purchase necessary items. However, shockingly few realize the consequences of making only the required minimum payments on their credit card balances.[1]

Let's say John and Jane each have $2,000 in debt on their credit cards, which require a minimum payment of 3%, or $10, whichever is higher. Both are strapped for cash, but Jane manages to pay an extra $10 on top of her minimum *monthly payments*. John pays only the minimum. Every month, John and Jane are charged a 20% annual percentage rate (APR) on each card's outstanding balance. So, when John and Jane make payments, part of those payments goes to paying interest and part goes to the *principal*.

[1] "Understanding Credit Card Interest," May 20, 2011, Investopedia.com. www.investopedia.com/article/01/061301.asp.

- John pays $4,240 in total over 15 years to absolve the $2,000 in credit card debt. The interest that John pays over the 15 years totals $2,240, higher than the original credit card debt.

- Since Jane paid an extra $10 a month, she pays a total of $3,276 over seven years to pay off the $2,000 in credit card debt. Jane pays a total of $1,276 in interest.

The extra $10 a month saves Jane almost $1,000 and cuts her repayment period by more than seven years! Every little bit counts. Paying twice your minimum, or more, can drastically cut down the time it takes to pay off the balance, which in turn leads to lower interest charges.

However, as we will see soon, rather than pay the minimum due or even just a little more than the minimum, it is best simply not to carry a balance at all. Clearly, credit cards are an important part of our day-to-day lives, which is why it is critical for consumers to truly understand the effect of that interest on them. As you can see in the following table,[2] the credit card interest rates vary with creditworthiness—the more creditworthy you are, the lower the interest rate is.

CreditCards.com's Weekly Rate Report

	Avr. APR	Last week	6 months ago
National average	14.91%	14.91%	14.71%
Low interest	10.73%	10.73%	11.98%
Balance transfer	12.78%	12.78%	12.88%
Business	13.07%	13.07%	12.91%
Student	13.77%	13.77%	13.31%
Cash back	14.16%	14.16%	12.48%
Airline	14.31%	14.31%	14.24%
Reward	14.51%	14.51%	14.35%
Instant approval	15.99%	15.99%	15.99%
Bad credit	24.96%	24.96%	24.95%

Source: CreditCards.com (July 14, 2011).

[2] Kate Tomasino, "Rate Survey: Credit Card APRs Stay at Record High," CreditCards.com.

Can you explain the meaning of a 20% annual percentage rate (APR) quoted by the credit card company? And how the credit card company calculates the interest payment? In this chapter, we will consider several concepts crucial to managing money. In Chapter 2, we examined how time affects the value of money and developed various interest formulas for these calculations. Using these basic formulas, we will now extend the concept of equivalence to determine interest rates implicit in many financial contracts. To this end, we will introduce several examples in the area of loan transactions. For instance, many commercial loans require interest to compound more frequently than once a year—be it monthly or daily. To appreciate the effects of more frequent compounding, we must begin with an understanding of the concepts of nominal and effective interest.

3.1 Market Interest Rates

In Chapter 2, the market interest rate is defined as the interest rate established by the financial market, such as banks and financial institutions. This interest rate is supposed to reflect any anticipated changes in earning power as well as purchasing power in the economy. In this section, we will review the nature of this interest rate in more detail.

3.1.1 Nominal Interest Rates

Take a closer look at the billing statement for any credit card or the loan contract for a newly financed car. You should be able to find the interest that the bank charges on your unpaid balance. Even if a financial institution uses a unit of time other than a year—for example, a month or a quarter—when calculating interest payments, the institution usually quotes the interest rate on an *annual basis*. Many banks, for example, state the interest arrangement for credit cards in the following manner:

"18% compounded monthly."

This statement means simply that each month the bank will charge 1.5% interest (12 months per year × 1.5% per month = 18% per year) on the unpaid balance. As shown in Figure 3.1, we say that 18% is the **nominal interest rate** or **annual**

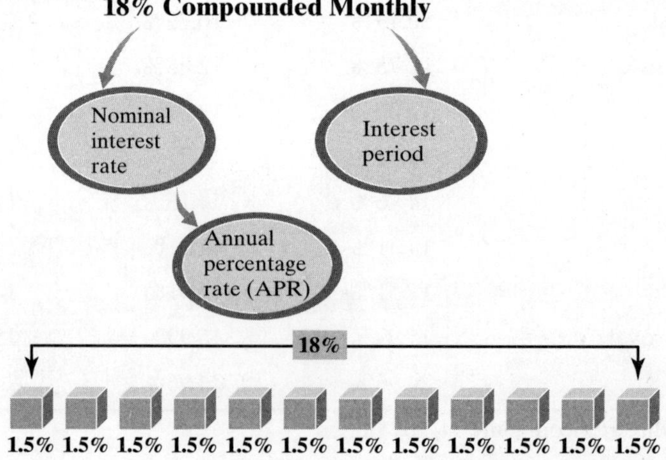

Figure 3.1 Relationship between APR and interest period

percentage rate (APR) and that the compounding frequency is monthly (12 times per year).

Although APR is commonly used by financial institutions and is familiar to many customers, the term does not explain precisely the amount of interest that will accumulate in a year. To explain the true effect of more frequent compounding on annual interest amounts, we will introduce the term *effective interest rate,* commonly known as *annual effective yield,* or annual percentage yield (APY).

3.1.2 Annual Effective Yields

The **annual effective yield** (or **effective annual interest rate**) is the one rate that truly represents the interest earned in a year. On a yearly basis, you are looking for a cumulative rate—1.5% each month for 12 times. This cumulative rate predicts the actual interest payment on your outstanding credit card balance.

We could calculate the total annual interest payment for a credit card debt of $1,000 by using the future value formula given in Eq. (2.3). If $P = \$1,000$, $i = 1.5\%$, and $N = 12$, we obtain

$$F = P(1 + i)^N$$
$$= \$1,000(1 + 0.015)^{12}$$
$$= \$1,195.62.$$

In effect, the bank is earning more than 18% on your original credit card debt. In fact, since you are paying $195.62, the implication is that, for each dollar owed, you are paying an equivalent annual interest of 19.56 cents. In terms of an effective annual interest rate (i_a), the interest payment can be rewritten as a percentage of the principal amount:

$$i_a = \$195.62/\$1,000 = 0.19562 \text{ or } 19.562\%.$$

In other words, paying 1.5% interest per month for 12 months is equivalent to paying 19.56% interest just one time each year. This relationship is depicted in Figure 3.2.

Table 3.1 shows effective interest rates at various compounding intervals for 4%–12% APRs. Depending on the frequency of compounding, the effective interest earned (or paid by the borrower) can differ significantly from the APR. Therefore,

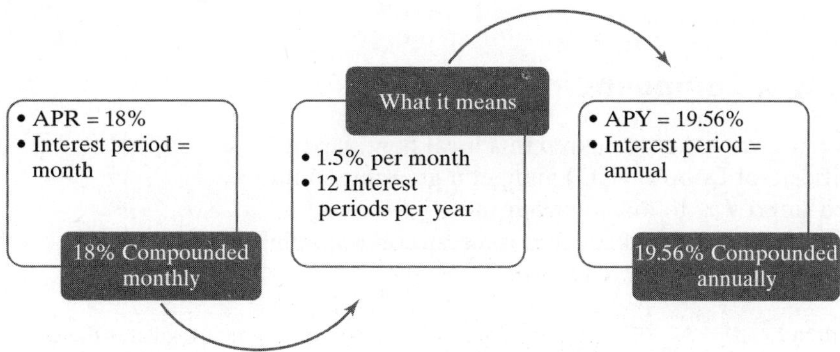

Figure 3.2   Relationship between nominal and effective interest rates

TABLE 3.1　Annual Effective Yields at Various Compounding Intervals

Nominal Rate	Compounding Frequency				
	Annually	Semiannually	Quarterly	Monthly	Daily
4%	4.00%	4.04%	4.06%	4.07%	4.08%
5%	5.00%	5.06%	5.09%	5.12%	5.13%
6%	6.00%	6.09%	6.14%	6.17%	6.18%
7%	7.00%	7.12%	7.19%	7.23%	7.25%
8%	8.00%	8.16%	8.24%	8.30%	8.33%
9%	9.00%	9.20%	9.31%	9.38%	9.42%
10%	10.00%	10.25%	10.38%	10.47%	10.52%
11%	11.00%	11.30%	11.46%	11.57%	11.63%
12%	12.00%	12.36%	12.55%	12.68%	12.75%

truth-in-lending laws[3] require that financial institutions quote both nominal and effective interest rates when you deposit or borrow money.

More frequent compounding increases the amount of interest paid over a year at the same nominal interest rate. Assuming that the nominal interest rate is r and that M compounding periods occur during the year, the annual effective yield i_a can be calculated as follows:

$$i_a = (1 + \frac{r}{M})^M - 1. \tag{3.1}$$

When $M = 1$, we have the special case of annual compounding. Substituting $M = 1$ into Eq. (3.1) reduces it to $i_a = r$. That is, when compounding takes place once annually, effective interest is equal to nominal interest. Thus, in most of our examples in Chapter 2, where only annual interest was considered, we were, by definition, using annual effective yields.

EXAMPLE 3.1　Determining a Compounding Period

Consider the following bank advertisement that appeared in a local newspaper:

"Open a Liberty Bank Certificate of Deposit (CD) and get a guaranteed rate of return on as little as $500. It's a smart way to manage your money for months."

In this advertisement, no mention is made of specific interest compounding frequencies. Find the compounding period for each CD.

[3] The Truth in Lending Act (TILA), passed in 1968, is a federal law that regulates the credit market and sets minimum standards for the information that a creditor must provide in an installment credit contract.

Type of Certificate	Interest Rate (APR)	Annual Percentage Yield (APY)	Minimum Required to Open
1-Year Certificate	2.23%	2.25%	$500
2-Year Certificate	3.06%	3.10%	$500
3-Year Certificate	3.35%	3.40%	$500
4-Year Certificate	3.45%	3.50%	$500
5- to 10-Year Certificates	4.41%	4.50%	$500

DISSECTING THE PROBLEM

Given: $r = 4.41\%$ per year, $i_a = 4.50\%$.
Find: M.

METHODOLOGY

Method 1: By Trial and Error.

Method 2: Using an Excel Function.

SOLUTION

First, we will consider the 5-to-10-year CD. The nominal interest rate is 4.41% per year, and the effective annual interest rate (or APY) is 4.50%. Using Eq. (3.1), we obtain the expression

$$0.0450 = (1 + 0.0441/M)^M - 1.$$

By trial and error, we find that $M = 12$. Thus, the 5-to-10-year CD earns 4.41% interest compounded monthly. Similarly, we can find that the interest periods for the other CDs are monthly as well.

We can also find the compounding period in much quicker way using one of the following financial functions in Excel.

Effective rate "=EFFECT(r,M)"
Nominal rate "=NOMINAL(i_a,M)"

Taking the 5-to-10-year CD example, we create a worksheet where Cell B3 is a function of M (Cell B4). We vary the value in B4 until we see a close match to the published APY.

	A	B
1		
2	Annual percentage rate (r)	0.0441
3	Effective annual rate (i_a)	0.045002
4	Number of compounding periods per year (M)	12
5		

3.2 Calculating Effective Interest Rates Based on Payment Periods

We can generalize the result of Eq. (3.1) to compute the effective interest rate for *any duration of time*. As you will see later, the effective interest rate is usually computed according to the payment (transaction) period. We will look into two types of compounding situations: (1) discrete compounding and (2) continuous compounding.

3.2.1 Discrete Compounding

If cash flow transactions occur *quarterly* but interest is compounded *monthly*, we may wish to calculate the effective interest rate on a *quarterly basis*. In this case, we may redefine Eq. (3.1) as

$$i = (1 + r/M)^C - 1$$
$$= (1 + r/CK)^C - 1, \tag{3.2}$$

where

$$M = \text{the number of interest periods per year,}$$
$$C = \text{the number of interest periods per payment period, and}$$
$$K = \text{the number of payment periods per year.}$$

Note that $M = CK$ in Eq. (3.2).

EXAMPLE 3.2 Effective Rate per Payment Period

Suppose that you make quarterly deposits into a savings account that earns 8% interest compounded monthly. Compute the effective interest rate per quarter.

DISSECTING THE PROBLEM	
	Given: $r = 8\%$ per year, $C = 3$ interest periods per quarter, $K = 4$ quarterly payments per year, and $M = 12$ interest periods per year. **Find:** i.
METHODOLOGY	**SOLUTION**
Method 1: Calculate the Effective Interest Rate Based on the Payment Period.	Using Eq. (3.2), we compute the effective interest rate per quarter as $$i = (1 + 0.08/12)^3 - 1$$ $$= 2.0134\%.$$

Method 2: Calculate the Effective Interest Rate per Payment Period Using Excel.

Using Excel,

	A	B
1	**Inputs**	
2		
3	(r) APR (%)	8%
4	(K) Payment periods per year	4
5	(C) Interest periods per payment period	3
6	**Output**	
7	(M) Compounding periods per year	12
8	(i) Effective interest rate per payment period	2.0134%
9		

COMMENTS: The annual effective interest rate i_a is $(1 + 0.02013)^4 - 1 = 8.30\%$. For the special case of annual payments with annual compounding, we obtain $i = i_a$ with $C = M$ and $K = 1$. Figure 3.3 illustrates the relationship between the nominal and effective interest rates per payment period.

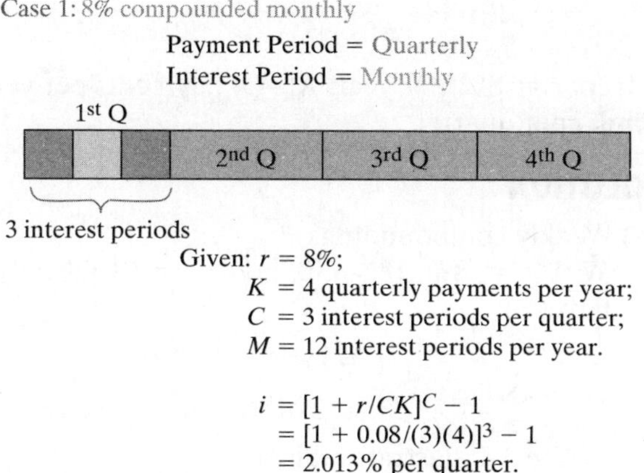

Figure 3.3   Computing the effective interest rate per quarter

3.2.2 Continuous Compounding

To be competitive in the financial market, or to entice potential depositors, some financial institutions offer more frequent compounding. As the number of compounding periods (M) becomes very large, the interest rate per compounding period (r/M)

becomes very small. As M approaches infinity and r/M approaches zero, we approximate the situation of **continuous compounding**.

By taking limits on the right side of Eq. (3.2), we obtain the effective interest rate per payment period as

$$i = \lim_{CK \to \infty} \left[(1 + r/CK)^C - 1 \right]$$

$$= \lim_{CK \to \infty} (1 + r/CK)^C - 1$$

$$= (e^r)^{1/K} - 1.$$

In sum, the effective interest rate per payment period is

$$i = (e)^{r/K} - 1. \tag{3.3}$$

To calculate the effective *annual* interest rate for continuous compounding, we set K equal to 1, resulting in

$$i_a = e^r - 1. \tag{3.4}$$

As an example, the effective annual interest rate for a nominal interest rate of 12% compounded continuously is $i_a = e^{0.12} - 1 = 12.7497\%$.

EXAMPLE 3.3 Calculating an Effective Interest Rate

Find the effective interest rate per quarter at a nominal rate of 8% compounded
(a) weekly, (b) daily, and (c) continuously.

DISSECTING THE PROBLEM	
	Given: $r = 8\%$ per year, $K = 4$ payments per year. **Find:** i per quarter.

METHODOLOGY	SOLUTION
Calculate the effective interest rate, altering the period value.	(a) Weekly compounding: With $r = 8\%$, $M = 52$, and $C = 13$ periods per quarter, we have

$$i = (1 + 0.08/52)^{13} - 1$$

$$= 2.0186\% \text{ per quarter}.$$

Figure 3.4 illustrates this result.

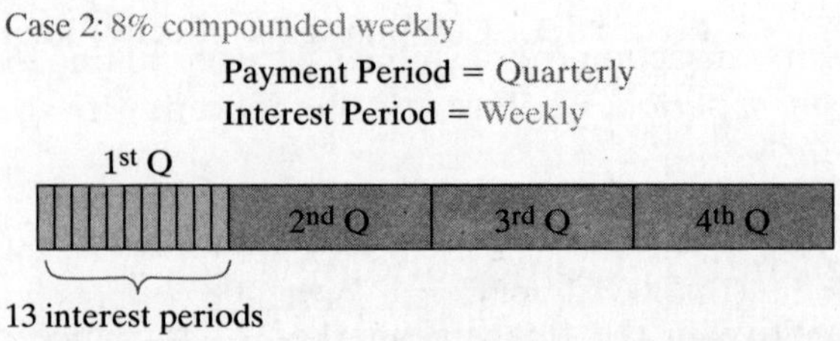

Figure 3.4 Effective interest rate per payment period: quarterly payments with weekly compounding

(b) Daily compounding:

With $r = 8\%$, $M = 365$, and $C = 91.25$ per quarter, we have

$$i = (1 + 0.08/365)^{91.25} - 1$$
$$= 2.0199\% \text{ per quarter.}$$

(c) Continuous compounding:

With $r = 8\%$, $M \to \infty$, $C \to \infty$, and $K = 4$ using Eq. (3.3), we obtain

$$i = e^{0.08/4} - 1 = 2.0201\% \text{ per quarter.}$$

COMMENTS: Note that the difference between daily compounding and continuous compounding is often negligible. Many banks offer continuous compounding to entice deposit customers, but the extra benefits are small. Table 3.2 summarizes the varying effective interest rates per payment period (quarterly, in this case) under various compounding frequencies.

TABLE 3.2   **Effective Interest Rates per Payment Period**

	Base	Case 1	Case 2	Case 3	Case 4
Interest Rate	8% compounded quarterly	8% compounded monthly	8% compounded weekly	8% compounded daily	8% compounded continuously
Payment Period	Payments occur quarterly	Payments occur quarterly	Payments occur quarterly	Payments occur quarterly	Payments occur quarterly
Effective Interest Rate per Payment Period	2.000% per quarter	2.013% per quarter	2.0186% per quarter	2.0199% per quarter	2.0201% per quarter

3.3 Equivalence Calculations with Effective Interest Rates

When calculating equivalent values, we need to identify both the interest period and the payment period. If the time interval for compounding is different from the time interval for cash transaction (or payment), we need to find *the effective interest rate that covers the payment period*. We illustrate this concept with specific examples.

3.3.1 Compounding Period Equal to Payment Period

All examples in Chapter 2 assumed annual payments and annual compounding. Whenever a situation occurs where the compounding and payment periods are equal ($M = K$), no matter whether the interest is compounded annually or at some other interval, the following solution method can be used:

1. Identify the number of compounding (or payment) periods ($M = K$) per year.
2. Compute the effective interest rate per payment period; that is,

$$i = (1 + r/M)^C - 1$$
$$= r/M \, (\text{with } C = 1).$$

3. Determine the number of payment periods:

$$N = M \times (\text{number of years}).$$

4. Use i and N in the appropriate formulas in Table 2.11.

EXAMPLE 3.4 Calculating Auto Loan Payments

Suppose you want to buy a car. You have surveyed the dealers' newspaper advertisements, and the one in Figure 3.5 has caught your attention. You can afford to make a down payment of $2,678.95, so the net amount to be financed is $20,000.

(a) What would the monthly payment be?
(b) After the 25th payment, you want to pay off the remaining loan in a lump-sum amount. What is this lump sum?

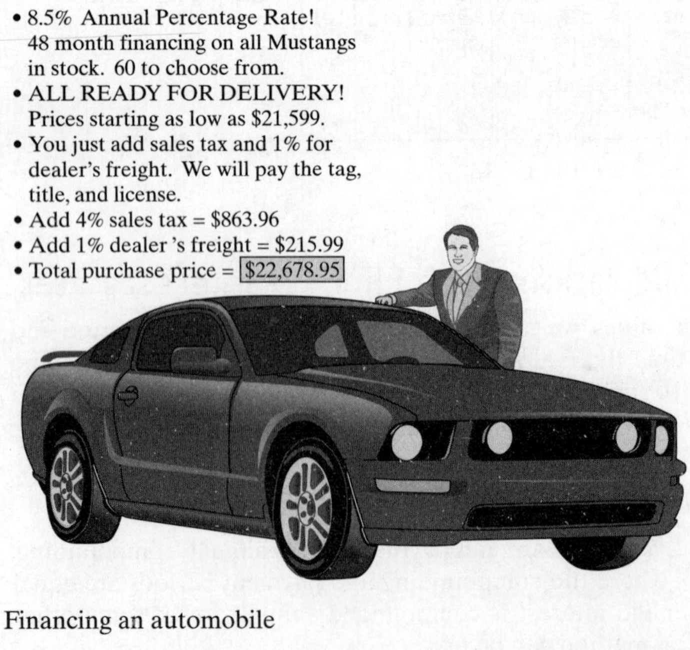

Figure 3.5 Financing an automobile

DISSECTING THE PROBLEM

The advertisement does not specify a compounding period, but in automobile financing, the interest and the payment periods are almost always monthly.

In the second part of the example, we need to calculate the remaining balance after the 25th payment.

Given: $P = \$20{,}000$, $r = 8.5\%$ per year, $K = 12$ payments per year, $N = 48$ months, and $C = 1$, and $M = 12$.

Find: A.

Given: $A = \$492.97$, $i = 0.7083\%$, and $N = 23$ months.

Find: Remaining balance after 25 months (B_{25}).

METHODOLOGY

Step 1: In this situation, we can easily compute the monthly payment by using Eq. (2.9). The 8.5% APR means 8.5% compounded monthly.

SOLUTION

$$i = \left(1 + \frac{0.085}{12}\right)^1 - 1 = 0.7083\% \text{ per month}$$

and

$$N = (12)(4) = 48 \text{ months},$$

we have

$$A = \$20{,}000\,(A/P, 0.7083\%, 48) = \$492.97.$$

Figure 3.6 shows the cash flow diagram for this part of the example.

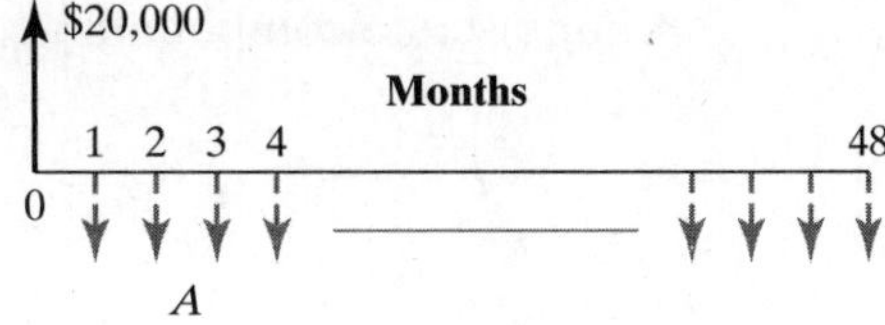

Figure 3.6   Cash flow diagram for part (a)

Step 2: We can compute the amount you owe after you make the 25th payment by calculating the equivalent worth of the remaining 23 payments at the end of the 25th month, with the time scale shifted by 25 months.

The balance is calculated as follows:

$$B_{25} = \$492.97(P/A, 0.7083\%, 23) = \$10{,}428.96.$$

So, if you desire to pay off the remainder of the loan at the end of the 25th payment, you must come up with \$10,428.96, in addition to the payment for that month of \$492.97. (See Figure 3.7.)

Suppose you want to pay off the remaining loan in a lump sum right after making the 25th payment. How much would this payoff amount be?

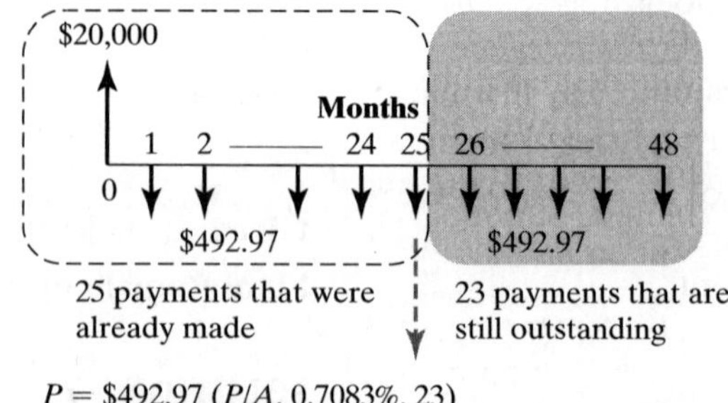

$$P = \$492.97 \, (P/A, 0.7083\%, 23)$$
$$= \$10,428.96.$$

Figure 3.7 Process of calculating the remaining balance of the auto loan

3.3.2 Compounding Occurs at a Different Rate than That at Which Payments Are Made

The computational procedure for dealing with compounding periods and payment periods that cannot be compared is as follows:

1. Identify the number of compounding periods per year (M), the number of payment periods per year (K), and the number of interest periods per payment period (C).

2. Compute the effective interest rate per payment period:
   - For discrete compounding, compute

$$i = (1 + r/M)^C - 1.$$

   - For continuous compounding, compute

$$i = e^{r/K} - 1.$$

3. Find the total number of payment periods:

$$N = K \times (\text{number of years}).$$

4. Use i and N in the appropriate formulas in Table 2.11.

EXAMPLE 3.5 Compounding Occurs More Frequently than Payments Are Made

Suppose you make equal quarterly deposits of $1,000 into a fund that pays interest at a rate of 12% compounded monthly. Find the balance at the end of year 3.

DISSECTING THE PROBLEM

Given: $A = \$1,000$ per quarter, $r = 12\%$ per year, $M = 12$ compounding periods per year, $N = 12$ quarters, and the cash flow diagram in Figure 3.8.

Find: F.

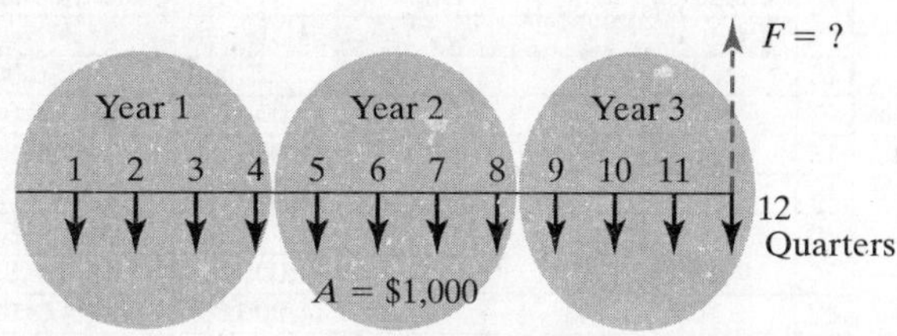

Figure 3.8   Cash flow diagram

METHODOLOGY

Method 1: Noncomparable Compounding and Payment Periods

We follow the procedure for noncomparable compounding and payment periods, as described previously.

SOLUTION

1. Identify the parameter values for M, K, and C, where

$$M = 12 \text{ compounding periods per year,}$$
$$K = 4 \text{ payment periods per year, and}$$
$$C = 3 \text{ interest periods per payment period.}$$

2. Use Eq. (3.2) to compute effective interest:

$$i = (1 + 0.12/12)^3 - 1$$
$$= 3.030\% \text{ per quarter.}$$

3. Find the total number of payment periods, N, where

$$N = K(\text{number of years}) = 4(3) = 12 \text{ quarters.}$$

4. Use i and N in the appropriate equivalence formulas:

$$F = \$1,000\,(F/A, 3.030\%, 12) = \$14,216.24.$$

Method 2: Excel Worksheet
Table 3.3 illustrates the process of obtaining the future worth of the quarterly payment series in Excel format.

TABLE 3.3 An Excel Worksheet to Illustrate the Process of Accumulating the Future Worth

	A	B	C	D	E	F	G
1	**Equal-Payment Cash Flows (Future Worth)**						
2							
3		**Inputs**				**Output**	
4							
5	(*A*) Annuity ($)		1,000.00		(*F*) Future Worth ($)		$14,216.32
6	(*r*) APR (%)		12%				
7	(*K*) Payment periods per year		4		**Cash Balance Over Time**		
8	(*M*) Compounding periods per year		12				
9	(C) Interest periods per payment period		3				
10							
11	(*i*) Effective interest rate per payment period		3,03%				
12	(*N*) Total number of payment periods		12				
13							
14	Periods (*n*)	Deposit	Cash Balance				
15							
16	0	$0.00	$0.00				
17	1	(1,000.00)	$1,000.00				
18	2	(1,000.00)	$2,030.30				
19	3	(1,000.00)	$3,091.82				
20	4	(1,000.00)	$4,185.51				
21	5	(1,000.00)	$5,312.33				
22	6	(1,000.00)	$6,473.30				
23	7	(1,000.00)	$7,669.45				
24	8	(1,000.00)	$8,901.84				
25	9	(1,000.00)	$10,171.57				
26	10	(1,000.00)	$11,479.78				
27	11	(1,000.00)	$12,827.63				
28	12	(1,000.00)	$14,216.32				
29							
30							

=FV($C$11,$C$12,-$C$5)

=(1+C6/C8)^C9-1

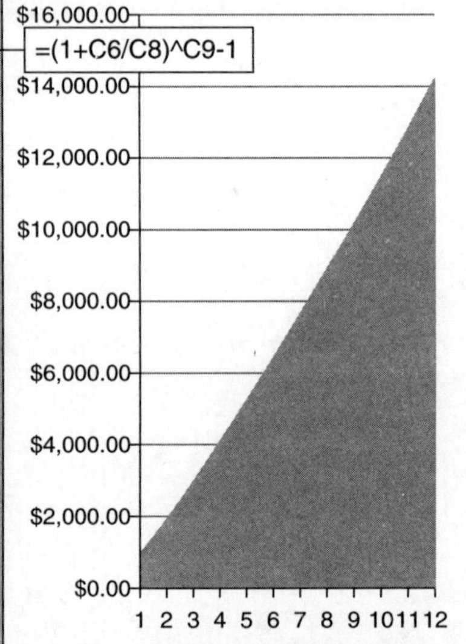

COMMENTS: Appendix B does not provide interest factors for $i = 3.030\%$, but the interest factor can still be evaluated by $F = \$1{,}000(A/F, 1\%, 3)(F/A, 1\%, 36)$, where the first interest factor finds its equivalent monthly payment and the second interest factor converts the monthly payment series to an equivalent lump-sum future payment. If continuous compounding is assumed, the accumulated balance would be $14,228.37, which is about $12 more than the balance for the monthly compounding situation. (See Figure 3.9.)

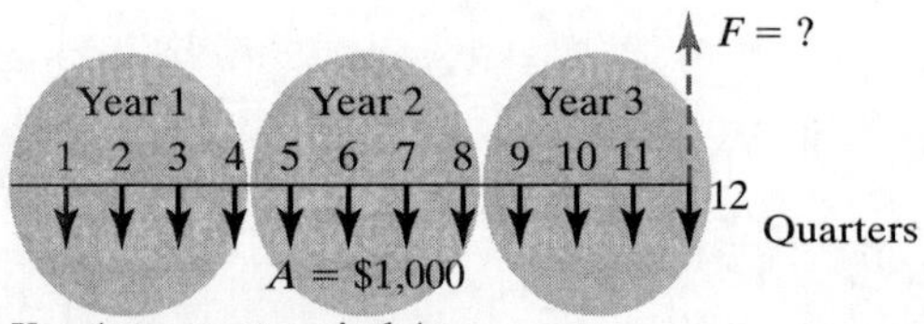

Step 1: $K = 4$ payment periods/year;
$C = \infty$ interest periods per quarter.

Step 2: $i = e^{0.12/4} - 1$
$= 3.045\%$ per quarter.

Step 3: $N = 4(3) = 12$.

Step 4: $F = \$1{,}000\,(F/A, 3.045\%, 12)$
$= \$14{,}228.37$.

Figure 3.9 Equivalence calculation for continuous compounding

EXAMPLE 3.6 Equivalence Calculations with Changing Interest Rates

Compute the future worth (F) for the cash flows with the different interest rates specified in Figure 3.10. The cash flows occur at the end of each year over four years.

DISSECTING THE PROBLEM

Given: $r_1 = 8\%$ per year, $r_2 = 6\%$ per year, $N = 4$ years, and payment period = annual.

Find: F.

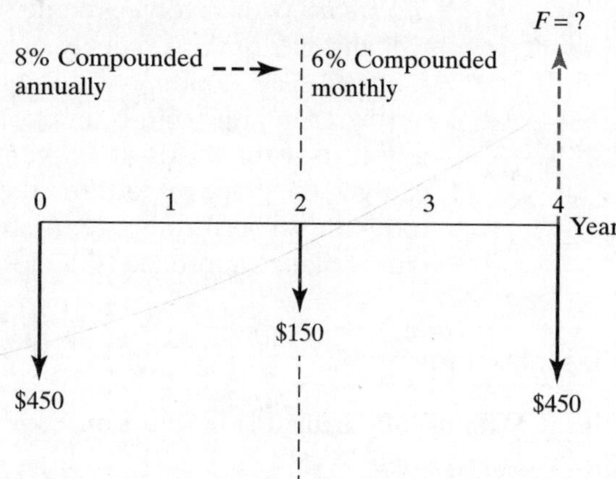

Figure 3.10   Cash flow diagram for a deposit series with changing interest rates

METHODOLOGY

Calculate the effective interest rates per payment period, altering the nominal interest rate. Then, calculate the balance at the end of each deposit period.

SOLUTION

(a) Years 0–2:

With $r_1 = 8\%$, $M = 1$, and $C = 1$, we have

$$i = i_a = (1 + 0.08/1)^1 - 1 = 8\% \text{ per year.}$$

The balance at the end of year 2 is

$$B_2 = \$450(F/P, 8\%, 2) + \$150 = \$674.88.$$

(b) Years 2–4:

With $r_2 = 6\%$, $M = 12$, and B_2, we have

$$i = i_a = (1 + 0.06/12)^{12} - 1$$
$$= 6.168\% \text{ per year.}$$

The balance at the end of year 4 will be

$$F = B_4 = \$674.88(F/P, 6.168\%, 2) + \$450$$
$$= \$1,210.70.$$

3.4 Debt Management

Credit card debt and commercial loans are easily among the most significant and familiar financial obligations that involve interest. Many types of loans are available, but here we will focus on those most frequently used by individuals and in business.

3.4.1 Borrowing with Credit Cards

When credit cards were introduced in 1959, they offered people the ability to handle their personal finances in a dramatically different way. From a consumer's perspective, your ability to use credit cards means that you do not have to wait for a paycheck to reach the bank before you can make a purchase. Most credit cards operate on *revolving credit*. With revolving credit, you have a line of borrowing that you can tap into at will and pay back as quickly or slowly as you want—as long as you pay the minimum required each month.

Your monthly bill is an excellent source of information about what your card really costs. Four things affect your card-based credit costs: the annual fees, the finance charges, the grace period, and the method of calculating interest. In fact, there are three different ways to compute interest charges, as summarized in Table 3.4. The average-daily-balance approach is the most common.

TABLE 3.4 **Methods of Calculating Interests on Your Credit Cards**

Method	Description	Example of the Interest You Owe, Given a Beginning Balance of $3,000 at 18%
Adjusted Balance	The bank subtracts the amount of your payment from the beginning balance and charges you interest on the remainder. This method costs you the least.	With a $1,000 payment, your new balance will be $2,000. You pay 1.5% interest for the month on this new balance, which comes out to $(1.5\%)(\$2,000) = \$30$.
Average Daily Balance	The bank charges you interest on the average of the amount you owe each day during the period. So, the larger the payment you make, the lower the interest you pay.	With a $1,000 payment on the 15th day, your balance reduced to $2,000. Therefore, the interest on your average daily balance for the month will be $(1.5\%)(\$3,000 + \$2,000)/2 = \$37.50$.
Previous Balance	The bank does not subtract any payments you make from your previous balance. You pay interest on the total amount you owe at the beginning of the period. This method costs you the most.	The annual interest rate is 18% compounded monthly. Regardless of your payment amount, the bank will charge 1.5% on your beginning balance of $3,000. Therefore, your interest for the month will be $(1.5\%)(\$3,000) = \$45$.

EXAMPLE 3.7 Paying Off Cards Saves a Bundle

Suppose that you owe $2,000 on a credit card that charges 18% APR and you pay either the minimum 10% or $20, whichever is higher, every month. How long will it take you to eliminate the debt? Assume that the bank uses the previous-balance method to calculate your interest, meaning that the bank does not subtract the amount of your payment from the beginning balance but charges you interest on the previous balance.

DISSECTING THE PROBLEM

Given: APR $= 18\%$ (or 1.5% per month), beginning balance $= \$2,000$, and monthly payment $= 10\%$ of outstanding balance or $20, whichever is higher.

Find: The number of months to pay off the loan, assuming that no new purchases are made during this payment period.

METHODOLOGY

Use Excel to calculate the number of payments.

SOLUTION

With the initial balance of $2,000 ($n = 0$), the interest for the first month will be $30 ($=\$2,000(0.015)$), so you will be billed $2,030. Then you make a $203 payment (10% of the outstanding balance), so the remaining balance will be $1,827. At the end of the second month, the billing statement will show that you owe the bank the amount of $1,854.41 of which $27.41 is interest. With a $185.44 payment, the balance is reduced to $1,668.96. This process repeats until the 26th payment. For the 27th payment and all those thereafter, 10% of the outstanding balance is less than $20, so you pay $20. As shown in Table 3.5, it would take 37 months to pay off the $2,000 debt with total interest payments of $330.42.

In developing the Excel worksheet in Table 3.5, you may use a nested IF function, one of Excel's most useful functions. What it does is test to see whether a certain condition is true or false. In our example, the values in column E are obtained by using the nested IF function. For example, to calculate the value in Cell E6, the IF logic function looks like

$$= IF(D6*0.1>20, D6*0.1, IF(F5<20, D6, 20))$$

The reason why you need a nested IF function is to avoid the situation where you do not want to pay more than what you owe, like in Cell E42.

TABLE 3.5 Creating a Loan Repayment Schedule

	A	B	C	D	E	F
1						
2	Period	Beg.	Interest	Amount	Payment	End.
3	(*n*)	Balance	Charged	Billed	Required	Balance
4						
5	0					$2,000.00
6	1	$2,000.00	$30.00	$2,030.00	$203.00	$1,827.00
7	2	$1,827.00	$27.41	$1,854.41	$185.44	$1,668.96
8	3	$1,668.96	$25.03	$1,694.00	$169.40	$1,524.60
9	4	$1,524.60	$22.87	$1,547.47	$154.75	$1,392.72
10	5	$1,392.72	$20.89	$1,413.61	$141.36	$1,272.25
11	6	$1,272.25	$19.08	$1,291.33	$129.13	$1,162.20
12	7	$1,162.20	$17.43	$1,179.63	$117.96	$1,061.67
13	8	$1,061.67	$15.93	$1,077.60	$107.76	$969.84
14	9	$969.84	$14.55	$984.38	$98.44	$885.95
15	10	$885.95	$13.29	$899.23	$89.92	$809.31
16	11	$809.31	$12.14	$821.45	$82.15	$739.31
17	12	$739.31	$11.09	$750.40	$75.04	$675.36
18	13	$675.36	$10.13	$685.49	$68.55	$616.94
19	14	$616.94	$9.25	$626.19	$62.62	$563.57
20	15	$563.57	$8.45	$572.03	$57.20	$514.82
21	16	$514.82	$7.72	$522.55	$52.25	$470.29
22	17	$470.29	$7.05	$477.35	$47.73	$429.61
23	18	$429.61	$6.44	$436.06	$43.61	$392.45
24	19	$392.45	$5.89	$398.34	$39.83	$358.50
25	20	$358.50	$5.38	$363.88	$36.39	$327.49
26	21	$327.49	$4.91	$332.40	$33.24	$299.16
27	22	$299.16	$4.49	$303.65	$30.37	$273.29
28	23	$273.29	$4.10	$277.39	$27.74	$249.65
29	24	$249.65	$3.74	$253.39	$25.34	$228.05
30	25	$228.05	$3.42	$231.47	$23.15	$208.33
31	26	$208.33	$3.12	$211.45	$21.15	$190.31
32	27	$190.31	$2.85	$193.16	$20.00	$173.16
33	28	$173.16	$2.60	$175.76	$20.00	$155.76
34	29	$155.76	$2.34	$158.09	$20.00	$138.09
35	30	$138.09	$2.07	$140.17	$20.00	$120.17
36	31	$120.17	$1.80	$121.97	$20.00	$101.97
37	32	$101.97	$1.53	$103.50	$20.00	$83.50
38	33	$83.50	$1.25	$84.75	$20.00	$64.75
39	34	$64.75	$0.97	$65.72	$20.00	$45.72
40	35	$45.72	$0.69	$46.41	$20.00	$26.41
41	36	$26.41	$0.40	$26.80	$20.00	$6.80
42	37	$6.80	$0.10	$6.91	$6.91	$0.00
43						

```
=IF(D41*0.1>20,D41*0.1,IF(F40<20,D41,20))
```

COMMENTS: If the bank uses the average-daily-balance method and charges you interest on the average of the amount you owe each day during the period, it would take a little longer to pay off the debt. For example, if you make a $200 payment on the 15th day, your balance is reduced to $1,800. Therefore, the interest on your average daily balance for the month will be (1.5%) ($2,000 + $1,800)/2= $28.50, and the ending balance will be $1,828.50 instead of $1,827.00.

3.4.2 Commercial Loans—Calculating Principal and Interest Payments

One of the most important applications of compound interest involves loans that are paid off in **installments** over time. If a loan is to be repaid in equal periodic amounts (e.g., weekly, monthly, quarterly, or annually), it is said to be an **amortized loan**. Examples include automobile loans, loans for appliances, home mortgage loans, and most business debts other than very short-term loans. Most commercial loans have interest that is compounded monthly. With a car loan, for example, a local bank or a dealer advances you the money to pay for the car, and you repay the principal plus interest in monthly installments, usually over a period of three to five years. The car is your collateral. If you don't keep up with your payments, the lender can repossess, or take back, the car and keep all the payments you have made.

Two factors determine what borrowing will cost you: the finance charge and the length of the loan. The cheapest loan is not necessarily the loan with the lowest payments or even the loan with the lowest interest rate. Instead, you have to look at the total cost of borrowing, which depends on the interest rate, fees, and the term (i.e., the length of time it takes you to repay the loan). While you probably cannot influence the rate and fees, you may be able to arrange for a shorter term.

So far, we have considered many instances of amortized loans in which we calculated present or future values of the loans or the amounts of the installment payments. Also of great interest to us is calculating the amount of interest contained versus the portion of the principal that is paid off in each installment. As we shall explore more fully in Chapter 10, the interest paid on a loan is an important element in calculating taxable income. We will further show how we may calculate the interest and principal paid at any point in the life of a loan using Excel's financial functions. As Example 3.8 illustrates, the amount of interest owed for a specified period is calculated on the *remaining balance* of the loan at the beginning of the period.

EXAMPLE 3.8 Using Excel to Determine a Loan's Balance, Principal, and Interest

Suppose you secure a home improvement loan in the amount of $5,000 from a local bank. The loan officer gives you the following loan terms:

- Contract amount = $5,000
- Contract period = 24 months
- Annual percentage rate = 12%
- Monthly installment = $235.37

Figure 3.11 shows the cash flow diagram for this loan. Construct the loan payment schedule by showing the remaining balance, interest payment, and principal payment at the end of each period over the life of the loan.

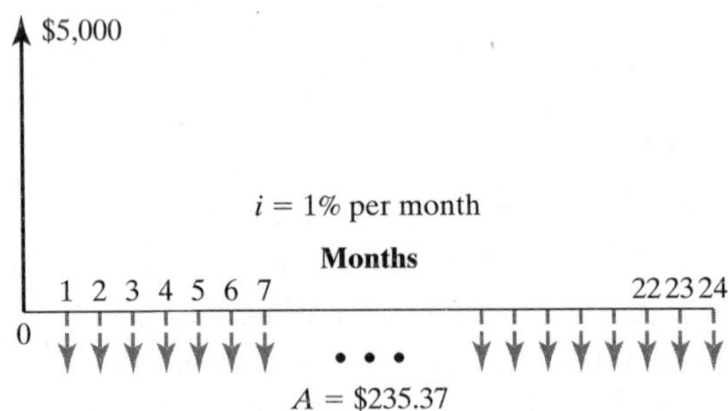

Figure 3.11   Cash flow diagram

DISSECTING THE PROBLEM	
	Given: $P = \$5,000$, $A = \$235.37$ per month, $r = 12\%$ per year, $M = 12$ compounding periods per year, and $N = 24$ months.
	Find: B_n and I_n for $n = 1$ to 24.

METHODOLOGY	SOLUTION
We can easily see how the bank calculated the monthly payment of $235.37.	Since the effective interest rate per payment period on this loan transaction is 1% per month, we establish the following equivalence relationship:

$$\$5,000(A/P, 1\%, 24) = \$5,000\,(0.0471) = \$235.37.$$

The loan payment schedule can be constructed in Excel as in Table 3.6. The interest due at $n = 1$ is $50.00, 1% of the $5,000 outstanding during the first month. The $185.37 left over is applied to the principal, reducing the amount outstanding in the second month to $4,814.63. The interest due in the second month is 1% of $4,814.63, or $48.15, leaving $187.22 for repayment of the principal. At $n = 24$, the last $235.37 payment is just sufficient to pay the interest on the unpaid loan principal and to repay the remaining principal.

COMMENTS: We can use the special financial functions provided in Excel to determine the total interest (or principal) paid between any two payment periods. Two financial functions are "=CUMIPMT(.)" and "=CUMPRINC(.)." Using the functional arguments in Table 3.7, you may determine the total interest and principal paid in the second year as follows:

- =CUMIPMT(1%,24,5000,13,24,0) → (175.33)

- =CUMPRINC(1%,24,5000,13,24,0) → (2,649.08)

TABLE 3.6 Loan Repayment Schedule Generated by Excel

	A	B	C	D	E	F	G
1		Example 3.8		Loan Repayment Schedule			
2							
3							
4		Contract amount	$ 5,000.00		Total payment		$ 5,648.82
5		Contract period	24		Total interest		$648.82
6		APR (%)	12				
7		Monthly Payment	($235.37)				
8							
9							
10			Payment No.	Payment Size	Principal Payment	Interest Payment	Loan Balance
11			1	($235.37)	($185.37)	($50.00)	$4,814.63
12			2	($235.37)	($187.22)	($48.15)	$4,627.41
13			3	($235.37)	($189.09)	($46.27)	$4,438.32
14		=PMT($C$6/1200,$C$5,$C$4,0)	4	($235.37)	($190.98)	($44.38)	$4,247.33
15			5	($235.37)	($192.89)	($42.47)	$4,054.44
16			6	($235.37)	($194.82)	($40.54)	$3,859.62
17			7	($235.37)	($196.77)	($38.60)	$3,662.85
18			8	($235.37)	($198.74)	($36.63)	$3,464.11
19			9	($235.37)	($200.73)	($34.64)	$3,263.38
20			10	($235.37)	($202.73)	($32.63)	$3,060.65
21			11	($235.37)	($204.76)	($30.61)	$2,855.89
22			12	($235.37)	($206.81)	($28.56)	$2,649.08
23			13	($235.37)	($208.88)	($26.49)	$2,440.20
24			14	($235.37)	($210.97)	($24.40)	$2,229.24
25			15	($235.37)	($213.08)	($22.29)	$2,016.16
26			16	($235.37)	($215.21)	($20.16)	$1,800.96
27			17	($235.37)	($217.36)	($18.01)	$1,583.60
28			18	($235.37)	($219.53)	($15.84)	$1,364.07
29			19	($235.37)	($221.73)	($13.64)	$1,142.34
30			20	($235.37)	($223.94)	($11.42)	$918.40
31			21	($235.37)	($226.18)	($9.18)	$692.21
32			22	($235.37)	($228.45)	($6.92)	$463.77
33			23	($235.37)	($230.73)	($4.64)	$233.04
34			24	($235.37)	($233.04)	($2.33)	$0.00
35							
36							
37							
38		=PPMT($C$6/1200,C33,$C$5,$C$4,0)					
39						=G32+E33	
40		=IPMT($C$6/1200,C33,$C$5,$C$4,0)					
41							

TABLE 3.7 Excel's Financial Functions to Determine a Loan's Principal and Interest Payments between Two Payment Periods

	A	B
1		
2	**EXCEL FUNCTIONS**	**DESCRIPTION**
3		
4	=IMPT(i%,n,N,P)	Interest payment
5		
6	=PPMT(i%,n,N,P)	Principal payment
7		
8	=CUMIPMT(i%,N,P, start_period,end_period,type)	Cumulative interest payment
9		
10	=CUMPRINC(i%,N,P, start_period,end_period,type)	Cumulative principal payment
11		
12	**Data**	**DESCRIPTION**
13	12%	Annual percentage rate
14	5	Period for which you want to find the interest
15	2	Years of loan
16	$5,000.00	Present value of loan
17	**Result**	**DESCRIPTION**
18	($42.47) =IPMT(A13/12,A14,A15*12,A16)	Interest due in the fifth month for a loan with the terms above
19	($192.93) =PPMT(A13/12,A14,A15*12,A16,1)	Principal payment due in the fifth month for a loan with the terms above
20	($175.33) =CUMIPMT(A13/12,A15*12,A16,13,24,0)	Total Interest paid in the 2nd year for a loan with the terms above, where payments are made monthly
21	=CUMPRINC(A13/12,A15*12,A16,13,24,0) ($2,649.08)	Total principal paid in the 2nd year for a loan with the terms above, where payments are mode monthly
22		

3.4.3 Comparing Different Financing Options

When you choose a car, you also choose how to pay for it. If you do not have the cash on hand to buy a new car outright—as most of us do not—you can consider taking out a loan or leasing the car in order to spread out the payments over time. Your decision to pay cash, take out a loan, or sign a lease depends on a number of personal as well as economic factors. Leasing is an option that lets you pay for the portion of a vehicle you expect to use over a specified term plus rent charge, taxes, and fees. For example, you might want a $20,000 vehicle. Assume that the vehicle might be worth about $9,000 (its residual value) at the end of a three-year lease. Your options are as follows:

- If you have enough money to buy the car, you could purchase the car with cash. If you pay cash, however, you will lose the opportunity to earn interest on the amount you spend. That could be substantial if you have access to investments paying good returns.
- If you purchase the vehicle via debt financing, your monthly payments will be based on the entire $20,000 value of the vehicle. You will own the vehicle at the end of your financing term, but the interest you will pay on the loan will drive up the real cost of the car ownership.
- If you lease the vehicle, your monthly payments will be based on the amount of the vehicle you expect to "use up" over the lease term. This value ($11,000 in our example) is the difference between the original cost ($20,000) and the estimated value at lease end ($9,000). With leasing, the length of your agreement, the monthly payments, and the yearly mileage allowance can be tailored to your driving needs. The greatest financial appeal for leasing is its low initial outlay costs: usually, you pay only an administrative fee, one month's lease payment, and a refundable security deposit. The terms of your lease will include a specific mileage allowance; if you use additional miles, you will have to pay an additional charge for each extra mile. Of course, you can make some cash down payment up-front to reduce the lease payment.

Which Interest Rate Do We Use in Comparing Different Financing Options?

The dealer's (bank's) interest rate is supposed to reflect the time value of money of the dealer (or the bank) and is factored into the required payments. However, the correct interest rate for us to use when comparing financing options is the interest rate that reflects *your* earning opportunity. For most individuals, this interest rate is equivalent to the savings rate from their deposits. To illustrate, we provide two examples. Example 3.8 compares two different financing options for an automobile. Example 3.9 explores a lease-versus-buying decision on an automobile.

EXAMPLE 3.9 Buying a Car: Paying in Cash versus Taking a Loan

Consider the following two options proposed by an auto dealer:

- **Option A:** Purchase the vehicle at the normal price of $26,200 and pay for the vehicle over 36 months with equal monthly payments at 1.9% APR financing.
- **Option B:** Purchase the vehicle at a discounted price of $24,048 to be paid immediately. The funds that would be used to purchase the vehicle are presently earning 5% annual interest compounded monthly.

Which option is more economically sound?

DISSECTING THE PROBLEM

In calculating the net cost of financing the car, we need to decide which interest rate to use in discounting the loan repayment series. Note that the 1.9% APR represents the dealer's interest rate to calculate the loan payments. With the 1.9% interest, your monthly payments will be $A = \$26,200\,(A/P, 1.9\%/12, 36) = \$749.29$. On the other hand, the 5% APR represents your earning opportunity rate. Thus, if you do not buy the car, your money continues to earn 5% APR. Therefore, this 5% rate also represents your opportunity cost of purchasing the car. Which interest rate should we use in this analysis? Since we wish to calculate each option's present worth to you, given your money and financial situation, we must use your 5% interest rate to value these cash flows.

Given: The loan payment series shown in Figure 3.12, $r = 5\%$ per year, payment period = monthly, and compounding period = monthly.

Find: The most economical financing option.

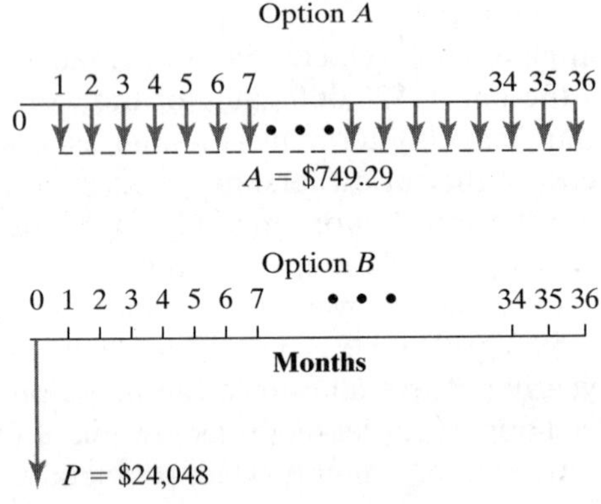

Figure 3.12   Cash flow diagram

METHODOLOGY

For each option, we will calculate the net equivalent cost (present worth) at $n = 0$. Since the loan payments occur monthly, we need to determine the effective interest rate per month, which is 5%/12.

SOLUTION

- Option A (conventional financing): The equivalent present cost of the total loan repayments is calculated as

$$P_A = \$749.29(P/A, 5\%/12, 36)$$
$$= \$25,000.$$

- Option B (cash payment): Since the cash payment is a lump sum to be paid presently, its equivalent present cost is equal to its value:

$$P_B = \$24,048.$$

Thus, there would be $952 of savings in present value with the cash payment option.

EXAMPLE 3.10 Buying versus Leasing a Car

Two types of financing options are offered for an automobile by a local dealer, as shown in the following table. The calculations are based on special financing programs available at participating dealers for a limited time. For each option, license, title, registration fees, taxes, and insurance are extra. For the lease option, the lessee must come up with $731.45 at signing. This cash due at signing includes the first month's lease payment of $236.45 and a $495 administrative fee. No security deposit is required. However, a $300 disposition fee is due at lease end. The lessee has the option to purchase the vehicle at lease end for $8,673.10. The lessee is also responsible for excessive wear and use. If your earning interest rate is 6% compounded monthly, which financing option is a better choice?

Buying versus Leasing

	Option 1 Debt Financing	Option 2 Lease Financing
Price	$14,695	$14,695
Down payment	$2,000	$0
APR (%)	3.6%	
Monthly payment	$372.55	$236.45
Length	36 months	36 months
Fees		$495
Cash due at lease end		$300
Purchase option at lease end		$8,673.10
Cash due at signing	$2,000	$731.45

DISSECTING THE PROBLEM

With a lease payment, you pay for the portion of the vehicle you expect to use. At the end of the lease, you simply return the vehicle to the dealer and pay the agreed-upon disposal fee. With traditional financing, your monthly payment is based on the entire $14,695 value of the vehicle, and you will own the vehicle at the end of your financing terms. Since you are comparing the options over three years, you must explicitly consider the unused portion (resale value) of the vehicle at the end of the term. For comparison purposes, you must consider the resale value of the vehicle in order to figure out the net cost of owning the vehicle. You could use the $8,673.10 quoted by the dealer in the lease option as the resale value. Then you have to ask yourself if you can get that kind of resale value after three years of ownership. (See Figure 3.13.)

Given: The lease payment series shown in Figure 3.13, $r = 6\%$ per year, payment period = monthly, and compounding period = monthly.

Find: The most economical financing option, assuming that you will be able to sell the vehicle for $8,673.10 at the end of three years.

For each option, we will calculate the net equivalent total cost at $n = 0$. Since the loan payments occur monthly, we need to determine the effective interest rate per month, which is 0.5%.

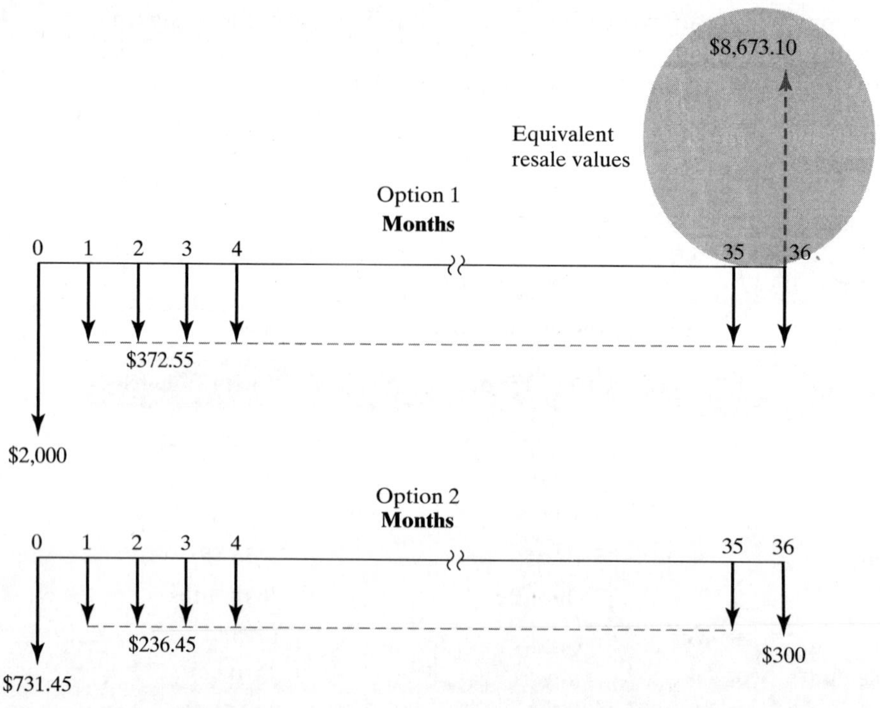

Figure 3.13   Cash flow diagrams for buying and leasing the car

METHODOLOGY	SOLUTION

METHODOLOGY

Method 1: Conventional Financing

SOLUTION

The equivalent present cost of the total loan payments is calculated as

$$P_1 = \$2,000 + \$372.55\,(P/A, 0.5\%, 36)$$
$$= \$14,246.10.$$

The equivalent present worth of the resale value is calculated as

$$P_2 = \$8,673.10(P/F, 0.5\%, 36) = \$7,247.63.$$

The equivalent present net financing cost is therefore

$$P = P_1 - P_2 = \$14,246.10 - \$7,247.63$$
$$= \$6,998.47.$$

Method 2: Lease Financing

The equivalent present cost of the total lease payments is calculated as

$$P_1 = \$731.45 + \$236.45\,(P/A, 0.5\%, 35)$$
$$= \$731.45 + \$7,574.76$$
$$= \$8,306.21.$$

The equivalent present cost of the disposition fee is calculated as

$$P_2 = \$300(P/F, 0.5\%, 36) = \$250.69.$$

The equivalent present net lease cost is therefore

$$P = P_1 + P_2 = \$8,306.21 + \$250.69$$
$$= \$8,556.90.$$

It appears that the traditional financing program to purchase the car is more economical at 6% interest compounded monthly.

COMMENTS: By varying the resale value S, we can find the break-even resale value that makes traditional financing equivalent to lease financing for this case:

$$\$8,556.90 = \$14,246.10 - S(P/F, 0.5\%, 36).$$

Thus, the break-even resale value is

$$S = (\$14,246.10 - \$8,556.90)/0.8356$$
$$= \$6,808.14.$$

So, at a resale value greater than $6,808.14, the conventional financing plan would be the more economical choice. Table 3.8 illustrates how we may create an Excel worksheet to determine the break-even resale value by using the **Goal Seek** function. To perform this function, we calculate the equivalent debt financing cost at cell B18 and the equivalent leasing financing cost at cell D20. Next, we enter the differential amount in cell B22. Then we are looking for a resale value (by changing cell B17) to make this differential cost (set cell B22) to be zero (To value). When you click OK, Excel will find the break-even resale value at $6,808.14.

SUMMARY

- Interest is most frequently quoted by financial institutions as an **APR**. However, compounding often occurs more frequently. Simply multiplying the APR by the amount of debt does not account for the effect of this more frequent compounding. This situation leads to the distinction between nominal and effective interest.

- **Nominal interest** is a stated rate of interest for a given period (usually, a year).

- **Effective interest** is the actual rate of interest, which accounts for the interest amount accumulated over a given period. The **effective rate** is related to the APR by

$$i = (1 + r/M)^M - 1,$$

TABLE 3.8 An Excel Worksheet to Determine the Break-Even Resale Value

	A	B	C	D	E	F	G	H
		Option 1		Option 2			Option 1	Option 2
		Debt Financing		Lease Financing		Period	Debt Financing	Lease Financing
1								
2		Option 1		Option 2			Option 1	Option 2
3		Debt Financing		Lease Financing		Period	Debt Financing	Lease Financing
4								
5	Price	$14,695.00		$14,695.00		0	$2,000.00	$731.45
6	Down payment	$2,000.00				1	$372.55	$236.45
7	APR(%)	3.60%				2	$372.55	$236.45
8	Length (months)	36		36		3	$372.55	$236.45
9	Monthly payment	$372.55		$236.45		4	$372.55	$236.45
10	Fees			$495.00		5	$372.55	$236.45
11	Cash Due at lease end			$300.00		6	$372.55	$236.45
12	Purchase option at lease end			$8,673.10		7	$372.55	$236.45
13	Cash due at signing	$2,000.00		$731.45		8	$372.55	$236.45
14						9	$372.55	$236.45
15						10	$372.55	$236.45
16	Interest rate per month	0.50%				11	$372.55	$236.45
17	Estimated resale value	$6,808.14				12	$372.55	$236.45
18	Equivalent debt financing cost	$8,556.91				13	$372.55	$236.45
19						14	$372.55	$236.45
20	Equivalent lease financing cost			$8,556.91		15	$372.55	$236.45
21						16	$372.55	$236.45
22	Differential cost	$0.00				17	$372.55	$236.45
23						18	$372.55	$236.45
24						19	$372.55	$236.45
25	=NPV(0.5%,G6:G41)+G5					20	$372.55	$236.45
26						21	$372.55	$236.45
27						22	$372.55	$236.45
28						23	$372.55	$236.45
29						24	$372.55	$236.45
30						25	$372.55	$236.45
31		Set cell: $B$22				26	$372.55	$236.45
32		To value: 0				27	$372.55	$236.45
33		By changing cell: $B$17				28	$372.55	$236.45
34						29	$372.55	$236.45
35						30	$372.55	$236.45
36						31	$372.55	$236.45
37						32	$372.55	$236.45
38						33	$372.55	$236.45
39						34	$372.55	$236.45
40		=NPV(0.5%,H6:H41)+H5				35	$372.55	$236.45
41						36	($6,435.59)	$300.00
42								

where r = the APR, M = the number of compounding periods, and i = the effective interest rate.

- In any equivalence problem, the interest rate to use is the effective interest rate per payment period, which is expressed as

$$i = [1 + r/CK]^C - 1,$$

where C = the number of interest periods per payment period, K = the number of payment periods per year, and r/K = the nominal interest rate per payment period.

- The equation for determining the effective interest of continuous compounding is as follows:

$$i = e^{r/K} - 1.$$

- The difference in accumulated interest between continuous compounding and daily compounding is relatively small.

■ Whenever payment and compounding periods differ from each other, it is recommended to compute the effective interest rate per payment period. The reason is that, to proceed with equivalency analysis, the compounding and payment periods must be the same.

■ The cost of a loan will depend on many factors, such as loan amount, loan term, payment frequency, fees, and interest rate.

■ In comparing different financing options, the interest rate we use is the one that reflects the decision maker's time value of money, not the interest rate quoted by the financial institution(s) lending the money.

SELF-TEST QUESTIONS

3s.1. You are making $5,000 monthly deposits into a fund that pays interest at a rate of 6% compounded *monthly*. What would be the balance at the end of 15 years?
(a) $1,063,879
(b) $1,358,169
(c) $1,452,053
(d) $1,459,423

3s.2. Two banks offer the following interest rates on your deposit:
■ Bank A : 9% interest compounded *quarterly*
■ Bank B : 8.5% interest compounded *continuously*
Which of the following statements is *not* true?
(a) The annual percentage yield (APY) for Bank A is 9.30%.
(b) The effective annual interest rate for Bank B is 8.87%.
(c) Bank A offers a better deal.
(d) The annual percentage rate (APR) for Bank B is 8.5%.

3s.3. You are making semiannual deposits into a fund that pays interest at a rate of 9% compounded *continuously*. What is the effective *semiannual* interest rate?
(a) 4.000%
(b) 4.708%
(c) 4.164%
(d) 4.175%

3s.4. Calculate the future worth of 20 annual $4,000 deposits in a savings account that earns 8% compounded monthly. Assume all deposits are made at the beginning of each year.
(a) $196,010
(b) $188,196
(c) $190,162
(d) $199,279

3s.5. You borrow $15,000 from a bank to be repaid in monthly installments for three years at 15% interest compounded monthly. What is the portion of interest payment for the 15th payment?
(a) $150
(b) $188

    (c) $180

    (d) $124

3s.6. You borrowed $25,000 from a bank at an interest rate of 12%, compounded *monthly*. This loan will be repaid in 48 equal monthly installments over four years. Immediately after your 20th payment, if you want to pay off the remainder of the loan in a single payment, the amount is close to

    (a) $15,723

    (b) $15,447

    (c) $15,239

    (d) $16,017

3s.7. You borrowed $120,000, agreeing to pay the balance in 12 equal annual installments at 9% annual interest. Determine the remaining loan balance right after the fifth payment.

    (a) $84,373

    (b) $68,894

    (c) $59,503

    (d) $49,360

3s.8. Consider the following two cash flow transactions. If they are economically equivalent at 10% interest, find the value of *C*.

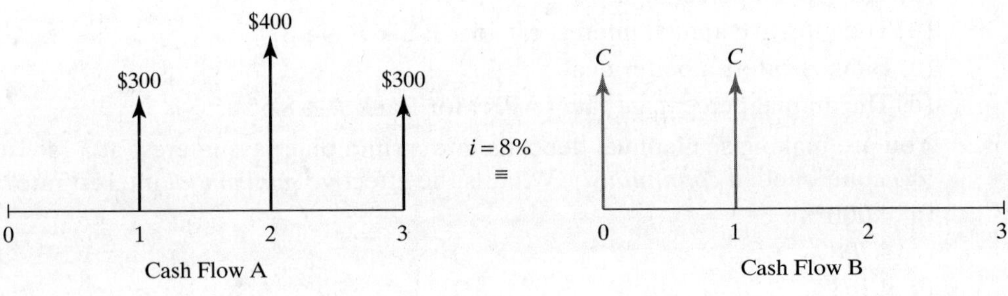

    (a) $C = \$325$

    (b) $C = \$282$

    (c) $C = \$455$

    (d) $C = \$277$

3s.9 Compute the present worth (*P*) for the cash flows with the different periodic interest rates specified. The cash flows occur at the end of each year over six years.

    (a) $P = \$2,140$

    (b) $P = \$2,154$

    (c) $P = \$2,234$

    (d) $P = \$2,249$

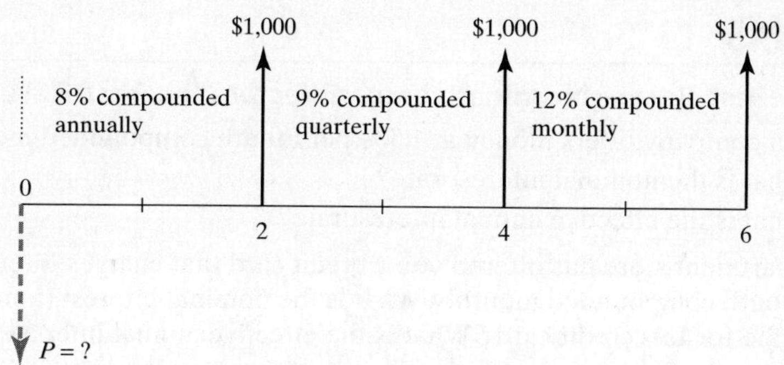

3s.10 Suppose you purchased a corporate bond with a 10-year maturity, a $1,000 par value, a 9% coupon rate ($45 interest payment every six months), and semiannual interest payments. Five years after the bonds were purchased, the going rate of interest on new bonds fell to 6% (or 6% compounded semiannually). What is the current market value (P) of the bond (five years after the purchase)?

(a) $P = \$890$

(b) $P = \$1,223$

(c) $P = \$1,090$

(d) $P = \$1,128$

3s.11. Your company borrowed $180,000, agreeing to pay the balance in 18 equal monthly installments at 8% compounded monthly. Determine the remaining loan balance right after the 12th payment.

(a) $81,816

(b) $90,751

(c) $96,876

(d) $95,928

3s.12 You are considering either buying or leasing a vehicle. The following data have been compiled:

	Buying	Leasing
Price of vehicle	$22,000	$22,000
Down payment required at year 0	$2,000	0
Value of vehicle at the end of year 3 (unknown)	S	
36 Monthly payments	$608 (*end* of each month)	$420 (*beginning* of each month)
Documentation fee (one time, nonrecurring expense, not refundable)		$400 (payable at the beginning of lease)

If your interest rate is 6% compounded monthly, at what value of the vehicle at the end of 3 years (S) would make the both options economically equivalent?

(a) $7,711

(b) $8,980

(c) $9,228

(d) $9,310

PROBLEMS

Market Interest Rates (Nominal versus Effective Interest Rates)

3.1 A loan company offers money at 1.5% per month compounded monthly.
(a) What is the nominal interest rate?
(b) What is the effective annual interest rate?

3.2 A department store has offered you a credit card that charges interest at 1.75% per month compounded monthly. What is the nominal interest (annual percentage) rate for this credit card? What is the effective annual interest rate?

3.3 A discount interest loan is a loan arrangement where the interest and any other related charges are calculated at the time the loan is closed. Suppose a one-year loan is stated as $10,000 and the interest rate is 14%. Then, the borrower pays $1,400 interest up front, thereby receiving net funds of $8,600 and repaying $10,000 in a year. What is the effective interest rate on this one-year loan?

3.4 A California bank, Berkeley Savings and Loan, advertised the following information: 7% interest and effective annual yield 7.22%. No mention is made of the interest period in the advertisement. Can you figure out the compounding scheme used by the bank?

3.5 American Eagle Financial Sources, which makes small loans to college students, offers to lend a student $600. The borrower is required to pay $4 at the end of each week for 13 weeks. Find the interest rate per week. What is the nominal interest rate per year? What is the effective interest rate per year?

3.6 A financial institution is willing to lend you $800. However, you must repay $802 at the end of one week.
(a) What is the nominal interest rate?
(b) What is the effective annual interest rate?

3.7 A loan of $22,000 is to be financed to assist a person's college education. Based upon monthly compounding for 24 months, the end-of-the-month equal payment is quoted as $250. What nominal interest rate is being charged?

3.8 You are purchasing a $18,000 used automobile, which is to be paid for in 36 monthly installments of $525. What nominal interest rate are you paying on this financing arrangement?

3.9 To finance your car, you have decided to take a car loan in the amount of $20,000 from your credit union. You will pay off this loan over 60 months. If the required monthly payment is $400, what is the effective annual interest rate on this car loan?

3.10 You obtained a loan of $25,000 to finance your home improvement project. Based on monthly compounding over 24 months, the end-of-the-month equal payment was figured to be $1200. What is the APR used for this loan?

3.11 Bank A charges 12% compounded monthly on its business loan. Bank B charges 11.8% compounded daily. If you want to borrow money, which bank would you choose?

Calculating an Effective Interest Rate Based on a Payment Period

3.12 Find the effective interest rate per payment period for an interest rate of 8% compounded monthly for each of the given payment schedule:

(a) Monthly
(b) Quarterly
(c) Semiannually
(d) Annually

3.13 What is the effective interest rate per quarter if the interest rate is 10% compounded monthly?

3.14 What is the effective interest rate per month if the interest rate is 9% compounded continuously?

3.15 What is the effective interest rate per quarter if the interest rate is 8% compounded continuously?

3.16 James Hogan is purchasing a $30,000 automobile, which is to be paid for in 48 monthly installments of $650. What is the effective interest rate per month for this financing arrangement?

3.17 Find the APY in each of the following cases:
(a) 10% compounded annually.
(b) 9% compounded semiannually.
(c) 12% compounded quarterly.
(d) 7% compounded daily.

Equivalence Calculations Using Effective Interest Rates

3.18 What will be the amount accumulated by each of the given present investments?
(a) $6,000 in 12 years at 8% compounded semiannually.
(b) $14,500 in 18 years at 6% compounded quarterly.
(c) $12,500 in 7 years at 8% compounded monthly.

3.19 What is the future worth of each of the given series of payments?
(a) $12,000 at the end of each six-month period for 12 years at 8% compounded semiannually.
(b) $8,000 at the end of each quarter for 6 years at 12% compounded quarterly.
(c) $6,000 at the end of each month for 5 years at 6% compounded monthly.

3.20 What equal series of payments must be paid into a sinking fund in order to accumulate each given amount?
(a) $1,700 in 10 years at 8% compounded semiannually when payments are semiannual.
(b) $9,000 in 6 years at 3% compounded quarterly when payments are quarterly.
(c) $4,000 in 2 years at 12% compounded monthly when payments are monthly.

3.21 What is the present worth of each of the given series of payments?
(a) $2,700 at the end of each six-month period for 10 years at 8% compounded semiannually.
(b) $10,000 at the end of each quarter for five years at 12% compounded quarterly.
(c) $14,000 at the end of each month for eight years at 6% compounded monthly.

3.22 What is the amount C of quarterly deposits such that you will be able to withdraw the amounts shown in the accompanying cash flow diagram if the interest rate is 8% compounded quarterly?

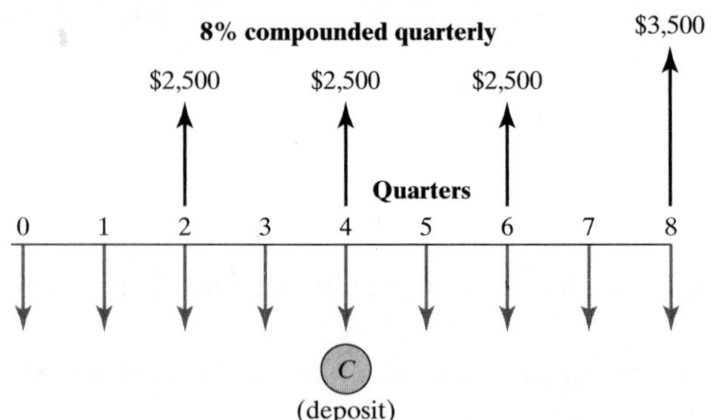

3.23 A series of equal quarterly deposits of $8,000 extends over a period of three years. It is desired to compute the future worth of this quarterly deposit series at 8% compounded monthly. Which of the equations shown is correct for this operation?

(a) $F = \$8,000\ (F/A, 8\%, 3)$.

(b) $F = \$8,000\ (F/A, 2.01\%, 12)$.

(c) $F = \$8,000\ (F/A, 1\%, 12)$.

(d) $F = \$8,000\ (F/A, 3.03\%, 12)$.

3.24 Suppose you deposit $4,000 at the end of each quarter for five years at an interest rate of 8% compounded monthly. Which of the formulas given next will determine the equal annual end-of-year deposit amount that would accumulate the same balance over five years, under the same interest compounding, as the $4,000 deposited quarterly?

(a) $A = [\$4,000\ (F/A, 2.01\%, 20)] \times (A/F, 8\%, 5)$.

(b) $A = \$4,000\ (F/A, 9\%, 5)$.

(c) $A = \$4,000\ (F/A, 9\%, 20) \times (A/F, 9\%, 5)$.

(d) None of the above.

3.25 Suppose a newlywed couple is planning to buy a home two years from now. To save the down payment required at the time of purchasing a home worth $400,000 (let's assume this required down payment is 25% of the sales price, or $100,000), the couple has decided to set aside some money from their salaries at the end of each month. If the couple can earn 9% interest (compounded monthly) on their savings, determine the equal amount the couple must deposit each month so that they may buy the home at the end of two years.

3.26 Georgi Rostov deposits $4,000 in a savings account that pays 8% interest compounded monthly. Three years later, he deposits $5,000. Two years after the $5,000 deposit, he makes another deposit in the amount of $7,000. Four years after the $7,000 deposit, half of the accumulated money is transferred to a fund that pays 9% interest compounded quarterly. How much money will be in each account six years after the transfer?

3.27 A man is planning to retire in 25 years. He wishes to deposit a regular amount every three months until he retires so that, beginning one year following his retirement, he will receive annual payments of $50,000 for the next 10 years. How much must he deposit if the interest rate is 9% compounded quarterly?

3.28 Consider the cash flow series shown below. Determine the required annual deposits (end of year) that will generate the cash flows from years 4 to 7. Assume the interest rate is 9%, compounded *monthly*.

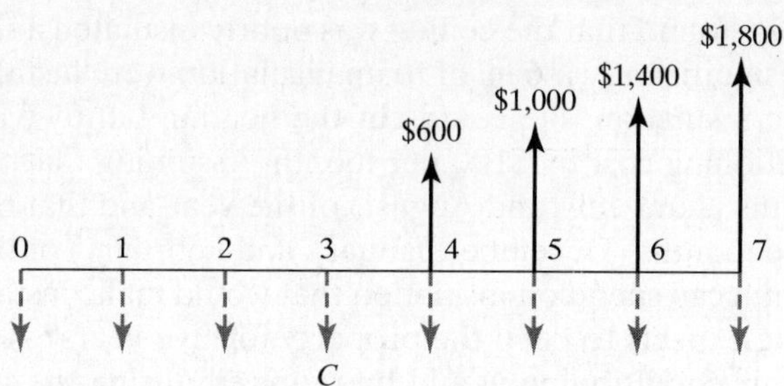

3.29 You are in financial trouble and are delinquent on your mortgage payment. Your bank has agreed to a repayment schedule of $1,000 per month, and it will charge 0.5% per month interest on the outstanding balance. If the current outstanding balance is $300,000, how long will it take for you to pay off the loan?

3.30 A building is priced at $300,000. If a buyer makes a down payment of $100,000 and a payment of $2,000 every month thereafter, how many months will it take for the buyer to completely pay for the building? Interest is charged at a rate of 8% compounded monthly.

3.31 Today is your birthday and you decide to start saving for your retirement. You will retire on your 60th birthday and need $40,000 per year at the end of each of following 15 years. You will make a first deposit one year from today in an account paying 9% interest annually and continue to make an equal amount of deposit each year up to the year before you plan to retire. If an annual deposit of $967.28 will allow you to reach your goal, what birthday are you celebrating today?

3.32 A couple is planning to finance its three-year-old son's college education. The couple can deposit money at 12% compounded quarterly. What quarterly deposit must be made from the son's 3rd birthday to his 18th birthday in order to provide $30,000 on each birthday from the 18th to the 21st? (Note that the last deposit is made on the date of the first withdrawal.)

3.33 Sam Musso is planning to retire in 20 years. He can deposit money at 12% compounded quarterly. What deposit must he make at the end of each quarter until he retires so that he can make a withdrawal of $55,000 semiannually over five years after his retirement? Assume that his first withdrawal occurs at the end of six months after his retirement.

3.34 Suppose you borrowed $12,000 at an interest rate of 8%, compounded monthly over 36 months. At the end of the first year (after 12 payments), you want to negotiate with the bank to pay off the remainder of the loan in eight equal quarterly payments. What is the amount of this quarterly payment, if the interest rate and compounding frequency remain the same?

3.35 Tamara Massey received $1,500,000 from an insurance company after her husband's death. She wants to deposit this amount in a savings account that earns interest at a rate of 8% compounded monthly. Then she would like to make 48 equal monthly withdrawals over four years such that, when she makes the last withdrawal, the savings account will have a balance of zero. How much should she withdraw each month?

3.36 Anita Hayes, who owns a travel agency, bought an old house to use as her business office. She found that the ceiling was poorly insulated and that the heat loss could be cut significantly if 6 in. of foam insulation were installed. She estimated that, with the insulation, she could cut the heating bill by $160 per month and the air-conditioning cost by $100 per month. Assuming that the summer season is three months (June, July, and August) of the year and that the winter season is another three months (December, January, and February) of the year, what is the most that Anita can spend on insulation that would make installation worthwhile given that she expects to keep the property for five years? Assume that neither heating nor air conditioning would be required during the fall and spring seasons. If she decides to install the insulation, it will be done at the beginning of May. Anita's interest rate is 9% compounded monthly.

3.37 You want to open a savings plan for your future retirement. You are considering the following two options:

- Option 1: You deposit $1,000 at the end of each quarter for the first 10 years. At the end of 10 years, you make no further deposits, but you leave the amount accumulated at the end of 10 years for the next 15 years.

- Option 2: You do nothing for the first 10 years. Then you deposit $6,000 at the end of each year for the next 15 years.

If your deposits or investments earn an interest rate of 6% compounded quarterly and you choose Option 2 over Option 1, then at the end of 25 years from now, you will have accumulated

(a) $7,067 more.

(b) $8,523 more.

(c) $14,757 less.

(d) $13,302 less.

3.38 Maria Anguiano's current salary is $80,000 per year, and she is planning to retire 25 years from now. She anticipates that her annual salary will increase by 3% each year. (That is, in the first year she will earn $82,400, in the second year $84,872, in the third year $87,418.16, and so forth.) She plans to deposit 6% of her yearly salary into a retirement fund that earns 8% interest compounded monthly. What will be the amount accumulated at the time of her retirement?

Equivalence Calculations with Continuous Compounding

3.39 How many years will it take an investment to *triple* if the interest rate is 8% compounded

(a) quarterly?

(b) monthly?

(c) continuously?

3.40 A series of equal quarterly payments of $6,000 for 10 years is equivalent to what present amount at an interest rate of 12% compounded

(a) quarterly?

(b) monthly?

(c) continuously?

3.41 What is the future worth of an equal-payment series of $5,000 per year for ten years if the interest rate is 8% compounded continuously?

3.42 Suppose that $1,500 is placed in a bank account at the end of each quarter over the next 20 years. What is the account's future worth at the end of 20 years when the interest rate is 8% compounded
(a) semiannually?
(b) monthly?
(c) continuously?

3.43 If the interest rate is 7% compounded continuously, what is the required quarterly payment to repay a loan of $20,000 in five years?

3.44 What is the future worth of a series of equal monthly payments of $2,000 if the series extends over a period of six years at 9% interest compounded
(a) quarterly?
(b) monthly?
(c) continuously?

3.45 What is the required quarterly payment to repay a loan of $30,000 in six years? If the interest rate is 9% compounded continuously?

3.46 A series of equal quarterly payments of $2,500 extends over a period of four years. What is the present worth of this quarterly-payment series at 8% interest compounded continuously?

3.47 A series of equal quarterly payments of $5,000 for 10 years is equivalent to what future lump-sum amount at the end of 15 years at an interest rate of 6% compounded continuously?

Borrowing with Credit Cards

3.48 Your bank calculates the interest based on 15% APR on your credit card balance (monthly compounding). Suppose that your current outstanding balance is $5,000 and you skip payments for two months. What would be the total balance two months from now?

3.49 You have just received credit card applications from two banks, *A* and *B*. The interest terms on your unpaid balance are stated as follows:
1. Bank *A*: 20% compounded quarterly.
2. Bank *B*: 19.5% compounded daily.

Which of the following statements is *incorrect*?
(a) The effective annual interest rate for Bank A is 18.25%.
(b) The nominal annual interest rate for Bank B is 19.5%.
(c) Bank B's term is a better deal, because you will pay less interest on your unpaid balance.
(d) Bank A's term is a better deal, because you will pay less interest on your unpaid balance.

3.50 You received a credit card application from Sun Bank offering an introductory rate of 3% per year compounded monthly for the first six months, increasing thereafter to 18% compounded monthly. This offer is good as long as you transfer your current debt from your existing card. Assuming that you will transfer $5,000 balance, you will continue to make $150 monthly payment (without making any subsequent purchases), what would be the credit card balance at the end of the first year?

3.51 Jennifer Lee, an engineering major in her junior year, has received in the mail two guaranteed-line-of-credit applications from two different banks. Each bank offers a different annual fee and finance charge. Jennifer expects her average monthly balance after payment to be $500 and plans to keep the card she chooses for only 24 months. (After graduation, she will apply for a new card.) Jennifer's interest rate (on her savings account) is 8% compounded daily.

Terms	Bank *A*	Bank *B*
Annual fee	$25	Free
Finance charge	1.65% monthly interest rate	20% annual percentage rate

(a) Compute the effective annual interest rate for each card.
(b) Which bank's credit card should Jennifer choose?

Commercial Loans

3.52 Suppose you take out a car loan of $15,000 with an interest rate of 15% compounded monthly. You will pay off the loan over 36 months with equal monthly payments.
(a) What is the monthly interest rate?
(b) What is the amount of the equal monthly payment?
(c) What is the interest payment for the 15th payment?
(d) What is the total interest paid over the life of the loan?

3.53 An automobile loan of $15,000 at a nominal rate of 9% compounded monthly for 36 months requires equal end-of-month payments of $477. Complete the following table for the first six payments as you would expect a bank to calculate the values:

End of Month (n)	Interest Payment	Repayment of Principal	Remaining Loan Balance
1			$14,635.50
2		$367.23	
3		$369.99	
4	$104.24		
5	$101.44		
6			$12,771.58

3.54 You borrow $200,000 with a 25-year payback term and a variable APR that starts at 8% and can be changed every five years.
(a) What is the initial monthly payment?
(b) If, at the end of five years, the lender's interest rate changes to 9% (APR), what will the new monthly payment be?

3.55 Sarah Maddox wants to buy a new car that will cost $15,000. She will make a down payment in the amount of $3,000. She would like to borrow the remainder from a bank at an interest rate of 8% compounded monthly. She agrees to make monthly payments for a period of two years in order to pay off the loan. Select the correct answer for each of the following questions:

(a) What is the amount of the monthly payment (A)?

1. $A = \$12,000\ (A/P,\ 0.75\%,\ 24)$.
2. $A = \$12,000\ (A/F,\ 0.66\%,\ 24)$.
3. $A = \$12,000\ (A/P,\ 0.66\%,\ 24)$.
4. $A = \$12,000\ (A/F,\ 9\%,\ 2)/12$.

(b) Sarah has made 12 payments and wants to figure out the remaining balance immediately after the 12th payment. What is that remaining balance?

1. $B_{12} = 12A$.
2. $B_{12} = A(P/A,\ 9\%,\ 1)/12$.
3. $B_{12} = A(P/A,\ 0.66\%,\ 12)$.
4. $B_{12} = 10{,}000 - 12A$.

3.56 Talhi Hafid is considering the purchase of a used car. The price, including the title and taxes, is $10,500. Talhi is able to make a $2,500 down payment. The balance, $8,000, will be borrowed from his credit union at an interest rate of 10% compounded daily. The loan should be paid in 48 equal monthly payments. Compute the monthly payment. What is the total amount of interest Talhi has to pay over the life of the loan?

3.57 Janie Curtis borrowed $25,000 from a bank at an interest rate of 12% compounded monthly. This loan is to be repaid in 48 equal monthly installments over four years. Immediately after her 20th payment, Janie desires to pay the remainder of the loan in a single payment. Compute the total amounts she must pay at that time.

3.58 You are buying a home for $500,000. If you make a down payment of $80,000 and take out a mortgage on the rest at 10% compounded monthly, what will be your monthly payment if the mortgage is to be paid off in 12 years?

3.59 For a $425,000 home mortgage loan with a 20-year term at 8% APR compounded monthly, compute the total payments on principal and interest over the first five years of ownership.

3.60 A lender requires that monthly mortgage payments be no more than one third of gross monthly income, with a maximum term of 20 years. If you can make only a 20% down payment, what is the minimum monthly income you would need in order to purchase a $420,000 house when the interest rate is 12% compounded monthly?

3.61 To buy an $180,000 condominium, you put down $30,000 and take out a mortgage for $150,000 at an APR of 9% compounded monthly. Five years later, you sell the house for $205,000 (after all selling expenses are factored in). What equity (the amount that you can keep before any taxes are taken out) would you realize with a 30-year mortgage repayment term? (Assume that the loan is paid off when the condo is sold in lump sum.)

3.62 Just before the 20th payment,
- Family A had a balance of $150,000 on a 9%, 30-year mortgage.
- Family B had a balance of $150,000 on a 9%, 15-year mortgage.
- Family C had a balance of $150,000 on a 9%, 20-year mortgage.

All of the APRs are compounded monthly. How much interest did each family pay on its 20th payment?

3.63 Home mortgage lenders often charge points on a loan in order to avoid exceeding a legal limit on interest rates or to make their rates appear competitive with those of other lenders. As an example, with a two-point loan, the lender would loan only $98 for each $100 borrowed. The borrower would receive only $98 but would have to make payments just as if he or she had received $100. In this way, the lender can make more money while keeping his or her interest rate lower. Suppose that you receive a loan of $260,000 payable at the end each month for 30 years with an interest rate of 9% compounded monthly, but you have been charged three points. What is the effective interest rate on this home mortgage loan?

3.64 A restaurant is considering purchasing the lot adjacent to its business to provide adequate parking space for its customers. The restaurant needs to borrow $44,000 to secure the lot. A deal has been made between a local bank and the restaurant such that the restaurant would pay the loan back over a five-year period with the following payment terms: 15%, 20%, 25%, 30%, and 35% of the initial loan at the end of the first, second, third, fourth, and fifth years, respectively.

(a) What rate of interest is the bank earning from this loan transaction?

(b) What would be the total interest paid by the restaurant over the five-year period?

3.65 Alice Harzem wanted to purchase a new car for $18,400. A dealer offered her financing through a local bank at an interest rate of 13.5% compounded monthly. The dealer's financing required a 10% down payment and 48 equal monthly payments. Because the interest rate was rather high, Alice checked with her credit union for other possible financing options. The loan officer at the credit union quoted her 10.5% interest for a new-car loan and 12.25% for a used-car loan. But to be eligible for the loan, Alice had to have been a member of the credit union for at least six months. Since she joined the credit union two months ago, she has to wait four more months to apply for the loan. Alice decides to go ahead with the dealer's financing and, four months later, refinances the balance through the credit union at an interest rate of 12.25% over 48 months (because the car is no longer new).

(a) Compute the monthly payment to the dealer.

(b) Compute the monthly payment to the credit union.

(c) What is the total interest payment for each loan transaction?

3.66 David Kapamagian borrowed money from a bank to finance a small fishing boat. The bank's loan terms allowed him to defer payments (interest is still being charged even though payment is deferred) for six months and then to make 36 equal end-of-month payments thereafter. The original bank note was for $9,600 with an interest rate of 12% compounded monthly. After 16 monthly payments, David found himself in a financial bind and went to a loan company for assistance in lowering his monthly payments. Fortunately, the loan company offered to pay his debts in one lump sum, provided that he pays the company $208 per month for the next 36 months. What monthly rate of interest is the loan company charging on this transaction?

3.67 A loan of $18,000 is to be financed over a period of 24 wmonths. The agency quotes a nominal interest rate of 8% for the first 12 months and a nominal interest rate of 9% for any remaining unpaid balance after 12 months with both rates compounded monthly. At these rates, what equal end-of-the-month payment for 24 months would be required in order to repay the loan?

3.68 Robert Carré financed his office furniture through the furniture dealer from which he bought it. The dealer's terms allowed him to defer payments (with interest being charged) for six months and then to make 36 equal end-of-month payments thereafter. The original note was for $12,000 with interest at 12% compounded monthly. After 26 monthly payments, Robert found himself in a financial bind and went to a loan company for assistance. The loan company offered to pay his debts in one lump sum, provided that he will pay the company $204 per month for the next 30 months.

(a) Determine the original monthly payment made to the furniture store.

(b) Determine the lump-sum payoff amount the loan company will make.

(c) What monthly rate of interest is the loan company charging on this loan?

Comparing Different Financing Options

3.69 Suppose you are in the market for a new car worth $18,000. You are offered a deal to make a $1,800 down payment now and to pay the balance in equal end-of-month payments of $421.85 over a 48-month period. Consider the following situations:

(a) Instead of going through the dealer's financing, you want to make a down payment of $1,800 and take out an auto loan from a bank at 11.75% compounded monthly. What would be your monthly payment to pay off the loan in four years?

(b) If you were to accept the dealer's offer, what would be the effective rate of interest per month charged by the dealer on your financing?

3.70 A local dealer is advertising a 24-month lease of a sport utility vehicle for $520 payable at the beginning of each month. The lease requires a $2,500 down payment plus a $500 refundable security deposit. As an alternative, the company offers a 24-month lease with a single up-front payment of $12,780 plus a $500 refundable security deposit. The security deposit will be refunded at the end of the 24-month lease. Assuming you have access to a deposit account that pays an interest rate of 6% compounded monthly, which lease is more favorable?

3.71 You want to purchase a house for $85,000, and you have $17,000 cash available for a down payment. You are considering the following two financing options:

- Option 1: Get a new standard mortgage with 4.5% (APR) interest compounded monthly and a 30-year term.

- Option 2: Assume the seller's old mortgage (FHA loan) that has an interest rate of 4.0% (APR) compounded monthly, a remaining term of 25 years (from an original term of 30 years), a remaining balance of $45,578, and payments of $253.34 per month. You can obtain a second mortgage for the remaining balance, $22,422, from your credit union at 6.5% (APR) compounded monthly with a 10-year repayment period.

(a) What is the effective interest rate for Option 2?

(b) Compute the monthly payments for each option over the life of the mortgage.

(c) Compute the total interest payment for each option.

(d) What homeowner's interest rate (homeowner's time value of money) makes the two financing options equivalent?

Short Case Studies with Excel

3.72 Kevin Moore received his monthly credit card statement from his bank. His current outstanding balance is $3,168.97. The minimum monthly payment due is 1% of the outstanding balance or $20, whichever is higher. The bank uses the Average Daily Balance method to calculate the periodic interest charges. Show how the bank calculated the total estimated payments for the two scenarios: (a) the minimum payment only option and (b) $111 per month.

Payment Information		
New Balance		$3,168.97
Minimum Payment Due (Current Month)		$32.00
Minimum Payment Due (Past Due)		$0.00
Total New Minimum Payment Due		**$32.00**
Payment Due Date		Jun 22, 2011

Late Payment Warning: If we do not receive your minimum payment by the date listed above, you may have to pay up to a $35.00 Late Fee.

Minimum Payment Warning: If you make only the minimum payment each period, you will pay more in interest and it will take you longer to pay off your balance. For example:

If you make no additional charges using this card and each month you pay...	You will pay off the balance shown on this statement in about...	And you will end up paying an estimated total of...
Only the minimum payment	9 years	$5,408
$111	3 years	$4,010 *(Savings = $1,398)*

3.73 Suppose you purchased a corporate bond with a 10-year maturity, a $1,000 par value, a 10% coupon rate, and semiannual interest payments. What all this means that you receive $50 interest payment at the end of each six-month period for 10 years (20 times). Then, when the bond matures, you will receive the principal amount (the face value) in a lump sum. Three years after the bonds were purchased, the going rate of interest (coupon rate) on new bonds fell to 6% (or 6% compounded semiannually). What is the current market value (P) of the bond (3 years after the purchase)?

3.74 Consider Gizmo, a small manufacturing company whose management wishes to reduce overhead by installing a new, energy-efficient heating system. The new system costs $100,000. Due to the company's insufficient cash reserves, the management has decided that borrowing money is the only way to finance the desired improvement. A problem arises when Gizmo's accountant points out that a standard direct reduction loan would severely strain the firm's cash flow during the heating season. In order to overcome this difficulty, the accountant suggests a periodic linear gradient series repayment scheme with the gradient $G = \$75$ in a skip payment loan. The accountant proposed the following repayment schedule:

Length of Loan: Four Years

Month	Repay
Jan–Aug	Yes
Sep–Apr	Skip
May–Sep	Yes
Oct–Mar	Skip
Apr–Oct	Yes
Nov–Feb	Skip
Mar–Dec	Yes

The lender has quoted an APR of 12%. Determine the repayment schedule over four years.

(*Source:* R.A. Formato, "Generalized Formula for the Periodic Payment in a Skip Payment Loan with Arbitrary Skips," *The Engineering Economist,* 37(4), Summer 1992.)

3.75 You are considering buying a new car worth $15,000. You can finance the car either by withdrawing cash from your savings account, which earns 8% interest compounded monthly, or by borrowing $15,000 from your dealer for four years at 11% interest compounded monthly. You could earn $5,635 in interest from your savings account in four years if you leave the money in the account. If you borrow $15,000 from your dealer, you pay only $3,609 in interest over four years, so it makes sense to borrow for your new car and keep your cash in your savings account. Do you agree or disagree with the foregoing statement? Justify your reasoning with a numerical calculation.

3.76 Suppose you are going to buy a home worth $110,000, making a down payment in the amount of $50,000. The balance will be borrowed from the Capital Savings and Loan Bank. The loan officer offers the following two financing plans for the property:

- Option 1: A conventional fixed loan at an interest rate of 13% compounded monthly over 30 years with 360 equal monthly payments.
- Option 2: A graduated payment schedule (FHA 235 plan) at 11.5% interest compounded monthly with the following monthly payment schedule:

Year (n)	Monthly Payment	Monthly Mortgage Insurance
1	$497.76	$25.19
2	$522.65	$25.56
3	$548.78	$25.84
4	$576.22	$26.01
5	$605.03	$26.06
6–30	$635.28	$25.96

For the FHA 235 plan, mortgage insurance is a must.

(a) Compute the monthly payment for Option 1.

(b) What is the effective annual interest rate you would pay under Option 2?

(c) Compute the outstanding balance for each option at the end of five years.

(d) Compute the total interest payment for each option.

(e) Assuming that your only investment alternative is a savings account that earns an interest rate of 6% compounded monthly, which option is a better deal?

3.77 Ms. Kennedy borrowed $4,909 from a bank to finance a car at an add-on interest rate[4] of 6.105%. The bank calculated the monthly payments as follows:

- Contract amount = $4,909 and contract period = 42 months (or 3.5 years). Thus, add-on interest is = $4,909 (0.06105)(3.5) = $1,048.90.

- Acquisition fee = $25; thus, total loan charge = $1,048.90 + $25 = $1,073.90.

- Total of payments = $4,909 + 1,073.90 = $5,982.90, and monthly installment = $5,982.90/42 = $142.45.

After making the seventh payment, Ms. Kennedy wants to pay off the remaining balance just before making the eighth payment. The following is the letter from the bank explaining the net balance Ms. Kennedy owes:

Dear Ms. Kennedy,

The following is an explanation of how we arrived at the payoff amount on your loan account:

Original note amount	$5,982.90
Less 7 payments @ $142.45 each	997.15
	4,985.75
Loan charge (interest)	1,073.90
Less acquisition fee	25.00
	$1,048.90

---

[4] The add-on loan is totally different from the popular amortized loan. In this type of loan, the total interest to be paid is precalculated and added to the principal. The principal plus the precalculated interest amount is then paid in equal installments. In such a case, the interest rate quoted is not the effective interest rate but what is known as *add-on interest*.

Rebate factor from Rule of 78s chart is 0.6589. (Loan ran 8 months on a 42-month term.)

$1,048.90 multiplied by 0.6589 is $691.12.

$691.12 represents the unearned interest rebate.

Therefore, your payoff amount is computed as follows:

Balance	$4,985.75
Less unearned interest rebate	691.12
Payoff amount	$4,294.63

If you have any further questions concerning these matters, please contact us.

Sincerely,
S. Govia
Vice President

Hint: The Rule of 78s is used by some financial institutions to determine the outstanding loan balance. According to the Rule of 78s, the interest charged during a given month is figured out by applying a changing fraction to the total interest over the loan period. For example, in the case of a one-year loan, the fraction used in determining the interest charge for the first month would be 12/78, 12 being the number of remaining months of the loan and 78 being the sum of $1 + 2 + \cdots + 11 + 12$. For the second month, the fraction would be 11/78, and so on. In the case of a two-year loan, the fraction during the first month is 24/300, because there are 24 remaining payment periods and the sum of the loan periods is $300 = 1 + 2 + \cdots + 24$.

(a) Compute the effective annual interest rate for this loan.

(b) Compute the annual percentage rate (APR) for this loan.

(c) Show how would you derive the rebate factor (0.6589).

(d) Verify the payoff amount by using the Rule of 78s formula.

(e) Compute the payoff amount by using the interest factor $(P/A, i, N)$.

CHAPTER FOUR

Equivalence Calculations under Inflation

How Much Will It Cost to Buy Football Tickets in 2011?
When was the last time you bought a ticket for a professional football game? With almost everything going up in price due to inflation, football tickets are no exception. In 2005, it cost about $66.20 to purchase a ticket for a Dallas Cowboys game. In 2011, it cost $110.20, representing an almost 166% increase in price. TMR's (Team Marketing Report, Inc.) exclusive Fan Cost Index™[1] (FCI) survey tracks the cost of attendance for a family of four. The FCI comprises the prices of four (4) adult average-price tickets, two (2) small draft beers, four (4) small soft drinks, four (4) regular size hot dogs, parking for one (1) car, two (2) game programs, and two (2) least expensive, adult-size caps.

[1] Team Marketing Report, Inc. Chicago, Illinois. ©2011.

In developing the average ticket price, TMR uses a weighted average of season ticket prices for general seating categories determined by factoring the tickets in each price range as a percentage of the total number of seats in each ballpark. The 2011 FCIs for both Dallas Cowboys and league average were as follows:

Team	Avg. Ticket	Avg. Premium Ticket	Beer	Soda	Hot Dog	Parking	Program	Cap	FCI	Percent Change over 2008
Dallas Cowboys	$110.20	$340	$8.00	$6.00	$5.50	$75.00	$10.00	$10.00	$613.80	40.94%
NFL Average	77.34	242.34	7.20	4.36	4.77	25.77	4.03	16.55	427.21	7.78%

The NFL average price increase over 2008 is just 7.78%. Essentially, fans would buy 7.78% less with the same amount of dollars in 2011. If this trend continues, the purchasing power of future dollars will also continue to decline. Here the purchasing power reflects the value of a currency expressed in terms of the amount of goods or services that one unit of money can buy. Purchasing power is important because, all else being equal, inflation decreases the amount of goods or services that the same amount of money can normally purchase. Our interest in this case is how we may incorporate this loss of purchasing power into our dollar comparison from Chapters 2 and 3.

Up to this point, we have demonstrated how to compute equivalence values under constant conditions in the general economy. We have assumed that prices remain relatively unchanged over long periods. As you know from personal experience, this is not a realistic assumption. In this chapter, we define and quantify the loss of purchasing power, or **inflation**, and then go on to apply it in several equivalence analyses.

4.1 Measure of Inflation

Historically, the general economy has usually fluctuated in such a way as to experience **inflation**, a loss in the purchasing power of money over time. Inflation means that the cost of an item tends to increase over time; or, to put it another way, the same dollar amount buys less of an item over time. **Deflation** is the opposite of inflation, in that prices decrease over time, and hence a specified dollar amount gains purchasing power. Inflation is far more common than deflation in the real world, so our consideration in this chapter will be restricted to accounting for inflation in economic analyses.

4.1.1 Consumer Price Index

Before we can introduce inflation into an equivalence calculation, we need a means of isolating and measuring its effect. Consumers usually have a relative and imprecise sense of how their purchasing power is declining based on their experience of shopping for food, clothing, transportation, and housing over the years. Economists have developed a measure called the **consumer price index** (CPI), which is based on a typical **market basket** of goods and services required by the average consumer. This market basket normally consists of items from eight major groups: (1) food and alcoholic beverages, (2) housing, (3) apparel, (4) transportation, (5) medical care, (6) entertainment, (7) personal care, and (8) other goods and services.

The CPI compares the cost of the typical market basket of goods and services in a current month with its cost at a previous time, such as one month ago, one year ago, or 10 years ago. The point in the past with which current prices are compared is called the **base period**. The index value for this base period is set at $100. There are two different types of CPIs kept by the Bureau of Labor and Statistics (BLS) of the U.S. Department of Labor:

- **Original Measure (Base Period = 1967):** The original base period used by the BLS for the CPI index is 1967. For example, let us say that, in 1967, the prescribed market basket could have been purchased for $100. Suppose the same combination of goods and services costs $669.41 in 2011. We can then compute the CPI for 2011 by multiplying the ratio of the current price to the base-period price by 100. In our example, the price index is ($669.41/$100)100 = 669.41, which means that the 2011 price of the contents of the market basket is 669.41% of its base-period price. (See Figure 4.1.)
- **Revised Measure (Base Period = 1982–1984):** The revised CPI introduced by the BLS in 1987 includes indices for two populations: (1) urban wage earners and clerical workers (CW) and (2) all urban consumers (CU). This change reflected the fact that differing populations had differing needs and thus differing market baskets. Both the CW and the CU indices use updated expenditure weights based upon data tabulated from the three years of the Consumer Expenditure Survey (1982, 1983, and 1984) and incorporate a number of technical improvements. As shown in Figure 4.1, the new CPI measure for 2011 is 223.47.

Basically, these two indices measure the same degree of changes in purchasing power as long as we use them consistently in any economic study. For example, the CPIs for 2001 and 2011 are 176.2 and 223.47, respectively. For the same period, the original CPIs are 528.0 and 669.41, respectively. So, the price change over a 10-year period is 26.78% and 26.83%, which is basically the same value.

However, the BLS method of assessing inflation does not imply that consumers actually purchase the same goods and services year after year. Consumers tend to adjust their shopping practices to changes in relative prices and to substitute other items for those whose prices have greatly increased in relative terms. We must understand that the CPI does not take into account this sort of consumer behavior because it is predicated on the purchase of a fixed market basket of the same goods and services in the same proportions, month after month. For this reason, the CPI is called a **price index** rather than a **cost-of-living index**, although the general public often refers to it as a cost-of-living index.

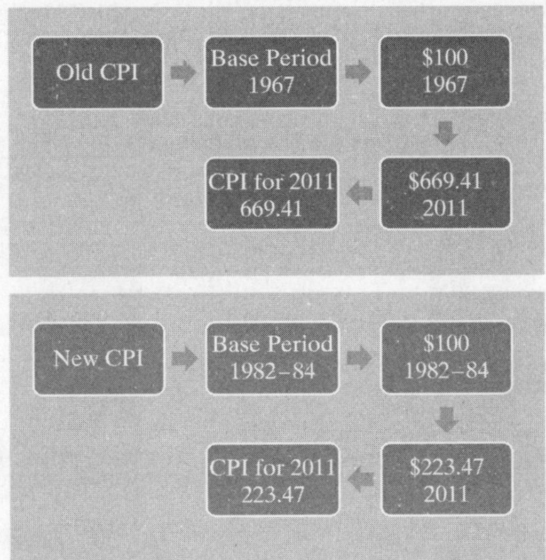

Figure 4.1   Comparison between old CPI
and new CPI measures

4.1.2 Producer Price Index

The consumer price index is a good measure of the general price increase of consumer products, but it is not a good measure of industrial price increases. When performing engineering economic analysis, the appropriate price indices must be selected to accurately estimate the price increases of raw materials, finished products, and operating costs. For example, the cost to produce and deliver gasoline to consumers includes the cost of crude oil to refiners, refinery processing costs, marketing and distribution costs, and finally, the retail station costs and taxes. As shown in Figure 4.2, the prices paid by consumers at the pump reflect these costs as well as the profits (and sometimes losses) of refiners, marketers, distributors, and retail station owners.

In 2011, the price of crude oil averaged \$109.92 per barrel, and crude oil accounted for about 69% of the cost of a gallon of regular-grade gasoline. In comparison, the average price for crude oil in 2005 was \$50.23 per barrel, and it composed 53% of the cost of a gallon of regular gasoline.

The producer price index is calculated to capture this type of price changes over time for a specific commodity or industry. The *Survey of Current Business,* a monthly publication prepared by the BLS, provides the industrial-product price index for various industrial goods. Table 4.1 lists the CPI together with several price indexes over a number of years.[2]

From Table 4.1, we can easily calculate the price index (or inflation rate) of gasoline from 2010 to 2011 as follows:

$$\frac{303.6 - 244.8}{244.8} = 0.2402 = 24.02\%.$$

---

[2] Most up-to-date CPI data are available at http://stats.bls.gov.

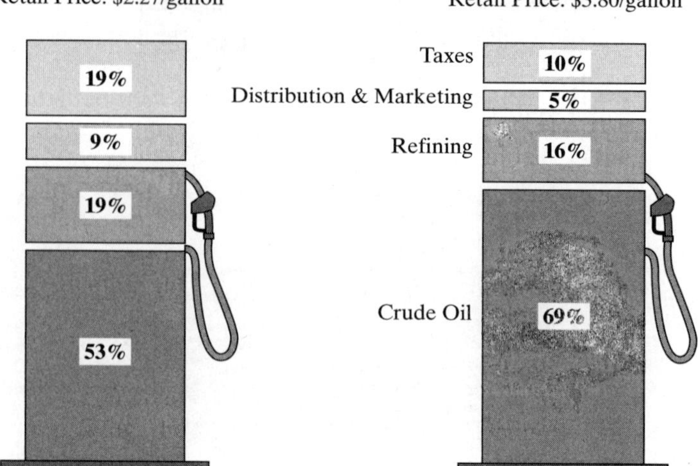

Figure 4.2 Various cost components that affect the retail gasoline price in the United States (*Source:* Energy Information Administration, Washington, DC.)

TABLE 4.1 Selected Price Indices between 2002 and 2011

Year (Base Period)	New CPI (1982–84)	Old CPI (1967)	Gasoline (1982)	Steel (1982)	Automobile (1982)
2002	178.9	535.8	89.0	114.1	134.9
2003	183.8	550.5	100.1	121.5	135.1
2004	188.0	563.2	126.1	162.4	136.5
2005	194.6	582.9	162.5	171.1	135.1
2006	201.5	600.9	217.7	186.6	130.6
2007	206.7	619.1	232.7	193.4	136.6
2008	214.8	643.5	294.3	207.5	135.2
2009	213.2	638.8	177.3	156.5	134.9
2010	218.0	653.1	244.8	195.8	138.2
2011	223.5	669.4	303.6	216.0	140.9

Source: U.S. Bureau of Labor Statistics.

Since the price index calculated is positive, the price of gasoline actually increased at an annual rate of 24.02% over the year 2010, which was one of the worst years for consumers who drive. However, in 2011, the price of automobiles increased barely at an annual rate of 1.95% over the price in 2010.

4.1.3 Average Inflation Rate

To account for the effect of varying yearly inflation rates over a period of several years, we can compute a single rate that represents an **average inflation rate**. Since each year's inflation rate is based on the previous year's rate, these rates have a compounding effect. Suppose we want to calculate the average inflation rate for a two-year period. The first year's inflation rate is 4%, and the second year's rate is 8%, with a base price of $100. To calculate the average inflation rate for the two years, we employ the following procedure:

- **Step 1:** To find the price at the end of the second year, we use the process of compounding:

$$\overbrace{\$100(1 + 0.04)}^{\text{First year}}\underbrace{(1 + 0.08)}_{\text{Second year}} = \$112.32.$$

- **Step 2:** To find the average inflation rate f, we establish the following equivalence equation:

$$\$100(1 + f)^2 = \$112.32, \text{ or } \$100(F/P, f, 2) = \$112.32.$$

Solving for f yields

$$f = 5.98\%.$$

Thus, we can say that the price increases in the last two years are equivalent to an average rate of 5.98% per year. Note that the average is a geometric average, not an arithmetic average, over a several-year period. *Why do we need to calculate this average inflation rate?* If we want to estimate the future prices on the basis of the historical data, it simplifies our economic analysis to have a single average rate such as this rather than a different rate for each year's price.

EXAMPLE 4.1 Calculating an Average Inflation Rate

Consider the price increases for the 11 items in the following table over the last 11 years:

Category	2011 Price	2000 Price	Average Inflation Rate
Postage	$0.44	$0.33	2.65%
Homeowners insurance (per year)	$674.00	$500.00	2.75%
Auto insurance (per year)	$872.00	$687.00	2.19%
Private college tuition and fees	$27,293.00	$15,518.00	5.27%
Gasoline (per gallon)	$3.64	$1.56	8.01%
Haircut	$21.00	$10.50	6.50%
Car (Toyota Camry)	$22,590.00	$21,000.00	0.67%
Natural gas (per million BTUs)	$11.99	$3.17	12.86%
Baseball tickets (family of four)	$197.35	$131.88	3.73%
Movies (average ticket)	$7.50	$5.39	3.05%
Health care (per year)	$3,365.08	$1,656.00	6.66%
Consumer price index (CPI)	**223.47**	**171.20**	**2.45%**

Base period: 1982–84 = 100

Explain how the average inflation rates are calculated in the table.

DISSECTING THE PROBLEM	
Let's take the fourth item, the cost of private college tuition, for a sample calculation. Since we know the prices during both 2000 and 2011, we can use the appropriate equivalence formula (single-payment compound amount factor or growth formula).	**Given:** $P = \$15{,}518$, $F = \$27{,}293$, and $N = 2011 - 2000 = 11$. **Find:** f.

METHODOLOGY	**SOLUTION**
Compute for average inflation rate.	We use the equation $F = P(1 + f)^N$:

$$\$27{,}293 = \$15{,}518(1 + f)^{11}.$$

Solving for f yields

$$f = \sqrt[11]{1.7588} - 1$$
$$= 0.05267 = 5.27\%.$$

This 5.27% means that the private college tuition has outpaced the overall inflation (2.45%) by 215% over the last 11 years. If the past trend continues into the future, the private college tuition in 2020 may be estimated as follows:

$$\text{Private tuition in year 2020} = \$27{,}293(1 + 0.05267)^9$$
$$= \$43{,}319.$$

In a similar fashion, we can obtain the average inflation rates for the remaining items as shown in the table. Clearly, the cost of natural gas increased the most among the items listed in the table.

4.1.4 General Inflation Rate ($\bar{f}$) versus Specific Inflation Rate (f_j)

When we use the CPI as a base to determine the average inflation rate, we obtain the **general inflation rate**. We need to distinguish carefully between the general inflation rate and the average inflation rate for specific goods:

- **General inflation rate ($\bar{f}$):** This average inflation rate is calculated on the basis of the CPI for all items in the market basket. The market interest rate is expected to respond to this general inflation rate.

  In terms of CPI, we define the general inflation rate as

$$\text{CPI}_n = \text{CPI}_0(1 + \bar{f})^n, \tag{4.1}$$

or

$$\bar{f} = \left[\frac{\text{CPI}_n}{\text{CPI}_0}\right]^{1/n} - 1, \tag{4.2}$$

where $\bar{f} = $ the general inflation rate,

CPI_n = the consumer price index at the end period n, and

CPI_0 = the consumer price index for the base period.

If we know the CPI values for two consecutive years, we can calculate the annual general inflation rate as

$$\bar{f}_n = \frac{\text{CPI}_n - \text{CPI}_{n-1}}{\text{CPI}_{n-1}}, \tag{4.3}$$

where $\bar{f}_n$ = the general inflation rate for period n.

As an example, let us calculate the general inflation rate for the year 2011, where $\text{CPI}_{2010} = 218.0$ and $\text{CPI}_{2011} = 223.5$:

$$\frac{223.5 - 218.0}{218.0} = 0.0252 = 2.52\%.$$

This calculation demonstrates that 2011 was an unusually good year for the U.S. consumers, as its 2.52% general inflation rate is slightly lower than the average general inflation rate of 2.94% over the last 29 years.[3]

- **Specific inflation rate (f_j)**: This rate is based on a price index (other than the CPI) specific to segment j of the economy. For example, we often must estimate the future cost for an item such as labor, material, housing, or gasoline. (When we refer to the average inflation rate for just one item, we will drop the subscript j for simplicity.) All average inflation rates calculated in Example 4.1 are specific inflation rates for each individual price item.

EXAMPLE 4.2 Developing Specific Inflation Rate for Baseball Tickets

The accompanying table shows the average cost since 2005 for a family of four to attend a Boston Red Sox game. Determine the specific inflation rate for each period, and calculate the average inflation rate over the six years.

Year	Cost	Yearly Inflation Rate
2005	$276.24	
2006	$287.84	4.20%
2007	$313.83	9.03%
2008	$320.71	2.19%
2009	$326.45	1.79%
2010	$334.78	2.55%
2011	$339.01	1.26%

[3] To calculate the average general inflation rate from the base period (1982) to 2011, we need to know the CPI for year 1982, which is 96.5.

$$f = \left[\frac{223.5}{96.5}\right]^{1/29} - 1 = 2.94\%.$$

DISSECTING THE PROBLEM

Given: History of baseball ticket prices.

Find: The yearly inflation rate (f_j) and the average inflation rate over the six-year time period (f).

METHODOLOGY

Calculate the inflation rate for each year and the average inflation rate over the six-year period.

SOLUTION

The inflation rate between year 2005 and year 2006 (f_1) is
$$(\$287.84 - \$276.24)/\$276.24 = 4.20\%.$$
The inflation rate during year 2006 and year 2007 (f_2) is
$$(\$313.83 - \$287.84)/\$287.84 = 9.03\%.$$
The inflation rate during year 2007 and year 2008 (f_3) is
$$(\$320.71 - \$313.83)/\$313.83 = 2.19\%.$$
Continue these calculations through 2009–2011. The average inflation rate over the six years is
$$f = \left(\frac{\$339.01}{\$276.24}\right)^{1/6} - 1 = 0.0347 = 3.47\%.$$

Note that, although the average inflation rate is 3.47% for the period taken as a whole, none of the years within the period had this rate.[4]

COMMENTS: Let's see how FCI works out for National Football League. The average FCI was $420.54 for 2010 and $329.91 for 2005, respectively. The average inflation rate is 4.97% over five-year period.

4.2 Actual Versus Constant Dollars

Due to inflation, the purchasing power of the dollar changes over time. To compare dollar values of different purchasing power from one period to another, they need to be converted to dollar values of *common* purchasing power—converting from actual to constant dollars or from constant to actual dollars. To introduce the effect of inflation into our economic analysis, we need to define the following two inflation-related terms:[5]

- **Actual (current) dollars (A_n):** Actual dollars are estimates of future cash flows for year n that take into account any anticipated changes in amount caused by inflationary or deflationary effects. Actual dollars are the number of dollars that will be paid or received, regardless of how much these dollars are worth. Usually, these numbers are determined by applying an inflation rate to base-year dollar estimates.
- **Constant (real) dollars (A'_n):** Constant dollars reflect constant purchasing power independent of the passage of time. Constant dollars are a measure of worth, not an indicator of the number of dollars paid or received. In situations where inflationary effects were assumed when cash flows were estimated, we can convert these estimates to constant dollars (base-year dollars) by adjustment, using some

---

[4] Since we obtained this average rate on the basis of costs that are specific to the baseball industry, this rate is not the general inflation rate. It is a specific inflation rate for the Boston Red Sox.

[5] Based on the ANSI Z94 Standard Committee on Industrial Engineering Terminology, *The Engineering Economist,* 33(2), 1988, pp. 145–171.

readily accepted **general inflation rate**. *Unless specified otherwise, we will always assume that the base year is at time zero.*

4.2.1 Conversion from Constant to Actual Dollars

Since constant dollars represent dollar amounts expressed in terms of the purchasing power of the base year (see Figure 4.3), we may find the equivalent dollars in year n by using the general inflation rate $\bar{f}$ in the equation

$$A_n = A'_n(1 + \bar{f})^n = A'_n(F/P, \bar{f}, n),\qquad(4.4)$$

where A'_n = the constant-dollar expression for the cash flow occurring at the end of year n and A_n = the actual-dollar expression for the cash flow occurring at the end of year n.

If the future price of a specific cost element (j) is not expected to follow the general inflation rate, we will need to use the appropriate average inflation rate applicable to this cost element, f_j instead of $\bar{f}$.

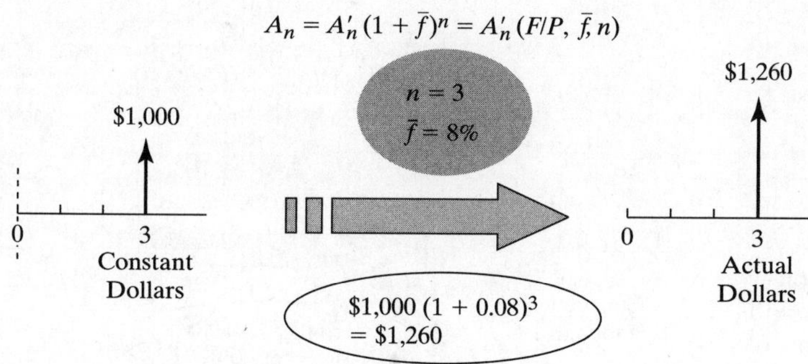

Figure 4.3 Conversion from constant to actual dollars

EXAMPLE 4.3 Conversion from Constant to Actual Dollars

What would $30,000 earned in 1995 be equal to in 2011? The CPIs for the two years are 152.4 and 223.47, respectively.

DISSECTING THE PROBLEM	
	Given: $30,000 in 1995, $CPI_{1995} = 152.4$, and $CPI_{2011} = 223.47$. **Find:** The actual dollar amount in 2011.
METHODOLOGY	**SOLUTION**
Compute the equivalent actual dollars.	By Eq. (4.2), the general inflation rate is calculated as $$\bar{f} = \left[\frac{CPI_{2011}}{CPI_{1995}}\right]^{1/16} - 1 = \left[\frac{223.47}{152.40}\right]^{1/16} - 1 = 2.4211\%,$$ and the equivalent actual dollars in 2011 is $$\$30,000(1 + 0.024211)^{16} = \$43,990.16.$$

4.2.2 Conversion from Actual to Constant Dollars

As shown in Figure 4.4, this process is the reverse of converting from constant to actual dollars. Instead of using the compounding formula, we use a discounting formula (single-payment present-worth factor):

$$A'_n = \frac{A_n}{(1 + \bar{f})^n} = A_n(P/F, \bar{f}, n).\tag{4.5}$$

Once again, we may substitute f_j for $\bar{f}$ if future prices are not expected to follow the general inflation rate.

The constant dollar is often used by companies to compare the performance of recent years with past performance. Governments also use the constant dollar to track changes in economic indicators, such as wages, over time. Any kind of financial data that is represented in dollar terms can be converted into constant dollars based on the CPIs of various years. As an example, consider Figure 4.5, which tracks U.S. gasoline prices between 1960 and 2010. Since the actual prices and the consumer price indices

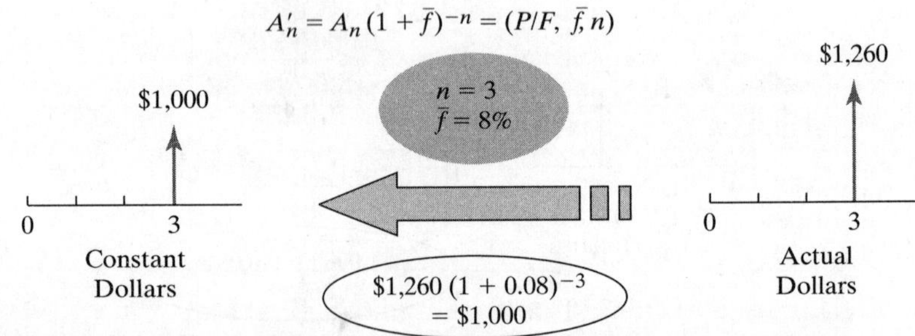

Figure 4.4 Conversion from actual to constant dollars: $1,260 three years from now will have a purchasing power of $1,000 in terms of base dollars (year 0)

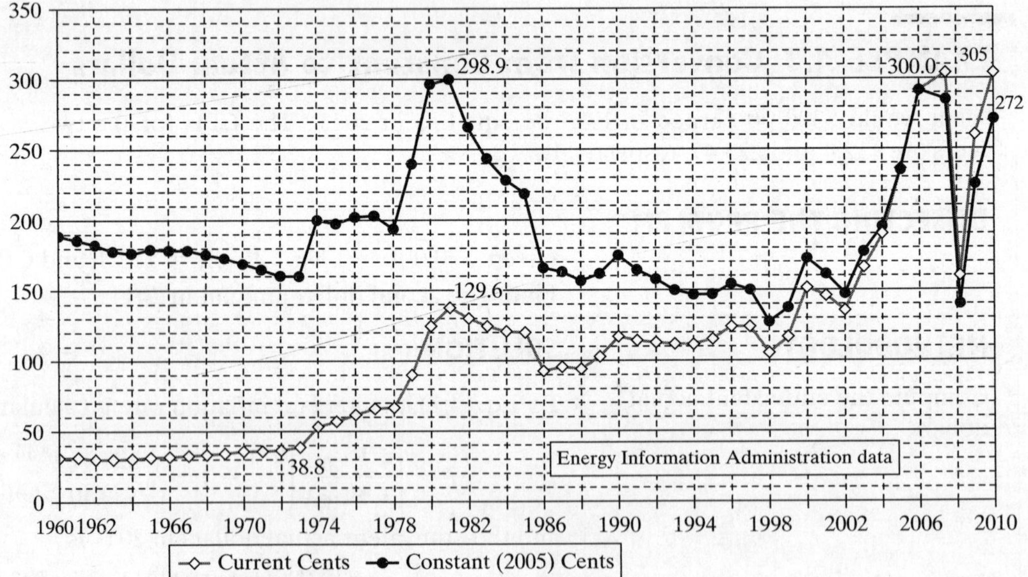

Figure 4.5 U.S. gasoline prices, 1960 to 2010, in actual and constant (year 2005) cents per gallon (*Source:* http://oregonstate.edu/Dept/pol_sci/fac/sahr/GASoline.xls)

are available over this period, we can develop a chart in which the gasoline prices are expressed in both actual dollars and constant dollars (expressed in terms of 2005 dollars) from 1960 to 2010. Even though consumers experienced a sharp price increase in 2010, the price, in fact, closely matches the 1981 price, which rose sharply due to an oil embargo imposed by some Middle Eastern countries.

In Examples 4.4 and 4.5, we will illustrate how we may convert actual dollars into constant dollars of the base year or vice versa.

EXAMPLE 4.4 Comparing Prize Monies Earned at Different Points in Time

The next table lists the winners and their prize monies in actual dollars from the Masters Golf Championship from 2006 to 2011. Convert the prize monies into equivalent dollars of 2011.

Prize Money of the Masters Golf Championship

Year	Winner	Prize Money (in Actual Dollars)
2006	Phil Mickelson	$1,260,000
2007	Zach Johnson	$1,305,000
2008	Trevor Immelman	$1,350,000
2009	Angel Cabrera	$1,350,000
2010	Phil Mickelson	$1,350,000
2011	Charl Schwartzel	$1,440,000

In doing so,

(a) Determine the growth rate of the prize money in actual dollars over the five-year period.
(b) Find the equivalent prize money for each, stated in terms of year 2011 dollars.
(c) Determine the growth rate of the prize money in constant (real) dollars.
(d) If the current trend continues, what would the expected prize money be in actual dollars for the winner in 2015?

DISSECTING THE PROBLEM

You need to find out the specific inflation rate for each past year to determine the loss of purchasing power. This requires the CPI information from 2006 to 2011.

Given: Prize history.

Find: Growth rate of the prize monies in actual as well as constant dollars and projection of the prize money for year 2015.

METHODOLOGY

Calculate the growth rate of prize monies in actual and constant dollars and project the 2015 prize money value.

SOLUTION

(a) Growth of the prize money in actual dollars:

$$\$1,440,000 = \$1,260,000(1 + f)^5$$
$$f = 2.7066\%.$$

(b) Prize money, stated in terms of 2011 dollars. In doing so, you need to calculate the general inflation rate for each year:

- Phil Mickelson (2010):

$$\$1,350,000(1 + 0.0252) = \$1,384,060.$$

- Angel Cabrera (2009):

$$\$1,350,000(1 + 0.0225)(1 + 0.0252) = \$1,415,220.$$

Other Masters Champions' prize monies can be converted into the base year dollars of 2011 as shown in the table below.

(c) Real growth of the prize money:

$$\$1,440,000 = \$1,397,568(1 + g)^5$$
$$g = 0.60\%.$$

(d) Anticipated 2015 prize money in actual dollars:

$$F_{2015} = \$1,440,000(1 + 0.027066)^4$$
$$= \$1,602,345.$$

Year	Winner	Prize Money (in Actual Dollars)	Consumer Price Index	Inflation Rate	Equivalent Prize Money (in 2011 Dollars)
2006	Phil Mickelson	$1,260,000	201.5		$1,397,568
2007	Zach Johnson	$1,305,000	206.7	2.58%	$1,411,067
2008	Trevor Immelman	$1,350,000	214.8	3.92%	$1,404,679
2009	Angel Cabrera	$1,350,000	213.2	–0.74%	$1,415,220
2010	Phil Mickelson	$1,350,000	218.0	2.25%	$1,384,060
2011	Charl Schwartzel	$1,440,000	223.5	2.52%	$1,440,000

COMMENTS: The annual growth rate of the prize monies between 2006 and 2011 is merely 2.7066%. However, if you look at the entire history of the prize monies over 77 years and know that the prize money for the first winner in 1934 was $1,500, the growth rate is 9.33%.

EXAMPLE 4.5 How Much Does It Cost to Go to College?

Tuition and fees for colleges and universities across the United States have consistently risen higher per year than inflation over the same period of time. The following table summarizes tuition and fees for four-year public institutions for the last 10 years. Cost is the value in actual dollars. With 2000 as the base year, adjust the college cost in actual dollars to the college cost in constant dollars of 2000 (2000$).

DISSECTING THE PROBLEM

The first task is to determine the general inflation $(\bar{f})$ between each period. Then we convert the actual dollars in each period into the respective constant 2000$ using this periodic general inflation rate.

Given: College costs in actual dollars.

Find: Equivalent constant dollars in year 2000.

	A	B	C	D	E
1					
2		Public		CPI	
3		Four-Year		Base Year (1982-84)	
4					
5	Year	Cost	% Inc	Index	% Inc
6					
7	00-01	$ 3,508		171.2	
8	01-02	$ 3,766	7.35%	176.6	3.15%
9	02-03	$ 4,098	8.82%	178.9	1.30%
10	03-04	$ 4,645	13.35%	183.8	2.74%
11	04-05	$ 5,126	10.36%	188.0	2.29%
12	05-06	$ 5,492	7.14%	194.6	3.51%
13	06-07	$ 5,904	7.50%	201.5	3.55%
14	07-08	$ 6,191	4.86%	206.7	2.58%
15	08-09	$ 6,591	6.46%	214.8	3.92%
16	09-10	$ 7,020	6.51%	213.2	-0.75%
17	10-11	$ 7,605	8.33%	218.0	2.25%
18					

METHODOLOGY

Calculate the equivalent college cost in constant 2000$ for each year.

SOLUTION

Using Eq. (4.5), we determine the equivalent college tuition and fees in constant dollars as follows:

	G	H	I	J	K	L
1						
2		CPI			Public	
3		Base Year (1982-84)			Four-Year	
4			General	Equivalent		
5			Inflation	Discounting	Actual	Constant
6	Year	Index	Rate	Factor	Cost	(2000$)
7						
8	00-01	171.2		1.0000	$ 3,508	$ 3,508
9	01-02	176.6	3.15%	0.9694	$ 3,766	$ 3,651
10	02-03	178.9	1.30%	0.9570	$ 4,098	$ 3,922
11	03-04	183.8	2.74%	0.9314	$ 4,645	$ 4,327
12	04-05	188.0	2.29%	0.9106	$ 5,126	$ 4,668
13	05-06	194.6	3.51%	0.8798	$ 5,492	$ 4,832

	G	**H**	**I**	**J**	**K**	**L**
14	06-07	201.5	3.55%	0.8496	$ 5,904	$ 5,016
15	07-08	206.7	2.58%	0.8283	$ 6,191	$ 5,128
16	08-09	214.8	3.92%	0.7970	$ 6,591	$ 5,253
17	09-10	213.2	-0.75%	0.8030	$ 7,020	$ 5,637
18	10-11	218.0	2.25%	0.7853	$ 7,605	$ 5,972
19						

For example, public four-year colleges charged, on average, $7,605 in tuition and fees in actual dollars for the 2010–2011 year. To determine its equivalent constant dollars in the year 2000, we need to discount the actual dollars using the multiple inflation rates, as follows:

$$A'_{2000} = \frac{\$7,605}{(1 + 0.0252)(1 - 0.0075)(1 + 0.0392) \cdots (1 + 0.0315)}$$
$$= \frac{\$7,605}{1.2735}$$
$$= \$7,605(0.7853)$$
$$= \$5,972.$$

The average general inflation rate over a 10-year period is

$$\bar{f} = \left[\frac{\text{CPI}_{2010}}{\text{CPI}_{2000}} \right]^{1/10} - 1 = \left[\frac{218.0}{171.2} \right]^{1/10} - 1 = 2.446\%.$$

The average price index for public four-year colleges over the same period is

$$f = \left[\frac{7,605}{3,508} \right]^{1/10} - 1 = 8.0445\%.$$

This indicates that the average price of public college tuition and fees has been increasing at a much faster rate than the general inflation in the economy.

COMMENTS: In determining the equivalent college cost in constant dollars, we used the periodic annual general inflation rates, instead of the average general inflation rate of 2.446%. This is possible only because we know precisely the actual costs in each year. However, if our task is to estimate the future college costs in, say, 2015, then we need to use the average inflation rate of 8.0445%. For example, the projected public four-year college tuition and fees in year 2015 is $7,605(1 + 0.080445)^5 = \$11,197$ in actual dollars. If we want to use the price of 2000 as a base ($3,508), the projected price in year 2015 is $3,508(1 + 0.080445)^{15} = \$11,197$, which is the same value we obtained previously.

4.3 Equivalence Calculations under Inflation

In previous chapters, our equivalence analyses took changes in the **earning power** of money into consideration. To factor in changes in **purchasing power**—that is, inflation— we may use either (1) constant-dollar analysis or (2) actual-dollar analysis. Either method produces the same solution; however, each method requires the use of a different interest rate and procedure. Before presenting the two procedures for integrating earning and purchasing power, we will give a precise definition of the two interest rates used in them.

4.3.1 Market and Inflation-Free Interest Rates

Two types of interest rates are used in equivalence calculations: (1) the market interest rate and (2) the inflation-free interest rate. The difference between the two is analogous to the relationship between actual and constant dollars.

- **Market interest rate (i):** This rate, commonly known as the **nominal interest rate**, takes into account the combined effects of the earning value of capital (earning power) and any anticipated inflation or deflation (purchasing power). Virtually all interest rates stated by financial institutions for loans and savings accounts are market interest rates. Most firms use a market interest rate (also known as **inflation-adjusted required rate of return**) in evaluating their investment projects, as well.
- **Inflation-free interest rate (i'):** This rate is an estimate of the true earning power of money when the effects of inflation have been removed. Commonly known as the **real interest rate**, it can be computed if the market interest rate and the inflation rate are known. In fact, all the interest rates mentioned in previous chapters are market interest rates. As you will see later in this chapter, in the absence of inflation, the market interest rate is the same as the inflation-free interest rate.

In calculating any cash flow equivalence, we need to identify the nature of the cash flows. The three common cases are as follows:

    Case 1: All cash flow elements are estimated in constant dollars.

    Case 2: All cash flow elements are estimated in actual dollars.

    Case 3: Some of the cash flow elements are estimated in constant dollars, and others are estimated in actual dollars.

For Case 3, we simply convert all cash flow elements into one type—either constant or actual dollars. Then we proceed with either constant-dollar analysis, as for Case 1, or actual-dollar analysis, as for Case 2. Constant-dollar analysis is common in the evaluation of many long-term public projects because governments do not pay income taxes. Typically, income taxes are levied on the basis of taxable incomes in actual dollars, so actual-dollar analysis is more common in the private sector.

4.3.2 Constant-Dollar Analysis

Suppose that all cash flow elements are already given in constant dollars and that we want to compute the equivalent present worth of the constant dollars (A'_n) in year n. In the absence of any inflationary effect, we should use i' to account for only the earning power of the money. To find the present-worth equivalent of this constant-dollar amount at i', we use

$$P_n = \frac{A'_n}{(1 + i')^n}. \tag{4.6}$$

4.3.3 Actual-Dollar Analysis

Now let us assume that all cash flow elements are estimated in actual dollars. To find the equivalent present worth of this actual-dollar amount (A_n) in year n, we may use two steps to convert actual dollars into equivalent present-worth dollars. First, we convert actual dollars into equivalent constant dollars by discounting with the general inflation rate, a step that removes the inflationary effect. Now we can use i' to find the equivalent present worth. However, the two-step process can be greatly streamlined by the efficiency of the **market interest rate**, which performs deflation and discounting in one step. Mathematically, the two steps can be expressed as

$$P_n = \overbrace{A_n(1+\bar{f})^{-n}}^{\text{Convert to constant \$}}\underbrace{(1+i')^{-n}}_{\text{Discount the constant \$}}$$

$$= A_n[(1+\bar{f})(1+i')]^{-n} \tag{4.7}$$

$$= A_n\left(1 + \underbrace{i' + \bar{f} + i'\bar{f}}_{\text{market interest rate}}\right)^{-n}$$

$$= A_n(1+i)^{-n}.$$

This equation leads to the following relationship among $\bar{f}$, i', and i:

$$i = i' + \bar{f} + i'\bar{f}. \tag{4.8}$$

This equation also implies that the market interest rate is a function of two terms, i' and $\bar{f}$.

Note that, without an inflationary effect, the two interest rates are the same. (If $\bar{f} = 0$, then $i = i'$.) As either i' or $\bar{f}$ increases, i also increases. When prices increase due to inflation, bond rates climb because promises of future payments from debtors are worth relatively less to lenders (i.e., banks, bondholders, money market investors, CD holders, etc.). Thus, lenders demand and set higher interest rates. Similarly, if inflation were to remain at 3%, we might be satisfied with an interest rate of 7% on a bond because our return would more than beat inflation. If inflation were running at 10%, however, we would not buy a 7% bond; we might insist instead on a return of at least 14%. On the other hand, when prices are coming down or at least are stable, lenders do not fear the loss of purchasing power with the loans they make, so they are satisfied to lend at lower interest rates.

In practice, we often approximate the market interest rate i by simply adding the inflation rate $\bar{f}$ to the real interest rate i' and ignoring the product term $(i'\bar{f})$. *This practice is okay as long as either i' or $\bar{f}$ is relatively small.* With continuous compounding, however, the relationship among i, i', and $\bar{f}$ becomes precisely

$$i' = i - \bar{f}. \tag{4.9}$$

So, if we assume a nominal annual percentage rate (APR) (market interest rate) of 6% per year compounded continuously and an inflation rate of 4% per year compounded continuously, the inflation-free interest rate is exactly 2% per year compounded continuously.

EXAMPLE 4.6 Equivalence Calculations under Inflation— Constant- and Actual-Dollar Analysis

Chena Hot Springs Resort built the very first ice museum in the United States. Chena is located 60 miles (100 km) northeast of Fairbanks, Alaska, which is the traditional world capital of ice art. To save the cooling cost for the ice museum in 2011, Chena installed an absorption chiller, which requires 148 HP (horsepower) to operate. This saves $244,560 in fuel costs per year at the 2011 diesel fuel price of $4.11 per gallon. The expected life of the plant is 15 years, and the diesel price is expected to increase at an annual rate of 5% during the life of operation of the absorption chiller. If Chena's market interest rate is 12%, which would account for the expected general inflation rate of 3% during this project period, what is the value of installing the absorption chiller in 2011 dollars? In solving this problem, we demonstrate that we will obtain the same result whether we use the constant-dollar analysis or the actual-dollar analysis.

DISSECTING THE PROBLEM

Given: Cash flows stated in constant dollars, $i = 12\%$ per year.
Find: Equivalent present worth of the cash flow series.

METHODOLOGY

Method 1: Constant-Dollar Analysis

SOLUTION

Since the diesel fuel price increases at a different rate (5%) from the general inflation rate (3%), we first need to find the fuel savings in actual dollars at each period. For example, equivalent fuel savings in actual dollars are determined by

$$A_1 = \$244,560(1 + 0.05) = \$\$256,788$$

$$A_2 = \$244,560(1 + 0.05)^2 = \$269,627$$

$$\vdots$$

$$A_{15} = \$244,560(1 + 0.05)^{15} = \$508,423.$$

Then we convert these fuel savings in actual dollars into equivalent constant dollars.

$$A'_1 = \$256,788(1 + 0.03)^{-1} = \$249,309$$

$$A'_2 = \$269,627(1 + 0.03)^{-2} = \$254,150$$

$$\vdots$$

$$A'_{15} = \$508,423(1 + 0.03)^{-15} = \$326,337.$$

We may attempt to find the equivalent fuel savings in 2011 dollars by first finding the inflation-free interest rate and then applying this inflation-free rate to obtain the present values of the fuel savings in constant dollars. Using Eq. (4.8), we find i' as follows:

$$0.12 = i' + 0.03 + 0.03i'$$

$$i' = 8.74\%.$$

<table>
<tr><th>METHODOLOGY</th><th>SOLUTION</th></tr>
</table>

METHODOLOGY

SOLUTION

Then, the total present equivalent fuel savings in 2011 can be calculated using the geometric series present-worth factor with g calculated as

$$g = \frac{1 + 0.05}{1 + 0.03} - 1 = 1.94\%,$$
$$P = \$249{,}309 \, (P/A_1, 1.94\%, 8.74\%, 15)$$
$$= \$2{,}275{,}096.$$

Table 4.2 illustrates the process of computing the equivalent present worth when all cash flows are given in actual dollars. Once the fuel savings figures in actual dollars are entered in cells B12 through B27, we need to convert them into equivalent constant dollars as shown in cells C12 through C27. Once the cash flow series is expressed in constant dollars, we use the inflation-free (real) interest rate to find the equivalent present worth. This is shown in column D, or cells D12 through D27. We can also easily plot the expected fuel savings in terms of both constant and actual dollars.

Method 2: Actual-Dollar Analysis

Since fuel savings are given in actual dollars of 2011, we need to convert them into equivalent present worth using the market interest rate. Since the fuel savings are growing at the annual rate of 5%, the fuel savings series in actual dollars forms a geometric gradient series. To find the equivalent total savings in 2011 dollars, we use the market interest rate of 12% to discount this geometric series:

$$P = \$256{,}788(P/A_1, 5\%, 12\%, 15)$$

$$= \$2{,}275{,}096 \text{ (in year 2011 dollars)}.$$

Note that the result is essentially the same as before. (We might observe some slight discrepancy due to rounding errors introduced when we apply the different interest factors.) Table 4.3 illustrates the tabular approach to obtaining the equivalent present worth in Excel. We first enter the fuel savings in actual dollars in cells B12 through B27. We could calculate the present worth of the cash flow series in actual dollars, using the market interest rate. This is shown in cells C12 through C27. We may also display the cumulative PW of fuel savings as a function of operating year as shown in cells D12 through D27. So, the figure in cell D27 represents the total fuel savings in present worth over 15 years.

TABLE 4.2 An Excel Worksheet to Perform a Constant-Dollar Analysis

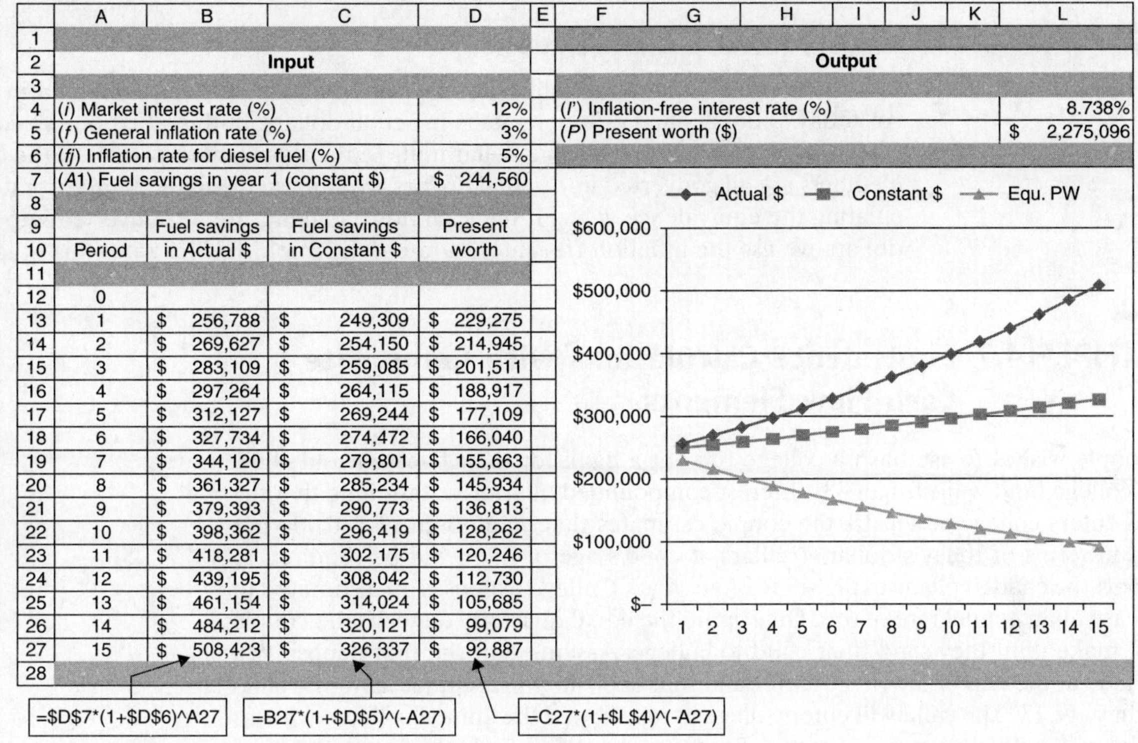

	A	B	C	D	E	F	G	H	I	J	K	L
1												
2			Input					Output				
3												
4	(i) Market interest rate (%)			12%		(I') Inflation-free interest rate (%)						8.738%
5	(f) General inflation rate (%)			3%		(P) Present worth ($)						$ 2,275,096
6	(f_j) Inflation rate for diesel fuel (%)			5%								
7	($A1$) Fuel savings in year 1 (constant $)			$ 244,560								
8												
9		Fuel savings	Fuel savings	Present								
10	Period	in Actual $	in Constant $	worth								
11												
12	0											
13	1	$ 256,788	$ 249,309	$ 229,275								
14	2	$ 269,627	$ 254,150	$ 214,945								
15	3	$ 283,109	$ 259,085	$ 201,511								
16	4	$ 297,264	$ 264,115	$ 188,917								
17	5	$ 312,127	$ 269,244	$ 177,109								
18	6	$ 327,734	$ 274,472	$ 166,040								
19	7	$ 344,120	$ 279,801	$ 155,663								
20	8	$ 361,327	$ 285,234	$ 145,934								
21	9	$ 379,393	$ 290,773	$ 136,813								
22	10	$ 398,362	$ 296,419	$ 128,262								
23	11	$ 418,281	$ 302,175	$ 120,246								
24	12	$ 439,195	$ 308,042	$ 112,730								
25	13	$ 461,154	$ 314,024	$ 105,685								
26	14	$ 484,212	$ 320,121	$ 99,079								
27	15	$ 508,423	$ 326,337	$ 92,887								
28												

`=$D$7*(1+$D$6)^A27`   `=B27*(1+$D$5)^(-A27)`   `=C27*(1+$L$4)^(-A27)`

TABLE 4.3 An Excel Worksheet to Perform an Actual-Dollar Analysis

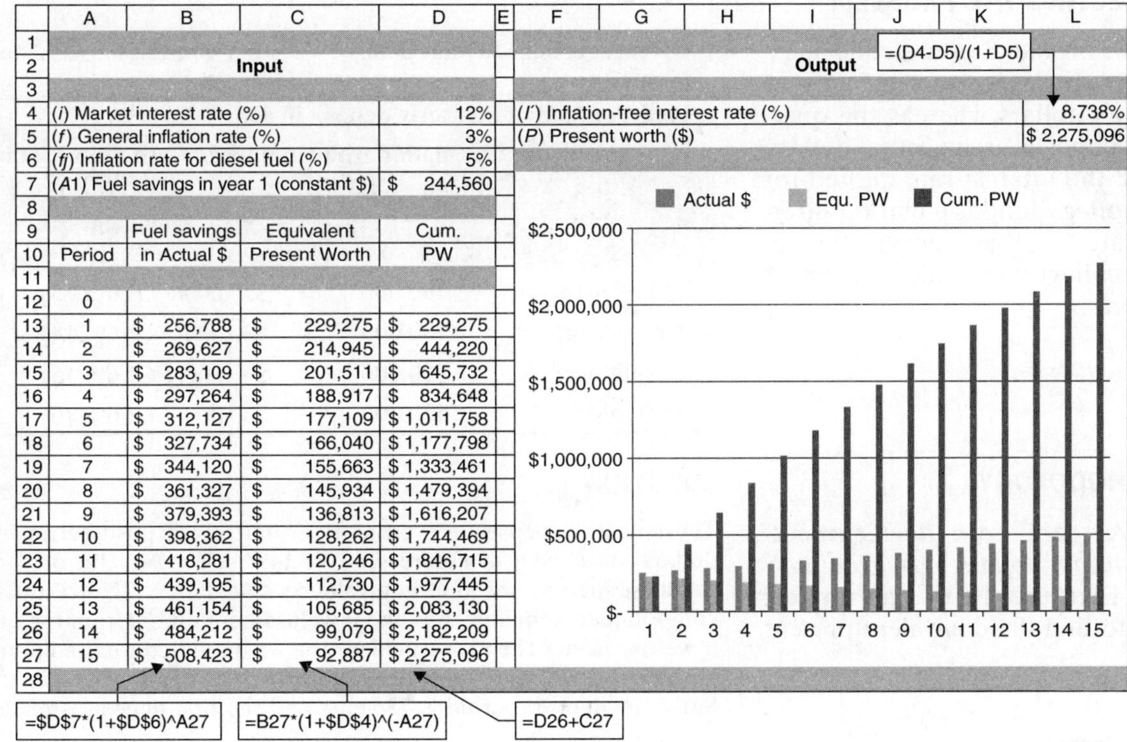

	A	B	C	D	E	F	G	H	I	J	K	L
1												
2			Input					Output				
3												
4	(i) Market interest rate (%)			12%		(I') Inflation-free interest rate (%)						8.738%
5	(f) General inflation rate (%)			3%		(P) Present worth ($)						$ 2,275,096
6	(f_j) Inflation rate for diesel fuel (%)			5%								
7	($A1$) Fuel savings in year 1 (constant $)			$ 244,560								
8												
9		Fuel savings	Equivalent	Cum.								
10	Period	in Actual $	Present Worth	PW								
11												
12	0											
13	1	$ 256,788	$ 229,275	$ 229,275								
14	2	$ 269,627	$ 214,945	$ 444,220								
15	3	$ 283,109	$ 201,511	$ 645,732								
16	4	$ 297,264	$ 188,917	$ 834,648								
17	5	$ 312,127	$ 177,109	$ 1,011,758								
18	6	$ 327,734	$ 166,040	$ 1,177,798								
19	7	$ 344,120	$ 155,663	$ 1,333,461								
20	8	$ 361,327	$ 145,934	$ 1,479,394								
21	9	$ 379,393	$ 136,813	$ 1,616,207								
22	10	$ 398,362	$ 128,262	$ 1,744,469								
23	11	$ 418,281	$ 120,246	$ 1,846,715								
24	12	$ 439,195	$ 112,730	$ 1,977,445								
25	13	$ 461,154	$ 105,685	$ 2,083,130								
26	14	$ 484,212	$ 99,079	$ 2,182,209								
27	15	$ 508,423	$ 92,887	$ 2,275,096								
28												

`=(D4-D5)/(1+D5)`

`=$D$7*(1+$D$6)^A27`   `=B27*(1+$D$4)^(-A27)`   `=D26+C27`

4.3.4 Mixed-Dollar Analysis

Let's examine a situation in which some cash flow elements are expressed in constant (or today's) dollars and other elements in actual dollars. In this situation, we convert all cash flow elements into the same dollar units (either constant or actual). If the cash flow elements are all converted into actual dollars, we can use the market interest rate i in calculating the equivalence value. If the cash flow elements are all converted into constant dollars, we use the inflation-free interest rate i'. Example 4.7 illustrates this situation.

EXAMPLE 4.7 Equivalence Calculations with Composite Cash Flow Elements

A couple wishes to establish a college fund at a bank for their five-year-old child. The college fund will earn an 8% interest compounded quarterly. Assuming that the child enters college at age 18, the couple estimates that an amount of $30,000 per year, in terms of today's dollars (dollars at child's age of five), will be required to support the child's college expenses for four years. College expenses are estimated to increase at an annual rate of 6%. Determine the equal quarterly deposits the couple must make until they send their child to college. Assume that the first deposit will be made at the end of the first quarter and that deposits will continue until the child reaches age 17. The child will enter college at age 18, and the annual college expense will be paid at the beginning of each college year. In other words, the first withdrawal will be made when the child is 18.

DISSECTING THE PROBLEM

In this problem, future college expenses are expressed in terms of today's dollars whereas the quarterly deposits are in actual dollars. Since the interest rate quoted for the college fund is a market interest rate, we may convert the future college expenses into actual dollars.

Given: A college savings plan, $i = 2\%$ per quarter, $f = 6\%$, and $N = 12$ years.

Find: Amount of quarterly deposit in actual dollars.

Equivalence Calculation with Composite Cash Flow Elements

Age	College Expenses (in Today's Dollars)	College Expenses (in Actual Dollars)
18 (freshman)	$30,000	$30,000(F/P,6\%,13) = \$63,988$
19 (sophomore)	$30,000	$30,000(F/P,6\%,14) = \$67,827$
20 (junior)	$30,000	$30,000(F/P,6\%,15) = \$71,897$
21 (senior)	$30,000	$30,000(F/P,6\%,16) = \$76,211$

METHODOLOGY

Convert any *cash flow elements* in *constant dollars* into *actual dollars*. Then use the market interest rate to find the equivalent present value.

SOLUTION

The college expenses as well as the quarterly deposit series in actual dollars are shown in Figure 4.6. We first select $n = 12$, or age 17, as the base period for our equivalence calculation. (Note: Inflation is compounded annually; thus, the n we use here differs from the quarterly n we use next.) Then we calculate the accumulated total amount at the base period at 2% interest per quarter (8% APR/4 = 2% per quarter). Since the deposit period is 12 years and the first deposit is made at the end of the first quarter, we have a 48-quarter deposit period. Therefore, the total balance of the deposits when the child is 17 would be

$$V_1 = C(F/A, 2\%, 48)$$
$$= 79.3535C.$$

The equivalent lump-sum worth of the total college expenditure at the base period would be

$$V_2 = \$63,988(P/F, 2\%, 4) + \$67,827(P/F, 2\%, 8)$$
$$+ \$71,897(P/F, 2\%, 12) + \$76,211(P/F, 2\%, 16)$$
$$= \$229,211.$$

By setting $V_1 = V_2$ and solving for C, we obtain $C = \$2,888.48$.

COMMENTS: This is a good example for which Excel would help us understand the effects of variations in the circumstances of the situation. For example, how does changing the inflation rate affect the required quarterly savings plan? To begin, we must set up an Excel spreadsheet and utilize the Goal Seek function. Table 4.4 is a sample spreadsheet that shows the deposit and withdrawal schedule for this scenario. After specifying the interest rate in E6 and using Excel functions to calculate equivalent total deposits and withdrawals in present-worth terms, we designate cell E58 as the difference between E56 and E57 (i.e., E56−E57). To ensure that the accumulated balance of deposits is exactly sufficient to meet projected withdrawals, we specify that this target cell be zero (i.e., E56−E57 = 0) and command Goal Seek to adjust the quarterly deposit (E55) accordingly. Note that the quarterly deposit is linked to the schedule of deposits in column B. The Goal Seek function finds the required quarterly deposit amount to be $2,888.47, in Cell E55.

Sensitivity Analysis: Using the spreadsheet displayed in Table 4.4, we can then adjust the interest rate and see the change in quarterly deposits required. If we adjust annual inflation from 6% to 4%, we will find that the required quarterly deposit amount is $2,192.96, which is $695.51 less than in the 6% case. The result is shown in Table 4.5.

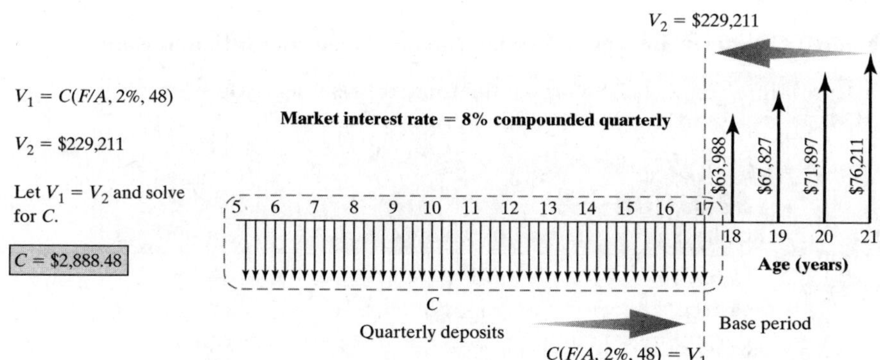

Figure 4.6   Establishing a college fund under an inflationary economy for a five-year-old child by making 48 quarterly deposits

TABLE 4.4 Excel Solution for Finding the Required Quarterly Deposits (Example 4.7)

	A	B	C	D	E
1					
2	Quarter	Deposits	Withdrawals	Intput	
3					
4	0			College Expense in Constant $	$30,000.00
5	1	($2,888.47)		Inflation Rate	6.00%
6	2	($2,888.47)		Interest Rate per Quarter	2.00%
7	3	($2,888.47)			
8	4	($2,888.47)		College Expense in Actual $	
9	5	($2,888.47)		18 (Freshman)	$63,988
41	37	($2,888.47)		19 (Sophomore)	$67,827
42	38	($2,888.47)		20 (Junior)	$71,897
43	39	($2,888.47)		21 (Senior)	$76,211
44	40	($2,888.47)			
45	41	($2,888.47)			
46	42	($2,888.47)		=FV(E5,16,,-E4)	
47	43	($2,888.47)			
48	44	($2,888.47)			
49	45	($2,888.47)			
50	46	($2,888.47)		Base Period	
51	47	($2,888.47)			
52	48	($2,888.47)			
53	49			Output	
54	50				
55	51			Required Quarterly Deposit	$2,888.47
56	52		$63,988	Equ. Total Deposit	$229,210.02
57	53			Equ. Total Withdrawals	$229,210.02
58	54			Target cell	$0.00
59	55				
60	56		$67,827	=FV($E$6,48,-1*E55)	
61	57				
62	58				
63	59				
64	60		$71,897	=PV($E$6,4,,-C56)	
65	61			+PV($E$6,8,,-C60)	
66	62			+PV($E$6,12,,-C64)	
67	63			+PV($E$6,16,,-C68)	
68	64		$76,211		
69					
70	Note: Row 10 through Row 40 are hidden.				
71					

=E56-E57

TABLE 4.5 Required Quarterly Savings at Varying Interest Rates and Inflation Rates

Varying the annual inflation rate when the savings rate is fixed at 2% per quarter		Varying the quarterly savings rate when the inflation rate is fixed at 6% per year	
Annual Inflation Rate	Required Deposit Amount	Quarterly Savings Rate	Required Deposit Amount
2%	$1,657	1%	$4,131
4%	$2,193	1.5%	$3,459
6%	$2,888	2.0%	$2,888
8%	$3,787	2.5%	$2,404
10%	$4,942	3.0%	$1,995

SUMMARY

■ The **Consumer Price Index (CPI)** is a statistical measure of change, over time, of the prices of goods and services in major expenditure groups—such as food, housing, apparel, transportation, and medical care—typically purchased by urban consumers. The CPI compares the cost of a sample "market basket" of goods and services in a specific period with the cost of the same market basket in an earlier reference period. This reference period is designated as the **base period**.

■ **Inflation** is the term used to describe a **decline in purchasing power** evidenced in an economic environment of rising prices.

■ **Deflation** is the opposite of inflation: It is an increase in purchasing power evidenced by falling prices.

■ The **general inflation rate** $\bar{f}$ is an average inflation rate based on the CPI. An annual general inflation rate $\bar{f}_n$ can be calculated by the following equation:

$$\bar{f}_n = \frac{\text{CPI}_n - \text{CPI}_{n-1}}{\text{CPI}_{n-1}}.$$

■ The price changes of specific, individual commodities do not always reflect the general inflation rate. We can calculate an **average inflation rate** $\bar{f}$ for a specific commodity (j) if we have an index (i.e., a record of historical costs) for that commodity.

■ Project cash flows may be stated in one of two forms:
1. **Actual dollars (A_n):** Dollar amounts that reflect the inflation or deflation rate.
2. **Constant dollars (A'_n):** Dollar amounts that reflect the purchasing power of year zero dollars.

■ Interest rates for the evaluation of cash flows may be stated in one of two forms:
1. **Market interest rate (i):** A rate that combines the effects of interest and inflation; this rate is used with actual-dollar analysis. Unless otherwise mentioned, the interest rates used in the remainder of this text are the market interest rates.
2. **Inflation-free interest rate (i'):** A rate from which the effects of inflation have been removed; this rate is used with constant-dollar analysis.

■ To calculate the present worth of actual dollars, we can use either a two-step or a one-step process:

   ■ **Deflation method—two steps:**

   1. Convert actual dollars to constant dollars by deflating with the general inflation rate of $\bar{f}$.
   2. Calculate the present worth of constant dollars by discounting at i'.

   ■ **Adjusted-discount method—one step (use the market interest rate):**

   $$P_n = \frac{A_n}{[(1 + \bar{f})(1 + i')]^n}$$

   $$= \frac{A_n}{(1 + i)^n},$$

   where

   $$i = i' + \bar{f} + i'\bar{f}.$$

   Alternatively, just use the market interest rate to find the net present worth.

TABLE 4.6 Summary of Inflation Terminologies

Category	Terms Used in This Text	Other Terms Used
Dollars	Actual dollars	Current dollars
	Constant dollars	Real dollars
Cash flow	Cash flow in actual dollars	Nominal cash flow
	Cash flow in constant dollars	Real cash flow
Interest rate	Market interest rate	Nominal interest rate
	Inflation-free interest rate	Real interest rate
Inflation rate	General inflation rate	Average rate of inflation, annual rate of inflation
	Average inflation rate	Escalation rate, growth rate

■ In this chapter we have introduced many inflation-related terminologies. Since some of them are different from those commonly found in other publications, Table 4.6 summarizes other terms used in other publications or business.

SELF-TEST QUESTIONS

4s.1 How many years will it take for the dollar's purchasing power to be one-third what it is now, if the general inflation rate is expected to continue at the rate of 7% for an indefinite period?

(a) About 10 years

(b) About 12 years

(c) About 13 years

(d) About 16 years

4s.2 An engineer's salary was $50,000 in 2006. The same engineer's salary in 2011 is $80,000. If the company's salary policy dictates that a yearly raise in salaries reflect the cost of living increase due to inflation, what is the average inflation rate for the period 2002–2011?

(a) 7.45%

(b) 8.94%

(c) 9.80%

(d) 10.95%

4s.3 Suppose that you borrow $60,000 at 9% compounded monthly over five years. Knowing that the 9% represents the market interest rate, you compute the monthly payment in actual dollars as $1245.51. If the average monthly general inflation rate is expected to be 0.25%, determine the equivalent equal monthly payment series in constant dollars.

(a) $1159

(b) $1375

(c) $1405

(d) $1415

4s.4 A couple wants to save for their daughter's college expense. The daughter will enter college eight years from now, and she will need $50,000, $51,000, $52,000, and $53,000 in *actual dollars* over four school years. Assume that these college payments will be made at the beginning of each school year. The future general inflation rate is estimated to be 7% per year, and the annual inflation-free interest rate is 6%. What is the equal amount, in *actual dollars,* the couple must save each year until their daughter goes to college?

(a) $21,838

(b) $21,945

(c) $22,323

(d) $22,538

4s.5 You just signed a business consulting contract with one of your clients. The client will pay you $80,000 a year for five years for the service you will provide over this period. You anticipate the general inflation rate over this period to be 5%. If your desired inflation-free interest rate (real interest rate) is to be 3%, what is the worth of the fifth payment in present dollars? The client will pay the consulting fee at the end of each year.

(a) $53,506

(b) $54,070

(c) $59,498

(d) $59,320

4s.6 The annual fuel costs to operate a small solid-waste treatment plant are projected to be $1.8 million, without consideration for any future inflation. The best estimates indicate that the annual inflation-free interest rate (i') will be 7% and the general inflation rate $f = 4\%$. If the plant has a remaining useful life of five years, what is the present equivalent value of its fuel costs, using actual-dollar analysis?

(a) $ 6.606 million

(b) $ 3.567 million

(c) $10.095 million

(d) $ 8.317 million

4s.7 A series of five constant-dollar (or real-dollar) payments, beginning with $8,000 at the end of the first year, are increasing at the rate of 5% per year. Assume that the average general inflation rate is 5% and the market interest rate is 12% during this inflationary period. What is the equivalent present worth of the series?

(a) $24,259

(b) $25,892

(c) $36,413

(d) $29,406

4s.8 "At a market interest rate of 7% per year and an inflation rate of 5% per year, a series of three equal annual receipts of $100 in constant dollars is equivalent to a series of three annual receipts of $108 in actual dollars." Which of the following statements is correct?

(a) The amount of actual dollars is overstated.

(b) The amount of actual dollars is understated.

(c) The amount of actual dollars is about right.

(d) Sufficient information is not available to make a comparison.

4s.9 A father wants to save in advance for his eight-year-old daughter's college expenses. The daughter will enter the college 10 years from now. An annual amount of $20,000 in today's dollars (constant dollars) will be required to support her college expenses for four years. Assume that these college payments will be made at the *beginning* of each school year. (The first payment occurs at the end of 10 years.) The future general inflation rate is estimated to be 5% per year, and the interest rate on the savings account will be 8% compounded quarterly (market interest rate) during this period. If the father has decided to save only $500 (actual dollars) each quarter, how much will the daughter have to borrow to cover her freshman expenses?

(a) $1,920

(b) $2,114

(c) $2,210

(d) $2,377

PROBLEMS

Note: In these problems, the term "market interest rate" represents the inflation-adjusted interest rate for equivalence calculations or the APR quoted by a financial institution for commercial loans. Unless otherwise mentioned, all stated interest rates will be compounded annually.

Measure of Inflation

4.1 The average unleaded-gasoline price for residents of a city on May 30, 2011, was $5.20 per gallon. Assuming that the base period (price index=100) is 1996 and that the unleaded-gasoline price for that year was $2.10 per gallon, compute the average price index for the unleaded-gasoline price for the year 2011.

4.2 The average cost of a gallon of gas was $0.80 per gallon in 1995. In 2011, the average cost of a gallon of gas is $3.50. What is the average inflation rate for the period 1998–2011?

4.3 The following data indicate the price indices of lumber (price index for the base period (1982–1984 = 100) during the last 10 years:

Period	Price Index
2001	164.5
2011	185.1

(a) If the base period (price index = 100) is reset to the year 2001, compute the inflation rate for lumber between 2001 and 2009.

(b) If the past trend is expected to continue, how would you estimate the price of lumber in 2014?

4.4 Prices are increasing at an annual rate of 6% the first year and 10% the second year. Determine the average inflation rate $(\bar{f})$ over these two years.

4.5 The accompanying table shows a utility company's cost to supply a fixed amount of power to a new housing development; the indices are specific to the utility industry. Assume that year 0 is the base period. Determine the specific inflation for each period and calculate the average inflation rate over the three-year period.

Year	Cost
0	$624,000
1	$638,400
2	$677,000
3	$729,500

4.6 Because of general price inflation in our economy, the purchasing power of the dollar shrinks with the passage of time. If the average general inflation rate is expected to be 8% per year for the foreseeable future, how many years will it take for the dollar's purchasing power to be one-third of what it is now?

4.7 An engineer's salary was $40,000 in 2004. The same engineer's salary in 2011 is $75,000. If the company's salary policy dictates that a yearly raise in salaries reflect the cost of living increase due to inflation, what is the average inflation rate for the period 2004–2012?

4.8 The average starting salary for engineers was $8,000 a year in 1985. John, a mechanical engineer, got an offer for $48,000 a year in 2012. Knowing that the CPIs for 1985 and 2012 are 36.87 and 205.43, respectively, what is John's real salary in terms of constant 1985 dollars?

4.9 If you are looking for a 4% real return (inflation-free interest) on your investment, would you be interested in an investment opportunity that produce a 9% return on investment (market interest rate) if the inflation rate is 5%?

4.10 If you deposit $12,000 in a bank account that pays a 4% interest compounded monthly for five years, what would be your economic loss if the general inflation rate is 5% during that period?

4.11 An annuity provides for 10 consecutive end-of-year payments of $15,000. The average general inflation rate is estimated to be 6% annually, and the market interest rate is 8% annually. What is the annuity worth in terms of a single equivalent amount of today's dollars?

4.12 A company is considering buying workstation computers to support its engineering staff. In today's dollars, it is estimated that the maintenance costs for the computers (paid at the end of each year) will be $20,000, $26,000, $34,000, $38,000, and $42,000 for years one through five, respectively. The general inflation rate ($\bar{f}$) is estimated to be 10% per year, and the company will receive 16% per year on its invested funds during the inflationary period. The company wants to pay for maintenance expenses in equivalent equal payments (in actual dollars) at the end of each of the five years. Find the amount of the company's annual payment.

4.13 Given the cash flows in actual dollars provided in the following table, convert the cash flows to equivalent cash flows in constant dollars if the base year is time 0. Assume that the market interest rate is 16% and that the general inflation rate ($\bar{f}$) is estimated at 4% per year.

n	Cash Flow (in Actual Dollars)
0	$20,500
4	$41,500
5	$36,500
7	$55,500

4.14 The purchase of a car requires a $15,000 loan to be repaid in monthly installments for four years at 10% interest compounded monthly. If the general inflation rate is 6% compounded monthly, find the actual and constant dollar value of the 15th payment of this loan.

4.15 A series of four annual constant-dollar payments beginning with $50,000 at the end of the first year is growing at the rate of 8% per year. Assume that the base year is the current year ($n = 0$). If the market interest rate is 16% per year and the general inflation rate ($\bar{f}$) is 10% per year, find the present worth of this series of payments, based on

(a) constant-dollar analysis.

(b) actual-dollar analysis.

4.16 Consider a situation, where (a) the equal-payment cash flow of $1,500 in constant dollars over three years is converted from the (b) equal-payment cash flow in actual dollars over three years, at an annual general inflation rate of $f = 4\%$. Also, $i = 8.5\%$. What is the amount A in actual dollars equivalent $A' = \$1,500$ in constant dollars?

4.17 A 10-year $2,000 bond pays a nominal rate of 8% compounded semiannually. If the market interest rate is 9% compounded annually and the general inflation rate is 5% per year, find the actual and constant dollar amount (time = year zero dollars) of the 14th interest payment on the bond.

4.18 The following table represents the thallium production and apparent consumption in the United States for the years 2004 through 2010. Unit value is the value in actual dollars of one metric ton (t) of thallium apparent consumption. With 2004 as the base year, adjust the unit value in actual U.S. dollars to the unit value in constant 2004 U.S. dollars (2004$).

Year	Thallium Production	Imports	Exports	Apparent Consumption	Unit Value ($/ton)	Total Consumption (in Actual Dollars)
2004	685,000	150,000	42,000	793,000	31.90	$25,296,700
2005	711,000	144,000	47,000	808,000	33.40	$26,987,200
2006	672,000	180,000	43,000	809,000	33.80	$27,344,200
2007	588,000	175,000	43,000	720,000	36.30	$26,136,000
2008	521,000	224,000	42,000	703,000	36.50	$25,659,500
2009	493,000	245,000	37,000	701,000	38.00	$26,638,000
2010	508,000	238,000	37,000	709,000	41.00	$29,069,000

Equivalence Calculation under Inflation

4.19 You will receive $60 interest every six months from your investment in a corporate bond. The bond will mature in five years from now and it has a face value of $2,000. This means that if you hold the bond until its maturity, you will continue to receive $150 interest semiannually and $2,000 face value at the end of five years.

(a) What is the present value of the bond in the absence of inflation if the market interest rate is 9%?

(b) What would happen to the value of the bond if the inflation rate over the next five years is expected to be 4%?

4.20 You just signed a business consulting contract with one of your clients. The client will pay you $80,000 a year for five years for the service you will provide over this period. You anticipate the general inflation rate over this period to be 5%. If your desired inflation-free interest rate (real interest rate) is to be 3%, what is the worth of the fifth payment in present dollars? The client will pay the consulting fee at the end of each year.

4.21 Suppose that you borrow $60,000 at 9% compounded monthly over five years. Knowing that the 9% represents the market interest rate, you compute the monthly payment in actual dollars as $1,245.51. If the average monthly general inflation rate is expected to be 0.25%, determine the equivalent equal monthly payment series in constant dollars.

4.22 The annual fuel costs to operate a small solid-waste treatment plant are projected to be $1.8 million, without consideration for any future inflation. The best estimates indicate that the annual inflation-free interest rate (i') will be 7% and the general inflation rate $f = 4\%$. If the plant has a remaining useful life of five years, what is the present equivalent value of its fuel costs, using actual-dollar analysis?

4.23 Suppose that you just purchased a used car worth $14,000 in today's dollars. Assume also that, to finance the purchase, you borrowed $12,000 from a local bank at 8% compounded monthly over two years. The bank calculated your monthly payment at $542.36. Assume that average general inflation will run at 1% per month over the next two years.

(a) Determine the annual inflation-free interest rate (i') for the bank.

(b) What equal monthly payments, in terms of constant dollars over the next two years, are equivalent to the series of actual payments to be made over the life of the loan?

4.24 A man is planning to retire in 20 years. He can deposit money for his retirement at 8% compounded monthly. It is estimated that the future general inflation ($\bar{f}$) rate will be 3% compounded annually. What deposit must be made each month until the man retires so that he can make annual withdrawals of $20,000, in terms of today's dollars, over the 15 years following his retirement? (Assume that his first withdrawal occurs at the end of the first six months after his retirement.)

4.25 On her 23rd birthday, an engineer decides to start saving toward building up a retirement fund that pays 9% interest compounded quarterly (market interest rate). She feels that $800,000 worth of purchasing power in today's dollars will be adequate to see her through her sunset years after her 63rd birthday. Assume a general inflation rate of 5% per year.

(a) If she plans to save by making 160 equal quarterly deposits, what should be the amount of each quarterly deposit in actual dollars?

(b) If she plans to save by making end-of-the-year deposits, increasing by $1,000 over each subsequent year, how much would her first deposit be, in actual dollars?

4.26 A couple wants to save for their daughter's college expense. The daughter will enter college eight years from now, and she will need $50,000, $51,000, $52,000, and $53,000 in *actual dollars* for four school years. Assume that these college payments will be made at the *beginning* of each school year. The future general inflation rate is estimated to be 7% per year, and the annual inflation-free interest rate is 6%.

(a) What is the market interest rate to use in the analysis?

(b) What is the equal amount, in *actual dollars,* the couple must save each year until their daughter goes to college?

4.27 A father wants to save for his eight-year-old son's college expenses. The son will enter college 10 years from now. An annual amount of $40,000 in constant dollars will be required to support the son's college expenses for four years. Assume that these college payments will be made at the *beginning* of each school year. The future general inflation rate is estimated to be 6% per year, and the market interest rate on the savings account will average 8% compounded annually.

(a) What is the amount of the son's freshman-year expense in terms of actual dollars?

(b) What is the equivalent single-sum amount at the present time for these college expenses?

(c) What is the equal amount, in actual dollars, the father must save each year until his son goes to college?

4.28 Consider the following project's after-tax cash flow and the expected annual general inflation rate during the project period:

End of Year	Expected Cash Flow (in Actual Dollars)	General Inflation Rate
0	−$45,000	
1	$36,000	6.5%
2	$46,000	7.7%
3	$26,000	8.1%

(a) Determine the average annual general inflation rate over the project period.

(b) Convert the cash flows in actual dollars into equivalent constant dollars with year 0 as the base year.

(c) If the annual inflation-free interest rate is 5%, what is the present worth of the cash flow?

Short Case Studies with Excel

4.29 Suppose you have three goals in your financial planning for saving money. First, you would like to be able to retire 25 years from now with a retirement income of $10,000 (today's dollar) per month for 20 years. Second, you would like to purchase a vacation home in Sedona in 10 years at an estimated cost of $500,000 (today's dollars). Third, assuming that you will live until your life expectancy, say 20 years after your retirement, you would like to leave a cash contribution to your college in the amount of $1,000,000 (actual dollars). You can afford to save $2,000 (actual dollars) per month for the next 10 years. Assume that the general inflation rate is 4% and the property value in Sedona increases at an annual rate of 5%. Your first retirement withdrawal will be made 25 years and 1 month from now. Before retirement, you would be able to invest your money at an annual rate of 10%. But after retirement, you will invest your assets in more conservative financial assets at an annual rate of 6%. What is the required savings in each month in years 11 through 25?

4.30 If we were to invest $10,000 in an S&P 500 index fund, pay 0.2% annual fees, and add $100 a month to it for 40 years, receiving 10.4% annual returns, what, theoretically, would happen to our investment with 3.43% annual inflation? What would it be worth in terms of today's dollars? That's 10.4% − 0.2% − 3.43% = 6.77% over 40 years.

4.31 You have $10,000 cash that you want to invest. Normally, you would deposit the money in a savings account that pays an annual interest rate of 6%. However, you are now considering the possibility of investing in a bond. Your alternatives are either a nontaxable municipal bond paying 9% or a taxable corporate bond paying 12%. Your marginal tax rate is 30% for both ordinary income and capital gains. (The marginal tax rate of 30% means that you will keep only 70% of your bond interest income.) You expect the general inflation rate to be 3% during the investment period. You can buy a high-grade municipal bond costing $10,000 that pays interest of 9% ($900) per year. This interest is not taxable. A comparable high-grade corporate bond for the same price is also available. This bond is just as safe as the municipal bond but pays an interest rate of 12% ($1,200) per year. The interest for this bond is taxable as ordinary income. Both bonds mature at the end of year 5.

(a) Determine the real (inflation-free) rate of return for each bond.

(b) Without knowing your earning-interest rate, what choice would you make between these two bonds?

4.32 *Businessweek* magazine currently offers the following subscription options: one year for $39; two years for $72; three years for $103. These rates are expected to increase at the general inflation rate. You may expect the general inflation rate to be between 3% and 7%. What is your optimal strategy for subscribing at the lowest possible cost, assuming you intend to be a lifetime subscriber? What other assumptions are required in order to make your purchase?

Evaluating Business and Engineering Assets

CHAPTER FIVE

Present-Worth Analysis

China Market Presents Large Opportunity for Corning[1]

Corning® Incorporated announced that its board of directors has approved a capital expenditure plan to expand the company's LCD glass and Gorilla® glass manufacturing in China. In response to strong demand, Corning's $1 billion in new investments includes a plan to build the company's first LCD glass melting facility and expand its light-duty substrate manufacturing operation. "Our total China sales exceeded $800 million in 2010. We are forecasting sales of at least $1.2 billion in 2011, and we could reach $2 billion in revenue by 2014," Eric Musser, chief executive officer of Corning Greater China, said.

China's market trends are creating growth opportunities across Corning's diverse businesses, he said. "We believe that China's LCD TV

[1] Corning News Releases, "China Market Presents Large Opportunity for Corning," February 04, 2011, www.corning.com/news_center/news_releases/2011/2011020402.aspx.

end market represents more than 20% of the worldwide total. Consequently, LCD panel manufacturers have been investing in China-based production for the past several years. Corning is making significant investments in its LCD glass manufacturing capabilities to meet this increasing market demand."

China has been Corning's largest market for optical fiber in recent years. Corning expects China to continue making significant investments in building out the nation's wireless, FTTH, and enterprise networks for several additional years. "We anticipate China's fiber-to-the-home subscriber base could grow at a compound annual rate of more than 150% and optical solutions in the data center space may continue at a 20% compound growth rate, both through 2014," Musser said.

Corning's decision to expand in China is primarily based on an improved outlook (continued higher-than-expected retail demand) for LCD televisions, laptops, and desktop computers. Then our immediate question is: Would there be enough annual demand from Chinese consumers to recoup the initial investment? Even if Corning believes that annual LCD glass demand could be at the higher end of its forecasted range of 2.9 billion square feet to 3.1 billion square feet this year, we can also pose the following questions:

- How long would it take to recover the initial investment?
- If the projected glass demand never materializes, what is the extent of financial risk?
- If a new competitor enters into the Chinese market in the near future that could bring more intense price pressure, how would that affect the future investment decisions?

These are the essential types of questions to address in evaluating any business investment decision, where financial risk is by far the most critical element to consider.

The investments a company chooses today determines its future success. Project ideas can originate from many different levels in an organization; procedures for screening projects to ensure that the right investments are made, need to be established. As mentioned in Chapter 1, many large companies have a specialized project analysis division that actively searches for new ideas, projects, and ventures. The generation and evaluation of creative investment proposals is far too important a task to be left to just this project analysis group; instead, the task is the ongoing responsibility of all managers and engineers throughout the organization. A key aspect of the process is the financial evaluation of investment proposals.

Our treatment of measures of investment worth is divided into four chapters. This chapter begins with a consideration of the payback period, a project-screening tool that was the first formal method used to evaluate investment projects. Then we introduce two measures based on the basic cash flow equivalence technique of present-worth (PW) analysis or commonly known as discounted cash flow techniques. Since the annual-worth approach has many useful engineering applications related to estimating the unit cost, Chapter 6 is devoted to annual cash flow analysis. Chapter 7 presents measures of investment worth based on yield; these measures are known as rate-of-return analysis. Chapter 8 presents another measure based on index, known as benefit–cost ratio.

5.1 Loan versus Project Cash Flows

An investment made in a fixed asset is similar to an investment made by a bank when it lends money. The essential characteristic of both transactions is that funds are committed today in the expectation of their earning a return in the future. In the case of the bank loan, the future return takes the form of interest plus repayment of the principal. This return is known as the **loan cash flow**. In the case of the fixed asset, the future return takes the form of cash generated by productive use of the asset. The representation of these future earnings, along with the capital expenditures and annual expenses (such as wages, raw materials, operating costs, maintenance costs, and income taxes), is the **project cash flow**. The similarity between the loan cash flow and the project cash flow (see Figure 5.1) brings us to an important conclusion—that is, we can use the same equivalence techniques developed in earlier chapters to measure economic worth.

In Chapters 2 through 4, we presented the concept of the time value of money and developed techniques for establishing cash flow equivalence with compound-interest factors. This background provides the foundation for accepting or rejecting a capital investment—that is, for economically evaluating a project's desirability. The coverage of investment worthiness discussed in this chapter will allow us to step beyond accepting or rejecting an investment to making comparisons of alternative investments. We will determine how to compare alternatives on an equal basis and select the alternative that is wisest from an economic standpoint.

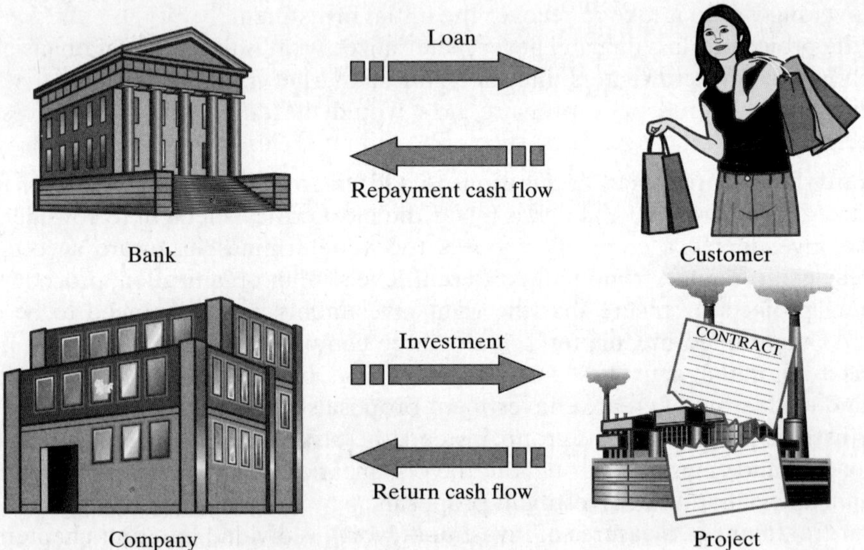

Figure 5.1 Loan versus project cash flows

We must also recognize that one of the most important parts of this capital-budgeting process is the estimation of relevant cash flows. For all examples in this chapter, as well as those in Chapters 6 and 7, net cash flows can be viewed as before-tax values or after-tax values for which tax effects have been recalculated. Since some organizations (e.g., governments and nonprofit organizations) are not subject to tax, the before-tax situation provides a valid base for this type of economic evaluation. Taking this view will allow us to focus on our main area of concern, the economic evaluation of investment projects. The procedures for determining after-tax net cash flows in taxable situations are developed in Part III. We will also assume that all cash flows are estimated in *actual dollars* unless otherwise mentioned. Also, all interest rates used in project evaluation are assumed to be *market interest rates* where any future inflationary effect has been reflected in this interest rate.

5.2 Initial Project Screening Methods

Before studying the four measures of investment attractiveness, we will introduce a simple method that is commonly used to screen capital investments. One of the primary concerns of most businesspeople is whether, and when, the money invested in a project can be recovered. The **payback method** screens projects on the basis of how long it takes for net receipts to equal investment outlays:

- The payback period is calculated by adding the expected cash flows for each year until the sum is equal to or greater than zero. The cumulative cash flow equals zero at the point where cash inflows exactly match, or pay back, the cash outflows; thus, the project has reached the payback point. Once the cumulative cash flows exceed zero, the project has begun to generate a profit.

- This calculation can take one of two forms by either ignoring time-value-of-money considerations or including them. The former case is usually designated as the **conventional-payback method**, whereas the latter case is known as the **discounted-payback method**.

- A project does not merit consideration unless its payback period is *shorter* than some specified period of time. (This time limit is largely determined by management policy.)

For example, a high-tech firm, such as a computer chip manufacturer, would set a short time limit for any new investment because high-tech products rapidly become obsolete. If the payback period is within the acceptable range, a formal project evaluation (such as a present-worth analysis, which is the subject of this chapter) may begin. It is important to remember that **payback screening** is not an *end* in itself but a method of screening out certain obviously unacceptable investment alternatives before progressing to an analysis of potentially acceptable ones.

EXAMPLE 5.1 Conventional-Payback Period

A machine shop is considering combining machining and turning centers into a single Mazak Multi-Tasking® machine center. Multitasking in the machine world is the combining of processes that were traditionally processed on multiple machines onto one machine. The ultimate goal is to turn, mill, drill, tap, bore, and finish the part in a single setup. The total investment cost is $1.8M with following anticipated cost savings:

	Current Cost (% Saved)	Savings
Setup	$335,000 (70%)	$234,500
Scrap/Rework	58,530 (85%)	49,750
Operators	220,000 (100%)	220,000
Fixturing	185,000 (85%)	157,250
Programming Time	80,000 (60%)	48,000
Floor Space	35,000 (65%)	22,750
Maintenance	45,000 (60%)	27,000
Coolant	15,000 (50%)	7,500
Inspection	120,000 (100%)	120,000
Documentation	5,000 (50%)	2,500
Expediting	25,000 (75%)	18,750
Total Annual Savings		**$908,000**

Determine how long it would take to recover the initial investment.

DISSECTING THE PROBLEM

It is necessary to determine how long you can expect to reap benefit from the investment. Most machine shops typically use seven years and assume a 20% residual value at the end of the project life. It is also very common for a learning curve to take place in operating a complex new machine. To allow for the learning curve, assume that only 50% of the full potential savings of $908,000 occur during the first year and 75% occur during the second year. With these assumptions, the project cash flows are summarized in the table at the right.

Given: Initial cost = $1,800,000; cash flow series as shown in the table below.

Find: Conventional-payback period.

Period	Cash Flow	Cumulative Cash Flow
0	–$1,800,000	–$1,800,000
1	454,000	–1,346,000
2	681,000	–665,000
3	908,000	243,000
4	908,000	1,151,000
5	908,000	2,059,000
6	908,000	2,967,000
7	1,268,000	4,235,000

METHODOLOGY

Create a chart reflecting the conventional payback period.

SOLUTION

See Figure 5.2.

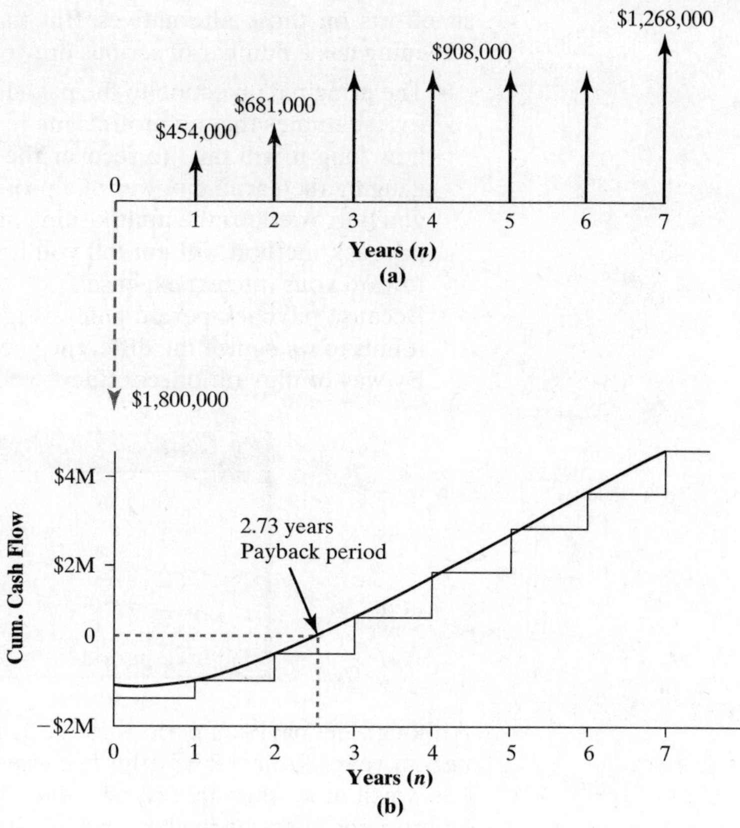

Figure 5.2 Illustration of conventional payback period—(a) annual project cash flow over the life of the project and (b) cumulative project cash flows over time

As we see from the cumulative cash flow series in Figure 5.2(b), the total investment is recovered at the end of year 3. If the firm's stated maximum payback period is two years, the project would not pass the initial screening stage.

COMMENTS: In this example, we assumed that cash flows occur only in discrete lumps at the end of years. If cash flows occur continuously throughout the year, our calculation of the payback period needs adjustment. A negative balance of $665,000 remains at the end of year 2. If the $908,000 is reasonably expected to be a continuous flow during year 3, then the total investment will be recovered about three-quarters ($665,000/$908,000) of the way through the third year. In this situation, the prorated payback period is thus 2.73 years.

5.2.1 Benefits and Flaws of Payback Screening

The simplicity of the payback method is one of its most appealing qualities. Initial project screening by the payback method reduces the information search by focusing on that time at which the firm expects to recover the initial investment. The method may also eliminate some alternatives, thus reducing a firm's need to make further analysis efforts on those alternatives. But the much-used payback method of investment screening has a number of serious drawbacks as well:

- The principal objection to the payback method is that it fails to measure profitability; it assumes that no profit is made during the payback period. Simply measuring how long it will take to recover the initial investment outlay contributes little to gauging the earning power of a project. (For instance, if you know that the money you borrowed for the multitasking machine center is costing you 15% per year, the payback method will not tell you how much your invested money is contributing toward your interest expense.)
- Because payback-period analysis ignores differences in the timing of cash flows, it fails to recognize the difference between the present and future value of money. By way of illustration, consider two investment projects:

n	Project 1	Project 2
0	–$10,000	–$10,000
1	$1,000	$9,000
2	$9,000	$1,000
3	$1,000	$2,000
Payback period:	2 years	2 years

Although the payback periods for both investments can be the same in terms of numbers of years, Project 2 is better because most investment recovered at the end of year 1 is worth more than that to be gained later. Because payback screening also ignores all proceeds after the payback period, it does not allow for the possible advantages of a project with a longer economic life.

5.2.2 Discounted-Payback Period

To remedy one of the shortcomings of the payback period described previously, we modify the procedure to consider the time value of money—that is, the cost of funds (interest) used to support the project. This modified payback period is often referred to as the **discounted-payback period**. In other words, we may define the discounted-payback period as the number of years required to recover the investment from *discounted* cash flows.

EXAMPLE 5.2 Discounted-Payback Periods

Consider the cash flow data given in Example 5.1. Assuming the firm's cost of funds to be 15%, compute the discounted-payback period.

DISSECTING THE PROBLEM

Given: $i = 15\%$ per year; cash flow data in Example 5.1.

Find: Discounted-payback period.

METHODOLOGY

Construct a table.

SOLUTION

To determine the period necessary to recover both the capital investment and the cost of funds required to support the investment, we construct Table 5.1, which shows the cash flows and costs of funds to be recovered over the project's life. The cost of funds shown can be thought of as interest payments if the initial investment is financed by loan or as the opportunity cost of committing capital (commonly known as the cost of capital).

To illustrate, let's consider the cost of funds during the first year. With $1,800,000 committed at the beginning of the year, the interest in year 1 would be $270,000 ($1,800,000 \times 0.15$). Therefore, the total commitment grows to $2,070,000, but the $454,000 cash flow in year 1 leaves a net commitment of $1,616,000. The cost of funds during the second year would be $242,400 ($1,616,000 \times 0.15$). But with the $681,000 receipt from the project, the net commitment reduces to $1,177,400. When this process repeats for the remaining project years, we find that the net commitment to the project ends during year 4. Depending on the cash flow assumption, the project must remain in use for about 3.56 years (continuous cash flows) or four years (year-end cash flows) in order for the company to cover its cost of capital and recover the funds invested in the project.

TABLE 5.1 **Payback Period Calculation Considering the Cost of Funds at 15%**

Period	Cash Flow	Cost of Funds (15%)	Cumulative Cash Flow
0	−$1,800,000	0	−$1,800,000
1	454,000	$-1,800,000\,(0.15) = -270,000$	−1,616,000
2	681,000	$-1,616,000\,(0.15) = -242,400$	−1,177,400
3	908,000	$-1,177,400\,(0.15) = -176,610$	−446,010
4	908,000	$-446,010\,(0.15) = -66,902$	395,089
5	908,000	$395,089\,(0.15) = 59,263$	1,362,352
6	908,000	$1,362,352\,(0.15) = 204,353$	2,474,705
7	1,268,000	$2,474,705\,(0.15) = 371,206$	4,113,911

COMMENTS: Inclusion of time-value-of-money effects has increased the payback period calculated for this example by 9.96 months (0.83 years) compared with the conventional payback period. Certainly, this modified measure is an improved one, but it, too, does not show the complete picture of the project's profitability.

5.3 Present-Worth Analysis

Until the 1950s, the payback method was widely used for making investment decisions. As flaws in this method were recognized, however, businesspeople began to search for methods to improve project evaluations. The result was the development of **discounted cash flow techniques (DCFs)**, which take into account the time value of money. One of the DCFs is the net-present-worth (or net-present-value) (NPW or NPV) method.

A capital-investment problem is essentially a matter of determining whether the anticipated cash inflows from a proposed project are sufficiently attractive to invest funds in the project. In developing the NPW criterion, we will use the concept of cash flow equivalence discussed in Chapter 2. As we observed there, the most convenient point at which to calculate the equivalent values is often at time zero. Under the PW criterion, the present worth of all cash inflows associated with an investment project is compared with the present worth of all cash outflows associated with that project. The difference between the two of these cash flows, referred to as the **net present worth** (NPW), determines whether the project is an acceptable investment. When two or more projects are under consideration, NPW analysis further allows us to select the best project by comparing their NPW figures directly.

5.3.1 Net-Present-Worth Criterion

We will first summarize the basic procedure for applying the net-present-worth criterion to a typical investment project, as well as for comparing alternative projects.

- **Evaluating a Single Project**

  Step 1: Determine the interest rate that the firm wishes to earn on its investments. The interest rate you determine represents the rate at which the firm can always invest the money in its **investment pool**, the value of capital available for lending and investing. This interest rate is often referred to as either a *required rate of return* or a *minimum attractive rate of return* (MARR). Usually, this selection is a policy decision made by top management. It is possible for the MARR to change over the life of a project, but for now we will use a single rate of interest when calculating PW.

  Step 2: Estimate the service life of the project.

  Step 3: Estimate the cash inflow for each period over the service life.

  Step 4: Estimate the cash outflow for each period over the service life.

  Step 5: Determine the net cash flows for each period (Net cash flow = Cash inflow − Cash outflow).

  Step 6: Find the present worth of each net cash flow at the MARR. Add up these present-worth figures; their sum is defined as the project's NPW. That is,

$$
\begin{aligned}
\mathrm{PW}(i) &= \frac{A_0}{(1+i)^0} + \frac{A_1}{(1+i)^1} + \frac{A_2}{(1+i)^2} + \cdots + \frac{A_N}{(1+i)^N} \\
&= \sum_{n=0}^{N} \frac{A_n}{(1+i)^n} \\
&= \sum_{n=0}^{N} A_n (P/F, i, n),
\end{aligned}
\tag{5.1}
$$

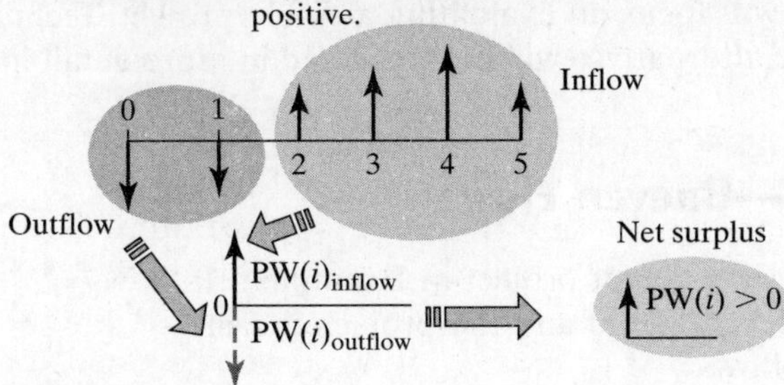

Figure 5.3   Illustration of how NPW decision rules work

where

$$PW(i) = \text{NPW calculated at } i,$$
$$A_n = \text{net cash flow at the end of period } n,$$
$$i = \text{MARR (or cost of capital), and}$$
$$n = \text{service life of the project.}$$

A_n will be positive if the corresponding period has a net cash inflow and negative if the period has a net cash outflow.

Step 7: In this context, a positive NPW means that the equivalent worth of the inflows is more than the equivalent worth of the outflows so that the project makes a profit. Therefore, if the PW(i) is positive for a single project, the project should be accepted; if it is negative, the project should be rejected. The process of applying the NPW measure is shown in Figure 5.3 and is implemented with the following decision rule:

$$\text{If } PW(i) > 0, \text{ accept the investment.}$$
$$\text{If } PW(i) = 0, \text{ remain indifferent.}$$
$$\text{If } PW(i) < 0, \text{ reject the investment.}$$

- **Comparing More than One Alternative**

Note that the foregoing decision rule is for evaluation of a single project for which you can estimate the revenues as well as the costs.[2] The following guidelines should be used for evaluating and comparing more than one project:

1. If you need to select the best alternative, based on the net-present-worth criterion, select the one with the highest NPW, as long as all the alternatives have the same service lives. Comparison of alternatives with unequal service lives requires special assumptions as will be detailed in Section 5.4.

2. As you will find in Section 5.4, comparison of mutually exclusive alternatives with the same revenues is performed on a *cost-only basis*. In this situation, you should

[2] Some projects cannot be avoided—e.g., the installation of pollution-control equipment to comply with government regulations. In such a case, the project would be accepted even though its PW(i) < 0.

accept the project that results in the smallest PW of costs, or the least negative PW (because you are minimizing costs rather than maximizing profits).

For now, we will focus on evaluating a single project. Techniques on how to compare multiple alternatives will be addressed in more detail in Section 5.4.

EXAMPLE 5.3 Net Present Worth—Uneven Flows

Consider the Multi-Tasking® machine center investment project in Example 5.1. Recall that the required initial investment of $1,800,000 and the projected cash savings over a seven-year project life are as follows:[3]

End of Year	Cash Flow
0	–$1,800,000
1	454,000
2	681,000
3	908,000
4	908,000
5	908,000
6	908,000
7	1,268,000

You have been asked by the president of the company to evaluate the economic merit of the acquisition. The firm's MARR is known to be 15% per year.

DISSECTING THE PROBLEM

Given: Cash flows as tabulated; MARR = 15% per year.

Find: NPW.

METHODOLOGY

Calculate the present value of the Multi-Tasking® machine center.

SOLUTION

If we bring each flow to its equivalent at time zero as shown in Figure 5.4, we find that

$$PW(15\%) = -\$1,800,000 + \$454,000\,(P/F, 15\%, 1)$$
$$+ \$681,000\,(P/F, 15\%, 2)$$
$$+ \$908,000\,(P/A, 15\%, 4)\,(P/F, 15\%, 2)$$
$$+ \$1,268,000\,(P/F, 15\%, 7)$$
$$= \$1,546,571.$$

Since the project results in a surplus of $1,546,571, the project is acceptable. It is returning a profit greater than 15%.

[3] As we stated at the beginning of this chapter, we treat net cash flows in actual dollars as before-tax values or as having their tax effects precalculated. Explaining the process of obtaining cash flows requires an understanding of income taxes and the role of depreciation, which are discussed in Chapters 9 and 10.

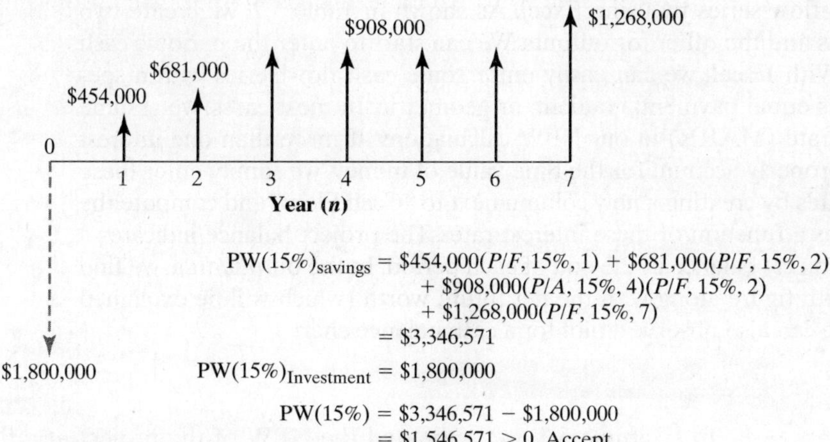

$$PW(15\%)_{savings} = \$454,000(P/F, 15\%, 1) + \$681,000(P/F, 15\%, 2)$$
$$+ \$908,000(P/A, 15\%, 4)(P/F, 15\%, 2)$$
$$+ \$1,268,000(P/F, 15\%, 7)$$
$$= \$3,346,571$$

$$\$1,800,000 \quad PW(15\%)_{Investment} = \$1,800,000$$

$$PW(15\%) = \$3,346,571 - \$1,800,000$$
$$= \$1,546,571 > 0, \text{ Accept}$$

Figure 5.4 Calculating the net present value of the Multi-Tasking® machine center project

TABLE 5.2 An Excel Worksheet to Illustrate the Process of Computing the NPW

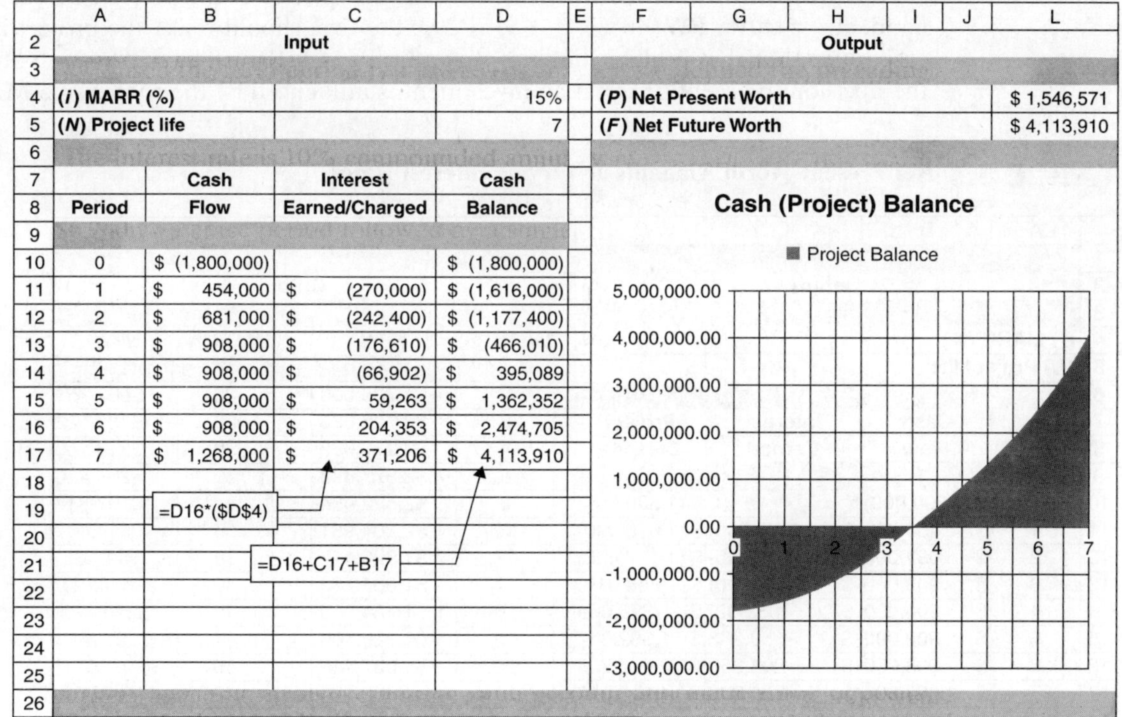

	A	B	C	D	E	F	G	H	I	J	L
2			Input					Output			
3											
4	(*i*) MARR (%)			15%		(*P*) Net Present Worth					$ 1,546,571
5	(*N*) Project life			7		(*F*) Net Future Worth					$ 4,113,910
6											
7		Cash	Interest	Cash							
8	Period	Flow	Earned/Charged	Balance				Cash (Project) Balance			
9											
10	0	$ (1,800,000)		$ (1,800,000)							
11	1	$ 454,000	$ (270,000)	$ (1,616,000)							
12	2	$ 681,000	$ (242,400)	$ (1,177,400)							
13	3	$ 908,000	$ (176,610)	$ (466,010)							
14	4	$ 908,000	$ (66,902)	$ 395,089							
15	5	$ 908,000	$ 59,263	$ 1,362,352							
16	6	$ 908,000	$ 204,353	$ 2,474,705							
17	7	$ 1,268,000	$ 371,206	$ 4,113,910							
18											
19		=D16*($D$4)									
20											
21		=D16+C17+B17									
22											
23											
24											
25											
26											

COMMENTS: We could easily automate the process of computing the net present worth of any project cash flow series by using Excel. As shown in Table 5.2, we create two areas: one for inputs and the other for outputs. We can start to enter the periodic cash flows in cell B10. With Excel, we can easily enter some cash flow series with a specific pattern, such as equal payment, gradient, or geometric. In most cases, we assume a constant interest rate (MARR) in our NPW calculations. If more than one interest rate may apply to properly account for the time value of money, we simply enter these changing interest rates by creating a new column next to "Cash Flow" and compute the "Interest Earned" as a function of these interest rates. The project balance indicates a periodic cash (or project) balance at the end of each period. In the output area, we find the net present-worth figure along with the net future worth (which will be explained in Section 5.3.4). We can also observe a plot for a cash balance chart.

In Example 5.3, we computed the NPW of the project at a fixed interest rate of 15%. If we compute the NPW at varying interest rates, we obtain the data shown in Table 5.3. Plotting the NPW as a function of interest rate gives the graph in Figure 5.5, the present-worth profile.

Figure 5.5 indicates that the investment project has a positive NPW if the interest rate is below 36.32% and a negative PW if the interest rate is above 36.32%. As we will see in Chapter 7, this **break-even interest rate** is known as the **internal rate of return**. If the firm's MARR is 15%, the project's NPW is $1,546,571, so the $1.8M capital expenditure may be easily justified. The figure of $1,546,571 measures the equivalent immediate gain in present worth to the firm following the acceptance of the project. On the other hand, at $i = 40\%$, $PW(40\%) = -\$151,293$, the firm should reject the project in this case (even though it is highly unlikely that a firm's MARR will be this high). Note that the decision to accept or reject an investment is influenced by the choice of a MARR,

TABLE 5.3 Net Present-Worth Amounts at Varying Interest Rates

	A	B	C	D	E	F	G	H	I	J
1										
2			Input					Output		
3										
4	(*i*) MARR (%)			15%		MARR (%)	NPW		MARR (%)	NPW
5	(*N*) Project life			7						
6						0	$4,235,000		26	$567,751
7		Cash	Interest	Project		2	$3,726,686		28	$437,522
8	Period	Flow	Earned	Balance		4	$3,277,023		30	$318,140
9						6	$2,877,892		32	$208,470
10	0	$ (1,800,000)		$ (1,800,000)		8	$2,522,454		34	$107,518
11	1	$ 454,000	$ (270,000)	$ (1,616,000)		10	$2,204,931		36	$14,407
12	2	$ 681,000	$ (242,400)	$ (1,177,400)		12	$1,920,417		38	($71,636)
13	3	$ 908,000	$ (176,610)	$ (466,010)		14	$1,664,735		40	($151,293)
14	4	$ 908,000	$ (66,902)	$ 395,089		16	$1,434,319		42	($225,170)
15	5	$ 908,000	$ 59,263	$ 1,362,352		18	$1,226,106		44	($293,803)
16	6	$ 908,000	$ 204,353	$ 2,474,705		20	$1,037,466		46	($357,671)
17	7	$ 1,268,000	$ 371,206	$ 4,113,910		22	$866,128		48	($417,201)
18						24	$710,125		50	($472,772)

=D16*($D$4)

=D16+C17+B17

=NPV(F18%,$B$11:$B$17)+$B$10

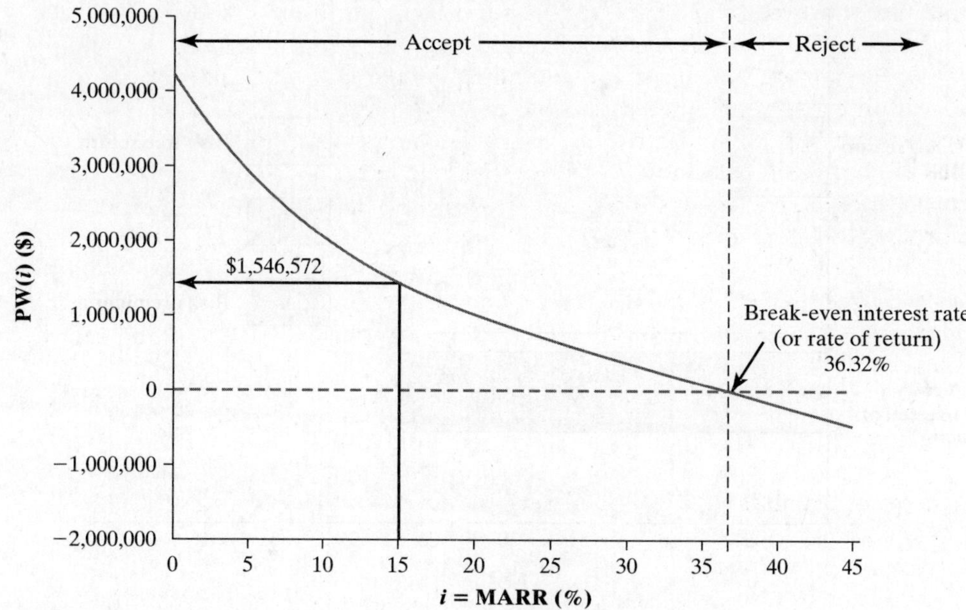

Figure 5.5   Net present-worth profile described in Example 5.3

so it is crucial to estimate the MARR correctly. We will briefly describe the elements to consider when setting this interest rate for project evaluation.

5.3.2 Guidelines for Selecting a MARR

Return is what you get back in relation to the amount you invested. Return is one way to evaluate how your investments in financial assets or projects do in relation to each other and in relation to the performance of investments in general. Let us look first at how we may derive rates of return. Conceptually, the rate of return that we realistically expect to earn on any investment is a function of three components:

- Risk-free real return
- Inflation factor
- Risk premium(s)

Suppose you want to invest in a stock. First, you would expect to be compensated in some way for not being able to use your money while you hold the stock. Second, you would expect to be compensated for decreases in purchasing power between the time you invest and the time your investment is returned to you. Finally, you would demand additional rewards for having taken the risk of losing your money if the stock did poorly. If you did not expect your investment to compensate you for these factors, why would you tie up your money in this investment in the first place?

For example, if you were to invest $1,000 in risk-free U.S. Treasury bills for a year, you would expect a real rate of return of about 2%. Your risk premium would be zero. You probably think that this does not sound like much. However, to that you have to add an allowance for inflation. If you expect inflation to be about 4% during the investment period, you should realistically expect to earn 6% during that interval

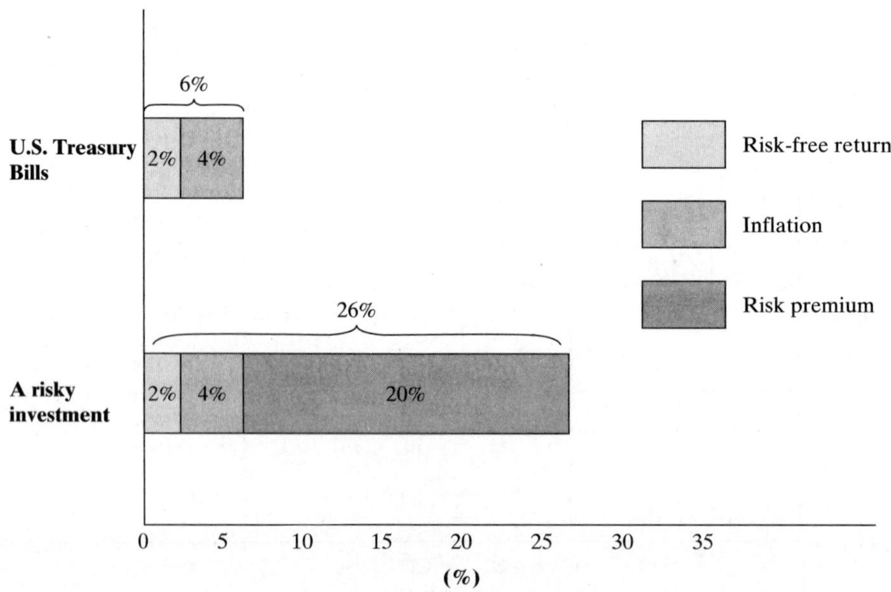

Figure 5.6 Elements of required return—establishing a MARR

(2% real return + 4% inflation factor + 0% for risk premium). This concept is illustrated in Figure 5.6.

How would it work out for a riskier investment, say, an Internet stock? As you would consider the investment to be a very volatile one, you would increase the risk premium to, say, 20%. So, you will not invest your money in such a stock unless you are reasonably confident of having it grow at an annual rate of 2% real return + 4% inflation factor + 20% risk premium = 26%. Again, the risk premium of 20% is a perceived value that can vary from one investor to another.

We use the same concept in selecting the interest rate for a project evaluation. If you consider a routine project where you can reasonably predict the future cash flows with a great deal of confidence, a lower interest (discount) will be prevailed. In Section 11.4, we will consider this special issue in more detail. For now, we will assume that the firm has established a single interest rate for project evaluation, considering all relevant risk inherent in the project, and we will use this rate to measure the project's worth.

5.3.3 Meaning of Net Present Worth

In present-worth analysis, we assume that all the funds in a firm's treasury can be placed in investments that yield a return equal to the MARR. We may view these funds as an *investment pool*. Alternatively, if no funds are available for investment, we assume that the firm can borrow them at the MARR from the capital markets. In this section, we will examine these two views when explaining the meaning of MARR in PW calculations.

Investment-Pool Concept

An investment pool is equivalent to a firm's treasury. It is where all fund transactions are administered and managed by the firm's comptroller. The firm may withdraw funds from this investment pool for other investment purposes, but if left in the pool, the funds will earn interest at the MARR. Thus, in investment analysis, net cash flows will be those that are relative to this investment pool. To illustrate the investment-pool concept, we consider again the project in Example 5.3, which required an investment of $1,800,000.

If the firm did not invest in the project and instead left the $1,800,000 in the investment pool for seven years, these funds would have grown as follows:

$$\$1,800,000\,(F/P, 15\%, 7) = \$4,788,036.$$

Suppose the company did decide to invest $1,800,000 in the project described in Example 5.3. Then the firm would receive a stream of cash inflows during the project life of seven years in the following amounts:

End of Year (n)	Cash Flow (A_n)
1	$454,000
2	681,000
3	908,000
4	908,000
5	908,000
6	908,000
7	1,268,000

Since the funds that return to the investment pool earn interest at a rate of 15%, it would be helpful to see how much the firm would benefit from this investment. For this alternative, the returns after reinvestment are as follows:

$$\$454,000\,(F/P, 15\%, 6) = \$1,050,130$$

$$\$681,000\,(F/P, 15\%, 5) = \$1,369,734$$

$$\$908,000\,(F/A, 15\%, 4)\,(F/P, 15\%, 1) = \$5,214,082$$

$$\$1,268,000\,(F/P, 15\%, 0) = \$1,268,000$$

$$\$8,901,946$$

These returns total $8,901,946. The additional cash accumulation at the end of seven years from investing in the project is

$$\$8,901,946 - \$4,788,036 = \$4,113,910.$$

This $4,113,910 surplus is also known as *net future worth of the project* at the project termination. If we compute the equivalent present worth of this net cash surplus at time 0, we obtain

$$\$4,113,910\,(P/F, 15\%, 7) = \$1,546,571,$$

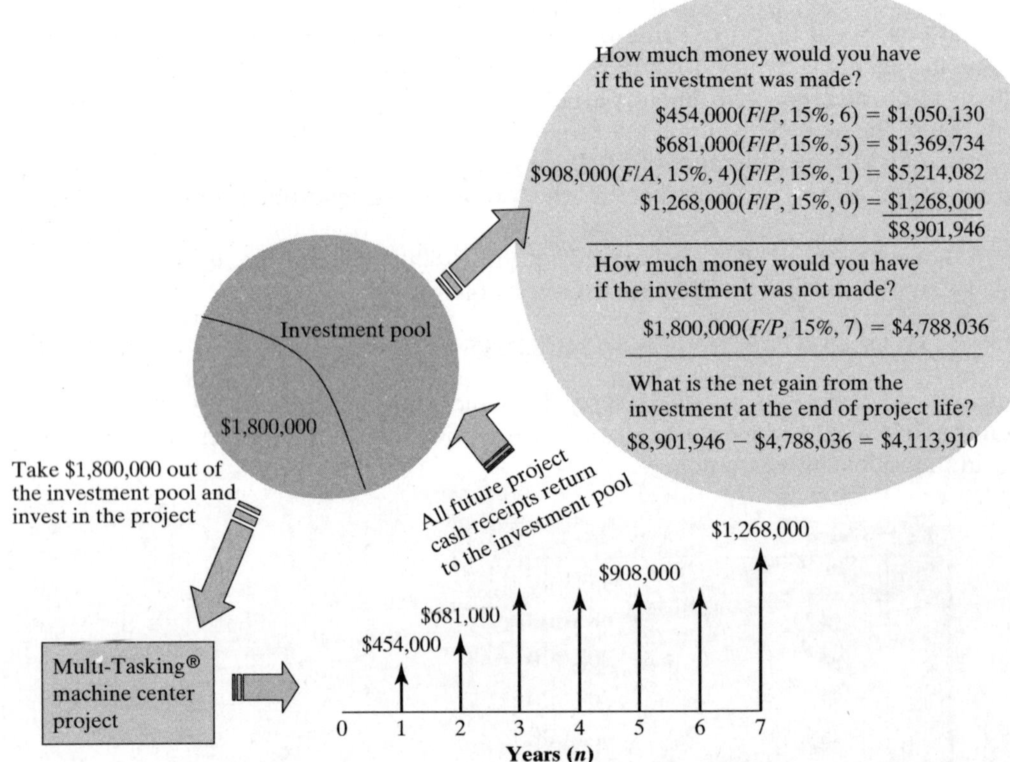

Figure 5.7 The concept of the investment pool with the company as a lender and the project as a borrower

which is exactly the same as the NPW of the project as computed by Eq. (5.1). Clearly, on the basis of its positive NPW, the alternative of purchasing the multitasking machine should be preferred to that of simply leaving the funds in the investment pool at the MARR. Thus, in NPW analysis, any investment is assumed to be returned at the MARR. If a surplus exists at the end of the project life, then we know that PW(MARR) > 0. Figure 5.7 summarizes the reinvestment concept as it relates to the firm's investment pool.

Borrowed-Funds Concept

Suppose that the firm does not have $1,800,000 at the outset. In fact, the firm does not have to maintain an investment pool at all. Let's further assume that the firm borrows all its capital from a bank at an interest rate of 15% per year, invests in the project, and uses the proceeds from the investment to pay off the principal and interest on the bank loan. How much is left over for the firm at the end of the project period?

At the end of the first year, the interest on the bank loan would be $1,800,000 (0.15) = $270,000. Therefore, the total loan balance grows to $1,800,000(1.15) = $2,070,000. Then the firm receives $454,000 from the project and applies the entire amount to repay the loan portion. This repayment leaves a balance due of

$$PB(15\%)_1 = -\$1,800,000(1 + 0.15) + \$454,000 = -\$1,616,000.$$

TABLE 5.4 Tabular Approach to Determining the Project Balances

	A	B	C	D	E	F	G	H	I
1									
2	End of Year (n)	0	1	2	3	4	5	6	7
3									
4	Beginning Project Balance		($1,800,000)	($1,616,000)	($1,177,400)	($446,010)	$395,089	$1,362,352	$2,474,705
5	Interest Charged (15%)		($270,000)	($242,400)	($176,610)	($66,902)	$59,263	$204,353	$371,206
6	Payment Received	($1,800,000)	$454,000	$681,000	$908,000	$908,000	$908,000	$908,000	$1,268,000
7									
8	Project Balance		($1,800,000)	($1,616,000)	($1,717,400)	($446,010)	$395,089	$1,362,352	$2,474,705	$4,113,910
9									
10				=PV(15%,7,0,-I8,0)					E8	
11	Net Present Worth (15%)	$1,546,571							
12	Net Future Worth (15%)	$4,113,910	=I8			=SUM(F4:F6)		=F4*0.15	
13									
14									

This amount is also known as the **project balance**. We will use $PB(i)_n$ to denote the cash balance at the end of period n. As summarized in Table 5.4, this amount becomes the net amount the project is borrowing at the beginning of year 2.

At the end of year 2, the debt to the bank grows to $1,616,000(1.15) = $1,858,400. But with the receipt of $681,000, the project balance reduces to

$$PB(15\%)_2 = -\$1,616,000(1 + 0.15) + \$681,000 = -\$1,177,400.$$

The process continues, and eventually, at the end of year 4, the debt to the bank becomes $446,010(1.15) = $512,912. With the receipt of $908,000 from the project, however, the firm should be able to pay off the remaining debt and come out with a surplus in the amount of $395,089.

$$-\$446,000(1 + 0.15) + \$908,000 = \$395,089.$$

Once the firm pays off the bank loan, we will assume that any surplus generated from the project will go into its investment pool and earn interest at the same rate of 15%. Therefore, the project balance at the end of year 5 will be calculated as

$$n = 5, \qquad \$395,089(1 + 0.15) + \$908,000 = \$1,362,352$$

$$n = 6, \qquad \$1,362,352(1 + 0.15) + \$908,000 = \$2,474,705$$

$$n = 7, \qquad \$2,474,705(1 + 0.15) + \$1,268,000 = \$4,113,910.$$

Note that the amount of the terminal project balance is $4,113,910, which is positive, indicating that the firm fully repays its initial bank loan and interest at the end of year 4, with a resulting profit of $4,113,910. Finally, if we compute the equivalent present worth of this net surplus at time 0, we obtain

$$PW(15\%) = \$4,113,910(P/F, 15\%, 7) = \$1,546,571.$$

The result is identical to the case where we directly computed the PW of the project at $i = 15\%$, shown in Example 5.3.

5.3.4 Net Future Worth and Project Balance Diagram

The terminal project balance in Table 5.4 ($4,113,910) is also known as the **net future worth** of the project, and we can use this number as a figure of investment worth to make an accept–reject decision on the project. In other words, if the net future worth is positive, indicating a surplus, we should accept the investment. Otherwise, we may reject the project. This decision rule will be consistent with the net present worth criterion, as we obtain the NPW of the project from its net future worth simply by applying the discounting factor, which is always nonnegative. Alternatively, we can show why the terminal project balance is equivalent to the net future worth of the project as follows:

$$n: 0 \rightarrow \mathrm{PB}(i)_0 = A_0$$

$$n: 1 \rightarrow \mathrm{PB}(i)_1 = \mathrm{PB}(i)_0(1 + i) + A_1$$
$$= A_0(1 + i) + A_1$$

$$n: 2 \rightarrow \mathrm{PB}(i)_2 = \mathrm{PB}(i)_1(1 + i) + A_2$$
$$= A_0(1 + i)^2 + A_1(1 + i) + A_2$$

$$n: N \rightarrow \mathrm{PB}(i)_N = \mathrm{PB}(i)_{N-1}(1 + i) + A_N$$
$$= A_0(1 + i)^N + A_1(1 + i)^{N-1} + \cdots + A_N$$
$$= \mathrm{FW}(i). \tag{5.2}$$

Therefore, in our example we can calculate the net future of the project by using Eq. (5.2):

$$\mathrm{FW}(15\%) = -\$1,800,000(1 + 0.15)^7 + \$454,000(1 + 0.15)^6$$
$$+ \$681,000(1 + 0.15)^5 + \cdots + \$1,268,000$$
$$= \$4,113,910.$$

Figure 5.8 illustrates the project balance as a function of time. In this diagram, we can observe four important investment characteristics of the project:

- **The exposure to financial risk:** A negative project balance indicates the amount of investment to be recovered or exposed to risk of loss if the project is terminated at this point. The negative project balance area will increase if the cash received from the project is less than the interest owed for the period. If the other situation prevails, the negative area will decrease. Therefore, if other things are equal, we prefer a smaller area of negative project balance.

- **The discounted payback period:** This indicates how long it will be before the project breaks even. This condition occurs when the project balance becomes nonnegative. (In our example, this occurs at $n = 4$.) If the project is terminated after this payback period, no economic loss is anticipated if there is no additional investment required to close the project. Clearly, we prefer a shorter payback period if other things are equal.

- **The profit potential:** The area in light green represents the area of positive project balance. Since the initial investment plus interest has been fully recovered at this phase of the project, any cash generated during this period directly contributes toward the final profitability of the project. Therefore, we prefer a larger area of positive project balance (if other things are equal) as this area indicates the magnitude of profits expected and the rate at which they will be accumulated. This information will be useful when we must decide on the right time to phase out the investment. (This decision is called the abandonment decision.)

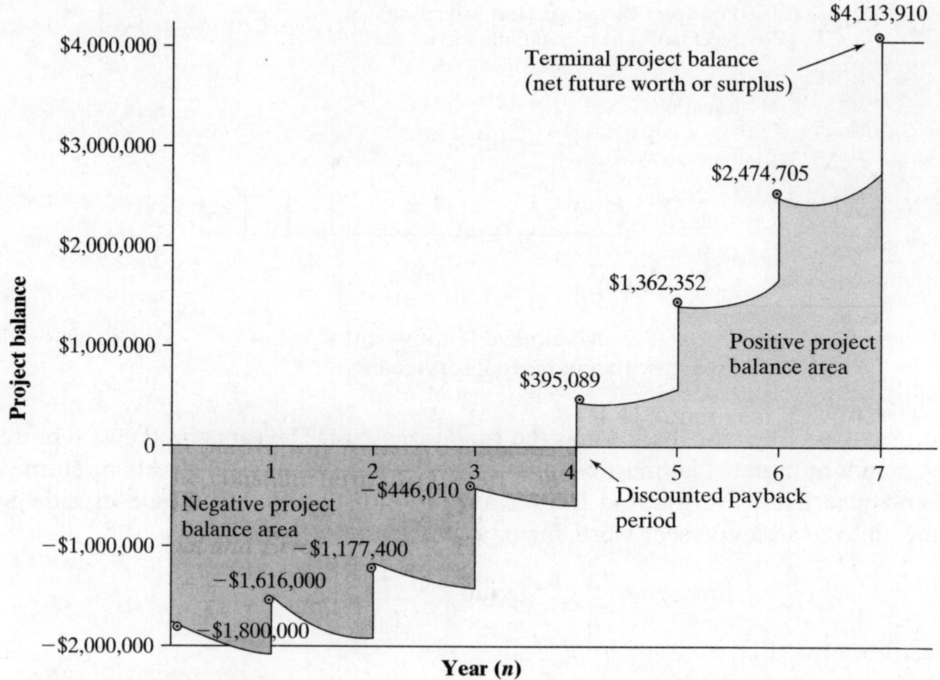

Figure 5.8   Project balance diagram as a function of investment period—(1) area of negative project balance, (2) discounted payback period, (3) area of positive project balance, and (4) terminal project balance (or net future worth of the investment)

- **The net future worth (surplus):** The terminal project balance indicates the surplus of the project at the end of the project life. If we borrowed money to finance the project, this figure would represent any additional cash generated from the project as well as reinvestment of the cash left over after we paid back the amount borrowed with all interest.

Clearly, a project balance diagram provides important insights into the desirability of the investment and the ultimate profitability of the project (net present value). This additional information will be even more important when we need to compare various projects having similar profitability.

5.3.5 Capitalized-Equivalent Method

Let's consider a situation where the life of a proposed project is **perpetual** or the planning horizon is extremely long (say, 40 years or more). Many public projects such as bridge and waterway construction, irrigation systems, and hydroelectric dams are expected to generate benefits over an extended period of time (or forever). How do we calculate the PW for these projects? In this section, we examine the **capitalized-equivalent** $[\mathrm{CE}(i)]$ method, a special case of the NPW criterion, for evaluating such projects.

Perpetual Service Life

Consider the cash flow series shown in Figure 5.9. How do we determine the PW for an infinite (or almost infinite) uniform series of cash flows or a repeated cycle of cash flows? The process of computing the PW for this infinite series is referred to as the **capitalization**

Principle: PW for a project with an annual
receipt of A over an infinite service life

Equation:
$$CE(i) = A(P/A, i, \infty) = A/i$$

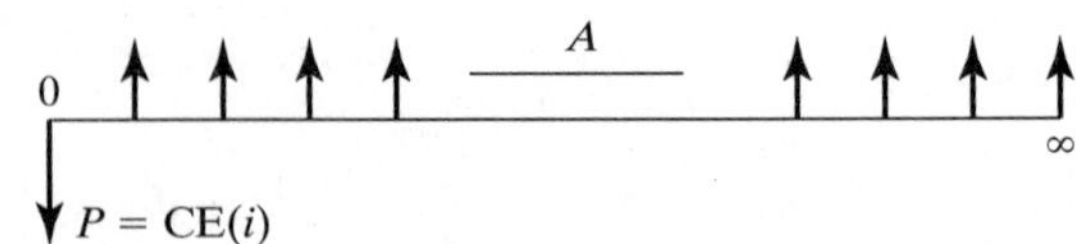

$P = CE(i)$

Figure 5.9 Capitalized-equivalent worth—a
project with a perpetual service life

of project cost. The cost is known as the **capitalized cost**. The capitalized cost represents
the amount of money that must be invested today in order to yield a certain return A at
the end of each and every period, forever, assuming an interest rate of i. Observe the limit
of the uniform-series present-worth factor as N approaches infinity:

$$\lim_{N \to \infty} (P/A, i, N) = \lim_{N \to \infty} \left[\frac{(1 + i)^N - 1}{i(1 + i)^N} \right] = \frac{1}{i}.$$

Thus, it follows that

$$PW(i) = A(P/A, i, N \to \infty) = \frac{A}{i}. \tag{5.3}$$

This is the same result shown in Section 2.5.5. Another way of looking at this concept
is to ask what constant income stream could be generated by $PW(i)$ dollars today in
perpetuity. Clearly, the answer is $A = iPW(i)$. If withdrawals were higher than A, you
would be eating into the principal, which would eventually reduce it to zero.

EXAMPLE 5.4 Capitalized-Equivalent Cost

An engineering school has just completed a new engineering complex worth $50 mil-
lion. A campaign targeting alumni is planned to raise funds for future maintenance
costs, which are estimated at $2 million per year. Any unforeseen costs above $2 million per year would be obtained by raising tuition. Assuming that the school can create a trust fund that earns 8% interest annually, how much has to be raised now to
cover the perpetual string of $2 million annual costs?

DISSECTING THE PROBLEM

Given: $A = \$2$ million, $i = 8\%$ per year, and $N = \infty$.
Find: CE(8%).

METHODOLOGY

Calculate capitalized cost.

SOLUTION

The capitalized-cost equation is

$$CE(i) = \frac{A}{i}.$$

Substituting in our given values, we obtain

$$CE(8\%) = \$2{,}000{,}000/0.08$$
$$= \$25{,}000{,}000.$$

COMMENTS: It is easy to see that this lump-sum amount should be sufficient to pay maintenance expenses for the school forever. Suppose the school deposited $25 million at a bank that paid 8% interest annually. At the end of the first year, the $25 million would earn $8\%\,(\$25\,\text{million}) = \$2\,\text{million}$ interest. If this interest were withdrawn, the $25 million would remain in the account. At the end of the second year, the $25 million balance would again earn $8\%(\$25\,\text{million}) = \$2\,\text{million}$. The annual withdrawal could be continued forever, and the endowment (gift funds) would always remain at $25 million.

5.4 Methods to Compare Mutually Exclusive Alternatives

Until now, we have considered situations involving only a single project or projects that were independent of each other. In both cases, we made the decision to accept or reject each project individually according to whether it met the MARR requirements, evaluated by using the PW.

In the real world of engineering practice, however, it is typical for us to have two or more choices of projects for accomplishing a business objective. (As we shall see, even when it appears that we have only one project to consider, the implicit "do-nothing" alternative must be factored into the decision-making process.)

In this section, we extend our evaluation techniques to consider multiple projects that are mutually exclusive. Often, various projects or investments under consideration do not have the same duration or do not match the desired study period. Adjustments must be made when we compare multiple options in order to properly account for such differences. We also explain the concepts of an analysis period and the process of accommodating for different lifetimes as important considerations in selecting among several alternatives. In the first few subsections of this section, all available options in a decision problem are assumed to have equal lifetimes. In Section 5.4.4, this restriction is relaxed.

When alternatives are **mutually exclusive**, any one of them will fulfill the same need, and the selection of one alternative implies that the others will be excluded. Take, for example, buying versus leasing an automobile for business use: When one alternative is accepted, the other is excluded. We use the terms **alternative** and **project** interchangeably to mean decision option. *One of the fundamental principles in comparing mutually exclusive alternatives is that they must be compared over an equal time span (or analysis period).* In this section, we will present some of the fundamental principles that should be applied in comparing mutually exclusive investment alternatives. In doing so, we will consider two cases: (1) one where the analysis period equals the project lives and (2) the other where the analysis period differs from the project lives. In each case, the required assumption for analysis can be varied. First, we will define some of the relevant terminology, such as "do-nothing alternative," "revenue project," and "service project."

5.4.1 Doing Nothing Is a Decision Option

Investment projects fall within two types. A project either is aimed at replacing (or improving) an existing asset or system or is a new endeavor. In either case, a do-nothing alternative may exist. If a process or system already in place to accomplish our business objectives is still adequate, then we must determine which, if any, new proposals are economical replacements. If none are feasible, then we do nothing. On the other hand, if the existing system has terminally failed, the choice among proposed alternatives is mandatory (i.e., doing nothing is not an option).

New endeavors occur as alternatives to the do-nothing situation, which has zero revenues and zero costs. For most new endeavors, doing nothing is generally an alternative because we will not proceed unless at least one of the proposed alternatives is economically sound. In fact, undertaking even a single project entails making a decision between two alternatives when the project is optional because the do-nothing alternative is implicitly included. Occasionally, a new initiative *must* be undertaken, cost notwithstanding, and in this case, the goal is to choose the most economical alternative since doing nothing is not an option.

When the option of retaining an existing asset or system is available, there are two ways to incorporate it into the evaluation of the new proposals. One way is to treat the do-nothing option as a distinct alternative; this approach will be covered primarily in Chapter 12, where methodologies specific to replacement analysis are presented. The second approach, used in this chapter, is to generate the incremental cash flows of the new proposals relative to those of the do-nothing alternative—what additional costs and benefits can we expect from the new proposals? That is, for each new alternative, the **incremental costs** (and incremental savings or revenues if applicable) relative to those of the do-nothing alternative are used for the economic evaluation.

For a replacement-type problem, we calculate the incremental cash flow by subtracting the do-nothing cash flows from those of each new alternative. For new endeavors, the incremental cash flows are the same as the absolute amounts associated with each alternative since the do-nothing values are all zero.

5.4.2 Service Projects versus Revenue Projects

When comparing mutually exclusive alternatives, we need to classify investment projects as either service or revenue projects.

Service Projects

Suppose an electric utility company is considering building a new power plant to meet the peak-load demand during either hot summer or cold winter days. Two alternative service projects could meet this peak-load demand: a combustion turbine plant or a fuel-cell power plant. No matter which type of plant is selected, the firm will generate the same amount of revenue from its customers. The only difference is how much it will cost to generate electricity from each plant. If we were to compare these service projects, we would be interested in knowing which plant could provide cheaper power (lower production cost). Therefore, **service projects** are projects that generate revenues that do not depend on the choice of project but *must produce the same amount of output (revenue)*. In this situation, we certainly want to choose an alternative with the least input (or cost). Further, if we were to use the PW criterion to compare these alternatives to minimize expenditures, *we would choose the alternative with the lower present-value production cost over the service life*.

Revenue Projects

Suppose that a computer-monitor manufacturer is considering marketing two types of high-resolution monitors. With its present production capacity, the firm can market only one of them. Distinct production processes for the two models could incur very different manufacturing costs, and the revenues from each model would be expected to differ, due to divergent market prices and potentially different sales volumes. Clearly, these projects' revenues depend on the choice of alternative. For such **revenue projects**, we are not limiting the amount of input to the project or the amount of output that the project would generate. Therefore, we want to select the alternative with the largest net gains (output − input). In this situation, if we were to use the PW criterion, *we would select the model that promises to bring in the largest net present worth*.

5.4.3 Analysis Period Equals Project Lives

Let us begin our analysis with the simplest situation in which the project lives equal the analysis period. In this case, we compute the PW for each project and select the one with the highest PW. Example 5.5 illustrates this point.

EXAMPLE 5.5 A Service Project with a "Do-Nothing" Alternative

Ansell, Inc., a medical-device manufacturer, uses compressed air in solenoids and pressure switches in its machines to control various mechanical movements. Over the years, the manufacturing floor layout has changed numerous times. With each new layout, more piping was added to the compressed-air delivery system in order to accommodate new locations of manufacturing machines. None of the extra, unused old piping was capped or removed; thus, the current compressed-air delivery system is inefficient and fraught with leaks. Because of the leaks in the current system, the compressor is expected to run 70% of the time that the plant will be in operation during the upcoming year. The compressor will require 260 kW of electricity at a rate of $0.05/kWh. The plant runs 250 days a year, 24 hours per day. Ansell may address this issue in one of two ways:

- **Option 1:** Continue current operation. If Ansell continues to operate the current air delivery system, the compressor's run time will increase by 7% per year for the next five years because of ever-worsening leaks. (After five years, the current system will not be able to meet the plant's compressed-air requirement, so it will have to be replaced.)

- **Option 2:** Replace old piping now. If Ansell decides to replace all of the old piping now, new piping will cost $28,570. The compressor will still run for the same number of days; however, it will run 23% less (or will incur $70\%(1 - 0.23) = 53.9\%$ usage per day) because of the reduced air-pressure loss.

If Ansell's interest rate is 12% compounded annually, is it worth fixing the air delivery system now?

DISSECTING THE PROBLEM

Given: Current power consumption, $g = 7\%$, $i = 12\%$ per year, and $N = 5$ years.

Find: A_1 and P.

METHODOLOGY

Construct a chart comparing the options. In doing so, first determine the required annual power consumption with the current system. Then, calculate the estimated energy loss due to leaks from old the piping system.

SOLUTION

- **Step 1:** We need to calculate the cost of power consumption of the current piping system during the first year. The power consumption is determined as follows:

$$\text{Annual power cost} = \% \text{ of day operating} \times \text{days operating per year}$$
$$\times \text{ hours per day} \times \text{kW} \times \$/\text{kWh}$$
$$= (70\%) \times (250\,\text{days/year}) \times (24\,\text{hours/day})$$
$$\times (260\,\text{kW}) \times (\$0.05/\text{kWh})$$
$$= \$54{,}600.$$

- **Step 2:** Each year, if the current piping system is left in place, the annual power cost will increase at the rate of 7% over the previous year's cost. The anticipated power cost over the five-year period is summarized in Figure 5.10. The equivalent present lump-sum cost at 12% interest for this geometric gradient series is

$$P_{\text{Option 1}} = \$54{,}600\,(P/A_1, 7\%, 12\%, 5)$$
$$= \$54{,}600\left[\frac{1 - (1 + 0.07)^5(1 + 0.12)^{-5}}{0.12 - 0.07}\right]$$
$$= \$222{,}937.$$

- **Step 3:** If Ansell replaces the current compressed-air delivery system with the new one, the annual power cost will be 23% less during the first year and will remain at that level over the next five years. The equivalent present lump-sum cost at 12% interest is

$$P_{\text{Option 2}} = \$54{,}600\,(1 - 0.23)\,(P/A, 12\%, 5)$$
$$= \$42{,}042\,(3.6048)$$
$$= \$151{,}553.$$

- **Step 4:** The net cost of not replacing the old system now is $71{,}384\,(= \$222{,}937 - \$151{,}553)$. Since the new system costs only $28{,}570$, the replacement should be made now.

- Option 1:
  $g = 7\%$
  $i = 12\%$
  $N = 5$ years
  $A_1 = \$54{,}600$

$$P_{\text{Option 1}} = \$54{,}600 \left[\frac{1 - (1+0.07)^5\,(1+0.12)^{-5}}{0.12 - 0.07} \right]$$
$$= \$222{,}937$$

- Option 2:
$$P_{\text{Option 2}} = \$54{,}600(1 - 0.23)(P/A, 12\%, 5)$$
$$= \$42{,}042(P/A, 12\%, 5)$$
$$= \$151{,}553$$

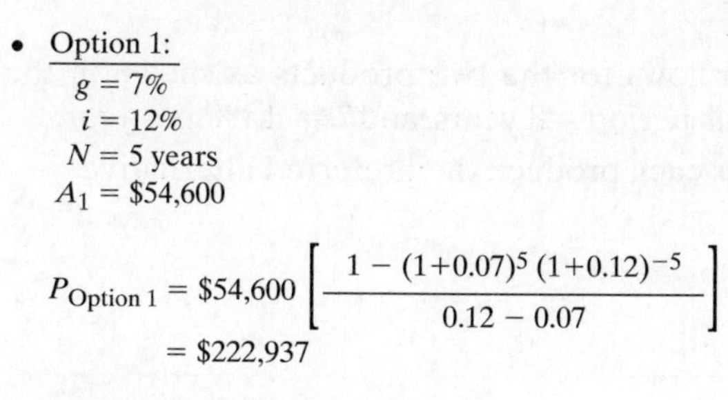

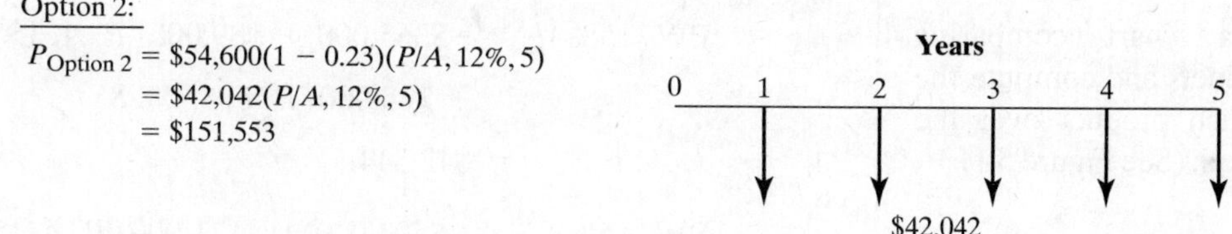

Figure 5.10   Comparing two mutually exclusive options

EXAMPLE 5.6 Comparing Two Mutually Exclusive Revenue Projects

Monroe Manufacturing owns a warehouse that has been used for storing finished goods for electro-pump products. As the company is phasing out the electro-pump product line, the company is considering modifying the existing structure to use for manufacturing a new product line. Monroe's production engineer feels that the warehouse could be modified to handle one of two new product lines. The cost and revenue data for the two product alternatives are as follows:

	Product A	Product B
Initial cash expenditure:		
• Warehouse modification	$115,000	$189,000
• Equipment	$250,000	$315,000
Annual revenues	$215,000	$289,000
Annual O&M costs	$126,000	$168,000
Product life	8 years	8 years
Salvage value (equipment)	$25,000	$35,000

After eight years, the converted building will be too small for efficient production of either product line. At that time, Monroe plans to use it as a warehouse for storing raw materials as before. Monroe's required return on investment is 15%. Which product should be manufactured?

DISSECTING THE PROBLEM

Note that these are revenue projects, so we need to estimate the revenue streams for both product lines. Since the converted building will be used as a warehouse by the firm, there will be no salvage value associated with the building.

Given: Cash flows for the two products as shown in the proceeding table, analysis period = 8 years, and $i = 15\%$ per year.

Find: PW for each product; the preferred alternative.

METHODOLOGY

Construct a chart comparing the two products and compute the NPW for each product over the analysis period. (See Figure 5.11.)

SOLUTION

$$PW(15\%)_A = -\$365,000 + \$89,000\,(P/A, 15\%, 8)$$
$$+ \$25,000\,(P/F, 15\%, 8)$$
$$= \$42,544.$$

$$PW(15\%)_B = -\$504,000 + \$121,000\,(P/A, 15\%, 8)$$
$$+ \$35,000\,(P/F, 15\%, 8)$$
$$= \$50,407.$$

For revenue projects, we select the one with the largest NPW, so producing product B is more economical.

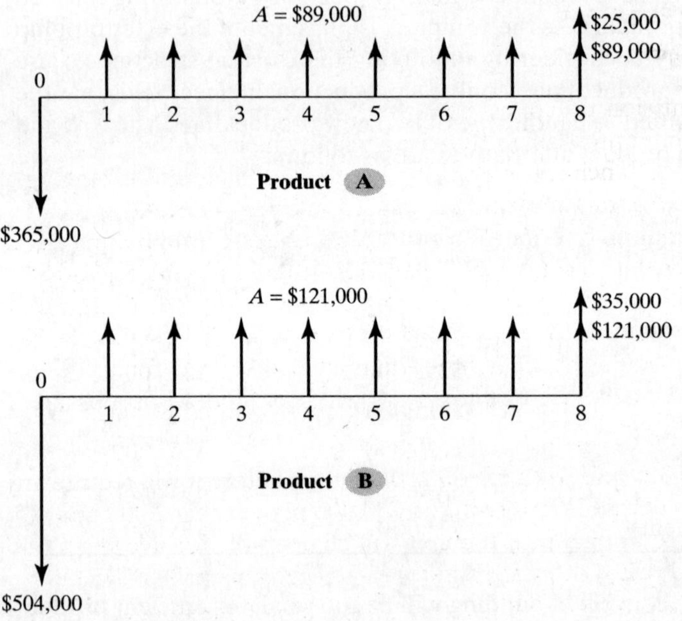

Figure 5.11 Cash flows associated with producing products A and B (revenue projects)

5.4.4 Analysis Period Differs from Project Lives

In Example 5.6, we assumed the simplest scenario possible when analyzing mutually exclusive projects. The projects had useful lives equal to each other and to the required service period. In practice, this is seldom the case. Often project lives do not match the required analysis period or do not match each other. For example, two machines may perform exactly the same function, but one lasts longer than the other, and both of them last longer than the analysis period for which they are being considered. In the upcoming sections and examples, we will develop some techniques for dealing with these complications.

Case I: Project's Life Is Longer than Analysis Period

Consider the case of a firm that undertakes a five-year production project (or plans to phase out the production at the end of five years) when all of the alternative equipment choices have useful lives of seven years. In such a case, we analyze each project only for as long as the required service period (in this case, five years). We are then left with some unused portion of the equipment (in this case, two years' worth), which we include as salvage value in our analysis. **Salvage value** is the amount of money for which the equipment could be sold after its service to the project has been rendered or the dollar measure of its remaining usefulness.

We often find this scenario (project lives that are longer than the analysis period) in the construction industry, where a building project may have a relatively short completion time, but the equipment purchased (power tools, tractors, etc.) has a much longer useful life.

EXAMPLE 5.7 Present-Worth Comparison: Project Lives Longer than the Analysis Period

Allan Company got permission to harvest southern pines from one of its timberland tracts. It is considering purchasing a feller-buncher, which has the ability to hold, saw, and place trees in bunches to be skidded to the log landing. The logging operation on this timberland tract must be completed in *three years*. Allan could speed up the logging operation, but doing so is not desirable because the market demand of the timber does not warrant such haste. Because the logging operation is to be done in wet conditions, this task requires a specially made feller-buncher with high-flotation tires and other devices designed to reduce site impact. There are two possible models of feller-buncher that Allan could purchase for this job: Model A is a two-year old used piece of equipment whereas Model B is a brand-new machine.

- Model A costs $205,000 and has a life of 10,000 hours before it will require any major overhaul. The operating cost will run $50,000 per year for 2,000 hours of operation. At this operational rate, the unit will be operable for five years, and at the end of that time, it is estimated that the salvage value will be $75,000.
- The more efficient Model B costs $275,000, has a life of 14,000 hours before requiring any major overhaul and costs $32,500 to operate for 2,000 hours per year in order to complete the job within three years. The estimated salvage value of Model B at the end of seven years is $95,000.

Since the lifetime of either model exceeds the required service period of three years, Allan Company has to assume some things about the used equipment at the end of that time. Therefore, the engineers at Allan estimate that, after three years, the Model A unit could be sold for $130,000 and the Model B unit for $180,000. After considering all tax effects, Allan summarized the resulting cash flows (in thousands of dollars) for the projects as follows:

Period	Model A		Model B	
0		−$205,000		−$275,000
1		−50,000		−32,500
2		−50,000		−32,500
3	130,000	−50,000	180,000	−32,500
4		−50,000		−32,500
5	75,000	−50,000		−32,500
6				−32,500
7			95,000	−32,500

Here, the figures in the boxes represent the estimated salvage values at the end of the analysis period (end of year 3). Assuming that the firm's MARR is 15%, which option is more acceptable?

DISSECTING THE PROBLEM

First, note that these projects are service projects, so we can assume the same revenues for both configurations. Since the firm explicitly estimated the market values of the assets at the end of the analysis period (three years), we can compare the two models directly. Since the benefits (timber harvesting) are equal, we can concentrate on the costs.

Given: Cash flows for the two alternatives as shown in the preceding table, $i = 15\%$ per year.

Find: PW for each alternative and the preferred alternative.

METHODOLOGY

Construct a chart comparing the options, and compute the NPW for each model over the analysis period (three years).

SOLUTION

Concentrate the costs:

$$PW(15\%)_A = -\$205,000 - \$50,000(P/A, 15\%, 3)$$
$$+ \$130,000(P/F, 15\%, 3)$$
$$= -\$233,684;$$
$$PW(15\%)_B = -\$275,000 - \$32,500(P/A, 15\%, 3)$$
$$+ \$180,000(P/F, 15\%, 3)$$
$$= -\$230,852.$$

Model B is cheaper to operate and thus would be preferred. (See Figure 5.12.)

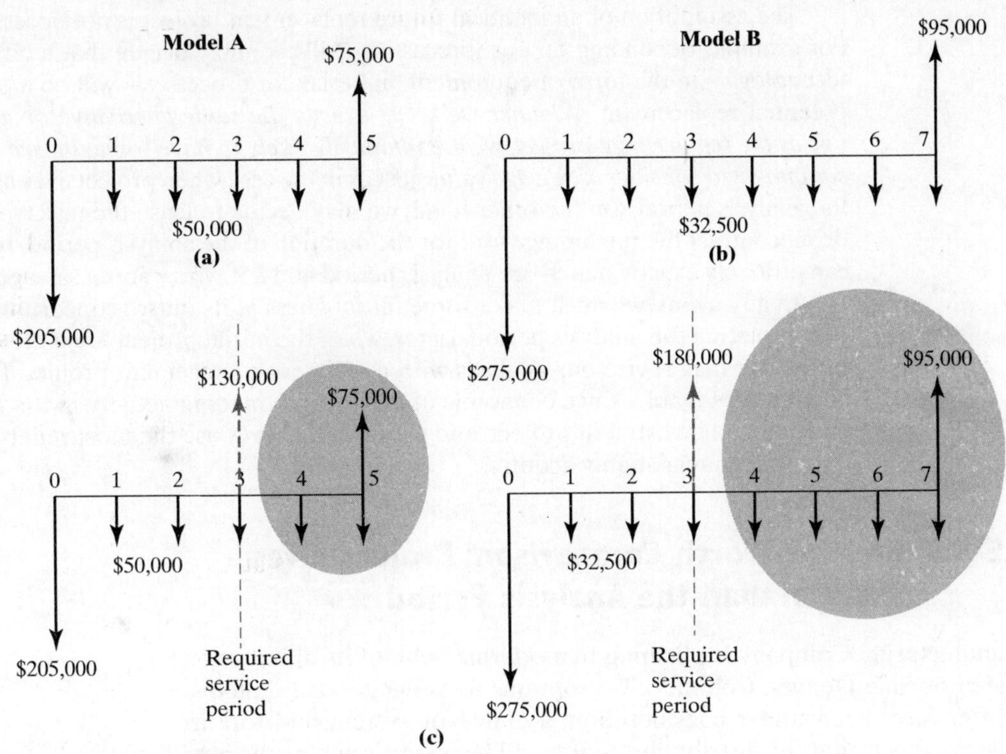

Figure 5.12 (a), (b) If models are not sold after the required service period; (c) if models are sold after the required service period

COMMENTS: The decision heavily depends on the salvage value estimates at the end of the analysis period. Commonly, information about the salvage value of used equipment can be obtained from the equipment vendors because they are familiar with the secondary market for their equipment.

Case II: Project's Life Is Shorter than Analysis Period

When project lives are shorter than the required service period, we must consider how, at the end of a project's life, we will satisfy the rest of the required service period. Replacement projects—implemented when the initial project has reached the limits of its useful life—are needed in such a case. Sufficient replacement projects must be analyzed to match or exceed the required service period.

To simplify our analysis, we could assume that the replacement project will be exactly the same as the initial project with the same corresponding costs and benefits. In the case of an indefinitely ongoing service project, we typically select a finite analysis period by using the **lowest common multiple** of the project's life. For example, if alternative A has a three-year useful life and alternative B has a four-year useful life, we may select 12 years as the analysis period. Because this assumption is rather unrealistic in most real-world problems, we will not advocate the method in this book. However, if such an analysis is warranted, we will demonstrate how the annual-equivalent approach would simplify the mathematical aspect of the analysis in Example 6.7.

The assumption of an identical future replacement project is not necessary, however. For example, depending on our forecasting skills, we may decide that a different kind of technology—in the form of equipment, materials, or processes—will be a preferable and potential replacement. *Whether we select exactly the same alternative or a new technology as the replacement project, we are ultimately likely to have some unused portion of the equipment to consider as salvage value,* just as in the case when project lives are longer than the analysis period. On the other hand, we may decide to lease the necessary equipment or subcontract the remaining work for the duration of the analysis period. In this case, we can probably exactly match our analysis period and not worry about salvage values.

In any event, we must make some initial guess at its outset concerning the method of completing the analysis period. Later, when the initial project life is closer to its expiration, we may revise our analysis with a different replacement project. This approach is quite reasonable, since economic analysis is an ongoing activity in the life of a company and an investment project, and we should always use the most reliable, up-to-date data we can reasonably acquire.

EXAMPLE 5.8 Present-Worth Comparison: Project Lives Shorter than the Analysis Period

Phoenix Manufacturing Company is planning to modernize one of its distribution centers located outside Denver, Colorado. Two options to move goods in the distribution center have been under consideration: a conveyor system and forklift trucks. The firm expects that the distribution center will be operational for the next 10 years, and then it will be converted into a factory outlet. The conveyor system would last eight years whereas the forklift trucks would last only six years. The two options will be designed differently but will have identical capacities and will do exactly the same job. The expected cash flows for the two options, including maintenance costs, salvage values, and tax effects, are as follows:

n	Conveyor System	Lift Trucks
0	−$68,000	−$40,000
1	−$13,000	−$15,000
2	−$13,000	−$15,000
3	−$13,000	−$15,000
4	−$13,000	−$15,000
5	−$13,000	−$15,000
6	−$13,000	−$15,000 + $4,000
7	−$13,000	
8	−$13,000 + $5,000	

With this scenario, which option should the firm select at MARR = 12%?

DISSECTING THE PROBLEM

Given: Cash flows for the two alternatives, analysis period of 10 years, and MARR = 12% per year.

Find: PW for each alternative and the preferred alternative.

METHODOLOGY

Compute cash flows for both models and conduct PW analysis.

SOLUTION

Since each option has a shorter life than the required service period (10 years), we need to make an explicit assumption of how the service requirement is to be met.

- If the company goes with the conveyor system, it will spend $18,000 to overhaul the system to extend its service life beyond eight years. The expected salvage value of the system at the end of the required service period (10 years) will be $6,000. The annual operating and maintenance costs will be $13,000.

- If the company goes with the lift truck option, the company will consider leasing a comparable lift truck that has an annual lease payment of $8,000, payable at the *beginning* of each year, with an annual operating cost of $15,000 for the remaining required service period.

The anticipated cash flows for both models under this scenario are as shown in Figure 5.13. Table 5.5 is an Excel solution to the decision problem. As shown in Table 5.5, note that both alternatives now have the same required service period of 10 years.

Therefore, we can use PW analysis:

$$PW(12\%)_{Conveyor} = -\$68,000 - \$13,000\,(P/A, 12\%, 10)$$
$$- \$18,000\,(P/F, 12\%, 8)$$
$$+ \$6,000\,(P/F, 12\%, 10)$$
$$= -\$146,791;$$

$$PW(12\%)_{Lift\,Trucks} = -\$40,000 - \$15,000\,(P/A, 12\%, 10)$$
$$- \$8,000\,(P/A, 12\%, 4)\,(P/F, 12\%, 5)$$
$$+ \$4,000\,(P/F, 12\%, 6)$$
$$= -\$136,515.$$

Since these projects are service projects, the lift truck option is the better choice.

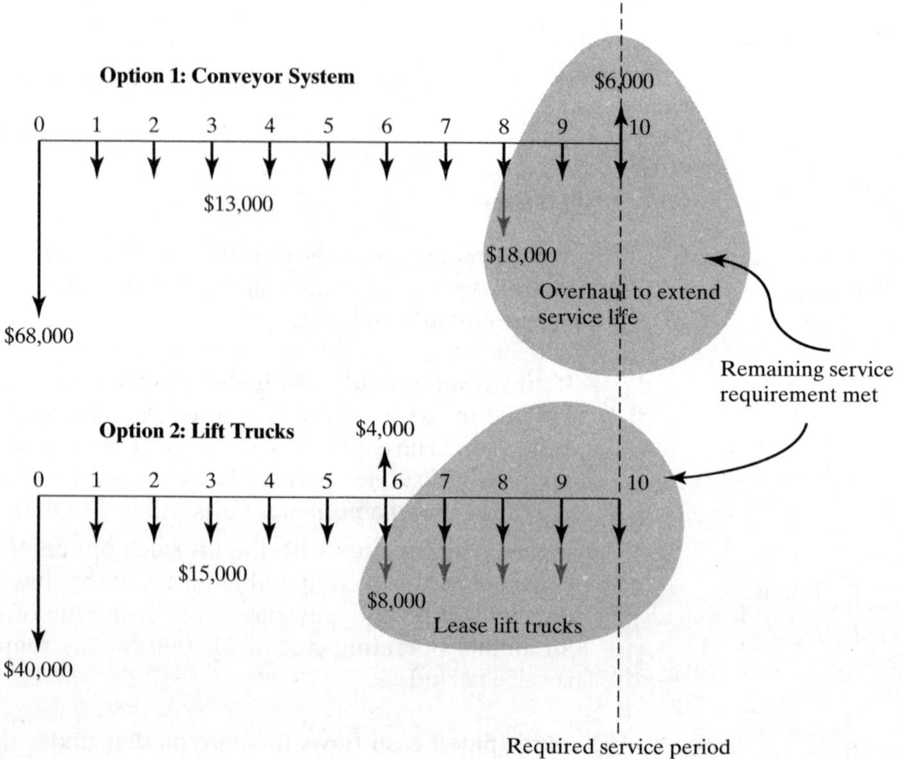

Figure 5.13 Comparison for mutually exclusive service projects with unequal lives when the required service period is longer than the individual project life

TABLE 5.5 An Excel Worksheet to Compare Two Mutually Exclusive Alternatives

	A	B	C	D	E	F	G	H	I	J	K
2		Cash Flow									
3		Conveyor			Lift Trucks				Net Cash Flow		
4	Period	Investment	O&M	Overhaul	Investment	O&M	Lease		Period	Conveyor	Lift trucks
5	0	$ (68,000)			$ (40,000)				0	$ (68,000)	$ (40,000)
6	1		$ (13,000)			$ (15,000)			1	$ (13,000)	$ (15,000)
7	2		$ (13,000)			$ (15,000)			2	$ (13,000)	$ (15,000)
8	3		$ (13,000)			$ (15,000)			3	$ (13,000)	$ (15,000)
9	4		$ (13,000)			$ (15,000)			4	$ (13,000)	$ (15,000)
10	5		$ (13,000)			$ (15,000)			5	$ (13,000)	$ (15,000)
11	6		$ (13,000)		$ 4,000	$ (15,000)	$ (8,000)		6	$ (13,000)	$ (19,000)
12	7		$ (13,000)			$ (15,000)	$ (8,000)		7	$ (13,000)	$ (23,000)
13	8		$ (13,000)	$ (18,000)		$ (15,000)	$ (8,000)		8	$ (31,000)	$ (23,000)
14	9		$ (13,000)			$ (15,000)	$ (8,000)		9	$ (13,000)	$ (23,000)
15	10	$ (6,000)	$ (13,000)			$ (15,000)			10	$ (7,000)	$ (15,000)
16									PW(12%)	$ (146,791)	$ (136,515)
17											

=NPV(12%,J6:J15)+J5

=NPV(12%,K6:K15)+K5

SUMMARY

In this chapter, we presented the concept of present-worth analysis based on cash flow equivalence along with the payback period. We observed the following important results:

- Present worth is an equivalence method of analysis in which a project's cash flows are discounted to a single present value. It is perhaps the most efficient analysis method we can use for determining project acceptability on an economic basis. Other analysis methods, which we will study in Chapters 6 and 7, are built on a sound understanding of present worth.

- The MARR, or minimum attractive rate of return, is the interest rate at which a firm can always earn or borrow money. It is generally dictated by management and is the rate at which PW analysis should be conducted.

- Revenue projects are projects for which the income generated depends on the choice of project. Service projects are projects for which income remains the same regardless of which project is selected.

- The term **mutually exclusive** as applied to a set of alternatives that meet the same need means that when one of the alternatives is selected, the others will be rejected.

- When not specified by management or company policy, the analysis period for use in a comparison of mutually exclusive projects may be chosen by an individual analyst. Several efficiencies can be applied when we select an analysis period. In general, the analysis period should be chosen to cover the required service period.

SELF-TEST QUESTIONS

5s.1 An investment project costs $100,000. It is expected to have an annual net cash flow of $40,000 for 5 years. What is the project's payback period?

(a) 2.5 years

(b) 3.5 year

(c) 4.5 years

(d) 5 years

5s.2 Find the net present worth of the following cash flow series at an interest rate of 8%.

End of Period	Cash Flow
0	–$1,000
1	–2,000
2	3,000
3	4,500
4	1,500

(a) $4,067

(b) $6,000

(c) $4,394

(d) $6,549

5s.3 You are considering buying a CNC machine. This machine will have an estimated service life of 10 years with a salvage value of 5% of the investment cost. Its annual net revenues are estimated to be $40,000. To expect a 15% rate of return on investment, what would be the maximum amount that you are willing to pay for the machine?

(a) $213,065

(b) $203,240

(c) $249,998

(d) $276,860

5s.4 What is the future worth in year 10 of $5,000 at $n = 0$, $10,000 at $n = 3$ years, and $8,000 at $n = 5$ years if the interest rate is 12% per year?

(a) $16,657

(b) $51,735

(c) $71,435

(d) $40,533

5s.5 You invested $100,000 in a project and received $40,000 at $n = 1$, $40,000 at $n = 2$, and $30,000 at $n = 3$ years. You need to terminate the project at the end of year 3. Your interest rate is 10%; what is the project balance at the time of termination?

(a) Gain of $10,000

(b) Loss of $8,039

(c) Loss of $10,700

(d) Just break even

5s.6 Find the capitalized equivalent worth for the project cash flow series with repeating cycles at an interest rate of 10%.

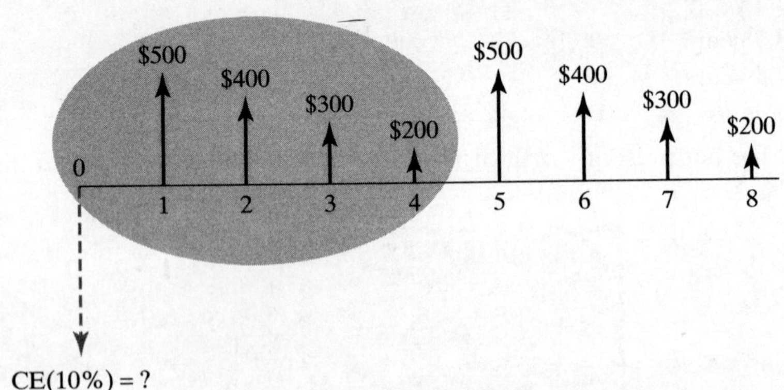

(a) $1,147

(b) $1,679

(c) $3,619

(d) $6,381

5s.7   The following table contains a summary of expected changes to a project's balance over its five-year service life at 10% interest.

End of Period	Project Balance
0	−$1,000
1	−1,500
2	600
3	900
4	1,500
5	2,000

Which of the following statements is incorrect?
(a) The required additional investment at the end of period 1 is $500.
(b) The net present worth of the project at 10% interest is $1,242.
(c) The net future of the project at 10% interest is $2,000.
(d) Within two years, the company will recover all its investments and the cost of funds (interest) from the project.

5s.8   A&M Corporation purchased a vibratory finishing machine for $20,000 in year 0. The machine's useful life is 10 years at the end of which the machine is estimated to have a zero salvage value. The machine generates net annual revenues of $6,000. The annual operating and maintenance expenses are estimated to be $1,000. If A&M's MARR is 15%, how many years does it take before this machine becomes profitable?
(a) 3 years $<n \leq 4$ years
(b) 4 years $<n \leq 5$ years
(c) 5 years $<n \leq 6$ years
(d) 6 years $<n \leq 7$ years

5s.9   You are considering buying an old warehouse that you will convert into an office building for rental. Assuming that you will own the property for 10 years, how much would you be willing to pay for the old house now given the following financial data?
- Remodeling cost at period 0 = $550,000;
- Annual rental income = $800,000;
- Annual upkeep costs (including taxes) = $80,000;
- Estimated net property value (after taxes) at the end of 10 years = $2,225,000;
- The time value of your money (interest rate) = 8% per year.
(a) $4,445,770
(b) $5,033,400
(c) $5,311,865
(d) $5,812,665

5s.10 Alpha Company is planning to invest in a machine, the use of which will result in the following:

- Annual revenues of $10,000 in the first year and increases of $5,000 each year, up to year 9. From year 10, the revenues will remain constant ($52,000) for an indefinite period.
- The machine is to be overhauled every 10 years. The expense for each overhaul is $40,000.

If Alpha expects a present worth of at least $100,000 at a MARR of 10% for this project, what is the maximum investment that Alpha should be prepared to make?

(a) $250,140

(b) $674,697

(c) $350,100

(d) $509,600

5s.11 Consider the following two mutually exclusive investment alternatives:

	Net Cash Flow	
End of Year	**Machine A**	**Machine B**
0	−$2,000	−$1,000
1	−$600	−$900
2	−$700	−$1,000 + $200
3	−$800 + $500	

Suppose that your firm needs either machine for only two years. The net proceeds from the sale of machine B are estimated to be $200. What should be the required net proceeds from the sale of machine A in two years so that both machines could be considered economically indifferent at an interest rate of 10%?

(a) $750

(b) $780

(c) $800

(d) $850

PROBLEMS

Note: Unless otherwise stated, all cash flows are in *actual dollars* with tax effects considered. The interest rate (MARR) is also given on an after-tax basis, considering the effects of inflation in the economy. This interest rate is equivalent to the market interest rate. Also, all interest rates are assumed to be compounded *annually*.

Identifying Cash Inflows and Outflows

5.1 K&J Enterprise Inc. has purchased a small motor engine line to go in golf carts. The total purchase cost was $1.5 million, which can generate revenues of $650,000 per year. Direct manufacturing costs are expected to run $220,000 a year and other fixed cost expenditures would be somewhere near $80,000 a year. The O&M cost would be around $45,000 a year, and K&J expects to pay various taxes including income taxes of $58,000. The project would last about 10 years and at that time, the business could be sold for $1 million. Determine the project cash flows over a 10-year period.

5.2   Delaware Chemicals is considering the installation of a computer process control system in one of its processing plants. This plant is used about 40% of the time, or 3,500 operating hours per year, to produce a proprietary demulsification chemical; during the remaining 60% of the time, it is used to produce other specialty chemicals. The annual production of the demulsification chemical amounts to 30,000 kilograms per year, and it sells for $15 per kilogram. The proposed computer process control system will cost $65,000 and is expected to provide specific benefits in the production of the demulsification chemical as follows:

- First, the selling price of the product could be increased by $2 per kilogram because the product would be of higher purity, which translates into better demulsification performance.

- Second, production volumes would increase by 4,000 kilograms per year as a result of higher reaction yields, without any increase in requirements for raw material quantities or production time.

- Finally, the number of process operators could be reduced by one per shift, which represents a savings of $25 per hour. The new control system would result in additional maintenance costs of $53,000 per year and has an expected useful life of eight years.

While the system is likely to provide similar benefits in the production of the other specialty chemicals manufactured in the process plant, these have not been quantified as yet.

(a) Identify the cash inflows over the life of the project.

(b) Identify the cash outflows over the life of the project.

(c) Determine the net cash flows over the life of the project.

5.3   As a chief engineer, you need to come up with the cash flow estimate for a newly proposed production line. Initially, the system is designed to have a maximum capacity (C_{max}) of six million parts to produce per year, but the demand is expected to grow at an annual compound rate of 10%. Whenever the annual demand reaches 80% of the maximum designed capacity, the maximum designed capacity must be doubled in the subsequent year. The cost of meeting these future demands, as well as other projected financial data, are as follows:

- Cost of building the production system as a function of maximum designed capacity:

$$1.5\,M + 0.5\,(C_{max})^{0.7}.$$

- Initial demand = 3 million parts per year.
- Demand growth rate = 10% per year.
- Project life = 15 years.
- Revenues per year = demand during year $n \times (5)^{1.05}$.
- Expenses per year = $120,000 + demand during year $n \times (2)^{1.08}$.

Estimate the project cash flows over the project life.

Payback Period

5.4 An investment project provides cash inflows of $3,000 per year for five years. What is the payback period if the project requires $5,000 at the beginning of the project?

5.5 Consider a project with the following cash flows:

End of Year (n)	Cash Flows ($)
0	−$22,400
1	4,500
2	12,670
3	14,780
4	13,650
5	11,440
6	7,800

(a) At an interest rate of 18%, what is the discounted payback period?

(b) What is the discounted payback period if the interest rate is 0%?

5.6 Refer to Problem 5.2 in answering the following questions:

(a) How long does it take to recover the investment?

(b) If the firm's interest rate is 15%, what would be the discounted-payback period for this project?

5.7 J&M Manufacturing plans on purchasing a new assembly machine for $32,000 to automate one of its current manufacturing operations. It will cost an additional $3,500 to have the new machine installed. With the new machine, J&M expects to save $12,000 in annual operating and maintenance costs. The machine will last five years with an expected salvage value of $5,000.

(a) How long will it take to recover the investment (plus installation cost)?

(b) If J&M's interest rate is known to be 17%, determine the discounted payback period.

5.8 You are given the following financial data about a new system to be implemented at a company:

- Investment cost at $n = 0$: $23,000
- Investment cost at $n = 1$: $18,000
- Useful life: 10 years
- Salvage value (at the end of 11 years): $7,000
- Annual revenues: $19,000 per year
- Annual expenses: $6,000 per year
- MARR: 10%

Note: The first revenues and expenses will occur at the end of year 2.

(a) Determine the conventional-payback period.

(b) Determine the discounted-payback period.

5.9 Consider the following cash flows, for four different projects:

Project Cash Flows

n	A	B	C	D
0	−$2,500	−$6,000	−$13,000	−$14,500
1	$600	$2,500	$3,000	$6,000
2	$500	$1,000	$4,000	$9,000
3	$500	$1,500	$5,000	−$4,000
4	$700	$500	$6,000	$5,000
5	$800	$500	$7,000	$1,000
6	$400	$1,500		$2,000
7	$400			$3,000
8	$400			

(a) Calculate the conventional payback period for each project.
(b) Determine whether it is meaningful to calculate a payback period for Project D.
(c) Assuming $i = 10\%$ calculate the discounted-payback period for each project.

NPW Criterion

5.10 The Northern Investment Group is considering investing $2.5 million in a new shopping plaza in Atlanta. The company has estimated that the shopping plaza, once built, will generate $500,000 per year for 10 years. If the firm is looking for a return of 12% on its investment, is it worth undertaking? Assume that the shopping plaza will retain about 60% of its initial investment as salvage value.

5.11 Due to a high demand for corn as a source of ethanol fuel production, a farmer is considering planting more corn, which requires the purchase of a new, larger row crop planter. The planter will cost $25,000 and has an expected service life of six years with salvage value of 10% of the initial purchase price. The new planter allows the farmer to plant the crop in less time and to increase average crop yields. The net cash flow from this more efficient planter is as follows:

n	A_n
0	−$25,000
1	$6,800
2	$6,350
3	$8,735
4	$7,500
5	$4,300
6	$7,000 + $1,800

What is the net present value for this purchase if the farmer's interest rate is 9%?

5.12 You are considering producing a new golf ball for sale in China to meet a growing demand in the country. This golf ball is less expensive to manufacture compared with a better known brand, but it meets all requirements set by the United States Golf Association (USGA) for play at any competitive event. Production will require an initial outlay for the purchase of equipment worth $1,500,000. The equipment has a six-year life with an expected salvage value of $100,000. You already own the land on which the project will be located. The land has a current market value of $100,000, and its price is expected to grow by 5% per year. If you decide not to produce the golf balls, you will sell the land. You have also gathered the following information:

- You expect revenue of $500,000 per year for each year of operation. Your direct cost of producing the golf ball is expected to be 30% of the revenue.
- The operating cost, including marketing, is another 15% of the revenue.
- You will need to pay a license fee in the amount of $25,000 plus 3% of revenue, to the company that originally came up with the special dimple design of the golf ball.

(a) Is this project worthwhile at an interest rate of 15%?

(b) How long will it take to recover the initial investment and cost of funds at 15%?

5.13 Consider the following set of investment projects, all of which have a three-year investment life:

Project Cash Flows

n	A	B	C	D
0	-$1,200	-$1,800	-$1,000	-$6,500
1	$0	$600	-$1,200	$2,500
2	$0	$900	$900	$1,900
3	$3,000	$1,700	$3,500	$2,800

(a) Compute the net present worth of each project at $i = 10\%$.

(b) Plot the present worth as a function of the interest rate (from 0% to 30%) for Project B.

5.14 You have been asked to evaluate the profitability of building a new distribution center under the following conditions:

- The proposal is for a distribution center costing $1,500,000. The facility has an expected useful life of 35 years and a net salvage value (net proceeds from its sale after tax adjustments) of $225,000.
- Annual savings (due to a better strategic location) of $227,000 are expected, annual maintenance and administrative costs will be $114,000, and annual income taxes are $43,000.

Suppose that the firm's MARR is 12%. Determine the net present worth of the investment.

5.15 You are considering the purchase of a parking deck close to your office building. The parking deck is a 15-year old structure with an estimated remaining service life of 25 years. The tenants have recently signed long-term leases, which leads you to believe that the current rental income of $250,000 per year will remain constant for the first five years. Then the rental income will increase by 10% for every five-year interval over the remaining asset life. Thus, the annual rental income would be $275,000 for years 6 through 10, $302,500 for years 11 through 15, $332,750 for years 16 through 20, and $366,025 for years 21 through 25. You estimate that operating expenses, including income taxes, will be $65,000 for the first year and that they will increase by $6,000 each year thereafter. You estimate that razing the building and selling the lot on which it stands will realize a net amount of $200,000 at the end of the 25-year period. If you had the opportunity to invest your money elsewhere and thereby earn interest at the rate of 15% per annum, what would be the maximum amount you would be willing to pay for the parking deck and lot at the present time?

5.16 Consider the following investment project:

n	A_n	i
0	−$8,500	9%
1	$4,400	12%
2	$4,400	10%
3	$1,500	13%
4	$3,500	12%
5	$4,300	10%

Suppose, as shown in the preceding table, that the company's reinvestment opportunities (that is, its MARR) change over the life of the project. For example, the company can invest funds available now at 9% for the first year, 12% for the second year, and so forth. Calculate the net present worth of this investment, and determine its acceptability.

5.17 You are in the mail-order business, selling computer peripherals, including high-speed Internet cables, various storage devices such as memory sticks, and wireless networking devices. You are considering upgrading your mail ordering system to make your operations more efficient and to increase sales. The computerized ordering system will cost $250,000 to install and $50,000 to operate each year. The system is expected to last eight years with no salvage value at the end of the service period. The new order system will save $120,000 in operating costs (mainly, reduction in inventory carrying cost) each year and bring in additional sales revenue in the amount of $40,000 per year for the next eight years. If your interest rate is 12%, justify your investment using the NPW method.

5.18 A large food-processing corporation is considering using laser technology to speed up and eliminate waste in the potato-peeling process. To implement the system, the company anticipates needing $3 million to purchase the industrial-strength lasers. The system will save $1,200,000 per year in labor and materials. However, it will incur an additional operating and maintenance cost of $250,000 per year. Annual income taxes will also increase by $150,000. The system is expected to have a 10-year service life and a salvage value of about $200,000. If the company's MARR is 18%, justify the economics of the project using the PW method.

5.19 A university is trying to determine how much it should charge for tickets to basketball games to help offset the expenses of the new arena. The cost to build the arena including labor, materials, etc. was $92 million. Each year the maintenance cost is expected to increase by 5% as the building gets older. The maintenance cost for the first year is $150,000. Utilities are expected to average about $200,000 per year and labor costs $300,000. The average attendance at basketball games over the year is expected to be 100,000 people (or 100,000 tickets sold to events). Assuming the arena has no other source of income besides regular ticket sales (not including student tickets) for basketball games, what should the university charge so that it can recover at least 6% cost of borrowing on its investment? The university expects the arena to be used for 40 years and to have no appreciable salvage value.

Future Worth and Project Balance

5.20 Consider the following sets of investment projects, each of which has a three-year investment life:

Period	Project Cash Flows			
n	A	B	C	D
0	−$6,000	−$2,500	$4,800	−$4,100
1	$5,800	−$4,400	−$6,000	$1,000
2	$12,400	$7,000	$2,000	$5,000
3	$8,200	$3,000	$4,000	$6,000

Compute the net future worth of each project at $i = 16\%$.

5.21 Consider the following information for a typical investment project with a service life of five years:

n	Cash Flow	Project Balance
0	−$1,000	−$1,000
1	$200	−$900
2	$490	−$500
3	$550	$0
4	−$100	−$100
5	$200	$90

What interest rate is used in the project-balance calculation?

5.22 Consider the following project balances for a typical investment project with a service life of four years:

n	A_n	Project Balance
0	−$1,000	−$1,000
1	( )	−$1,100
2	( )	−$800
3	$460	−$500
4	( )	$0

(a) Construct the original cash flows of the project.

(b) Determine the interest rate used in computing the project balance.

(c) Would this project be acceptable at a MARR of 12%?

5.23 Consider the following project-balance profiles for proposed investment projects:

Project Balances

n	Project A	Project B	Project C
0	−$600	−$500	−$200
1	$200	$300	$0
2	$300	$650	$150
PW	?	$416	?
Rate used	15%	?	?

Now consider the following statements:

 Statement 1: For Project A, the cash flow at the end of year 2 is $100.

 Statement 2: The future value of Project C is $0.

 Statement 3: The interest rate used in the Project B balance calculations is 25%.

Which of the preceding statements is (are) correct?

(a) Just statement 1.

(b) Just statement 2.

(c) Just statement 3.

(d) All of them.

5.24 A project has a service of five years with the initial investment outlay of $180,000. If the discounted payback period occurs at the end of project service life (say five years) at an interest rate of 8%, what can you say about the NFW of the project?

5.25 Consider the following cash flows and present-worth profiles on Page 218:

Net Cash Flows

Year	Project 1	Project 2
0	−$100	−$100
1	$40	$30
2	$80	$Y
3	$X	$80

(a) Determine the values for X and Y.

(b) Calculate the terminal project balance of Project 1 at MARR = 24%.

(c) Find the values for $a, b,$ and c in the PW plot.

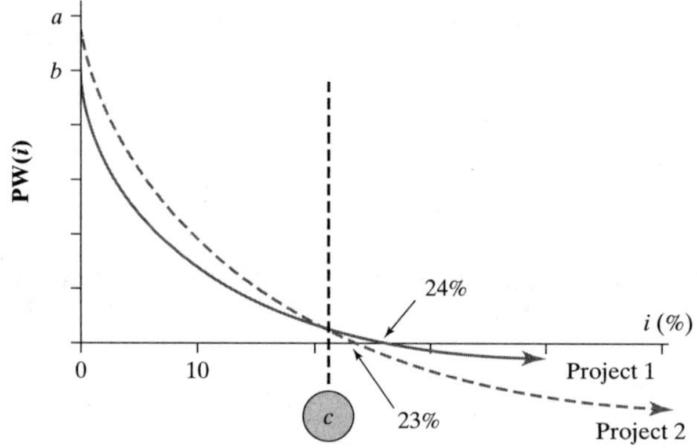

5.26 Consider the following project balances for a typical investment project with a service life of five years:

n	A_n	Project Balance
0	−$1,000	−$1,000
1	( )	−$900
2	$490	−$500
3	( )	$0
4	( )	−$100
5	$200	( )

(a) Fill in the blanks by constructing the original cash flows of the project and determining the terminal balance.

(b) Determine the interest rate used in the project-balance calculation, and compute the present worth of this project at the computed interest rate.

5.27 Consider the following sets of investment projects:

	Project Cash Flows				
n	A	B	C	D	E
0	−$6,000	−$6,000	−$6,000	−$6,000	−$6,000
1	$500	$2,000	$0	$500	$1,000
2	$900	−$3,000	$0	$2,000	$3,000
3	$1,000	$5,000	$3,000	$3,000	$2,000
4	$2,000	$5,000	$7,000	$4,000	
5	−$500	$3,500	$13,000	$1,250	

(a) Compute the future worth at the end of life for each project at $i = 15\%$.
(b) Determine the area of negative project balance for each project.
(c) Determine the discounted payback period for each project.
(d) Determine the area of positive project balance for each project.

5.28 Consider the following set of independent investment projects:

Project Cash Flows

n	A	B	C
0	−$200	−$100	$120
1	$50	$40	−$40
2	$50	$40	−$40
3	$50	$40	−$40
4	−$100	$10	
5	$400	$10	
6	$400		

(a) For a MARR of 10%, compute the net present worth for each project, and determine the acceptability of each project.

(b) For a MARR of 10%, compute the net future worth of each project at the end of each project period, and determine the acceptability of each project.

(c) Compute the future worth of each project at the end of six years with variable MARRs as follows: 10% for $n = 0$ to $n = 3$ and 15% for $n = 4$ to $n = 6$.

5.29 Consider the following project-balance profiles for proposed investment projects, where the project-balance figures are rounded to the nearest dollar:

Project Balances

n	A	B	C
0	−$1,000	−$1,000	−$1,000
1	−$800	−$680	−$530
2	−$600	−$302	$X
3	−$400	−$57	−$211
4	−$200	$233	−$89
5	$0	$575	$0
Interest rate used	0%	18%	12%

(a) Compute the net present worth of each investment.

(b) Determine the project balance at the end of period 2 for Project C if $A_2 = 500.

(c) Determine the cash flows for each project.

(d) Identify the net future worth of each project.

Capitalized-Equivalent Worth

5.30 Maintenance money for a new building at a college is being solicited from potential alumni donors. You would like to make a donation to cover all future expected maintenance costs for the building. These maintenance costs are expected to be $40,000 each year for the first five years, $50,000 for each of years 6 through 10, and $60,000 each year after that. (The building has an indefinite service life.)

(a) If the money is placed in an account that will pay 13% interest compounded annually, how large should the gift be?

(b) What is the equivalent annual maintenance cost over the infinite service life?

5.31 Consider an investment project for which the cash flow pattern repeats itself every four years indefinitely, as shown in the accompanying figure. At an interest rate of 12% compounded annually, compute the capitalized-equivalent amount for this project.

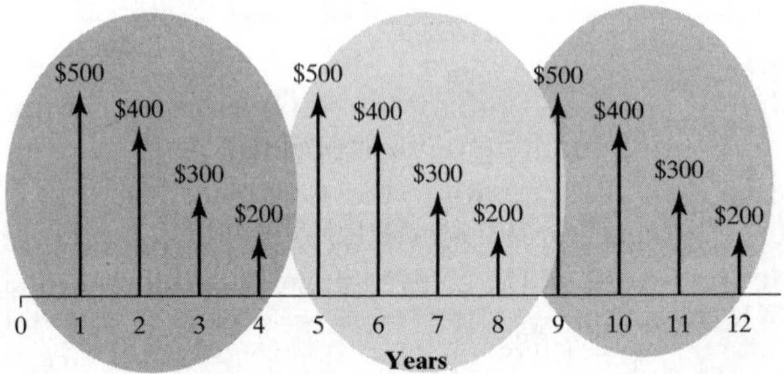

5.32 A group of concerned citizens has established a trust fund that pays 6% interest compounded monthly to preserve a historical building by providing annual maintenance funds of $25,000 forever. Compute the capitalized-equivalent amount for these building maintenance expenses.

5.33 A newly constructed bridge costs $10,000,000. The same bridge is estimated to need renovation every 10 years at a cost of $1,000,000. Annual repairs and maintenance are estimated to be $100,000 per year.

(a) If the interest rate is 5%, determine the capitalized-equivalent cost of the bridge.

(b) Suppose that the bridge must be renovated every 15 years, not every 10 years. What is the capitalized cost of the bridge if the interest rate is the same as in (a)?

(c) Repeat (a) and (b) with an interest rate of 10%. What can you say about the effect of interest on the results?

5.34 To decrease the costs of operating a lock in a large river, a new system of operation is proposed. The system will cost $650,000 to design and build. It is estimated that it will have to be reworked every 10 years at a cost of $100,000. In addition, an expenditure of $50,000 will have to be made at the end of the fifth year for a new type of gear that will not be available until then. Annual operating costs are expected to be $30,000 for the first 15 years and $35,000 a year thereafter. Compute the capitalized cost of perpetual service at $i = 8\%$.

5.35 Consider a retired gentleman who starts to collect his Social Security benefits at the age of 66. The monthly check would be close to $2,460. Assuming that his interest rate is 6% compounded monthly, answer the following questions:

(a) If he lives 20 years after retirement, what would be the equivalent total Social Security benefit collected?

(b) If he lives 40 years after retirement, what would be the equivalent total Social Security benefit collected?

(c) Suppose he lives forever. What would be the total amount collected? Now, comparing this answer with that in (b), what can you conclude?

Comparing Mutually Exclusive Alternatives

5.36 Consider the following two mutually exclusive projects:

	Net Cash Flow	
End of Year	**Project A**	**Project B**
0	−$1,000	−$1,000
1	$912	$284
2	$684	$568
3	$456	$852
4	$228	$1,136

(a) At an interest rate of 25%, which project would you recommend choosing?

(b) Compute the area of negative project balance, discounted payback period, and area of positive project balance for each project. Which project is exposed to a higher risk of loss if either project terminates at the end of year 2?

5.37 Consider the following cash flow data for two competing investment projects:

	Cash Flow Data (thousands of $)	
n	**Project A**	**Project B**
0	−$1,000,000	−$1,200,000
1	$700,000	$700,000
2	$700,000	$1,000,000

(a) At $i = 12\%$, which of the two projects would be a better choice?

(b) At $i = 22\%$, which project is chosen by the NPW rule?

5.38 Consider the following two mutually exclusive investment projects:

	Project Cash Flows	
n	**A**	**B**
0	−$5,000	−$3,200
1	$2,610	$1,210
2	$2,930	$1,720
3	$2,300	$1,500

Assume that the MARR $= 12\%$.

(a) Which alternative would you select by using the NPW criterion?

(b) Which alternative would you select by using the net-future-worth criterion?

5.39 Consider the following two mutually exclusive investment projects:

Project Cash Flows

n	A	B
0	−$4,000	−$8,500
1	$400	$11,500
2	$7,000	$400

Assume that the MARR $= 15\%$.

(a) Using the NPW criterion, which project would you select?

(b) On the same chart, sketch the PW(i) function for each alternative for $i = 0\%$ and 50%. For what range of i would you prefer Project B?

5.40 Consider the following two investment alternatives:

The firm's MARR is known to be 15%.

(a) Compute the PW (15%) for Project A.

Project Cash Flows

n	A	B
0	−$15,000	−$25,000
1	$9,500	$0
2	$12,500	$X
3	$7,500	$X
PW(15%)	?	$9,300

(b) Compute the unknown cash flow X in years 2 and 3 for Project B.

(c) Compute the project balance (at 15%) for Project A at the end of year 3.

(d) If these two projects are mutually exclusive alternatives, which project would you select?

5.41 Consider the following two mutually exclusive projects:

n	A	B
0	−$12,000	−$10,000
1	$4,000	$X
2	$6,000	$3,000
3	$8,000	$X

What value of X would make the decision maker indifferent between A and B at an interest rate of 12%?

5.42 Consider the following after-tax cash flows:

Project Cash Flows

n	A	B	C	D
0	−$2,500	−$7,000	−$5,000	−$5,000
1	$650	−$2,500	−$2,000	−$500
2	$650	−$2,000	−$2,000	−$500
3	$650	−$1,500	−$2,000	$4,000
4	$600	−$1,500	−$2,000	$3,000
5	$600	−$1,500	−$2,000	$3,000
6	$600	−$1,500	−$2,000	$2,000
7	$300		−$2,000	$3,000
8	$300			

(a) Compute the project balances for Projects A and D, as a function of project year, at $i = 10\%$.

(b) Compute the future worth values for Projects A and D at $i = 10\%$ at the end of service life.

(c) Suppose that Projects B and C are mutually exclusive. Assume also that the required service period is eight years and that the company is considering leasing comparable equipment that has an annual lease expense of $3,000 for the remaining years of the required service period. Which project is the better choice?

5.43 Consider the following two mutually exclusive investment projects:

Project Cash Flows

n	A	B
0	−$11,000	−$25,000
1	$7,500	$14,500
2	$8,000	$18,000
3	$5,000	

Which project would you select if you used the infinite planning horizon with project repeatability likely (same costs and benefits) based on the PW criterion? Assume that $i = 12\%$.

5.44 Consider the following two mutually exclusive investment projects that have unequal service lives:

Project Cash Flows

n	A	B
0	−$1,200	−$2,100
1	−$400	−$300
2	−$400	−$300
3	−$400 + $200	−$300

(continued)

n	A	B
4		−$300
5		−$300
6		−$300
7		−$300
8		−$300 + $500

(a) What assumption(s) do you need in order to compare a set of mutually exclusive investments with unequal service lives?

(b) With the assumption(s) defined in (a) and using $i = 10\%$, determine which project should be selected.

(c) If your analysis period (study period) is just three years, what should be the salvage value of Project B at the end of year 3 in order to make the two alternatives economically indifferent?

5.45 Consider the following two mutually exclusive investment projects:

	A		B	
n	Cash Flow	Salvage Value	Cash Flow	Salvage Value
0	−$12,000		−$10,000	
1	−$2,000	$6,000	−$2,100	$6,000
2	−$2,000	$4,000	−$2,100	$3,000
3	−$2,000	$3,000	−$2,100	$1,000
4	−$2,000	$2,000		
5	−$2,000	$2,000		

Salvage values represent the net proceeds (after tax) from the disposal of assets if they are sold at the end of the year listed. Both projects will be available (and can be repeated) with the same costs and salvage values for an indefinite period.

(a) With an infinite planning horizon, which project is a better choice at MARR = 12%?

(b) With a 10-year planning horizon, which project is a better choice at MARR = 12%?

5.46 Two methods of carrying away surface runoff water from a new subdivision are being evaluated:

■ Method A: Dig a ditch. The initial cost would be $30,000, and $10,000 of redigging and shaping would be required at five-year intervals forever.

■ Method B: Lay concrete pipe. The initial cost would be $75,000, and replacement pipe would be required at 50-year intervals at a net cost of $90,000 indefinitely.

At $i = 12\%$, which method is the better one? (*Hint*: Use the capitalized-equivalent-worth approach.)

5.47 A local car dealer is advertising a standard 24-month lease of $1,150 per month for its new XT 3000 series sports car. The standard lease requires a down payment of $4,500 plus a $1,000 refundable initial deposit now. The first lease payment is due at the end of month 1. Alternatively, the dealer offers a 24-month lease plan that has a single up-front payment of $30,500 plus a refundable initial deposit of $1,000. Under both options, the initial deposit will be refunded at the end of month 24. Assume an interest rate of 6% compounded monthly. With the present-worth criterion, which option is preferred?

5.48 Two alternative machines are being considered for a manufacturing process. Machine A has an initial cost of $75,200, and its estimated salvage value at the end of its six years of service life is $21,000. The operating costs of this machine are estimated to be $6,800 per year. Extra income taxes are estimated at $2,400 per year. Machine B has an initial cost of $44,000, and its salvage value at the end of its six years of service life is estimated to be negligible. Its annual operating costs will be $11,500. Compare these two alternatives by the present-worth method at $i = 13\%$.

5.49 An electric motor is rated at 10 horsepower (HP) and costs $800. Its full-load efficiency is specified to be 85%. A newly designed, high-efficiency motor of the same size has an efficiency of 90%, but costs $1,200. It is estimated that the motors will operate at a rated 10-HP output for 1,500 hours a year, and the cost of energy will be $0.07 per kilowatt-hour. Each motor is expected to have a 15-year life. At the end of 15 years, the first motor will have a salvage value of $50, and the second motor will have a salvage value of $100. Consider the MARR to be 8%. (Note: $1\,\text{HP} = 0.7457\,\text{kW}$.)

(a) Determine which motor should be installed based on the PW criterion.

(b) What if the motors operated 2,500 hours a year instead of 1,500 hours a year? Would the motor selected in (a) still be the choice?

5.50 Consider the following cash flows for two types of models:

Project Cash Flows

n	Model A	Model B
0	−$6,600	−$16,500
1	$3,500	$11,000
2	$4,500	$12,000
3	$5,500	

Both models will have no salvage value upon their disposal (at the end of their respective service lives). The firm's MARR is known to be 15%.

(a) Notice that both models have different service lives. However, Model A will be available in the future with the same cash flows. Model B is available now only. If you select Model B now, you will have to replace it with Model A at the end of year 2. If your firm uses the present worth as a decision criterion, which model should be selected, assuming that your firm will need one of the two models for an indefinite period?

(b) Suppose that your firm will need either model for only two years. Determine the salvage value of Model A at the end of year 2 that makes both models indifferent (equally likely).

5.51 An electric utility company is taking bids on the purchase, installation, and operation of microwave towers:

Cost per Tower

	Bid A	Bid B
Equipment cost	$65,000	$58,000
Installation cost	$15,000	$20,000
Annual maintenance and inspection fee	$1,000	$1,250
Annual extra income taxes		$500
Life	40 years	35 years
Salvage value	$0	$0

Which is the most economical bid if the interest rate is 11%? Both towers will have no salvage value after 20 years of use.

5.52 A bi-level mall is under construction. Installation of only nine escalators is planned at the start although the ultimate design calls for 16. The question arises whether to provide necessary facilities that would permit the installation of the additional escalators (e.g., stair supports, wiring conduits, and motor foundations) at the mere cost of their purchase and installation now or to defer investment in these facilities until the escalators need to be installed. The two options are detailed as follows:

- **Option 1:** Provide these facilities now for all seven future escalators at $200,000.

- **Option 2:** Defer the investment as needed. Installation of two more escalators is planned in two years, three more in five years, and the last two in eight years. The installation of these facilities at the time they are required is estimated to cost $100,000 in year 2, $160,000 in year 5, and $140,000 in year 8. Additional annual expenses are estimated at $3,000 for each escalator facility installed.

5.53 A large refinery and petrochemical complex is planning to manufacture caustic soda, which will use 10,000 gallons of feed water per day. Two types of feed-water storage installation are being considered to serve over 40 years of useful life:

- **Option 1:** Build a 20,000-gallon tank on a tower. The cost of installing the tank and tower is estimated to be $164,000. The salvage value is estimated to be negligible.

- **Option 2:** Place a 20,000-gallon tank of equal capacity on a hill that is 150 yards away from the refinery. The cost of installing the tank on the hill, including the extra length of service lines, is estimated to be $120,000 with negligible salvage value. Because of its hill location, an additional investment of $12,000 in pumping equipment is required. The pumping equipment is expected to have a service life of 20 years with a salvage value of $1,000 at the end of that time. The annual operating and maintenance cost (including any income-tax effects) for the pumping operation is estimated at $1,000.

If the firm's MARR is known to be 12%, which option is better, calculated on the basis of the present-worth criterion? At an interest rate of 12%, compare the net present worth of each option over eight years.

5.54 Consider the following two mutually exclusive service projects with project lives of three years and two years, respectively. (The mutually exclusive service projects will have identical revenues for each year of service.) The interest rate is known to be 12%.

	Net Cash Flow	
End of Year	**Project A**	**Project B**
0	−$1,000	−$800
1	−400	−200
2	−400	−200 + 0
3	−400 + 200	

If the required service period is six years and both projects can be repeated with the given costs and better service projects are unavailable in the future, which project is better and why? Choose from the following options:

(a) Select Project B because it will save you $344 in present worth over the required service period.

(b) Select Project A because it will cost $1,818 in NPW each cycle, with only one replacement, whereas Project B will cost $1,138 in NPW each cycle with two replacements.

(c) Select Project B because its NPW exceeds that of Project A by $680.

(d) None of the above.

Short Case Studies with Excel

5.55 An electrical utility is experiencing sharp power demand, which continues to grow at a high rate in a certain local area. Two alternatives to address this situation are under consideration. Each alternative is designed to provide enough capacity during the next 25 years. Both alternatives will consume the same amounts of fuel, so fuel cost is not considered in the analysis. The alternatives are detailed as follows:

- **Alternative *A*:** Increase the generating capacity now so that the ultimate demand can be met with additional expenditures later. An initial investment of $30 million would be required, and it is estimated that this plant facility would be in service for 25 years and have a salvage value of $0.85 million. The annual operating and maintenance costs (including income taxes) would be $0.4 million.

- **Alternative *B*:** Spend $10 million now, and follow this expenditure with additions during the 10th year and the 15th year. These additions would cost $18 million and $12 million, respectively. The facility would be sold 25 years from now with a salvage value of $1.5 million. The annual operating and maintenance costs (including income taxes) initially will be $250,000 increasing to $350,000 after the first addition (from the 11th year to the 15th year) and to $450,000 during the final 10 years. (Assume that these costs begin one year subsequent to the actual addition.)

If the firm uses 15% as a MARR, which alternative should be undertaken based on the present-worth criterion?

5.56 Apex Corporation requires a chemical finishing process for a product under contract for a period of six years. Three options are available. Neither Option 1 nor Option 2 can be repeated after its process life. However, Option 3 will always be available from H&H Chemical Corporation at the same cost during the contract period. The details of each option are as follows:

- **Option 1:** Process device A, which costs $100,000, has annual operating and labor costs of $60,000, and has a useful service life of four years with an estimated salvage value of $10,000.

- **Option 2:** Process device B, which costs $150,000, has annual operating and labor costs of $50,000, and has a useful service life of six years with an estimated salvage value of $30,000.

- **Option 3:** Subcontract the process out at a cost of $100,000 per year.

According to the present-worth criterion, which option would you recommend at $i = 12\%$?

5.57 H-Robotic Incorporated (HRI), a world leader in the robotics industry, produces a line of industrial robots and peripheral equipment that performs many routine assembly-line tasks. However, increased competition, particularly from Japanese firms, has caused HRI's management to be concerned about the company's growth potential in the future. HRI's research and development department has been applying the industrial robot technology to develop a line of household robots. The household robot is designed to function as a maid, mainly performing such tasks as vacuuming floors and carpets. This effort has now reached the stage where a decision on whether to go forward with production must be made. The engineering department has estimated that the firm would need a new manufacturing plant with the following construction schedule:

- The plant would require a 35-acre site, and HRI currently has an option to purchase a suitable tract of land for $2.5 million. The building construction would begin in early 2012 and continue through 2013. The building would cost $10.5 million in total, but a $3.5 million payment would be made to the contractor on December 31, 2012, and another $7 million payable on December 31, 2013.

- The necessary manufacturing equipment would be installed late in 2013 and would be paid for on December 31, 2013. The equipment would cost $18.5 million, including transportation, plus another $500,000 for installation.

- As of December 31, 2011, the company has spent $12 million on research and development associated with the household robot.

(a) What is the equivalent total investment cost (future worth) at the time of completion (December 31, 2013), assuming that HRI's MARR is 15%?

(b) If the product life is 10 years, what is the required minimum annual net cash flow (after all expenses) that must be generated to just break even? (Ignore any tax considerations.)

CHAPTER SIX

Annual Equivalence Analysis

Owning a Corporate Jet Lambert Manufacturing Corporation (LMC) wants to investigate fractional ownership as opposed to purchasing a business jet for domestic travels for their executives. Currently, the company uses a chartered aircraft for most executive travels or lets them fly in a first class on commercial airlines. A 2011 Beechcraft® Baron Model G58 has been proposed for consideration. The company record reveals that the average flight hours logged by the executives on chartered aircraft were 200 hours per year in the last three years.

- **Fractional Jet Ownership.**[1] Fractional ownership in private aviation works slightly differently in that ownership emulates a membership club, offering access to a large fleet. Owners can purchase shares starting at 1/16 of an aircraft (about 50 flying hours per year)

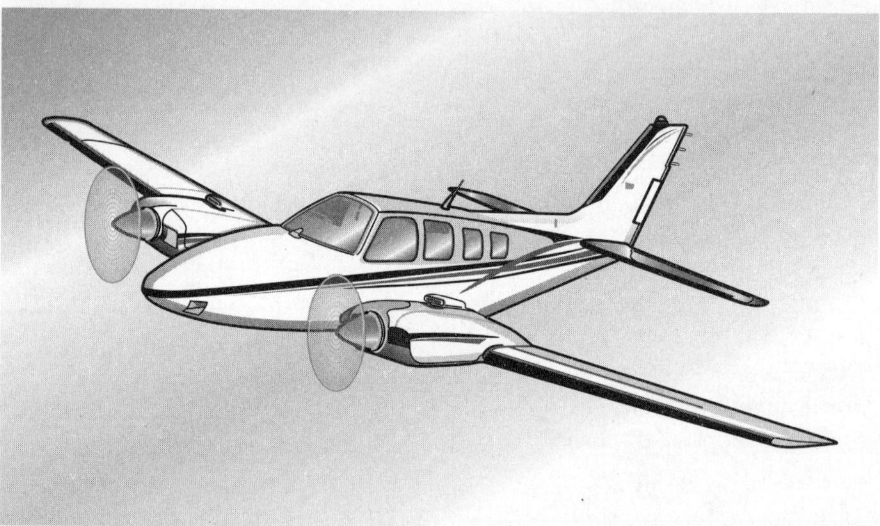

[1] "Fractional Ownership Is on the Rise, so Power Up that Corporate Jet," *Reuters Money,* July 14, 2011.

under a typical five-year contract. Depending on the deal, fractional owners may sell their stake or can exercise a put option, which the company
will honor at fair market value, when the contract expires.

- **Full ownership.** The 2011 Baron Model G58 carries a price tag of
$1,282,035, and the annual operating and maintenance costs are estima-
ted at $575 per hour based on 200 flight hours.[2]

Is there any other cost to consider if Lambert owns the plane? The
main issue is: *How much will it really cost per hour to own and operate
the Beechcraft Baron Model G58?* How does the hourly cost of flying
change with increased flight hours per year? We need to consider both

	Beechcraft® Baron Model G58
Actual Price in June 2011	$1,282,035
Variable Costs per Flight Hour	
Fuel ($4.92/gallon, 36 gallons per hour)	$178
Scheduled and Unscheduled Maintenance	
Parts (include shipping)	$40
Labor	$45
Propeller Overhaul	$9
Total Variable Costs per Flight Hour	$272
Annual Fixed Costs	
Insurance	$31,530
Jeppesen Electronic NavData and Approach Charts	$1,640
XM WX Satellite Weather Aviation Edition	$600
Recurrent Training	$6,320
Rental Engine Liability Insurance ($10M coverage)	$20,500
Total Fixed Costs per Year	$60,590
Total Fixed Costs per Hour (200 Flight Hours)	$302.95
Total Operating Costs per Hour	$574.95

[2] *Source:* Cost data has been compiled based on various sources including **Economics Comparison Chart**, Eclipse Aviation (www.eclipseaviation.com/eclipse_500/comparisons).

the ownership cost (or commonly known as capital costs) along with the operating costs. This information will be necessary for the company to determine the value of owning, chartering, or having a fractional ownership of a business jet to meet the executives' travel needs.

S uppose you are considering buying a new car. If you expect to drive 12,000 miles per year, can you figure out the cost of owning and operating the car per mile? You would have good reason to want to know this cost if you were being reimbursed by your employer on a per-mile basis for the business use of your car. Or consider a real-estate developer who is planning to build a shopping center of 500,000 square feet. What would be the minimum annual rental fee per square foot required in order to recover the initial investment?

Annual cash flow analysis is the method by which these and other unit costs can be calculated. Annual-equivalence analysis (along with present-worth analysis) is the second major equivalence technique for translating alternatives into a common basis of comparison. In this chapter, we develop the annual-equivalence criterion and demonstrate a number of situations in which annual-equivalence analysis is preferable to other methods of comparison.

6.1 Annual-Equivalent Worth Criterion

The **annual-equivalent worth (AE) criterion** provides a basis for measuring investment worth by determining equal payments on an annual basis. Knowing that any lump-sum amount can be converted into a series of equal annual payments, we may first find the net present worth of the original series and then multiply this amount by the capital-recovery factor:

$$AE(i) = PW(i) (A/P, i, N). \tag{6.1}$$

We use this formula to evaluate the investment worth of projects as follows:

- **Evaluating a Single Project:** The accept–reject decision rule for a single *revenue* project is as follows:

  If $AE(i) > 0$, accept the investment.
  If $AE(i) = 0$, remain indifferent to the investment.
  If $AE(i) < 0$, reject the investment.

  Notice that the factor $(A/P, i, N)$ in Eq. (6.1) is positive for $-1 < i < \infty$, which indicates that the $AE(i)$ value will be positive if and only if $PW(i)$ is positive. In other words, accepting a project that has a positive $AE(i)$ value is equivalent to accepting a project that has a positive $PW(i)$ value. Therefore, the AE criterion provides a basis for evaluating a project that is consistent with the PW criterion.

- **Comparing Multiple Alternatives.** When you compare mutually exclusive revenue projects, you select the project with the largest AE value. If you are comparing mutually exclusive *service* projects that have equivalent revenues, you may compare them on a *cost-only* basis. In this situation, the alternative with the least annual equivalent cost (AEC) or least negative annual equivalent worth is selected.

EXAMPLE 6.1 Finding Annual Equivalent Worth by Conversion from Net Present Worth (NPW)

A hospital uses four coal-fired boilers to supply steam for space heating, domestic hot water, and the hospital laundry. One boiler is operated at times of low load and on weekends, two are operated during the week, and the third boiler is normally off-line. The design efficiency on a steady load is generally about 78%. The boilers at the hospital were being run at between 70% and 73% efficiency, due to inadequate instrumentation and controls. Engineers have proposed that the boiler controls be upgraded. The upgrade would consist of installing variable-speed drives for the boiler fans and using the fans in conjunction with oxygen trim equipment for combustion control.

- The cost of implementing the project is $159,000. The boilers have a remaining service life of 12 years. Any upgrade will have no salvage value at the end of 12 years.

- The annual electricity use in the boiler house is expected to be reduced from 410,000 kWh to 180,000 kWh as a result of variable speed control of the boiler fan (because with the variable-speed drives, the fan motors draw only the power actually required to supply air to the boilers). This is equivalent to $14,000 per year. This savings is expected to increase at an annual rate of 4% as the cost of electricity increases over time.

- Coal use will be 2% lower due to the projected improvement in boiler efficiency. This corresponds to a cost reduction of $40,950 per year. This savings is projected to increase as the coal price increases at an annual rate of 5%.

If the hospital uses a 10% interest rate for any project justification, what would be the annual equivalent energy savings due to the improvement?

DISSECTING THE PROBLEM

When a cash flow has no special pattern, it is easiest to find the AE in two steps: (1) Find the PW of the flow and (2) find the AE of the PW. We use this method in the solution to this example. You might want to try another method with this type of cash flow in order to discover how tedious using another method can be.

Given: The cash flow diagram in Figure 6.1; $i = 10\%$ per year.
Find: The AE.

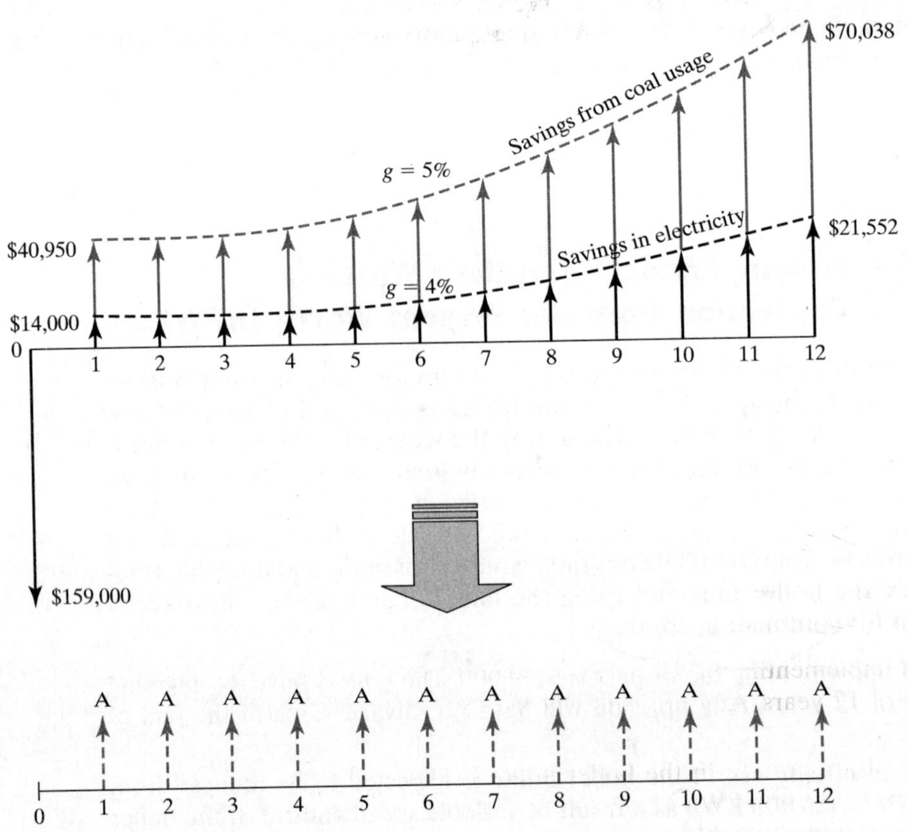

Figure 6.1 Computing equivalent annual worth—First convert each of the two different geometric gradient series into its equivalent present worth, determine the NPW of the boiler improvement project, and then find the equivalent annual worth of the energy savings

METHODOLOGY

Find the present worth of the flow, and then find the AE of the present worth.

SOLUTION

Since energy savings are in two different geometric gradient series, we calculate the equivalent present worth in the following steps:

- Savings in electricity:

$$P_{\text{Savings in electricity}} = \$14,000\,(P/A_1,4\%,10\%,12)$$

$$= \$14,000\left[\frac{1 - (1 + 0.04)^{12}(1 + 0.10)^{-12}}{0.10 - 0.04}\right]$$

$$= \$114,301.$$

- Savings in coal usage:

$$P_{\text{Savings in coal usage}} = \$40{,}950\,(P/A_1, 5\%, 10\%, 12)$$

$$= \$40{,}950\left[\frac{1 - (1 + 0.05)^{12}(1 + 0.10)^{-12}}{0.10 - 0.05}\right]$$

$$= \$350{,}356.$$

- Net present worth calculation:

$$\text{PW}(10\%) = \$114{,}301 + \$350{,}356 - \$159{,}000$$

$$= \$305{,}657.$$

Since $\text{PW}(10\%) > 0$, the project would be acceptable under the PW analysis.

Now, spreading the NPW over the project life gives

$$\text{AE}(10\%) = \$305{,}657\,(A/P, 10\%, 12)$$

$$= \$44{,}859.$$

Since $\text{AE}(10\%) > 0$, the project is also worth undertaking. The positive AE value indicates that the project is expected to bring in a net annual benefit of $44,859 over the life of the project.

TABLE 6.1   **An Excel Worksheet to Calculate the Annual Equivalent Worth (Example 6.1)**

	A	B	C	D	E	F	G	H	I	J	K	M
1												
2			Input						Output			
3												
4	(*I*) Investment				$ 159,000		Net Present Worth					$ 305,657
5	(*i*) MARR (%)				10%		Net Future Worth					$ 959,282
6	(*N*) Project life				12		Annual Equivalent Worth					$ 44,859
7												
8			Fuel Savings		Net	Project						
9	Period	Electricity	Coal Usage		Cash Flow	Balance						
10												
11	0				$ (159,000)	$ (159,000)						
12	1	$ 14,000	$ 40,950		$ 54,950	$ (119,950)						
13	2	$ 14,560	$ 42,998		$ 57,558	$ (74,388)						
14	3	$ 15,142	$ 45,147		$ 60,290	$ (21,536)						
15	4	$ 15,748	$ 47,405		$ 63,153	$ 39,463						
16	5	$ 16,378	$ 49,775		$ 66,153	$ 109,562						
17	6	$ 17,033	$ 52,264		$ 69,297	$ 189,815						
18	7	$ 17,714	$ 54,877		$ 72,591	$ 281,388						
19	8	$ 18,423	$ 57,621		$ 76,044	$ 385,571						
20	9	$ 19,160	$ 60,502		$ 79,662	$ 503,789						
21	10	$ 19,926	$ 63,527		$ 83,453	$ 637,622						
22	11	$ 20,723	$ 66,703		$ 87,427	$ 788,810						
23	12	$ 21,552	$ 70,038		$ 91,591	$ 59,282.17						
24												

=E22*(1+$E$5)+D23

COMMENTS: Table 6.1 illustrates how we might calculate the annual equivalent value by using Excel. To speed up the cash flow input process, we may enter the two different geometric series by using Columns B and C. In Column D, these two cash flows are combined and the project balances are calculated in Column E. Then, we calculate the net present worth first at 10%, followed by the annual equivalent value. These are shown in the outputs section.

6.1.1 Benefits of AE Analysis

Example 6.1 should look familiar to you. It is exactly the situation we encountered in Chapter 2 when we converted an uneven cash flow series into a single present value and then into a series of equivalent cash flows. In the case of Example 6.1, you may wonder why we bother to convert NPW to AE at all, since we already know from the NPW analysis that the project is acceptable. In fact, the example was mainly an exercise to familiarize you with the AE calculation.

In the real world, a number of situations can occur in which AE analysis is preferred, or even demanded, over NPW analysis. Some of typical situations include the following:

1. **When life-cycle-cost analysis is desired.** A life-cycle-cost analysis is useful when project alternatives fulfill the same performance requirements but differ with respect to initial costs and operating costs. Life-cycle-cost analysis enables the analysts to make sure that the selection of a design alternative is not based solely on the lowest initial costs but also to take into account all the future costs over the project's useful life.

2. **When there is a need to determine unit costs or profits.** In many situations, projects must be broken into unit costs (or profits) for ease of comparison with alternatives. Outsourcing decisions such as "make-or-buy" and pricing the usage of an asset (rental charge per hour) reimbursement analyses are key examples of such situations and will be discussed in this chapter.

3. **When project lives are unequal.** As we saw in Chapter 5, comparison of projects with unequal service lives is complicated by the need to determine the common lifespan. For the special situation of an indefinite service period and replacement with identical projects, we can avoid this complication by using AE analysis. This situation will also be discussed in more detail in this chapter.

6.1.2 Capital (Ownership) Costs versus Operating Costs

When only costs are involved, the AE method is sometimes called the **annual-equivalent cost method**. In this case, revenues must cover two kinds of costs: **operating costs** and **capital costs**. Normally, capital costs are nonrecurring (i.e., one-time costs) whereas operating costs recur for as long as an asset is being utilized.

Capital (Ownership) Costs

Capital costs (or *ownership costs*) are incurred by the purchase of assets to be used in production and service. Because capital costs tend to be one-time costs (buying and selling), when conducting an annual equivalent cost analysis, we must translate these one-time costs into their annual equivalent over the life of the project. Suppose you purchased an equipment costing $10,000. If you keep the asset for 5 years, your cost

- Definition: The cost of owning a piece of equipment is associated with two amounts: (1) the equipment's initial cost (I) and (2) its salvage value (S).

- Capital costs: Taking these amounts into account, we calculate the capital costs as follows:

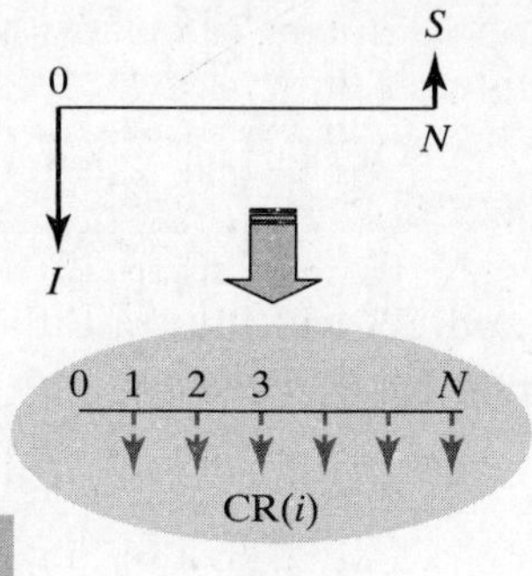

$$CR(i) = I(A/P, i, N) - S(A/F, i, N)$$
$$= (I - S)(A/P, i, N) + iS$$

Figure 6.2   Calculation of capital-recovery cost (with return)

of owning the asset should include the opportunity cost of $10,000. So, the capital cost is defined as the net cost of purchasing (after any salvage value adjustment) plus the interest cost over the life of the ownership.

The annual equivalent of a capital cost is given a special name: **capital-recovery cost**, designated $CR(i)$. As shown in Figure 6.2, two general monetary transactions are associated with the purchase and eventual retirement of a capital asset: the asset's initial cost (I) and its salvage value (S). Taking these amounts into account, we calculate the capital-recovery cost as follows:

$$CR(i) = I(A/P, i, N) - S(A/F, i, N).$$

If we recall the algebraic relationships between factors shown in Table 2.11 and notice that the $(A/F, i, N)$ factor can be expressed as

$$(A/F, i, N) = (A/P, i, N) - i,$$

then we may rewrite the expression for $CR(i)$ as

$$CR(i) = I(A/P, i, N) - S[(A/P, i, N) - i]$$
$$= (I - S)(A/P, i, N) + iS. \tag{6.2}$$

Basically, to obtain the machine, one borrows a total of I dollars, S dollars of which are returned at the end of the Nth year. The first term, $(I - S)(A/P, i, N)$, implies that the balance $(I - S)$ will be paid back in equal installments over the N-year period at a rate of i, and the second term implies that *simple interest* in the amount iS is paid on S until S is repaid. Many auto leases are based on this arrangement, in that most require a guarantee of S dollars in salvage (or market value at the time of restocking the returned vehicle).

Equivalent Annual Operating Costs

Once you place an asset in service, *operating costs* will incur by the operation of physical plants or equipment needed to provide service; examples include the costs of items such as labor and raw materials. Because operating costs recur over the life of a project, they tend to be estimated on an annual basis; so, for the purposes of annual-equivalent cost analysis, no special calculation is required unless the annual amount keeps changing. In that case, we need to find the *equivalent* present worth of the operating costs and spread the present worth over the asset life on an annual basis.

$$\text{OC}(i) = \underbrace{\left(\sum_{n=1}^{N} \text{OC}_n (1 + i)^{-n} \right)}_{\text{Total present worth of operating cost}} \overbrace{\phantom{\left(\sum_{n=1}^{N} \text{OC}_n (1 + i)^{-n} \right)}}^{\text{Equivalent annual operating cost}} (A/P, i, N). \qquad (6.3)$$

Examples 6.2 and 6.3 will illustrate the process of computing the capital costs and equivalent annual operating costs.

EXAMPLE 6.2 Will Your Car Hold Its Value? Costs of Owning a Vehicle

Consider two vehicles whose values are expected to hold during five years of ownership:

		Percent of Total Value Retained			
Type of Vehicles	MSRP	After two years	After three years	After four years	After five years
2010 BMW M3	$58,400	70%	60%	51%	43%
2010 Hyundai-Accent GLS	$14,365	40%	30%	24%	18%

MSRP: Manufacturer's suggested retail price.

Determine the annual ownership cost of each vehicle, assuming an interest rate of 6% compounded annually.

DISSECTING THE PROBLEM

Given: $I = \$58,400, S = \$25,112, N = 5$ years, and $i = 6\%$ per year.

Find: CR(6%) for each vehicle after five years of ownership.

METHODOLOGY

SOLUTION

For a BMW M3, buying it at $58,400 and selling it at $25,112 (43% of MSRP) after five years, your annual ownership cost (capital cost) would be:

$$\text{CR}(6\%) = \underbrace{(\$58,400 - \$25,112)(A/P, 6\%, 5)}_{\$7,902} + (0.06)\,\$25,112$$

$$= \$9,409.$$

Costs of owning the vehicles as a function of ownership period are then as follows:

| | | CR(6%) | | | |
Type of Vehicles	MSRP	After two years	After three years	After four years	After five years
2010 BMW M3	$58,400	$12,009	$10,842	$10,045	$9,409
2010 Hyundai-Accent GLS	$14,365	$5,046	$4,020	$3,357	$2,951

Clearly, the longer you keep the vehicle, the smaller the ownership cost.

From an industry viewpoint, $CR(i)$ is the annual cost to the firm of owning the asset. With this information, the amount of annual savings required in order to recover the capital and operating costs associated with a project can be determined. As an illustration, consider Example 6.3.

EXAMPLE 6.3 Required Annual Savings to Justify the Purchase of Equipment

Ferguson Company is considering an investment in computer-aided design equipment. The equipment will cost $110,000 and will have a five-year useful economic life. It has a salvage value of $10,000. The expected annual operating costs for the equipment would be $20,000 for the first two years and $25,000 for the remaining three years. Assuming that Ferguson's desired return on its investment (MARR) is 15%, what is required annual savings to make the investment worthwhile?

DISSECTING THE PROBLEM

Given: $I = \$110,000$, $S = \$10,000$, yearly operating costs, $N = 5$ years, and $i = 15\%$ per year.

Find: AEC, and determine whether the firm should or should not purchase the machine.

METHODOLOGY

Separate cash flows from operating cash flow

SOLUTION

As shown in Figure 6.3, we separate cash flows associated with the asset acquisition and disposal from the normal operating cash flows. Since the operating cash flows are not uniform, we need to convert the series into equivalent annual flows.

- Capital costs:

$$CR(15\%) = (\$110,000 - \$10,000)(A/P, 15\%, 5)$$
$$+ (0.15)\$10,000$$
$$= \$31,332.$$

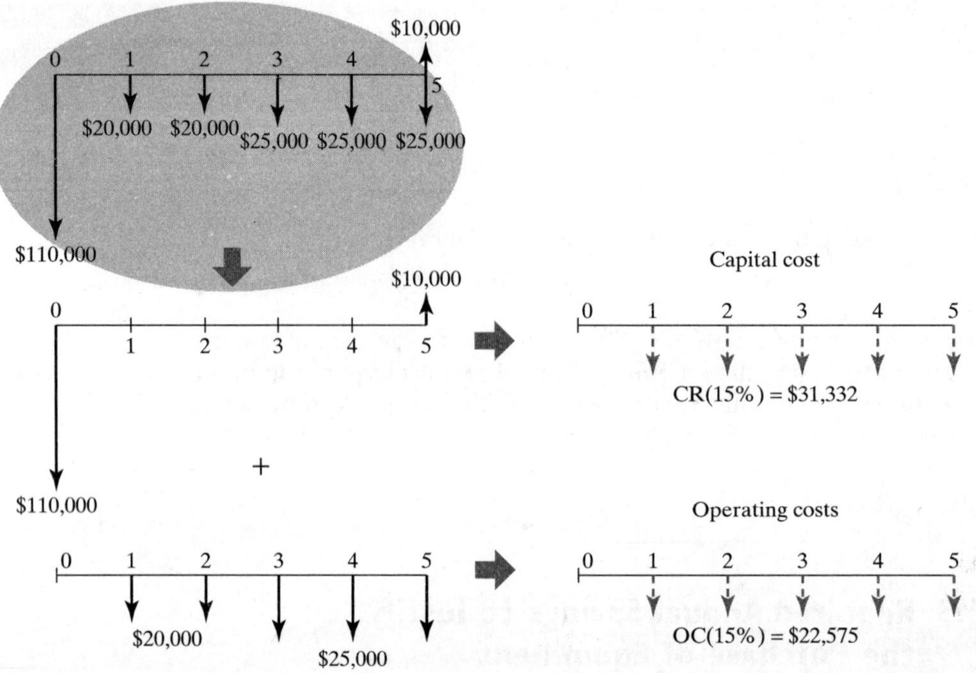

Figure 6.3 Computing the required the annual savings to cover the capital and operating costs

- Operating costs:

$$\text{OC}(15\%) = \left[\overbrace{\left(\begin{array}{l} \$20,000(P/A, 15\%, 2) \\ +\$25,000 \, (P/A, 15\%, 3)(P/F, 15\%, 2) \end{array} \right)}^{\text{Total present worth of operating cash flows}} \right]_{\$75,675}$$

$$\times \, (A/P, 15\%, 5)$$
$$= \$22,575.$$

- Annual equivalent cost:

$$\text{AEC}(15\%) = \text{CR}(15\%) + \text{OC}(15\%)$$
$$= \$31,332 + \$22,575$$
$$= \$53,907.$$

The required annual savings must be at least $53,907 to recover the investment made in the asset and cover the annual operating expenses.

6.2 Applying Annual-Worth Analysis

In general, most engineering economic analysis problems can be solved by the present-worth methods that were introduced in Chapter 5. However, some economic analysis problems can be solved more efficiently by annual-worth analysis. In this section, we introduce several applications that call for annual-worth analysis techniques.

6.2.1 Unit-Profit or Unit-Cost Calculation

In many situations, we need to know the *unit profit* (or *unit cost*) of operating an asset. To obtain a unit profit (or cost), we may proceed as follows:

Step 1: Determine the number of units to be produced (or serviced) each year over the life of the asset.

Step 2: Identify the cash flow series associated with production or service over the life of the asset.

Step 3: Calculate the present worth of the project's cash flow series at a given interest rate, and then determine the equivalent annual worth.

Step 4: Divide the equivalent annual worth by the number of units to be produced or serviced during each year. When the number of units varies each year, you may need to convert the units into equivalent annual units.

To illustrate the procedure, we will consider Example 6.4, in which the annual-equivalence concept is useful in estimating the savings per machine-hour for a proposed machine acquisition.

EXAMPLE 6.4 Unit Profit per Machine-Hour with Constant or Varying Annual Operating Hours

Harrison Company experiences frequent industrial accidents involving workers who perform spot-welding. The firm is looking into the possibility of investing in a specific robot for welding tasks. The required investment will cost Harrison $1 million upfront, and this robot has a five-year useful life and a salvage value of $100,000. The robot will reduce labor costs, worker insurance costs, and materials usage cost and will eliminate accidents involving workers at the spot-welding operations. The savings figure translates into a total of $800,000 a year. The additional operating and maintenance costs associated with the robot amount to $300,000 annually. Compute the equivalent savings per machine-hour at $i = 15\%$ compounded annually for the following two situations:

(a) Suppose that this robot will be operated for 2,000 hours per year.

(b) Suppose that the robot will be operated according to varying hours: 1,500 hours in the first year, 2,500 hours in the second year, 2,500 hours in the third year, 2,000 hours in the fourth year, and 1,500 hours in the fifth year. The total number of operating hours is still 10,000 over five years.

DISSECTING THE PROBLEM

Given: $I = \$1,000,000, S = \$100,000, N = 5\,\text{years}$, net savings per year $= \$500,000$, and there are 10,000 machine-hours over five years.

Find: Equivalent savings per machine-hour.

METHODOLOGY

(a) *Annual operating hours remain constant:* First compute the annual equivalent savings, and then calculate the equivalent savings per machine-hour.

SOLUTION

We first compute the annual equivalent savings from the use of the robot.

$$\text{PW}\,(15\%) = -\$1,000,000 + \$500,000\,(P\,/\,A,15\%,5)$$
$$+ \$100,000\,(P/F,15\%,5)$$
$$= \$725,795.$$
$$\text{AE}\,(15\%) = \$725,795\,(A/P,15\%,5)$$
$$= \$216,516.$$

With an annual usage of 2,000 hours, the equivalent savings per machine-hour would be calculated as follows:

Savings per machine-hour $= \$216,516/2,000\,\text{hours} = \$108.26/\text{hour}$.

See Figure 6.4.

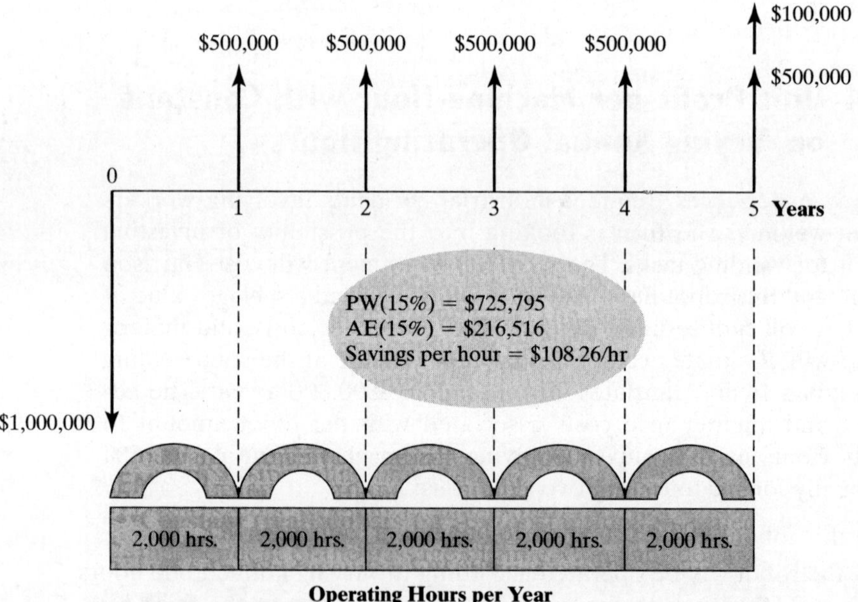

Figure 6.4 Computing equivalent savings per machine-hour (Example 6.4)

(b) *Annual operating hours fluctuate:* Calculate the equivalent annual savings as a function *C*.

SOLUTION

Let C denote the equivalent annual savings per machine-hour that need to be determined. Now, with varying annual usages of the machine, we can set up the equivalent annual savings as a function of C:

$$\text{Equivalent annual savings} = C\big[\,(1{,}500)\,(P/A,15\%,5)$$
$$+ (1{,}000)\,(P/A,15\%,2)\,(P/F,15\%,1)$$
$$+ (500)\,(P/F,15\%,4)\,\big]\,(A/P,15\%,5)$$
$$= 2{,}006.99C.$$

We can equate this amount to $216,516 and solve for C. This operation gives us

$$C = \$216{,}516/2{,}006.99 = \$107.88/\text{hour},$$

which is about $0.38 less than in the situation in Example 6.4(a).

COMMENTS: Note that we cannot simply divide the NPW amount ($725,795) by the total number of machine-hours over the five-year period (10,000 hours), which would result in $72.58/hour. This $72.58/hour figure represents the instant savings in present worth for each hour of use of the robot but *does not* consider the time over which the savings occur. Once we have the annual equivalent worth, we can divide by the desired time unit if the compounding period is one year. If the compounding period is shorter, then the equivalent worth should be calculated for the compounding period.

EXAMPLE 6.5 Cost to Fly per Hour

Revisit the chapter opening story about LMC's consideration of purchasing a business airplane for domestic travels. Key financial data are as follows:

- Cost of aircraft: $1,282,035
- Market value of the aircraft after five years: $832,000
- Total variable cost per hour: $272 first year and increases at 6% per year thereafter
- Total fixed operating cost per hour: $302.95 first year and increases at 4% per year
- Annual operating hours: 200 hours

Compute the equivalent annual cost of owning and operating the aircraft per flying hour over five years at an annual interest rate of 12%.

DISSECTING THE PROBLEM

Given: Financial data as summarized in Figure 6.5, and $i = 12\%$ per year.

Find: Hourly cost of owning and operating the business airplane.

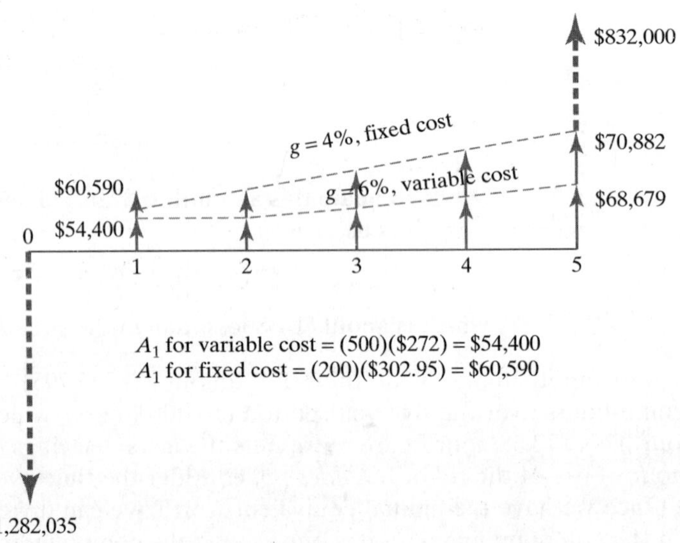

Figure 6.5   Cash flows associated with owning and operating a business airplane (Example 6.5)

METHODOLOGY

First compute the annual equivalent cost, then calculate the equivalent cost per flying hour.

SOLUTION

The two cost components are capital cost and operating cost. We calculate the annual equivalent cost for each as follows:

- **Capital costs:**

$$\mathrm{CR}(12\%) = (\$1,282,035 - \$832,000)(A/P, 12\%, 5)$$
$$+ 0.12(\$832,000)$$
$$= \$224,684.$$

- **Operating costs:**
  - Variable cost:

$$\mathrm{OC}(12\%)_{\text{Variable}} = (200)(\$272)(P/A_1, 6\%, 12\%, 5)$$
$$\times (A/P, 12\%, 5)$$
$$= \$60,529.$$

  - Fixed cost:

$$\mathrm{OC}(12\%)_{\text{Fixed}} = (200)(\$302.95)(P/A_1, 4\%, 12\%, 5)$$
$$\times (A/P, 12\%, 5)$$
$$= \$65,056.$$

- Total operating costs:

$$OC(12\%) = OC(12\%)_{\text{Variable}} + OC(12\%)_{\text{Fixed}}$$
$$= \$125{,}585.$$

Then, the cost of flying is

$$\text{Flying cost per hour} = \frac{\$224{,}684 + \$125{,}585}{200}$$
$$= \$1{,}751.35.$$

COMMENTS: Note that the flying cost per hour when we considered the ownership cost (capital costs) along with the operating costs is much higher than \$575, the initial estimate of operating cost. Now LMC needs to look at how much it has budgeted for its executives' travels next five years and can decide whether it is worth owning a corporate airplane.

6.2.2 Make-or-Buy Decision

Outsourcing decisions such as make-or-buy problems are among the most common business decisions. At any given time, a firm may have the option of either buying an item or producing it. *If either the "make" or the "buy" alternative requires the acquisition of machinery or equipment besides the item itself, then the problem becomes an investment decision.* Since the cost of an outside service (the "buy" alternative) is usually quoted in terms of dollars per unit, it is easier to compare the two alternatives if the differential costs of the "make" alternative are also given in dollars per unit. This unit-cost comparison requires the use of annual-worth analysis. The specific procedure is as follows:

- **Step 1:** Determine the time span (planning horizon) for which the part (or product) will be needed.
- **Step 2:** Determine the required annual quantity of the part (or product).
- **Step 3:** Obtain the unit cost of purchasing the part (or product) from the outside firm.
- **Step 4:** Determine the cost of the equipment, manpower, and all other resources required to make the part (or product).
- **Step 5:** Estimate the net cash flows associated with the "make" option over the planning horizon.
- **Step 6:** Compute the annual equivalent cost of producing the part (or product).
- **Step 7:** Compute the unit cost of making the part (or product) by dividing the annual equivalent cost by the required annual quantity.
- **Step 8:** Choose the option with the smallest unit cost.

EXAMPLE 6.6 Unit Cost: Make or Buy

B&S Company manufactures several lines of pressure washers. One unique part, an axial cam, requires specialized tools and equipment that need to be replaced. Management has decided that the only alternative to replacing these tools is to acquire the axial cam from an outside source. B&S's average usage of the axial cam is 120,000 units each year over the next five years.

- **Buy Option:** A supplier is willing to provide the axial cam at a unit sales price of $35 if at least 100,000 units are ordered annually.
- **Make Option:** If the specialized tools are purchased, they will cost $2,200,000 and will have a salvage value of $120,000 after their expected economic life of five years. With these new tools, the direct labor and variable factory overhead will be reduced, resulting in the following estimated unit production cost:

Direct material	$8.50
Direct labor	$5.50
Variable factory overhead	$4.80
Fixed factory overhead	$7.50
Total unit cost	$26.30

Assuming that the firm's interest rate is 12% per year, calculate the unit cost under each option and determine whether the company should replace the old tools or purchase the axial cam from an outside source.

DISSECTING THE PROBLEM

Given: Cash flows for both options as shown in Figure 6.6; $i = 12\%$.
Find: Unit cost for each option and which option is preferred.

METHODOLOGY

First determine the AEC for each option and then calculate the unit cost for each option.

SOLUTION

The required annual production volume is 120,000 units. We now need to calculate the annual equivalent cost under each option.

- **Buy Option:** Since we already know how much it would cost to buy the axial cam, we can easily find the annual equivalent cost:

$$\text{AEC}(12\%)_{\text{Buy}} = (\$35/\text{unit}) \times (120{,}000\,\text{units}/\text{year})$$

$$= \$4{,}200{,}000/\text{year}.$$

- **Make Option:** The two cost components are capital cost and operating cost.

  We calculate the annual equivalent cost for each as follows:

  Capital cost:
  The capital-recovery cost is

$$\text{CR}(12\%) = (\$2{,}200{,}000 - \$120{,}000)(A/P, 12\%, 5)$$

$$+ (0.12)(\$120{,}000) = \$591{,}412.$$

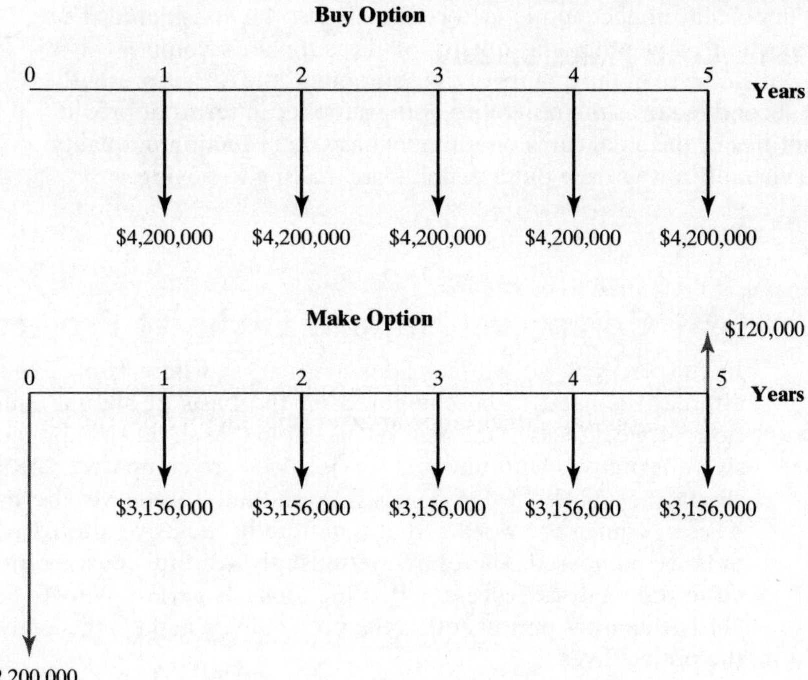

Figure 6.6   Cash flows associated with make-or-buy option in manufacturing axial cams

Production cost:

The annual production cost is

$$OC(12\%)_{\text{Make}} = (\$26.30/\text{unit}) \times (120,000\,\text{units/year})$$
$$= \$3,156,000/\text{year}.$$

Total annual equivalent cost:

Therefore, the total annual equivalent cost is

$$AEC(12\%)_{\text{Make}} = \$591,412 + \$3,156,000 = \$3,747,412.$$

Obviously, this annual-equivalence calculation indicates that B&S would be better off making the axial cam in-house rather than buying it from the outside vendor. However, B&S wants to know the unit costs in order to set a price for the product. For this situation, we need to calculate the unit cost of producing the axial cam under each option. We do this calculation by dividing the magnitude of the annual-equivalent cost for each option by the annual quantity required:

- **Buy Option:**

$$\text{Unit cost} = \$35.00/\text{unit}.$$

- **Make Option:**

$$\text{Unit cost} = \$3,747,412/120,000 = \$31.23/\text{unit}.$$

Making the axial cam in-house by replacing the tools and equipment will save B&S $3.77 per unit before any tax consideration.

COMMENTS: Two important noneconomic factors should also be considered. The first factor is the question of whether the quality of the supplier's component is better than, equal to, or worse than the quality of the component the firm is presently manufacturing. The second factor is the reliability of the supplier in terms of providing the needed quantities of the axial cams on a timely basis. A reduction in quality or reliability should virtually always rule out a switch from making to buying.

6.3 Comparing Mutually Exclusive Projects

In this section, we will consider a situation where two or more mutually exclusive alternatives need to be compared on the basis of annual equivalent worth. In Section 5.4, we discussed the general principle that should be applied when mutually exclusive alternatives with unequal service lives are compared. The same general principle should be applied when comparing mutually exclusive alternatives on annual—the basis of equivalent worth—that is, mutually exclusive alternatives in equal time spans must be compared. Therefore, we must give careful consideration to the time expended in the analysis process, called the **analysis period**. We will consider two situations: (1) The analysis period equals the project lives, and (2) the analysis period differs from the project lives.

6.3.1 Analysis Period Equals Project Lives

Let us begin our comparison with a simple situation where the length of the projects' lives equals the length of the analysis period. In this situation, we compute the AE value for each project and select the project that has the least AEC (for service projects) or the largest AE value (for revenue projects).

In many situations, we need to compare different design alternatives, each of which would produce the same number of units (constant revenues) but would require different amounts of investment and operating costs (because of different degrees of mechanization). This is commonly known as **life-cycle-cost analysis**. Example 6.7 illustrates the use of the annual equivalent cost concept to compare the cost of operating a conventional electric motor with that of operating a premium-efficiency motor in a strip-processing mill.

EXAMPLE 6.7 Life-Cycle Cost Analysis—How Premium Efficiency Motors Can Cut Your Electric Costs

Birmingham Steel Corporation is considering replacing 20 conventional 25-HP, 230-V, 60-Hz, 1,800-rpm induction motors in its plant with modern premium-efficiency (PE) motors. Both types of motors have power outputs of 18.650 kW per motor (25 HP $\times$ 0.746 kW/HP). Conventional motors have a published efficiency of 89.5%, while the PE motors are 93% efficient. The initial cost of the conventional motors is $13,000 while the initial cost of the proposed PE motors is $15,600. The motors are operated 12 hours per day, 5 days per week, 52 weeks per year with a local utility cost of $0.07 per kilowatt-hour (kWh). The life cycle of both the conventional motor and the PE motor is 20 years with no appreciable salvage value.

(a) At an interest rate of 13% compounded annually, what is the amount of savings per kWh gained by switching from the conventional motors to the PE motors?

(b) At what operating hours are the two types of motors equally economical?

DISSECTING THE PROBLEM

Whenever we compare machines with different efficiency ratings, we need to determine the input powers required to operate the machines. Since percent efficiency is equal to the ratio of output power to input power, we can determine the required input power by dividing the output power by the motor's percent efficiency:

$$\text{Input power} = \frac{\text{ourput power}}{\text{percent efficiency}}.$$

For example, a 30-HP motor with 90% efficiency will require an input power calculated as follows:

$$\text{Input power} = \frac{(30\,\text{HP} \times 0.746\,\text{kW/HP})}{0.90}$$
$$= 24.87\,\text{kW}.$$

Given: Types of motors $= (\text{standard}, \text{PE})$, $I = (\$13,000, \$15,600)$, $S = (0, 0)$, $N = (20\ \text{years}, 20\ \text{years})$, rated power output $= (18.65\,\text{kW}, 18.65\,\text{kW})$, efficiency rating $= (89.5\%, 93\%)$, $i = 13\%$, utility rate $= \$0.07/\text{kWh}$, operating hours $= 3{,}120$ hours per year, and number of motors required $= 20$.

Find: (a) The amount saved per kWh by operating the PE motor and (b) the break-even number of operating hours for the PE motor.

Mutually Exclusive Alternatives with Equal Project Lives		
	Standard Motor	**Premium-Efficiency Motor**
Size	18.65 kW	18.65 kW
Cost	$13,000	$15,600
Life	20 years	20 years
Salvage Value	$0	$0
Efficiency	89.5%	93%
Energy Cost	$0.07/kWh	$0.07/kWh
Operating Hours	3,120 hrs/yr	3,120 hrs/yr

METHODOLOGY

First, calculate the operating cost per kWh per unit, and then determine the break-even number of operating hours for the PE motors.

SOLUTION

(a) Execute the following steps to determine the operating cost per kWh per unit:

- Determine total input power for both motor types.

  Conventional motor:

$$\text{Input power} = \frac{18.650\,\text{kW}}{0.895} = 20.838\,\text{kW}.$$

  PE motor:

$$\text{Input power} = \frac{18.650\,\text{kW}}{0.93} = 20.054\,\text{kW}.$$

Note that each PE motor requires 0.784 kW less input power (or 15.68 kW for 20 motors), which results in energy savings.

- Determine the total kWh per year for each type of motor, assuming a total of 3,120 hours per year in motor operation.

Conventional motor:

$$3,120 \, \text{hrs/year} \times 20.838 \, \text{kW} = 65,015 \, \text{kWh/year}.$$

PE motor:

$$3,120 \, \text{hrs/year} \times 20.054 \, \text{kW} = 62,568 \, \text{kWh/year}.$$

- Determine the annual energy costs for both motor types. Since the utility rate is $0.07/kWh, the annual energy cost for each type of motor is calculated as follows:

Conventional motor:

$$\$0.07/\text{kWh} \times 65,015 \, \text{kWh/year} = \$4,551/\text{year}.$$

PE motor:

$$\$0.07/\text{kWh} \times 62,568 \, \text{kWh/year} = \$4,380/\text{year}.$$

- Determine the capital costs for both types of motors. Recall that we assumed that the useful life for both motor types is 20 years. To determine the annualized capital cost at 13% interest, we use the capital-recovery factor.

Conventional motor:

$$(\$13,000)(A/P, 13\%, 20) = \$1,851.$$

PE motor:

$$(\$15,600)(A/P, 13\%, 20) = \$2,221.$$

- Determine the total equivalent annual cost, which is equal to the capital cost plus the annual energy cost. Then calculate the unit cost per kWh on the basis of output power. Note that the total output power is 58,188 kWh per year (25 HP $\times$ 0.746 kW/HP $\times$ 3120 hours/year). We execute these steps as follows:

Conventional motor:

We calculate that

$$\text{AEC}(13\%) = \$4,551 + \$1,851 = \$6,402.$$

So,

$$\text{Cost per kWh} = \$6{,}402/58{,}188\,\text{kWh}$$
$$= 11.00\,\text{cents/kWh}.$$

PE motor:
We calculate that

$$\text{AEC}(13\%) = \$4{,}380 + \$2{,}221 = \$6{,}601.$$

So,

$$\text{Cost per kWh} = \$6{,}601/58{,}188\,\text{kWh}$$
$$= 11.34\,\text{cents/k Wh}.$$

Clearly, conventional motors are cheaper to operate if the motors are expected to run only 3,120 hours per year.

- Determine the savings (or loss) per operating hour obtained by switching from conventional to PE motors.

  Additional capital cost required from switching from conventional to PE motors:

  $$\text{Incremental capital cost} = \$2{,}221 - \$1{,}851 = \$370.$$

  Additional energy-cost savings from switching from conventional to PE motors:

  $$\text{Incremental energy savings} = \$4{,}551 - \$4{,}380 = \$171.$$

  At 3,120 annual operating hours, it will cost the company an additional $370 to switch to PE motors, but the energy savings are only $171, which results in a $199 loss from each motor. In other words, for each operating hour, you lose about 6.38 cents.

(b) Determine the break-even number of operating hours for the PE motors:

- Would the result found in part (a) change if the same motor were to operate 5,000 hours per year? If a motor is to run around the clock, the savings in kWh would result in a substantial annual savings in electricity bills, which are an operating cost. As we calculate the annual equivalent cost by varying the number of operating hours, we obtain the situation shown in Table 6.2. Observe that if Birmingham Steel Corporation used the PE motors for more than 6,742 hours annually, replacing the conventional motors with the PE motors would be justified.

TABLE 6.2 Break-Even Number of Operating Hours as Calculated by Using Excel

	A	B	C	D	E	F	G
		Conventional Motor	**Premium Efficiency Motor**		**Operating Hours**	**Conventional Motor**	**PE Motor**
1							
6	Output power (hp)	25	25		0	$ 1,851	$ 2,221
7	Operating hours per year	6,742	6,742		500	$ 2,580	$ 2,923
8	Efficiency (%)	89.5	93		1000	$ 3,309	$ 3,624
9					1500	$ 4,039	$ 4,326
10	Initial cost ($)	$ 13,000	$ 15,600		2000	$ 4,768	$ 5,028
11	Salvage value ($)	0	0		2500	$ 5,497	$ 5,730
12	Service life (year)	20	20		3000	$ 6,227	$ 6,432
13	Utility rate ($/kWh)	0.07	0.07		3500	$ 6,956	$ 7,134
14	interest rate (%)	13	13		4000	$ 7,685	$ 7,836
15	=C13*(C6*0.746/(C8/100)*C7)				4500	$ 8,415	$ 8,538
16					5000	$ 9,144	$ 9,240
17	Capital cost ($/year)	$ 1,850.60	$ 2,220.72		5500	$ 9,873	$ 9,941
18	Energy cost ($/year)	$ 9,834.28	$ 9,464.17		6000	$ 10,603	$ 10,643
19	Total Equ. annual cost	$ 11,684.88	$ 11,684.89		6500	$ 11,332	$ 11,345
20	Cost per kWh	$ 0.09	$ 0.09		7000	$ 12,061	$ 12,047
21					7500	$ 12,791	$ 12,749
22			=C17+C18		8000	$ 13,520	$ 13,451
23					8500	$ 14,249	$ 14,153
24					8750	$ 14,614	$ 14,504

Chart formula annotations:

=B19/(B6*0.746*B7)

=-(PMT(B14/100,B12,B10-B11)+(B14/100)*B11)

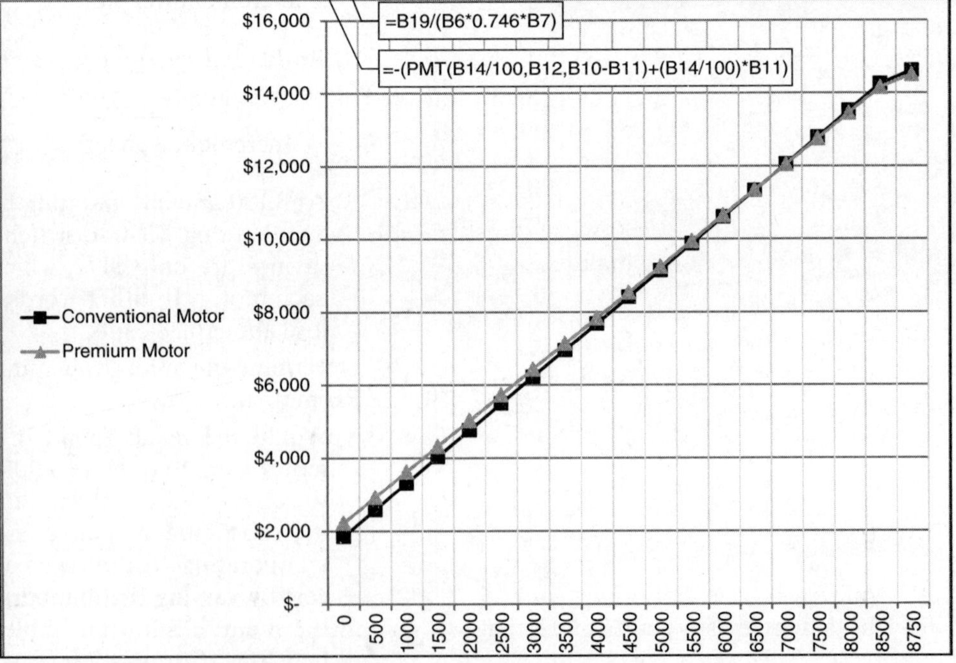

6.3.2 Analysis Period Differs from Project Lives

In Section 5.4, we learned that, in present-worth analysis we must have a common analysis period when mutually exclusive alternatives are compared. One of the approaches is the **replacement chain method** (or least common multiple), which assumes that each project can be repeated as many times as necessary to reach a common life span; the NPWs over this life span are then compared, and the project with the higher common life NPW is chosen. Annual-worth analysis also requires establishing common analysis periods, but AE offers some computational advantages over present-worth analysis, provided the following criteria are met:

1. The service of the selected alternative is required on a continuous basis.
2. Each alternative will be replaced by an *identical* asset that has the same costs and performance.

When these two criteria are met, we may solve for the AE of each project on the basis of its initial life span rather than on the basis of the infinite streams of project cash flows.

EXAMPLE 6.8 Annual Equivalent Cost Comparison— Unequal Project Lives

You are running a small machine shop where you need to replace a worn-out sanding machine. Two different models have been proposed:

- Model A is semiautomated, requires an initial investment of $150,000, and has an annual operating cost of $55,000 for each of three years, at which time it will have to be replaced. The expected salvage value of the machine is just $15,000.
- Model B is an automated machine with a five-year life and requires an initial investment of $230,000 with an estimated salvage value of $35,000. Expected annual operating and maintenance cost of the B machine is $30,000.

Suppose that the current mode of operation is expected to continue for an indefinite period. You also think that these two models will be available in the future without significant changes in price and operating costs. At MARR = 15%, which model should you select? Apply the annual-equivalence approach to select the most economical machine.

DISSECTING THE PROBLEM

A required service period of infinity may be assumed if we anticipate that an investment project will be ongoing at roughly the same level of production for some indefinite period. This assumption certainly is possible mathematically although the analysis is likely to be complicated and tedious.

Given: Cash flows for Model A and Model B, and $i = 15\%$ compounded annually.

Find: AE cost and which model is the preferred alternative.

Therefore, in the case of an indefinitely ongoing investment project, we typically select a finite analysis period by using the **lowest common multiple** of project lives (15 years). We would consider alternative A through five life cycles and alternative B through three life cycles; in each case, we would use the alternatives completely. We then accept the finite model's results as a good prediction of the economically wisest course of action for the foreseeable future. This example is a case in which we conveniently use the lowest common multiple of project lives as our analysis period. (See Figure 6.7.)

n	Model A	Model B
0	−$150,000	−$230,000
1	−$55,000	−$30,000
2	−$55,000	−$30,000
3	+$15,000 − $55,000	−$30,000
4		−$30,000
5		+$35,000 − $30,000

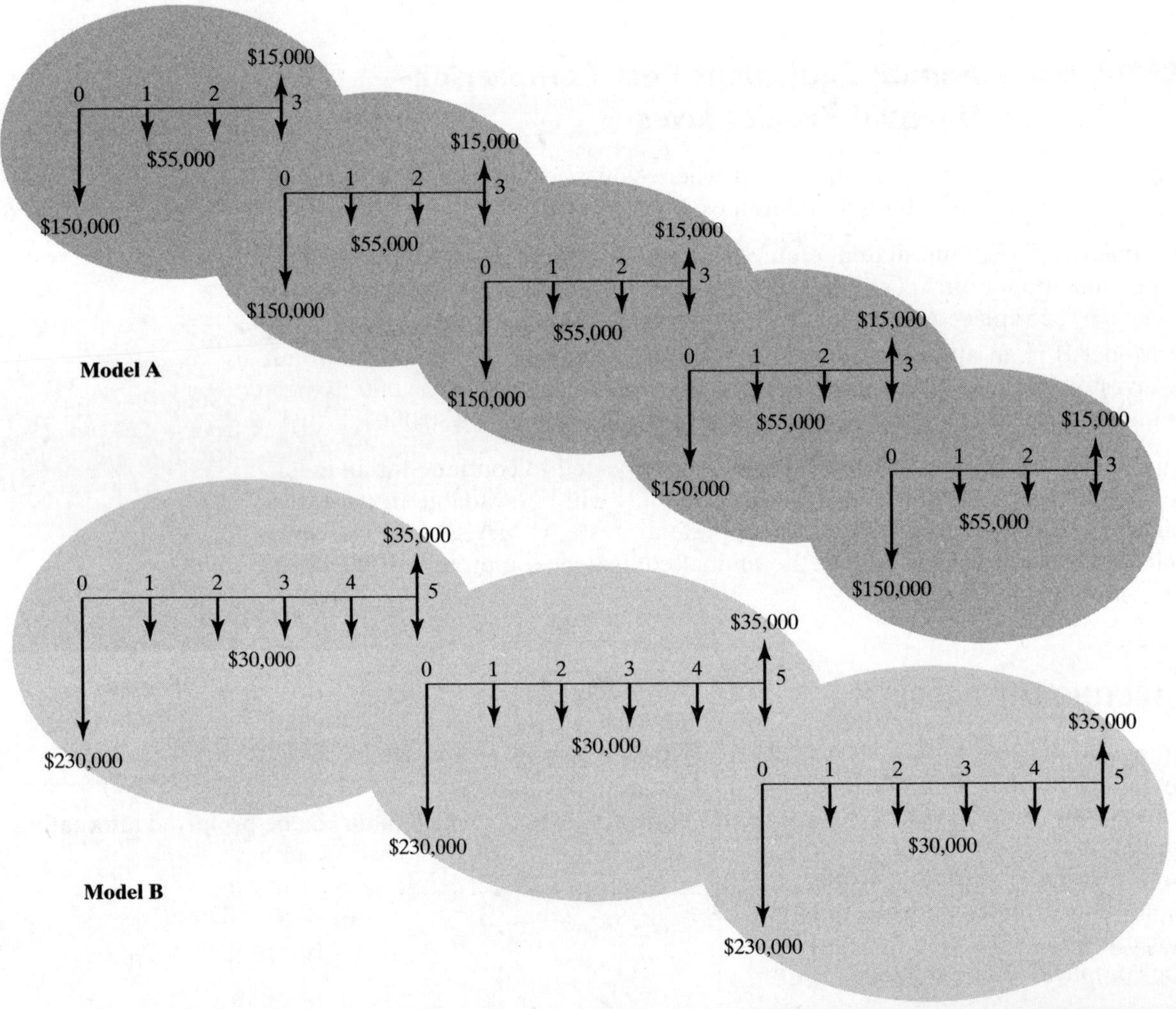

Figure 6.7 Comparing unequal-lived projects on the basis of the replacement chain approach—least common multiple service period of 15 years

METHODOLOGY

Our objective is to determine the AE cost of each model over the lowest common multiple period of 15 years. In doing so, we will compute the PW cost of the first cycle, and then we convert it into its equivalent AE cost. We do the same for the entire cycle.

SOLUTION

Model A:

- For a three-year period (first cycle):

$$PW(15\%)_{\text{first cycle}} = -\$150{,}000 - \$55{,}000\,(P/A,15\%,3)$$
$$+ \$15{,}000\,(P/F,15\%,3)$$
$$= -\$265{,}715.$$

$$AEC(15\%)_{\text{first cycle}} = \$265{,}715\,(A/P,15\%,3)$$
$$= \$116{,}377.$$

- For a 15-year period (five replacement cycles):

$$PW(15\%)_{\text{15-year period}} = -\$265{,}715\big[1 + (P/F,15\%,3)$$
$$+ (P/F,15\%,6) + (P/F,15\%,9) + (P/F,15\%,12)\big]$$
$$= -\$680{,}499.$$

$$AEC(15\%)_{\text{15-year period}} = \$680{,}499\,(A/P,15\%,15)$$
$$= \$116{,}377.$$

Model B:

- For a five-year life (first cycle):

$$PW(15\%)_{\text{first cycle}} = -\$230{,}000 - \$30{,}000\,(P/A,15\%,5)$$
$$+ \$35{,}000\,(P/F,15\%,5)$$
$$= -\$313{,}163.$$

$$AEC(15\%)_{\text{first cycle}} = \$313{,}163\,(A/P,15\%,5)$$
$$= \$93{,}422.$$

- For a 15-year period (three replacement cycles):

$$PW(15\%)_{\text{15-year period}} = -\$313{,}163\big[1 + (P/F,15\%,5)$$
$$+ (P/F,15\%,10)\big]$$
$$= -\$546{,}270.$$

$$AEC(15\%)_{\text{15-year period}} = \$546{,}270\,(A/P,15\%,15)$$
$$= \$93{,}422.$$

We can see that the AE cost of Model A is much higher ($116,377 > $93,422); thus, we select Model B, despite its higher initial cost.

COMMENTS: Notice that the AE costs calculated on the basis of the lowest common multiple period are the same as those that were obtained over the initial life spans. Thus, for alternatives with unequal lives, comparing the AE cost of each project over its first cycle is sufficient in determining the best alternative.

SUMMARY

■ Annual equivalent worth analysis, or AE, and present-worth analysis are the two main analysis techniques determined on the concept of equivalence. The equation for AE is

$$AE(i) = PW(i)(A/P,i,N).$$

AE analysis yields the same decision result as PW analysis.

■ The capital-recovery cost factor, or $CR(i)$, is one of the most important applications of AE analysis in that it allows managers to calculate an annual equivalent cost of capital for ease of itemization with annual operating costs. The equation for $CR(i)$ is

$$CR(i) = (I - S)(A/P,i,N) + iS,$$

where I = initial cost and S = salvage value.

■ AE analysis is recommended over PW analysis in many key real-world situations for the following reasons:

1. In many financial reports, an annual-equivalence value is preferred over a present-worth value for ease of use and its relevance to annual results.
2. Calculation of unit costs is often required in order to determine reasonable pricing for sale items.
3. Calculation of cost per unit of use is required in order to reimburse employees for business use of personal cars.
4. Make-or-buy decisions usually require the development of unit costs so that "make" costs can be compared with prices for "buying."
5. Comparisons of options with unequal service lives is facilitated by the AE method, assuming that the future replacements of the project have the same initial and operating costs. In general, this method is not practical, because future replacement projects typically have quite different cost streams. It is recommended that you consider various future replacement options by estimating the cash flows associated with each of them.

SELF-TEST QUESTIONS

6s.1   You are considering making an $80,000 investment in a process improvement project. Revenues are expected to grow from $50,000 in year 1 by $30,000 each year for next four years ($50,000 first year, $80,000 second year, $110,000 third year, and so forth) while costs are expected to increase from $20,000 in year 1 by $10,000 each year. If there is no salvage value at the end of five years, what is the annual equivalent worth of the project assuming an MARR of 12%?
(a) $65,492
(b) $53,300
(c) $47,785
(d) $43,300

6s.2   You are considering buying a 30-HP electric motor which has an efficiency rating of 89%. The motor costs $10,000 and will be used for 10 years. The expected salvage value at that time is $1,000. The cost to run the electric motor is $0.09 per kWh for 2,000 hours a year. ($1\,HP = 0.7457\,kW$.) What is the total equivalent cost (present worth) of owning and operating the motor for 10 years at an interest rate of 12% per year?

(a) $35,242

(b) $25,884

(c) $32,426

(d) $22,425

6s.3   You purchased a drill press machine for $50,000. It is expected to have a useful life of 8 years. The accounting department tells you that the annual capital cost is $9,740 at $i = 12\%$. What salvage value is used in obtaining the annual capital cost of this machine?

(a) $3,010

(b) $4,000

(c) $4,997

(d) $4,200

6s.4   You are considering a project with the following financial data:

■ Required initial investment at $n = 0$: $50M

■ Project life: 10 years

■ Estimated annual revenue: $X (unknown)

■ Estimated annual operating cost: $15M

■ Required minimum return: 20% per year

■ Salvage value of the project: 15% of the initial investment

What *minimum* annual revenue (in $M) must be generated to make the project worthwhile?

(a) $X = \$26.64\,M$

(b) $X = \$28.38\,M$

(c) $X = \$32.47\,M$

(d) $X = \$35.22\,M$

6s.5   Consider manufacturing equipment that has an installed cost of $120,000. The equipment is expected to generate $45,000 of the annual energy savings during its first year of installation. The value of these annual savings is expected to increase by 5% per year (over previous year) because of increased fuel costs. Assume that the equipment has a service life of 10 years (or 5,000 operating hours per year) with $20,000 worth of salvage value. Determine the equivalent dollar savings per each operating hour at $i = 10\%$ per year.

(a) $6.99 per hour

(b) $7.24 per hour

(c) $4.45 per hour

(d) $4.29 per hour

6s.6   The city of Atlanta is considering adding new buses for its current mass-transit system that links Hartsfield International Airport to major city destinations on nonstop basis. The total investment package is worth $8 million and is expected to last 10 years with a $750,000 salvage value. The annual operating and maintenance costs for buses would be $2 million. If the system is used for 600,000 trips per year, what would be the fair price to charge per trip? Assume that the city of Atlanta uses 5% interest rate for any city-sponsored projects.

(a) $3.50 per trip

(b) $4.00 per trip

(c) $4.50 per trip

(d) $5.00 per trip

6s.7 You are considering a luxury apartment building project that requires an investment of $12,500,000. The building has 50 units. You expect the maintenance cost for the apartment building to be $250,000 in the first year, $300,000 in the second year, and increasing by $50,000 in subsequent years. The cost to hire a manager for the building is estimated to be $80,000 per year. After five years of operation, the apartment building can be sold for $14,000,000. What is the annual rent per apartment unit that will provide a return on investment of 15% per year? Assume the building will remain fully occupied during the five years.

(a) $36,445

(b) $38,567

(c) $41,373

(d) $44,980

6s.8 Two options are available for painting your house: (1) Oil-based painting, which costs $5,000, and (2) water-based painting, which costs $3,000. The estimated lives are 10 years and 5 years, respectively. For either option, no salvage value will remain at the end of respective service lives. Assume that you will keep and maintain the house for 10 years. If your personal interest rate is 10% per year, which of the following statements is correct?

(a) On an annual basis, Option 1 will cost about $850

(b) On an annual basis, Option 2 is about $22 less than Option 1

(c) On an annual basis, both options cost about the same

(d) On an annual basis, Option 2 will cost about $820.

6s.9 A consumer product company is considering introducing a new shaving system called DELTA-4 in the market. The company plans to manufacture 75 million units of DELTA-4 a year. The investment at time 0 that is required for building the manufacturing plant is estimated as $500 million, and the economic life of the project is assumed to be 10 years. The annual total operating expenses, including manufacturing costs and overhead, are estimated at $175 million. The salvage value that can be realized from the project is estimated at $120 million. If the company's MARR is 25%, determine the price that the company should charge for a DELTA-4 shaving system to break even.

(a) $3.15

(b) $4.15

(c) $5.15

(d) $2.80

PROBLEMS

Note 1: Unless otherwise stated, all cash flows given in the problems represent after-tax cash flows in *actual dollars*. The MARR also represents a market interest rate, which considers any inflationary effects in the cash flows.

Note 2: Unless otherwise stated, all interest rates presented in this set of problems are based on annual compounding.

6.1   An engineering design firm needs to borrow $400,000 from a local bank at an interest rate of 8% over five years. What is the required annual equal payment to retire the loan in five years?

6.2   You are considering an investment costing $300,000. If you want to recover the initial investment, and also earn 10% interest while your money is being tied up, within four years, what is the required equal annual net revenue that must be generated from the investment?

6.3   Consider the cash flow series shown below. Determine the required annual deposits (end of year) that will generate the cash flows from years 4 to 7. Assume the interest rate is 8%.

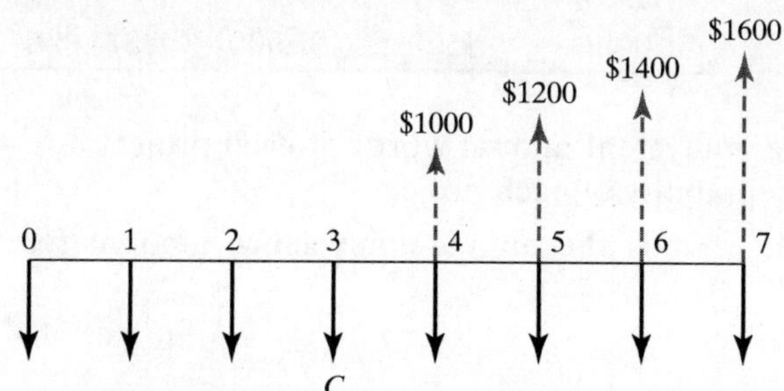

6.4   Consider the following cash flows and compute the equivalent annual worth at $i = 12\%$:

n	Investment	Revenue
		A_n
0	−$34,000	
1	−$10,000	$15,000
2		$14,000
3		$13,000
4		$13,000
5		$8,000
6		$5,500

6.5   The investment shown in the following figure has an annual equivalent worth of $200 at $i = 8\%$. Determine the cash flows in periods 2, 3, 5 and 6.

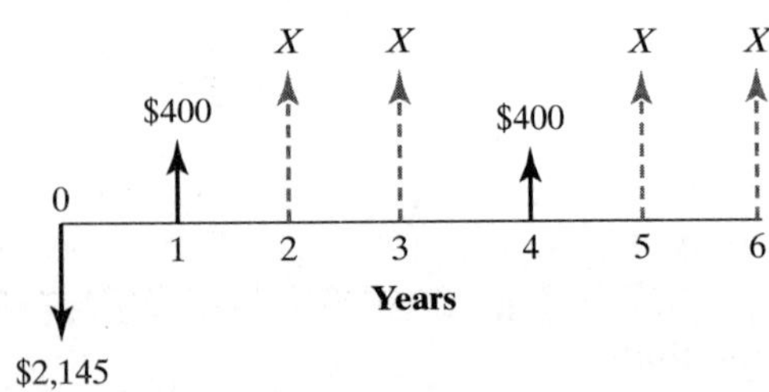

6.6   Consider the following sets of investment projects:

		Project Cash Flows		
n	A	B	C	D
0	−$3,500	−$5,800	−$5,200	−$40,000
1	$600	$3,000	−$2,000	$12,000
2	$600	$2,000	$4,000	$14,000
3	$1,000	$1,000	$2,000	$18,000
4	$1,000	$500	$4,000	$18,000
5	$1,000	$500	$2,000	$14,000

Compute the equivalent annual worth of each project at $i = 10\%$, and determine the acceptability of each project.

6.7   At $i = 12\%$, what is the annual-equivalence amount for the infinite series shown next?

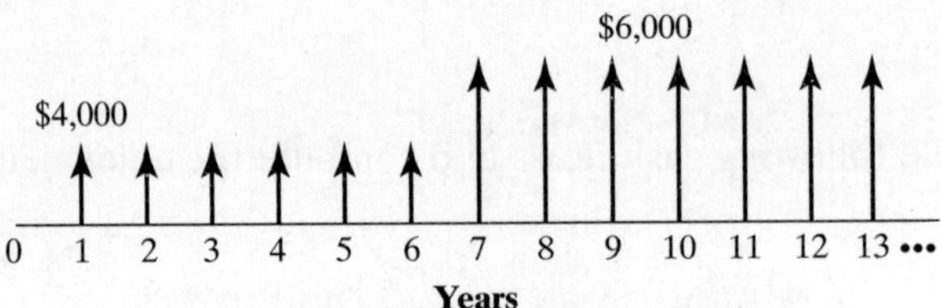

6.8   Compute the annual-equivalence amount for the following cash flow series at $i = 10\%$:

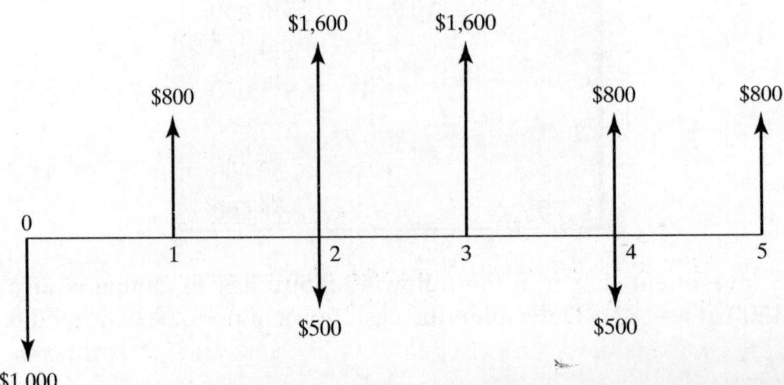

6.9 Consider the following sets of investment projects:

Period	Project Cash Flows			
n	A	B	C	D
0	−$4,300	−$3,500	−$5,500	−$3,800
1	$0	$1,500	$3,000	$1,800
2	$0	$1,800	$2,000	$1,800
3	$5,500	$2,100	$1,000	$1,800

Compute the equivalent annual worth of each project at $i = 13\%$, and determine the acceptability of each project.

6.10 Consider an investment project with the following repeating cash flow pattern every four years forever:

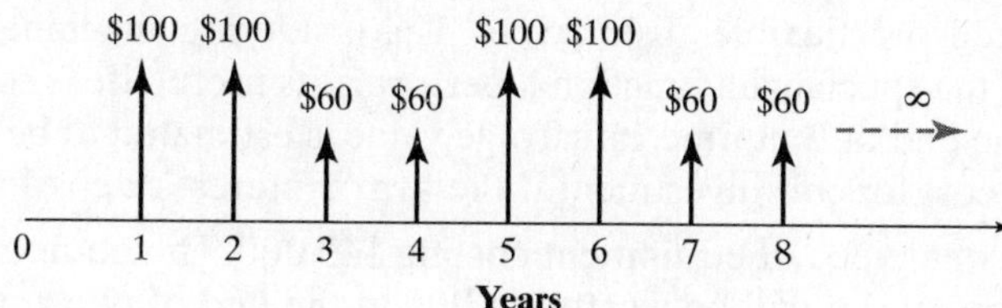

What is the annual-equivalence amount of this project at an interest rate of 14%?

6.11 A newly constructed water treatment facility cost $2 million. It is estimated that the facility will need revamping to maintain the original design specification every 30 years at a cost of $1 million. Annual repairs and maintenance costs are estimated to be $100,000. At an interest rate of 8%, determine the capitalized cost of the facility, assuming that it will be used for an indefinite period.

6.12 An airline is planning to make iPads® available on some of its Boeing 747 aircrafts with in-flight e-mail and Internet service on transoceanic flights. Passengers on these flights will be able to rent iPads from the airline and use them to browse webs or to send and receive e-mail no matter where they are in the skies. A nominal charge of approximately $30 will be instituted for each rental. The airline has estimated the projected cash flows (in millions of dollars) for the systems in the first 10 aircraft as follows:

Year	A_n (Unit: Million Dollars)
2012	−$5.0
2013	$1.5
2014	$5.0
2015	$9.0
2016	$12.0
2017	$10.0

Determine whether this project can be justified at MARR = 15%, and calculate the annual benefit (or loss) that would be generated after installation of the systems.

Capital Recovery (Ownership) Cost

6.13 A drill press was purchased for $300,000. It was expected to last 10 years and to have a salvage value of $30,000. If the firm's interest rate is 18%, what would be the capital cost for each year during a 12-year ownership?

6.14 You purchased a CNC machine for $50,000. It is expected to have a useful life of 8 years and a salvage value of $4,000. At $i = 12\%$, what is the annual capital cost of this machine?

6.15 Susan is considering buying a 2011 Smart ForTwo costing $21,635 and finds that the retaining values of the vehicle over next five years are as follows:

- Percent of the total value retained after 36 months: 28%
- Percent of the total value retained after 60 months: 17%

If her interest rate is 6% compounded annually, what is the ownership cost of the vehicle over three years? five years?

6.16 Nelson Electronics, Inc., just purchased a soldering machine to be used in its assembly cell for flexible disk drives. This soldering machine costs $150,000. Because of the specialized function it performs, its useful life is estimated to be six years. At the end of that time, its salvage value is estimated to be $20,000. What is the capital cost for this investment if the firm's interest rate is 15%?

6.17 You invest in a piece of equipment costing $40,000. The equipment will be used for two years, and it will be worth $15,000 at the end of two years. The machine will be used for 4,000 hours during the first year and 6,000 hours during the second year. The expected savings associated with the use of the piece of equipment will be $28,000 during the first year and $40,000 during the second year. Your interest rate is 10%.

(a) What is the capital recovery cost?

(b) What is the annual equivalent worth?

(c) What is net savings generated per machine-hour?

6.18 You are considering purchasing a dump truck. The truck will cost $45,000 and have operating and maintenance costs that start at $15,000 the first year and increase by $2,000 per year thereafter. Assume that the salvage value at the end of five years is $9,000 and interest rate is 12%. Determine the equivalent annual cost of owning and operating the truck.

6.19 An auto-parts manufacturer is considering establishing an engineering computing center. This center will be equipped with three engineering workstations each of which would cost $25,000 and have a service life of five years. The expected salvage value of each workstation is practically zero. The annual operating and maintenance cost for each workstation would be $15,000. If the MARR is 15%, determine the equivalent annual cost of operating the engineering center.

6.20 Beginning next year, a foundation will support an annual seminar on campus by using the interest earnings on a $100,000 gift it received this year. It is determined that 6% interest will be realized for the first 10 years, but that plans should be made to anticipate an interest rate of only 4% after that time. What amount should be added to the foundation now in order to fund the seminar at a level of $10,000 per year into infinity?

6.21 A machine tool company is considering a new investment in a punch press machine that will cost $100,000 and has an annual maintenance cost of $10,000.

There is also an additional overhauling cost of $20,000 for the equipment once every four years. Assuming that this equipment will last 12 years under these conditions, what is the cost of owning and maintaining the punch press at an interest rate of 10%?

6.22 The owner of a business is considering investing $55,000 in new equipment. He estimates that the net cash flows will be $5,000 during the first year and will increase by $2,500 per year each year thereafter. The equipment is estimated to have a 10-year service life and a net salvage value at the end of this time of $6,000. The firm's interest rate is 12%.

(a) Determine the annual capital cost (ownership cost) for the equipment.

(b) Determine the equivalent annual savings (revenues).

(c) Determine whether this investment is wise.

Annual Equivalent Worth Criterion

6.23 Company X has been contracting its overhauling work to Company Y for $40,000 per machine per year. Company X estimates that by building a $500,000 maintenance facility with a life of 15 years and a salvage value of $100,000 at the end of its life, it could handle its own overhauling at a cost of only $30,000 per machine per year. What is the minimum annual number of machines that Company X must operate to make it economically feasible to build its own facility, assuming an interest rate of 10%?

6.24 Consider the cash flows for the following investment projects:

	Project Cash Flows	
n	A	B
0	−$5,500	$7,900
1	$1,500	−$1,200
2	$X	−$1,500
3	$1,500	−$1,800
4	$1,500	−$2,100

(a) For Project A, find the value of X that makes the equivalent annual receipts equal the equivalent annual disbursement at $i = 13\%$.

(b) Would you accept Project B at $i = 15\%$ based on the AE criterion?

6.25 An industrial firm is considering purchasing several programmable controllers and automating their manufacturing operations. It is estimated that the equipment will initially cost $150,000, and the labor to install it will cost $45,000. A service contract to maintain the equipment will cost $5,000 per year. A trained machine operator will have to be hired at an annual salary of $40,000. Also estimated is an approximate $15,000 annual income-tax savings (cash inflow). How much will this investment in equipment and services have to increase the annual revenues after taxes in order for the firm to break even? The equipment is estimated to have an operating life of 10 years with no salvage value (because of obsolescence). The firm's MARR is 12%.

6.26 A certain factory building has an old lighting system. To light this building costs, on average, $30,000 a year. A lighting consultant tells the factory supervisor that the lighting bill could be reduced to $8,000 a year if $55,000 were invested in a new lighting system for the factory building. If the new lighting system is installed, an incremental maintenance cost of $4,000 per year must be considered. If the old lighting system has zero salvage value and the new lighting system is estimated to have a life of 20 years, what is the net annual benefit for this investment in new lighting? Consider the MARR to be 12%. Also consider that the new lighting system has zero salvage value at the end of its life.

Unit-Profit or Unit-Cost Calculation

6.27 Consider a piece of industrial equipment that has an installed cost of $100,000. The equipment is expected to generate $30,000 worth of annual energy savings during its first year of installation. The value of these annual savings is expected to increase at the rate of 5% per year because of increased fuel costs. Assume that the equipment has a service life of five years (or 3,000 operating hours per year) with no appreciable salvage value. Determine the equivalent dollar savings per each operating hour at $i = 14\%$.

6.28 You have purchased an equipment costing $20,000. The equipment will be used for two years, and at the end of two years, its salvage value is expected to be $10,000. The equipment will be used 6,000 hours during the first year and 8,000 hours during the second year. The expected annual net savings will be $30,000 during the first year and $40,000 during the second year. If your interest rate is 10%, what would be the equivalent net savings per machine-hour?

6.29 You just purchased a pin-inserting machine to relieve some bottleneck problems that have been created in manufacturing a PC board. The machine cost $56,000 and has an estimated service life of five years. At that time, the estimated salvage value would be $5,000. The machine is expected to operate 2,500 hours per year. The expected annual operating and maintenance cost would be $6,000. If your firm's interest rate is 15%, what would be the machine cost (owning and operating) per hour?

6.30 Georgia Mills Company (GMC) purchased a milling machine, which it intends to use for the next five years, for $180,000. This machine is expected to save GMC $35,000 during the first operating year. Then, the annual savings are expected to decrease by *3% each subsequent year over the previous year* due to increased maintenance costs. Assuming that GMC would operate the machine for an average of 5,000 hours per year and that the machine would have no appreciable salvage value at the end of the five-year period, determine the equivalent dollar savings per operating hour at 15% interest compounded annually.

6.31 You invest in a piece of equipment costing $30,000. The equipment will be used for two years, at the end of which time the salvage value of the machine is expected to be $10,000. The machine will be used for 5,000 hours during the first year and 8,000 hours during the second year. The expected annual net savings in operating costs will be $25,000 during the first year and $40,000 during the second year. If your interest rate is 10%, what would be the equivalent net savings per machine-hour?

6.32 A company is currently paying its employees $0.51 per mile to drive their own cars when on company business. However, it is considering supplying employees with cars, which would involve the following cost components: car purchase at $22,000 with an estimated three-year life; a net salvage value of $5,000; taxes and insurance at a cost of $1,000 per year; and operating and maintenance expenses of $0.25 per mile. If the interest rate is 10% and the company anticipates an employee's annual travel to be 30,000 miles, what is the equivalent cost per mile (without considering income tax)? Which plan is better?

6.33 Santa Fe Company, a farm-equipment manufacturer, currently produces 20,000 units of gas filters for use in its lawnmower production annually. The following costs are reported according to the previous year's production:

Item	Expense
Direct materials	$60,000
Direct labor	$180,000
Variable overhead (power and water)	$135,000
Fixed overhead (light and heat)	$70,000
Total cost	**$445,000**

It is anticipated that gas-filter production will last five years. If the company continues to produce the product in-house, annual direct-material costs will increase at a rate of 5%. (For example, the annual direct-material costs during the first production year will be $63,000.) In addition, direct-labor costs will increase at a rate of 6% per year, and variable-overhead costs will increase at a rate of 3% while fixed-overhead costs will remain at the current level over the next five years. Tompkins Company has offered to sell Santa Fe Company 20,000 units of gas filters for $25 per unit. If Santa Fe accepts the offer, some of the facilities currently used to manufacture the gas filters could be rented to a third party at an annual rate of $35,000. In addition, $3.50 per unit of the fixed-overhead costs applied to gas-filter production would be eliminated. The firm's interest rate is known to be 15%. What is the unit cost of buying the gas filters from the outside source? Should Santa Fe accept Tompkins's offer? Why or why not?

6.34 An electric automobile can be purchased for $25,000. The automobile is estimated to have a life of 12 years with annual mileage of 20,000 miles. Every three years, a new set of batteries will have to be purchased at a cost of $3,000. The $3,000 cost of the batteries is a net value with the old batteries traded in for the new ones. Annual maintenance of the vehicle is estimated to cost $700. The cost of recharging the batteries is estimated at $0.015 per mile. The salvage value of the batteries and the vehicle at the end of 12 years is estimated at $2,000. Consider the MARR to be 7%. What is the cost per mile to own and operate this vehicle according to these estimates?

6.35 A California utility firm is considering building a 50-megawatt geothermal plant that generates electricity from naturally occurring underground heat. The binary geothermal system will cost $85 million to build and $6 million (including any income-tax effect) to operate per year. (Unlike a conventional fossil-fuel plant, this system will require virtually no fuel costs.) The geothermal plant is to last 25 years. At the end of that time, the expected salvage value will be about the same as the cost to remove the plant. The plant will be in operation for 70% (the plant-utilization factor) of the year (or 70% of 8,760 hours per year). If the firm's MARR is 14% per year, determine the cost of generating electricity per kilowatt-hour.

Break-Even Analysis

6.36 A city has decided to build a softball complex, and the city council has already voted to fund the project at the level of $800,000 (initial capital investment). The city engineer has collected the following financial information for the complex project:

- Annual upkeep costs: $120,000
- Annual utility costs: $13,000
- Renovation costs: $50,000 for every five years
- Annual team user fees (revenues): $32,000
- Useful life: Infinite
- Interest rate: 8%

If the city can expect 40,000 visitors to the complex each year, what should be the minimum ticket price per person so that the city can break even?

6.37 J&M Company is a real-estate developer considering a 40-unit apartment complex in a growing college town. As the area is also booming with foreign automakers locating their U.S. assembly plants, the firm expects that the apartment complex, once built, will enjoy a 90% occupancy for an extended period. The firm already compiled some of the critical financial information related to the development project as follows:

- Land price (1 acre) = $1,200,000
- Building (40 units of single bedroom) = $4,800,000
- Project life = 25 years
- Building maintenance per unit per month = $100
- Annual property taxes and insurance = $400,000

Assuming that the land will appreciate at an annual rate of 5%, but the building will have no value at the end of 25 years (it will be torn down and a new structure would be built), determine the minimum monthly rent that should be charged if a 12% return (or 0.9489% per month) before tax is desired.

6.38 The estimated cost of a completely installed and ready-to-operate 40-kilowatt generator is $30,000. Its annual maintenance costs are estimated at $500. The energy that can be produced annually, at full load, is estimated to be 100,000 kilowatt-hours. If the value of the energy produced is considered to be $0.08 per kilowatt-hour, how long will it take before this generator becomes profitable? Consider the MARR to be 9% and the salvage value of the machine to be $2,000 at the end of its estimated life of 15 years.

6.39 A large state university, currently facing a severe parking shortage on its campus, is considering constructing parking decks off campus. A shuttle service composed of minibuses could pick up students at the off-campus parking deck and quickly transport them to various locations on campus. The university would charge a small fee for each shuttle ride, and the students could be quickly and economically transported to their classes. The funds raised by the shuttle would be used to pay for minibuses, which cost about $150,000 each. Each minibus has a 12-year service life with an estimated salvage value of $3,000. To operate each minibus, the following additional expenses must be considered:

Item	Annual Expenses
Driver	$40,000
Maintenance	$7,000
Insurance	$2,000

If students pay 10 cents for each ride, determine the annual ridership (i.e., the number of shuttle rides per year) required to justify the shuttle project, assuming an interest rate of 6%.

6.40 Two 180-horsepower water pumps are being considered for installation in a farm. Financial data for these pumps are as follows:

Item	Pump I	Pump II
Initial cost	$6,000	$4,000
Efficiency	86%	80%
Useful life	12 years	12 years
Annual operating cost	$500	$440
Salvage value	$0	$0

If power cost is a flat 6 cents per kWh over the study period, determine the minimum number of hours of full-load operation per year that would justify the purchase of the more expensive pump at an interest rate of 8% ($1\,\text{HP} = 746$ watts $= 0.746$ kilowatts).

6.41 Eradicator Food Prep, Inc., has invested $7 million to construct a food irradiation plant, which would destroy organisms that cause spoilage and disease, thus extending the shelf life of fresh foods and the distances over which they can be shipped. The plant can handle about 200,000 pounds of produce in an hour and will be operated for 3,600 hours a year. The net expected operating and maintenance costs (considering any income-tax effects) would be $4 million per year. The plant is expected to have a useful life of 15 years with a net salvage value of $700,000. The firm's interest rate is 15%.

(a) If investors in the company want to recover the plant investment within six years of operation (rather than 15 years), what would be the equivalent after-tax annual revenues that must be generated?

(b) To generate the annual revenues determined in part (a), what minimum processing fee per pound should the company charge to its customers?

6.42 You are considering developing an 18-hole championship golf course that requires an investment of $20,000,000. This investment cost includes the course development, club house, and golf carts. Once constructed, you expect the maintenance cost for the golf course to be $650,000 in the first year, $700,000 in the second year and continue to increase by $50,000 in subsequent years. The net revenue generated from selling food and beverage will be about 15% of greens fees paid by the players. The cart fee per player is $15, and 40,000 rounds of golf are expected per year. You will own and operate the course complex for 10 years and expect to sell it for $25,000,000. What is the greens fee per round that will provide a return on investment of 15%? Assume that the greens fee will be increased at an annual rate of 5%.

6.43 A corporate executive jet with a seating capacity of 20 has the following cost factors:

Item	Cost
Initial cost	$12,000,000
Service life	15 years
Salvage value	$2,000,000
Crew costs per year	$225,000
Fuel cost per mile	$1.10
Landing fee	$250
Maintenance costs per year	$237,500
Insurance costs per year	$166,000
Catering cost per passenger round trip	$75

The company flies three round trips from Boston to London and back per week, a distance of 3,280 miles one way. How many passengers must be carried on an average round trip in order to justify the use of the jet if the alternative commercial airline first-class round-trip fare is $3,400 per passenger? The firm's MARR is 15%. (Ignore income-tax consequences.)

Using the AE Method to Compare Mutually Exclusive Alternatives

6.44 An industrial firm can purchase a certain machine for $40,000. A down payment of $4,000 is required, and the balance can be paid in five equal year-end install-ments at 7% interest on the unpaid balance. As an alternative, the machine can be purchased for $36,000 in cash. If the firm's MARR is 10%, determine which alternative should be accepted using the annual-equivalence method.

6.45 Peabody Transport Service is considering the purchase of a helicopter for con-necting services between its base airport and the new intercounty airport being built about 30 miles away. It is believed that the helicopter will be needed only for six years until the rapid transit connection is phased in. The estimates on two types of helicopters under consideration, Model A and Model B, are given:

	Model A	Model B
First Cost	$95,000	$120,000
Annual Maintenance	$3,000	$9,000
Salvage Value	$12,000	$25,000
Useful life in years	3	6

Assuming that the Model A will be available in the future, with identical costs, what is the annual cost advantage of selecting the Model B? (Use an interest rate of 10%.)

6.46 You are asked to decide between two projects based on annual equivalent worth.

A	B
−$10,000	−$12,000
$6,000	$7,000
$5,000	$8,000
$4,000	

(a) What assumptions do you need to make in comparing these mutually exclusive revenue projects?

(b) Based on the assumptions in (a), which project should you choose at $i = 10\%$?

6.47 You are considering two types of electric motors for your paint shop. Financial information and operating characteristics are summarized as follows:

Summary Info and Characteristics	Brand X	Brand Y
Price	$4,500	$3,600
O&M cost per year	$300	$500
Salvage value	$250	$100
Capacity	150 HP	150 HP
Efficiency	83%	80%

If you plan to operate the motor for 2,000 hours annually, what would be the total cost savings per operating hour associated with the more efficient brand (Brand X) at an interest rate of 12%? The motor will be needed for 10 years. Assume that power costs are 5 cents per kilowatt-hour ($1\,\text{HP} = 0.746\,\text{kW}$).

6.48 The following cash flows represent the potential annual savings associated with two different types of production processes, each of which requires an investment of $22,000:

n	Process A	Process B
0	−$22,000	−$22,000
1	$9,120	$7,350
2	$7,840	$7,350
3	$6,560	$7,350
4	$3,280	$7,350

Assuming that the interest rate is 15%, complete the following tasks:

(a) Determine the equivalent annual savings for each process.

(b) Determine the hourly savings for each process, assuming 2,000 hours of operation per year.

(c) Determine which process should be selected.

6.49 Two 150-horsepower (HP) motors are being considered for installation at a municipal sewage-treatment plant. The first costs $4,500 and has an operating efficiency of 83%. The second costs $3,600 and has an operating efficiency of 80%. Both motors are projected to have zero salvage value after a life of

10 years. All the annual charges, such as insurance and maintenance, amount to a total of 15% of the original cost of each motor. If power cost is a flat 5 cents per kilowatt-hour, which alternative should be chosen at 5,000 operating hours per year? Assume an interest rate of 6%. (A conversion factor you might find useful is 1HP = 746 watts = 0.746 kilowatts.)

6.50 A chemical company is considering two types of incinerators to burn solid waste generated by a chemical operation. Both incinerators have a burning capacity of 20 tons per day. The following data have been compiled for comparison of the two incinerators:

Item	Incinerator A	Incinerator B
Installed cost	$1,200,000	$750,000
Annual O&M costs	$50,000	$80,000
Service life	20 years	10 years
Salvage value	$60,000	$30,000
Income taxes	$40,000	$30,000

If the firm's MARR is known to be 13%, determine the processing cost per ton of solid waste for each incinerator. Assume that incinerator *B* will be available in the future at the same cost.

6.51 An airline is considering two types of engine systems for use in its planes:
- System A costs $100,000 and uses 40,000 gallons of fuel per 1,000 hours of operation at the average load encountered in passenger service.
- System B costs $200,000 and uses 32,000 gallons of fuel per 1,000 hours of operation at the average load encountered in passenger service.

Both engine systems have the same life and the same maintenance and repair record, and both have a three-year life before any major overhaul is required. Each system has a salvage value of 10% of the initial investment. If jet fuel costs $4.80 per gallon currently and fuel consumption is expected to increase at the rate of 6% per year because of degrading engine efficiency, which engine system should the firm install? Assume 2,000 hours of operation per year and an MARR of 10%. Use the AE criterion. What is the equivalent operating cost per hour for each engine?

6.52 Norton Auto Parts, Inc., is considering two different forklift trucks for use in its assembly plant:
- Truck A costs $15,000 and requires $3,000 in annual operating expenses. It will have a $5,000 salvage value at the end of its three-year service life.
- Truck B costs $20,000 but requires only $2,000 in annual operating expenses; its service life is four years after which its expected salvage value is $8,000.

The firm's MARR is 12%. Assuming that the truck is needed for 12 years and that no significant changes are expected in the future price and functional capacity of both trucks, select the most economical truck based on AE analysis.

6.53 A small manufacturing firm is considering the purchase of a new machine to modernize one of its current production lines. Two types of machines are available on the market. The lives of Machine A and Machine B are four years and six years, respectively, but the firm does not expect to need the service of either machine for more than five years. The machines have the following expected receipts and disbursements:

Item	Machine A	Machine B
Initial cost	$6,500	$8,500
Service life	4 years	6 years
Estimated salvage value	$600	$1,000
Annual O&M costs	$800	$520
Cost to change oil filter every other year	$100	None
Engine overhaul	$200 (every 3 years)	$280 (every 4 years)

After four years of use, the salvage value for Machine B will be $1,000. The firm always has another option: to lease a machine at $3,000 per year, fully maintained by the leasing company. The lease payment will be made at the beginning of each year.

(a) How many decision alternatives are there?

(b) Which decision appears to be the best at $i = 10\%$?

6.54 A plastic-manufacturing company owns and operates a polypropylene-production facility that converts the propylene from one of its cracking facilities to polypropylene plastics for outside sale. The polypropylene-production facility is currently forced to operate at less than capacity due to lack of enough propylene-production capacity in its hydrocarbon-cracking facility. The chemical engineers are considering alternatives for supplying additional propylene to the polypropylene-production facility. Some of the feasible alternatives are as follows:

- Option 1: Build a pipeline to the nearest outside supply source.
- Option 2: Provide additional propylene by truck from an outside source.

The engineers also gathered the following projected cost estimates:

- Future costs for purchased propylene, excluding delivery: $0.215 per lb
- Cost of pipeline construction: $200,000 per pipeline mile
- Estimated length of pipeline: 180 miles
- Transportation costs by tank truck: $0.05 per lb, using a common carrier
- Pipeline operating costs: $0.005 per lb, excluding capital costs
- Projected additional propylene needs: 180 million lbs per year
- Projected project life: 20 years
- Estimated salvage value of the pipeline: 8% of the installed costs

Determine the propylene cost per pound under each option if the firm's MARR is 18%. Which option is more economical?

Short Case Studies with Excel

6.55 The city of Peachtree is comparing the following two plans for supplying water to a newly developed subdivision:

- Plan A will manage requirements for the next 15 years; at the end of that period, the initial cost of $1,500,000 will have to be doubled to meet the requirements of subsequent years. The facilities installed in years 0 and 15 may be considered permanent; however, certain supporting equipment will have to be replaced every 30 years from the installation dates at a cost of $200,000. Operating costs are $91,000 a year for the first 15 years and $182,000 thereafter. Beginning in the 21st year, they will increase by $3,000 a year.

■ Plan B will supply all requirements for water indefinitely into the future, although it will operate at only half capacity for the first 15 years. Annual costs over this period will be $105,000 and will increase to $155,000 beginning in the 16th year. The initial cost of Plan B is $1,950,000; the facilities can be considered permanent, although it will be necessary to replace $350,000 of equipment every 30 years after the initial installation.

The city will charge the subdivision the use of water calculated on the equivalent annual cost. At an interest rate of 10%, determine the equivalent annual cost for each plan and make a recommendation to the city as to the amount that should be charged to the subdivision.

6.56 Capstone Turbine Corporation is the world's leading provider of microturbine-based MicroCHP (combined heat and power) systems for clean, continuous, distributed-generation electricity. The MicroCHP unit is a compact turbine generator that delivers electricity on-site or close to the point where it is needed. This form of distributed-generation technology, designed to operate on a variety of gaseous and liquid fuels, first debuted in 1998. The microturbine is expected to operate on demand or continuously for up to a year between recommended maintenance (filter cleaning/replacement). The generator is cooled by airflow into the gas turbine, thus eliminating the need for liquid cooling. It can make electricity from a variety of fuels—natural gas, kerosene, diesel oil, and even waste gases from landfills, sewage plants, and oil fields.

Capstone's focus applications include combined heat and power, resource recovery of waste fuel from wellhead and biogas sites, and hybrid electric vehicles. And, unlike traditional backup power, this solution can support everyday energy needs and generate favorable payback. With the current design, which has a 60-kW rating, one of Capstone's generators would cost about $84,000. The expected annual expenses, including capital costs as well as operating costs, would run close to $19,000. These expenses yield an annual savings of close to $25,000 compared with the corresponding expenses for a conventional generator of the same size. The investment would pay for itself within three to four years.

One of the major questions among the Capstone executives is: How low does the microturbine's production cost need to be for it to be a sensible option in some utility operations? To answer this question, Capstone must first determine the cost per kilowatt of its generators.

How does Capstone come up with the capital cost of $1,400 per kilowatt? Suppose you plan to purchase the 60-kW microturbine and expect to operate it continuously for 10 years. How would you calculate the operating cost per kilowatt-hour?

6.57 Empex Corporation currently produces both videocassette cases (bodies) and metal-particle magnetic tape for commercial use. An increased demand for metal-particle videotapes is projected, and Empex is deciding between increasing the internal production of both empty cassette cases and magnetic tape or purchasing empty cassette cases from an outside vendor. If Empex purchases the cases from a vendor, the company must also buy specialized equipment to load the magnetic tape into the empty cases, since its current loading machine is not compatible with the cassette cases produced by the vendor under consideration. The projected production rate of cassettes is 79,815 units per week for 48 weeks of operation per year. The planning horizon is seven years. After considering the effects of income taxes, the accounting department has itemized the costs associated with each option as follows:

■ "Make" Option:

Annual Costs	
Labor	$1,445,633
Materials	$2,048,511
Incremental overhead	$1,088,110
Total annual cost	$4,582,254

■ "Buy" Option:

Capital Expenditure	
Acquisition of a new loading machine	$405,000
Salvage value at end of seven years	$45,000

Annual Operating Costs:	
Labor	$251,956
Purchase of empty cassette cases ($0.85/unit)	$3,256,452
Incremental overhead	$822,719
Total annual operating costs	$4,331,127

(Note the conventional assumption that cash flows occur in discrete lumps at the ends of years, as shown in Figure 6.5.) Assuming that Empex's MARR is 14%, calculate the unit cost under each option.

6.58 A Veterans Administration (VA) hospital needs to decide which type of boiler fuel system will most efficiently provide the required steam energy output for heating, laundry, and sterilization purposes. The present boilers were installed in the early 1970s and are now obsolete. Much of the auxiliary equipment is also old and requires repair. Because of these general conditions, an engineering recommendation was made to replace the entire plant with a new boiler-plant building that would house modern equipment. The cost of demolishing the old boiler plant would be almost a complete loss, as the salvage value of the scrap steel and used brick is estimated to be only about $1,000. The VA hospital's engineer finally selected two alternative proposals as being worthy of more intensive analysis. The hospital's annual energy requirement, measured in terms of steam output, is approximately 145,000,000 pounds of steam. As a general rule for analysis, 1 pound of steam is approximately 1,000 BTUs, and 1 cubic foot of natural gas is approximately 1,000 BTUs. The two alternatives are as follows:

■ Proposal 1: Build a new coal-fired boiler plant, which would cost $2,570,300. To meet the requirements for particulate emission as set by the Environmental Protection Agency (EPA), the new coal-fired boiler, even if it burned low-sulfur coal, would need an electrostatic precipitator, which would cost approximately $145,000. The new plant would last for 20 years. One pound of dry coal yields about 14,300 BTUs. To convert the 145,000,000 pounds of steam energy into the common unit of BTUs, it is necessary to multiply by 1,000. To find BTU input requirements, it is necessary to divide by the relative boiler efficiency for type of fuel. The boiler efficiency for coal is 0.75. The coal price is estimated to be $125 per metric ton.

■ Proposal 2: Build a gas-fired boiler plant with No. 2 fuel oil as a standby. This system would cost $1,289,340 with an expected service life of 20 years. Since small household or commercial users entirely dependent on gas for energy have priority, large plants must have oil switch-over capabilities. It has been estimated that 6% of 145,000,000 pounds (or 8,700,000 pounds) of steam energy would result from the switch between oil and gas. The boiler efficiency would be 0.78 for gas and 0.81 for oil. The heat value of natural gas is approximately 1,000,000 BTU/MCF (million cubic feet), and for No. 2 fuel oil it is 139,400 BTU/gal. The estimated gas price is $14.50/MCF, and the No. 2 fuel-oil price is $2.93 per gallon.

(a) Calculate the annual fuel costs for each proposal.

(b) Determine the unit cost per steam pound for each proposal. Assume $i = 10\%$.

(c) Which proposal is more economical?

CHAPTER SEVEN

Rate-of-Return Analysis

What's a Degree Really Worth?[1] For years, higher education was touted as a safe path to professional and financial success. Easy money, in the form of student loans, flowed to help parents and students finance degrees with the implication that in the long run, a bachelor's degree was a good bet. The numbers appeared to back it up. In recent years, the nonprofit College Board touted the difference in lifetime earnings of college grads over high-school graduates at $800,000, a widely circulated figure. Other estimates topped $1 million.[2]

With this ever-itching curiosity, Investor's Business Daily[3] compiled an interesting statistic—the typical cumulative pay for graduates 30 years after they earn their bachelor's degree. It is net pay, beyond what it cost them to get their degree. Some of the private engineering graduates do display an impressive number; say the top median net income was $1.7 million for grads for Caltech as of 2010, but the typical price tag at this institution is about $200,000.

What happens when you look at earnings per dollar spent to get an education? Leading is Georgia Tech's 13.9% return on investment, next is the University of Virginia's 13.3%. The top returns on investment (ROI) get a boost from the relatively modest costs for in-state students who spent $77,980 to earn a degree at state-supported Georgia Tech as of 2010.

What does the 13.9% rate-of-return figure represent for the Georgia Tech graduates? If you look at your college degree from purely an investment point of view, what we are saying here is "investing $77,980" in four years will bring in additional earnings of $1,129,000 over 30 years. This is equivalent to generating 13.9% interest earned by your savings account. Is this a good investment?

---

[1] Mary Pilon, "What Is a Degree Really Worth?" *The Wall Street Journal*, February 20, 2010.
[2] "College: Big Investment, Paltry Return," *Bloomberg Businessweek*, June 28, 2010.
[3] Paul Katzeff, "Colleges with Top Investment Returns on Degree Costs," Investors.com, May 27, 2011.

Biggest Bang For Your College Buck

Colleges ranked by return on investment, based on first 30 years of net median pay beyond costs of education

School	Cost to complete degree	30-year net income	Annual ROI
Ga. Inst. of Technology	$77,980	$1,129,000	13.9%
Univ. of Virginia	80,440	968,700	13.3
Colo. School of Mines	92,820	1,045,000	13.1
Virginia Tech	78,920	876,700	13.0
UC-Berkeley	110,000	1,167,000	12.9
Univ. of Fla.	64,530	687,600	12.9
College of William and Mary	81,680	857,400	12.8
Texas A&M	84,140	842,600	12.7
U. of Ill., Urbana-Champaign	99,160	964,800	12.6
Brigham Young Univ.	73,210	730,600	12.6
UC-San Diego	99,410	950,100	12.5
Binghamton Univ.	73,700	712,300	12.5
Univ. of Mich.	92,710	870,900	12.4
Cal Poly	88,530	825,100	12.4

Source: PayScale.com

How do we compute the figure? And once we have computed this figure, how do we use it when evaluating an investment alternative? Our consideration of the concept of rate of return in this chapter will answer these and other questions.

Along with the PW and AE concepts, the third primary measure of investment worth is **rate of return (ROR)**. As shown in Chapter 5, the PW measure is easy to calculate and apply. Nevertheless, many engineers and financial managers prefer rate-of-return analysis to the PW method because they find it intuitively more appealing to analyze investments in terms of percentage rates of return rather than in dollars of PW. Consider the following statements regarding an investment's profitability:

- This project will bring in a 15% rate of return on the investment.
- This project will result in a net surplus of $10,000 in terms of PW.

Neither statement describes the nature of an investment project in any complete sense. However, the rate-of-return figure is somewhat easier to understand because many of us are familiar with savings and loan interest rates, which are in fact rates of return.

In this chapter, we will examine four aspects of rate-of-return analysis: (1) the concept of return on investment; (2) calculation of a rate of return; (3) development of an internal rate-of-return criterion; and (4) comparison of mutually exclusive alternatives, based on rate of return.

7.1 Rate of Return

Many different terms are used to refer to **rate of return**, including **yield** (e.g., yield to maturity, commonly used in bond valuation), **internal rate of return**, and **marginal efficiency of capital**. We will first review three common definitions of rate of return. Then we will use the definition of internal rate of return as a measure of profitability for a single investment project, throughout the text.

7.1.1 Return on Investment

There are several ways of defining the concept of rate of return on investment. We will show two of them: the first is based on a typical loan transaction, and the second is based on the mathematical expression of the present-worth function.

> **Definition 1.** *Rate of return is the interest earned on the unpaid balance of an amortized loan.*

Suppose that a bank lends $10,000, which is repaid in installments of $4,021 at the end of each year for three years. How would you determine the interest rate that the bank charges on this transaction? As we learned in Chapter 3, you would set up the following equivalence equation and solve for i:

$$\$10,000 = \$4,021\,(P/A, i, 3).$$

It turns out that $i = 10\%$. In this situation, the bank will earn a return of 10% on its investment of $10,000. The bank calculates the loan balances over the life of the loan as follows:

Year	Unpaid Balance at Beginning of Year	Return on Unpaid Balance (10%)	Payment Received	Unpaid Balance at End of Year
0				−$10,000
1	−$10,000	−$1,000	$4,021	−$6,979
2	−$6,979	−$698	$4,021	−$3,656
3	−$3,656	−$366	$4,021	$0

A negative balance indicates an unpaid balance.

Observe that, for the repayment schedule shown, the 10% interest is calculated only for each year's outstanding balance. In this situation, only part of the $4,021 annual payment represents interest; the remainder goes toward repaying the principal. In other words, the three annual payments repay the loan itself and provide a return of 10% on the *amount still outstanding each year.*

Note also that, when the last payment is made, the outstanding principal is eventually reduced to zero.[4] If we calculate the NPW of the loan transaction at its rate of return (10%), we see that

$$PW(10\%) = -\$10{,}000 + \$4{,}021\,(P/A, 10\%, 3) = 0,$$

which indicates that the bank can break even at a 10% rate of interest. In other words, the rate of return becomes the rate of interest that equates the present value of future cash repayments to the amount of the loan. This observation prompts the second definition of rate of return:

Definition 2. *Rate of return is the break-even interest rate i^* at which the net present worth of a project is zero, or*

$$PW(i^*) = PW_{\text{Cash inflows}} - PW_{\text{Cash outflows}} = 0.$$

Note that the foregoing expression is equivalent to

$$PW(i^*) = \frac{A_0}{(1+i^*)^0} + \frac{A_1}{(1+i^*)^1} + \cdots + \frac{A_N}{(1+i^*)^N} = 0. \tag{7.1}$$

Here, we know the value of A_n for each period, but not the value of i^*. Since it is the only unknown, we can solve for i^*. As we will discuss momentarily, this solution is not always straightforward due to the nature of the PW function in Eq. (7.1); it is certainly possible to have more than one rate of return for certain types of cash flows.[5]

Note that the i^* formula in Eq. (7.1) is simply the PW formula in Eq. (5.1) solved for the particular interest rate (i^*) at which $PW(i)$ is equal to zero. By multiplying both sides of Eq. (7.1) by $(1+i^*)^N$, we obtain

$$PW(i^*)(1+i^*)^N = FW(i^*) = 0.$$

If we multiply both sides of Eq. (7.1) by the capital-recovery factor, $(A/P, i^*, N)$, we obtain the relationship $AE(i^*) = 0$. *Therefore, the i^* of a project may also be defined as the rate of interest that equates the net present worth, future worth, and annual equivalent worth of the entire series of cash flows to zero.* Or,

$$PW(i^*) = FW(i^*) = AE(i^*) = 0.$$

7.1.2 Return on Invested Capital

Investment projects can be viewed as analogous to bank loans. We will now introduce the concept of rate of return based on the return on invested capital in terms of a project

---

[4] As we learned in Section 5.3.4, the terminal balance is equivalent to the net future worth of the investment. If the net future worth of the investment is zero, its PW should also be zero.

[5] You will always have N rates of return. The issue is whether these rates are real or imaginary numbers. If they are real, the question of whether they are in the $(-100\%, \infty)$ interval should be asked. A **negative rate of return** implies that you never recover your initial investment fully.

investment. A project's return is referred to as the internal rate of return (IRR), or the **yield** promised by an **investment project** over its **useful life**.

> **Definition 3.** *The internal rate of return is the interest rate charged on the unrecovered project balance of the investment such that, when the project terminates, the unrecovered project balance is zero.*

Suppose a company invests $10,000 in a computer with a three-year useful life and equivalent annual labor savings of $4,021. Here, we may view the investing firm as the lender and the project as the borrower. The cash flow transaction between them would be identical to the amortized loan transaction described under Definition 1:

Year	Beginning Project Balance	Return on Invested Capital (10%)	Cash Generated from Project	Project Balance at End of Year
0				−$10,000
1	−$10,000	−$1,000	$4,021	−$6,979
2	−$6,979	−$698	$4,021	−$3,656
3	−$3,656	−$366	$4,021	$0

In our project-balance calculation, we see that 10% is earned (or charged) on $10,000 during year 1, 10% is earned on $6,979 during year 2, and 10% is earned on $3,656 during year 3. This information indicates that the firm earns a 10% rate of return on funds that remain *internally* invested in the project. Since it is a return *internal* to the project, we refer to it as the **internal rate of return**, or IRR. This means that the computer project under consideration brings in enough cash to pay for itself in three years and to provide the firm with a return of 10% on its invested capital. To put it differently, if the computer is financed with funds costing 10% annually, the cash generated by the investment will be exactly sufficient to repay the principal and the annual interest charge on the fund in three years.

Notice also that only one cash outflow occurs in year 0, and the present worth of this outflow is simply $10,000. There are three equal receipts, and the present worth of these inflows is $4,021 (P/A, 10%, 3) = $10,000. Since $PW = PW_{Inflow} - PW_{Outflow} = \$10,000 - \$10,000 = 0$, 10% also satisfies Definition 2 for rate of return. Even though this simple example implies that $i*$ coincides with IRR, only Definitions 1 and 3 correctly describe the true meaning of internal rate of return. As we will see later, if the cash expenditures of an investment are not restricted to the initial period, several break-even interest rates may exist that satisfy Eq. (7.1). However, there may not be a rate of return *internal* to the project.

7.2 Methods for Finding Rate of Return

We may find $i*$ by using several procedures, each of which has its advantages and disadvantages. To facilitate the process of finding the rate of return for an investment project, we will first classify the types of investment cash flow.

7.2.1 Simple versus Nonsimple Investments

We can classify an investment project by counting the number of sign changes in its net cash flow sequence. A change from either "−" to "+" or "+" to "−" is counted as one sign change. (We ignore a zero cash flow.) We can then establish the following categories:

- A **simple (or conventional) investment** is simply when one sign change occurs in the net cash flow series. If the initial cash flows are negative, we call them **simple-investment** cash flows. If the initial flows are positive, we call them **simple-borrowing** cash flows.
- A **nonsimple (or nonconventional) investment** is an investment in which more than one sign change occurs in the cash flow series.

Multiple i^*s, as we will see later, occur only in nonsimple investments. If there is no sign change in the entire cash flow series, no rate of return exists. The different types of investment possibilities may be illustrated as follows:

Investment Type	Cash Flow Sign at Period						The Number of Sign Changes
	0	1	2	3	4	5	
Simple	−	+	+	+	+	+	1
Simple	−	−	+	+	0	+	1
Nonsimple	−	+	−	+	+	−	4
Nonsimple	−	+	+	−	0	+	3

EXAMPLE 7.1 Investment Classification

Classify the following three cash flow series as either simple or nonsimple investments:

Net Cash Flow

Period n	Project A	Project B	Project C
0	−$1,000	−$1,000	$1,000
1	−$500	$3,900	−$450
2	$800	−$5,030	−$450
3	$1,500	$2,145	−$450
4	$2,000		

DISSECTING THE PROBLEM

Given: Cash flow sequences provided in the foregoing table.

Find: Classify the sequences as either simple or nonsimple investments.

METHODOLOGY

Create a classification of investment chart.

SOLUTION

- Project A represents many common simple investments. This type of investment reveals the PW profile shown in Figure 7.1(a). The curve crosses the i-axis only once.
- Project B represents a nonsimple investment. The PW profile for this investment has the shape shown in Figure 7.1(b). The i-axis is crossed at 10%, 30%, and 50%.

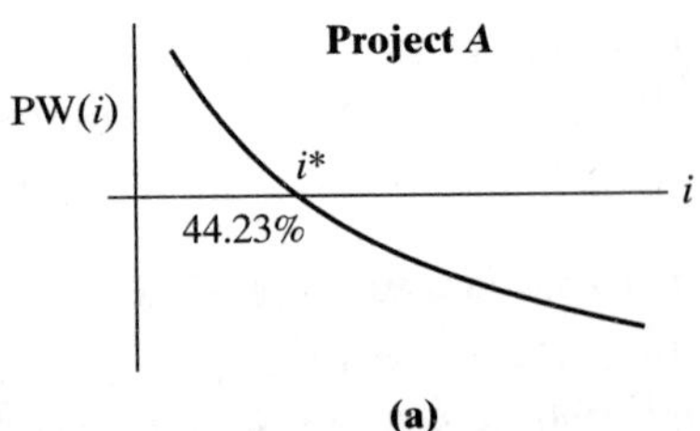

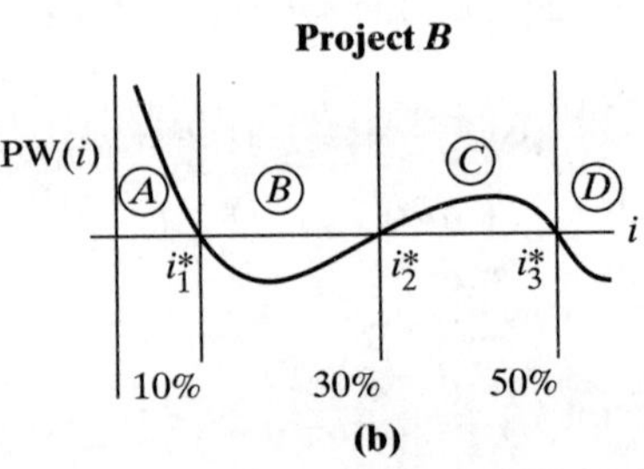

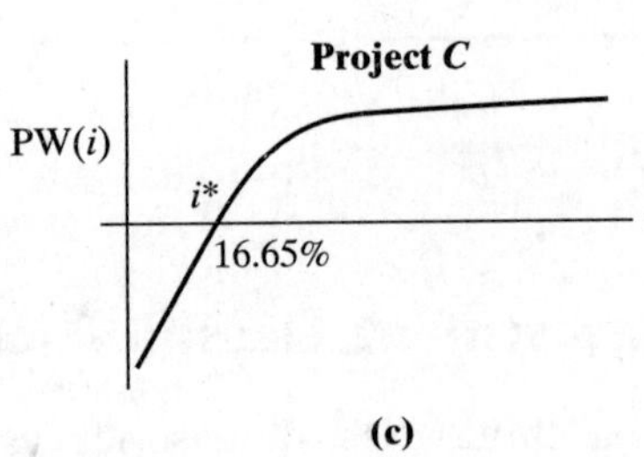

Period (n)	Project A	Project B	Project C
0	−$1,000	−$1,000	$1,000
1	−$500	$3,900	−$450
2	$800	−$5,030	−$450
3	$1,500	$2,145	−$450
4	$2,000		

Project A is a simple investment.
Project B is a nonsimple investment.
Project C is a simple-borrowing cash flow.

Figure 7.1 Classification of investments

- Project C represents neither a simple nor a nonsimple investment, even though only one sign change occurs in the cash flow sequence. Since the first cash flow is positive, this flow is a **simple-borrowing** cash flow, not an investment flow. The PW profile for this type of investment looks like the one in Figure 7.1(c).

7.2.2 Computational Methods

Once we identify the type of an investment cash flow, there are several ways to determine its rate of return. We will discuss some of the most practical methods here. They are as follows:

- Direct-solution method
- Trial-and-error method
- Excel method

Direct-Solution Method

For the very special case of a project with only a two-flow transaction (an investment followed by a single future payment) or a project with a service life of two years of return, we can seek a direct analytical solution for determining the rate of return. These two cases are examined in Example 7.2.

EXAMPLE 7.2 Finding i^* by Direct Solution: Two Flows and Two Periods

Consider two investment projects with the following cash flow transactions:

n	Project 1	Project 2
0	−$3,000	−$2,000
1	$0	$1,300
2	$0	$1,500
3	$0	
4	$4,500	

Compute the rate of return for each project.

DISSECTING THE PROBLEM

Given: Cash flows for two projects.

Find: i^* for each project.

METHODOLOGY

Write out the net present (or future) worth expression and solve for i.

SOLUTION

Project 1: Solving for i^* in $PW(i^*) = 0$ is identical to solving for i^* in $FW(i^*) = 0$, because FW equals PW times a constant. We could use either method here, but we choose $FW(i^*) = 0$. Using the single-payment future-worth relationship, we obtain

$$FW(i) = -\$3,000(F/P, i, 4) + \$4,500 = 0.$$

Setting $FW(i) = 0$, we obtain

$$\$4,500 = \$3,000(F/P, i, 4) = \$3,000(1 + i)^4,$$

or

$$1.5 = (1 + i)^4.$$

Solving for i yields

$$i^* = \sqrt[4]{1.5} - 1 = 0.1067, \text{ or } 10.67\%.$$

Project 2: We may write the PW expression for this project as follows:

$$PW(i) = -\$2,000 + \frac{\$1,300}{(1 + i)} + \frac{\$1,500}{(1 + i)^2} = 0.$$

Let

$$X = \frac{1}{(1 + i)}.$$

We may then rewrite the $PW(i)$ expression as a function of X and set it equal to zero, as follows:

$$PW(i) = -\$2,000 + \$1,300X + \$1,500X^2 = 0.$$

This expression is a quadratic equation that has the following solution:[6]

$$X = \frac{-1{,}300 \pm \sqrt{1{,}300^2 - 4(1{,}500)(-2{,}000)}}{2(1{,}500)}$$

$$= \frac{-1{,}300 \pm 3{,}700}{3{,}000}$$

$$= 0.8 \text{ or } -1.667.$$

Replacing the X values and solving for i gives us

$$0.8 = \frac{1}{(1+i)} \rightarrow i = 25\%$$

and

$$-1.667 = \frac{1}{(1+i)} \rightarrow i = -160\%.$$

Since an interest rate less than -100% has no economic significance, we find that the project's unique i^* is 25%.

COMMENTS: In both projects, one sign change occurred in the net cash flow series, so we expected a unique i^*. Also, these projects had very simple cash flows. Generally, when cash flows are more complex, we must use a trial-and-error method or a computer program to find i^*.

Trial-and-Error Method

The first step in the trial-and-error method is to make an estimated guess at the value of i^*.[7] For a simple investment, we use the guessed interest rate to compute the present worth of net cash flows and observe whether the result is positive, negative, or zero:

- **Case 1:** $\text{PW}(i) < 0$. Since we are aiming for a value of i that makes $\text{PW}(i) = 0$, we must raise the present worth of the cash flow. To do this, we lower the interest rate and repeat the process.
- **Case 2:** $\text{PW}(i) > 0$. We raise the interest rate in order to lower $\text{PW}(i)$. The process is continued until $\text{PW}(i)$ is approximately equal to zero.

Whenever we reach the point where $\text{PW}(i)$ is bounded by one negative value and one positive value, we use **linear interpolation** to approximate i^*. This technique was discussed in Chapter 2. This process is somewhat tedious and inefficient. (The trial-and-error method does not work for nonsimple investments in which the PW function is not, in general, a monotonically decreasing function of interest rate.)

---

[6] Given $aX^2 + bX + c = 0$, the solution of the quadratic equation is $X = \dfrac{-b \pm \sqrt{b^2 - 4ac}}{2a}$.

[7] As we will see later in this chapter, the ultimate objective of finding i^* is to compare it with the MARR. Therefore, it is a good idea to use the MARR as the initial guess value.

EXAMPLE 7.3 Finding *i** by Trial and Error

ACME Corporation distributes agricultural equipment. The board of directors is considering a proposal to establish a facility to manufacture an electronically controlled "intelligent" crop sprayer invented by a professor at a local university. This crop-sprayer project would require an investment of $10 million in assets and would produce an annual after-tax net benefit of $1.8 million over a service life of eight years. All costs and benefits are included in these figures. When the project terminates, the net proceeds from the sale of the assets would be $1 million (Figure 7.2). Compute the rate of return of this project.

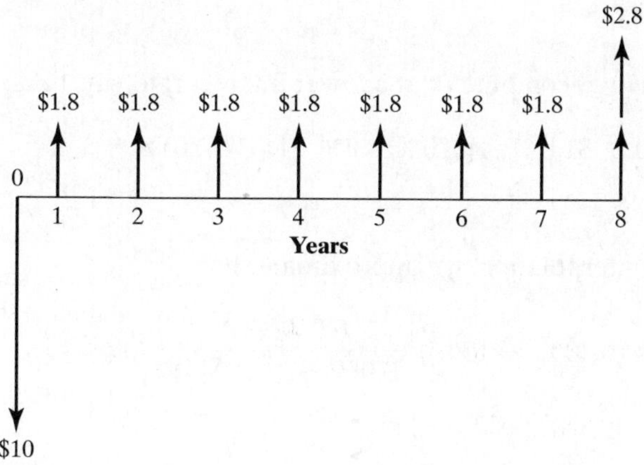

Figure 7.2 Cash flow diagram for a simple investment; all dollar amounts are in millions of dollars

---

DISSECTING THE PROBLEM	
	Given: I = $10 million, A = $1.8 million, S = $1 million, and N = 8 years. **Find:** i^*.
METHODOLOGY Find i^* by trial and error.	**SOLUTION** We start with a guessed interest rate of 8%. The net present worth of the cash flows in millions of dollars is $$\text{PW}(8\%) = -\$10 + \$1.8(P/A, 8\%, 8) + \$1(P/F, 8\%, 8) = \$0.88.$$ Since this net present worth is positive, we must raise the interest rate in order to bring this value toward zero. When we use an interest rate of 12%, we find that $$\text{PW}(12\%) = -\$10 + \$1.8(P/A, 12\%, 8)$$ $$+ \$1(P/F, 12\%, 8) = -\$0.65.$$

We have bracketed the solution. $PW(i)$ will be zero at i somewhere between 8% and 12%. Using straight-line interpolation, we approximate that

$$i^* \approx 8\% + (12\% - 8\%)\left[\frac{0.88 - 0}{0.88 - (-0.65)}\right]$$

$$= 8\% + 4\%(0.5752)$$

$$= 10.30\%.$$

Now we will check to see how close this value is to the precise value of i^*. If we compute the net present worth at this interpolated value, we obtain

$$PW(10.30\%) = -\$10 + \$1.8(P/A, 10.30\%, 8) + \$1(P/F, 10.30\%, 8)$$

$$= -\$0.045.$$

As this result is not zero, we may recompute i^* at a lower interest rate, say, 10%:

$$PW(10\%) = -\$10 + \$1.8(P/A, 10\%, 8) + \$1(P/F, 10\%, 8)$$

$$= \$0.069.$$

With another round of linear interpolation, we approximate that

$$i^* \approx 10\% + (10.30\% - 10\%)\left[\frac{0.069 - 0}{0.069 - (-0.045)}\right]$$

$$= 10\% + 0.30\%(0.6053)$$

$$= 10.18\%.$$

At this interest rate,

$$PW(10.18\%) = -\$10 + \$1.8(P/A, 10.18\%, 8) + \$1(P/F, 10.18\%, 8)$$

$$= \$0.0007,$$

which is practically zero, so we may stop here. In fact, there is no need to be more precise about these interpolations because the final result can be no more accurate than the basic data, which ordinarily are only rough estimates. Incidentally, computing the i^* for this problem on a computer gives us 10.1819%.

Rate-of-Return Calculation with Excel

Fortunately, we do not need to do laborious manual calculations to find i^*. Many financial calculators have built-in functions for calculating i^*. It is worth noting that many spreadsheet packages have i^* functions that solve Eq. (7.1) very rapidly. Spreadsheets usually apply functions by entering the cash flows via a computer keyboard or by reading a cash flow data file. For example, Microsoft Excel has an IRR financial function that analyzes investment cash flows, namely, $= \text{IRR}(\text{range}, \text{guess})$. We will demonstrate the IRR function with an example involving an investment in a corporate bond.

EXAMPLE 7.4 Yield to Maturity

Consider buying a $1,000-denomination corporate bond at the market price of $996.25. The interest will be paid semiannually at an interest rate per payment period of 4.8125%. Twenty interest payments over 10 years are required. We show the resulting cash flow to the investor in Figure 7.3. Find the return on this bond investment (or yield to maturity).

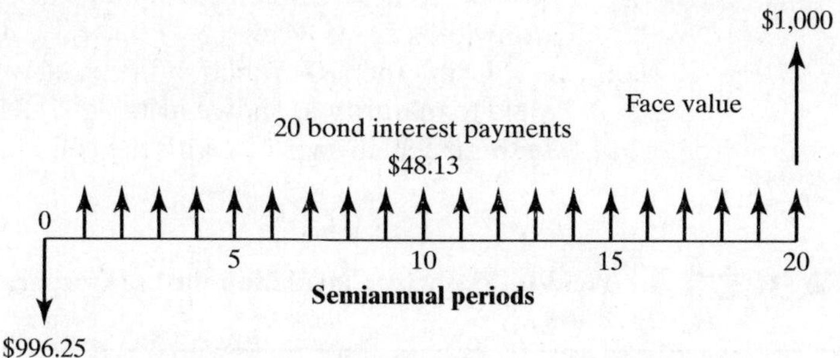

Figure 7.3   A typical cash flow transaction associated with an investment in the corporate bond

DISSECTING THE PROBLEM

You can trade bonds on the market just like stocks. Once you have purchased a bond, you can keep the bond until it reaches maturity or sell at any interest period before maturity. You can purchase or sell bonds at prices other than face value, depending on the economic environment, as bond prices change over time because of the risk of nonpayment of interest or face value, supply and demand, and the outlook for economic conditions. These factors affect the **yield to maturity** (or **return on investment**). The **yield to maturity** represents the actual interest earned from a bond over the holding period. In other words, the yield to maturity on a bond is the interest rate that establishes the equivalence between all future interest and face-value receipts and the market price of the bond. Some specific bond terms to understand are summarized as follows:

- **Face (par) value:** The corporate bond has a face value of $1,000.
- **Maturity date:** The bonds that were issued on January 30, 2011, will mature on January 31, 2021; thus, they have a 10-year maturity at time of issue.
- **Coupon rate:** The bond's coupon rate is 9.625%, and interest is payable semiannually. For example, the bonds have a $1,000 face value, and they pay $96.25 in simple interest ($9\frac{5}{8}$%) each year (or $48.13 every six months).
- **Discount bond:** The bonds are offered at less than the face value at 99.625%, or 0.375% discount. For example, a bond with a face value of $1,000 can be purchased for just $996.25, which is known as the **market price** (or value) of the bond.

Given: Initial purchase price = $996.25, coupon rate = 9.625% per year paid semiannually, and 10-year maturity with a face value of $1,000.

Find: Yield to maturity.

METHODOLOGY

Determine the interest rate that makes the PW of receipts equal to the bond's market price.

SOLUTION

We find the yield to maturity by determining the interest rate that makes the present worth of the receipts equal to the market price of the bond:

$$\$996.25 = \$48.13\,(P/A, i, 20) + \$1000\,(P/F, i, 20).$$

The value of i that makes the present worth of the receipts equal to \$996.25 lies between 4.5% and 5%. Solving for i by interpolation yields $i = 4.84\%$.

Using the IRR function in Excel, we may easily calculate the yield to maturity, as shown in Table 7.1. The initial guess value used in this calculation is 4% with the cell range of B10:B30.

TABLE 7.1 Yield-to-Maturity Calculation for the Corporate Bond

	A	B	C	D
1	**Example 7.4 Yield to Maturity Calculation**			
2				
3	Market price			$ 996.25
4	Maturity (semiannual periods)			20
5	Face value			$ 1,000.00
6	Coupon rate (per semiannual period)			4.813%
7	Yield to maturity			4.842%
8				
9	Period	Cash Flow		
10	0	$ (996.25)		
11	1	$ 48.13		
12	2	$ 48.13	=IRR(B10:B30,4%)	
13	3	$ 48.13		
14	4	$ 48.13		
15	5	$ 48.13		
16	6	$ 48.13		
17	7	$ 48.13		
18	8	$ 48.13		
19	9	$ 48.13		
20	10	$ 48.13		
21	11	$ 48.13		
22	12	$ 48.13		
23	13	$ 48.13		
24	14	$ 48.13		
25	15	$ 48.13		
26	16	$ 48.13		
27	17	$ 48.13		
28	18	$ 48.13		
29	19	$ 48.13		
30	20	$ 1,048.13		
31				

COMMENTS: Note that this result is a 4.84% yield to maturity per semiannual period. The nominal (annual) yield is $2(4.84) = 9.68\%$ compounded semiannually. When compared with the coupon rate of $9\frac{5}{8}\%$ (or 9.625%), purchasing the bond with the price discounted at 0.375% brings about an additional 0.055% yield. The effective annual coupon rate is then

$$i_a = (1 + 0.0484)^2 - 1 = 9.91\%.$$

This 9.91% represents the **effective annual yield** to maturity on the bond. Notice that when you purchase a bond at face value and sell at face value, the yield to maturity will be the *same* as the coupon rate of the bond.

7.3 Internal-Rate-of-Return Criterion

Now that we have classified investment projects and learned methods to determine the i^* value for a given project's cash flows, our objective is to develop an accept-or-reject decision rule that gives results consistent with those obtained from PW analysis.

7.3.1 Relationship to the PW Analysis

As we already observed in Chapter 5, PW analysis is dependent on the rate of interest used for the PW computation. A different rate may change a project from being considered acceptable to being considered unacceptable, or it may change the priority of several projects.

Consider again the PW profile as drawn for the simple project in Figure 7.1(a). For interest rates below i^*, this project should be accepted, as PW > 0; for interest rates above i^*, it should be rejected.

On the other hand, for certain nonsimple projects, the PW may look like the one shown in Figure 7.1(b). Use of PW analysis would lead you to accept the projects in regions A and C but reject those in regions B and D. Of course, this result goes against intuition: A higher interest rate would change an unacceptable project into an acceptable one. The situation graphed in Figure 7.1(b) is one of the cases of multiple i^*s mentioned earlier.

For the simple investment situation in Figure 7.1(a), the i^* can serve as an appropriate index for either accepting or rejecting the investment. However, for the nonsimple investment in Figure 7.1(b), it is not clear which i^* to use in order to make an accept-or-reject decision. Therefore, the i^* value fails to provide an appropriate measure of profitability for an investment project with multiple rates of return.

7.3.2 Decision Rule for Simple Investments

Suppose we have a simple investment. Why should we be interested in finding the interest rate that equates a project's cost with the present worth of its receipts? Again, we may easily answer this question by examining Figure 7.1(a). In this figure, we notice two important characteristics of the PW profile. First, as we compute the project's $PW(i)$ at a varying interest rate i, we see that the PW is positive for $i < i^*$, indicating that the project would be acceptable under the PW analysis for those values of i. Second, the PW is negative for $i > i^*$, indicating that the project is unacceptable for those values of i.

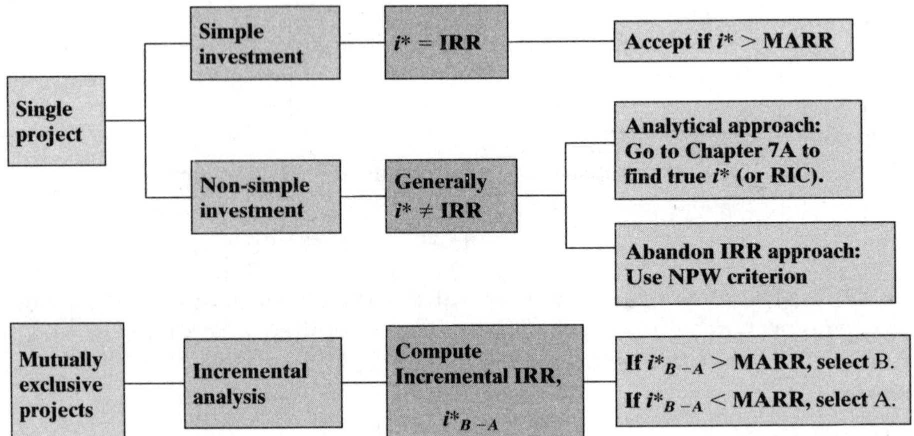

Figure 7.4 Project selection rules under the IRR criterion

Therefore, the i^* serves as a **benchmark** interest rate. By knowing this benchmark rate, we will be able to make an accept-or-reject decision consistent with the PW analysis:

- **Evaluating a Single Project:** For a simple investment, i^* is indeed the IRR of the investment. (See Section 7.1.2.) Merely knowing i^* is not enough to apply this method, however. Because firms typically wish to do better than break even (recall that at PW $= 0$, we were indifferent to the project), a minimum acceptable rate of return (MARR) is indicated by company policy, management, or the project decision maker. If the IRR exceeds this MARR, we are assured that the company will more than break even. Thus, the IRR becomes a useful gauge against which to judge project acceptability (see Figure 7.4), and the decision rule for a simple project is as follows:

  If IRR $>$ MARR, accept the project.

  If IRR $=$ MARR, remain indifferent.

  If IRR $<$ MARR, reject the project.

- **Evaluating Mutually Exclusive Projects:** Note that the foregoing decision rule is designed to be applied for a single-project evaluation. When we have to compare mutually exclusive investment projects, we need to apply the **incremental analysis approach**, as we shall see in Section 7.4.2. For now, we will consider the single-project evaluations.

EXAMPLE 7.5 Investment Decision for a Simple Investment—Economics of Wind

An energy firm is betting on wind power's long-term viability in Texas and plans to erect what would be one of the biggest wind farms in the world with 200 wind turbines costing some $1.69 million each. Energy companies investing in wind power are also expecting governments to toughen rules relating to traditional energy sources, as part of long-term efforts to reduce global-warming emissions. But generating power from wind is not profitable for companies without government tax breaks. The following financial and technical data have been compiled for further consideration:

- Number of wind turbines to be built: 200 units
- Power capacity: 310,000 kW
- Capital investment required: $338,000,000
- Project life: 20 years
- Salvage value of the wind turbines after 20 years: $0
- Annual net cash flows (after all deductions): $41,391,160

According to the data provided, answer the following questions:

(a) What is the projected IRR on this investment?
(b) If the company's MARR is known to be 10%, is the investment justified?

DISSECTING THE PROBLEM

We assumed the following in obtaining the annual net cash flows ($41,391,160):

- Average load factor: 35% (site specific, but use this value for analysis purposes)
- Power generated per year:

$$\text{Power generated per year} = 310{,}000\,\text{kW} \times 0.35$$
$$\times\ 24\,\text{hrs/day} \times 365\,\text{days/yr}$$
$$= 950{,}460{,}000\,\text{kWh/yr}$$

- Selling price of power generated from the wind turbines: $0.034/kWh:

$$\text{Operating revenues} = \$0.034/\text{kWh} \times 950{,}460{,}000\,\text{kWh/yr}$$
$$= \$32{,}315{,}640/\text{yr}$$

- Federal tax credit: $0.018/kWh sold to utility customers:

$$\text{Tax credit} = \$0.018/\text{kWh} \times 950{,}460{,}000\,\text{kWh/yr}$$
$$= \$17{,}108{,}280/\text{yr}$$

- Annual easement cost: $4,000 per turbine per year (or $800,000)
- Annual operating and maintenance cost: $16,300 per turbine per year or ($3,260,000)
- Annual taxes paid: $3,972,760 (We will discuss how we calculate this amount in Chapter 9.)

Given: Financial as well as the technical data as given above; MARR = 10%.

Find: (a) IRR and (b) whether to accept or reject the investment.

METHODOLOGY

Use Excel to calculate IRR.

SOLUTION

(a) Since only one sign change occurs in the net cash flow series, the project is a simple investment. This factor indicates that there will be a unique rate of return that is internal to the project:

$$PW(i) = -\$338,000,000 + \$41,391,160(P/A, i, 20) = 0.$$

We could use the trial-and-error approach outlined in Section 7.2.2 to find the IRR, but the IRR function in Excel would be a more convenient way to calculate the internal rate of return. Table 7.2 shows that the rate of return for the project is 10.62%, which barely exceeds the MARR of 10%. (This project is not economical without the federal tax credit.)

(b) The IRR figure exceeds the required MARR, indicating that the project is an economically attractive one and could proceed. However, there is no doubt that the installation of the wind turbines system would pose a great deal of financial risk to the firm if any climate changes in the region lowered the capacity (or load) factor.

TABLE 7.2 **An Excel Worksheet to Illustrate How to Determine the IRR (Example 7.5)**

	A	B	C	D	E	F	G	H	I	J	K	L
1	(*I*) Investment			$ 338,000,000		Net Present Worth						$ 14,386,278
2	(*i*) MARR (%)			10%		Internal Rate of Return						▲10.62%
3												
4		Cash	Cash	Net		MARR		=NPV(F10%,$D$8:$D$27)+$D$7				
5	*n*	Inflows	Outflows	Cash Flows		(%)	NPW	NPW as a Function of Interest Rate				
6												
7	0			$ (338,000,000)		0	$ 489,823,200					
8	1	$ 49,423,920	$ 8,032,760	$ 41,391,160		1	$ 408,926,370			=IRR(D7:D27,10%)		
9	2	$ 49,423,920	$ 8,032,760	$ 41,391,160		2	$ 338,804,794					
10	3	$ 49,423,920	$ 8,032,760	$ 41,391,160		3	$ 277,795,942					
11	4	$ 49,423,920	$ 8,032,760	$ 41,391,160		4	$ 224,519,372					
12	5	$ 49,423,920	$ 8,032,760	$ 41,391,160		5	$ 177,825,342					
13	6	$ 49,423,920	$ 8,032,760	$ 41,391,160		6	$ 136,753,344					
14	7	$ 49,423,920	$ 8,032,760	$ 41,391,160		7	$ 100,498,539					
15	8	$ 49,423,920	$ 8,032,760	$ 41,391,160		8	$ 68,384,510					
16	9	$ 49,423,920	$ 8,032,760	$ 41,391,160		9	$ 39,841,094					
17	10	$ 49,423,920	$ 8,032,760	$ 41,391,160		10	$ 14,386,278					
18	11	$ 49,423,920	$ 8,032,760	$ 41,391,160		11	$ (8,388,612)					
19	12	$ 49,423,920	$ 8,032,760	$ 41,391,160		12	$ (28,831,064)					
20	13	$ 49,423,920	$ 8,032,760	$ 41,391,160		13	$ (47,237,383)					
21	14	$ 49,423,920	$ 8,032,760	$ 41,391,160		14	$ (63,860,944)					
22	15	$ 49,423,920	$ 8,032,760	$ 41,391,160		15	$ (78,919,009)					
23	16	$ 49,423,920	$ 8,032,760	$ 41,391,160		16	$ (92,598,398)					
24	17	$ 49,423,920	$ 8,032,760	$ 41,391,160		17	$ (105,060,182)					
25	18	$ 49,423,920	$ 8,032,760	$ 41,391,160		18	$ (116,443,613)					
26	19	$ 49,423,920	$ 8,032,760	$ 41,391,160		19	$ (126,869,399)					
27	20	$ 49,423,920	$ 8,032,760	$ 41,391,160		20	$ (136,442,446)					
28												

7.3.3 Decision Rule for Nonsimple Investments

When applied to simple projects, the i^* provides an unambiguous criterion for measuring profitability. However, when multiple rates of return occur, none of them is an accurate portrayal of project acceptability or profitability. Clearly, then, we should place a high priority on discovering this situation early in our analysis of a project's cash flows. The quickest way to predict the existence of multiple i^*s is to generate a PW profile on the computer and check if it crosses the horizontal axis more than once.

In addition to the PW profile, there are good—although somewhat more complex—analytical methods for predicting the existence of multiple i^*s. Perhaps more importantly, there is a good method, discussed in Chapter 7A, that uses an **external interest rate** for refining our analysis when we do discover that there are multiple i^*s. An external rate of return allows us to calculate a single true rate of return.

If you choose to avoid these more complex applications of rate-of-return techniques, you must be able to predict the existence of multiple i^*s via the PW profile and, when they occur, select an alternative method, such as PW or AE analysis, for determining project acceptability.

EXAMPLE 7.6 Investment Decision for a Nonsimple Project

By outbidding its competitors, Turbo Image Processing (TIP), a defense contractor, has received a contract worth $7,300,000 to build navy flight simulators for U.S. Navy pilot training over two years. For some defense contracts, the U.S. government makes an advance payment when the contract is signed, but in this case, the government will make two progressive payments: $4,300,000 at the end of the first year and the $3,000,000 balance at the end of the second year. The expected cash outflows required in order to produce these simulators are estimated to be $1,000,000 now, $2,000,000 during the first year, and $4,320,000 during the second year. The expected net cash flows from this project are summarized as follows:

Year	Cash Inflow	Cash Outflow	Net Cash Flow
0		$1,000,000	−$1,000,000
1	$4,300,000	$2,000,000	$2,300,000
2	$3,000,000	$4,320,000	−$1,320,000

In normal situations, TIP would not even consider a marginal project such as this one in the first place. However, hoping that TIP can establish itself as a technology leader in the field, management felt that it was worth outbidding its competitors by providing the lowest bid. Financially, what is the economic worth of outbidding the competitors for this project?

(a) Compute the values of the i^*s for this project.
(b) Make an accept-or-reject decision on the basis of the results of part (a). Assume that the contractor's MARR is 15%.

DISSECTING THE PROBLEM

Given: Cash flow shown in the foregoing table; $\text{MARR} = 15\%$.

Find: (a) i^* and (b) determine whether to accept the project.

METHODOLOGY

Quadratic method.

SOLUTION

(a) Since this project has a two-year life, we may solve the NPW equation directly via the quadratic-formula method:

$$-\$1,000,000 + \frac{\$2,300,000}{(1 + i^*)} - \frac{\$1,320,000}{(1 + i^*)^2} = 0.$$

If we let $X = 1/(1 + i^*)$, we can rewrite the expression as

$$-1,000,000 + 2,300,000X - 1,320,000X^2 = 0.$$

Solving for X gives $X = \frac{10}{11}$ and $\frac{10}{12}$ or $i^* = 10\%$ and 20%, respectively.

(b) As shown in Figure 7.5, the PW profile intersects the horizontal axis twice, once at 10% and again at 20%. The investment is obviously not a simple one, and thus neither 10% nor 20% represents the true internal rate of return of this government project.

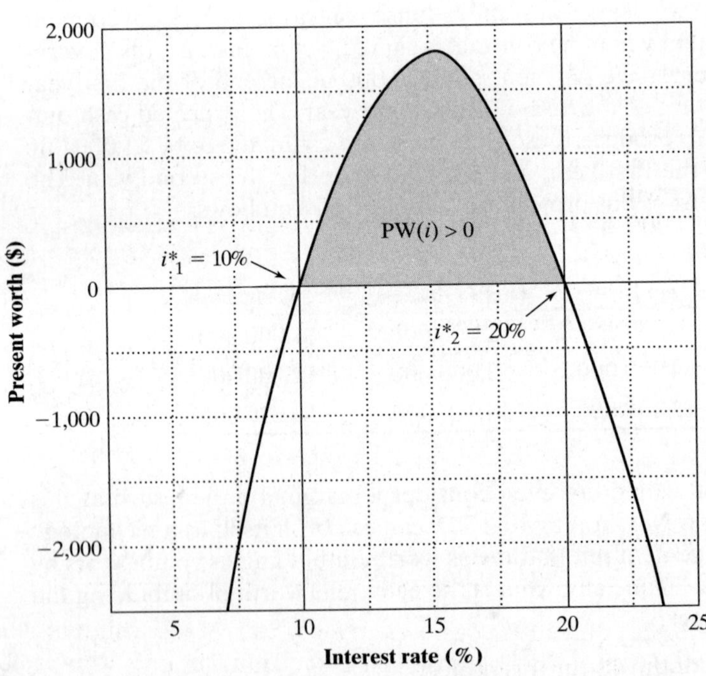

Figure 7.5 NPW plot for a nonsimple investment with multiple rates of return

Since the project is a nonsimple project, we may abandon the IRR criterion for practical purposes and use the PW criterion. If we use the present-worth method at MARR = 15%, we obtain

$$PW(15\%) = -\$1,000,000 + \$2,300,000\,(P/F, 15\%, 1)$$
$$-\$1,320,000\,(P/F, 15\%, 2)$$
$$= \$1,890,$$

which verifies that the project is marginally acceptable, and it is thus not as bad as we initially believed.

7.4 Incremental Analysis for Comparing Mutually Exclusive Alternatives

In this section, we present the decision procedures that should be used when comparing two or more mutually exclusive projects on the basis of the rate-of-return measure. We will consider two situations: (1) alternatives that have the same economic service life and (2) alternatives that have unequal service lives.

7.4.1 Flaws in Project Ranking by IRR

Under PW or AE analysis, the mutually exclusive project with the highest worth figure was preferred. (This approach is known as the "total investment approach.") Unfortunately, the analogy does not carry over to IRR analysis. The project with the highest IRR may *not* be the preferred alternative. To illustrate the flaws of comparing IRRs when selecting between mutually exclusive projects, suppose you have two mutually exclusive alternatives, each with a one-year service life. One requires an investment of $1,000 with a return of $2,000, and the other requires $5,000 with a return of $7,000. You have already obtained the IRRs and PWs at MARR = 10% as follows:

Comparing Mutually Exclusive Alternatives, Based on IRR

• Issue: Can we rank the mutually exclusive projects by the magnitude of IRR?			
n	Project A1		Project A2
0	−$1,000		−$5,000
1	$2,000		$7,000
IRR	100%	>	40%
PW(10%)	$818	<	$1,364

Assuming that you have exactly $5,000 in your investment pool to select either project, would you prefer the first project simply because you expect a higher rate of return?

We can see that Project A2 is preferred over Project A1 by the PW measure. On the other hand, the IRR measure gives a numerically higher rating for Project A1. This inconsistency in ranking occurs because the PW, FW, and AE are **absolute (dollar)** measures of investment worth, whereas the IRR is a **relative (percentage)** measure and cannot be applied in the same way. Consequently, the IRR measure ignores the scale of the investment. Clearly, the answer is no; instead, you would prefer the second project with the lower rate of return but higher PW. Either the PW or the AE measure would lead to that choice, but comparison of IRRs would rank the smaller project higher. Another approach, referred to as **incremental analysis**, is needed.

7.4.2 Incremental-Investment Analysis

In our previous example, the costlier option requires $4,000 more than the other option while it provides an additional return of $5,000. To compare these directly, we must look at the total impact on our investment pool using common terms. Here we look at each project's impact on an investment pool of $5,000. You must consider the following factors:

- If you decide to invest in Project $A1$, you will need to withdraw only $1,000 from your investment pool. The remaining $4,000 that is not committed will continue to earn 10% interest. One year later, you will have $2,000 from the outside investment and $4,400 from the investment pool. Thus, with an investment of $5,000, in one year you will have $6,400 (or a 28% return on the $5,000). The equivalent present worth of this wealth change is

$$\text{PW}(10\%) = -\$5,000 + \$6,400(P/F, 10\%, 1) = \$818.$$

- If you decide to invest in Project $A2$, you will need to withdraw $5,000 from your investment pool, leaving no money in the pool, but you will have $7,000 from your outside investment. Your total wealth changes from $5,000 to $7,000 in a year. The equivalent present worth of this wealth change is

$$\text{PW}(10\%) = -\$5,000 + \$7,000(P/F, 10\%, 1) = \$1,364.$$

In other words, if you decide to take the more costly option, certainly you would be interested in knowing that this additional investment can be justified at the MARR. The MARR value of 10% implies that you can always earn that rate from other investment sources (e.g., $4,400 at the end of one year for a $4,000 investment). However, in the second option, by investing the additional $4,000, you would make an additional $5,000, which is equivalent to earning at the rate of 25%. Therefore, the higher-cost investment can be justified. Figure 7.6 summarizes the process of performing incremental-investment analysis.

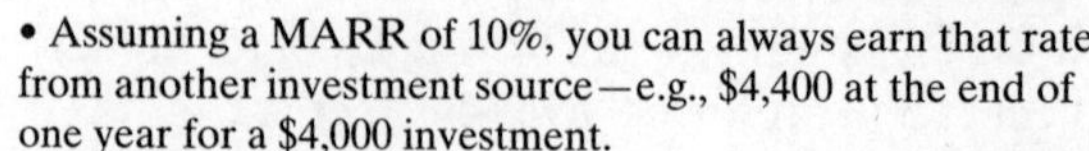

n	Project $A1$	Project $A2$	Incremental Investment $(A2 - A1)$
0	−$1,000	−$5,000	−$4,000
1	$2,000	$7,000	$5,000
IRR	100%	40%	25%
PW(10%)	$818	$1,364	$546

- Assuming a MARR of 10%, you can always earn that rate from another investment source—e.g., $4,400 at the end of one year for a $4,000 investment.

- By investing the additional $4,000 in $A2$, you would make an additional $5,000, which is equivalent to earning at the rate of 25%. Therefore, the incremental investment in $A2$ is justified.

Figure 7.6 Illustration of incremental analysis

Now we can generalize the decision rule for comparing mutually exclusive projects. For a pair of mutually exclusive projects (A and B, with B defined as a more costly option), we may rewrite B as

$$B = A + (B - A).$$

In other words, B has two cash flow components: (1) the same cash flow as A and (2) the incremental component $(B - A)$. Therefore, the only situation in which B is preferred to A is when the rate of return on the incremental component $(B - A)$ exceeds the MARR. Therefore, for two mutually exclusive projects, we use rate-of-return analysis by computing the *internal rate of return on incremental investment* (IRR_{B-A}) between the projects. Since we want to consider increments of investment, we compute the cash flow for the difference between the projects by subtracting the cash flow for the lower investment-cost project (A) from that of the higher investment-cost project (B). Then the decision rule is as follows, where $(B - A)$ is an investment increment. (The sign of the first cash flow should be always negative.)

If $IRR_{B-A} >$ MARR, select B (higher first-cost alternative).

If $IRR_{B-A} =$ MARR, select either one.

If $IRR_{B-A} <$ MARR, select A (lower first-cost alternative).

If a "do-nothing" alternative is allowed, the smaller cost option must be profitable (its IRR must be higher than the MARR) at first. This means that we compute the rate of return for each alternative in the mutually exclusive group and then eliminate the alternatives that have IRRs less than the MARR before applying the incremental-investment analysis. It may seem odd to you how this simple rule allows us to select the right project. Example 7.7 will illustrate the incremental-investment decision rule for you.

EXAMPLE 7.7 IRR on Incremental Investment: Two Alternatives

John Covington, a college student, wants to start a small-scale painting business during his off-school hours. To economize the start-up business, he decides to purchase some used painting equipment. He has two mutually exclusive options: ($B1$) Do most of the painting by himself by limiting his business to only residential painting jobs or ($B2$) purchase more painting equipment and hire some helpers to do both residential and commercial painting jobs. He expects option $B2$ will have a higher equipment cost but provide higher revenues as well. In either case, he expects to fold the business in three years when he graduates from college.

The cash flows for the two mutually exclusive alternatives are given as follows:

n	$B1$	$B2$	$B2 - B1$
0	-$3,000	-$12,000	-$9,000
1	$1,350	$4,200	$2,850
2	$1,800	$6,225	$4,425
3	$1,500	$6,330	$4,830
IRR	25%	17.43%	

With the knowledge that both alternatives are revenue projects, which project would John select at MARR $= 10\%$? (Note that both projects are profitable at 10%.)

DISSECTING THE PROBLEM

Given: Incremental cash flow between two alternatives; $\text{MARR} = 10\%$.

Find: (a) The IRR on the increment and (b) which alternative is preferable.

METHODOLOGY

Compute incremental cash flow, then IRR.

SOLUTION

(a) To choose the best project, we compute the incremental cash flow for $B2 - B1$. Then we compute the IRR on this increment of investment by solving

$$-\$9{,}000 + \$2{,}850\,(P/F, i, 1) + \$4{,}425\,(P/F, i, 2)$$
$$+ \$4{,}830\,(P/F, i, 3) = 0.$$

(b) We obtain $i^*_{B2-B1} = 15\%$ as plotted in Figure 7.7. By inspection of the incremental cash flow, we know it is a simple investment; so, $\text{IRR}_{B2-B1} = i^*_{B2-B1}$. Since $\text{IRR}_{B2-B1} > \text{MARR}$, we select B2, which is consistent with the PW analysis. Note that, at $\text{MARR} > 25\%$ neither project would be acceptable.

n	$B1$	$B2$	$B2 - B1$
0	$-\$3,000$	$-\$12,000$	$-\$9,000$
1	$\$1,350$	$\$4,200$	$\$2,850$
2	$\$1,800$	$\$6,225$	$\$4,425$
3	$\$1,500$	$\$6,330$	$\$4,830$
IRR	25%	17.43%	15%

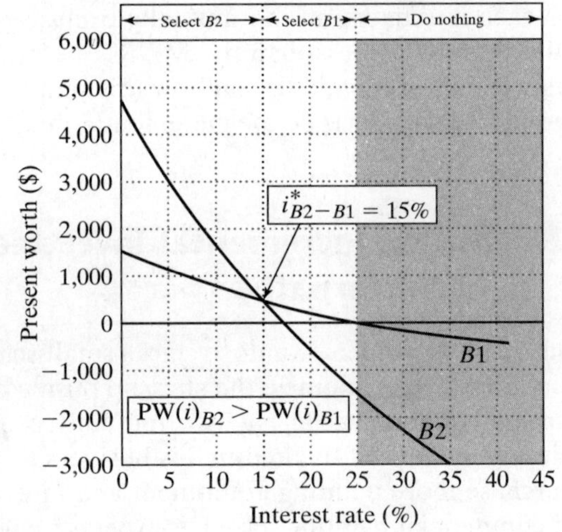

Given $\text{MARR} = 10\%$, which project is a better choice?
Since $\text{IRR}_{B2-B1} = 15\% > 10\%$ and $\text{IRR}_{B2} > 10\%$, select $B2$.

Figure 7.7 NPW profiles for $B1$ and $B2$

COMMENTS: Why did we choose to look at the increment $B2 - B1$ instead of $B1 - B2$? We want the first flow of the incremental cash flow series to be negative (investment flow) so that we can calculate an IRR. By subtracting the lower initial-investment project from the higher, we guarantee that the first increment will be an investment flow. If we ignore the investment ranking, we might end up with an increment that involves borrowing cash flow and has no rate of return internal to the investment.

The next example indicates that the ranking inconsistency between PW and IRR can also occur when differences in the timing of a project's future cash flows exist, even if their initial investments are the same.

EXAMPLE 7.8 IRR on Incremental Investment When Initial Flows Are Equal

Consider the following two mutually exclusive investment projects that require the same amount of investment:

n	C1	C2
0	−$9,000	−$9,000
1	$480	$5,800
2	$3,700	$3,250
3	$6,550	$2,000
4	$3,780	$1,561
IRR	18%	20%

Which project would you select on the basis of rate of return on incremental investment, assuming that MARR = 12%? (Once again, both projects are profitable at 12%.)

DISSECTING THE PROBLEM

Given: Cash flows for two mutually exclusive alternatives as shown; MARR = 12%.

Find: (a) The IRR on incremental investment and (b) which alternative is preferable.

METHODOLOGY

SOLUTION

(a) When initial investments are equal, we progress through the cash flows until we find the first difference and then set up the increment so that this first nonzero flow is negative (i.e., an investment). Thus, we set up the incremental investment by taking $(C1 - C2)$:

n	$C1 - C2$
0	$0
1	−$5,320
2	$450
3	$4,550
4	$2,219

We next set the PW equation equal to zero, as follows:

$$-\$5,320 + \$450(P/F, i, 1) + \$4,550(P/F, i, 2)$$
$$+ \$2,219(P/F, i, 3) = 0.$$

(b) Solving for i yields $i^* = 14.71\%$, which is also an IRR, since the increment is a simple investment. Since $\text{IRR}_{C1-C2} = 14.71\% > \text{MARR}$, we would select $C1$. If we used PW analysis, we would obtain $\text{PW}(12\%)_{C1} = \$1,443$ and $\text{PW}(12\%)_{C2} = \$1,185$, confirming the preference of $C1$ over $C2$.

COMMENTS: When you have more than two mutually exclusive alternatives, they can be compared in pairs by successive examination, as shown in Figure 7.8.

n	D1	D2	D3
0	−$2,000	−$1,000	−$3,000
1	$1,500	$800	$1,500
2	$1,000	$500	$2,000
3	$800	$500	$1,000
IRR	34.37%	40.76%	24.81%

Step 1: Examine the IRR for each project in order to eliminate any project that fails to meet the MARR($= 15\%$).

Step 2: Compare $D1$ and $D2$ in pairs:
$$IRR_{D1-D2} = 27.61\% > 15\%,$$
so select $D1$.

Step 3: Compare $D1$ and $D3$:
$$IRR_{D3-D1} = 8.8\% < 15\%,$$
so select $D1$.

Here, we conclude that $D1$ is the best alternative.

Figure 7.8 IRR on incremental investment: Three alternatives

EXAMPLE 7.9 Incremental Analysis for Cost-Only Projects

Falk Corporation is considering two types of manufacturing systems to produce its shaft couplings over six years: (1) a cellular manufacturing system (CMS) and (2) a flexible manufacturing system (FMS). The average number of pieces to be produced on either system would be 544,000 per year. Operating costs, initial investment, and salvage value for each alternative are estimated as follows:

Items	CMS Option	FMS Option
Investment	$4,500,000	$12,500,000
Total annual operating costs	$7,412,920	$5,504,100
Net salvage value	$500,000	$1,000,000

The firm's MARR is 15%. Which alternative would be a better choice based on the IRR criterion?

DISSECTING THE PROBLEM

Since we can assume that both manufacturing systems would provide the same level of revenues over the analysis period, we can compare these alternatives on the basis of cost only. (These systems are service projects.) Although we cannot compute the IRR for each option without knowing the revenue figures, we can still calculate the IRR on incremental cash flows. Since the FMS option requires a higher initial investment than that of the CMS, the incremental cash flow is the difference (FMS − CMS).

Given: Cash flows shown in Figure 7.9 and $i = 15\%$ per year.

Find: Incremental cash flows, and select the better alternative based on the IRR criterion.

n	CMS Option	FMS Option	Incremental (FMS − CMS)
0	−$4,500,000	−$12,500,000	−$8,000,000
1	−$7,412,920	−$5,504,100	$1,908,820
2	−$7,412,920	−$5,504,100	$1,908,820
3	−$7,412,920	−$5,504,100	$1,908,820
4	−$7,412,920	−$5,504,100	$1,908,820
5	−$7,412,920	−$5,504,100	$1,908,820
6	−$7,412,920 + $500,000	−$5,504,100 + $1,000,000	$2,408,820

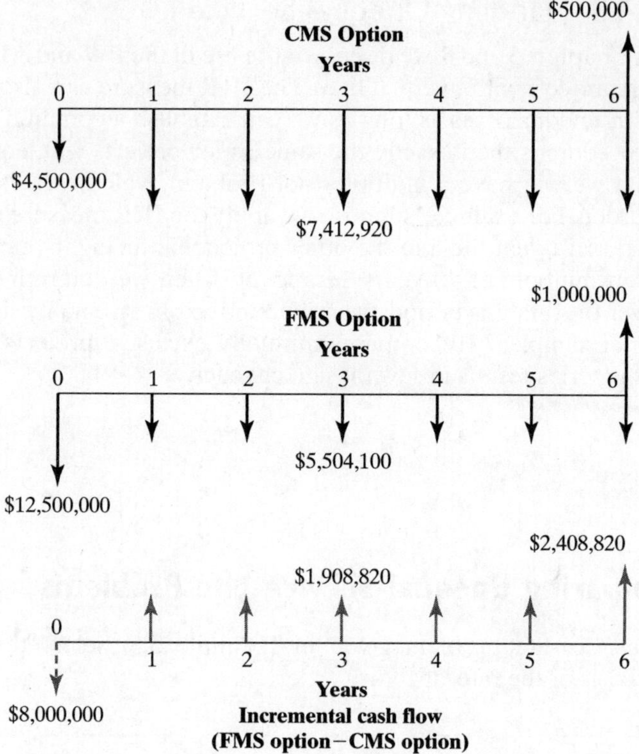

Figure 7.9 Cash flow diagrams for comparing cost-only projects

$$PW(i)_{\text{FMS–CMS}} = -\$8,000,000 + \$1,908,820(P/A, i, 5)$$
$$+\$2,408,820(P/F, i, 6) = 0.$$

METHODOLOGY	SOLUTION
Solve for i using Excel.	Solving for i by Excel yields 12.43%. Since $\text{IBR}_{\text{FMS–CMS}} = 12.43\% < 15\%$, we would select CMS. Although the FMS would provide an incremental annual savings of \$1,908,820 in operating costs, the savings do not justify the incremental investment of \$8,000,000.

COMMENTS: Note that the CMS option was marginally preferred to the FMS option. However, there are dangers in relying solely on the easily quantified savings in input factors—such as labor, energy, and materials—from FMS and in not considering gains from improved manufacturing performance that are more difficult and subjective to quantify. Factors such as improved product quality, increased manufacturing flexibility (rapid response to customer demand), reduced inventory levels, and increased capacity for product innovation are frequently ignored in financial analysis because we have inadequate means for quantifying their benefits. If these intangible benefits were considered, as they ought to be, however, the FMS option could come out better than the CMS option.

7.4.3 Handling Unequal Service Lives

In Chapters 5 and 6, we discussed the use of the PW and AE criteria as bases for comparing projects with unequal lives. The IRR measure can also be used to compare projects with unequal lives as long as we can establish a common analysis period. The decision procedure is then exactly the same as for projects with equal lives. It is likely, however, that we will have a multiple-root problem, which creates a substantial computational burden. For example, suppose we apply the IRR measure to a case in which one project has a five-year life and the other project has an eight-year life, resulting in a least common multiple of 40 years. Moreover, when we determine the incremental cash flows over the analysis period, we are bound to observe many sign changes.[8]

Example 7.10 compares mutually exclusive projects where the incremental cash flow series results in several sign changes.

EXAMPLE 7.10 Comparing Unequal-Service-Life Problems

Reconsider the unequal-service-life problem given in Example 5.8. Select the desired alternative on the basis of the rate-of-return criterion.

DISSECTING THE PROBLEM	
	Given: Cash flows for unequal-service-life projects as shown in Figure 5.13, and MARR = 12%.
	Find: Which project should be selected?

METHODOLOGY	SOLUTION
Use an Excel worksheet to prepare incremental cash flows.	Since each model has a shorter life than the required service period (five years), we need to make an explicit assumption of how the service requirement is to be met. With the leasing assumption given in Figure 7.10, the incremental cash flows would look like Table 7.3.
	Note that there are three sign changes in the incremental cash flows, indicating a possibility of multiple rates of return. However, there is a unique rate of return on this incremental cash flow series, namely, 3.90%.[9] Since this rate of return on incremental cash flow is less than the MARR of 12%, Option 2 is a better choice. This was the same conclusion that we reached in Example 5.8.

---

[8] This factor leads to the possibility of having many i^*s. Once again, if you desire to find the true rate of return on this incremental cash flow series, you need to refer to Chapter 7A.

[9] In Chapter 7A, a project with this type of cash flow series is known as a **pure investment**.

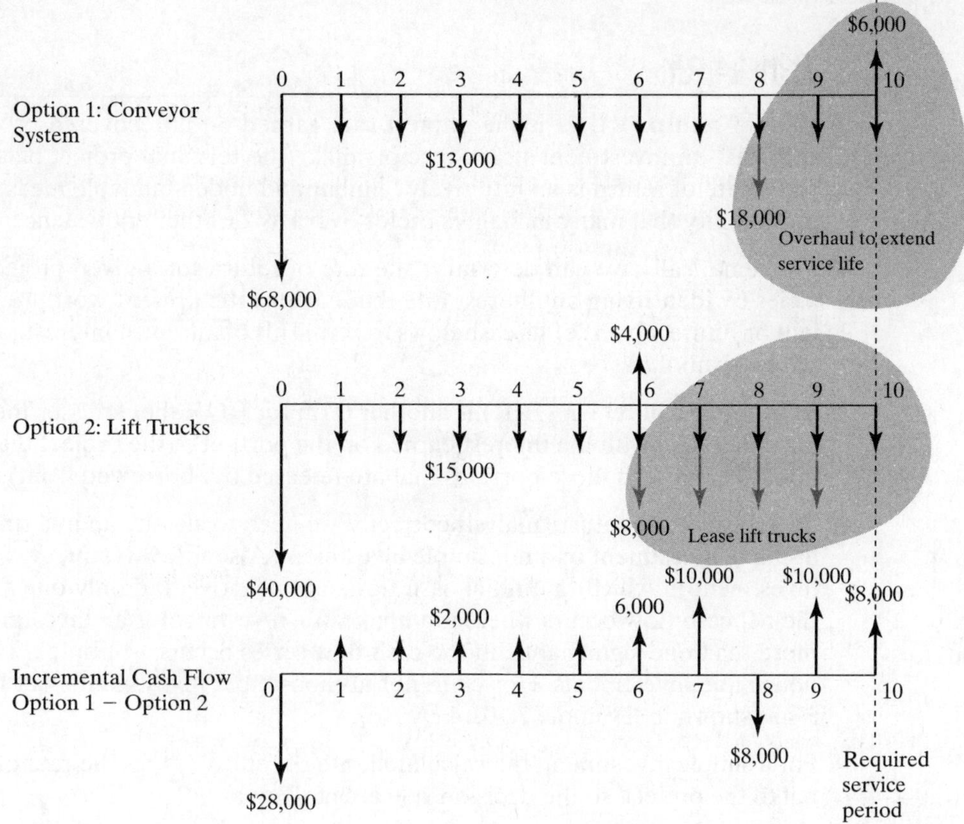

Figure 7.10 Incremental analysis (Option 1 – Option 2)—here we subtract Option 2 from Option 1 because Option 1 is a more costly alternative

TABLE 7.3 **An Excel Worksheet to Illustrate How to Prepare the Incremental Cash Flows**

	A	B	C	D
1		Example 7.10 - Comparing Unequal-Service-Life Problems		
2				
3		**Option 1**	**Option 2**	**Incremental**
4		**Conveyor Systems**	**Lift Trucks**	**Option 1 – Option 2**
5				
6	0	$ (68,000)	$ (40,000)	$ (28,000)
7	1	$ (13,000)	$ (15,000)	$ 2,000
8	2	$ (13,000)	$ (15,000)	$ 2,000
9	3	$ (13,000)	$ (15,000)	$ 2,000
10	4	$ (13,000)	$ (15,000)	$ 2,000
11	5	$ (13,000)	$ (15,000)	$ 2,000
12	6	$ (13,000)	$ (19,000)	$ 6,000
13	7	$ (13,000)	$ (23,000)	$ 10,000
14	8	$ (31,000)	$ (23,000)	$ (8,000)
15	9	$ (13,000)	$ (23,000)	$ 10,000
16	10	$ (7,000)	$ (15,000)	$ 8,000
17				
18			**Incremental IRR**	**3.90%**
19				
20			=IRR(D6:D16,15%)	
21				

SUMMARY

- **Rate of return (ROR)** is the interest rate earned on unrecovered project balances such that an investment's cash receipts make the terminal project balance equal to zero. Rate of return is an intuitively familiar and understandable measure of project profitability that many managers prefer over PW or other equivalence measures.

- Mathematically, we can determine the rate of return for a given project's cash flow series by identifying an interest rate that equates the present worth (annual equivalent or future worth) of its cash flows to zero. This break-even interest rate is denoted by the symbol i^*.

- **Internal rate of return (IRR)** is another term for ROR that stresses the fact that we are concerned with the interest earned on the portion of the project that is *internally* invested, not with those portions that are released by (borrowed from) the project.

- To apply rate-of-return analysis correctly, we need to classify an investment as either a simple investment or a nonsimple investment. A **simple investment** is defined as an investment in which the initial cash flows are negative and only one sign change in the net cash flow occurs whereas a **nonsimple investment** is an investment for which more than one sign change in the cash flow series occurs. Multiple i^*s occur only in nonsimple investments. However, not all nonsimple investments will have multiple i^*s as shown in Example 7.10.

- For a simple investment, the calculated rate of return (i^*) is the rate of return internal to the project, so the decision rule is as follows:

  If IRR > MARR, accept the project.
  If IRR = MARR, remain indifferent.
  If IRR < MARR, reject the project.

  IRR analysis yields results consistent with PW and other equivalence methods.

- For a nonsimple investment, because of the possibility of having multiple rates of return, it is recommended that the IRR analysis be abandoned and either the PW or AE analysis be used to make an accept-or-reject decision. Procedures are outlined in Chapter 7A for determining the rate of return internal to nonsimple investments. Once you find the IRR (or return on invested capital), you can use the same decision rule for simple investments.

- When properly selecting among alternative projects by IRR analysis, you must use **incremental investment**.

- Our purpose is not to encourage you to use the IRR approach to compare projects with unequal lives; rather, it is to show the correct way to compare them if the IRR approach must be used.

SELF-TEST QUESTIONS

7s.1 Google Inc. went public on August 20, 2004. The initial public offering price was $108 per share. If the stock traded at $490.92 on August 19, 2011, what would the compound annual return on investment be for the investors who purchased the stock and held it for eight years?

(a) 354%

(b) 44.31%

(c) 20.89%

(d) 71%

7s.2   You are considering an open-pit mining operation. The cash flow pattern is somewhat unusual since you must invest in some mining equipment, conduct operations for two years, and then restore the sites to their original condition. You estimate the net cash flows to be as follows:

n	Cash Flows
0	–$1,600,000
1	1,500,000
2	1,500,000
3	–700,000

What is the approximate rate of return of this investment?

(a) 25%

(b) 38%

(c) 42%

(d) 62%

7s.3   The following infinite cash flow has a rate of return of 20%. Compute the unknown value of X.

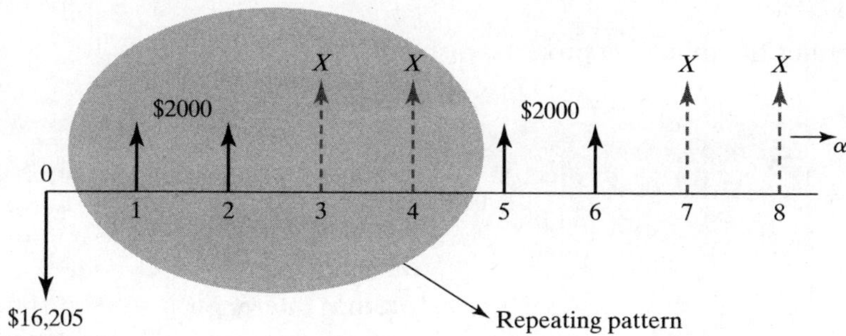

(a) $3,028

(b) $5,510

(c) $5,028

(d) $5,236

7s.4   Consider the investment project with the net cash flows as shown in the following table. What would be the value of X if the project's IRR is 23%?

End of Year (n)	Net Cash Flow
0	–$12,000
1	$2,500
2	$5,500
3	X
4	X

(a) $4,500

(b) $4,750

(c) $6,890

(d) $6,500

7s.5 You purchased a stamping machine for $100,000 to produce a new line of products. The stamping machine will be used for five years, and the expected salvage value of the machine is 20% of the initial cost. The annual operating and maintenance costs amount to $30,000. If each part stamped generates $12 revenue, how many parts should be stamped each year just to break even? Assume that you require a 15% return on your investment.

(a) 5,000

(b) 4,739

(c) 4,488

(d) 2,238

7s.6 You are considering purchasing a new punch press machine. This machine will have an estimated service life of 10 years. The expected after-tax salvage value at the end of service life will be 10% of the purchase cost. Its annual after-tax operating cash flows are estimated to be $60,000. If you can purchase the machine at $308,758, what is the expected rate of return on this investment?

(a) 12%

(b) 13.6%

(c) 15%

(d) 17.2%

7s.7 Consider the following projects' cash flows:

End of Year (n)	Project A	Project B	Project C	Project D
0	−$1,000	−$3,000	$2,000	−$4,000
1	$200	$2,000	−$600	−$1,000
2	$500	$2,000	−$600	$6,000
3	$600	−$1,500	−$600	0
4	$400	$2,000	−$600	$2,000

Which of the following statements is *correct*?

(a) Project *A* is the only simple investment.

(b) Project *A* and *D* are the only projects that will have a unique positive rate of return.

(c) Project *B* is the only nonsimple investment.

(d) None of the above.

7s.8 You are evaluating five investment projects. You have already calculated the rate of return for each alternative investment and incremental rate of return for the two alternatives. In calculating the incremental rate of return, a lower cost investment project is subtracted from the higher cost investment project. All rate of return figures are rounded to the nearest integers.

Investment Alternative	Initial Investment ($)	Rate of Return (%)	Rate of Return on Incremental Investment (%) When Compared with Alternative				
			A	B	C	D	E
A	35,000	12		28	20	36	27
B	45,000	15			12	40	22
C	50,000	13				42	25
D	65,000	20					−5
E	80,000	18					

If all investment alternatives are mutually exclusive and the MARR is 12%, which alternative should be chosen?

(a) D

(b) E

(c) B

(d) Do nothing

7s.9 Consider the following *project balance profiles* for proposed investment projects.

Project Balances

n	Project A	Project B	Project C
0	−$600	−$500	−$200
1	200	300	0
2	300	650	150
NPW	—	$416.00	—
Rate used	15%	?	—

Statement 1—For Project A, the cash flow at the end of year 2 is $100.

Statement 2—For Project C, its net future worth at the end of year 2 is $150.

Statement 3—For Project B, the interest rate used is 25%.

Statement 4—For Project A, the rate of return should be greater than 15%.

Which of the statement(s) above is (are) *correct*?

(a) Just Statements 1 and 2

(b) Just Statements 2 and 3

(c) Just Statements 1 and 3

(d) Just Statements 2, 3, and 4

7s.10 Consider the following investment projects.

Year (n)	Net Cash Flow	
	Project 1	Project 2
0	−$1,200	−$2,000
1	600	1,500
2	1,000	1,000
IRR	19.65%	17.54%

Determine the range of MARR for which Project 2 would be preferred over Project 1.

(a) MARR $\leq 12.5\%$

(b) $13\% \leq$ MARR $\leq 15\%$

(c) $16\% \leq$ MARR

(d) Not enough information to determine

7s.11 The following information on two mutually exclusive projects is given below:

n	Project A	Project B
0	−3,000	−5,000
1	1,350	1,350
2	1,800	1,800
3	1,500	5,406
IRR	25%	25%

Which of the following statements is *correct?*

(a) Since the two projects have the same rate of return, they are indifferent.

(b) Project A would be a better choice because the required investment is smaller with the same rate of return.

(c) Project B would be a better choice as long as the investor's MARR is less than 25%.

(d) Project B is a better choice regardless of the investor's MARR.

PROBLEMS

Note: The symbol i^* represents the interest rate that makes the present worth of the project equal to zero. The acronym IRR represents the *internal rate of return* of the investment. For a simple investment, IRR $= i^*$. For a nonsimple investment, i^* generally is not equal to IRR.

Concept of Rate of Return

7.1 If you invest $2,000 in a stock and its value is doubled in five years, what is the return on your stock investment?

7.2 You purchased a piece of property at $450,000 six years ago. You can sell the property at $650,000. What is the rate of return on this real estate investment?

7.3 Suppose you deposited $1,200 five years ago and another $800 three years ago in your savings account. If your current account balance shows $2,800, what is the rate of return on your deposit?

7.4 Assume that you are going to buy a new car worth $28,000. You will be able to make a down payment of $5,000. The remaining $23,000 will be financed by the dealer. The dealer computes your monthly payment to be $1540, for 60 months of financing. What is the dealer's annual rate of return on this car loan?

7.5 Mr. Smith wishes to sell a bond that has a face value of $1,000. The bond bears an interest rate (coupon rate) of 7.5%, with bond interest payable semiannually. Four years ago, the bond was purchased at $900. At least a 9% annual return

(APR) on the investment is desired. What must be the minimum selling price now for the bond in order for Mr. Smith to make the desired return on the investment after making eight interest payments?

7.6 The city of Houston made a $10 million public investment in the arts five years ago and the citizens of Houston are getting a 54% rate of return on their tax investment. What kind of proceeds from the investment in the arts is being made?

7.7 John Whitney Payson, who purchased a painting by Vincent van Gogh for $80,000 in 1947, sold it for $53.9 million in 1988. If Mr. Payson had invested his $80,000 in another investment vehicle (such as stock), how much annual interest would he need to have earned in order to accumulate the same wealth as he did from the painting investment? Assume for simplicity that the investment period is 40 years and that the interest is compounded annually.

Methods for Finding Rate of Return

7.8 You are purchasing a factory at $550,000. Your projected cash flow streams from the factory will be $135,000 in year 1, $152,000 in year 2, and $285,000 in year 3. What is the rate of return on this factory investment?

7.9 Best Foods forecasts the following cash flows on a special meat packing operation under consideration.

A_0	A_1	A_2	A_3
($15,000)	$0	$8,200	$9,500

What is the rate of return on this investment?

7.10 Consider a project that will bring in upfront cash inflows for the first two years but require paying some money to close the project in the third year.

A_0	A_1	A_2
$6,500	$4,500	($13,000)

This is a simple borrowing project. Determine the borrowing rate of return.

7.11 Consider four projects with the following sequences of cash flows:

n	Net Cash Flow			
	Project A	Project B	Project C	Project D
0	−$25,000	−$23,000	$43,233	−$56,500
1	$12,000	$32,000	−$18,000	−$2,500
2	$23,000	$32,000	−$18,000	−$6,459
3	$34,000	−$25,000	−$18,000	$88,345

(a) Identify all the simple investments.

(b) Identify all the nonsimple investments.

(c) Compute the i^* for each project using Excel.

(d) Which project has no rate of return?

7.12 Consider an investment project with the following net cash flows:

Year	Net Cash Flow
0	−$1,500
1	X
2	$650
3	X

What would be the value of X if the project's IRR is 10%?

7.13 Consider the investment project with the following net cash flows:

End of Year (n)	Net Cash Flow
0	−$12,000
1	$2,500
2	$5,500
3	X
4	X

What would be the value of X if the project's IRR is 25%?

7.14 An investor bought 100 shares of stock at a cost of $10 per share. He held the stock for 15 years and then sold it for a total of $4,000. For the first three years, he received no dividends. For each of the next seven years, he received total dividends of $50 per year. For the remaining period, he received total dividends of $100 per year. What rate of return did he make on the investment?

7.15 Consider the following sets of investment projects:

	Net Cash Flow				
n	A	B	C	D	E
0	−$250	−$200	−$70	−$300	−$90
1	$60	$90	$20	$220	−$100
2	$970	$90	$10	$40	−$50
3		$60	$5	$40	$0
4		$60	−$180	−$20	$150
5			$60	$40	$150
6			$50	$30	$100
7			$40		$100
8			$30		
9			$20		
10			$10		

(a) Classify each project as either simple or nonsimple.
(b) Compute the i^* for Project A, using the quadratic equation.
(c) Obtain the rate(s) of return for each project by plotting the PW as a function of interest rate.

7.16 Consider the following projects:

	Net Cash Flow			
n	A	B	C	D
0	−$1,800	−$1,900	−$2,200	−$3,000
1	$500	$800	$5,600	$360
2	$100	$600	$4,900	$4,675
3	$100	$500	−$3,000	$2,288
4	$1,000	$700	−$7,000	
5			−$1,400	
6			$2,100	
7			$900	

(a) Classify each project as either simple or nonsimple.
(b) Identify all positive i^*s for each project.
(c) Plot the present worth as a function of interest rate (i) for each project.

7.17 Consider the following financial data for a project:

Initial investment	$20,000
Project life	8 years
Salvage value	$0
Annual revenue	$9,500
Annual expenses (including income taxes)	$3,400

(a) What is the i^* for this project?
(b) If the annual expenses increase at a 7% rate over the previous year's expenses, but annual revenue is unchanged, what is the new i^*?

Internal-Rate-of-Return Criterion

7.18 A corporation is considering purchasing a machine that will save $200,000 per year before taxes. The cost of operating the machine, including maintenance, is $80,000 per year. The machine, costing $150,000, will be needed for five years after which it will have a salvage value of $25,000. If the firm wants a 15% rate of return before taxes, what is the net present value of the cash flows generated from this machine?

7.19 Consider an investment project with the following cash flows:

n	Cash Flow
0	−$5,000
1	$0
2	$4,840
3	$1,331

Compute the IRR for this investment. Is this project acceptable at MARR $= 10\%$?

7.20 Consider the following project's cash flows:

n	Net Cash Flow
0	−$3,000
1	$800
2	$900
3	X

Assume that the project's IRR is 10%.
(a) Find the value of X.
(b) Is this project acceptable at MARR = 8%?

7.21 You are considering a luxury apartment building project that requires an investment of $12,500,000. The building has 50 units. You expect that the maintenance cost for the apartment building will be $250,000 in the first year, and to rise to $300,000 in the second year, and to continue to increase by $50,000 in subsequent years. The cost to hire a manager for the building is estimated to be $80,000 per year. After five years of operation, the apartment building can be sold for $14,000,000. What annual rent per apartment unit will provide a return on investment of 15%? Assume that the building will remain fully occupied during the five years.

7.22 A machine costing $25,000 to buy and $3,000 per year to operate will save mainly labor expenses in packaging over six years. The anticipated salvage value of the machine at the end of six years is $5,000. For the machine to recoup a 12% return on investment (rate of return), what minimum required annual savings in labor must this machine provide?

7.23 You are considering a CNC machine. This machine will have an estimated service life of 10 years with a salvage value of 10% of the investment cost. Its expected savings from annual operating and maintenance costs are estimated to be $60,000. To expect a 15% rate of return on investment, what would be the maximum amount that you are willing to pay for the machine?

7.24 Your firm has purchased an injection molding machine at a cost of $100,000. The machine's useful life is estimated to be eight years. Your accounting department has estimated the capital cost for this machine at about $25,455 per year. To expect a 15% return on your investment, how much additional annual revenue (after deducting any operating expenses) must be generated?

7.25 Champion Chemical Corporation is planning to expand one of its propylene manufacturing facilities. At $n = 0$, a piece of property costing $1.5 million must be purchased for the expanded plant site. The building, which needs to be expanded at the beginning of the first year, costs $3 million. At the end of the first year, the company needs to spend about $4 million on equipment and other start-up needs. Once the plant becomes operational, it will generate revenue in the amount of $3.5 million during the first operating year. This amount will increase at an annual rate of 5% over the previous year's revenue for the next nine years. After 10 years, the sales revenue will stay constant for another 3 years before the operation is phased out. (The plant will have a project life of 13 years after construction.) The expected salvage value of the land would be about

$2 million, the building about $1.4 million, and the equipment about $500,000. The annual operating and maintenance costs are estimated to be about 40% of the sales revenue each year. What is the IRR for this investment? If the company's MARR is 15%, determine whether this expansion is a good investment. (Assume that all figures include the effect of income tax.)

7.26 Recent technology has made possible a computerized vending machine that can grind coffee beans and brew fresh coffee on demand. The computer also makes possible such complicated functions as changing $5 and $10 bills and tracking the age of an item and then moving the oldest stock to the front of the line, thus cutting down on spoilage. With a price tag of $4,500 for each unit, Easy Snack has estimated the cash flows in millions of dollars over the product's six-year useful life, including the initial investment, as follows:

n	Net Cash Flow
0	−$20
1	$8
2	$17
3	$19
4	$18
5	$10
6	$3

(a) If the firm's MARR is 18%, is this product worth marketing according to the IRR criterion?

(b) If the required investment remains unchanged but the future cash flows are expected to be 10% higher than the original estimates, how much increase in IRR do you expect?

(c) If the required investment has increased from $20 million to $22 million but the expected future cash flows are projected to be 10% smaller than the original estimates, how much decrease in IRR do you expect?

7.27 InterCell Company wants to participate in the upcoming World's Fair in Korea. To participate, the firm needs to spend $1.5 million in year 0 to develop a showcase. The showcase will produce a cash flow of $3.75 million at the end of year 1. Then at the end of year 2, $2.31 million must be expended to restore the land on which the showcase was presented to its original condition. Therefore, the project's expected net cash flows are as follows (in thousands of dollars):

n	Net Cash Flow
0	−$1,500
1	$3,750
2	−$2,310

(a) Plot the present worth of this investment as a function of i.

(b) Compute the i^*s for this investment. Is this a pure investment?

(c) Would you accept this investment at MARR $= 14\%$?

Incremental-Investment Analysis for Comparing Mutually Exclusive Alternatives

7.28 Consider two investments with the following sequences of cash flows:

	Net Cash Flow	
n	Project A	Project B
0	-$30,000	-$15,000
1	$2,000	$10,000
2	$6,000	$10,000
3	$12,000	$10,000
4	$24,000	$10,000
5	$28,000	$5,000

(a) Compute the i^* for each investment.

(b) Plot the present-worth curve for each project on the same chart and find the interest rate that makes the two projects equivalent.

(c) If A and B are mutually exclusive investment projects, which project is more economically desirable at MARR of 15%?

7.29 Consider two investments with the following sequences of cash flows:

	Net Cash Flow	
n	Project A	Project B
0	-$3,000	-$3,000
1	$1,500	$300
2	$1,200	$600
3	$600	$600
4	$600	$1,200
5	$300	$2,100

At MARR of 12%, which project would you select?

7.30 Consider two investments with the following sequences of cash flows:

	Net Cash Flow	
n	Project A	Project B
0	-$150,000	-$120,000
1	$30,000	$25,000
2	$25,000	$15,000
3	$120,000	$110,000

(a) Compute the IRR for each investment.

(b) At MARR = 15%, determine the acceptability of each project.

(c) If A and B are mutually exclusive projects, which project would you select on the basis of the rate of return on incremental investment?

7.31 Consider two investments with the following sequences of cash flows:

	Net Cash Flow	
n	Project A	Project B
0	−$100,000	−$100,000
1	$10,500	$70,000
2	$60,000	$50,000
3	$80,000	$20,500

(a) Compute the IRR for each investment.

(b) At MARR = 10%, determine the acceptability of each project.

(c) If *A* and *B* are mutually exclusive projects, which project would you select on the basis of the rate of return on incremental investment?

7.32 With $10,000 available, you have two investment options. The first option is to buy a certificate of deposit from a bank at an interest rate of 10% annually for five years. The second choice is to purchase a bond for $10,000 and invest the bond's interest payments in the bank at an interest rate of 9%. The bond pays 10% interest annually and will mature at its face value of $10,000 in five years. Which option is better? Assume your MARR is 9% per year.

7.33 Consider the following two mutually exclusive investment projects:

	Net Cash Flow	
Year (n)	Project 1	Project 2
0	−$2,200	−$2,000
1	1,200	1,200
2	1,650	1,400
IRR	18.07%	18.88%

Determine the range of MARR where Project 2 would be preferred over Project 1 with "do-nothing" alternative.

(a) MARR ≤ 11.80%

(b) MARR ≥ 11.80%

(c) 11.80% ≤ MARR ≤ 18.88%

(d) MARR ≤ 18.88%

7.34 A manufacturing firm is considering the following mutually exclusive alternatives:

	Net Cash Flow	
n	Project A	Project B
0	−$2,000	−$3,000
1	$1,400	$2,400
2	$1,640	$2,000

Determine which project is a better choice at MARR = 15% on the basis of the IRR criterion.

7.35 Consider the following two mutually exclusive alternatives:

	Net Cash Flow	
n	**Project A1**	**Project A2**
0	−$10,000	−$12,000
1	$5,000	$6,100
2	$5,000	$6,100
3	$5,000	$6,100

(a) Determine the IRR on the incremental investment in the amount of $2,000.
(b) If the firm's MARR is 10%, which alternative is the better choice?

7.36 Consider the following two mutually exclusive investment alternatives:

	Net Cash Flow	
n	**Project A1**	**Project A2**
0	−$16,000	−$20,000
1	$7,500	$5,000
2	$7,500	$15,000
3	$7,500	$8,000
IRR	19.19%	17.65%

(a) Determine the IRR on the incremental investment in the amount of $4,000. (Assume that MARR = 10%.)
(b) If the firm's MARR is 10%, which alternative is the better choice?

7.37 Consider the following two investment alternatives:

	Net Cash Flow	
n	**Project A**	**Project B**
0	−$10,000	−$20,000
1	$5,500	$0
2	$5,500	$0
3	$5,500	$40,000
IRR	30%	?
PW(15%)	?	$6,300

The firm's MARR is known to be 15%.
(a) Compute the IRR of Project B.
(b) Compute the PW of Project A.
(c) Suppose that Projects A and B are mutually exclusive. Using the IRR, which project would you select?

7.38 You are considering two types of automobiles. Model A costs $18,000, and Model B costs $15,624. Although the two models are essentially the same, Model A can be sold for $9,000 after four years of use while Model B can be sold for $6,500 after the same amount of time. Model A commands a better resale value because its styling is popular among young college students. Determine the rate of return on the incremental investment of $2,376. For what range of values of your MARR is Model *A* preferable?

7.39 A plant engineer is considering two types of solar water-heating systems:

Item	Model *A*	Model *B*
Initial cost	$5,000	$7,000
Annual savings	$700	$1,000
Annual maintenance	$100	$50
Expected life	20 years	20 years
Salvage value	$400	$500

The firm's MARR is 10%. On the basis of the IRR criterion, decide which system is the better choice.

7.40 Fulton National Hospital is reviewing ways of cutting the costs for stocking medical supplies. Two new stockless systems are being considered to lower the hospital's holding and handling costs. The hospital's industrial engineer has compiled the relevant financial data for each system, as follows, where dollar values are in millions:

Item	Current Practice	Just-in-Time System	Stockless Supply
Start-up cost	$0	$2.5	$5
Annual stock-holding cost	$3	$1.4	$0.2
Annual operating cost	$2	$1.5	$1.2
System life	8 years	8 years	8 years

The system life of eight years represents the contract period with the medical suppliers. If the hospital's MARR is 10%, which system is more economical?

7.41 Consider the following investment projects:

	Net Cash Flow		
n	Project 1	Project 2	Project 3
0	−$1,000	−$5,000	−$2,000
1	$500	$7,500	$1,500
2	$2,500	$600	$2,000

Assume that MARR = 15%.

(a) Compute the IRR for each project.

(b) If the three projects are mutually exclusive investments, which project should be selected according to the IRR criterion?

7.42 Consider the following two investment situations:

■ In 1980, when W.M. Company went public, 100 shares cost $1,650. That investment was worth $12,283,904 after 32 years (2012) with a rate of return of around 32%.

■ In 1990, if you bought 100 shares of First Mutual Funds it would have cost $5,245. That investment would have been worth $289,556 after 22 years.

Which of the following statements is correct?

(a) If you had bought only 50 shares of the W.M. Company stock in 1980 and kept them for 32 years, your rate of return would be 0.5 times 32%.

(b) If you had bought 100 shares of First Mutual Funds in 1990, you would have made a profit at an annual rate of 30% on the funds remaining invested.

(c) If you had bought 100 shares of W.M. Company in 1980 but sold them after 10 years (assume that the W.M. Company stock value increased at an annual rate of 32% for the first 10 years) and immediately put all the proceeds into First Mutual Funds, then after 22 years the total worth of your investment would be around $1,462,885.

(d) None of the above.

7.43 The GeoStars Company, a leading wireless communication device manufacturer, is considering three cost-reduction proposals in its batch-job shop manufacturing operations. The company has already calculated rates of return for the three projects along with some incremental rates of return. A_0 denotes the do-nothing alternative. The required investments are $420,000 for A_1, $550,000 for A_2, and $720,000 for A_3. If the firm's MARR is 15%, which system should be selected?

Incremental Investment	Incremental Rate of Return
$A_1 - A_0$	18%
$A_2 - A_0$	20%
$A_3 - A_0$	25%
$A_2 - A_1$	10%
$A_3 - A_1$	22%
$A_3 - A_2$	23%

7.44 An electronic circuit board manufacturer is considering six mutually exclusive cost-reduction projects for its PC-board manufacturing plant. All have lives of 10 years and zero salvage value. The required investment, the estimated after-tax reduction in annual disbursements, and the gross rate of return are given for each alternative in the following table:

Proposal A_j	Required Investment	After-Tax Savings	Rate of Return
A_1	$60,000	$22,000	34.8%
A_2	$100,000	$28,200	25.2%
A_3	$110,000	$32,600	26.9%
A_4	$120,000	$33,600	25.0%
A_5	$140,000	$38,400	24.3%
A_6	$150,000	$42,200	25.1%

The rate of return on incremental investments is given for each project as follows:

Incremental Investment	Incremental Rate of Return
$A_2 - A_1$	8.9%
$A_3 - A_2$	42.7%
$A_4 - A_3$	0.0%
$A_5 - A_4$	20.2%
$A_6 - A_5$	36.3%

Which project would you select according to the rate of return on incremental investment if it is stated that the MARR is 15%?

7.45 Suppose we have four mutually exclusive projects, $D1$, $D2$, $D3$, and $D4$, whose internal rates of return on incremental investment between the projects is given as follows:

$$\text{IRR } (D1 - D2) = 27.62\%$$
$$\text{IRR } (D1 - D3) = 14.26\%$$
$$\text{IRR } (D1 - D4) = 25.24\%$$
$$\text{IRR } (D3 - D2) = 30.24\%$$
$$\text{IRR } (D2 - D4) = 17.34\%$$
$$\text{IRR } (D3 - D4) = 16.14\%$$

Which project should be selected at MARR 15%?

7.46 Baby Doll Shop currently manufactures wooden parts for dollhouses. Its sole worker is paid $8.10 an hour and, using a handsaw, can produce a year's required production (1,600 parts) in just eight weeks of 40 hours per week. That is, the worker averages five parts per hour when working by hand. The shop is considering the purchase of a power band saw with associated fixtures in order to improve the productivity of this operation. Three models of power saw could be purchased: Model A (economy version), Model B (high-powered version), and Model C (deluxe high-end version). The major operating difference between these models is their speed of operation. The investment costs, including the required fixtures and other operating characteristics, are summarized as follows:

Category	By Hand	Model A	Model B	Model C
Production rate (parts/hour)	5	10	15	20
Labor hours required (hours/year)	320	160	107	80
Annual labor cost (@ $8.10/hour)	$2,592	$1,296	$867	$648
Annual power cost		$400	$420	$480
Initial investment		$4,000	$6,000	$7,000
Salvage value		$400	$600	$700
Service life (years)		20	20	20

Assume that MARR = 10%. Are there enough potential savings to make it economical to purchase any of the power band saws? Which model is most economical according to the rate-of-return principle? (Assume that any effect of income tax has already been considered in the dollar estimates.) (*Source*: This problem is adapted with the permission of Professor Peter Jackson of Cornell University.)

7.47 An oil company is considering changing the size of a small pump that currently is in operation in an oil field. If the current pump is kept, it will extract 50% of the known crude oil reserve in the first year of operation and the remaining 50% in the second year. A pump larger than the current pump will cost $1.6 million, but it will extract 100% of the known reserve in the first year. The total oil revenues over the two years are the same for both pumps: $20 million. The advantage of the large pump is that it allows 50% of the revenue to be realized a year earlier than the small pump. The two options are summarized as follows:

Item	Current Pump	Larger Pump
Investment, year 0	$0	$1.6 million
Revenue, year 1	$10 million	$20 million
Revenue, year 2	$10 million	$0

If the firm's MARR is known to be 20%, what do you recommend, according to the IRR criterion?

Unequal Service Lives

7.48 Consider the following two mutually exclusive investment projects:

	Net Cash Flow	
n	Project A	Project B
0	−$100	−$200
1	$60	$120
2	$50	$150
3	$50	
IRR	28.89%	21.65%

Assume that MARR = 15%. Which project would be selected under an infinite planning horizon with project repeatability likely, according to the IRR criterion?

7.49 A company has to decide between two machines that do the same job but have different lives.

Net Cash Flow	
Machine A	Machine B
−$40,000	−$55,000
−$15,000	−$10,000
−$15,000	−$10,000
−$15,000	−$10,000
	−$10,000

Which machine should the company buy, at an interest rate of 10%, based on the principle of internal rate of return?

7.50 Consider the following two mutually exclusive investment projects:

	Net Cash Flow	
n	Project A1	Project A2
0	−$10,000	−$15,000
1	$5,000	$20,000
2	$5,000	
3	$5,000	

(a) To use the IRR criterion, what assumption must be made in order to compare a set of mutually exclusive investments with unequal service lives?

(b) With the assumption defined in part (a), determine the range of MARR that will indicate the selection of Project $A1$.

Short Case Studies with Excel

7.51 Merco, Inc., a machinery builder in Louisville, Kentucky, is considering making an investment of $1,250,000 in a complete structural-beam-fabrication system. The increased productivity resulting from the installation of the drilling system is central to the project's justification. Merco estimates the following figures as a basis for calculating productivity:

- Increased fabricated-steel production: 2,000 tons/year
- Average sales price per ton of fabricated steel: $2,566.50
- Labor rate: $10.50/hour
- Tons of steel produced in a year: 15,000
- Cost of steel per ton (2,205 lb): $1,950
- Number of workers on layout, hole making, sawing, and material handling: 17
- Additional maintenance cost: $128,500/year

With the cost of steel at $1,950 per ton and the direct-labor cost of fabricating 1 lb at 10 cents, the cost of producing a ton of fabricated steel is about $2,170.50. With a selling price of $2,566.50 per ton, the resulting contribution to overhead and profit becomes $396 per ton. Assuming that Merco will be able to sustain an increased production of 2,000 tons per year by purchasing the system, the projected additional contribution has been estimated to be 2,000 tons $\times$ $396 = $792,000.

Since the drilling system has the capacity to fabricate the full range of structural steel, two workers can run the system, one operating the saw and the other operating the drill. A third worker is required to operate a crane for loading and unloading materials. Merco estimates that to perform equivalent work with a conventional manufacturing system would require, on average, an additional 14 people for center punching, hole making with a radial or magnetic drill, and material handling. This factor translates into a labor savings in the amount of $294,000 per year ($14 \times 10.50×40 hours/week $\times 50$ weeks/year). The system can last for 15 years with an estimated after-tax salvage value of $80,000. However, after an annual deduction of $226,000 in corporate income taxes, the net investment costs, as well as savings, are as follows:

- Project investment cost: $1,250,000
- Projected annual net savings:

$$(\$792,000 + \$294,000) - \$128,500 - \$226,000 = \$731,500$$

- Projected after-tax salvage value at the end of year 15: $80,000

(a) What is the projected IRR on this investment?

(b) If Merco's MARR is known to be 18%, is this investment justifiable?

7.52 Critics have charged that the commercial nuclear power industry does not consider the cost of "decommissioning," or "mothballing," a nuclear power plant when doing an economic analysis and that the analysis is therefore unduly optimistic. As an example, consider the Tennessee Valley Authority's Bellefont twin nuclear generating facility under construction at Scottsboro in northern Alabama. The initial cost is $1.5 billion, and the estimated life is 40 years. The annual operating and maintenance costs the first year are assumed to be 4.6% of the first cost in the first year and are expected to increase at the fixed rate of 0.05% of the first cost each year. Annual revenues have been estimated to be three times the annual operating and maintenance costs throughout the life of the plant. From this information, comment on the following statements:

(a) The criticism of excessive optimism in the economic analysis caused by the omission of mothballing costs is not justified since the addition of a cost to mothball the plant equal to 50% of the initial cost decreases the 10% rate of return only to approximately 9.9%.

(b) If the estimated life of the plant is more realistically taken as 25 years instead of 40 years, then the criticism is justified. When the life is reduced to 25 years, the rate of return of approximately 9% without a mothballing cost drops to approximately 7.7% with a cost to mothball the plant equal to 50% of the initial cost added to the analysis.

7.53 The B&E Cooling Technology Company, a maker of automobile air conditioners, faces an impending deadline to phase out the traditional chilling technique, which uses chlorofluorocarbons (CFCs), a family of refrigerant chemicals believed to attack the earth's protective ozone layer. B&E has been pursuing other means of cooling and refrigeration. As a near-term solution, its engineers recommend a cooling technology known as an absorption chiller, which uses plain water as a refrigerant and semiconductors that cool down when charged with electricity. B&E is considering two options:

■ Option 1: Retrofit the plant now to adopt the absorption chiller and continuing to be a market leader in cooling technology.

■ Option 2: Defer the retrofit until the federal deadline, which is three years away. With expected improvement in cooling technology and technical know-how, the retrofitting cost will be cheaper then. But there will be tough market competition, and revenues would be less than that from Option 1.

The financial data for the two options are as follows:

Item	Option 1	Option 2
Investment timing	Now	3 years from now
Initial investment	$6 million	$5 million
System life	8 years	8 years
Salvage value	$1 million	$2 million
Annual revenue	$15 million	$11 million
Annual O&M costs	$6 million	$7 million

(a) What assumptions must be made in order to compare these two options?

(b) If B&E's MARR is 15%, which option is the better choice according to the IRR criterion?

7.54 Reconsider the chapter opening story about the return on investment on college education. According to a recent study, attending a university full-time costs the average student more than $17,000 a year. But here's the magic number that makes it all worthwhile: Over the years, university graduates earn an average of almost \$10,000 a year more than high-school graduates do—and that's an after-tax figure. One recent attempt was made to estimate the median future earnings by two groups—high-school graduates and college graduates. Suppose that net incomes after n years from high-school graduation are as follows:

- High-school graduates: Net income = \$13,529 $\ln(n+17)$ − \$14,788
- College graduates: Net income = \$36,529 $\ln(n + 17)$ − \$64,021, $(n > 4)$

Here n represents the year after high school graduation. Now estimate your college expenses for four years and determine the rate of return on your college education.

But you would expect that some degrees to lead to more lucrative occupations than others. It is the right time of year to take a fresh look at an old question: Why bother going to college? With all the accompanying fees and debts, is doing so still worth it?

CHAPTER 7A

Resolution of Multiple Rates of Return

To comprehend the nature of multiple i^*s, we need to understand the investment situation represented by any cash flow. The net-investment test will indicate whether the i^* computed represents the true rate of return earned on the money invested in a project while the money is actually in the project. As we shall see, the phenomenon of multiple i^*s occurs only when the net-investment test fails. When multiple positive rates of return for a cash flow are found, in general, none is suitable as a measure of project profitability, and we must proceed to the next analysis step: introducing an external rate of return.

7A-1 Net-Investment Test

A project is said to be a **net investment** when the project balances computed at the project's i^* values, $\text{PB}(i^*)_n$, are all less than or equal to zero throughout the life of the investment with $A_0 < 0$. The investment is *net* in the sense that the firm does not overdraw on its return at any point and hence is *not indebted* to the project. This type of project is called a **pure investment**. [On the other hand, **pure borrowing** is defined as the situation where $\text{PB}(i^*)_n$ values are all positive or zero throughout the life of the loan, with $A_0 > 0$.] *Simple investments will always be pure investments.* Therefore, if a nonsimple project passes the net-investment test (i.e., it is a pure investment), then the accept-or-reject decision rule will be the same as in the simple-investment case given in Section 7.3.2.

If any of the project balances calculated at the project's i^* is positive, the project is not a pure investment. A positive project balance indicates that, at some time during the project life, the firm acts as a borrower $[\text{PB}(i^*)_n > 0]$ rather than an investor $[\text{PB}(i^*)_n < 0]$ in the project. This type of investment is called a **mixed investment**.

EXAMPLE 7A.1 Pure versus Mixed Investments

Consider the following four investment projects with known i^* values:

n	A	B	C	D
0	−$1,000	−$1,000	−$1,000	−$1,000
1	−$1,000	$1,600	$500	$3,900
2	$2,000	−$300	−$500	−$5,030
3	$1,500	−$200	$2,000	$2,145
i^*	33.64%	21.95%	29.95%	(10%, 30%, 50%)

Determine which projects are pure investments.

SOLUTION

Given: Four projects with cash flows and i^*s as shown in the preceding table.

Find: Which projects are pure investments.

We will first compute the project balances at the projects' respective i^*s. If multiple rates of return exist, we may use the largest value of i^* greater than zero. (In fact, it does not matter which rate we use in applying the net-investment test. If one value passes the net-investment test, they will all pass. If one value fails, they will all fail.)

Project A:

$\text{PB}(33.64\%)_0 = -\$1,000;$

$\text{PB}(33.64\%)_1 = -\$1,000(1 + 0.3364) + (-\$1,000) = -\$2,336.40;$

$\text{PB}(33.64\%)_2 = -\$2,336.40(1 + 0.3364) + \$2,000 = -\$1,122.36;$

$\text{PB}(33.64\%)_3 = -\$1,122.36(1 + 0.3364) + \$1,500 = 0.$

$(-, -, -, 0)$: Passes the net-investment test (pure investment).

Project B:

$\text{PB}(21.95\%)_0 = -\$1,000;$

$\text{PB}(21.95\%)_1 = -\$1,000(1 + 0.2195) + \$1,600 = \$380.50;$

$\text{PB}(21.95\%)_2 = +\$380.50(1 + 0.2195) - \$300 = \$164.02;$

$\text{PB}(21.95\%)_3 = +\$164.02(1 + 0.2195) - \$200 = 0.$

$(-, +, +, 0)$: Fails the net-investment test (mixed investment).

Project C:

$\text{PB}(29.95\%)_0 = -\$1,000;$

$\text{PB}(29.95\%)_1 = -\$1,000(1 + 0.2995) + \$500 = -\$799.50;$

$\text{PB}(29.95\%)_2 = -\$799,50(1 + 0.2995) - \$500 = -\$1,538.95;$

$\text{PB}(29.95\%)_3 = -\$1,538.95(1 + 0.2995) + \$2,000 = 0.$

$(-, -, -, 0)$: Passes the net-investment test (pure investment).

Project D:

There are three rates of return. We can use any of them for the net-investment test. We use the third rate given, 50%, as follows:

$\text{PB}(50\%)_0 = -\$1,000;$

$\text{PB}(50\%)_1 = -\$1,000(1 + 0.50) + \$3,900 = \$2400;$

$\text{PB}(50\%)_2 = +\$2,400(1 + 0.50) - \$5,030 = -\$1,430;$

$\text{PB}(50\%)_3 = +\$1,430(1 + 0.50) - \$2,145 = 0.$

$(-, +, -, 0)$: Fails the net-investment test (mixed investment).

COMMENTS: As shown in Figure 7A.1, Projects *A* and *C* are the only pure investments. Project *B* demonstrates that the existence of a unique i^* is a necessary, but not sufficient, condition for a pure investment.

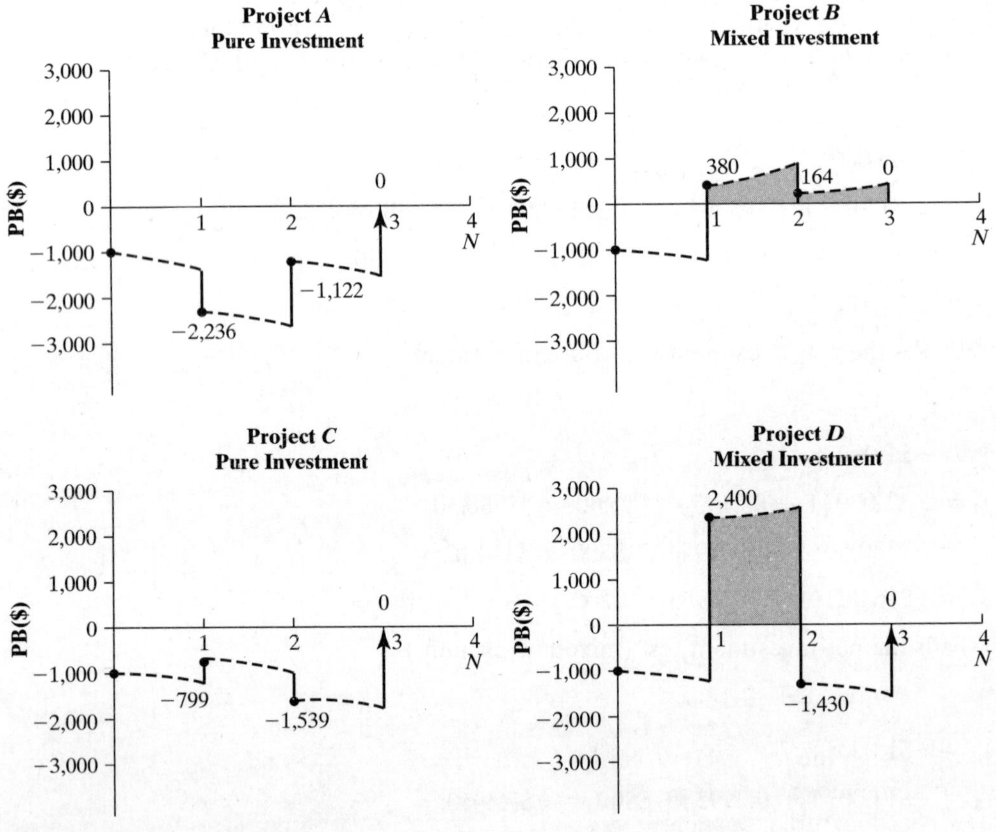

Figure 7A.1 Net-investment test

7A-2 The Need for an External Interest Rate

Even for a nonsimple investment, in which there is only one positive rate of return, the project may fail the net-investment test, as demonstrated by Project *B* in Example 7A.1. In this case, the unique i^* still may not be a true indicator of the project's profitability. That is, when we calculate the project balance at an i^* for mixed investments, we notice an important point. Cash borrowed (released) from the project is assumed to earn the same interest rate through external investment as money that remains internally invested. In other words, in solving for a cash flow for an unknown interest rate, it is assumed that money released from a project can be reinvested to yield a rate of return equal to that received from the project. In fact, we have been making this assumption whether a cash flow produces a unique positive i^* or not. Note that money is borrowed from the project only when $PB(i^*) > 0$, and the magnitude of the borrowed amount is the project balance. When $PB(i^*) < 0$, no money is borrowed even though the cash flow may be positive at that time.

In reality, it is not always possible for cash borrowed (released) from a project to be reinvested to yield a rate of return equal to that received from the project. Instead, it is likely that the rate of return available on a capital investment in the business is much different—usually higher—from the rate of return available on other external investments. Thus, it may be necessary to compute project balances for a project's cash flow at two different interest rates—one on the internal investment and one on the external investments. As we will see later, by separating the interest rates, we can measure the **true rate of return** of any internal portion of an investment project.

Because the net-investment test is the only way to accurately predict project borrowing (i.e., external investment), its significance now becomes clear. In order to calculate accurately a project's true IRR, we should always test a solution by the net-investment test and, if the test fails, take the further analytical step of introducing an external interest rate. Even the presence of a unique positive i^* is a necessary, but not sufficient, condition to predict net investment, so if we find a unique value, we should still subject the project to the net-investment test.

7A-3 Calculation of Return on Invested Capital for Mixed Investments

A failed net-investment test indicates a combination of internal and external investment. When this combination exists, we must calculate a rate of return on the portion of capital that remains invested internally. This rate is defined as the **true IRR** for the mixed investment and is commonly known as the **return on invested capital (RIC).**

How do we determine the true IRR of a mixed investment? Insofar as a project is not a net investment, the money from one or more periods when the project has a net outflow of money (positive project balance) must later be returned to the project. This money can be put into the firm's investment pool until such time when it is needed in the project. The interest rate of this investment pool is the interest rate at which the money can, in fact, be invested outside the project.

Recall that the PW method assumed that the interest rate charged to any funds withdrawn from a firm's investment pool would be equal to the MARR. In this book, we use the MARR as an established external interest rate (i.e., the rate earned by money invested outside of the project). We can then compute the true IRR, or RIC, as a function of the MARR by finding the value of IRR that will make the terminal project balance equal to zero. (This definition implies that the firm wants to fully recover any investment made in the project and pays off any borrowed funds at the end of the project life.) This way of computing rate of return is an accurate measure of the profitability of the project represented by the cash flow. The following procedure outlines the steps for determining the IRR for a mixed investment:

Step 1: Identify the MARR (or external interest rate).

Step 2: Calculate $PB(i, MARR)_n$ or simply PB_n, according to the following rule:

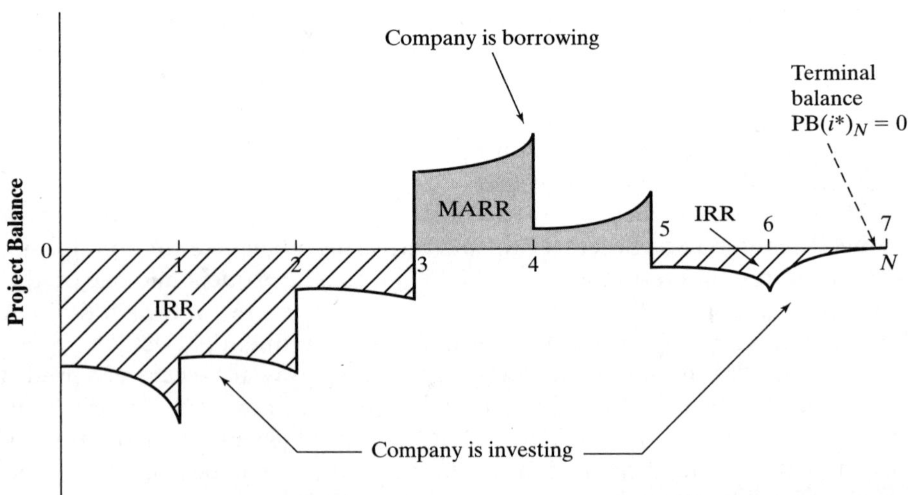

Figure 7A.2 Computational logic to find the true IRR for a mixed investment

$$PB(i, MARR)_0 = A_0.$$

$$PB(i, MARR)_1 = \begin{cases} PB_0(1 + i) + A_1, & \text{if } PB_0 < 0. \\ PB_0(1 + MARR) + A_1, & \text{if } PB_0 > 0. \end{cases}$$

$$\vdots$$

$$PB(i, MARR)_n = \begin{cases} PB_{n-1}(1 + i) + A_n, & \text{if } PB_{n-1} < 0. \\ PB_{n-1}(1 + MARR) + A_n, & \text{if } PB_{n-1} > 0. \end{cases}$$

(As defined in the text, A_n stands for the net cash flow at the end of period n. Note also that the terminal project balance must be zero.)

Step 3: Determine the value of i by solving the terminal-project-balance equation:

$$PB(i, MARR)_n = 0.$$

That interest rate is the IRR for the mixed investment.

Using the MARR as an external interest rate, we may accept a project if the IRR exceeds MARR and should reject the project otherwise. Figure 7A.2 summarizes the IRR computation for a mixed investment.

EXAMPLE 7A.2 IRR for a Nonsimple Project: Mixed Investment

Reconsider the defense contractor's flight-simulator project in Example 7.6. The project was a nonsimple and mixed investment. To simplify the decision-making process, we abandoned the IRR criterion and used the PW to make an accept-or-reject decision. Apply the procedures outlined in this chapter to find the true IRR, or return on invested capital, of this mixed investment:

(a) Compute the IRR (RIC) for this project, assuming MARR $= 15\%$.
(b) Make an accept-or-reject decision based on the results in part (a).

SOLUTION

Given: Cash flow shown in Example 7.6; MARR $= 15\%$.
Find: (a) IRR and (b) determine whether to accept the project.

(a) As calculated in Example 7.6, the project has multiple rates of return (10% and 20%). This project is obviously not a pure investment as shown in the following table:

Net-Investment Test Using $i^* = 20\%$

n	0	1	2
Beginning balance	$0	−$1,000	$1,100
Return on investment	$0	−$200	−$220
Payment	−$1,000	$2,300	−$1,320
Ending balance	−$1,000	$1,100	$0

(Unit: $1,000)

Because the net-investment test indicates external as well as internal investment, neither 10% nor 20% represents the true internal rate of return of this project. Since the project is a mixed investment, we need to find the true IRR by applying the steps shown previously.

At $n = 0$, there is a net investment for the firm so that the project-balance expression becomes

$$PB(i, 15\%)_0 = -\$1,000,000.$$

The net investment of $1,000,000 that remains invested internally grows at i for the next period. With the receipt of $2,300,000 in year 1, the project balance becomes

$$PB(i, 15\%)_1 = -\$1,000,000(1 + i) + \$2,300,000$$

$$= \$1,300,000 - \$1,000,000i$$

$$= \$1,000,000(1.3 - i).$$

At this point, we do not know whether $PB(i,15\%)_1$ is positive or negative. We need to know this information in order to test for net investment and the presence of a unique i^*. Net investment depends on the value of i, which we want to determine. Therefore, we need to consider two situations, (1) $i < 1.3$ and $i > 1.3$:

- **Case 1:** $i < 1.3 \rightarrow PB(i, 15)_1 > 0$.

Since this condition indicates a positive balance, the cash released from the project would be returned to the firm's investment pool to grow at the MARR until it is required to be put back into the project. By the end of year 2, the cash placed in the investment pool would have grown at the rate of 15%

$[$to $\$1,000,000(1.3 - i)(1 + 0.15)]$ and must equal the investment into the project of $\$1,320,000$ required at that time. Then the terminal balance must be

$$\mathrm{PB}(i, 15\%)_2 = \$1,000,000(1.3 - i)(1 + 0.15) - \$1,320,000$$
$$= \$175,000 - \$1,150,000i = 0.$$

Solving for i yields

$$\mathrm{IRR} = 0.1522, \text{ or } 15.22\%.$$

- **Case 2:** $i > 1.3 \rightarrow \mathrm{PB}(i, 15\%)_1 < 0.$

The firm is still in an investment mode. Therefore, the balance at the end of year 1 that remains invested will grow at a rate of i for the next period. Because of the investment of $\$1,320,000$ required in year 2 and the fact that the net investment must be zero at the end of the project life, the balance at the end of year 2 should be

$$\mathrm{PB}(i, 15\%)_2 = \$1,000,000(1.3 - i)(1 + i) - \$1,320,000$$
$$= -\$20,000 + \$300,000i - \$1,000,000i^2 = 0.$$

Solving for i gives

$$\mathrm{IRR} = 0.1 \text{ or } 0.2 < 1.3,$$

which violates the initial assumption $(i > 1.3)$. Therefore, Case 1 is the correct situation.

(b) Case 1 indicates that IRR $>$ MARR, so the project would be acceptable, resulting in the same decision obtained in Example 7.6 by applying the PW criterion.

COMMENTS: In this example, we could have seen by inspection that Case 1 was correct. Since the project required an investment as the final cash flow, the project balance at the end of the previous period (year 1) had to be positive in order for the final balance to equal zero. However, inspection does not typically work for more complex cash flows. In general, it is much easier to find the true IRR by using the Goal Seek function in Excel. Table 7A.1 illustrates how you may obtain the true IRR by using the Goal Seek function. In doing so, you may need the following steps:

- **Step 1:** Specify the MARR in cell B4 and the guessed RIC in cell B5. Enter cash flow information into the cells B9 through B11.
- **Step 2:** Designate cells C9 through C11 as project balance for each period. To calculate the project balance figure as a function of both MARR and RIC, we need an "IF" statement in Excel. In a formula, the arguments are separated by commas, so for this example, let us put our formula in cell C10:

$$=\mathrm{IF}(\mathrm{C9}{<}0,\mathrm{C9}^*(1{+}\$\mathrm{B}\$5){+}\mathrm{B10},\mathrm{C9}^*(1{+}\$\mathrm{B}\$4){+}\mathrm{B10}).$$

This says, IF the value in C9 is less than 0, calculate C9*(1+$B$5)+B10 and enter this value in C10 and if it is greater than zero, calculate C9*(1+$B$4)+B10 and enter this value in C10. Repeat the process for cell C11.

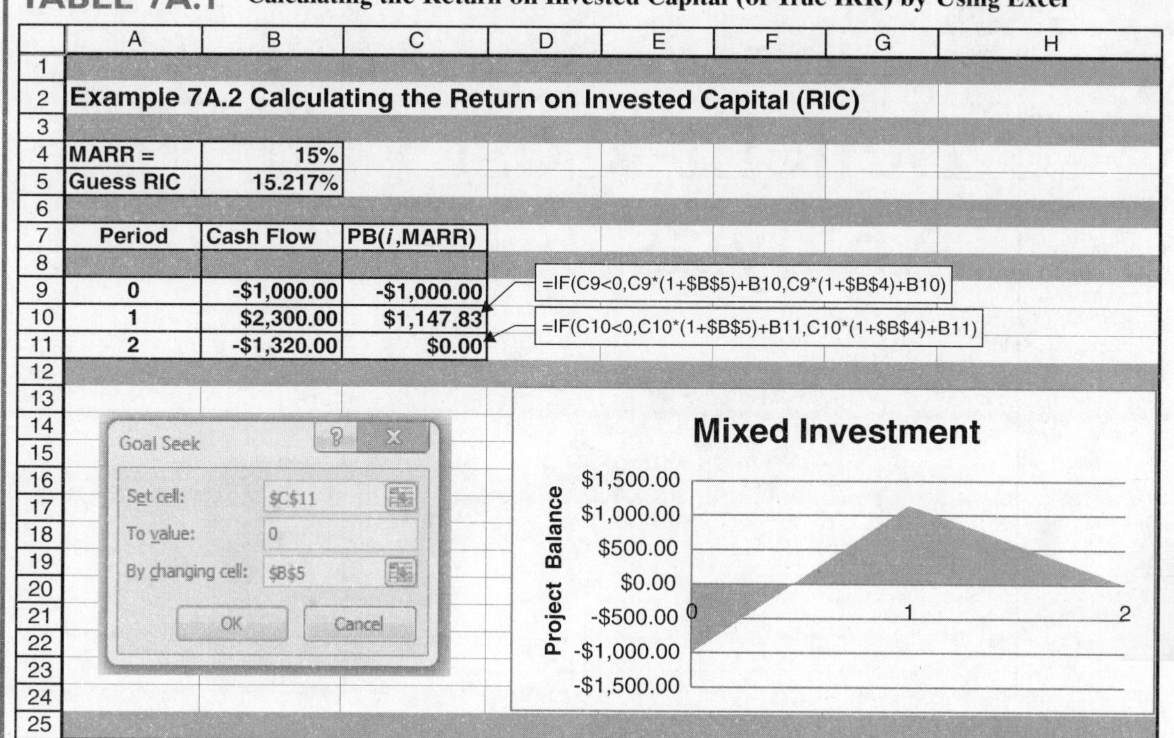

TABLE 7A.1 Calculating the Return on Invested Capital (or True IRR) by Using Excel

- **Step 3:** Go to the "Tools" menu, and click on the "Goal Seek" command. Then you will see the "Goal Seek" dialog box as shown in Table 7A.1. Make $C$11 as the "Set Cell," enter "0" to "To value," and $B$5 as "By changing cell." Then click "OK."

- **Step 4:** Check the RIC displayed in cell B5. In our example, this value is 15.22%. If this figure is the same as the rate of return, you will have a pure investment. For a mixed investment, the RIC will be different from any of the rate-of-return figures.

CHAPTER EIGHT

Benefit–Cost Analysis

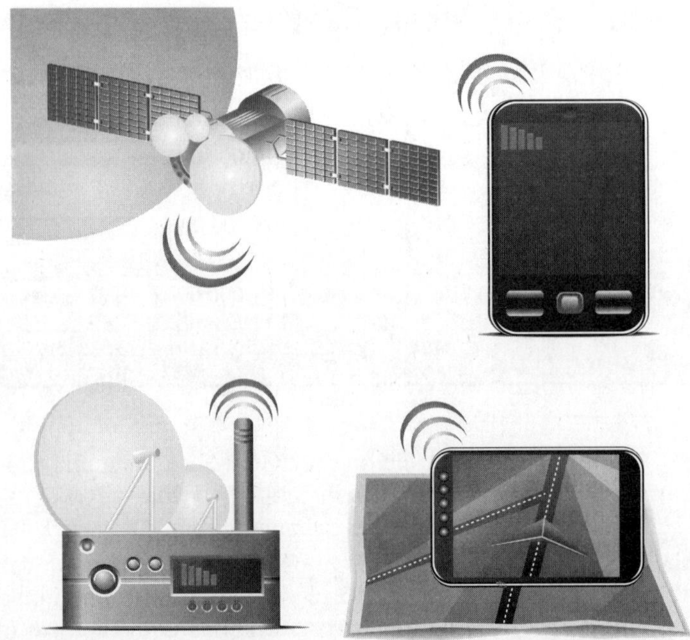

Broadband for All, Worth the Price? Is it worth $40 billion to provide an entire nation with access to broadband? To the Australian government, the simple answer is yes.

In 2009, the Australian government established The National Broadband Network Co. Limited (NBN Co.) and made plans to build a high-speed Internet network across the entire country. The plan will result in approximately 15,000 jobs and will span a period of ten years. It is considered an essential step in building the infrastructure of the nation and is meant to transform businesses, healthcare, and education.

Utilizing fixed fiber optic cables and satellite transmission, the NBN forecasts data transmission speeds of minimally 12 megabits per second. This will vary based on various factors, most notably the business/user's service plan provider, equipment setup, and in-premises connections.

The NBN has assured that taxpayers will get their money back and benefit from this project, with expected annual returns of 7%. Funding for the project involves approximately $27 billion of government capital; the balance of the expenditure is to be secured by the NBN through private investors whether local or overseas.

But the hefty price tag has caused quite a stir. While the government promises those who are opposed have a different view, many detractors believe the government should conduct a rigorous **benefit–cost analysis** of the project. They contend that such an analysis would result in definitive proof that this project would have little value to taxpayers in the long run.

Meanwhile, the process has already started, with only 4000 of potentially 13 million users hooked up. Only time—or possibly a further, more in-depth analysis—will tell whether this is a successful endeavor.

Many engineers are employed in public-works areas such as airport construction, highway construction, and water projects. One of the most important aspects of any public project is to quantify the benefits in dollar terms. For example, in any airport runway expansion, what is the economic benefit of reducing airport delay? From the airline's point of view, taxiing and arrival delays mean added fuel costs. From the airport's point of view, delays mean lost revenues in landing and departure fees. From the public's point of view, delays mean lost earnings, as people to spend more time traveling and less time earning a living. Comparison of the investment costs of a project with the project's potential benefits, a process known as **benefit–cost analysis**, is an important feature of the economic analysis method.

Up to this point, we have focused our attention on investment decisions in the private sector; the primary objective of these investments was to increase the wealth of corporations. In the public sector, federal, state, and local governments spend hundreds of billions of dollars annually on a wide variety of public activities, such as expanding airport runways. In addition, governments at all levels regulate the behavior of individuals and businesses by influencing the use of enormous quantities of productive resources. How can public decision makers determine whether their decisions, which affect the use of these productive resources, are, in fact, in the best public interest?

Benefit–cost analysis is a decision-making tool for systematically developing useful information about the desirable and undesirable effects of public projects. In a sense, we may view benefit–cost analysis in the public sector as profitability analysis in the private sector. In other words, benefit–cost analyses attempt to determine whether the social benefits of a proposed public activity outweigh the social costs. Usually, public investment decisions involve a great deal of expenditure, and their benefits are expected to occur over an extended time. Examples of benefit–cost analyses include studies of public transportation systems, environmental regulations, public safety programs, education and training programs, public health programs, flood control systems, water resource development projects, and national defense programs.

Benefit–cost analysis problems have three goals: (1) maximize the benefits for any given set of costs (or budgets), (2) maximize the net benefits when both benefits and costs vary, and (3) minimize costs in order to achieve any given level of benefits (often called cost-effectiveness analysis). These types of decision problems will be considered in this chapter.

8.1 Evaluation of Public Projects

To evaluate public projects designed to accomplish widely differing tasks, we need to measure the benefits or costs in the same units in all projects so that we have a common perspective by which to judge them. In practice, this requirement means expressing benefits and costs in monetary units, a process that often must be performed without accurate data. In performing benefit–cost analysis, we define **users** as the public and **sponsors** as the government.

The general framework for benefit–cost analysis can be summarized as follows:

1. Identify all users' **benefits** (favorable outcomes) and **disbenefits** (unfavorable outcomes) expected to arise from the project.
2. Quantify, as well as possible, these benefits and disbenefits in dollar terms so that different benefits and the respective costs of attaining them may be compared.
3. Identify the sponsor's costs and quantify them.
4. Determine the equivalent net benefits and net costs at the base period; use a discount rate appropriate for the project.
5. Accept the project if the equivalent users' net benefits exceed the equivalent sponsor's net costs.

We can use benefit–cost analysis to choose among alternatives in allocating funds for such projects as the construction of a mass-transit system, building an irrigation dam, highway maintenance, or implementing an air-traffic control system. If the projects are on the same scale with respect to cost, it is merely a question of choosing the project where the benefits exceed the costs by the greatest amount. The steps previously outlined are for a single (or independent) project evaluation. As in the case for the internal rate of return criterion, when comparing mutually exclusive alternatives, an **incremental benefit–cost ratio** must be used. Section 8.2.2 illustrates this important issue in detail.

8.1.1 Valuation of Benefits and Costs

In the abstract, the framework we just developed for benefit–cost analysis is no different from the one we have used throughout this text to evaluate private investment projects. The complications, as we shall discover in practice, arise in trying to identify and assign values to all the benefits and costs of a public project.

8.1.2 Users' Benefits

To begin a benefit–cost analysis, we identify all project benefits and disbenefits to the users, bearing in mind the indirect consequences resulting from the project—the so-called **secondary effects**. For example, the construction of a new highway will create new businesses such as gas stations, restaurants, and motels (benefits), but it will also divert some traffic from the old roads, and, as a consequence, some businesses may be lost (disbenefits). Once the benefits and disbenefits are quantified, we define the overall user's benefit B as follows:

$$B = \text{benefits} - \text{disbenefits}.$$

In identifying the user's benefits, we classify each as a **primary benefit**—a benefit directly attributable to the project—or a **secondary benefit**—a benefit indirectly attributable to the project. As an example, the U.S. government at one time was considering building a superconductor research laboratory in Texas. Such a move would bring many scientists and engineers, along with other supporting people, to the region. Primary national benefits may include the long-term benefits that accrue as a result of various applications of the research to U.S. businesses. Primary regional benefits may include economic benefits created by the research laboratory activities, which would generate many new supporting businesses. The secondary benefits might include the creation of new economic wealth as a consequence of any increase in international trade and the income of various regional producers attributable to a growing population.

The reason for making this distinction between primary and secondary benefits is that it may make our analysis more efficient. If primary benefits alone are sufficient to justify project costs, the secondary benefits need not be quantified.

8.1.3 Sponsor's Costs

We determine the cost to the sponsor by identifying and classifying the expenditures required and any savings (or revenues) to be realized. The sponsor's costs should include both capital investments and annual operating costs. Any sales of products or services that take place on completion of the project will generate some revenues—for example, toll revenues on highways. These revenues reduce the sponsor's costs. Therefore, we calculate the sponsor's costs by combining these cost and revenue elements:

Sponsor's costs = capital costs + operating and maintenance costs − revenues.

8.1.4 Social Discount Rate

As we briefly mentioned in Chapter 5, the selection of an appropriate MARR for evaluating an investment project is a critical issue in the private sector. In public-project analyses, we also need to select an interest rate, called the **social discount rate**, in order to determine equivalent benefits as well as the equivalent costs. Selection of the social discount rate in public-project evaluation is as critical as the selection of an MARR in the private sector.

Historically, present-worth calculations were initiated to evaluate public water resources and related land-use projects in the 1930s. Since then, the growing tendency has been for analysts to use relatively low rates of discount compared with the rates existing in markets for private assets. During the 1950s and into the 1960s, the rate for water resource projects was 2.63%, which, for much of this period, was even lower than the yield on long-term government securities. The persistent use of a lower interest rate for water resource projects has been a political issue.

In recent years, with the growing interest in performance budgeting and systems analysis that started in the 1960s, government agencies have begun to examine the appropriateness of the discount rate in the public sector in relation to the efficient allocation of resources in the economic system as a whole. Two views of the basis for determining the social discount rate prevail:

1. **Projects without private counterparts:** *The social discount rate should reflect only the prevailing government borrowing rate.* Projects such as dams designed purely for flood control, access roads for noncommercial uses, and reservoirs for community water supply may not have corresponding private counterparts. In such areas of government activity where benefit–cost analysis has been employed in evaluation, the rate of discount traditionally used has been the cost of government borrowing. In fact, water resource project evaluations follow this view exclusively.

2. **Projects with private counterparts:** *The social discount rate should represent the rate that could have been earned had the funds not been removed from the private sector.* If all public projects were financed by borrowing at the expense of private investment, we may have focused on the opportunity cost of capital in alternative investments in the private sector in order to determine the social discount rate. So, in the case of public capital projects similar to projects in the private sector that produce a commodity or a service to be sold on the market (such as electric power), the discount rate employed is the average cost of capital as will be discussed in Chapter 11. The reasons for using the private rate of return as the opportunity cost of capital for projects similar to those in the private sector are (1) to prevent the public sector from transferring capital from higher yielding to lower yielding investments and (2) to force public-project evaluators to employ market standards when justifying projects.

The Office of Management and Budget (OMB) holds the second view. Since 1972, the OMB has annually updated the discount rates to be used in various federal projects. For calendar year 2011, discount rates for public investment and regulatory analyses[2] are as follows:

- **Base-Case Analysis.** Constant-dollar benefit–cost analyses of proposed investments and regulations should report net present value and other outcomes

---

[2] The Office of Management and Budget, The White House, www.whitehouse.gov/omb/circulars_a094#8.

Step 1	Identify user's benefits

- Calculate all users' benefits in dollar terms
- Calculate all users' disbenefits in dollar terms
- Compute the net users' benefits (= benefit – disbenefits)

Step 2	Identify the sponsor's costs

- Determine the non-recurring costs such as capital expenditure and residual value at the end of project period
- Determine the recurring costs such as operating and maintenance costs, renovation costs
- Determine any annual revenues (fees) generated from the project such as toll revenues in providing service
- Calculate the net annual sponsor's cost (= non-recurring costs + recurring costs – revenues or fees charged – residual value)

Step 3	Perform the benefit–cost analysis

- Determine the interest rate to use in benefit–cost analysis
- Determine the equivalent net benefits
- Determine the equivalent sponsor's cost
- Calculate the benefit–cost ratio

Figure 8.1   Key steps in performing benefit–cost analysis for a typical public project

determined using *a real discount rate of 7%*. This rate approximates the marginal pretax rate of return on an average investment in the private sector in recent years. Significant changes in this rate will be reflected in future updates of this circular.

- **Other Discount Rates.** Analyses should show the sensitivity of the discounted net present value and other outcomes to variations in the discount rate. The importance of these alternative calculations will depend on the specific economic characteristics of the program under analysis. For example, in analyzing a regulatory proposal whose main cost is to reduce business investment, net present value should also be calculated using a discount rate higher than 7%.

Many state and city governments use discount rates different from the federal government, typically ranging from 3% to 8%, depending on the nature of the project. So, it is important to check the appropriate interest rate to use before conducting any public project analyses. Figure 8.1 summarizes the key steps involved in any benefit–cost analysis for a typical public project.

8.2 Benefit–Cost Analysis

An alternative way of expressing the worthiness of a public project is to compare the user's benefits (B) with the sponsor's costs (C) by taking the ratio B/C. In this section, we shall define the benefit–cost (B/C) ratio and explain the relationship between the conventional PW criterion and the B/C ratio.

8.2.1 Definition of Benefit–Cost Ratio

For a given benefit–cost profile, let B and C be the present worth of benefits and costs, defined by

$$B = \sum_{n=0}^{N} b_n (1 + i)^{-n},\tag{8.1}$$

$$C = \sum_{n=0}^{N} c_n (1 + i)^{-n},\tag{8.2}$$

where

$b_n =$ benefits at the end of period n,
$c_n =$ expenses at the end of period n,
$N =$ project life, and
$i =$ sponsor's interest rate (social discount rate).

The sponsor's costs (C) consist of the capital expenditure (I) and the annual operating costs (C') accrued in each successive period. (Note the sign convention we use in calculating a benefit–cost ratio: Since we are using a ratio, all benefit and cost flows are expressed in positive units. Recall that in previous equivalent worth calculations, our sign convention was to explicitly assign "+" for cash inflows and "−" for cash outflows.) Let us assume that a series of initial investments is required during the first K periods while annual operating and maintenance costs accrue in each following period. Then the equivalent present worth for each component is

$$I = \sum_{n=0}^{K} c_n (1 + i)^{-n},\tag{8.3}$$

$$C' = \sum_{n=K+1}^{N} c_n (1 + i)^{-n},\tag{8.4}$$

and $C = I + C'$.

The B/C ratio is defined as

$$\text{BC}(i) = \frac{B}{C} = \frac{B}{I + C'} \quad \text{where } I + C' > 0.\tag{8.5}$$

If we are to accept a project, $\text{BC}(i)$ must be higher than 1. Note that the acceptance rule by the B/C-ratio criterion is equivalent to that for the PW criterion as illustrated in Figure 8.2. Note also that we must express the values of B, C', and I in present-worth

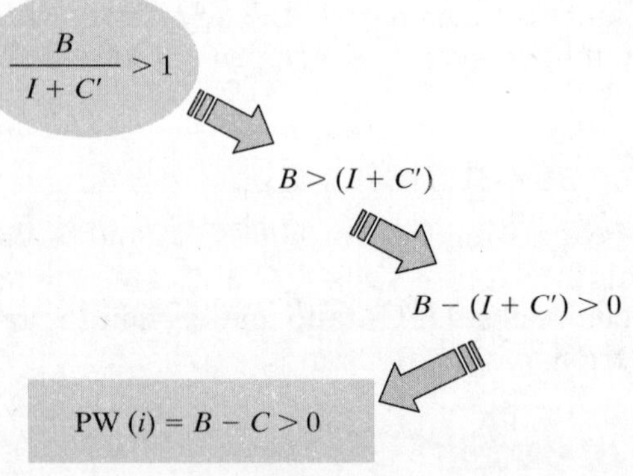

Figure 8.2 Relationship between B/C ratio and PW criterion

equivalents. Alternatively, we can compute these values in terms of annual equivalents and use them in calculating the B/C ratio. The resulting B/C ratio is not affected.

EXAMPLE 8.1 Benefit–Cost Ratio

A public project being considered by a local government has the following estimated benefit–cost profile (see Figure 8.3):

Assume that $i = 10\%$, $N = 5$ and $K = 1$. Compute B, C, I, C', and $BC(10\%)$.

n	b_n	c_n	A_n
0		$10	–$10
1		$10	–$10
2	$20	$5	$15
3	$30	$5	$25
4	$30	$8	$22
5	$20	$8	$12

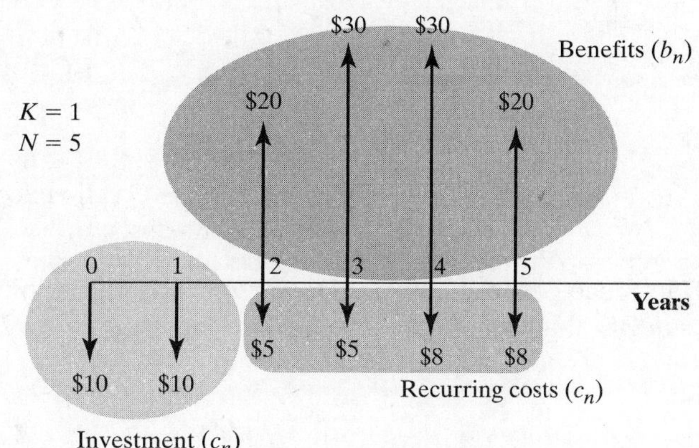

Figure 8.3   Classification of a project's cash flow elements into benefits and costs

---

DISSECTING THE PROBLEM

Given: b_n, c_n, $K = 1$, $N = 5$, and $i = 10\%$ per year.
Find: $BC(i)$.

METHODOLOGY

SOLUTION

We calculate B as follows:

$$B = \$20(P/F, 10\%, 2) + \$30(P/F, 10\%, 3)$$
$$+ \$30(P/F, 10\%, 4) + \$20(P/F, 10\%, 5)$$
$$= \$71.98.$$

We calculate C as follows:

$$C = \$10 + \$10(P/F, 10\%, 1) + \$5(P/F, 10\%, 2)$$
$$+ \$5(P/F, 10\%, 3) + \$8(P/F, 10\%, 4) + \$8(P/F, 10\%, 5)$$
$$= \$37.41.$$

We calculate I as follows:

$$I = \$10 + \$10\,(P/F, 10\%, 1)$$
$$= \$19.09.$$

We calculate C' as follows:

$$C' = C - I$$
$$= \$18.32.$$

Using Eq. (8.5), we can compute the B/C ratio as

$$BC(10\%) = \frac{\$71.98}{\$19.09 + \$18.32} = \frac{\$71.98}{\$37.41}$$
$$= 1.92 > 1.$$

The B/C ratio exceeds 1, so the user's benefits exceed the sponsor's costs.

COMMENTS: Since governments do not pay taxes, depreciation and income taxes are not issues in BC analysis.

8.2.2 Incremental B/C-Ratio Analysis

Let us now consider how we choose among mutually exclusive public projects. As we explained in Chapter 7, we must use the incremental-investment approach in comparing alternatives on the basis of any relative measure, such as IRR or B/C.

To apply incremental analysis, we compute the incremental differences for each term $(B, I,$ and $C')$ and take the B/C ratio based on these differences. To use $BC(i)$ on an incremental investment, we may proceed as follows:

1. Eliminate any alternatives with a B/C ratio less than 1.
2. Arrange the remaining alternatives in increasing order of the denominator $(I + C')$. Thus, the alternative with the smallest denominator should be the first (j), the alternative with the second smallest (k) should be the second, and so forth.
3. Compute the incremental differences for each term $(B, I,$ and $C')$ for the paired alternatives (j, k) in the list:

$$\Delta B = B_k - B_j;$$
$$\Delta I = I_k - I_j;$$
$$\Delta C' = C'_k - C'_j.$$

4. Compute $BC(i)$ on incremental investment by evaluating

$$BC(i)_{k-j} = \frac{\Delta B}{\Delta I + \Delta C'}.$$

If $BC(i)_{k-j} > 1$, select the k alternative. Otherwise, select the j alternative.

5. Compare the selected alternative with the next one on the list by computing the incremental benefit–cost ratio. Continue the process until you reach the bottom of the list. The alternative selected during the last pairing is the best one.

We may modify the decision procedures when we encounter the following situations:

- If $\Delta I + \Delta C' = 0$, we cannot use the benefit–cost ratio because this relationship implies that both alternatives require the same initial investment and operating expenditures. In such cases, we simply select the alternative with the largest B value.

- In situations where public projects with *unequal service lives* are to be compared but the alternative can be repeated, we may compute all component values (B, C' and I) on an *annual basis* and use them in incremental analysis.

EXAMPLE 8.2 Incremental Benefit–Cost Ratios

Consider three investment projects: $A1$, $A2$, and $A3$. Each project has the same service life, and the present worth of each component value (B, I, and C') is computed at 10% as follows:

	Projects		
	A1	**A2**	**A3**
B	$12,000	$35,000	$21,000
I	$5,000	$20,000	$14,000
C'	$4,000	$8,000	$1,000
PW(i)	$3,000	$7,000	$6,000

(a) If all three projects are independent, which projects would be selected, based on BC(i)?

(b) If the three projects are mutually exclusive, which project would be the best alternative? Show the sequence of calculations that would be required in order to produce the correct results. Use the B/C ratio on incremental investment.

DISSECTING THE PROBLEM

Given: I, B, and C' for each project, $i = 10\%$ per year.
Find: Select the best project.

METHODOLOGY

Calculate the BC(i) for each project and compare the projects incrementally.

SOLUTION

(a) Since $\text{PW}(i)_1$, $\text{PW}(i)_2$, and $\text{PW}(i)_3$ are positive, all of the projects would be acceptable if they were independent. Also, the BC(i) value for each project is higher than 1, so the use of the benefit–cost ratio criterion leads to the same accept–reject conclusion as under the PW criterion:

	A1	**A2**	**A3**
BC(i)	1.33	1.25	1.40

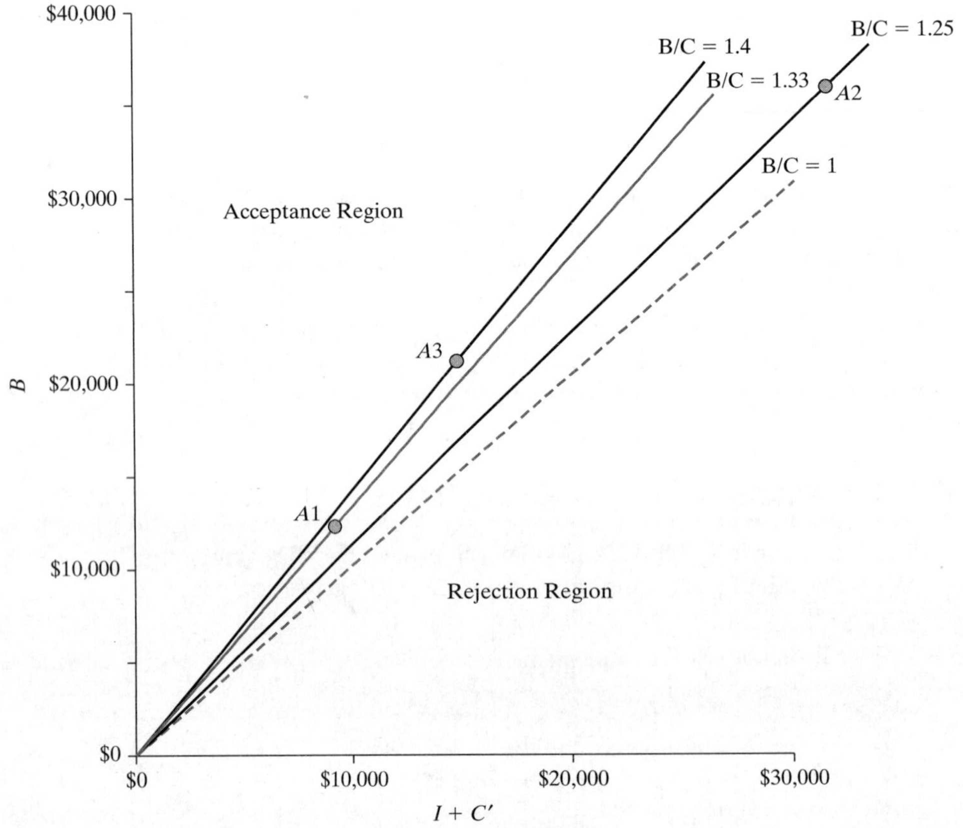

Figure 8.4 Benefit–cost ratio graph of Example 8.2

Benefit–cost analysis may be graphically illustrated as shown in Figure 8.4. B/C = 1 represents the 45° line where any project located above this line is selected. The slope made by connecting the origin $(0, 0)$ with each point of the project location represents the B/C ratio.

(b) If these projects are mutually exclusive, we must use the principle of incremental analysis as shown in Figure 8.5. If we attempt to rank the projects according to the size of the B/C ratio, obviously, we will observe a different project preference. For example, if we use BC(i) on the total investment, we see that $A3$ appears to be the most desirable and $A2$ the least desirable project; however, selecting mutually exclusive projects on the basis of B/C ratios is incorrect. Certainly, with $\text{PW}(i)_2 > \text{PW}(i)_3 > \text{PW}(i)_1$, project $A2$ would be selected under the PW criterion. By computing the incremental B/C ratios, we will select a project that is consistent with the PW criterion. We will first arrange the projects by increasing order of their denominator $(I + C')$ for the BC(i) criterion:

Ranking Base	A1	A3	A2
$I + C'$	$9,000	$15,000	$28,000

We now compare the projects incrementally as follows:

- $A1$ versus $A3$: With the do-nothing alternative, we first drop from consideration any project that has a B/C ratio smaller than 1. In our example, the B/C ratios of all three projects exceed 1, so the first incremental comparison is between $A1$ and $A3$:

$$\mathrm{BC}(i)_{3-1} = \frac{\$21,000 - \$12,000}{(\$14,000 - \$5,000) + (\$1,000 - \$4,000)}$$

$$= 1.50.$$

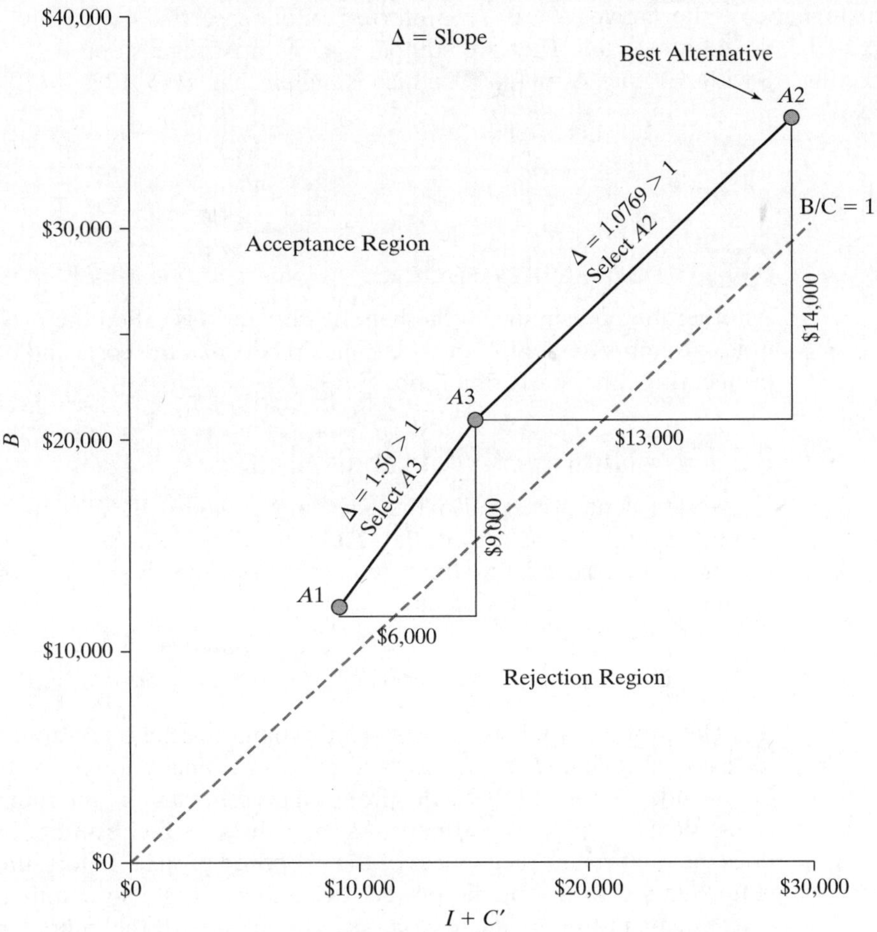

Figure 8.5 Incremental benefit–cost analyses. The slope of line $A3 - A1$ indicates a $\Delta B/\Delta C$ ratio > 1. This is also true for line $A2 - A3$, indicating $A2$ will be the ultimate choice

Since the ratio is higher than 1, we prefer $A3$ over $A1$. Therefore, $A3$ becomes the "current best" alternative.

- $A3$ versus $A2$: Next we must determine whether the incremental benefits to be realized from $A2$ would justify the additional expenditure. Therefore, we need to compare $A2$ and $A3$ as follows:

$$\text{BC}(i)_{2-3} = \frac{\$35{,}000 - \$21{,}000}{(\$20{,}000 - \$14{,}000) + (\$8{,}000 - \$1{,}000)}$$

$$= 1.0769.$$

The incremental B/C ratio again exceeds 1, and therefore, we prefer $A2$ over $A3$. With no further projects to consider, $A2$ becomes the ultimate choice.

COMMENTS: Figure 8.5 illustrates also elimination of inferior alternatives. When we compare $A3$ with $A1$, where $A3$ has a higher sum of $I + C'$, we are basically attempting to determine the slope (Δ) created by connecting $A1$ and $A3$. If this slope is higher than 1, the higher cost alternative $(I + C')$ is preferred. In our case, this slope happens to be $\Delta = 1.5$, so $A3$ is selected. Then we compare $A3$ with $A2$. The slope created by connecting $A3$ with $A2$ gives $\Delta = 1.0769$, which is higher than 1; so $A2$ is the better choice.

8.3 Profitability Index

Another method similar to the benefit–cost ratio is called the profitability index. This index attempts to identify the relationship between the costs and benfits of a proposed project through the use of a ratio.

8.3.1 Definition of Profitability Index

Unlike the benefit-cost ratio, the **profitability index**, $\text{PI}(i)$, considers only the initial capital expenditure as cash outlay, and annual net benefits are used—the ratio of the present value of the future expected cash flows after initial investment divided by the amount of the initial investment.

$$\text{PI}(i) = \frac{B - C'}{I}, I > 0. \tag{8.6}$$

The profitability index measures the bang for the buck invested. In a way, it is a measure of capital efficiency. A ratio of 1.0 is logically the lowest acceptable measure on the index. With a $\text{PI}(i) < 1$, the project's present value of the future cash flow streams is less than the initial investment. As the values on the profitability index increase, so does the financial attractiveness of the proposed project. In fact, this profitability index is not limited to the public project evaluation. It is also commonly used in ranking investments in the private sector. As is the case with the benefit–cost ratio, we select all independent projects whose PI ratio is higher than 1 as long as the budget permits. Figure 8.6 illustrates the conceptual differences between the benefit–cost ratio and the profitability index.

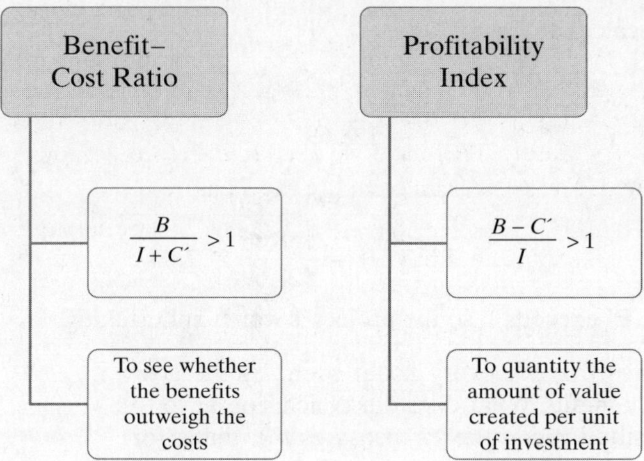

Figure 8.6 Conceptual difference between the benefit–cost ratio and the profitability index

EXAMPLE 8.3 Profitability Index Ratio

Assume a five-year program that will commit the government to the stream of real (or constant-dollar) expenditures to generate a series of real benefits for a public project. Assume that $i = 7\%$, $N = 5$ and $K = 1$. Compute PI (7%) and determine whether it is worth funding the program.

n	b_n	c_n	A_n
0		$10	−$10
1		$20	−$20
2	$35	$5	$30
3	$30	$5	$25
4	$20	$7	$13
5	$10	$7	$3

DISSECTING THE PROBLEM

Given: $b_n, c_n, N = 5$, and $i = 7\%$ per year.
Find: PI(i).

METHODOLOGY

Use Eq. (8.6).

SOLUTION

We calculate $B - C'$ as follows:

$$B - C' = \$30\,(P/F, 7\%, 2) + \$25\,(P/F, 7\%, 3)$$
$$+ \$13\,(P/F, 7\%, 4) + \$3\,(P/F, 7\%, 5)$$
$$= \$58.66.$$

We calculate I as follows:

$$I = \$10 + \$20(P/F, 7\%, 1)$$

$$= \$28.69.$$

Using Eq. (8,6), we can compute the PI as

$$PI(7\%) = \frac{\$58.66}{\$28.69} = 2.04 > 1.$$

The PI exceeds 1, so the project is worth undertaking.

COMMENTS: The PI value of 2.04 indicates that for every dollar spent by the government, the project will generate $2.04 benefits. What does our conclusion have to say about the PI rule? In the case of limited funds, the PI measures the "bang for the buck," so it could be used as a tool to rank the projects according to its capital efficiency.

8.3.2 Incremental PI Ratio Analysis for Mutually Exclusive Alternatives

Because PI is a ratio, like BC(i) and IRR, it ignores differences of scale for mutually exclusive projects. This, however, can be corrected by using incremental analysis. We write the incremental cash flows after subtracting lower cost investment alternative from the higher cost alternative. If the incremental PI is higher than 1, we choose the alternative with the higher cost of investment. This way of selecting the alternative will ensure that we will pick the same project that would be selected under the NPW analysis.

In situations where we need to compare projects with *unequal service lives*, we may compute all component values (B, C', and I) on an *annual basis* and use them in incremental analysis with the assumption that the alternative can be repeated.

EXAMPLE 8.4 Incremental Profitability Index

Reconsider the three investment projects: $A1$, $A2$, and $A3$ in Example 8.2. Each project has the same service life, and the present worth of each component value (B, I, and C') is computed at 10% as follows:

	Projects		
	A1	**A2**	**A3**
B	$12,000	$35,000	$21,000
I	$5,000	$20,000	$14,000
C'	$4,000	$8,000	$1,000
PW(i)	$3,000	$7,000	$6,000

(a) If all three projects are independent, which projects would be selected based on PI(i)?

(b) If the three projects are mutually exclusive, which project would be the best alternative? Show the sequence of calculations that would be required in order to produce the correct results. Use the PI on incremental investment.

DISSECTING THE PROBLEM

Given: I, B, and C' for each project, $i = 10\%$ per year.

Find: Select the best project based on PI.

METHODOLOGY

Calculate the PI(i) for each project and compare the projects incrementally.

SOLUTION

(a) As before, all of the projects would be acceptable if they were independent. Also, the PI(i) value for each project is higher than 1, so the use of the profitability index criterion leads to the same accept–reject conclusion as under the PW criterion:

	A1	A2	A3
PI(i)	1.6	1.35	1.43

(b) If these projects are mutually exclusive, we must use the principle of incremental analysis. If we attempt to rank the projects according to the size of the PI ratio, obviously, we will observe a different project preference. For example, if we use PI(i) on the total investment, we see that $A1$ appears to be the most desirable and $A2$ the least desirable project; however, selecting mutually exclusive projects on the basis of PI ratios is incorrect. Certainly, with $PW(i)_2 > PW(i)_3 > PW(i)_1$, project $A2$ would be selected under the PW criterion. By computing the incremental PI ratios, we will select a project that is consistent with the PW criterion. We will first arrange the projects by increasing order of their denominator I for the PI(i) criterion:

Ranking Base	A1	A3	A2
I	\$5,000	\$14,000	\$20,000

With the do-nothing alternative, we first drop from consideration any project that has a PI ratio less than 1. In our example, the PI ratios of all three projects exceed 1, so the first incremental comparison is between $A1$ and $A3$. We now compare the projects incrementally as follows:

- $A1$ versus $A3$:

$$\text{PI}(i)_{3-1} = \frac{(\$21{,}000 - \$1{,}000) - (\$12{,}000 - \$4{,}000)}{(\$14{,}000 - \$5{,}000)}$$

$$= 1.33 > 1.$$

Since the ratio is higher than 1, we prefer $A3$ over $A1$. Therefore, $A3$ becomes the "current best" alternative.

- *A3* versus *A2*: Next we must determine whether the incremental benefits to be realized from *A2* would justify the additional expenditure. Therefore, we need to compare *A2* and *A3* as follows:

$$\text{PI}(i)_{2-3} = \frac{(\$35,000 - \$8,000) - (\$21,000 - \$1,000)}{(\$20,000 - \$14,000)}$$

$$= 1.17 > 1.$$

The incremental PI ratio again exceeds 1, and therefore, we prefer *A2* over *A3*. With no further projects to consider, *A2* becomes the ultimate choice.

Note that this is exactly the same conclusion that we obtained under the benefit–cost analysis.

8.4 Highway Benefit–Cost Analysis[3]

In this section, we will examine how a benefit–cost analysis may be used in making investments in highway improvement projects. The improvement may reduce the number or severity of crashes, eliminate long delays during peak hours, or reduce travel time (by providing a shorter route). In highway benefit–cost analysis, the usual procedure is that benefits are first estimated in physical terms and then valued in economic terms. This means that the analyst has to first estimate the number of crashes eliminated, the amount of travel time saved, and/or the number of vehicle-miles reduced before assigning or calculating monetary values.

8.4.1 Define the Base Case and the Proposed Alternatives

Every analysis requires a definition of the base case and proposed alternative(s).

- The **base case** is not necessarily a "do-nothing" alternative, but it is generally the "lowest" capital cost alternative that maintains the serviceability of the existing facility. In other words, the base case should include an estimate of any physical and operational deterioration in the condition of the facility and the costs associated with the periodic need to rehabilitate the major elements of the facility through the analysis period.

- The **proposed alternatives** are specific and discrete sets of highway improvements that can be undertaken. These improvements generally change travel times, vehicle operating costs, and/or safety characteristics from the base case. Proposed alternatives must also be reasonably distinct from one another, and each alternative should be specified with as much detail as possible to estimate costs (capital and maintenance) and effects on travel time, operating costs, and safety.

- We also need to define the **analysis period** that will be used in the benefit–cost analysis. For many highway improvement projects, it is quite common to use an analysis period of 20 years or longer.

---

[3] This section is based on materials from "Benefit–Cost Analysis for Transportation Projects," *Benefit Cost Analysis Guidance*, Minnesota Department of Transportation, June 2005.

8.4.2 Highway User Benefits

The benefits of a transportation investment are typically estimated by comparing the amount of travel time, vehicle miles traveled, and expected number of crashes for the alternative with the base case. Specifically, consider the following:

1. **Travel-Time Savings:** These typically generate the greatest benefit. Savings are calculated on the basis of the difference in travel time between the base case and an alternative. Travel time is often expressed as vehicle-hours traveled (VHT) and can be estimated with various computer models. The estimation of travel-time savings should include both the driver and passengers (vehicle occupancy rates). In many cases, vehicle occupancy rates vary between peak and off-peak hours as well as between alternatives. The valuation of travel-time savings is calculated by standardized cost-per-hour-person figures for different types of vehicles (auto or truck).

2. **Vehicle Operating Cost Savings:** When transportation improvements are made, the cost of operating vehicles along a particular facility or set of facilities can change. Operating costs can change because the number of miles driven varies (as in the case of a shorter bypass or a reduction in diversion of trips) or because of variation in the number of stops or speed-cycle changes. The number of vehicle-miles traveled (VMT) is the most common variable that affects vehicle operating costs. Once the change in vehicle miles is estimated, the valuation of vehicle operating costs is calculated for standardized cost-per-mile figures for different types of vehicles (auto or truck).

3. **Safety Benefits:** Safety benefits are one of the principal benefits that can result from transportation improvements. Benefits occur when the number of crashes is reduced and/or the severity of the crashes is diminished on a facility or set of facilities because of the transportation improvement. Standard engineering methods can be used to evaluate both the potential crash reductions and/or changes in severity.

8.4.3 Sponsors' Costs

In economic terms, the transportation investment cost is determined by the amount of resources used/consumed over the course of a project. The total value of construction and any additional maintenance costs must be estimated. It is important to note that the analysis does not emphasize who incurs the cost but rather aims to include any and all costs that are involved in developing the project.

1. **Capital Costs:** These costs make up the total investment required to prepare a highway improvement for service from engineering through landscaping. When possible, capital costs should be grouped into similar life-cycle categories, including engineering, right of way, major structures, grading, subbase and base, surfacing, and miscellaneous items.

2. **Major Rehabilitation Costs:** Within a benefit–cost analysis period, future investments may be needed to maintain the serviceability of a major transportation facility. For example, with a new or reconstructed highway, pavement overlays may be required 8, 12, or 15 years after the initial construction year. The cost of overlays or other major preservation activities should be included in the analysis and allocated to the year in which they are anticipated to occur.

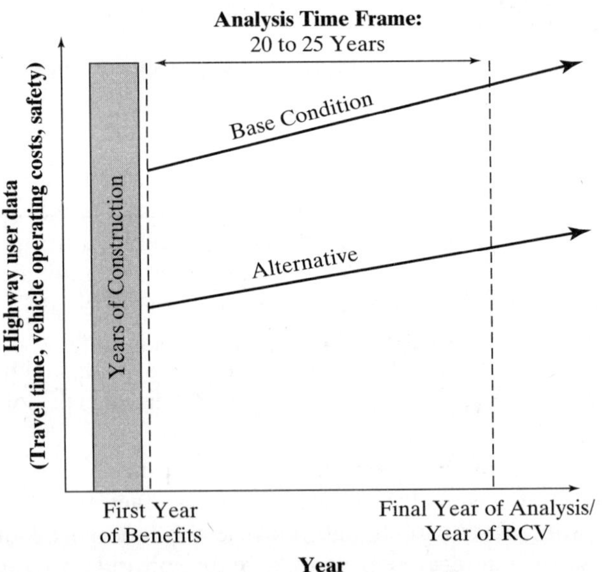

Figure 8.7 Time-dependent elements in a benefit–cost analysis

3. **Routine Annual Maintenance Costs:** When evaluating transportation investments, it is important to account for the future operating and maintenance costs of the facility. Bridges require preventive maintenance, and roadway lanes have to be plowed and patched each year. In the case of upgraded roadways, it is necessary to estimate the marginal or additional maintenance costs that would be required for the alternative, compared with the base case. For a new facility, the entire additional maintenance costs should be included as the incremental increase in costs.

4. **Remaining Capital Value (RCV):** Many components of a project retain some residual useful life beyond the benefit–cost analysis period (typically, 20 years). At the end of the analysis period, the infrastructure that has been put in place generally has not been completely worn out and will continue to provide benefits to drivers and travelers into the future. It is important to reflect this value in the analysis. Typically, we calculate the remaining capital value by determining the percentage of useful life remaining beyond the analysis period and multiplying that percentage by the construction cost for that component. Figure 8.7 summarizes the framework to be used in estimating the user's benefits and sponsor's cost in a highway improvement project.

8.4.4 Illustrating Case Example

This case example illustrates how the Minnesota Department of Transportation (Mn/DOT) made a decision to implement a highway improvement project. The base case was just maintaining the existing highway, and the proposed alternative case was to widen the existing highways from four lanes to six lanes. In doing economic analysis, Mn/DOT assumed that the construction would begin in 2007 and completed by the end of 2010. Mn/DOT used a study period of 20 years in justifying the improvement project.

- **Users' benefits:** In estimating the technical as well as financial data related to the project, we may proceed as follows:

TABLE 8.1 Example of a Total Highway User Benefit Tallying Spreadsheet[4]

	Year	VMT Benefits	VHT Benefits	Accident Reduction Savings	Present Value of Total User Benefits
		Present Value of User Benefits			
2011	1	$5,373,985	$22,348,044	$4,079,014	$31,801,043
2012	2	$5,222,634	$24,236,203	$3,774,352	$33,233,189
2013	3	$5,075,546	$26,049,598	$3,485,631	$34,610,775
2014	4	$4,932,600	$27,790,302	$3,212,120	$35,935,022
2015	5	$4,793,680	$29,460,334	$2,953,122	$37,207,136
2016	6	$4,658,672	$31,061,668	$2,707,967	$38,428,308
2017	7	$4,527,467	$32,596,229	$2,476,016	$39,599,712
2018	8	$4,399,957	$34,065,893	$2,256,656	$40,722,506
2019	9	$4,276,038	$35,472,493	$2,049,300	$41,797,832
2020	10	$4,155,609	$36,817,816	$1,853,388	$42,826,813
2021	11	$4,038,572	$38,103,604	$1,668,382	$43,810,559
2022	12	$3,924,831	$39,331,558	$1,493,770	$44,750,159
2023	13	$3,814,294	$40,503,338	$1,329,059	$45,646,690
2024	14	$3,706,869	$41,620,560	$1,173,779	$46,501,208
2025	15	$3,602,470	$42,684,802	$1,027,482	$47,314,754
2026	16	$3,501,011	$43,697,603	$889,737	$48,088,352
2027	17	$3,402,410	$44,660,465	$760,133	$48,823,008
2028	18	$3,306,585	$45,574,849	$638,277	$49,519,712
2029	19	$3,213,460	$46,442,185	$523,794	$50,179,438
2030	20	$3,122,957	$47,263,862	$416,323	$50,803,142
2011–2030		$83,049,648	$729,781,406	$38,768,303	$851,599,358

1. First, it is necessary to assemble highway user data from the database kept by the Mn/DOT (VMT, VHT, other operating costs and safety information) for the first year of benefits and the final year of analysis at a minimum. (If detailed annual estimates are not available, we could interpolate between these two data points to compute information for each year in the analysis time frame.)

2. Compute the difference in travel time, vehicle operating costs, and safety between the base case and the alternative for each year in the analysis. Table 8.1 summarizes the VMT benefits, VHT benefits, and accident reduction savings due to the proposed highway improvement project. Note that these benefit figures are incremental benefits over the base case.

---

[4] The detailed procedure to obtain these savings figures is not presented here but can be found in the Benefit–Cost Analysis Guidance by the State of Minnesota, Department of Transportation.

TABLE 8.2 Calculate Total Present Cost for the Base Case and Alternative(s)

| | | PRESENT VALUE OF COSTS | | | | | | |
| | | Capital Cost | | Maintenance Cost | | Remaining Capital Value | | Present Value of Net Annual Costs |
Year		Base Case	Alternative	Base Case	Alternative	Base Case	Alternative	
2008	-	$0	$94,115,754	$0	$0	$0	$0	$94,115,754
2009	-	$0	$90,933,096	$0	$0	$0	$0	$90,933,096
2010	-	$0	$87,858,064	$0	$0	$0	$0	$87,858,064
2011	**1**	**$0**	**$0**	**$391,887**	**$218,226**	**$0**	**$0**	**−$173,662**
2012	2	$0	$0	$378,635	$210,846	$0	$0	−$167,789
2013	3	$0	$0	$384,120	$203,716	$0	$0	−$180,404
2014	4	$0	$0	$353,460	$196,827	$0	$0	−$156,633
2015	5	$0	$0	$341,507	$190,171	$0	$0	−$151,336
2016	6	$0	$0	$329,959	$183,740	$0	$0	−$146,218
2017	7	$0	$0	$470,084	$177,527	$0	$0	−$292,557
2018	8	$0	$0	$448,041	$171,523	$0	$0	−$276,518
2019	9	$0	$0	$297,604	$165,723	$0	$0	−$131,881
2020	10	$7,497,177	$0	$37,080	$160,119	$0	$0	−$7,374,138
2021	11	$7,243,649	$0	$27,075	$154,704	$0	$0	−$7,116,019
2022	12	$0	$0	$268,421	$149,473	$0	$0	−$118,949
2023	13	$0	$0	$259,344	$144,418	$0	$0	−$114,926
2024	14	$0	$0	$250,574	$139,534	$0	$0	−$111,040
2025	15	$0	$0	$242,101	$134,816	$0	$0	−$107,285
2026	16	$0	$0	$503,821	$130,257	$0	$0	−$373,564
2027	17	$0	$0	$226,004	$125,852	$0	$0	−$100,152
2028	18	$0	$0	$218,361	$121,596	$0	$0	−$96,765
2029	19	$0	$0	$364,368	$117,484	$0	$0	−$246,883
2030	**20**	**$0**	**$0**	**$203,842**	**$113,511**	**$9,673,099**	**$91,944,562**	**−$82,361,793**
	2011–2030	$14,740,826	$272,906,915	$5,996,288	$3,210,064	$9,673,099	$91,944,562	**$173,108,403**

- **Total Sponsor's Costs:** In estimating the sponsor's cost (in this case, the state of Minnesota), the following procedures are assumed:

  1. Construction costs for the proposed alternative are estimated and allocated to the anticipated year of expenditure. In this case example, it is assumed that the base case has construction costs in the 10th and 11th years to maintain the existing traffic flows.

  2. Maintenance costs for each year are estimated over the analysis period, as the proposed alternative has a significant effect on maintenance costs (much different from the base case).

  3. Existing infrastructure typically retains some remaining capital value (RCV) at the end of the benefit–cost analysis period. When calculating the remaining capital value, we must estimate the useful life of the investment elements. The capital costs are broken into elements such as preliminary engineering, right of way, major structures, roadway grading and drainage, roadway sub-base and base, and roadway surface. The remaining capital values are estimated at the end of their useful lives. Since all investment elements last more than the analysis period of 20 years, we estimated these values at the end of 20 years, using the guideline suggested by the Mn/DOT.

  4. Table 8.2 shows the total present cost as the sum of the discounted annual costs found for each year in the analysis period. We calculate annual costs by adding the construction and recurring maintenance costs and subtracting the discounted remaining capital value for each year in the analysis.

- **Benefit–Cost Ratio Calculation:** With the benefits and sponsor's costs determined, we are ready to calculate the benefit–cost ratio by using Eq. (8.5). This is summarized in Table 8.3. The B/C ratio is 6.10, indicating that for each dollar of expenditure, it is generating $6.10 of benefits in present worth. This is an exceptionally good highway improvement project in terms of spending taxpayers' money. Of course, there are many uncertain parameters assumed in this analysis, so it is important to conduct a series of sensitivity as well as risk analyses before undertaking a large-scale investment such as this highway project.

TABLE 8.3 **Summary of Benefit–Cost Analysis for the Proposed Highway Improvement Project**

<table>
<tr><td colspan="4" align="center">BENEFIT–COST ANALYSIS
SUMMARY RESULTS</td></tr>
<tr><td>Net Cost of Project (mil. $)</td><td align="right">$173.11</td><td>PRESENT VALUE OF ITEMIZED BENEFITS (mil. $)</td><td></td></tr>
<tr><td>Present Value of Benefits (mil. $)</td><td align="right">$1,055.86</td><td>VMT Savings</td><td align="right">$96.97</td></tr>
<tr><td>Net Present Value (mil. $)</td><td align="right">$882.75</td><td>VHT Savings</td><td align="right">$915.47</td></tr>
<tr><td>Benefit / Cost Ratio</td><td align="right">6.10</td><td>Accident Reduction Benefits</td><td align="right">$43.42</td></tr>
<tr><td></td><td></td><td>PRESENT VALUE OF TOTAL BENEFITS (mil. $)</td><td align="right">$1,055.86</td></tr>
<tr><td></td><td></td><td>PRESENT VALUE OF ITEMIZED COSTS (mil. $)</td><td></td></tr>
<tr><td></td><td></td><td>Capital Cost Differential</td><td align="right">$258.17</td></tr>
<tr><td></td><td></td><td>Maintenance Cost Differential</td><td align="right">−$2.79</td></tr>
<tr><td></td><td></td><td>Remaining Capital Value Differential</td><td align="right">$82.27</td></tr>
<tr><td></td><td></td><td>PRESENT VALUE OF TOTAL COSTS (mil. $)</td><td align="right">$173.11</td></tr>
</table>

SUMMARY

■ **Benefit–cost analysis** is commonly used to evaluate public projects. Several facets unique to public-project analysis are neatly addressed by benefit–cost analysis:

1. Benefits of a nonmonetary nature can be quantified and factored into the analysis.
2. A broad range of project users distinct from the sponsor are considered; benefits and disbenefits to *all* these users can (and should) be taken into account.

■ Difficulties involved in public-project analysis include

1. Identifying all the users of the project.
2. Identifying all the benefits and disbenefits of the project.
3. Quantifying all the benefits and disbenefits in dollars or some other unit of measure.
4. Selecting an appropriate interest rate at which to discount benefits and costs to a present value.

■ The B/C ratio is defined as

$$BC(i) = \frac{B}{C} = \frac{B}{I + C'} \text{ where } I + C' > 0.$$

The decision rule is that, if $BC(i) > 1$, the project is acceptable.

■ The profitability index is defined as

$$PI(i) = \frac{B - C'}{I}, I > 0.$$

The profitability index measures the bang for the buck invested. In a way, it is a measure of capital efficiency.

■ When comparing mutually exclusive projects based on either B/C or PI, we need to use the incremental analysis.

SELF-TEST QUESTIONS

8s.1 A city is trying to decide whether to build a parking garage. An engineering plan calculates that the building will cost $2 million with costs of $200,000 per year to operate. Our analysis of operating revenue determines that the garage will start to earn revenues of $500,000 per year in the second year. The city is interested in knowing whether this project will be profitable over the next eight years at 6%. The project's B/C ratio is closest to

(a) 1

(b) 0.87

(c) 1.33

(d) 2.50

8s.2 A city government is considering increasing the capacity of the current waste-water treatment plant. The estimated financial data for the project are as follows:

Description	Data
Capital investment	$1,200,000
Project life	25 years
Incremental annual benefits	$250,000
Incremental annual costs	$100,000
Salvage value	$50,000
Discount rate	6%

What would be the benefit–cost ratio for this expansion project?
(a) 3.26
(b) 3.12
(c) 1.30
(d) 2.23

8s.3 Auburn Recreation and Parks Department is considering two mutually exclusive proposals for a new softball complex on a city-owned lot.

Alternative Design	Seating Capacity	Annual Benefits	Annual Costs	Required Investment
A1	3,000	$194,000	$87,500	$800,000
A2	4,000	$224,000	$105,000	$1,000,000

The complex will be useful for 30 years and has no appreciable salvage value (regardless of seating capacity). Assuming an 8% discount rate, which of the following statements is *incorrect*?
(a) Select A1 because it has the largest B/C ratio.
(b) Select A1 because it has the most benefits per seating capacity.
(c) Select A1 because it has the largest PW.
(d) Select A1 because the incremental benefits generated from A2 are not large enough to offset the additional investment ($200,000 more than A1).

8s.4 The city of Jefferson is reviewing the benefits and costs of a potential universal water-metering program. Two options are considered:
- **Option 1: Treated Surface Water Only** Benefits of Deferring/Downsizing Water and Sewer Projects—$28.1 million
Costs of Metering—$9.3 million Benefit–Cost Ratio—3.02
- **Option 2: Treated Surface Water Supplemented By 40 ML/Day Groundwater** Benefits of Deferring/Downsizing Water and Sewer Projects—$38.9 million
Costs of Metering (and groundwater development)—$14.7 million
Benefit–Cost Ratio—2.65

Which option should the city implement, assuming that the city has enough money to fund either project?
(a) Option 1.
(b) Option 2.
(c) Neither.
(d) Both options.

8s.5 The Texas Department of Transportation is considering in improving accident prevention countermeasures on the state's accident-prone public highways and bridges. The following set of projects has been recommended for evaluation at three different locations and assumes the budget is $20 million. All alternatives are mutually *independent* projects.

Location	Alternative	Benefit ($B - C'$)	Cost (I)	B/C Ratio
I	I-A	$45	12	3.75
	I-B	30	9	3.33
II	II-A	35	6	5.83
	II-B	20	12	1.67
III	III-A	25	2	12.5
	III-B	30	7	4.29

Determine the best combination of projects within the budget constraint.
(a) II-B and III-B only
(b) I-A, II-A, and III-B
(c) I-B, III-A, and III-B
(d) II-B and III-B

8s.6 The Ulrich Corporation is trying to choose between the following two mutually exclusive design projects. If the required rate of return is 10%, which of the following statements is correct?

Period	Project A1	Project A2
0	−$55,000	−$18,500
1	$38,000	$15,000
2	$38,000	$15,000
PI index	1.19	1.40
ROR	24.56%	39.29%

(a) Select A2 because it has a higher PI.
(b) Select A2 because it has a higher ROR.
(c) Select A1 because its incremental PI exceeds 1.
(d) Not enough information to decide.

8s.7 A regional airport is considering installing a new baggage handling system. Two different vendors submitted bids on the system. The airport is to replace its current system. The cash flows that describe each baggage handling system with respect to the current system are given below.

Years (n)	Vendor A	Vendor B	Vendor B – Vendor A
0	−$500,000	−$600,000	−$100,000
1 – 15	$48,170	$65,880	$17,710
ROR	5%	7%	15.73%
PI (4%)	1.07	1.22	1.97

Which of the following statements is correct?

(a) Vendor B is preferred as long as the airport's interest rate is less than or equal to 15.73%

(b) Vendor B is preferred as long as the airport's interest rate is more than 5%.

(c) Vendor B is preferred as long as the airport's interest rate is less than 7%.

(d) Vendor A is preferred if the airport's interest rate is more than 15.73%.

PROBLEMS

Benefits–Cost Analyses

8.1   A local government is considering promoting tourism in the city. It will cost $8,000 to develop a plan. The anticipated annual benefits and costs are as follows:

Annual benefits: Increased local income and tax collections	$125,000
Annual support service: Parking lot expansion, rest room, patrol car, and street repair	$50,000

If the city government uses a discount rate of 8% and a study period of five years, is this tourism project justifiable according to the benefit–cost analysis?

8.2   A city government is considering increasing the capacity of the current waste water treatment plant. The estimated financial data for the project are as follows:

Description	Data
Capital investment	$1,000,000
Project life	20 years
Incremental annual benefits	$220,000
Incremental annual costs	$80,000
Salvage value	$40,000
Discount rate	5%

Calculate the benefit–cost ratio for this capacity expansion project.

8.3   A city government is considering two types of town-dump sanitary systems. Design A requires an initial outlay of $400,000 with annual operating and maintenance costs of $50,000 for the next 15 years; design B calls for an investment of $300,000 with annual operating and maintenance costs of $80,000 per year for the next 15 years. Fee collections from the residents would be $85,000 per year. The interest rate is 8%, and no salvage value is associated with either system.

(a) By the benefit–cost ratio ($BC(i)$), which system should be selected?

(b) If a new design (design C), which requires an initial outlay of $350,000 and annual operating and maintenance costs of $65,000, is proposed, would your answer to (a) change?

Incremental Benefit–Cost Analysis

8.4   The U.S. government is considering building apartments for its employees working in a foreign country and currently living in locally owned housing.

A comparison of two possible buildings indicates the following:

	Building X	Building Y
Original investment by government agencies	$8,000,000	$12,000,000
Estimated annual maintenance costs	$240,000	$180,000
Savings in annual rent now being paid to house employees	$1,960,000	$1,320,000

Assume the salvage or sale value of the apartments to be 60% of the first investment. Use 10% and a 20-year study period to compute the B/C ratio on incremental investment, and make a recommendation as to the best option. (Do not assume a do-nothing alternative.)

8.5 Two different routes are under consideration for a new interstate highway:

	Length of Highway	First Cost	Annual Upkeep Cost
The "long" route	22 miles	$21 million	$140,000
Transmountain shortcut	10 miles	$45 million	$165,000

For either route, the volume of traffic will be 400,000 cars per year. These cars are assumed to operate at $0.25 per mile. Assuming a 40-year life for each road and an interest rate of 10%, determine which route should be selected.

8.6 Three public investment alternatives are available: $A1$, $A2$, and $A3$. Their respective total benefits, costs, and first costs are given in present worth as follows:

Present Worth	Proposals		
	$A1$	$A2$	$A3$
B	$400	$700	$500
I	$100	$300	$200
C'	$100	$200	$150

These alternatives have the same service life. Assuming that there is no do-nothing alternative, which project would you select, calculating on the basis of the benefit–cost ratio on incremental investment (BC(i))?

8.7 A city that operates automobile parking facilities is evaluating a proposal to erect and operate a structure for parking in its downtown area. Three designs for a facility to be built on available sites have been identified as follows, where all dollar figures are in thousands:

	Design A	Design B	Design C
Cost of site	$240	$180	$200
Cost of building	$2,200	$700	$1,400
Annual fee collection	$830	$750	$600
Annual maintenance cost	$410	$360	$310
Service life	30 years	30 years	30 years

At the end of the estimated service life, the selected facility would be torn down and the land would be sold. It is estimated that the proceeds from the resale of the land will be equal to the cost of clearing the site. If the city's interest rate is known to be 10%, which design alternative would be selected on the basis of the benefit–cost criterion?

8.8 The federal government is planning a hydroelectric project for a river basin. In addition to producing electric power, this project will provide flood control, irrigation, and recreational benefits. The estimated benefits and costs expected to be derived from the three alternatives under consideration are listed as follows:

	Decision Alternatives		
	A	B	C
Initial cost	$8,000,000	$10,000,000	$15,000,000
Annual benefits:			
Power sales	$1,000,000	$1,200,000	$1,800,000
Flood-control savings	$250,000	$350,000	$500,000
Irrigation benefits	$350,000	$450,000	$600,000
Recreation benefits	$100,000	$200,000	$350,000
O&M costs	$200,000	$250,000	$350,000

The interest rate is 10%, and the life of each project is estimated to be 50 years.
(a) Find the benefit–cost ratio for each alternative.
(b) Select the best alternative, according to BC(i).

8.9 A local government is considering four possible countermeasures to reduce crimes in the municipal park. Since each option has a different program length of duration, all benefits and costs are expressed in terms of *equivalent annual values*. Because of a limited budget, only one countermeasure will be implemented. Which countermeasure would you recommend based on the B/C analysis?

Countermeasure	Annual Benefit	Annual Cost	B/C Ratio
Program 1	$14,350	$1,430	10.03
Program 2	$11,350	$1,835	6.19
Program 3	$35,000	$19,500	1.79
Program 4	$42,000	$24,000	1.75

8.10 The government is considering undertaking one of the four projects $A1$, $A2$, $A3$, and $A4$. These projects are mutually exclusive, and the estimated present values of their costs and of their benefits are shown in millions of dollars as follows:

Projects	PW of Benefits	PW of Costs
$A1$	$40	$85
$A2$	$150	$110
$A3$	$70	$25
$A4$	$120	$73

All of the projects have the same duration. Assuming that there is no do-nothing alternative, which alternative would you select? Justify your choice by using a benefit–cost ratio on incremental investment (BC(i)).

Profitability Index

8.11 Consider the following two projects:

	Project A1	Project A2
Investment Required at $n = 0$	$900,000	$1,200,000
1	$400,000	$200,000
2	$340,000	$300,000
3	$300,000	$350,000
4	$240,000	$440,000
5	$200,000	$400,000
6	$150,000	$350,000

(a) Calculate the profitability index for A1 and A2 at an interest rate of 6%.
(b) Determine which project(s) you should accept (1) if you have enough money to undertake both and (2) if you could take only one due to a budget limit.

8.12 Consider the following two mutually exclusive projects:

	Project A1	Project A2
Investment Required at $n = 0$	$750,000	$1,000,000
1	$100,000	$200,000
2	$100,000	$200,000
3	$100,000	$200,000
4	$240,000	$300,000
5	$200,000	$300,000
6	$180,000	$250,000
7	$180,000	$250,000
8	$180,000	$150,000
9	$180,000	$100,000
10	$180,000	$50,000

(a) Which project has the higher profitability index at $i = 7\%$?

(b) Which project would you choose if you can raise an unlimited amount of funds in financing either project at 7%? Use the profitability index rule.

Short Case Studies

8.13 The city of Portland Sanitation Department is responsible for the collection and disposal of all solid waste within the city limits. The city must collect and dispose of an average of 300 tons of garbage each day. The city is considering ways to improve the current solid-waste collection and disposal system:

- The present collection and disposal system uses Dempster Dumpmaster front-end loaders for collection and disposal. Each collecting vehicle has a load capacity of 10 tons, or 24 cubic yards, and dumping is automatic. The incinerator in use was manufactured in 1962. It was designed to incinerate 150 tons every 24 hours. A natural gas afterburner has been added in an effort to reduce air pollution; however, the incinerator still does not meet state air-pollution requirements. Prison-farm labor is used for the operation of the incinerator. Because the capacity of the incinerator is relatively low, some trash is not incinerated but is taken to the city landfill instead. The trash landfill and the incinerator are located approximately 11 miles and 5 miles, respectively, from the center of the city. The mileage and costs in person-hours for delivery to the disposal sites are excessive; a high percentage of empty vehicle miles and person-hours are required because separate methods of disposal are used and the destination sites are remote from the collection areas. The operating cost for the present system is $905,400. This figure includes $624,635 to operate the prison-farm incinerator, $222,928 to operate the existing landfill, and $57,837 to maintain the current incinerator.

- The proposed system calls for a number of portable incinerators, each with 100-ton-per-day capacity for the collection and disposal of refuse waste from three designated areas within the city. Collection vehicles will also be staged at these incineration disposal sites with the necessary plant and support facilities for incinerator operation and collection-vehicle fueling and washing, and with support building for stores as well as shower and locker rooms for collection and site personnel. The pickup and collection procedure remains essentially the same as in the existing system. The disposal-staging sites, however, are located strategically in the city according to the volume and location of wastes collected; thus, long hauls are eliminated and the number of miles the collection vehicles must travel from pickup to disposal site and back is reduced.

Four variations of the proposed system are being considered, containing one, two, three, and four incinerator-staging areas, respectively. The type of incinerator used in each variation is a modular prepackaged unit, which can be installed at several sites in the city. All of the four units meet state and federal standards on exhaust emissions. The city of Portland needs 24 units, each with a rated capacity of 8.5 tons of garbage per 24 hours. The price per unit is $137,600, which means a capital investment of about $3,302,000. The estimated plant facilities, such as housing and foundation, are estimated to cost $200,000 per facility. This figure is based on a plan incorporating four incinerator plants strategically located around the city. Each plant would house eight units and would be capable of handling 100 tons of garbage per day. Additional plant features, such as landscaping, are estimated to cost $60,000 per plant.

The annual operating cost of the proposed system would vary according to the type of system configuration. It takes about 1.5 to 1.7 MCF of fuel to incinerate 1 ton of garbage. The conservative 1.7 MCF figure was used for total cost, resulting in a fuel cost of $4.25 per ton of garbage at a cost of $2.50 per MCF. Electric requirements at each plant will be 230 kW per day. For a plant operating at full capacity, that requirement means a $0.48-per-ton cost for electricity. Two workers can easily operate one plant, but safety factors dictate that there will be three operators at a cost of $7.14 per hour per operator. This translates to a cost of $1.72 per ton. The maintenance cost of each plant is estimated to be $1.19 per ton. Since the proposal for three plants will require fewer transportation miles, it is necessary to consider the savings accruing from this operating advantage. For example, the configuration with three plant locations will save 6.14 miles per truck per day on average. At an estimated $0.30-per-mile cost, this would mean that an annual savings of $15,300 would be realized from minimum trips to the landfill. Labor savings are also realized because the shorter routes would permit more pickups per day. This plan thus offers an annual labor savings of $103,500 for three incinerators. The following table summarizes all costs, in thousands of dollars, associated with the present and proposed systems.

Costs for Proposed Systems (Unit-thousand)

Item	Present System	Number of Incinerator Sites			
		1	**2**	**3**	**4**
Capital costs					
Incinerators		$3,302	$3,302	$3,302	$3,302
Plant facilities		$600	$900	$1,260	$1,920
Annex buildings		$91	$102	$112	$132
Additional features		$60	$80	$90	$100
Total		$4,053	$4,384	$4,764	$5,454
Annual O&M costs	$905.4	$342	$480	$414	$408
Annual savings					
Pickup transportation		$13.2	$14.7	$15.3	$17.1
Labor		**$87.6**	$99.3	$103.5	$119.40

A bond will be issued to provide the necessary capital investment at an interest rate of 8% with a maturity date 20 years.

The proposed systems are expected to last 20 years with negligible salvage values. If the current system is to be retained, the annual O&M costs would be expected to increase at an annual rate of 10%. The city will use the bond interest rate as the interest rate for any public-project evaluation.

(a) Determine the operating cost of the current system in terms of dollars per ton of solid waste.

(b) Determine the economics of each solid-waste disposal alternative in terms of dollars per ton of solid waste.

(c) Select the best alternative based on the benefit–cost ratio.

8.14 Atlanta Regional Commission is considering expanding Hartsfield (Atlanta) International Airport. Three options have been proposed to handle the growth expected at Hartsfield:

- Option 1: Build five new runways, a new concourse adjacent to a new east-side terminal, and close-in parking. Cost estimate: $1.5 billion.

- Option 2: Construct a more expensive version of Option 1, putting the new concourse adjacent to the fifth runway. Cost estimate: $1.6 billion.

- Option 3: In addition to the five new runways in Options 1 and 2, build a sixth runway north of the current airport boundaries in the College Park–East Point–Hapeville corridor side terminal. Cost estimate: $5.9 billion.

A study indicates that a north runway (e.g., the sixth runway in Option 3) would displace more than 3,000 households and 978 businesses. A south runway (Option 2) could dislocate as many as 7,000 households and more than 900 businesses. Under any scenario of airport expansion, there still will be some flight delays. However, some plans project longer delays than others. Figure 8.8 illustrates the three options under consideration, and the accompanying table summarizes some projections for the year 2015 under the no-build scenario.

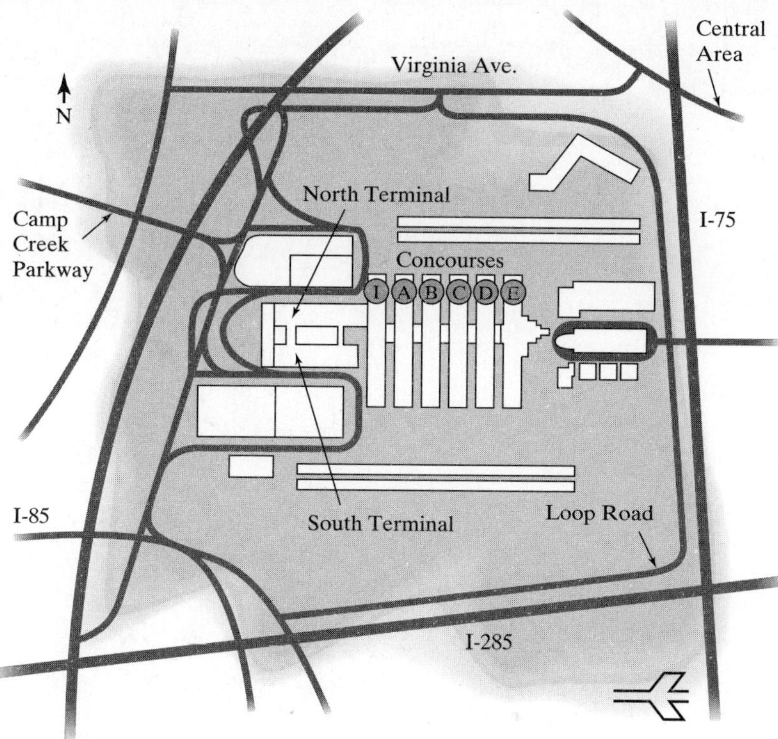

Figure 8.8 Proposed future expansion plan for Atlanta Hartsfield Airport

	Dealing with the Delays (Units in Minutes)			
	No Change	Option 1	Option 2	Option 3
Average departure delay	34.80	17.02	19.66	5.71
Average arrival delay	19.97	7.08	6.68	3.91
Average taxiing time	26.04	18.54	19.99	12.80

The committee has six months to study each option before making a final recommendation. What would you recommend?

Development of Project Cash Flows

Accounting for Depreciation and Income Taxes

Enjoy a Lump Sum Tax-Benefit Now or Take Deferred Benefits Over the Life of Equipment? In September 2010, in an effort to further speed along the ailing U.S. economy's recovery, President Obama proposed a new bill intended to save businesses money. Categorized by the administration as "the largest temporary investment incentive in American history," it would allow businesses to deduct any new equipment purchases from their incomes in 2011; the intent being to incentivize spending, increase the demands for goods, and create jobs.

While the government would be shelling out $200 billion to businesses owners, the Treasury would recoup this relief; estimates are that the overall price tag will drop to $30 billion over the next ten years. As businesses would eventually take deductions for the depreciated value, the plan is very simple: businesses spend their tax savings on equipment purchases now (which is equivalent to buying equipment at a discount), but give up their future annual depreciation allowances when the economy gets better.

So if a company decides to take advantage of this one-time offer and purchases state-of-the-art equipment at a discount, how does the loss of future deductions of the depreciated value affect the bottom line of the business? What will happen in a few years when more efficient machinery becomes available? Or the machinery starts to break down? Is it worth waiting?

Consider a manufacturer who purchased an industrial robot to be used in its spot-welding operation. It cost $220,000 and would qualify for the benefits of writing off the entire cost during the first year of

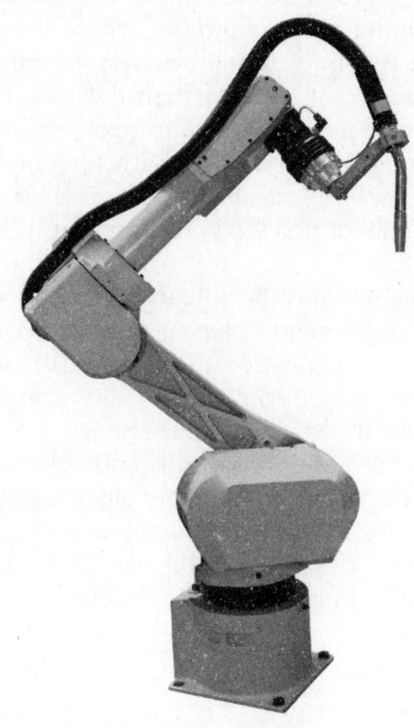

purchase. Now ask yourself: How does the cost of this system affect the financial position of the firm? In the long run, the system promises to create more wealth for the organization by increasing product quality and cutting down inspection time. In the short run, however, the high cost of the system will negatively impact the organization's bottom line because it involves high initial costs that are only gradually rewarded by the benefits of the system.

Another consideration should come to mind. This state-of-the-art equipment will inevitably wear out over time. Even if its productive service extends over many years, the cost of maintaining its high level of functioning will increase as the individual hardware pieces wear out and need to be replaced. Of even greater concern is the question of how long the system will be state-of-the-art. When will the competitive advantage the firm has just acquired become a competitive disadvantage due to obsolescence?

One of the facts of life that organizations must contend with is that fixed assets lose their value—even as they continue to function and contribute to the engineering projects that employ them. This loss of value, called **depreciation,** can involve deterioration and obsolescence. Why do engineers need to understand the concept of asset depreciation? All cash flows described in Chapters 5 through 7 are cash flows after taxes. In order to determine the effects of income taxes on project cash flows, we need to understand how a company calculates the profit (or net income) gained from undertaking a project, where depreciation expenses play a very critical role. The main function of **depreciation accounting** is to account for the cost of fixed assets in a pattern that matches their decline in value over time. The cost of the industrial robot we have just described, for example, will be allocated over several years in the firm's financial statements so that its pattern of costs roughly matches its pattern of service. In this way, as we shall see, depreciation accounting enables the firm to stabilize the statements of financial position that it distributes to stockholders and the outside world.

On a project level, engineers must be able to assess how the reality of depreciating fixed assets influences the investment value of a given project. To make this assessment, they need to estimate the allocation of capital costs over the life of the project; this requires an understanding of the conventions and techniques that accountants use to depreciate assets, which we'll review in this chapter.

We begin by discussing the nature of acquiring fixed assets, the significance of depreciation, and income taxes. We then focus our attention almost exclusively on the rules and laws that govern asset depreciation and the methods that accountants use to allocate depreciation expenses. Knowledge of these rules will prepare you to assess the depreciation of assets acquired in engineering projects.

9.1 Accounting Depreciation

The acquisition of fixed assets is an important activity for a business organization. This condition is true whether the organization is starting up or is acquiring new assets to remain competitive. In engineering economics, the term **cost** is used in many ways. Like other disbursements, the costs of fixed assets must be recorded as expenses on a firm's balance sheet and income statement. However, unlike costs such as maintenance, material, and labor, fixed assets are not treated simply as expenses to be accounted for during the year that they are acquired. Rather, these assets are **capitalized**; that is, their costs are distributed by subtracting them as expenses from gross income—one part at a time over a number of periods. The systematic allocation of the initial cost of an asset in parts over a time, known as its depreciable life, is what we mean by **accounting depreciation,** sometimes referred to more generally as **asset depreciation.**

The process of depreciating an asset requires that we make several preliminary determinations: (1) What is the cost of the asset? (2) What is the depreciable life of the asset? (3) What is the asset's value at the end of its useful life? (4) What method of depreciation do we choose? In this section, we will discuss each of these four factors.

9.1.1 Depreciable Property

As a starting point, it is important to recognize what constitutes a **depreciable asset**—that is, a property for which a firm may take depreciation deductions against income. For the purposes of U.S. tax law, any depreciable property must

1. be used in business or held for the production of income;
2. have a definite service life, which must be longer than one year; and
3. be something that wears out, decays, gets used up, becomes obsolete, or loses value from natural causes.

Depreciable property includes buildings, machinery, equipment, vehicles, and some intangible properties.[2] Inventories are not depreciable property, because they are held primarily for sale to customers in the ordinary course of business. If an asset has no definite service life, the asset cannot be depreciated. For example, you can never depreciate land. However, any land improvements such as driveways, parking lots, fences, landscaping, and lighting have limited useful lives, so they are subject to capitalization (depreciation).

As a side note, we should add that, while we have been focusing on depreciation within firms, individuals may also depreciate assets as long as the assets meet the conditions listed previously. For example, an individual may depreciate an automobile if the vehicle is used exclusively for business purposes.

9.1.2 Cost Basis

The **cost basis** of an asset represents the total cost that is claimed as an expense over an asset's life — the sum of the annual depreciation expenses. Cost basis generally includes the actual cost of an asset and all incidental expenses, such as freight, site preparation, and installation.[3] Total cost, rather than the cost of the asset only, must be the basis for depreciation charged as an expense over an asset's life. Besides being used in figuring depreciation deductions, an asset's cost basis is used in calculating the gain or loss to the firm if the asset is ever sold or salvaged.

EXAMPLE 9.1 Determining the Cost Basis

Raymond Stamping Services purchased a stamping machine priced at $21,500. The firm had to pay a sales tax of $1,200 on this purchase. Raymond also paid the inbound transportation charges of $525 on the new machine, as well as a labor cost of $1,350 to install the machine in the factory. In addition, Raymond had to prepare the site before installation at a cost of $2,125. Determine the cost basis for the new machine for depreciation purposes.

DISSECTING THE PROBLEM

Given: Invoice price = $22,700, freight = $525, installation cost = $1,350, and site preparation = $2,125.

Find: The cost basis.

---

[2] Intangible property is property that has value but cannot be seen or touched. Some intangible properties are (1) copyrights and patents, (2) customer and subscription lists, (3) designs and patterns, and (4) franchises. Generally, you can either amortize or depreciate intangible property.

[3] If you purchase an asset by trading in an old but similar asset, the cost basis for the new asset will be adjusted by the amount of gain or loss, or simply by its net book value. Example 9.6 will illustrate the process of calculating the cost basis with trade-in allowances.

METHODOLOGY	**SOLUTION**
Compute the cost basis.	The cost of the machine that is applicable for depreciation is computed as follows:

Cost of a new stamping machine	$22,700
Freight	$525
Installation labor	$1,350
Site preparation	$2,125
Cost of machine (cost basis)	$26,700

COMMENTS: Why do we include all the incidental charges relating to the acquisition of a machine in its cost? Why not treat these incidental charges as expenses of the period in which the machine is acquired? The matching of costs and revenue is a basic accounting principle. Consequently, the total costs of the machine should be viewed as an asset and allocated against the future revenue that the machine will generate. All costs incurred in acquiring the machine are costs of the services to be received from using the machine.

9.1.3 Useful Life and Salvage Value

How long will an asset be useful to the company? What do statutes and accounting rules mandate about assessing an asset's span of economic value? These questions must be answered when we are determining an asset's depreciable life, that is, the number of years over which the asset is to be depreciated.

Historically, depreciation accounting included choosing a depreciable life that based on the service life of an asset. Determining the service life of an asset, however, was often very difficult, and the uncertainty of these estimates frequently led to disputes between taxpayers and the Internal Revenue Service (IRS). To alleviate the problems, the IRS now publishes guidelines on lives for categories of assets, known as **asset depreciation ranges,** or **ADRs.** These guidelines specify a range of lives for classes of assets, based on historical data, allowing taxpayers to choose a depreciable life within the specified range for a given asset. An example of ADRs for some assets is given in Table 9.1.

An asset's estimated value at the end of its life is its **salvage value**; it is the amount eventually recovered through sale, trade-in, or salvage. The eventual salvage value of an asset must be estimated when the depreciation schedule for the asset is established. If this estimate subsequently proves to be inaccurate, then an adjustment must be made.

9.1.4 Depreciation Methods: Book and Tax Depreciation

One important distinction regarding the general definition of accounting depreciation must be introduced. Most firms calculate depreciation in two different ways, depending on whether the calculation is (1) intended for financial reports (**book depreciation method**), such as for the balance sheet or income statement, or (2) intended for the Internal Revenue Service (IRS) for the purpose of calculating taxes (**tax depreciation**

TABLE 9.1 Asset Depreciation Ranges (ADRs)

	Asset Depreciation Range (years)		
Assets Used	**Lower Limit**	**Midpoint Life**	**Upper Limit**
Office furniture, fixtures, and equipment	8	10	12
Information systems (computers)	5	6	7
Airplanes	5	6	7
Automobiles and taxis	2.5	3	3.5
Buses	7	9	11
Light trucks	3	4	5
Heavy trucks (concrete ready mixer)	5	6	7
Railroad cars and locomotives	12	15	18
Tractor units	5	6	7
Vessels, barges, tugs, and water transportation systems	14.5	18	21.5
Industrial steam and electrical generation or distribution systems	17.5	22	26.5
Manufacturer of electrical machinery	8	10	12
Manufacturer of electronic components, products, and systems	5	6	7
Manufacturer of motor vehicles	9.5	12	14.5
Telephone distribution plant	28	35	42

method). (See Figure 9.1.) In the United States, this distinction is totally legitimate under IRS regulations, as it is in many other countries. Calculating depreciation differently for financial reports and for tax purposes allows for the following benefits:

- The book depreciation enables firms to report depreciation to stockholders and other significant outsiders on the basis of the matching concept. Therefore, the actual loss in value of the assets is generally reflected.
- The tax depreciation method allows firms to benefit from the tax advantages of depreciating assets more quickly than would be possible under the matching concept. In many cases, tax depreciation allows firms to defer paying income taxes. *This deferral does not mean that they pay less tax overall because the total depreciation expense accounted for over time is the same in either case.* However, because tax depreciation methods generally permit a higher depreciation in earlier years than do book depreciation methods, the tax benefit of depreciation is enjoyed earlier, and firms usually pay lower taxes in the initial years of an investment project. Typically, this factor leads to a better cash flow position in early years with the added cash leading to increased future wealth because of the time value of the funds.

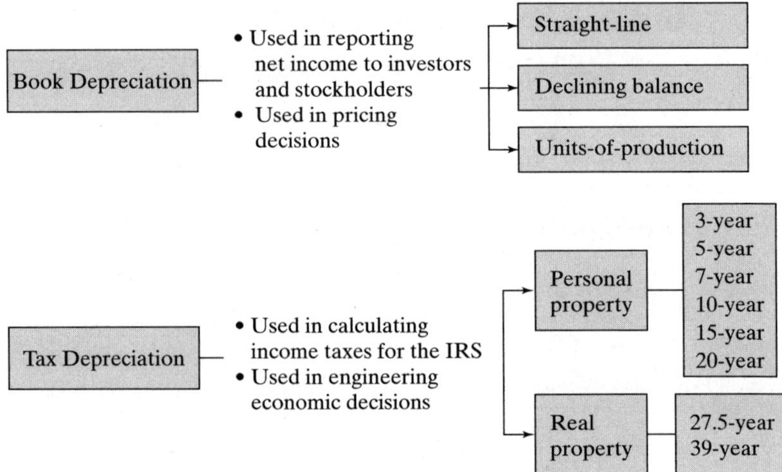

Figure 9.1 Types of accounting depreciation and their primary purposes

9.2 Book Depreciation Methods

Consider a machine purchased for $10,000 with an estimated life of five years and estimated salvage value of $2,000. The objective of depreciation accounting is to charge this net cost of $8,000 as an expense over the five-year period. How much should be charged as an expense each year? Three different methods can be used to calculate the periodic depreciation allowances for financial reporting: (1) the straight-line (SL) method, (2) the declining-balance (DB) method, and (3) the unit-of-production method. In engineering economic analysis, we are interested primarily in depreciation in the context of income-tax computation. Nonetheless, a number of reasons make the study of book depreciation methods useful:

- First, many product pricing decisions are based on book depreciation methods.
- Second, tax depreciation methods are based largely on the same principles that are used in book depreciation methods.
- Third, firms continue to use book depreciation methods for financial reporting to stockholders and outside parties.
- Finally, book depreciation methods are still used for state income-tax purposes in many states and foreign countries.

9.2.1 Straight-Line Method

The **straight-line (SL) method** of depreciation interprets a fixed asset as an asset that provides its services in a uniform fashion. That is, the asset provides an equal amount of service in each year of its useful life. In other words, the depreciation rate is $1/N$, where N is the depreciable life. Example 9.2 illustrates the straight-line depreciation concept.

EXAMPLE 9.2 Straight-Line Depreciation

Consider the following data on an automobile:

$$\text{Cost basis of the asset } (I) = \$10,000;$$
$$\text{Useful life } (N) = 5 \text{ years};$$
$$\text{Estimated salvage value } (S) = \$2,000.$$

Compute the annual depreciation allowances and the resulting book values using the straight-line depreciation method.

DISSECTING THE PROBLEM	
	Given: $I = \$10,000$, $S = \$2,000$, and $N = 5\,$years. **Find:** D_n and B_n for $n = 1$ to 5.

METHODOLOGY	SOLUTION
Create a straight-line depreciation table.	The straight-line depreciation rate is $\frac{1}{5}$ or 20%. Therefore, the annual depreciation charge is $$D_n = (0.20)(\$10,000 - \$2,000) = \$1,600.$$ Then the asset would have the following book values during its useful life, where B_n represents the book value after the depreciation charge for year n: $$B_n = I - (D_1 + D_2 + D_3 + \cdots + D_n).$$ Therefore, the depreciation schedule based on the straight-line method is as follows:

n	D_n	B_n
0		$10,000
1	$1,600	$8,400
2	$1,600	$6,800
3	$1,600	$5,200
4	$1,600	$3,600
5	$1,600	$2,000

COMMENTS: We can easily generate a depreciation schedule just like what we have shown by using a built-in financial command, **=SLN (cost, salvage, life)** in Excel. One way to automate the process of generating a depreciation schedule is to develop an Excel worksheet as the one shown in Table 9.2. First, we determine the type of depreciation method, such as, in this example, the straight-line method. Then we enter the cost basis in cell D2, the depreciable life in cell D3, and the salvage value in cell D4. Then, we can generate the depreciation schedule in cells C9–C13, and also plot the annual depreciation, as well as book value, as a function of age.

TABLE 9.2 An Excel Worksheet to Calculate the Depreciation Amounts by the Straight-Line Method

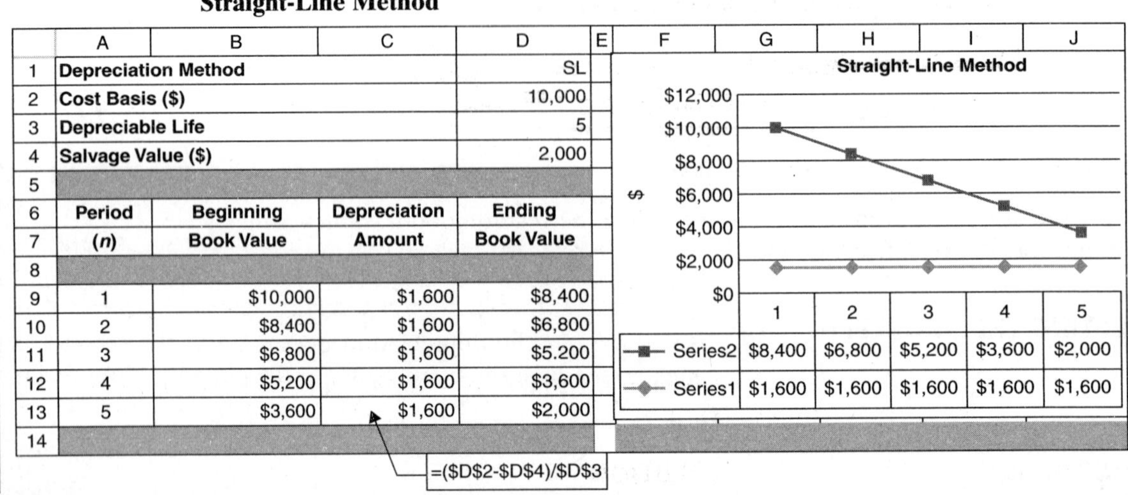

	A	B	C	D	E
1	Depreciation Method			SL	
2	Cost Basis ($)			10,000	
3	Depreciable Life			5	
4	Salvage Value ($)			2,000	
5					
6	Period	Beginning	Depreciation	Ending	
7	(n)	Book Value	Amount	Book Value	
8					
9	1	$10,000	$1,600	$8,400	
10	2	$8,400	$1,600	$6,800	
11	3	$6,800	$1,600	$5.200	
12	4	$5,200	$1,600	$3,600	
13	5	$3,600	$1,600	$2,000	
14					

=($D$2-$D$4)/$D$3

9.2.2 Declining-Balance Method

The second concept recognizes that the stream of services provided by a fixed asset may decrease over time; in other words, the stream may be greatest in the first year of an asset's service life and least in its last year. This pattern may occur because the mechanical efficiency of an asset tends to decline with age, because maintenance costs tend to increase with age, or because of the increasing likelihood that better equipment will become available and make the original asset obsolete. This reasoning leads to a method that charges a larger fraction of the cost as an expense of the early years than of the later years. This method, the **declining-balance method,** is the most widely used.

Depreciation Rate

The declining-balance method of calculating depreciation allocates a fixed fraction of the beginning book balance each year. The fraction α is obtained from the straight-line depreciation rate $(1/N)$ as a basis:

$$\alpha = (1/N)(\text{multiplier}). \tag{9.1}$$

The most commonly used multipliers in the United States are 1.5 (called 150% DB) and 2.0 (called 200% DDB, or double-declining-balance). So, a 200%-DB method specifies that the depreciation rate will be 200% of the straight-line rate. As N increases, α decreases, thereby resulting in a situation in which depreciation is highest in the first year and then decreases over the asset's depreciable life.

EXAMPLE 9.3 Declining-Balance Depreciation

Consider the following accounting information for a computer system:

Cost basis of the asset $(I) = \$10,000$;

Useful life $(N) = 5$ years;

Estimated salvage value $(S) = \$2,000$.

Compute the annual depreciation allowances and the resulting book values using the double-declining-balance depreciation method.

DISSECTING THE PROBLEM

Given: $I = \$10,000$, $S = \$2,000$, and $N = 5\,\text{years}$.

Find: D_n and B_n for $n = 1$ to 5.

METHODOLOGY

Create a double-declining-balance depreciation schedule in Excel.

SOLUTION

The book value at the beginning of the first year is \$10,000, and the declining-balance rate α is $\frac{1}{5}(2) = 40\%$. Then the depreciation deduction for the first year will be \$4,000 ($40\% \times \$10,000 = \$4,000$). To figure out the depreciation deduction in the second year, we must first adjust the book value for the amount of depreciation we deducted in the first year. The first year's depreciation is subtracted from the beginning book value ($\$10,000 - \$4,000 = \$6,000$). This amount is then multiplied by the rate of depreciation ($\$6,000 \times 40\% = \$2,400$). By continuing the process, we obtain D_3. However, in year 4, B_4 would be less than $S = \$2,000$ if the full deduction (\$864) were taken. *Tax law does not permit us to depreciate assets below their salvage value.* Therefore, we adjust D_4 to \$160, making $B_4 = \$2,000$. D_5 is zero, and B_5 remains at \$2,000. The following table provides a summary of these calculations:

End of Year	D_n	B_n
1	$0.4(\$10,000) = \$4,000$	$\$10,000 - \$4,000 = \$6,000$
2	$0.4(\$6,000) = \$2,400$	$\$6,000 - \$2,400 = \$3,600$
3	$0.4(\$3,600) = \$1,440$	$\$3,600 - \$1,440 = \$2,160$
4	$0.4(\$2,160) = \$864 \rightarrow \boxed{\$160}$	$\$2,160 - \$160 = \$2,000$
5	0	$\$2,000 - \$0 = \$2,000$
	Total $= \$8,000$	

TABLE 9.3 **An Excel Worksheet to Calculate the Depreciation Amounts by the Declining-Balance Method (Example 9.3)**

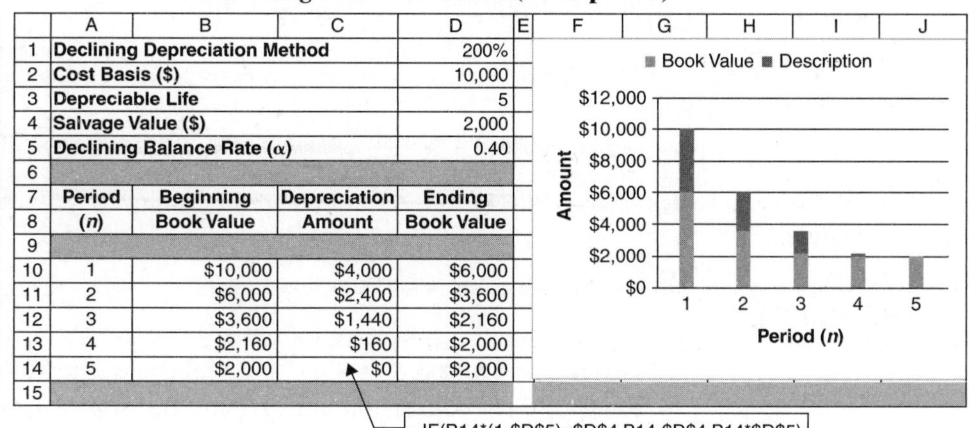

	A	B	C	D	E F	G	H	I	J
1	Declining Depreciation Method			200%					
2	Cost Basis ($)			10,000					
3	Depreciable Life			5					
4	Salvage Value ($)			2,000					
5	Declining Balance Rate (α)			0.40					
6									
7	Period	Beginning	Depreciation	Ending					
8	(*n*)	Book Value	Amount	Book Value					
9									
10	1	$10,000	$4,000	$6,000					
11	2	$6,000	$2,400	$3,600					
12	3	$3,600	$1,440	$2,160					
13	4	$2,160	$160	$2,000					
14	5	$2,000	$0	$2,000					
15									

=IF(B14*(1-$D$5)<$D$4,B14-$D$4,B14*$D$5)

Table 9.3 also illustrates the process of generating a depreciation schedule in Excel. This is basically the same worksheet, where we need to change only the depreciation method from the straight line to the declining balance using a 200% depreciation rate.

Switching Policy

When $B_N > S$, we are faced with a situation in which we have not depreciated the entire cost of the asset and thus have not taken full advantage of depreciation's tax-deferring benefits. If we would prefer to reduce the book value of an asset to its salvage value as quickly as possible, we can do so by switching from DB depreciation to SL depreciation whenever SL depreciation results in higher depreciation charges and, therefore, a more rapid reduction in the book value of the asset. The switch from DB to SL depreciation can take place in any of the n years, the objective being to identify the optimal year to switch. The switching rule is as follows: If DB depreciation in any year is less than (or equal to) the depreciation amount calculated by SL depreciation on the basis of the remaining years, switch to and remain with the SL method for the duration of the asset's depreciable life. The straight-line depreciation in any year n is calculated as:

$$D_n = \frac{\text{Book value at beginning of year } n - \text{Salvage value}}{\text{Remaining useful life at beginning of year } n}. \tag{9.2}$$

EXAMPLE 9.4 Declining Balance with Conversion to Straight-Line Depreciation ($B_N > S$)

Suppose the asset given in Example 9.3 has a zero salvage value instead of $2,000:

Cost basis of the asset $(I) = \$10,000$;

Useful life $(N) = 5$ years;

Salvage value $(S) = \$0$;

$$\alpha = (1/5)(2) = 40\%.$$

Determine the optimal time to switch from DB to SL depreciation and the resulting depreciation schedule.

DISSECTING THE PROBLEM

Given: $I = \$10,000, S = \$0, N = 5$ years, and $\alpha = 40\%$.

Find: Optimal conversion time; D_n and B_n for $n = 1$ to 5.

METHODOLOGY	SOLUTION
Create a table of depreciation amounts in Excel.	We will first proceed by computing the DDB depreciation for each year, as before. The result is shown in Table 9.4(a). Then we compute the SL depreciation for each year using Eq. (9.2). We compare the SL depreciation with the DDB depreciation for each year and use the decision rule to decide when to change. The result is shown in Table 9.4(b). The switching should take place in the fourth year.

COMMENTS: As we have seen in Table 9.4, the process of finding when to switch from DB to SL can be tedious if done manually. This is where we may use Excel to facilitate the calculation process. Table 9.5 demonstrates how we may design an Excel worksheet to accomplish this. Another benefit of Excel is its capability to plot the depreciation and book value as a function of asset age, just as we have seen in Table 9.3.

TABLE 9.4 **Switching Policy from DDB to SL Depreciation with $S = 0$**

	(a) Without switching			(b) With switching to SL depreciation	
n	Depreciation	Book Value	n	Depreciation	Book Value
1	$10,000(0.4) = $4,000	$6,000	1	$4,000	$6,000
2	$6,000(0.4) = $2,400	$3,600	2	$6,000/4 = $1,500 < $2,400	$3,600
3	$3,600(0.4) = $1,440	$2,160	3	$3,600/3 = $1,200 < $1,440	$2,160
4	$2,160(0.4) = $864	$1,296	4	$2,160/2 = $1,080 > $864	$1,080
5	$1,296(0.4) = $518	$778	5	$1,080/1 = $1,080 > $518	$0

Note: Without the switching policy, we do not depreciate the entire cost of the asset and thus do not take full advantage of depreciation's tax-deferring benefits.

TABLE 9.5 **An Excel Worksheet to Calculate the Depreciation Amounts with DB Switching to SL**

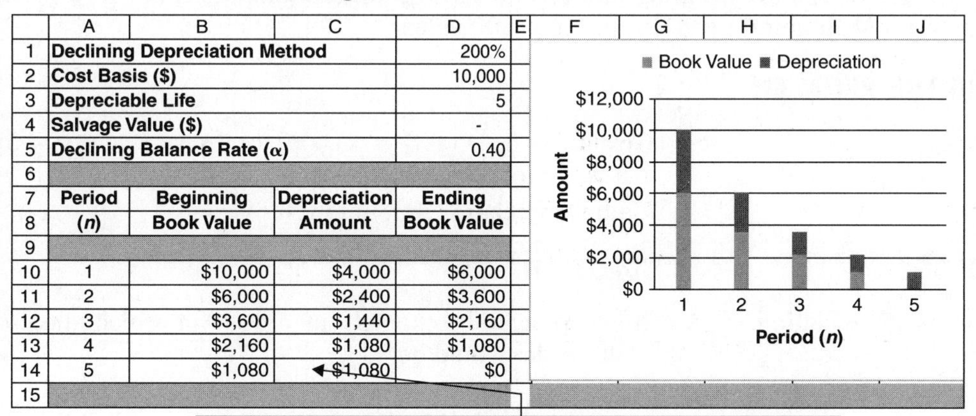

	A	B	C	D
1	Declining Depreciation Method			200%
2	Cost Basis ($)			10,000
3	Depreciable Life			5
4	Salvage Value ($)			-
5	Declining Balance Rate (α)			0.40
6				
7	Period	Beginning	Depreciation	Ending
8	(n)	Book Value	Amount	Book Value
9				
10	1	$10,000	$4,000	$6,000
11	2	$6,000	$2,400	$3,600
12	3	$3,600	$1,440	$2,160
13	4	$2,160	$1,080	$1,080
14	5	$1,080	◄ $1,080	$0
15				

```
=IF(B14*$D$5<(B14-$D$4)/($D$3-A13),(B14-$D$4)/($D$3-A13),B14*$D$5)
```

9.2.3 Units-of-Production Method

Straight-line depreciation can be defended only if the fixed asset—say, a machine—is used for exactly the same amount of time each year. What happens when a punch-press machine is run 1,670 hours one year and 780 the next, or when some of its output is shifted to a new machining center? This situation leads us to consider another depreciation concept that views the asset as a bundle of service units rather than as a single unit as in the SL and DB methods. However, this concept does not assume that the service units will be consumed in a time-phased pattern. The cost of each service unit is the net cost of the asset divided by the total number of such units. The depreciation charge for a period is then related to the number of service units consumed in that period. This definition leads to the **units-of-production method**. By this method, the depreciation in any year is given by

$$D_n = \frac{\text{Service units consumed during year } n}{\text{Total service units}}(I - S). \qquad (9.3)$$

With the units-of-production method, depreciation charges are made proportional to the ratio of actual output to the total expected output; usually, this ratio is figured in machine-hours. Advantages of using this method include the fact that depreciation varies with production volume, and therefore the method gives a more accurate picture of machine usage. A disadvantage of the units-of-production method is that the collection of data on machine use and the accounting methods are somewhat tedious. This method can be useful for depreciating equipment employed to exploit natural resources if the resources will be depleted before the equipment wears out. It is not, however, considered a practical method for general use in depreciating industrial equipment.

EXAMPLE 9.5 Units-of-Production Depreciation

A truck for hauling coal has an estimated net cost of $55,000 and is expected to give service for 250,000 miles, resulting in a $5,000 salvage value. Compute the allowed depreciation amount for truck usage of 30,000 miles.

DISSECTING THE PROBLEM	
	Given: $I = \$55,000, S = \$5,000$, total service units $= 250,000$ miles, and usage for this year $= 30,000$ miles.
	Find: Depreciation amount in this year.

METHODOLOGY	SOLUTION
Compute annual depreciation.	The depreciation expense in a year in which the truck traveled 30,000 miles would be

$$\frac{30{,}000 \text{ miles}}{250{,}000 \text{ miles}}(\$55{,}000 - \$5{,}000) = \left(\frac{3}{25}\right)(\$50{,}000) = \$6{,}000.$$

9.3 Tax Depreciation Methods

Prior to the Economic Recovery Act of 1981, taxpayers could choose among several methods when depreciating assets for tax purposes. The most widely used methods were the straight-line method and the declining-balance method. The subsequent imposition of the **accelerated cost recovery system** (ACRS) and the **modified accelerated cost recovery system** (MACRS) superseded these methods for use in tax purposes. Currently, the MACRS is the method used to determine the allowed depreciation amount in the calculation of income taxes. The foregoing history is summarized in Table 9.6.

9.3.1 MACRS Recovery Periods

Historically, for tax purposes as well as for accounting, an asset's depreciable life was determined by its estimated useful life; it was intended that an asset would be fully depreciated at approximately the end of its useful life. With the MACRS scheme, however, accountants totally abandoned this practice, and simpler guidelines were set that created several classes of assets, each with a more or less arbitrary lifespan called a **recovery period**. (*Note*: These recovery periods do not necessarily correspond to expected useful lives.)

As shown in Table 9.7, the MACRS scheme includes eight categories of assets: 3, 5, 7, 10, 15, 20, 27.5, and 39 years. Under MACRS, *the salvage value of property is always treated as zero*. MACRS guidelines are summarized as follows:

- Investments in some short-lived assets are depreciated over three years by 200% DB and then by a switch to SL depreciation.
- Computers, automobiles, and light trucks are written off over five years by 200% DB and then by switching to SL depreciation.
- Most types of manufacturing equipment are depreciated over seven years, but some long-lived assets are written off over 10 years. Most equipment write-offs are calculated by the 200% DB method and then by switching to SL depreciation, an approach that allows for faster write-offs in the first few years after an investment is made.
- Electric transmission property, any natural gas distribution line, sewage-treatment plants, and telephone-distribution plants are written off over 15 years by 150% DB and then by switching to SL depreciation.

TABLE 9.6 **History of Tax Depreciation Methods**

Tax Depreciation
• **Purpose:** To compute income taxes for the IRS.
• Assets placed in service prior to 1981:
Used book depreciation methods (SL, DB, or SOYD*).
• Assets placed in service from 1981 to 1986:
Used ACRS Table.
• Assets placed in service after 1986:
Use MACRS Table.

* SOYD: Sum-of-Years' Digit Method, no longer used as a book depreciation method.

TABLE 9.7 MACRS Property Classifications (ADR = Asset Depreciation Range)

Recovery Period	ADR Midpoint Class	Applicable Property
3 years	ADR ≤ 4	Special tools for manufacture of plastic products, fabricated metal products, and motor vehicles
5 years	4 < ADR ≤ 10	Automobiles, light trucks, high-tech equipment, equipment used for R&D, and computerized telephone-switching systems
7 years	10 < ADR ≤ 16	Manufacturing equipment, office furniture, and fixtures
10 years	16 < ADR ≤ 20	Vessels, barges, tugs, and railroad cars
15 years	20 < ADR ≤ 25	Wastewater plants, telephone-distribution plants, or similar utility property
20 years	25 ≤ ADR	Municipal sewers and electrical power plants
27.5 years		Residential rental property
39 years		Nonresidential real property, including elevators and escalators

- Farm buildings, municipal sewers, sewer pipes, and certain other very long-lived equipment are written off over 20 years by 150% DB and then by switching to SL depreciation.
- Investments in residential rental property are written off in straight-line fashion over 27.5 years. On the other hand, nonresidential real estate (commercial buildings) is written off by the SL method over 39 years.

9.3.2 MACRS Depreciation: Personal Property

Prior to 1986, the rate at which the value of an asset actually declined was estimated, and this rate was used for tax depreciation. Thus, different assets were depreciated along different paths over time. The MACRS method, however, establishes prescribed depreciation rates, called **recovery allowance percentages**, for all assets within each class. These rates, as set forth in 1986 and 1993, are shown in Table 9.8.

We determine the yearly recovery, or depreciation expense, by multiplying the asset's depreciation base by the applicable recovery-allowance percentage:

- **Half-Year convention:** The MACRS recovery percentages shown in Table 9.8 use the **half-year convention**; that is, it is assumed that all assets are placed in service at midyear and that they will have *zero* salvage value. As a result, only a half-year of depreciation is allowed for the first year that property is placed in service. With half of one year's depreciation being taken in the first year, a full year's depreciation is allowed in each of the remaining years of the asset's recovery period, and the remaining half-year's depreciation is incurred in the year following the end of the recovery period. A half-year of depreciation is also allowed for the year in which the property is disposed of, or is otherwise retired from service, any time before the end of the recovery period.
- **Switching from the DB method to the SL method:** The MACRS asset is depreciated initially by the DB method and then by the SL method. Consequently, the MACRS scheme adopts the switching convention illustrated in Section 9.2.2.

TABLE 9.8 MACRS Depreciation Schedules for Personal Property with Half-Year Convention

Year	Class Depreciation Rate	3 200% DB	5 200% DB	7 200% DB	10 200% DB	15 150% DB	20 150% DB
1		33.33	20.00	14.29	10.00	5.00	3.750
2		44.45	32.00	24.49	18.00	9.50	7.219
3		14.81*	19.20	17.49	14.40	8.55	6.677
4		7.41	11.52*	12.49	11.52	7.70	6.177
5			11.52	8.93*	9.22	6.93	5.713
6			5.76	8.92	7.37	6.23	5.285
7				8.93	6.55*	5.90*	4.888
8				4.46	6.55	5.90	4.522
9					6.56	5.91	4.462*
10					6.55	5.90	4.461
11					3.28	5.91	4.462
12						5.90	4.461
13						5.91	4.462
14						5.90	4.461
15						5.91	4.462
16						2.95	4.461
17							4.462
18							4.461
19							4.462
20							4.461
21							2.231

* Year to switch from declining balance to straight line. *Source*: IRS Publication 946, *How To Depreciate Property*, U.S. Government Printing Offices, Washington, DC, April 06, 2011.

To demonstrate how the MACRS depreciation percentages were calculated by the IRS using the half-year convention, let us consider Example 9.6.

EXAMPLE 9.6 MACRS Depreciation: Personal Property with Trade-In

An old automobile is traded for a new automobile with a list price of $30,000. The old automobile has a net book value of $5,000, but the dealer has given $6,000 trade-in allowance, so the total purchase price is $24,000. The automobile will be depreciated according to the five-year MACRS class. Determine the cost basis to use and compute the MACRS percentages and the depreciation amounts for the new automobile.

DISSECTING THE PROBLEM

If you purchase an asset by trading in an old but similar asset, the cost basis for the new asset will be adjusted by its net book value.

Given: Five-year asset, half-year convention, $\alpha = 40\%$, trade-in allowance = $6,000$, and $S = \$0$.

Find: (a) Cost basis and (b) MACRS depreciation percentages D_n for the new automobile.

METHODOLOGY

Create a table of MACRS depreciation amounts.

SOLUTION

(a) Cost basis with trade-in allowances:

$$\text{Cost basis} = \text{Cash paid} + \text{Book value}$$
$$= \$24,000 + \$5,000$$
$$= \$29,000.$$

(b) As shown in Figure 9.2, we can calculate the depreciation amounts using the percentages taken directly from Table 9.8, which is supplied by the IRS.

- Asset cost = $29,000$
- Recovery Period = 5-Year MACRS
- Depreciation Method = Half-year convention, zero salvage value, 200% DB switching to SL

20%	32%	19.20%	11.52%	11.52%	5.76%
$5,800	$9,280	$5,568	$3,341	$3,341	$1,167
		Full	Full	Full	Full	
1	2	3	4	5	6

Figure 9.2 Features of MACRS depreciation method

COMMENTS: Note that when an asset is disposed of before the end of the recovery period, only half of the normal depreciation is allowed. If, for example, the $29,000 asset were to be disposed of in year 2, the MACRS deduction for that year would be $4,640. Another way to calculate the MACRS depreciation allowances is to use Excel. Table 9.9 shows how you might develop an Excel worksheet to perform the tax depreciation calculations.

TABLE 9.9 An Excel Worksheet to Calculate Tax Depreciation Amounts by MACRS

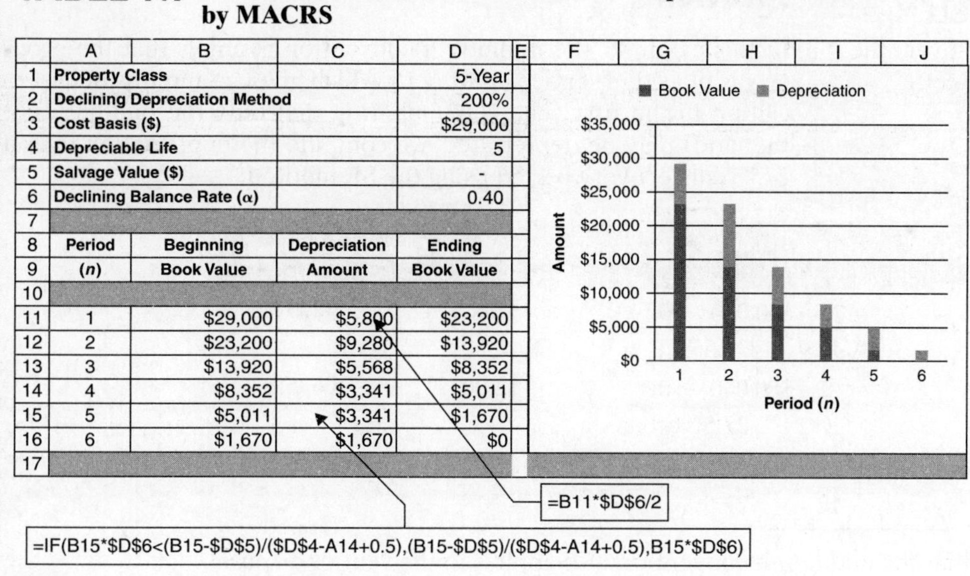

	A	B	C	D
1	Property Class			5-Year
2	Declining Depreciation Method			200%
3	Cost Basis ($)			$29,000
4	Depreciable Life			5
5	Salvage Value ($)			-
6	Declining Balance Rate (α)			0.40
7				
8	Period	Beginning	Depreciation	Ending
9	(*n*)	Book Value	Amount	Book Value
10				
11	1	$29,000	$5,800	$23,200
12	2	$23,200	$9,280	$13,920
13	3	$13,920	$5,568	$8,352
14	4	$8,352	$3,341	$5,011
15	5	$5,011	$3,341	$1,670
16	6	$1,670	$1,670	$0
17				

=B11*$D$6/2

=IF(B15*$D$6<(B15-$D$5)/($D$4-A14+0.5),(B15-$D$5)/($D$4-A14+0.5),B15*$D$6)

9.3.3 MACRS Depreciation: Real Property

Real properties are classified into two categories: (1) residential rental properties and (2) commercial buildings or properties. When depreciating such property, the straight-line method and the **midmonth convention** are used. For example, if you placed a property in service in March, you would get 9.5 months worth of depreciation for year 1. If it is disposed of before the end of the recovery period, the depreciation percentage must take into account the number of months the property was in service during the year of its disposal. Residential properties are depreciated over 27.5 years, and commercial properties are depreciated over 39 years.

EXAMPLE 9.7 MACRS Depreciation: Real Property

On May 1, Jack Costanza paid $100,000 for a residential rental property. This purchase price represents $80,000 for the cost of the building and $20,000 for the cost of the land. Nine years and five months later, on October 1, he sold the property for $130,000. Compute the MACRS depreciation for each of the 10 calendar years during which he owned the property.

DISSECTING THE PROBLEM

Given: Residential real property with cost basis = $80,000; the building was put into service on May 1.

Find: The depreciation in each of the 10 tax years the property was in service.

METHODOLOGY

Compute depreciation over the recovery period using Excel.

SOLUTION

In this example, the midmonth convention assumes that the property is placed in service on May 15, which gives 7.5 months of depreciation in the first year. Remembering that only the building (not the land) may be depreciated, we compute the depreciation over a 27.5-year recovery period using the SL method:

Year	Calculation	D_n	Recovery Percentages
1	$\left(\dfrac{7.5}{12}\right)\dfrac{\$80,000 - 0}{27.5} =$	$1,818	2.273%
2–9	$\dfrac{\$80,000 - 0}{27.5} =$	$2,909	3.636%
10	$\left(\dfrac{9.5}{12}\right)\dfrac{\$80,000 - 0}{27.5} =$	$2,303	2.879%

Notice that the midmonth convention also applies to the year of disposal.

COMMENTS: As for personal property, we can obtain depreciation calculations for real property by using Excel as shown in Table 9.10. Unlike the personal-property calculation, you need to specify the month in which the real property was placed in service in cell D5.

TABLE 9.10 **An Excel Worksheet to Generate a Depreciation Schedule for a Real Property (Example 9.7)**

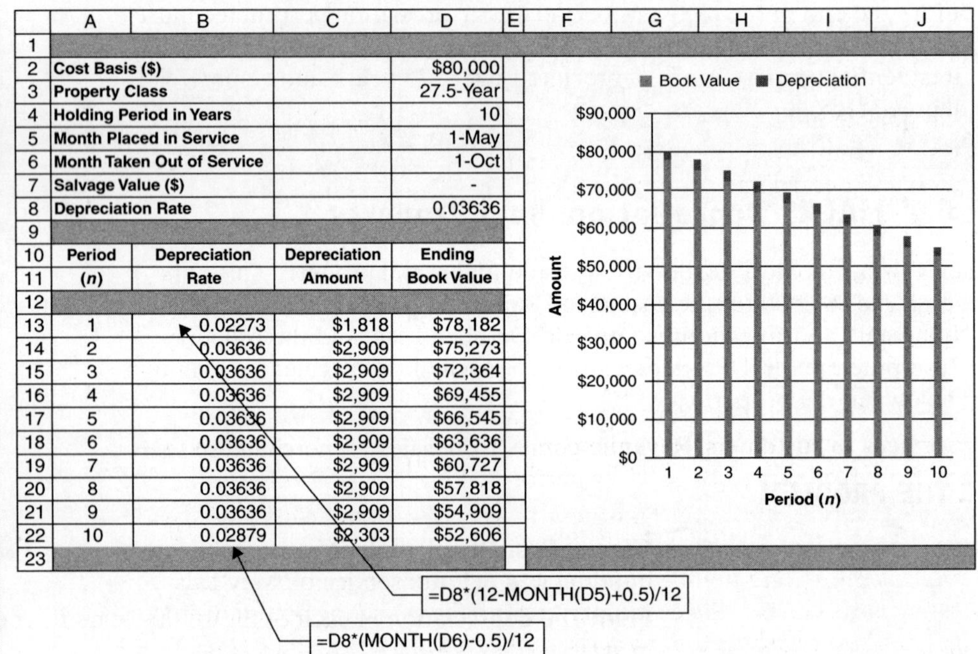

9.4 Corporate Taxes

As we have seen in Chapters 4 through 7, we make our investment decisions on the basis of the net project cash flows, that is, cash flows *after taxes*. In order to calculate the amount of taxes involved in project evaluation, we need to understand how businesses determine taxable income and thereby net income (profit).

9.4.1 How to Determine "Accounting Profit"

Firms invest in a project because they expect it to increase their wealth. If the project does this—that is, if project revenues exceed project costs—we say it has generated a **profit,** or **income**. If the project reduces a firm's wealth—that is, if project costs exceed project revenues—we say that the project has resulted in a **loss**. One of the most important roles of the accounting function within an organization is to measure the amount of profit or loss a project generates each year, or in any other relevant time period. Any profit generated will be taxed. The accounting measure of a project's after-tax profit during a particular time period is known as **net income**.

Treatment of Depreciation Expenses

Whether you are starting or maintaining a business, you will probably need to acquire assets (such as buildings and equipment). The cost of these assets becomes part of your business expenses. The accounting treatment of capital expenditures differs from the treatment of manufacturing and operating expenses, such as cost of goods sold and business operating expenses.

As mentioned earlier in the chapter, **capital expenditures must be capitalized,** or systematically allocated as expenses over their depreciable lives. Therefore, when you acquire a piece of property that has a productive life extending over several years, you cannot deduct the total costs from profits in the year the asset was purchased. Instead, a depreciation allowance is established over the life of the asset, and an appropriate portion of that allowance is included in the company's deductions from profit each year. Because it plays a role in reducing taxable income, depreciation accounting is of special concern to a company. In the next section, we will investigate the relationship between depreciation and net income.

Calculation of Net Income

Accountants measure the net income of a specified operating period by subtracting expenses from revenues for that period. For projects, these terms can be defined as follows:

1. **Gross revenues** are the incomes earned by a business as a result of providing products or services to customers. Revenue comes from sales of merchandise to customers and from fees earned by services performed for clients or others.
2. **Expenses** are costs incurred in doing business to generate the revenues of the specified operating period. Some common expenses are the cost of goods sold (labor, material, inventory, and supplies), depreciation, the cost of employees' salaries, the operating costs (such as the cost of renting buildings and the cost of insurance coverage), interest expenses for any business borrowing, and income taxes.

The aforementioned business expenses are accounted for in a straightforward fashion on a company's income statement and balance sheet; the amount paid by the organization for each item translates dollar for dollar into the expenses listed in financial reports for the period. One additional category of expenses, the purchase of new assets, is treated by depreciating the total cost gradually over time. Because capital goods are given this unique accounting treatment, depreciation is accounted for as a separate expense in financial reports. In the next section, we will discuss how depreciation accounting is reflected in net-income calculations. Once we define the gross incomes and expenses, the next step is to determine the corporate taxable income, which is defined as follows:

$$\text{Taxable income} = \text{Gross income (i.e., revenues)} - \text{Allowable deductions}.$$

The allowable deductions include the cost of goods sold, salaries and wages, rent, interest expenses, advertising, depreciation, amortization, depletion, and various tax payments other than federal income tax. Once taxable income is calculated, income taxes are determined as follows:

$$\text{Income taxes} = (\text{Tax rate}) \times (\text{Taxable income}).$$

(We will discuss how we determine the applicable tax rate in Section 9.4.2.) We then calculate net income as follows:

$$\text{Net income} = \text{Taxable income} - \text{Income taxes}.$$

A more common format is to present the net income in the tabular income statement, such as the one given in Figure 9.3. If the gross income and other expenses remain the same, any decrease in depreciation deduction will increase the amount of taxable income and thus the income taxes but result in a higher net income. On the other hand, any increase in depreciation deduction would result in a smaller amount of income taxes but a lower net income. If a firm borrows money to purchase assets or to finance a business operation, the interest payment is viewed as an operating expense that can be deducted from gross income.

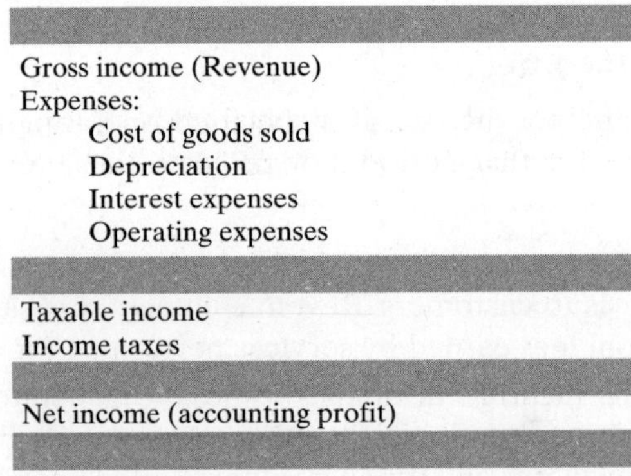

Figure 9.3 Tabular approach to finding the net income

TABLE 9.11 U.S. Corporate Tax Schedule (2011)

Taxable Income	Marginal Surtax Tax Rate	Tax Computation
0 – $50,000	15%	$0 + 0.15($\Delta$)
$50,001 – $75,000	25%	$7,500 + 0.25($\Delta$)
$75,000 – $100,000	34%	$13,750 + 0.34($\Delta$)
$100,001 – $335,000	34% + 5%	$22,250 + 0.39($\Delta$)
$335,001 – $10,000,000	34%	$113,900 + 0.34($\Delta$)
$10,000,001 – $15,000,000	35%	$3,400,000 + 0.35($\Delta$)
$15,000,001 – $18,333,333	35% + 3%	$5,150,000 + 0.38($\Delta$)
$18,333,334 and up	35%	$6,416,666 + 0.35($\Delta$)

(Δ) denotes the taxable income in excess of the lower bound of each tax bracket.

9.4.2 U.S. Corporate Income Tax Rates

Now that we have learned what elements constitute taxable income, we turn our attention to the process of computing income taxes. The U.S. corporate-tax-rate structure for 2011 is relatively simple. As shown in Table 9.11, there are four basic rate brackets (15%, 25%, 34%, and 35%) plus two surtax rates (5% and 3%) based on taxable incomes. U.S. tax rates are progressive; hence, businesses with lower taxable incomes are taxed at lower rates than those with higher taxable incomes.

Marginal Tax Rate

The rate applied to the last dollar of income earned is defined as **marginal tax rate**. Income of up to $50,000 is taxed at a 15% rate (meaning that, if your taxable income is less than $50,000, your marginal tax rate is 15%); income between $50,000 and $75,000 is taxed at a 25% rate; and income over $75,000 is taxed at a 34% rate. An additional 5% surtax (resulting in 39%) is imposed on a corporation's taxable income in excess of $100,000, the maximum additional tax being limited to $11,750 ($235,000 × 5%). This surtax provision phases out the benefit of graduated rates for corporations with taxable incomes between $100,000 and $335,000. Another 3% surtax rate is imposed on a corporate taxable income in the range $15,000,001 to $18,333,333. Corporations with incomes in excess of $18,333,333, in effect, pay a flat tax of 35%. As shown in Table 9.11, the corporate tax is also progressive up to $18,333,333 in taxable income but is essentially constant thereafter.

Average Tax Rates

The **average tax rate** is the total tax paid as a percentage of total income earned. This can be calculated from the data in Table 9.11. For example, if your corporation had a taxable income of $16,000,000 in 2011, then the income tax owed by the corporation for that year would be calculated as follows:

Marginal and Average Tax Rate for a Taxable Income of $16,000,000			
Taxable Income	**Marginal Tax Rate**	**Amount of Taxes**	**Cumulative Taxes**
First $50,000	15%	$7,500	$7,500
Next $25,000	25%	$6,250	$13,750
Next $25,000	34%	$8,500	$22,250
Next $235,000	39%	$91,650	$113,900
Next $9,665,000	34%	$3,286,100	$3,400,000
Next $5,000,000	35%	$1,750,000	$5,150,000
Remaining $1,000,000	38%	$380,000	$5,530,000

$$\text{Average tax rate} = \frac{\$5,530,000}{\$16,000,000} = 34.56\%$$

Or, using the tax formulas in Table 9.11, we obtain

$$\$5,150,000 + 0.38(\$16,000,000 - \$15,000,000) = \$5,530,000$$

for the total amount of taxes paid. The average tax rate would then be

$$\$5,530,000/\$16,000,000 = 0.3456, \text{ or } 34.56\%,$$

as opposed to the marginal rate of 38%. In other words, on average, the company paid 34.56 cents for each taxable dollar it generated during the accounting period.

EXAMPLE 9.8 How to Determine Corporate Taxes

A mail-order computer company sells personal computers and peripherals. The company leased showroom space and a warehouse for $20,000 a year and installed $290,000 worth of inventory-checking and packaging equipment. The allowed depreciation expense for this capital expenditure ($290,000 total) amounted to $58,000. The store was completed and operations began on January 1. The company had a gross income of $1,250,000 for the calendar year. Supplies and all operating expenses other than the lease expense were itemized as follows:

Merchandise sold in the year	$600,000
Employee salaries and benefits	$150,000
Other supplies and expenses	$90,000
	$840,000

Compute the taxable income for this company. How much will the company pay in federal income taxes for the year? What is its average corporate tax rate? What is the net income?

DISSECTING THE PROBLEM

Given: Income, foregoing cost information, and depreciation amount.
Find: Taxable income, amount paid in federal income taxes, and average corporate tax rate.

METHODOLOGY	**SOLUTION**
Compute taxable income, average corporate tax rate, and net income.	First, we compute the taxable income as follows:

Gross revenues	$1,250,000
Expenses	$840,000
Lease expense	$20,000
Depreciation	$58,000
Taxable income	$332,000

Note that capital expenditures are not deductible expenses. Since the company is in the 39% marginal tax bracket, the income tax can be calculated by the corresponding formula given in Table 9.11, $22,250 + 0.39(X - $100,000)$:

$$\text{Income tax} = \$22,250 + 0.39(\$332,000 - \$100,000) = \$112,730.$$

The firm's current marginal tax rate is 39%, but its average corporate tax rate is

$$\$112,730/\$332,000 = 33.95\%.$$

The net income is then

$$\text{Net income} = \$332,000 - \$112,730 = \$219,270.$$

9.4.3 Gain Taxes on Asset Disposals

When a depreciable asset used in business is sold for an amount that differs from its book value, the gains or losses have an important effect on income taxes. To calculate a gain or loss, we first need to determine the book value of the depreciable asset at the time of disposal.

Book Value Calculation

For a MACRS property, one important consideration at the time of disposal is whether the property is disposed of *during* or *before* its specified recovery period. Moreover, with the half-year convention, which is now mandated by all MACRS depreciation methods, the year of disposal is charged one-half of that year's annual depreciation amount, should the disposal occur during the recovery period. For example, let's consider a five-year MACRS property with a cost basis of $100,000. The book value calculation at the time of disposal looks like the following:

- **Case 1:** If you dispose of the asset *before* the recovery period, say, in year 3, then

$$\text{BV}_3 = \$100,000 - \$100,000 \left[0.20 + 0.32 + \frac{0.192}{2} \right] = \$38,400.$$

- **Case 2:** If you dispose of the asset *at the end* of its recovery period, say, in year 5, then

$$BV_5 = \$100,000 - \$100,000\left[0.20 + 0.32 + 0.192 + 0.1152 + \frac{0.1152}{2}\right]$$

$$= \$11,520.$$

- **Case 3:** If you dispose of the asset *after* the recovery period, say, in year 6, then

$$BV_6 = \$100,000 - \$100,000[0.20 + 0.32 + 0.192 + 0.1152 + 0.1152 + 0.0576]$$

$$= \$0.$$

Taxable Gains (or Losses)

Taxable gains are defined as the difference between the salvage value and the book value. If the salvage value is more than the cost basis, these taxable gains can be further divided into capital gains and ordinary gains. Specifically, we consider two cases as follows:

- **Case 1:** Salvage value $<$ Cost basis

    In this case,

$$\text{Gains(losses)} = \text{Salvage value} - \text{Book value},$$

   where the salvage value represents the proceeds from the sale (selling price) less any selling expense or removal cost. The gains, commonly known as **depreciation recapture,** are taxed as ordinary income under current tax law.

- **Case 2:** Salvage value $>$ Cost basis

    If an asset is sold for an amount more than its cost basis, the gain (salvage value − book value) is divided into two parts for tax purposes:

$$\text{Gains} = \text{Salvage value} - \text{Book value}$$
$$= \underbrace{(\text{Salvage value} - \text{Cost basis})}_{\text{Capital gains}} + \underbrace{(\text{Cost basis} - \text{Book value})}_{\text{Ordinary gains}}$$

As shown in Figure 9.4, this distinction is necessary only when capital gains are taxed at the capital-gains tax rate and ordinary gains (or depreciation recapture) are taxed at the ordinary income-tax rate. Current tax law does not provide a special low rate of taxation for capital gains for corporations. Currently, capital gains are treated as ordinary income, but the maximum tax rate is set at the U.S. statutory rate of 35%. Nevertheless, the statutory structure for capital gains has been retained in the tax code. This provision could allow Congress to restore preferential treatment for capital gains at some future time.

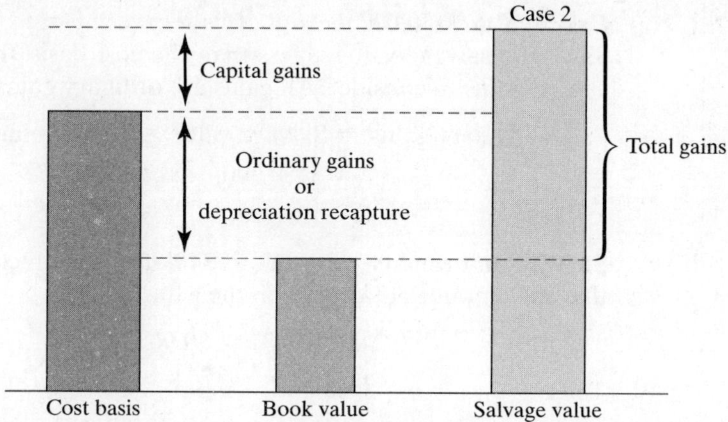

Figure 9.4 Determining ordinary gains and capital gains

EXAMPLE 9.9 Gains and Losses on Depreciable Assets

A company purchased a drill press costing $230,000 in year 0. The drill press, classified as seven-year recovery property, has been depreciated by the MACRS method. If it is sold at the end of three years for (1) $150,000 or (2) $100,000, compute the gains (losses) for each situation. Assume that both capital gains and ordinary income are taxed at 34%.

DISSECTING THE PROBLEM

Given: Seven-year MACRS asset, cost basis = $230,000, sold three years after purchase.

Find: Gains or losses, tax effects, and net proceeds from the sale if sold for $150,000 or $100,000.

METHODOLOGY

We first compute the current book value of the machine. From the MACRS depreciation schedule in Table 9.8, the allowed annual depreciation percentages for the first three years are 14.29%, 24.49%, and 17.49%, respectively. Since the asset is disposed of *before* the end of its recovery period, the depreciation amount in year 3 will be reduced by half.

SOLUTION

The total depreciation and final book value are calculated as follows:

$$\text{Total allowed depreciation} = \$230,000(0.1429 + 0.2449 + 0.1749/2)$$
$$= \$109,308;$$
$$\text{Book value} = \$230,000 - \$109,308$$
$$= \$120,692.$$

- **Case 1:** $S = \$150,000$.

  Since the salvage value is less than the cost basis, there are no capital gains to consider. All gains are ordinary gains:

  $$\text{Ordinary gains} = \text{Salvage value} - \text{Book value}$$
  $$= \$150,000 - \$120,692$$
  $$= \$29,308.$$

  So, with an ordinary-gains tax of 34% for this bracket, we find that the amount of tax paid on the gains is

  $$0.34(\$29,308) = \$9,965.$$

  Thus,

  $$\text{Net proceeds from sale} = \text{Salvage value} - \text{Gains tax}$$
  $$= \$150,000 - \$9,965$$
  $$= \$140,035.$$

  The computation process is summarized in Figure 9.5.

- **Case 2:** $S = \$100,000$.

  Since the book value is $120,692, the amount of loss will be $20,693. Since the loss can be applied to offset other gains or ordinary income from business to the extent of the loss, this has a tax-saving effect. The anticipated tax savings will be $120,692(0.34) = \$7,036$. Therefore, the net proceeds from sale will be $107,036.

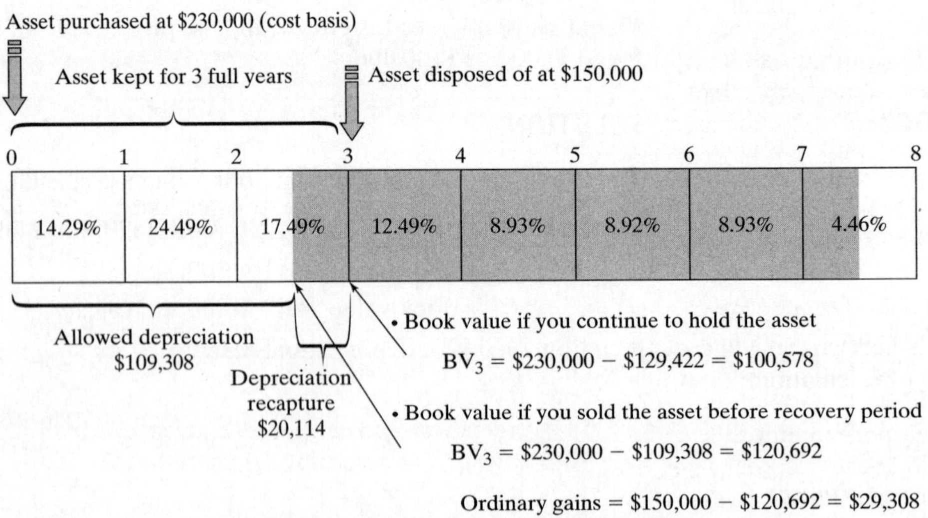

Figure 9.5 Gain or loss on a depreciable asset (Example 9.9)

SUMMARY

- Explicit consideration of taxes is a necessary aspect of any complete economic study of an investment project.

- Since we are interested primarily in the measurable financial aspects of depreciation, we consider the effects of depreciation on two important measures of an organization's financial position, **net income** and **cash flow from operations**. Once we understand that depreciation has a significant influence on the income and cash position of a firm, we will be able to appreciate fully the importance of using depreciation as a means to maximize the value both of engineering projects and of the organization as a whole.

- Machine tools and other manufacturing equipment and even factory buildings themselves are subject to wear over time. However, it is not always obvious how to account for the cost of their replacement. How we determine the estimated service life of a machine, and the method used to calculate the cost of operating it, can have significant effects on an asset's management.

- The entire cost of replacing a machine cannot be properly charged to any one year's production; rather, the cost should be spread (or capitalized) over the years in which the machine is in service. The cost charged to operations of an asset during a particular year is called **depreciation**. Several different meanings and applications of depreciation have been presented in this chapter. From an engineering economics point of view, our primary concern is with **accounting depreciation**—the systematic allocation of an asset's value over its depreciable life.

- Accounting depreciation can be broken into two categories:
  1. **Book depreciation** is the method of depreciation used for financial reports and pricing products.
  2. **Tax depreciation**, governed by tax legislation, is the method of depreciation used for calculating taxable income and income taxes.

- The four components of information required in order to calculate depreciation are
  1. The cost basis of the asset
  2. The salvage value of the asset
  3. The depreciable life of the asset
  4. The method of the asset's depreciation

- Because it employs accelerated methods of depreciation and shorter-than-actual depreciable lives, the **Modified Accelerated Cost Recovery System (MACRS)** gives taxpayers a break by allowing them to take earlier and faster advantage of the tax-deferring benefits of depreciation.

- Many firms select straight-line depreciation for book depreciation because of its relative ease of calculation.

- Given the frequently changing nature of depreciation and tax law, we must use whatever percentages, depreciable lives, and salvage values were mandated *at the time an asset was acquired*.

- Corporate taxable income is defined as

  Taxable income = Gross income (i.e., revenues) − Allowable deductions.

The allowable deductions include the cost of goods sold, salaries and wages, rent, interest, advertising, depreciation, amortization, depletion, and various tax payments other than federal income tax.

- For corporations, the U.S. tax system has the following characteristics:
  1. Tax rates are progressive: The more you earn, the more you pay.
  2. Tax rates increase in stair step fashion: There are four brackets and two additional surtax brackets, giving a total of six brackets.
  3. Allowable exemptions and deductions may reduce the overall tax assessment.

- Three distinct terms to describe taxes were used in this chapter: **marginal tax rate,** which is the rate applied to the last dollar of income earned; **average tax rate,** which is the ratio of income tax paid to net income; and **incremental tax rate,** which is the average rate applied to the incremental income generated by a new investment project.

- **Capital gains** are currently taxed as ordinary income, and the maximum rate is capped at 35%. **Capital losses** are deducted from capital gains; net remaining losses may be carried backward and forward for consideration in years other than the current tax year.

SELF-TEST QUESTIONS

9s.1   A machine, purchased for $50,000, has a depreciable life of five years. It will have an expected salvage value of $4,500 at the end of the depreciable life. Using the straight-line method, what is the book value at the end of year 2?
(a) $27,500
(b) $20,000
(c) $31,800
(d) $25,000

9s.2   Consider Problem 9s.1. If the double-declining balance (200% DB) method is used, what is the depreciation amount for year 2?
(a) $10,000
(b) $12,000
(c) $20,000
(d) $17,500

9s.3   Consider problem 9s.2. Suppose the salvage value at the end of year 4 is estimated to be $10,000 instead of $5,000. If the 200% method is used, what is the depreciation amount for year 3?
a. $5,625
b. $10,000
c. $12,000
d. $18,000

9s.4   A trucking company computes depreciation on its vehicles by a mileage basis. Suppose a delivery truck has a cost of $20,000, a salvage value of $2,000, and an estimated useful life of 200,000 miles. Determine the depreciation rate per mile.

(a) $0.08

(b) $0.09

(c) $0.10

(d) $0.11

9s.5   A company purchased a drill press priced at $170,000 in year 0. The company additionally incurred $30,000 for site preparation and labor to install the machine. The drill press was classified as a seven-year MACRS class property. The company is considering selling the drill press for $70,000 at the end of year 4. Compute the book value at the end of year 4 that should be used in calculating the taxable gains.

(a) $62,480

(b) $53,108

(c) $63,725

(d) $74,970

9s.6   Suppose that you placed a commercial building (warehouse) in service in January. The cost of property is $300,000, which includes the $100,000 value of land. Determine the amount of depreciation that is allowed during the first year of ownership.

(a) $7,692

(b) $5,128

(c) $7,372

(d) $4,915

9s.7   Centronix Corporation purchased new equipment with an estimated useful life of five years. The cost of the equipment was $200,000, and the residual (salvage) value was estimated to be $25,000. In purchasing the new equipment, an old machine was traded in that had an original cost of $180,000, and had been depreciated at the rate of $18,000 a year. The trade-in allowance was $21,000, and accumulated depreciation amounted to $144,000 at the time of the exchange. What should be the cost basis of the new equipment for tax depreciation purposes?

(a) $200,000

(b) $215,000

(c) $175,000

(d) $190,000

9s.8   Omar Shipping Company bought a tugboat for $75,000 (year 0) and expected to use it for five years after which it will be sold for $12,000. Suppose the company estimates the following revenues and expenses from the tugboat investment for the first operating year:

Operating revenue	$200,000
Operating expenses	$84,000
Depreciation	$4,000

If the company pays taxes at the rate of 30% on its taxable income, what is the net income during the first year?

(a) $28,700

(b) $81,200

(c) $78,400

(d) $25,900

9s.9 In Problem 9s.8, assume for the moment that (1) all sales were for cash and (2) all costs, except depreciation, were paid during year 1. How much cash would have been generated from operations?

(a) $82,400

(b) $32,700

(c) $85,200

(d) $3,400

9s.10 Minolta Machine Shop just purchased a computer-controlled vertical drill press for $100,000. The drill press is classified as a three-year MACRS property. Minolta is planning to use the press for five years. Then Minolta will sell the press at the end of its service life for $20,000. The annual revenues are estimated to be $110,000. If the estimated net cash flow at the end of year 5 is $30,000, what are the estimated operating and maintenance expenses in year 5? Minolta's income tax rate is 40%.

(a) $60,000

(b) $65,000

(c) $80,000

(d) $88,333

9s.11 Consider a five-year MACRS asset, which can be purchased at $80,000. The salvage value of this asset is expected to be $42,000 at the end of three years. What is the amount of gain (or loss) when the asset is disposed of at the end of three years?

(a) Gain $11,280

(b) Gain $9,860

(c) Loss $9,860

(d) Gain $18,960

9s.12 You purchased a stamping machine that cost $60,000 five years ago. At that time, the machine was estimated to have a service life of five years with salvage value of $5,000. These estimates are still good. The property has been depreciated according to a seven-year MACRS property class. Now (at the end of year 5 from purchase) you are considering selling the machine at $10,000. What book value should you use in determining the taxable gains?

(a) $10,000

(b) $13,386

(c) $16,065

(d) $17,520

PROBLEMS

Note: Unless otherwise specified, use current tax rates for corporate taxes. Check the IRS website for the most current tax rates for corporations.

Depreciation Concept

9.1 Identify which of the following expenditures is considered as a capital expenditure that must be capitalized (depreciated):

(a) Purchase land to build a warehouse at $300,000.

(b) Purchased a copy machine at $15,000.

(c) Installed a conveyor system at a cost of $55,000 to automate some part of production processes.

(d) Painted the office building, both interior and exterior, at a cost of $22,000.

(e) Repaved the parking lot at a cost of $25,000.

(f) Installed a purified water fountain in the employee lounge at a cost of $3,000.

(g) Purchased a spare part for a stamping machine at a cost of $3,800.

(h) Paid $12,000 to lease a dump truck for six months.

(i) Purchased a patent on an energy-saving device over five years at a cost of $30,000.

9.2 You purchased a machine four years ago at a cost of $5,000. It has a book value of $1,300. It can be sold now for $2,300, or it could be used for three more years, at the end of which time it would have no salvage value. Assuming it is kept for three more years, what is the amount of economic loss during this ownership?

Cost Basis

9.3 A builder paid $120,000 for a house and lot. The value of the land was appraised at $65,000, and the value of the house at $55,000. The house was then torn down at an additional cost of $8,000 so that a warehouse could be built on the lot at a cost of $50,000. What is the total value of the property with the warehouse? For depreciation purposes, what is the cost basis for the warehouse?

9.4 Nelson Company purchased equipment and incurred the following costs:

- Cash price = $55,000
- Sales taxes = $4,400
- Insurance during transit = $400
- Site preparation, installation, and testing = $2,300

What amount should be used as the cost basis of the equipment?

9.5 You purchased a new molding machine for $155,000 by trading in a similar machine that had a book value of $18,000. Assuming that the trade-in allowance was $20,000 and that $85,000 cash was paid for the new asset, what is the cost basis of the new molding machine for depreciation purposes?

9.6 You acquire a grinder priced at $65,000 by trading in a similar grinder and paying cash for the remaining balance. Assuming that the trade-in allowance is $11,000 and the book value of the asset traded in is $12,000, what is the cost basis of the new grinder for the computation of depreciation for tax purposes?

9.7 To automate one of its production processes, Milwaukee Corporation bought three flexible manufacturing cells at a price of $400,000 each. When they were delivered, Milwaukee paid freight charges of $30,000 and handling fees of $15,000. Site preparation for these cells cost $50,000. Six employees, each earning $15 an hour, worked five 40-hour weeks to set up and test the manufacturing cells. Special wiring and other materials applicable to the new manufacturing cells cost $2,000. Determine the cost basis (the amount to be capitalized) for these cells.

Book Depreciation Methods

9.8 El Dorado Machinery Company purchased a delivery truck at a cost of $35,000 on February 8, 2012. The truck has a useful life of six years with an estimated salvage value of $7,000. Compute the annual depreciation for the first two years using
(a) The straight-line method.
(b) The 150% declining-balance method.

9.9 Consider the following data on an asset:

Cost of the asset, I	$120,000
Useful life, N	5 years
Salvage value, S	$30,000

Compute the annual depreciation allowances and the resulting book values, using the following methods:
(a) The straight-line depreciation method
(b) The declining-balance method

9.10 Compute the declining-balance depreciation schedule for an asset with the following data:

Cost of the asset, I	$90,000
Useful life, N	7 years
Salvage value, S	$10,000

9.11 A firm is trying to decide whether to keep an item of construction equipment another year. The firm is using the DDB method for book purposes, and this is the fourth year of ownership of the equipment. The item cost $220,000 when it was new. What is the depreciation in year three? Assume that the depreciable life of the equipment is eight years, with zero salvage value.

9.12 Consider the following data on an asset:

Cost of the asset, I	$38,000
Useful life, N	6 years
Salvage value, S	$0

Compute the annual depreciation allowances and the resulting book values by using the DDB method and then switching to the SL method.

9.13 The double-declining-balance method is to be used for an asset with a cost of $90,000, estimated salvage value of $12,000, and estimated useful life of five years.

(a) What is the depreciation for the first three tax years, assuming that the asset was placed in service at the beginning of the year?

(b) If switching to the straight-line method is allowed, when is the optimal time to switch?

9.14 Compute the 175% DB depreciation schedule for an asset with the following data:

Cost of the asset, I	$25,000
Useful life, N	5 years
Salvage value, S	$3,000

(a) What is the value of α?

(b) What is the amount of depreciation for the first full year of use?

(c) What is the book value of the asset at the end of the fourth year?

9.15 Sanders LLC purchased new packaging equipment with an estimated useful life of five years. The cost of the equipment was $30,000, and the salvage value was estimated to be $3,000 at the end of five years. Compute the annual depreciation expenses through the five-year life of the equipment under each of the following methods of book depreciation:

(a) The straight-line method.

(b) The double-declining-balance method. (Limit the depreciation expense in the fifth year to an amount that will cause the book value of the equipment at year-end to equal the $3,000 estimated salvage value.)

9.16 You purchased a molding machine at a cost of $88,000. It has an estimated useful life of 12 years with a salvage value of $8,000. Determine the following:

(a) The amount of annual depreciation computed by the straight-line method.

(b) The amount of depreciation for the third year computed by using the double-declining-balance method.

Units-of-Production Method

9.17 New York Limousine Service owns 10 limos and uses the units-of-production method in computing depreciations on its limos. Each limo costing $32,000 is expected to be driven 200,000 miles and is expected to have a salvage value of $3,000. Limo #1 was driven 24,000 miles in year 1 and 28,000 miles in year 2. Determine the depreciation for each year and the book value at the end of year 2.

9.18 A truck for hauling coal has an estimated net cost of $85,000 and is expected to give service for 250,000 miles, resulting in a salvage value of $5,000. Compute the allowed depreciation amount for the truck usage at 55,000 miles.

9.19 A diesel-powered generator with a cost of $60,000 is expected to have a useful operating life of 50,000 hours. The expected salvage value of this generator is $8,000. In its first operating year, the generator was operated for 5,000 hours. Determine the depreciation for the year.

9.20 Ingot Land Company owns four trucks dedicated primarily to its landfill business. The company's accounting record indicates the following:

		Truck		
Description	**A**	**B**	**C**	**D**
Purchase cost	$50,000	$25,000	$18,500	$35,600
Salvage value	$5,000	$2,500	$1,500	$3,500
Useful life (miles)	200,000	120,000	100,000	200,000
Accumulated depreciation as year begins	$0	$1,500	$8,925	$24,075
Miles driven during year	25,000	12,000	15,000	20,000

Determine the amount of depreciation for each truck during the year.

9.21 A manufacturing company has purchased three assets:

	Asset Type		
Item	**Lathe**	**Truck**	**Building**
Initial cost	$45,000	$25,000	$800,000
Book life	12 years	200,000 miles	50 years
MACRS class	7 years	5 years	39 years
Salvage value	$3,000	$2,000	$100,000
Book depreciation	DDB	Unit production (UP)	SL

The truck was depreciated by the units-of-production method. Usage of the truck was 22,000 miles and 25,000 miles during the first two years, respectively.
(a) Calculate the book depreciation for each asset for the first two years.
(b) If the lathe is to be depreciated over the early portion of its life by the DDB method and then by a switch to the SL method for the remainder of its life, when should the switch occur?

9.22 Davis Machine Works purchased a stamping machine for $135,000 on February 1, 2012. The machine is expected to have a useful life of 10 years, salvage value of $12,000, production of 250,000 units, and number of working hours of 30,000. During 2012, Davis used the stamping machine for 2,450 hours to produce 23,450 units. From the information given, compute the book depreciation expense for 2012 under each of the following methods:
(a) Straight-line
(b) Units of production
(c) Working hours
(d) Double-declining-balance (without conversion to straight-line depreciation)

Tax Depreciation

9.23 A local private hospital has just purchased a new computerized patient information system with an installed cost of $220,000. The information system is treated as five-year MACRS property. The system would have a salvage value of about $20,000 at the end of five years. What are the yearly depreciation allowances?

9.24 Belmont Paving Company purchased a hauling truck on January 8, 2012, at a cost of $37,000. The truck has a useful life of eight years with an estimated salvage value of $6,000. The straight-line method is used for book purposes. For tax purposes, the truck would be depreciated by MACRS over its five-year class life. Determine the annual depreciation amount to be taken over the useful life of the hauling truck for both book and tax purposes.

9.25 AG&M Cutting Tools Company purchased a new abrasive jet-cutting machine in 2012 at a cost of $180,000. The company also paid $5,000 to have the equipment delivered and installed. The cutting machine has an estimated useful life of 12 years, but it will be depreciated by MACRS over its seven-year class life.

(a) What is the cost basis of the cutting equipment?

(b) What will be the depreciation allowance in each year of the seven-year class life for the cutting machine?

9.26 A stamping machine is classified as seven-year MACRS property. The cost basis for the machine is $120,000, and the expected salvage value is $10,000 at the end of 12 years. Compute the book value at the end of three years for tax purposes.

9.27 A hot-and-cold forming machine was purchased at a cost of $65,000. It has an estimated useful life of six years with salvage value of $8,000. It was placed in service on March 1 of the current fiscal year, which ends on December 31. The asset falls into a seven-year MACRS property category. Determine the annual depreciation amounts over the machinery's useful life.

9.28 In 2012, you purchased a spindle machine (seven-year MACRS property class) for $28,000, which you placed in service in January. Compute the depreciation allowances for the machine.

9.29 In 2012, three assets were purchased and placed in service by a firm:

Asset Type	Date Placed in Service	Cost Base	MACRS Property Class
Machine tools	March 17	$5,000	3 years
CNC machine	May 25	$125,000	7 years
Warehouse	June 19	$335,000	39 years

Compute the depreciation allowances for each asset.

9.30 On October 3, Kim Bailey paid $250,000 for a residential rental property. This purchase price represents $200,000 for the building and $50,000 for the land. Five years later, on June 25, she sold the property for $250,000. Compute the MACRS depreciation for each of the five calendar years during which she had the property.

9.31 On October 1, you purchased a residential home in which to locate your professional office for $180,000. The appraisal is divided into $30,000 for the land and $150,000 for the building.

(a) In your first year of ownership, how much can you deduct for depreciation for tax purposes?

(b) Suppose that you sold the property at $197,000 at the end of the fourth year of ownership. What is the book value of the property?

9.32 Ray Electric Company purchased a 10,000 ft^2 office space for $1,000,000 to relocate its engineering office on May 1, 2012. Determine the allowed depreciation in years 2012 and 2013.

(*Note:* There is no land value included in the purchase price.)

9.33 Consider the data in the following two tables:

First cost	$80,000
Book depreciation life	7 years
MACRS property class	7 years
Salvage value	$24,000

Depreciation Schedule

n	A	B	C	D
1	$8,000	$22,857	$11,429	$22,857
2	$8,000	$16,327	$19,592	$16,327
3	$8,000	$11,661	$13,994	$11,661
4	$8,000	$5,154	$9,996	$8,330
5	$8,000	$0	$7,140	$6,942
6	$8,000	$0	$7,140	$6,942
7	$8,000	$0	$7,140	$6,942
8	$0	$0	$3,570	$0

Identify the depreciation method used for each depreciation schedule as one of the following:

(a) Double-declining-balance depreciation

(b) Straight-line depreciation

(c) DDB with conversion to straight-line depreciation, assuming a zero salvage value

(d) MACRS seven-year depreciation with the half-year convention

(e) Double-declining-balance (with conversion to straight-line depreciation)

9.34 At the beginning of the fiscal year, G&J Company acquired new equipment at a cost of $100,000. The equipment has an estimated life of five years and an estimated salvage value of $10,000.

(a) Determine the annual depreciation (for financial reporting) for each of the five years of estimated useful life of the equipment, the accumulated depreciation at the end of each year, and the book value of the equipment at the end of each year by using (1) the straight-line method and (2) the double-declining-balance method.

(b) Determine the annual depreciation for tax purposes, assuming that the equipment falls into the seven-year MACRS property class.

(c) Assume that the equipment was depreciated under MACRS for a seven-year property class. In the first month of the fourth year, the equipment was traded in for similar equipment priced at $112,000. The trade-in allowance on the old equipment was $20,000, and cash was paid for the balance. What is the cost basis of the new equipment for computing the amount of depreciation for income-tax purposes?

9.35 A company purchased a new forging machine to manufacture disks for airplane turbine engines. The new press cost $3,800,000, and it falls into the seven-year MACRS property class. The company has to pay property taxes to the local township for ownership of this forging machine at a rate of 1.2% on the beginning book value of each year.

(a) Determine the book value of the asset at the beginning of each tax year.

(b) Determine the amount of property taxes over the machine's depreciable life.

Corporate Taxes and Accounting Profits (Net Income)

9.36 Lynn Construction Company had a gross income of $34,000,000 in tax-year 1, $5,000,000 in salaries, $4,000,000 in wages, $1,000,000 in depreciation expenses, a loan principal payment of $200,000, and a loan interest payment of $210,000.

(a) What is the marginal tax rate for Lynn Construction in tax-year 1?

(b) What is the average tax rate in tax-year 1?

(c) Determine the net income of the company in tax-year 1.

9.37 A consumer electronics company was formed to sell a portable handset system. The company purchased a warehouse and converted it into a manufacturing plant for $2,000,000 (including the purchase price of the warehouse). It completed installation of assembly equipment worth $1,500,000 on December 31. The plant began operation on January 1. The company had a gross income of $2,500,000 for the calendar year. Manufacturing costs and all operating expenses, excluding the capital expenditures, were $1,280,000. The depreciation expenses for capital expenditures amounted to $128,000.

(a) Compute the taxable income of this company.

(b) How much will the company pay in federal income taxes for the year?

9.38 ABC Corporation will commence operations on January 1, 2013. The company projects the following financial performance during its first year of operation:

■ Sales revenues are estimated at $2,500,000.

■ Labor, material, and overhead costs are projected at $800,000.

■ The company will purchase a warehouse worth $500,000 in February. To finance this warehouse, on January 1 the company will issue $500,000 of long-term bonds, which carry an interest rate of 10%. The first interest payment will occur on December 31.

■ For depreciation purposes, the purchase cost of the warehouse is divided into $100,000 for the land and $400,000 for the building. The building is classified into the 39-year MACRS real-property class and will be depreciated accordingly.

■ On January 5, the company will purchase $200,000 of equipment that has a five-year MACRS class life.

(a) Determine the total depreciation expenses allowed in 2013.

(b) Determine ABC's tax liability in 2013.

Gains or Losses

9.39 Consider a five-year MACRS asset that was purchased for $76,000. Compute the gain or loss amounts if the asset were disposed of in (a) year 3 with a salvage value of $20,000; (b) year 5 with a salvage value of $10,000; (c) year 6 with a salvage value of $5,000.

9.40 An electrical appliance company purchased an industrial robot costing $320,000 in year 0. The industrial robot, to be used for welding operations, is classified as a seven-year MACRS recovery property. If the robot is to be sold after five years, compute the amounts of gains (losses) for the following three salvage values, assuming that both capital gains and ordinary incomes are taxed at 35%:
(a) $15,000
(b) $125,460
(c) $200,000

9.41 Auburn Crane, Inc., a hydraulic crane service company, had sales revenues of $4,250,000 during tax year 2013. The following table provides other financial information relating to the tax year:

Labor expenses	$1,550,000
Material costs	$785,000
Depreciation	$332,500
Office supplies	$15,000
Debt interest expenses	$42,200
Rental expenses	$45,000
Proceeds from the sale of old cranes	$43,000

The sold cranes had a combined book value of $30,000 at the time of sale.
(a) Determine the taxable income for 2013.
(b) Determine the taxable gains for 2013.
(c) Determine the amount of income taxes and gains taxes (or loss credits) for 2013.

9.42 Electronic Measurement and Control Company (EMCC) has developed a laser speed detector that emits infrared light invisible to humans and radar detectors alike. For full-scale commercial marketing, EMCC needs to invest $5 million in new manufacturing facilities. The system is priced at $3,000 per unit. The company expects to sell 5,000 units annually over the next five years. The new manufacturing facilities will be depreciated according to a seven-year MACRS property class. The expected salvage value of the manufacturing facilities at the end of five years is $1.6 million. The manufacturing cost for the detector is $1,200 per unit excluding depreciation expenses. The operating and mainten-ance costs are expected to run to $1.2 million per year. EMCC has a combined federal and state income-tax rate of 35%, and undertaking this project will not change this current marginal tax rate.
(a) Determine the incremental taxable income, income taxes, and net income that would result from undertaking this new product for the next five years.
(b) Determine the gains or losses associated with the disposal of the manufac-turing facilities at the end of five years.

Short Case Studies with Excel

9.43 A machine now in use that was purchased three years ago at a cost of $4,000 has a book value of $2,000. It can be sold now for $2,500, or it could be used for three more years, at the end of which time it would have no salvage value. The annual O&M costs amount to $10,000 for the machine. If the machine is sold, a new machine can be purchased at an invoice price of $14,000 to replace the present equipment. Freight will amount to $800, and the installation cost will be $200. The new machine has an expected service life of five years and will have no salvage value at the end of that time. With the new machine, the expected direct cash savings amount to $8,000 the first year and $7,000 in O&M for each of the next two years. Corporate income taxes are at an annual rate of 40%, and the net capital gain is taxed at the ordinary income-tax rate. The present machine has been depreciated according to a straight-line method, and the proposed machine would be depreciated on a seven-year MACRS schedule. Consider each of the following questions independently:

(a) If the old asset is to be sold now, what would be the amount of its equivalent book value?

(b) For depreciation purposes, what would be the first cost of the new machine (depreciation base)?

(c) If the old machine is to be sold now, what would be the amount of taxable gains and the gains tax?

(d) If the old machine is sold for $5,000 now instead of $2,500, what would be the amount of the gains tax?

(e) If the old machine had been depreciated by 175% DB and then by a switch to SL depreciation, what would be the current book value?

(f) If the old machine were not replaced by the new one and has been depreciated by the 175% DB method, when would be the time to switch from DB to SL depreciation?

9.44 Phillip Zodrow owns and operates a small unincorporated plumbing service business, Zodrow Plumbing Service (ZPS). Phillip is married and has two children, so he claims four exemptions on his tax return. As business grows steadily, tax considerations are important to him. Therefore, Phillip is considering incorporation of the business. Under either form of the business (corporation or sole ownership), the family will initially own 100% of the firm. Phillip plans to finance the firm's expected growth by drawing a salary just sufficient for his family's living expenses and by retaining all other income in the business. He estimates the income and expenses over the next three years to be as follows:

	Year 1	Year 2	Year 3
Gross income	$200,000	$215,000	$230,000
Salary	$100,000	$110,000	$120,000
Business expenses	$25,000	$30,000	$40,000
Personal exemptions	$14,800	$14,800	$14,800
Itemized deductions	$16,000	$18,000	$20,000

Which form of business (corporation or sole ownership) will allow Phillip to pay the lowest taxes (and retain the most income) during the three years? Personal income-tax brackets and amounts of personal exemption are updated yearly, so you need to consult the IRS tax manual for the tax rates, as well as for the exemptions, that are applicable to the tax years.

9.45 Julie Magnolia has $50,000 cash to invest for three years. Two types of bonds are available for consideration. She can buy a tax-exempt Arizona state bond that pays interest of 9.5% per year, or she can buy a corporate bond. Julie's marginal tax rate is 25% for both ordinary income and capital gains. Assume that any investment decision considered will not change her marginal tax bracket.

(a) If Julie were looking for a corporate bond that was just as safe as the state bond, what interest rate on the corporate bond is required so that Julie would be indifferent between the two bonds? There would be no capital gains or losses at the time of her trading the bond.

(b) In (a), suppose at the time of trading (year 3) that the corporate bond is expected to be sold at a price 5% higher than its face value. What interest rate on the corporate bond is required so that Julie would be indifferent between the two bonds?

(c) Alternatively, Julie can invest the amount in a tract of land that could be sold at $75,000 (after she pays the real-estate commission) at the end of year 3. Is this investment better than the state bond?

Project Cash-Flow Analysis

Coke Leveraging Its Investment in Plant-Based Packaging[1] The Coca-Cola Company announced a partnership that will license the beverage giant's plant-based packaging to Heinz for use in its ketchup packaging. The bottle technology, which Coke launched in 2009, uses a plastic sourced from sugarcane waste to replace 30 percent of the plastic in beverage bottles. The company's goal is to eventually achieve 100 percent renewable sources for its packaging,[2] and licensing the technology to Heinz will no doubt help fund the research process.

[1] "Heinz and Coke Team up to Squeeze Ketchup into PlantBottles," GreenBiz.com, February 23, 2011.
[2] "The Coca-Cola Company's New PlantBottle® Packaging on Store Shelves Nationwide Today," *The New York Times*, April 4, 2011.

Heinz plans to introduce PlantBottled ketchup in the summer of 2011 across the United States, switching out about 120 million of its 20 ounce retail and food service bottles with the partly renewable packaging. The PlantBottles® will have a special label and environmental messages to communicate the benefits of the plant-based packaging to shoppers.

Coke has already planned to invest more than $150 million in the PlantBottle technology with a goal of reaching 100 percent renewable and recyclable packaging as soon as the technology allows. Although both CEOs declined to share financial details of the licensing agreement, adding a no-doubt-significant investment from Heinz into PlantBottle technology will also help Coke further its research into renewable packaging.

Although the PlantBottle technology currently costs slightly more to produce than traditional plastic—costs that both CEOs repeatedly said would not be passed on to shoppers—investing in renewably sourced and recyclable packaging provides both more future cost stability and helps achieve sustainability goals.

"Over time, depending where the price of nonrenewable fuels go," Heinz CEO Johnson said, "this could be a long-term cost savings because of stability. Long-term, we see this as cost benefit."

On what basis should Coke justify its $150 million investment in the PlantBottle technology? Clearly, Coke will continue to expend tens of millions dollars to develop the technology, and it will need to spend more to build the necessary manufacturing facilities. The question is how to estimate the projected cash flows from the PlantBottle—such as potential savings from replacing petroleum-based materials and licensing fees from transferring technology to other plastic industries. Certainly, Coke's use of PlantBottle technology can cut the company's carbon footprint by a 12% to 19%. And as plastic recycling rates increase, the carbon impacts of the bottles continue to decline. Then, how should Coke consider this savings?

To justify any investment, we need the detailed project cash flows over the estimated product life. Projecting cash flows is the most important—and the most difficult—step in the analysis of a capital project. Typically, a capital project will initially require investment outlays and only later produces annual net cash inflows. A great many variables are involved in forecasting cash flows, and many individuals, ranging from engineers to cost accountants and marketing people, participate in the process. This chapter provides the general principles on which the determination of a project's cash flows is based.

10.1 Understanding Project Cost Elements

First, we need to understand the types of costs that must be considered in estimating project cash flows. Because there are many types of costs, each is classified differently, according to the immediate needs of management. For example, engineers may want cost data in order to prepare external reports, prepare planning budgets, or make decisions. Also, different usage cost data demand a different classification and definition of cost. For example, the preparation of external financial reports requires the use of historical cost data whereas decision making may require current cost or estimated future cost data.

10.1.1 Classifying Costs for Manufacturing Environments

Our initial focus in this chapter is on manufacturing companies because their basic activities (such as acquiring raw materials, producing finished goods, and marketing) are commonly found in most other businesses.

Manufacturing Costs

The many manufacturing costs incurred by a typical manufacturer are exhibited and classified in Figure 10.1. In converting raw materials into finished goods, a manufacturer incurs the various costs of operating a factory. Most manufacturing companies divide manufacturing costs into three broad categories—direct materials, direct labor, and manufacturing overhead.

- **Direct Materials:** Direct raw materials are any materials that are used in the final product and that can be easily traced into it. Some examples are wood in furniture, steel in bridge construction, paper in printed products, and fabric in clothing. It is also important to conceptualize that the finished product of one company can become the raw materials of another company. For example, the computer chips produced by Intel® are a raw material used by Dell™ in its personal computers.
- **Direct Labor:** Just as the term "direct materials" refers to materials costs for the final product, "direct labor" refers to those labor costs that go into the fabrication of a product. The labor costs of assembly-line workers, for example, would be direct labor costs as would the labor costs of welders in metal-fabricating industries, carpenters and bricklayers in home-building businesses, and machine operators in various manufacturing operations.

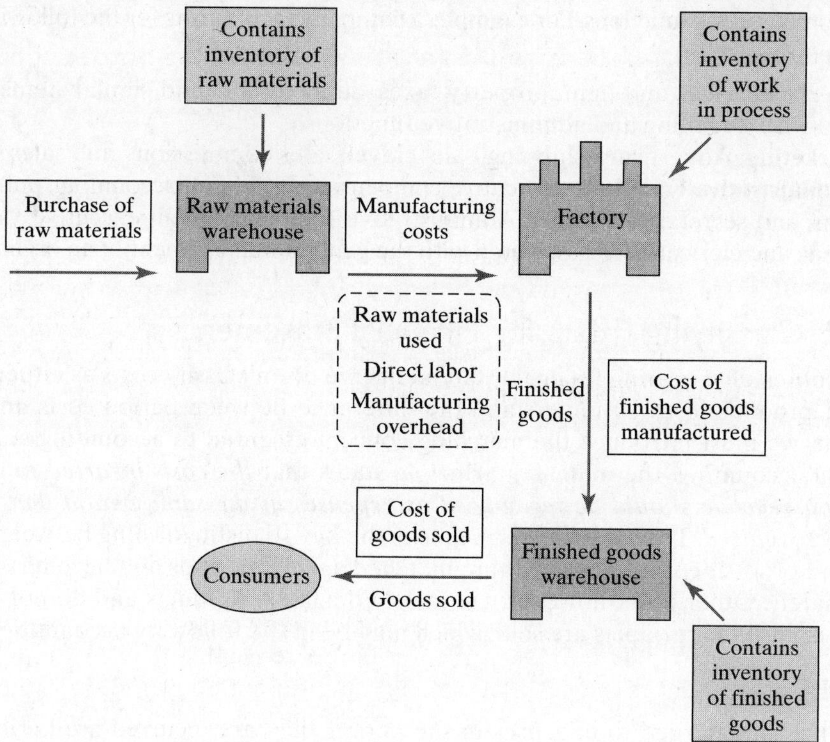

Figure 10.1 Various types of manufacturing costs

- **Manufacturing Overhead:** The third type of manufacturing cost, manufacturing overhead, includes all costs of manufacturing except direct materials and direct labor. In particular, it includes such items as indirect materials,[3] indirect labor,[4] maintenance and repairs on production equipment, heat and light, property taxes, depreciation, insurance on manufacturing facilities, and overtime premium. Unlike direct materials and direct labor, manufacturing overhead is not easily traceable to specific units of output. In addition, many manufacturing overhead costs do not change as output changes as long as the production volume stays within the capacity.

Nonmanufacturing Costs

There are two additional types of cost incurred to support any manufacturing: (1) operating costs, such as warehouse leasing and vehicle rentals and (2) marketing (or selling) and administrative costs. Marketing or selling costs include all expenses necessary to secure customer orders and get the finished product or service into the customer's operations. Cost breakdowns of these types provide data for control over selling and administrative functions in the same way that manufacturing-cost breakdowns provide data for control

---

[3] Sometimes, it may not be worth the effort to trace the costs of relatively insignificant materials to the finished products. Such minor items would include the solder used to make electrical connections in a computer circuit board or the glue used to bind this textbook. Materials such as solder and glue are called indirect materials and are included as part of manufacturing overhead.

[4] Sometimes, we may not be able to trace some of the labor costs to the creation of a product. We treat this type of labor cost as a part of manufacturing overhead along with indirect materials. Indirect labor includes the wages of janitors, supervisors, material handlers, and night security guards. Although the efforts of these workers are essential to production, it would be either impractical or impossible to trace their costs to specific units of product. Therefore, we treat such labor costs as indirect labor.

over manufacturing functions. For example, a company incurs costs for the following non-manufacturing items:

- **Overhead:** Heat and light, property taxes, depreciation, and similar items associated with its selling and administrative functions.
- **Marketing:** Advertising, shipping, sales travel, sales commissions, and sales salaries.
- **Administrative Functions:** Executive compensation, general accounting, public relations, and secretarial support. Administrative costs include all executive, organizational, and clerical costs associated with the general management of an organization.

10.1.2 Classifying Costs for Financial Statements

For purposes of preparing financial statements, we often classify costs as either period costs or product costs. To understand the difference between period costs and product costs, we must introduce the matching concept essential to accounting studies. In financial accounting, the **matching principle** states that *the costs incurred to generate particular revenue should be recognized as expenses in the same period that the revenue is recognized.* This matching principle is the key to distinguishing between period costs and product costs. Some costs are matched against periods and become expenses immediately. Other costs, however, are matched against products and do not become expenses until the products are sold, which may be in the following accounting period.

Period Costs

Costs that are charged to expenses in the period they are incurred are **period costs**. The underlying assumption is that the associated benefits are received in the same period as the expenses are incurred. Some specific examples of period costs are all general and administrative expenses, selling expenses, insurance, and income-tax expenses. Advertising costs, executive salaries, sales commissions, public-relations costs, and the other nonmanufacturing costs discussed earlier would also be period costs. Such costs are not related to the production and flow of manufactured goods but are deducted from revenue in the income statement. In other words, period costs will appear on the income statement as expenses in the time period in which they occur.

Product Costs

Some costs are better matched against products than they are against periods. Costs of this type, called **product costs**, include those involved in the purchase or manufacturing of goods. In the case of manufactured goods, these costs consist of direct materials, direct labor, and manufacturing overhead. Product costs are not viewed as expenses; rather, they are the cost of creating inventory. Thus, product costs are considered an asset until the related goods are sold. At this point of sale, the costs are released from inventory as expenses (typically called **cost of goods sold**) and matched against sales revenue. Since product costs are assigned to inventories, they are also known as *inventory costs*. In theory, product costs include all manufacturing costs—that is, all costs relating to the manufacturing process. Product costs appear on financial statements when the inventory (or final good) is sold, not when the product is manufactured.

Cost Flows in a Manufacturing Company

To understand product costs more fully, we now look briefly at the flow of costs in a manufacturing company. By doing so, we will be able to see how product costs move through the various accounts and affect the balance sheet and the income statement in the course of the manufacture and sale of goods. The flows of period costs and product

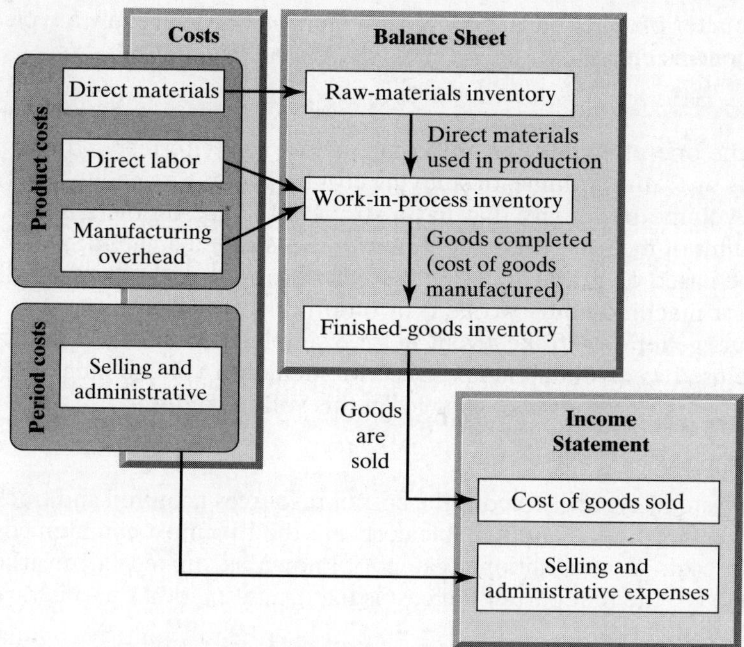

Figure 10.2 Cost flows and classifications in a manufacturing company

costs through the financial statements are illustrated in Figure 10.2. All product costs filter through the balance-sheet statement in the name of "inventory cost." If a product is sold, its inventory costs in the balance-sheet statement are transferred to the income statement in the name of "cost of goods sold." There are three types of inventory cost reflected in the balance sheet:

- **Raw-materials inventory** represents the unused portion of the raw materials on hand at the end of the fiscal year.
- **Work-in-process inventory** consists of the partially completed goods on hand in the factory at year-end. When raw materials are used in production, their costs are transferred to the work-in-process inventory account as direct materials. Note that direct-labor costs and manufacturing overhead costs are also added directly to the work-in-process entry. The work-in-process concept can be viewed as the assembly line in a manufacturing plant where workers are stationed and where products slowly take shape as they move from one end of the assembly line to the other.
- **Finished-goods inventory** shows the cost of finished goods on hand and awaiting sale to customers at year end. As goods are completed, accountants transfer the corresponding cost in the work-in-process account into the finished-goods account. Here, the goods await sale to a customer. As goods are sold, their cost is transferred from finished goods into cost of goods sold (or **cost of revenue**). At this point, we finally treat the various material, labor, and overhead costs that were involved in the manufacture of the units being sold as *expenses* in the income statement.

10.1.3 Classifying Costs for Predicting Cost Behavior

In project cash-flow analysis, we need to predict how a certain cost will behave in response to a change in activity. For example, a manager may want to estimate the impact that a 5% increase in production will have on the company's total wages before a decision to alter production is made. **Cost behavior** describes how a typical cost will react or respond to changes in the level of business activity.

Volume Index

In general, the operating costs of any company are likely to respond in some way to changes in its operating volume. In studying cost behavior, we need to determine some measurable volume or activity that has a strong influence on the amount of cost incurred. The unit of measure used to define volume is called a **volume index**. A volume index may be based on production inputs (such as tons of coal processed, direct labor-hours used, or machine-hours worked) or on production outputs (such as number of kilowatt-hours generated). Take a vehicle for example: the number of miles driven per year may be used as a volume index. Once we identify a volume index, we try to find out how costs vary in response to changes in this volume index.

Fixed and Variable Costs

Accounting systems typically record the cost of resources acquired and track their subsequent usage. Fixed costs and variable costs are the two most common cost behavior patterns. The costs in an additional category known as "mixed (semivariable) costs" contain two parts: the first part of the cost is fixed, and the other part is variable as the volume of output varies.

- *Fixed Costs:* The costs of providing a company's basic operating capacity are known as its **fixed costs** or **capacity costs**. For a cost item to be classified as fixed, it must have a relatively wide span of output for which costs are expected to remain constant. (See Figure 10.3.) This span is called the **relevant range**. In other words, fixed costs do not change within a given period although volume may change. For our previous automobile example, the annual insurance premium, property tax, and license fee are fixed costs, since they are independent of the number of miles driven per year. Some common examples of fixed costs are building rents; depreciation of buildings, machinery, and equipment; and salaries of administrative and production personnel.

- *Variable Costs:* In contrast to fixed operating costs, variable operating costs have a close relationship to the level of volume. (See Figure 10.4.) If, for example, volume increases 10%, a total variable cost will also increase by approximately 10%. Gasoline is a good example of a variable automobile cost, as fuel consumption

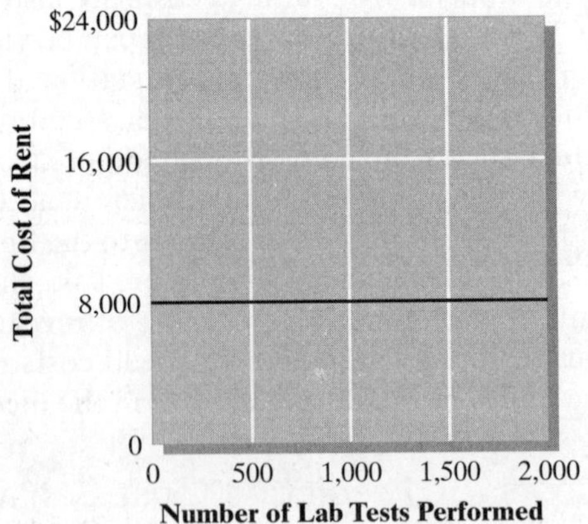

Figure 10.3   Fixed-cost behavior

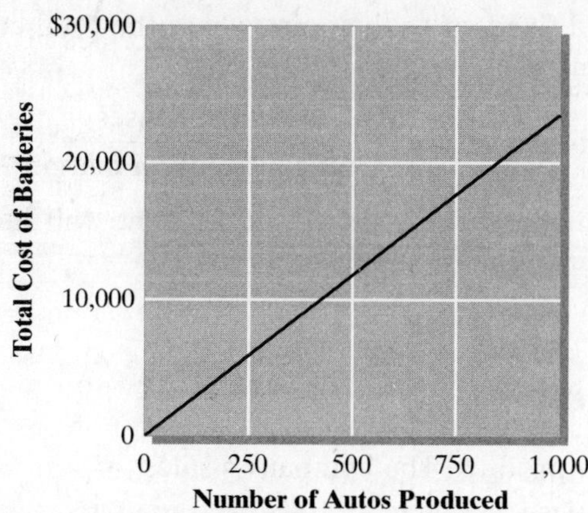

Figure 10.4 Variable-cost behavior

is directly related to miles driven. Similarly, the tire replacement cost will also increase as a vehicle is driven more. In a typical manufacturing environment, direct labor and material costs are major variable costs. The difference between the unit sales price and the unit variable cost is known as the **unit contribution margin**. We could express the contribution margin in two ways:

Unit contribution margin $=$ Unit sales price $-$ Unit variable cost.

Contribution margin $=$ Total sales revenue $-$ Total variable costs.

The first equation expresses the contribution margin on a unit basis whereas the second formula does so in terms of total volume. This means each unit sold contributes toward absorbing the company's fixed costs.

Mixed Costs

Some costs do not fall precisely into either the fixed or the variable category but contain elements of both. We refer to these costs as **mixed costs** (or **semivariable costs**). In our automobile example, **depreciation** (loss of value) is a **mixed cost**. Some depreciation occurs simply from the passage of time regardless of how many miles a car is driven, and this amount represents the fixed portion of depreciation. On the other hand, the more miles an automobile is driven a year, the faster it loses its market value, and this amount represents the variable portion of depreciation. A familiar example of a mixed cost in manufacturing is the cost of electric power. Some components of power consumption, such as lighting, are independent of operating volume while other components are likely to vary directly with volume (e.g., number of machine-hours operated).

Break-Even Sales Volume

As mentioned earlier, contribution margin is the amount remaining from sales revenue after variable expenses have been deducted. Thus, it is the amount available to cover fixed expenses—whatever remains becomes profit. If the contribution margin is not sufficient to cover the fixed expenses, a loss occurs for the period. Therefore, the **break-even point** can be defined either as the point where total sales revenue equals total expenses, variable and fixed, or as the point where the total contribution margin equals the total fixed expenses:

$$\text{Break-even point} = \frac{\text{Fixed expenses}}{\text{Unit contribution margin}}.$$

Once the break-even point has been reached, net income will increase by the unit contribution margin for each additional unit sold.

EXAMPLE 10.1 Break-Even Sales Volume

Ashland Company manufactures and sells a single product. The company's sales and expenses for a recent month are as follows:

	Total	Per Unit
Sales	$500,000	$20
Less variable expenses	$250,000	$10
Contribution margin	$250,000	$10
Less fixed expenses	$150,000	
Income (before tax)	$100,000	

(a) What is the monthly break-even point in units sold and in sales dollars?

(b) How many units would have to be sold each month to earn a minimum target net income of $50,000?

DISSECTING THE PROBLEM

Given: Financial data as provided in the preceding table.

Find: (a) The monthly break-even point and (b) the number of unit sales required to achieve the target income of $50,000 before tax.

METHODOLOGY

Compute the monthly break-even point and then the unit sales.

SOLUTION

(a) Monthly break-even point:

$$\text{Break-even point} = \frac{\$150,000}{\$10} = 15,000 \text{ units.}$$

(b) Number of units to be sold to make $50,000 profit before tax:

$$\text{Desired-profit point} = \frac{\$150,000 + \$50,000}{\$10} = 20,000 \text{ units.}$$

COMMENTS: We can express the relationships among revenue, cost, profit, and volume graphically by preparing a **cost–volume–profit graph** as shown in Figure 10.5. The break-even point (15,000 units) is where the total revenue and total expense lines cross. We can also read off the units sold to attain the target profit from the same chart (20,000 units). It shows clearly that once the fixed costs are covered, the unit contribution margin is fully available for meeting profit requirements.

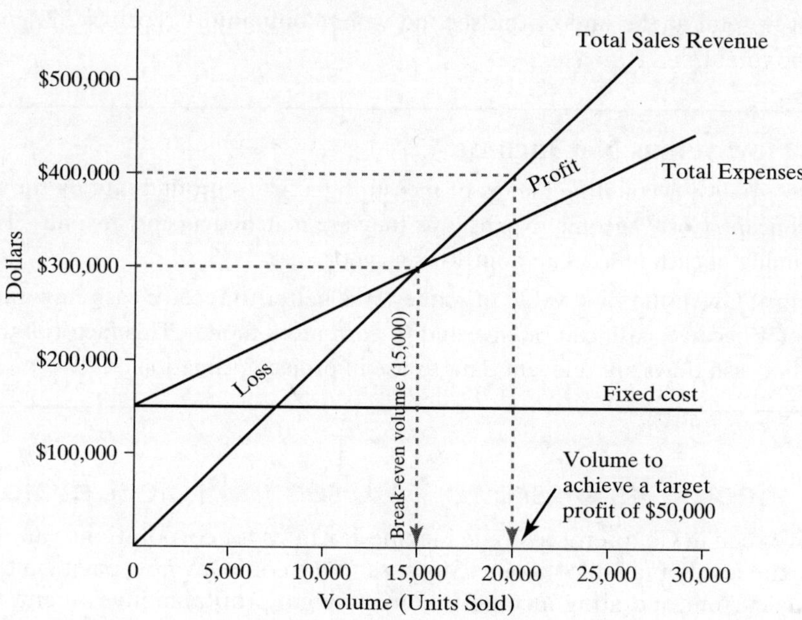

Figure 10.5   Cost–Volume–Profit graph showing that the break-even
point occurs at 15,000 units

10.2 Why Do We Need to Use Cash Flows in Economic Analysis?

Traditional accounting stresses net income as a means of measuring a firm's profitability, but it is also desirable to discuss why cash flows are relevant data to be used in project evaluation. As noted in Section 10.1.2, net income is an accounting measure based, in part, on the **matching concept**. Costs become expenses as they are matched against revenue. The actual timing of cash inflows and outflows is ignored.

Over the life of a firm, net aggregate incomes and net aggregate cash inflows will usually be the same. However, the timing of incomes and cash inflows can differ substantially. Remember the time value of money, it is better to receive cash now rather than later because cash can be invested to earn more cash. (You cannot invest net income.) For example, consider the following income and cash-flow schedules of two firms over two years:

		Company A	Company B
Year 1	Net income	$1,000,000	$1,000,000
	Cash flow	$1,000,000	$0
Year 2	Net income	$1,000,000	$1,000,000
	Cash flow	$1,000,000	$2,000,000

Both companies have the same amount of net income and cash sum over two years, but Company *A* returns $1 million cash yearly while Company *B* returns $2 million at the end of the second year. Company *A* could invest the $1 million it receives at the end of the first year at 10%, for example. In this case, while Company *B* receives only

$2 million in total at the end of the second year, Company *A* receives $2.1 million in total.

Cash Flow versus Net Income

Net income: An accounting means of measuring a firm's profitability by the matching concept. Costs become expenses as they are matched against revenue. The actual timing of cash inflows and outflows is ignored.

Cash flow: Given the time value of money, it is better to receive cash now rather than later because cash can be invested to earn more money. This factor is the reason that cash flows are relevant data to use in project evaluation.

10.3 Income-Tax Rate to Be Used in Project Evaluation

As we have seen in Chapter 9, average income-tax rates for corporations vary from 0 to 35% with the level of taxable income. Suppose that a company now paying a tax rate of 25% on its current operating income is considering a profitable investment. What tax rate should be used in calculating the taxes on the investment's projected income? As we will explain, the choice of the rate depends on the incremental effect the investment has on taxable income. In other words, *the tax rate to use is the rate that applies to the additional taxable income projected in the economic analysis.*

To illustrate, consider ABC Corporation whose taxable income from operations is expected to be $70,000 for the current tax year. ABC's management wishes to evaluate the incremental tax impact of undertaking a particular project during the same tax year. The revenues, expenses, and taxable incomes before and after the project are estimated as follows:

	Before	After	Incremental
Gross revenue	$200,000	$240,000	$40,000
Salaries	$100,000	$110,000	$10,000
Wages	$30,000	$40,000	$10,000
Taxable income	$70,000	$90,000	$20,000

Because the income-tax rate is progressive, the tax effect of the project cannot be isolated from the company's overall tax obligations. The base operations of ABC without the project are projected to yield a taxable income of $70,000. With the new project, the taxable income increases to $90,000. Using the tax computation formula in Table 9.11, we find that the corporate income taxes with and without the project, respectively, are as follows:

$$\text{Income tax with the project} = \$13,750 + 0.34(\$90,000 - \$75,000)$$

$$= \$18,850;$$

$$\text{Income tax without the project} = \$7,500 + 0.25(\$70,000 - \$50,000)$$

$$= \$12,500.$$

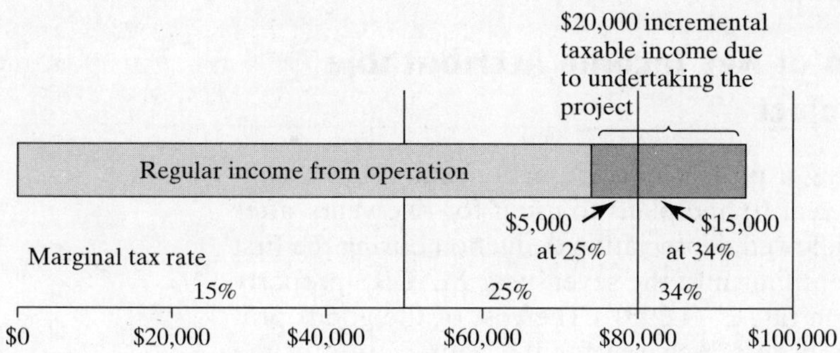

Figure 10.6   Illustration of incremental tax rate

The additional income tax is then $18,850 - $12,500 = $6,350$. The $6,350 tax on the additional $20,000 of taxable income, a rate of 31.75%, is an incremental rate. This is the rate we should use in evaluating the project in isolation from the rest of ABC's operations. As shown in Figure 10.6, the 31.75% is not an arbitrary figure but a weighted average of two distinct marginal rates. Because the new project pushes ABC into a higher tax bracket, the first $5,000 it generates is taxed at 25%; the remaining $15,000 it generates is taxed in the higher bracket, at 34%. Thus, we could have calculated the incremental tax rate as follows:

$$0.25(\$5,000/\$20,000) + 0.34(\$15,000/\$20,000) = 31.75\%.$$

The average tax rates before and after the new project being considered would be as shown in the following table:

	Before	After	Incremental
Taxable income	$70,000	$90,000	$20,000
Income taxes	$12,500	$18,850	$6,350
Average tax rate	17.86%	20.94%	
Incremental tax rate			31.75%

However, in conducting an economic analysis of an individual project, neither one of the companywide average rates is appropriate; we want the incremental rate applicable to just the new project to use in generating its cash flows.

A corporation with a continuing base of operations that places it consistently in the highest tax bracket will have both marginal and average federal tax rates of 35%. For such firms, the tax rate on an additional investment project is, naturally, 35%. If state income taxes are considered, the combined state and federal marginal tax rate may be close to 40%. But for corporations in lower tax brackets and those that fluctuate between losses and profits, marginal and average tax rates are likely to vary. For such corporations, estimating a prospective incremental tax rate for a new investment project may be difficult. The only solution may be to perform scenario analysis, which is to examine, for each potential situation, how much the income tax fluctuates from undertaking the project. (In other words, calculate the total taxes and the incremental taxes for each scenario.)

EXAMPLE 10.2 Calculation of Net Income Attributable to New Project

Tucker Enterprise Inc. is considering a project that requires a numerically controlled (NC) machine for $28,000 (year 0) and plans to use it for five years, after which time it will be scrapped. The allowed depreciation deduction during the first year is $4,000 because the equipment falls into the seven-year MACRS property category. (The first-year depreciation rate is 14.29%.) The cost of the goods produced by this NC machine should include a charge for the depreciation of the machine. Suppose the company estimates the following revenues and expenses, including the depreciation for the first operating year:

- Gross income = $50,000
- Cost of goods sold = $20,000
- Depreciation on the NC machine = $4,000
- Operating expenses = $6,000

Without the project, the company's taxable income from regular business operations amounts to $20 million, which places the company in the highest tax bracket of 35%. Compute the net income from the project during the first year.

DISSECTING THE PROBLEM

A corporation with $20 million taxable income from a continuing base of operations will have both marginal and average federal tax rates of 35%. That means the taxable income from the project will be taxed at 35%.

Given: Gross income and expenses as stated; income-tax rate = 35%.

Find: Net income.

METHODOLOGY

Compute net income.

SOLUTION

We consider the purchase of the machine to have been made at the end of year 0, which is also the beginning of year 1. (Note that our example explicitly assumes that the only depreciation charges for year 1 are those for the NC machine, a situation that may not be typical.)

Item	Amount
Gross income (revenues)	$50,000
Expenses	
Cost of goods sold	$20,000
Depreciation	$4,000
Operating expenses	$6,000
Taxable income	$20,000
Taxes (35%)	$7,000
Net income	$13,000

COMMENTS: In this example, the inclusion of a depreciation expense reflects the true cost of doing business. This expense is meant to correspond to the amount of the total cost of the machine that has been utilized, or "used up," during the first year. This example also highlights some of the reasons that income-tax laws govern the depreciation of assets. If the company were allowed to claim the entire $28,000 as a year 1 expense, a discrepancy would exist between the one-time cash outlay for the machine's cost and the gradual benefits of its productive use. This discrepancy would lead to dramatic variations in the firm's net income, and net income would become a less accurate measure of the organization's performance. On the other hand, failing to account for this cost at all would lead to increased reported profit during the accounting period. In this situation, the profit would be a "false profit" in that it would not accurately account for the usage of the machine. Capitalizing the purchase cost over time allows the company a logical distribution of costs that matches the utilization of the machine's value.

10.4 Incremental Cash Flows from Undertaking a Project

When a company purchases a fixed asset such as equipment, it makes an investment. The company commits funds today with the expectation of earning a return on those funds in the future. For a fixed asset, the future return is in the form of cash flows generated by the profitable use of the asset. In evaluating a capital investment, we are concerned only with those cash flows that result directly from the investment. These cash flows, called **differential**, or **incremental, cash flows**, represent the change in the firm's total cash flow that occurs as a direct result of the investment.

In this section, we will look into some of the cash flow elements common to most investments. Once the cash flow elements are determined (both inflows and outflows), we may group them into three areas according to their use or sources: (1) elements associated with operations, (2) elements associated with investment activities (such as capital expenditures), and (3) elements associated with project financing (such as borrowing). The main purpose of grouping cash flows in this way is to provide information about the operating, investing, and financing activities of a project.

10.4.1 Operating Activities

In general, cash flows from operations include current sales revenues, cost of goods sold, operating expenses, and income taxes. Cash flows from operations should generally reflect the cash effects of transactions entering into the determination of net income. The interest portion of a loan repayment is a deductible expense allowed when net income is determined and is included in the operating activities. Since we usually look only at yearly flows, it is logical to express all cash flows on a yearly basis.

Although depreciation has a direct impact on net income, it is *not* a cash outlay; as such, it is important to distinguish between annual income in the presence of depreciation and annual operating cash flow. The situation described in Example 10.2 demonstrates the difference between depreciation costs as expenses and the cash flow generated by the purchase of a fixed asset. In this example, cash in the amount

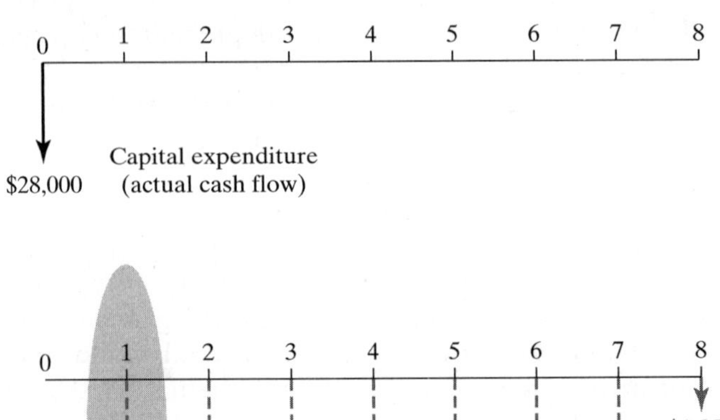

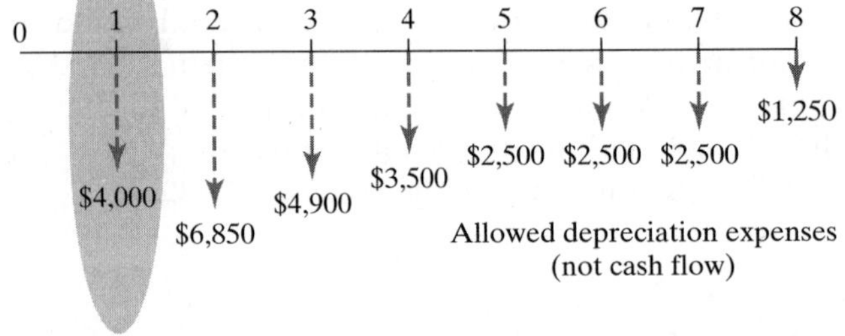

Figure 10.7 Capital expenditure versus depreciation expenses

of $28,000 was expended in year 0, but the $4,000 depreciation charged against the income in year 1 is not a cash outlay. Figure 10.7 summarizes the difference.

Therefore, we can determine the net cash flow from operations by using either (1) the net income or (2) the cash flow by computing income taxes in a separate step. When we use net income as the starting point for cash flow determination, we should add any noncash expenses (mainly, depreciation and amortization expenses) to net operating income in order to estimate the net cash flow from the operation. It is easy to show mathematically that the two approaches are identical:

$$\text{Cash flow from operation} = \text{Net income} + (\text{Depreciation and Amortization}).$$

EXAMPLE 10.3 Cash Flow from Operation

For the situation described in Example 10.2, assume that (1) all sales are cash sales and (2) all expenses except depreciation were paid during year 1. How much cash would be generated from operations?

DISSECTING THE PROBLEM

Depreciation and amortization are different from other expenses as they *are not* really cash outflows. Even though depreciation (or amortization expense) is deducted from revenue for tax or book purposes on a yearly basis, no cash is paid to anyone except when the asset was purchased.

Given: Net-income components as in Example 10.2.
Find: Cash flow from operation.

METHODOLOGY

Generate a cash-flow statement.

SOLUTION

We can generate a cash-flow statement by simply examining each item in the income statement and determining which items actually represent cash receipts or cash disbursements. Some of the assumptions listed in the statement of the problem make this process simpler. We summarize our findings as follows:

Item	Income	Cash Flow
Gross income (revenues)	$50,000	$50,000
Expenses		
Cost of goods sold	$20,000	−$20,000
Depreciation	$4,000	
Operating expenses	$6,000	−$6,000
Taxable income	$20,000	
Taxes (35%)	$7,000	−$7,000
Net income	$13,000	
Cash flow from operations		$17,000

The second column shows the income statement, and the third column shows the statement on a cash-flow basis. The sales of $50,000 are all cash sales. Costs other than depreciation were $26,000; these costs were paid in cash, leaving $24,000. Depreciation is not a cash flow; that is, the firm did not pay $4,000 in depreciation expenses. Taxes, however, are paid in cash, so the $7,000 for taxes must be deducted from the $24,000, leaving a net cash flow from operations of $17,000.

COMMENTS: Figure 10.8 illustrates how the net cash flow is related to the net income. The procedure for calculating net income is identical to that used for

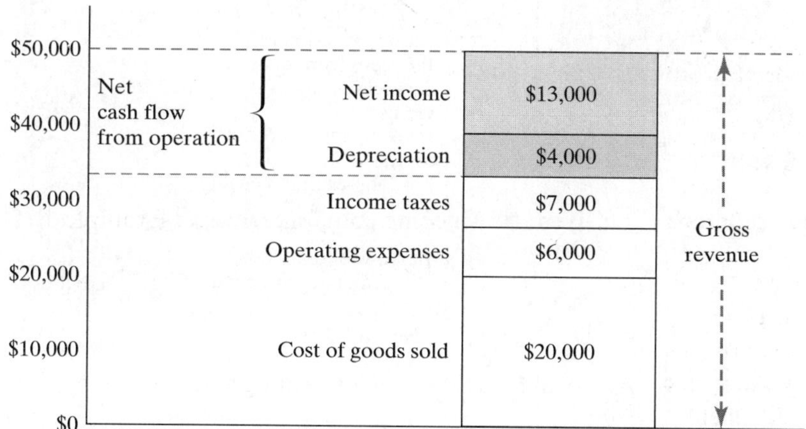

Figure 10.8 Relationship between net income and operating cash flow

obtaining net cash flow (after tax) from operations with the exception of depreciation, which is excluded from the net cash flow computation. Depreciation is needed only for computing income taxes.

10.4.2 Investing Activities

As shown in Figure 10.9, three types of investment flows are associated with buying a piece of equipment: (1) the original investment, (2) the salvage value at the end of the equipment's useful life, and (3) the **working-capital investment** (or recovery). Here, *the investment in working capital typically refers to the investment made in nondepreciable assets,* such as carrying raw-material inventories. The distinction between investment in physical assets and investment in working capital is as follows.

- *Investment in physical assets* should be capitalized (depreciated) over the depreciable life of the asset. Any salvage value of the asset exceeding its book value is subject to taxation as a gain.
- *Investment in working capital* should be treated as capital expenditure, but no depreciation deduction is allowed. Any recovery of working capital is not viewed as income, so there is no tax consequence.

We will assume that our outflows for both capital investment and working-capital investment take place in year 0. It is possible, however, that both investments will not occur instantaneously but over a few months as the project gets into gear; we could then use year 1 as an investment year. (Capital expenditures may occur over several years before a large investment project becomes fully operational. In this case, we should enter all expenditures as they occur.) For a small project, either method of timing these flows is satisfactory because the numerical differences are likely to be insignificant.

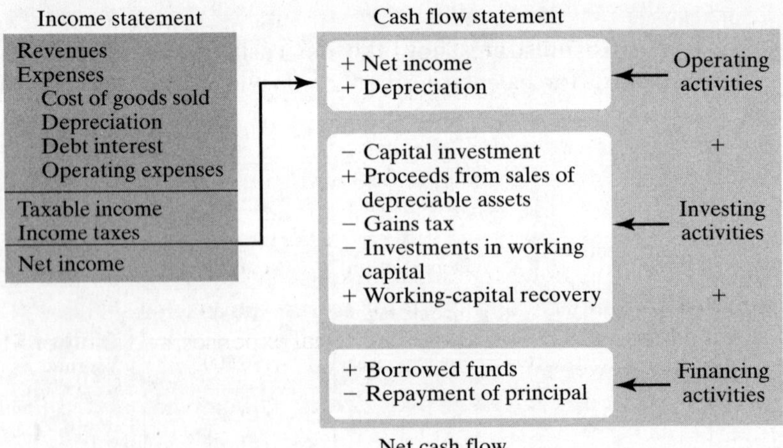

Figure 10.9   A typical format used in presenting a net cash flow statement

10.4.3 Financing Activities

Cash flows classified as financing activities include (1) the amount of borrowing and (2) the repayment of principal. Recall that interest payments are tax-deductible expenses, so they are classified as operating, not financing, activities.

The net cash flow for a given year is simply the sum of the net cash flows from operating, investing, and financing activities. Figure 10.9 can be used as a road map when you set up a cash flow statement because it classifies each type of cash flow element as an operating, investing, or financing activity.

10.5 Developing Project Cash Flow Statements

In this section, we will illustrate through a series of numerical examples how we actually prepare a project's cash flow statement; using a generic version in Figure 10.9, we first determine the net income from operations and then adjust the net income by adding any noncash expenses, mainly depreciation (or amortization). We will also consider a case in which a project generates a negative taxable income for an operating year.

10.5.1 When Projects Require Only Operating and Investing Activities

We will start with the simple case of determining after-tax cash flows for an investment project with only operating and investment activities. This is a situation in which the firm has enough funds to finance the entire investment, either using cash generated from its regular business operation or issuing common stock to investors (or simply known as **equity** financing). In the next section, we will add complexities to this problem by including financing borrowing activities.

EXAMPLE 10.4 Cash Flow Statement with Only Operating and Investing Activities

G&W Machine Shop is evaluating the proposed acquisition of a new milling machine. The milling machine costs $150,000 and would cost another $12,000 to modify it for special use by the company. The milling machine has an estimated service life of five years, with a salvage value of $45,000. With this milling machine, the firm will be able to generate additional annual revenues of $175,000. However, it requires a specially trained operator to run the machine. This will entail $60,000 in annual labor, $20,000 in annual material expenses, and another $10,000 in annual overhead (power and utility) expenses. It also requires an investment in working capital in the amount of $25,000, which will be recovered in full at the end of year 5.

The milling machine falls into the MACRS seven-year class. Find the year-by-year after-tax net cash flow for the project at a 40% marginal tax rate, and determine the net present worth of the project at the company's MARR of 15% (after tax).

DISSECTING THE PROBLEM

We will employ the business convention that no signs (positive or negative) be used in preparing the income statement except in the situation where we have a negative taxable income or tax savings. In this situation, we will use () to denote a negative entry. However, in preparing the cash-flow statement, we will observe explicitly the sign convention: A positive sign indicates a cash inflow; a negative sign, or (), indicates a cash outflow.

Given: Previously mentioned cash-flow information.
Find: After-tax cash flow.

METHODOLOGY

Compute after-tax cash flow.

SOLUTION

We can approach the problem in two steps by using the format shown in Figure 10.9 to generate an income statement and then a cash-flow statement. Table 10.1 summarizes the cash-flow statement associated with the milling machine project. The following notes explain the essential items in Table 10.1:

- **Revenue:** The revenues and costs are uniform annual flows in years 1 through 5. Annual revenues do not have to be uniform.
- **Expenses (excluding depreciation):** In our example, we assumed that the annual labor cost, materials cost, and overhead are all constant throughout the project period.
- **Depreciation calculation:** In year 0 (that is, at present), we have an investment cost of $162,000 for the equipment.[5] This cost will be depreciated in years 1 through 5. Since the equipment is held for only five years (shorter than the recovery period), the applicable depreciation amounts would be as follows:

Period	Dep. Rate (%)	Dep. Amount	Book Value
1	14.286%	$23,143	$138,857
2	24.490%	$39,673	$99,184
3	17.493%	$28,338	$70,845
4	12.495%	$20,242	$50,604
5	$\frac{8.925\%}{2}$	$7,229	$43,375

[5] We will assume that the asset is purchased and placed in service at the beginning of year 1 (or the end of year 0) and that the first year's depreciation will be claimed at the end of year 1.

TABLE 10.1   **Cash Flow Statement for the Milling Machine Project (Example 10.4)**

	A	B	C	D	E	F	G
1							
2	**Income Statement**						
3	End of Year	0	1	2	3	4	5
4							
5	Revenue		$ 175,000	$ 175,000	$ 175,000	$ 175,000	$ 175,000
6	Expenses:						
7	Labor		$ 60,000	$ 60,000	$ 60,000	$ 60,000	$ 60,000
8	Materials		$ 20,000	$ 20,000	$ 20,000	$ 20,000	$ 20,000
9	Overhead		$ 10,000	$ 10,000	$ 10,000	$ 10,000	$ 10,000
10	Depreciation		$ 23,143	$ 39,673	$ 28,338	$ 20,242	$ 7,229
11							
12	Taxable Income		$ 61,857	$ 45,327	$ 56,662	$ 64,758	$ 77,771
13	Income Taxes (40%)		$ 24,743	$ 18,131	$ 22,665	$ 25,903	$ 31,108
14							
15	Net Income		$ 37,114	$ 27,196	$ 33,997	$ 38,855	$ 46,663
16							
17	**Cash Flow Statement**						
18	Operating Activities:						
19	Net Income		$ 37,114	$ 27,196	$ 33,997	$ 38,855	$ 46,663
20	Depreciation		$ 23,143	$ 39,673	$ 28,338	$ 20,242	$ 7,229
21	Investment Activities:						
22	Milling machine	$ (162,000)					
23	Salvage Value						$ 45,000
24	Gains Tax						$ (650)
25	Working capital	$ (25,000)					$ 25,000
26							
27	Net Cash Flow	$ (187,000)	$ 60,257	$ 66,869	$ 62,335	$ 59,097	$ 123,242
28							
29							
30		PW(15%)=	$ 52,008				
31		IRR =	25.12%				
32							
33							
34							

Cell G23/G24 formula: `=-(G23-(-B22-SUM(C10:G10)))*0.4`

Cell C30 formula: `=NPV(15%,C27:G27)+B27`

Cell C31 formula: `=IRR(B27:G27,15%)`

Note that the fifth-year depreciation would ordinarily be $14,458 but is halved due to the half-year convention. We now have a value for our unknown D_n, which will enable us to complete the cell entries from C10 to G10.

- **Taxable income:** Once we find depreciation allowances for each year, we can easily compute the results for years 1 through 5, which have fixed revenue and expense entries, including the variable depreciation charges.

- **Salvage value and gains tax:** In year 5, we must deal with two aspects of the asset's disposal: salvage value and taxable gains. We list the estimated salvage value as a positive cash flow. Taxable gains are calculated as follows:

1. The total depreciation in years 1 through 5 is $118,625.
2. The book value at the end of year 5 is the cost basis minus the total depreciation, or $162,000 − $118,625 = $43,375.
3. The taxable gains on the sale are the salvage value minus the book value, or $45,000 − $43,375 = $1,625. (The salvage value is less than the cost basis, so these gains are ordinary gains.)
4. The tax on the ordinary gains is $1,625 × 40% = $650. This is the amount placed in the table in cell G24.

- **Working capital:** The investment in working capital is shown in cell B25, and its recovery appears in cell G25. As mentioned earlier, there are no tax consequences on the recovery amount even though it is a positive cash inflow.
- **Investment analysis:** Once we obtain the project's net cash flows after-tax, we can determine their equivalent present worth at the firm's discount rate. Since this series does not contain any patterns to simplify our calculations, we must find the net present worth of each payment. Using $i = 15\%$, we have

$$
\begin{aligned}
\text{PW}(15\%) = {} & -\$187,000 + \$60,257(P/F, 15\%, 1) \\
& + \$66,869(P/F, 15\%, 2) + \$62,335(P/F, 15\%, 3) \\
& + \$59,097(P/F, 15\%, 4) + \$123,242(P/F, 15\%, 5) \\
= {} & \$52,008.
\end{aligned}
$$

This result means that investing $187,000 in the milling machine project would bring in enough revenues to recover the initial investment and the cost of funds with a surplus of $52,008. Clearly, this is a good project to undertake.

TABLE 10.2 An Alternative Way of Preparing the Cash Flow Statement

	A	B	C	D	E	F	G	H	I	J	K
1											
2		Investment									
3	Year	Milling	Working	Revenue	Labor	Materials	Overhead	Depreciation	Taxable	Income	Net Cash
4	End	Machine	Capital						Income	Taxes	Flow
5											
6	0	($162,000)	($25,000)								($187,000)
7	1			$175,000	$60,000	$20,000	$10,000	$23,143	$61,857	$24,743	$60,257
8	2			$175,000	$60,000	$20,000	$10,000	$39,673	$45,327	$18,131	$66,869
9	3			$175,000	$60,000	$20,000	$10,000	$28,338	$56,662	$22,665	$62,335
10	4			$175,000	$60,000	$20,000	$10,000	$20,242	$64,758	$25,903	$59,097
11	5			$175,000	$60,000	$20,000	$10,000	$7,229	$77,771	$31,108	$123,242
12		$45,000	$25,000						$1,625	$650	
13											
14				=B12-(-B6-SUM(H7:H11))				=D11-SUM(E11:H11)			
15											
16											
17							=B10+C10+D10-SUM(E10:G10)-J10				
18											
19				=(B11+C11+D11-SUM(E11:G11)-J11)+(B12+C12+D12-SUM(E12:G12)-J12)							=I12*0.4
20											
21											
22											

COMMENTS: There is an alternative way of preparing the cash flow statement. A tabular format widely used in traditional engineering economics texts is shown in Table 10.2. Unlike the income-statement approach shown in Table 10.1, you may skip the entire process of computing the net income, thereby computing income taxes directly. However, most firms prepare the cash-flow statement according to a format similar to Table 10.1, as they want to know both net income as well as cash-flow figures. Therefore, we will use the cash-flow statement format from Table 10.1 whenever possible throughout this text.

10.5.2 When Projects Are Financed with Borrowed Funds

Many companies use a mixture of debt and equity to finance their physical plant and equipment. The ratio of total debt to total investment, generally called the **debt ratio**, represents the percentage of the total initial investment provided by borrowed funds. For example, a debt ratio of 0.3 indicates that 30% of the initial investment is borrowed and the rest is provided from the company's earnings (also known as **equity**). Since interest is a tax-deductible expense, companies in high tax brackets may incur lower after-tax interest costs by financing through debt. (The method of loan repayment can also have a significant impact on taxes.)

EXAMPLE 10.5 Cash Flow Statement with Financing (Borrowing) Activities

Rework Example 10.4, assuming that $64,800 of the $162,000 paid for the investment is obtained through debt financing (debt ratio $= 0.4$). The loan is to be repaid in equal annual installments at 12% interest over five years. The remaining $97,200 will be provided by equity (e.g., from retained earnings).

DISSECTING THE PROBLEM	
	Given: Same scenario as in Example 10.4, but $64,800 is borrowed and repaid in equal installments over five years at 12%.
	Find: Net after-tax cash flows in each year.
METHODOLOGY	**SOLUTION**
Compute after-tax cash flow.	We first need to compute the size of the annual loan repayment installments:

$$\$64,800(A/P, 12\%, 5) = \$17,976.$$

Next, we determine the repayment schedule of the loan by itemizing both the interest and the principal represented in each annual repayment.

The resulting after-tax cash flow is detailed in Table 10.3. The present-worth equivalent of the after-tax cash flow series is

TABLE 10.3   **Cash Flow Statement for the Milling Machine Project with Debt Financing (Example 10.5)**

	A	B	C	D	E	F	G
1							
2	**Income Statement**						
3	End of Year	0	1	2	3	4	5
4							
5	Revenue		$ 175,000	$ 175,000	$ 175,000	$ 175,000	$ 175,000
6	Expenses:						
7	Labor		$ 60,000	$ 60,000	$ 60,000	$ 60,000	$ 60,000
8	Materials		$ 20,000	$ 20,000	$ 20,000	$ 20,000	$ 20,000
9	Overhead		$ 10,000	$ 10,000	$ 10,000	$ 10,000	$ 10,000
10	Debt Interest		$ 7,776	$ 6,552	$ 5,181	$ 3,646	$ 1,926
11	Depreciation		$ 23,143	$ 39,673	$ 28,338	$ 20,242	$ 7,229
12							
13	Taxable Income		$ 54,081	$ 38,775	$ 51,481	$ 61,112	$ 75,845
14	Income Taxes (40%)		$ 21,632	$ 15,510	$ 20,592	$ 24,445	$ 30,338
15							
16	Net Income		$ 32,449	$ 23,265	$ 30,889	$ 36,667	$ 45,507
17				=IPMT(12%,2,5,-64800)			
18	**Cash Flow Statement**						
19	Operating Activities:						
20	Net Income		$ 32,449	$ 23,265	$ 30,889	$ 36,667	$ 45,507
21	Depreciation		$ 23,143	$ 39,673	$ 28,338	$ 20,242	$ 7,229
22	Investment Activities:						
23	Milling machine	$ (162,000)					
24	Salvage Value		=-(G24-(-B23-SUM(C11:G11)))*0.4				$ 45,000
25	Gains Tax						$ (650)
26	Working capital	$ (25,000)					$ 25,000
27	Financing Activities:		=PPMT(12%,D3,5,64800)				
28	Borrowed Funds	$ 64,800					
29	Principal Repayment		$ (10,200)	$ (11,424)	$ (12,795)	$ (14,330)	$ (16,050)
30							
31	Net Cash Flow	$ (122,200)	$ 45,392	$ 51,514	$ 46,432	$ 42,579	$ 106,036
32							
33							
34	PW(15%)=	$ 63,816	=NPV(15%,C31:G31)+B31				
35	IRR =	32.95%					
36		=IRR(B31:G31,15%)					

$$PW(15\%) = -\$122,200 + \$45,392(P/F, 15\%, 1) + \cdots$$

$$+ \$106,036(P/F, 15\%, 5)$$

$$= \$63,816.$$

When this amount is compared with the amount found in the case that involved no borrowing, $52,008, we see that debt financing actually increases the present worth by $11,808. This surprising result is caused entirely by the fact that the firm is able to borrow the funds at a lower rate, 12%, than its MARR (opportunity cost rate) of 15%. However, we should be careful in interpreting the result. It is true, to some extent, that firms can usually borrow money at lower rates than their MARR. However, if the firm can borrow money at a significantly lower rate, this factor also affects the firm's MARR because the borrowing rate is one of the elements used in determining the MARR as we will see in Section 11.4. Therefore, a significant difference between present values with borrowing and without borrowing is not always expected in practice.

Amount financed: $64,800, or 40% of total capital expenditure

Financing rate: 12% per year

Annual installment: $17,976, or A = $64,800 (A/P, 12%, 5)

End of Year	Beginning Balance	Interest Payment	Principal Payment	Ending Balance
1	$64,800	$7,776	$10,200	$54,600
2	$54,600	$6,552	$11,424	$43,176
3	$43,176	$5,181	$12,795	$30,381
4	$30,381	$3,646	$14,330	$16,051
5	$16,051	$1,926	$16,051	$0

$17,976

Note: The amount of interest and principal to be paid in each period can be easily obtained with Excel.

- Interest payment: = IMPT (rate, period, loan life, borrowing amount). For example, to find the interest payment in period 2, we use the following format: " = IMPT(12%,2,5,−64800)"
- Principal payment: = PPMT (rate, period, loan life, borrowing amount). For example, to find the principal payment in period 2, we use the following format: " = PPMT(12%,2,5,−64800)"

10.6 Effects of Inflation on Project Cash Flows

We will now consider the effects of inflation in determining the project cash flows. We are especially interested in three elements of project cash flows: (1) depreciation expenses, (2) interest expenses, and (3) investment in working capital. The first two elements are essentially immune to the effects of inflation, as they are always given in actual dollars. We will also consider the complication of how to proceed when multiple price indices have been used to generate various project cash flows. Capital projects requiring increased levels of **working capital** suffer from inflation because additional cash must be invested to maintain new price levels. For example, if the cost of inventory increases, additional cash infusions are required in order to maintain appropriate inventory levels over time. A similar phenomenon occurs with funds committed to account receivables. These additional working-capital requirements can significantly reduce a project's profitability or rate of return.

10.6.1 Depreciation Allowance under Inflation

Because depreciation expenses are calculated on some base-year purchase amount (historical cost), they do not increase over time to keep pace with inflation. Thus, they lose some of their value to defer taxes in real terms, because inflation drives up the general price level and, hence, taxable income. Similarly, the selling prices of depreciable assets can increase with the general inflation rate, and because any gains on salvage values are taxable, they can result in increased taxes. Example 10.6 illustrates how a project's profitability changes under an inflationary economy.

EXAMPLE 10.6 Effects of Inflation on Projects with Depreciable Assets

Reconsider Example 10.5 where 40% of the investment required by the milling machine center project was financed by a loan. A summary of the financial facts in the absence of inflation is shown in the following table.

Recall that the after-tax cash flow for the milling machine project was given in Table 10.3, and the net present worth of the project in the absence of inflation was calculated to be $63,816.

What will happen to this investment project if the general inflation rate $(\bar{f})$ during the next five years is expected to be 5% annually? Sales, operating costs, and working-capital requirements are assumed to increase accordingly. Depreciation and interest expenses will remain unchanged, but taxes, profits, and thus cash flow will be higher. The firm's inflation-free interest rate (i') is known to be 15%.

(a) Determine the PW of the project.

(b) Determine the real rate of return for the project.

Project Description	Milling Machine Project in the Absence of Inflation
Required investment:	$162,000
Investment in working capital:	$25,000
Debt ratio (0.40), meaning that 40% of the capital will be borrowed at 12% interest:	$64,800
Project life:	5 years
Salvage value:	$45,000
Depreciation method:	7-year MACRS
Annual revenues:	$175,000 per year
Annual expenses:	
Labor	$60,000 per year
Material	$20,000 per year
Overhead	$10,000 per year
Marginal tax rate:	40%
Inflation-free interest rate (i'):	15%

DISSECTING THE PROBLEM

Given: Financial data as shown in Table 10.3 but with a general inflation rate of 5%.

Find: (a) PW of the after-tax project cash flows and (b) real rate of return of the project.

METHODOLOGY	SOLUTION
Compute present worth and real rate of return.	(a) Table 10.4 shows the after-tax cash flows in actual dollars. Since we are dealing with cash flows in actual dollars, we need to find the market interest rate (see Section 4.3.3). The market interest rate to use is $i = 0.15 + 0.05 + (0.15)(0.05) = 20.75\%$.

(a) Table 10.4 shows the after-tax cash flows in actual dollars. Since we are dealing with cash flows in actual dollars, we need to find the market interest rate (see Section 4.3.3). The market interest rate to use is $i = 0.15 + 0.05 + (0.15)(0.05) = 20.75\%$.

$$PW(20.75\%) = -\$122,200 + \$46,692(P/F, 20.75\%, 1) + \cdots$$
$$+ \$132,974(P/F, 20.75\%, 5)$$
$$= \$60,957.$$

Since $PW(20.75\%) > 0$, the investment is still economically attractive.

(b) If you calculate the rate of return of the project on the basis of actual dollars, it will be 38.77% as shown in Table 10.4. Since the market interest rate is 20.75%, the project is still justifiable. To find the real (inflation-free) rate of return, you can use the following relationship from Eq. (4.8):

$$i' = \frac{i - \bar{f}}{1 + \bar{f}} = \frac{0.3877 - 0.05}{1 + 0.05} = 32.16\%.$$

Since the inflation-free MARR is 15%, the project also can be justified on the basis of real dollars.

COMMENTS: All cash flow elements, except depreciation and interest expenses, are assumed to be in constant dollars. Since income taxes are levied on actual taxable income, we will use the actual-dollar analysis, which requires that all cash flow elements be expressed in actual dollars. We make the following observations:

- For the purposes of this illustration, all inflationary calculations are made as of year-end.
- Cash flow elements such as sales, labor, material, overhead, and selling price of the asset will be inflated at the general inflation rate. For example, whereas annual sales had been estimated at $175,000, under conditions of inflation they become 5% higher in year 1 (or $183,750), 10.25% higher in year 2 ($192,938), and so forth.
- Future cash flows in actual dollars for other elements can be obtained in a similar way.
- No change occurs in the investment in year 0 or in the depreciation and interest expenses, since these items are unaffected by expected future inflation.
- Investment in working capital will change with inflation. Working-capital levels can be maintained only by an additional infusion of cash. For example, the $25,000 investment in working capital made in year 0 will be recovered at the end of the first year, assuming a one-year recovery cycle. However, because of 5% inflation, the required working capital for the second year increases to $26,250. Thus, in addition to reinvesting the $25,000 recovered at the end of year 1, $1,250 worth of new cash must be made. The $26,250 will be recovered at the end of the second year. However, the project will need a 5% increase in working capital, or $27,563, for the third year, and so forth. The deficit amount must be financed at the beginning of each year. Eventually, no investment in

TABLE 10.4 **Cash Flow Statement for the Milling Machine Project under Inflation (Example 10.6)**

	A	B	C	D	E	F	G	H
1								
2	**Income Statement**							
3	End of Year	Inflation Rate	0	1	2	3	4	5
4								
5	Revenue	5%		$ 183,750	$ 192,938	$ 202,584	$ 212,714	$ 223,349
6	Expenses:							
7	Labor	5%		$ 63,000	$ 66,150	$ 69,458	$ 72,930	$ 76,577
8	Materials	5%		$ 21,000	$ 22,050	$ 23,153	$ 24,310	$ 25,526
9	Overhead	5%		$ 10,500	$ 11,025	$ 11,576	$ 12,155	$ 12,763
10	Debt Interest			$ 7,776	$ 6,552	$ 5,181	$ 3,646	$ 1,926
11	Depreciation			$ 23,143	$ 39,673	$ 28,338	$ 20,242	$ 7,229
12								
13	Taxable Income			$ 58,331	$ 47,488	$ 64,879	$ 79,430	$ 99,329
14	Income Taxes (40%)			$ 23,332	$ 18,995	$ 25,952	$ 31,772	$ 39,732
15								
16	Net Income			$ 34,999	$ 28,493	$ 38,927	$ 47,658	$ 59,597
17								
18	**Cash Flow Statement**							
19	Operating Activities:							
20	Net Income			$ 34,999	$ 28,493	$ 38,927	$ 47,658	$ 59,597
21	Depreciation			$ 23,143	$ 39,673	$ 28,338	$ 20,242	$ 7,229
22	Investment Activities:							
23	Milling machine		$ (162,000)					
24	Salvage Value	5%				=-(H24-(-C23-SUM(D11:H11)))*0.4		$ 57,433
25	Gains Tax							$ (5,623)
26	Working capital	5%	$ (25,000)	($1,250)	($1,313)	($1,378)	($1,447)	$ 30,388
27	Financing Activities:							
28	Borrowed Funds		$ 64,800					
29	Principal Repayment			$ (10,200)	$ (11,424)	$ (12,795)	$ (14,330)	$ (16,050)
30								
31	Net Cash Flow (Actual Dollars)		$ (122,200)	$ 46,692	$ 55,429	$ 53,092	$ 52,123	$ 132,974
32								
33								
34			PW(20.75%)=	$ 60,957	=NPV(20.75%,D31:H31)+C31			
35			IRR =	38.77%				
36					=IRR(C31:H31,15%)			
37								
38								

working capital is required in year 5, as the project terminates. Therefore, the firm recovers all the investments it made in working capital in a lump sum ($30,338) at the end of year 5, and it can use this fund for other purposes.

End of Year	0	1	2	3	4	5
Recovered Working Capital		$25,000	$26,250	$27,563	$28,941	$30,388
Required Working Capital	($25,000)	($26,250)	($27,563)	($28,941)	($30,388)	$0
Balance	($25,000)	($1,250)	($1,313)	($1,378)	($1,447)	$30,388

- The depreciation expense is a charge against taxable income, which reduces the amount of taxes paid and, as a result, increases the cash flow attributable to an investment by the amount of taxes saved. But the depreciation expense under existing tax laws is based on historic cost. As time goes by, the depreciation expense is charged to taxable income in dollars of declining purchasing power; as a result, the "real" cost of the asset is not totally reflected in the depreciation expense. Depreciation costs are thereby understated, and the taxable income is thus overstated, resulting in higher taxes.

- On the other hand, the debt payment schedule with a fixed-interest rate is not going to change as the lender experiences inflation. Therefore, you are paying back with cheaper dollars, resulting in higher profitability. In our example, the increase in profit due to debt financing is smaller than the increase in taxes paid plus additional cash required to maintain proper working capital, so we still see overall loss in NPW.

- The resale price of the asset is expected to increase at the general inflation rate. Therefore, the salvage value in actual dollars will be

$$\$45,000(1 + 0.05)^5 = \$57,433.$$

This increase in salvage value will also increase the taxable gains, as the book value remains unchanged. The calculations for both the book value and gains tax are shown in Table 10.4.

- Note that the PW in the absence of inflation was $63,816 in Example 10.5. The $2,859 decrease (known as inflation loss) in the PW under inflation, illustrated in this example, is due entirely to income-tax considerations and *working-capital drains.*

10.6.2 Handling Multiple Inflation Rates

As we noted in Chapter 4, the inflation rate f_j represents a rate applicable to a specific segment j of the economy. For example, if we are estimating the future cost of a piece of machinery, we should use the inflation rate appropriate for that item. Furthermore, we may need to use several rates in order to accommodate the different costs and revenues in our analysis. Example 10.7 introduces the complexity of multiple inflation rates.

EXAMPLE 10.7 Applying Specific Inflation Rates

In this example, we will rework Example 10.6 using different annual indices (differential inflation rates) in the prices of cash-flow components. Suppose that we expect the general rate of inflation, $\bar{f}$, to average 6% during the next five years. We also expect that the selling price (salvage value) of the equipment will increase at 3% per year, that wages (labor) and overhead will increase at 5% per year, and that the cost of material will increase at 4% per year. The working-capital requirement will increase at 5% per year. We expect sales revenue to climb at the general inflation rate. Table 10.5 shows the relevant calculations according to the income-statement format. For simplicity, all cash flows and inflation effects are assumed to occur at year-end. Determine the net present worth of this investment.

TABLE 10.5 Cash Flow Statement for the Milling Machine Project under Inflation (Multiple Price Indices)

	A	B	C	D	E	F	G	H
1								
2	**Income Statement**				=D5*(1+$B$5)			
3	End of Year	Inflation Rate	0	1	2	3	4	5
4								
5	Revenue	6%		$ 185,500	$ 196,630	$ 208,428	$ 220,933	$ 234,189
6	Expenses:							
7	Labor	5%		$ 63,000	$ 66,150	$ 69,458	$ 72,930	$ 76,577
8	Materials	4%		$ 20,800	$ 21,632	$ 22,497	$ 23,397	$ 24,333
9	Overhead	5%		$ 10,500	$ 11,025	$ 11,576	$ 12,155	$ 12,763
10	Debt Interest			$ 7,776	$ 6,552	$ 5,181	$ 3,646	$ 1,926
11	Depreciation			$ 23,143	$ 39,673	$ 28,338	$ 20,242	$ 7,229
12								
13	Taxable Income			$ 60,281	$ 51,598	$ 71,378	$ 88,563	$ 111,362
14	Income Taxes (40%)			$ 24,112	$ 20,639	$ 28,551	$ 35,425	$ 44,545
15								
16	Net Income			$ 36,169	$ 30,959	$ 42,827	$ 53,138	$ 66,817
17								
18	**Cash Flow Statement**							
19	Operating Activities:							
20	Net Income			$ 36,169	$ 30,959	$ 42,827	$ 53,138	$ 66,817
21	Depreciation			$ 23,143	$ 39,673	$ 28,338	$ 20,242	$ 7,229
22	Investment Activities:							
23	Milling machine		$ (162,000)	=-(H24-(-C23-SUM(D11:H11)))*0.4				
24	Salvage Value	3%						$ 52,167
25	Gains Tax							$ (3,517)
26	Working capital	5%	$ (25,000)	($1,250)	($1,313)	($1,378)	($1,447)	$ 30,388
27	Financing Activities:							
28	Borrowed Funds		$ 64,800					
29	Principal Repayment			$ (10,200)	$ (11,424)	$ (12,795)	$ (14,330)	$ (16,050)
30								
31	Net Cash Flow (Actual Dollars)		$ (122,200)	$ 47,862	$ 57,895	$ 56,992	$ 57,603	$ 137,034
32								
33								
34			PW(21.90%)=	$ 64,485		=NPV(21.9%,D31:H31)+C31		
35			IRR =	41.15%				
36					=IRR(C31:H31,15%)			
37								

DISSECTING THE PROBLEM

Given: Financial data as shown in Table 10.5 but with multiple inflation rates.

Find: PW of the after-tax project cash flows.

METHODOLOGY

SOLUTION

Once we determine the project cash flows in actual dollars, we must adjust the original discount rate of 15%, which is an inflation-free interest rate, i'. The appropriate interest rate to use is the market interest rate:

$$i = i' + \bar{f} + i'\bar{f} = 0.15 + 0.06 + (0.15)(0.06) = 21.90\%.$$

The equivalent present worth is obtained as follows:

$$PW(21.90\%) = -\$122{,}200 + \$47{,}862(P/F, 21.90\%, 1)$$
$$+ \$57{,}895(P/F, 21.90\%, 2) + \cdots$$
$$+ \$137{,}034(P/F, 21.90\%, 5)$$
$$= \$64{,}485.$$

COMMENTS: Whenever you are dealing with multiple price indices in economic analysis, the price index that will affect the market interest rate set by many financial institutions is the consumer price index. In other words, the general inflation rate is used in calculating the market interest rate, which computes the equivalent net present worth.

SUMMARY

■ Most manufacturing companies divide **manufacturing costs** into three broad categories: *direct materials, direct labor,* and *manufacturing overhead.* **Nonmanufacturing costs** are classified into two categories: *marketing* or *selling costs* and *administrative costs.*

■ For the purpose of valuing inventories and determining expenses for the balance sheet and income statement, costs are classified as either **product costs** or **period costs**.

■ For the purpose of predicting **cost behavior**—how costs will react to changes in activity—managers commonly classify costs into two categories: variable and fixed costs.

■ Cash flow (not net income) must be considered to evaluate the economic merit of any investment project. Recall that depreciation (or amortization) is not a cash flow but is deducted, along with other operating expenses, from gross income to find taxable income and, therefore, taxes. Accountants calculate net income by subtracting taxes from taxable income. But depreciation was subtracted to find taxable income, so it must be added back into net income if we wish to use the net-income figure as an intermediate step along the path to determining after-tax cash flow.

■ The tax rate to use in economic analysis is the incremental tax rate resulting from undertaking the project in question, not the overall tax rate or average tax rate.

■ Identifying and estimating relevant project cash flows is perhaps the most challenging aspect of engineering economic analysis. All cash flows can be organized into one of the following three categories:
1. Operating activities
2. Investing activities
3. Financing activities

■ The **income-statement approach** is typically used in organizing project cash flows. This approach groups cash flows according to whether they are associated with operating, investing, or financing functions.

- Project cash flows may be stated in one of two forms:
  Actual dollars (A_n): dollars that reflect the inflation or deflation in economy
  Constant dollars (A'_n): year-0 dollars

- Interest rates for project evaluation may be stated in one of two forms:
  Market interest rate (i): a rate that combines the effects of interest and inflation and is used with **actual-dollar analysis**
  Inflation-free interest rate (i'): a rate from which the effects of inflation have been removed and is used with constant-dollar analysis

SELF-TEST QUESTIONS

10s.1 J&J Electric Company expects to have taxable income of $320,000 from its regular business over the next two years. The company is considering a new residential wiring project for a proposed apartment complex during year 0. This two-year project requires purchase of new equipment for $30,000. The equipment falls into the MACRS five-year class. The equipment will be sold after two years for $12,000. The project will bring in additional revenue of $100,000 each year, but it is expected to incur an additional operating cost of $40,000 each year. What is the income tax rate to use in year 1 for this project evaluation?

(a) 39%

(b) 34%

(c) 33.77%

(d) 35.39%

10s.2 Consider the following financial data for an investment project:

- Required capital investment at $n = 0$: $100,000
- Project service life: 10 years
- Salvage value at $n = 10$: $15,000
- Annual revenue: $150,000
- Annual O&M costs (not including depreciation): $50,000
- Depreciation method for tax purpose: seven-year MACRS
- Income tax rate: 40%.

Determine the project cash flow at the end of year 10.

(a) $69,000

(b) $73,000

(c) $66,000

(d) $67,000

10s.3 Suppose that in Problem 10s.2, the firm borrowed the entire capital investment at 10% interest over 10 years. If the required principal and interest payments in year 10 are

- Principal payment: $14,795
- Interest payment: $1,480,

what would be the net cash flow at the end of year 10?

(a) $46,725
(b) $63,000
(c) $62,112
(d) $53,317

10s.4 A new absorption chiller system costs $360,000 and will save $52,500 in each of the next 12 years. The asset is classified as a seven-year MACRS property for depreciation purpose. The expected salvage value is $20,000. The firm pays taxes at a combined rate of 40% and has an MARR of 12%. What is the net present worth of the system?

(a) $46,725
(b) $63,739
(c) $62,112
(d) $53,317

10s.5 A corporation is considering purchasing a machine that costs $120,000 and will save $X per year after taxes. The cost of operating the machine, including maintenance and depreciation, is $20,000 per year after taxes. The machine will be needed for four years after which it will have a zero salvage value. If the firm wants a 14% rate of return after taxes, what is the minimum after-tax annual savings that must be generated to realize a 14% rate of return after taxes?

(a) $50,000
(b) $61,184
(c) $91,974
(d) $101,974

10s.6 A corporation is considering purchasing a machine that will save $200,000 per year before taxes. The cost of operating the machine, including maintenance, is $80,000 per year. The machine costing $150,000 will be needed for five years, after which it will have a salvage value of $25,000. A straight-line depreciation with no half-year convention applies (i.e., 20% each year). If the firm wants 15% rate of return after taxes, what is the net present value of the cash flows generated from this machine? The firm's income tax rate is 40%.

(a) $137,306
(b) $218,313
(c) $199,460
(d) $375,000

10s.7 Which of the following statements is *incorrect* under inflationary economy?

(a) Borrowers will always come out ahead as they pay back with cheaper dollars.
(b) In general, a business that has depreciable assets will pay more taxes in real dollars.
(c) In general, there will be more drain in working capital.
(d) Bond interest rates will tend to be higher in the financial market so that it would cost more to finance a new project.

Problem Statement Questions for 10s.8–10s.10

A firm is trying to choose between two machines to manufacture a new line of office furniture. The financial data for each machine have been compiled as follows:

	Machine A	Machine B
Initial investment required	$20,000	$12,000
Service life	6 years	3 years
Salvage value	$5,000	$3,000
Annual operating expenses	$4,000	$2,500
Annual operating revenue	$15,000	$12,500
Depreciation method	5-year MACRS	5-year MACRS

The firm's marginal tax rate is 40% and uses a 15% discount rate to value the projects. Also, assume that the required service period is indefinite.

10s.8 What is the internal rate of return (after tax) of machine A?

(a) 28%

(b) 39%

(c) 35%

(d) 43%

10s.9 What is the net present worth of machine B after tax over 3 years?

(a) $6,394

(b) $6,233

(c) $5,562

(d) $7,070

10s.10 Using the replacement chain method (machine B can be replaced with an identical machine at the end of year 3), determine which project should be adopted after tax.

(a) Machine A.

(b) Machine B.

(c) Either machine.

(d) Neither machine.

10s.11 Phoenix Construction Ltd. is considering the acquisition of a new 18-wheeler.

- The truck's base price is $80,000, and it will cost another $20,000 to modify it for special use by the company.
- This truck falls into the MACRS five-year class.
- It will be sold after three years (project life) for $30,000.
- The truck purchase will have no effect on revenues, but it is expected to save the firm $45,000 per year in before-tax operating costs, mainly in leasing expenses.
- The firm's marginal tax rate (federal plus state) is 40%, and its MARR is 15%.

What is the net present worth of this acquisition?

(a) −$45,158 (loss)

(b) $532

(c) $1,677

(d) $2,742

10s.12 A special purpose machine tool set would cost $20,000. The tool set will be financed by a $10,000 bank loan repayable in two equal annual installments at 10% compounded annually. The tool is expected to provide annual savings (material) of $30,000 for two years and is to be depreciated by the three-year MACRS method. This special machine tool will require annual O&M costs in the amount of $5,000. The salvage value at the end of two years is expected to be $8,000. Suppose that it is expected a 6% annual inflation during the project period. Assuming a marginal tax rate of 40% and an MARR of 20% (inflation adjusted), what is the net present worth of this project?

(a) $16,301

(b) $24,558

(c) $23,607

(d) $18,562

PROBLEMS

Cost Behavior

10.1 Identify which of the following costs are fixed and which are variable:
(a) Wages paid to temporary workers
(b) Property taxes on a factory building
(c) Property taxes on an administrative building
(d) Sales commission
(e) Electricity for machinery and equipment in a plant
(f) Heat and air conditioning for a plant
(g) Salaries paid to design engineers
(h) Regular maintenance on machinery and equipment
(i) Basic raw materials used in production
(j) Factory fire insurance

10.2 Classify the following costs into either being product cost or period cost:
(a) Raw material costs
(b) Income taxes paid
(c) Interest expenses on borrowed funds
(d) Wages incurred in producing products
(e) Fire insurance premium paid on factory buildings
(f) Electric bill for the warehouse operation
(g) Salary paid for engineers
(h) Material handling cost related to production
(i) Salary paid for plant manager
(j) Leasing expense for forklift trucks in warehouse operation
(k) Mortgage payments on factory buildings

10.3 Some commonly known costs associated with manufacturing operations are listed below:
(a) Paint shop superintendent's salary
(b) Labor costs in assembling a product
(c) Rent on a factory building
(d) Radio-frequency identification (RFID) units embedded in the final product during shipping

(e) Depreciation on machinery

(f) Lubricants used for machines

(g) CPU chips used in notebook production

(h) Paint used in automobile production

(i) Janitorial and custodial salaries

(j) Coffee beans used in packaging roasted coffee

(k) Sugar used in icecream production

(l) Electricity for operation of machines

(m) Electricity for heating and cooling the factory building

(n) Glue used in electronic board production

Classify each cost as being either variable or fixed with respect to volume or level of activity.

10.4 The accompanying figures depict a number of cost behavior patterns that might be found in a company's cost structure. The vertical axis on each graph represents total cost, and the horizontal axis on each graph represents level of activity (volume). For each of the given situations, identify the graph that illustrates the cost pattern involved. Any graph may be used more than once. (Adapted originally from the CPA exam; also found in R. H. Garrison and E. W. Noreen, *Managerial Accounting,* 9th edition, Irwin, 2009.)

(a) Electricity bill—a flat-rate fixed charge plus a variable cost after a certain number of kilowatt-hours are used.

(b) City water bill, which is computed as follows:

First 1,000,000 gallons	$1,000 flat, or less
Next 10,000 gallons	$0.003 per gallon used
Next 10,000 gallons	$0.006 per gallon used
Next 10,000 gallons	$0.009 per gallon used
⋮	⋮

(c) Depreciation of equipment, where the amount is computed by the straight-line method. When the depreciation rate was established, it was anticipated that the obsolescence factor would be greater than the wear-and-tear factor.

(d) Rent on a factory building donated by the city, where the agreement calls for a fixed-fee payment unless 200,000 labor-hours or more are worked, in which case no rent need be paid.

(e) Cost of raw materials, where the cost decreases by 5 cents per unit for each of the first 100 units purchased after which it remains constant at $2.50 per unit.

(f) Salaries of maintenance workers, where one maintenance worker is needed for every 1,000 machine hours or less (that is, 0 to 1,000 hours require one maintenance worker, 1,001 to 2,000 hours require two maintenance workers, etc.).

(g) Cost of raw materials used.

(h) Rent on a factory building donated by the county, where the agreement calls for rent of $100,000 less $1 for each direct labor-hour worked in excess of 200,000 hours, but a minimum rental payment of $20,000 must be paid.

(i) Use of a machine under a lease, where a minimum charge of $1,000 is paid for up to 400 hours of machine time. After 400 hours of machine time, an additional charge of $2 per hour is paid up to a maximum charge of $2,000 per period.

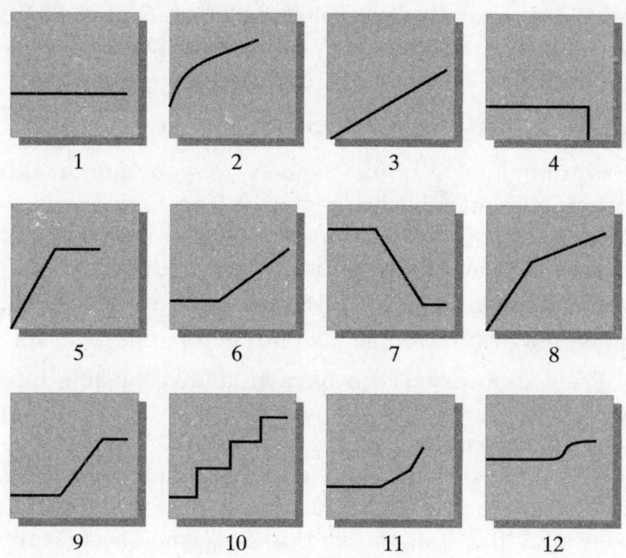

Contribution Margin and Break-Even Volume

10.5   Suppose that a company expects the following financial results from a project during its first year operation:

- Sales revenue: $250,000
- Variable costs: $80,000
- Fixed costs: $50,000
- Total unit produced and sold: 1,000 units

(a) Compute the contribution margin percentage.

(b) Compute the breakeven point in units sold.

10.6   Suppose ADI Corporation's breakeven sales volume is $450,000 with fixed costs of $200,000.

(a) Compute the contribution margin percentage.

(b) Compute the selling price if variable costs are $12 per unit.

10.7   Given the following information, answer the questions:

- The ratio of variable cost per unit divided by selling price per unit equals 0.25
- Fixed costs amount to $50,000

(a) Draw the cost-volume-profit diagram

(b) What is the break-even point?

(c) What effect would a 6% decrease in selling price have on the break-even point from part (b)?

10.8   The Austin Electric Company has three product lines of surge protectors commonly used in PC and other electronic devices—A, B, and C—having a contribution margin of $3, $2, and $1, respectively. The president foresees sales of 200,000 units in the coming period, consisting of 20,000 units of A, 100,000 units of B, and 80,000 units of C. The company's fixed costs for the period are $255,000.

(a) What is the company's break-even point in units, assuming that the given sales mix is maintained?

(b) If the mix is maintained, what is the total contribution margin when 200,000 units are sold? What is operating income?

(c) What would be operating income if 20,000 units of A, 80,000 units of B, and 100,000 units of C were sold? What is the new break-even point in units if these relationships persist in the next period?

Incremental (Marginal) Tax Rate in Project Evaluation

10.9 Buffalo Environmental Service expects to generate a taxable income of $350,000 from its regular business in 2012. The company is also considering a new venture: cleaning up oil spills made by fishing boats in lakes. This new venture is expected to generate an additional taxable income of $180,000.

(a) Determine the firm's marginal tax rates before and after the venture.

(b) Determine the firm's average tax rates before and after the venture.

10.10 Scottsdale Print Shop expects to have an annual taxable income of $300,000 from its regular business over the next two years. The company is also considering the proposed acquisition of a new printing machine to expand current business to offer in its product catalog. The machine's installed price is $105,000. The machine falls into the MACRS five-year class, and it will have an estimated salvage value of $30,000 at the end of six years. The machine is expected to generate additional before-tax revenue of $120,000 per year.

(a) Determine the company's annual marginal (incremental) tax rates over the next two years with the proposed investment in the printing machine.

(b) Determine the company's annual average tax rates over the next two years with the machine.

10.11 Delta Electric Company expects to have an annual taxable income of $500,000 from its residential accounts over the next two years. The company is also bidding on a two-year wiring service job for a large apartment complex. This commercial service requires the purchase of a new truck equipped with wire-pulling tools at a cost of $50,000. The equipment falls into the MACRS five-year class and will be retained for future use (instead of being sold) after two years, indicating no gain or loss on this property. The project will bring in additional annual revenue of $200,000, but it is expected to incur additional annual operating costs of $100,000. Compute the marginal tax rates applicable to the project's operating profits for the next two years.

10.12 A small manufacturing company has an estimated annual taxable income of $195,000. Due to an increase in business, the company is considering purchasing a new machine that will generate additional (before-tax) annual revenue of $80,000 over the next five years. The new machine requires an investment of $100,000, which will be depreciated under the five-year MACRS method.

(a) What is the increment in income tax caused by the purchase of the new machine in tax year 1?

(b) What is the incremental tax rate associated with the purchase of the new equipment in year 1?

10.13 Simon Machine Tools Company is considering the purchase of a new set of machine tools to process special orders over the next three years. The following financial information is available:

■ Without the project, the company expects to have a taxable income of $400,000 each year from its regular business over the next three years.

■ This three-year project requires the purchase of a new set of machine tools at a cost of $50,000. The equipment falls into the MACRS three-year class. The tools will be sold at the end of the project life for $10,000. The project will bring in additional annual revenue of $90,000, but it is expected to incur additional annual operating costs of $25,000.

(a) What are the additional taxable incomes (from undertaking the project) during years 1 through 3, respectively?

(b) What are the additional income taxes (from undertaking the new orders) during years 1 through 3, respectively?

Net Income versus Cash Flow

10.14 Jackson Heating & Air Company had sales revenue of $2,250,000 from operations during tax-year 1. Here are some operating data on the company for that year:

Labor expenses	$550,000
Materials costs	$385,000
Depreciation expenses	$132,500
Interest income on time deposit	$6,000
Bond interest income (nonoperating income)	$4,000
Interest expenses	$22,200
Rental expenses	$45,000
Proceeds from sale of old equipment with a book value of $20,000	$23,000

(a) What is Jackson's taxable gains?
(b) What is Jackson's taxable income?
(c) What are Jackson's marginal and average tax rates?
(d) What is Jackson's net cash flow after tax?

10.15 In 2012, Elway Aerospace Company had gross revenues of $1,200,000 from operations. The following financial transactions were posted during the year:

Manufacturing expenses (including depreciation of $45,000)	$450,000
Operating expenses (excluding interest expenses)	$120,000
A new short-term loan from a bank	$50,000
Interest expenses on borrowed funds (old and new)	$40,000
Old equipment sold	$60,000

The old equipment had a book value of $75,000 at the time of sale.
(a) What is Elway's income tax liability?
(b) What is Elway's operating income?
(c) What is the net cash flow?

Incremental Project Cash Flows

10.16 An asset in the five-year MACRS property class cost $100,000 and has a zero estimated salvage value after six years of use. The asset will generate annual revenues of $300,000 and will require $100,000 in annual labor costs and $50,000 in annual material expenses. There are no other revenues and expenses. Assume a tax rate of 40%.

(a) Compute the after-tax cash flows over the project life.

(b) Compute the NPW at MARR = 12%. Is this investment acceptable?

(c) Compute the IRR for this project.

10.17 An auto-part manufacturing company is considering the purchase of an industrial robot to do spot welding, which is currently done by skilled labor. The initial cost of the robot is $250,000, and the annual labor savings are projected to be $125,000. If purchased, the robot will be depreciated under MACRS as a seven-year recovery property. This robot will be used for five years after which the firm expects to sell it for $50,000. The company's marginal tax rate is 35% over the project period.

(a) Determine the net after-tax cash flows for each period over the project life.

(b) Is this a good investment at MARR of 15%?

10.18 You are considering purchasing a new injection molding machine. This machine will have an estimated service life of 10 years with a negligible after-tax salvage value. Its annual net after-tax operating cash flows are estimated to be $60,000. If you expect a 15% rate of return on investment, what would be the maximum amount that you should spend to purchase the injection molding machine?

10.19 A facilities engineer is considering a $50,000 investment in an energy management system (EMS). The system is expected to save $10,000 annually in utility bills for N years. After N years, the EMS will have a zero salvage value. In an after-tax analysis, how many years would N need to be in order for the engineer's company to earn a 10% return on the investment? Assume MACRS depreciation with a three-year class life and a 35% tax rate.

10.20 A corporation is considering a proposal for the purchase of a machine that will save $130,000 per year before taxes. The cost of operating the machine, including maintenance, is $20,000 per year. The machine will be needed for five years after which it will have a zero salvage value. MACRS depreciation will be used, assuming a three-year class life. The marginal income-tax rate is 40%. If the firm wants 12% IRR after taxes, how much can it afford to pay for this machine?

10.21 Atlanta Capital Leasing Company (ACLC) leases tractors to construction companies. The firm wants to set a three-year lease payment schedule for a tractor purchased at $53,000 from the equipment manufacturer. The asset is classified as a five-year MACRS property. The tractor is expected to have a salvage value of $22,000 at the end of three years of rental. ACLC will require the lessee to make a security deposit of $1,500 that is refundable at the end of the lease term. ACLC's marginal tax rate is 35%. If ACLC wants an after-tax return of 10%, what lease payment schedule should be set?

10.22 You are interested in purchasing a machine that will save $200,000 per year before taxes. The cost of operating the machine, including maintenance, is $80,000 per year. The machine, which costs $150,000, will be needed for five years after which it will have a salvage value of $25,000. The machine would qualify for a 7-year MACRS property. What is the net present value of the cash flows generated from this machine at 15%? The firm's income tax rate is 40%.

10.23 Peachtree Construction Company, a highway contractor, is considering the purchase of a new trench excavator that costs $300,000 and can dig a 3-foot-wide trench at the rate of 16 feet per hour. The contractor gets paid according to the usage of the equipment, $100 per hour. The expected average annual usage is 500 hours, and maintenance and operating costs will be $10 per hour. The contractor will depreciate the equipment by using a five-year MACRS, units-of-production method. At the end of five years, the excavator will be sold for $100,000.

(a) Assuming that the contractor's marginal tax rate is 35% per year, determine the annual after-tax cash flow.

(b) Is this a good investment if the contractor requires 15% return on investment?

10.24 Tucson Solar Company builds residential solar homes. Because of an anticipated increase in business volume, the company is considering the acquisition of a loader at a cost of $54,000. This acquisition cost includes delivery charges and applicable taxes. The firm has estimated that if the loader is acquired, the following additional revenues and operating expenses (excluding depreciation) should be expected:

End of Year	Additional Operating Revenue	Additional Operating Expenses, Excluding Depreciation	Allowed Tax Depreciation
1	$66,000	$29,000	$10,800
2	$70,000	$28,400	$17,280
3	$74,000	$32,000	$10,368
4	$80,000	$38,800	$6,221
5	$64,000	$31,000	$6,221
6	$50,000	$25,000	$3,110

The projected revenue is assumed to be in cash in the year indicated, and all the additional operating expenses are expected to be paid in the year in which they are incurred. The estimated salvage value for the loader at the end of the sixth year is $8,000. The firm's incremental (marginal) tax rate is 35%.

(a) What is the after-tax cash flow if the loader is acquired?

(b) What is the equivalent annual cash flow the firm can expect by owning and operating this loader at an interest rate of 12%?

10.25 An automaker is considering installing a three-dimensional (3-D) computerized styling system at a cost of $180,000 (including hardware and software). With the 3-D computer modeling system, designers will have the ability to view their design from many angles and to fully account for the space required for the engine and passengers. The digital information used to create the computer model can be revised in consultation with engineers, and the data can be used to run milling machines that make physical models quickly and precisely. The automaker expects to decrease turnaround time by 35% for new automobile models (from configuration to final design). The expected saving is $350,000 per year. The training and operating and maintenance cost for the new system is expected to be $80,000 per year. The system has a five-year useful life and can be depreciated as a five-year MACRS class. The system will have an estimated salvage value of $5,000. The automaker's marginal tax rate is 40%.

(a) Determine the annual cash flows for this investment.

(b) What is the return on investment for this project? The firm's MARR is 12%.

10.26 The Manufacturing Division of Ohio Vending Machine Company is considering its Toledo plant's request for a half-inch-capacity automatic screw-cutting machine to be included in the division's 2013 capital budget:

- Name of project: Mazda Automatic Screw Machine
- Project cost: $68,701
- Purpose of project: To reduce the cost of some of the parts that are now being subcontracted by this plant, to cut down on inventory by shortening lead time, and to better control the quality of the parts. The proposed equipment includes the following cost basis:

Machine cost	$48,635
Accessory cost	$8,766
Tooling	$4,321
Freight	$2,313
Installation	$2,110
Sales tax	$2,556
Total cost	$68,701

- Anticipated savings: as shown in the accompanying table.
- Tax depreciation method: seven-year MACRS.
- Marginal tax rate: 40%.
- MARR: 15%.

Item	Hours Present Machine Center Labor	Proposed Machine Center Labor	Present Method	Proposed Method
Setup		350 hrs		$7,700
Run	2,410 hrs	800 hrs		$17,600
Overhead				
Indirect labor				$3,500
Fringe benefits				$8,855
Maintenance				$1,350
Tooling				$6,320
Repair				$890
Supplies				$4,840
Power				$795
Taxes and insurance				$763
Other relevant costs:				
Floor space				$3,210
Subcontracting			$122,468	
Material				$27,655
Other				$210
Total			$122,468	$83,688
Operating advantage				$38,780

(a) Determine the net after-tax cash flows over the project life of six years. Assume a salvage value of $3,500.

(b) Is this project acceptable based on the PW criterion?

(c) Determine the IRR for this investment.

Effects of Working Capital

10.27 Reconsider Problem 10.17. Suppose that the project requires a $30,000 investment in working capital at the beginning of the project and the entire amount will be recovered at the end of project life. How does this investment in working capital change the net cash flows series?

10.28 Reconsider Problem 10.23. Suppose that the purchase also requires an investment in working capital in the amount of $50,000, which will be recovered in full at the end of year 5. Determine the net present worth of the project.

Effects of Borrowing on Project Cash Flows

10.29 Consider a project with an initial investment of $300,000, which must be financed at an interest rate of 12% per year. Assuming that the required repayment period is six years, determine the repayment schedule by identifying the principal as well as the interest payments for each of the following repayment methods:

(a) Equal repayment of the principal: $50,000 principal payment each year

(b) Equal repayment of the interest: $36,000 interest payment each year

(c) Equal annual installments: $72,968 each year

10.30 A special-purpose machine tool set would cost $30,000. The entire capital expenditure ($30,000) is to be borrowed with the stipulation that it be repaid by two equal end-of-year payments at 12% compounded annually. The tool is expected to provide annual savings (in material) of $45,000 for two years and is to be depreciated by the MACRS three-year recovery period. This special machine tool will require annual O&M costs in the amount of $12,000. The salvage value at the end of two years is expected to be $9,000. Assuming a marginal tax rate of 40% and MARR of 15%, what is the net present worth of this project?

10.31 The Balas Manufacturing Company is considering buying an overhead pulley system. The new system has a purchase price of $150,000, an estimated useful life and MACRS class life of five years, and an estimated salvage value of $10,000. The system is expected to enable the company to economize on electric power usage, labor, and repair costs, as well as to reduce the number of defective products made. A total annual savings of $95,000 will be realized if the new pulley system is installed. The company is in the 35% marginal tax bracket. The initial investment will be financed with 40% equity and 60% debt. The before-tax debt interest rate, which combines both short-term and long-term financing, is 12% with the loan to be repaid in equal annual installments over the project life.

(a) Determine the after-tax cash flows.

(b) Evaluate this investment project by using an MARR of 20%.

(c) Evaluate this investment project on the basis of the IRR criterion.

10.32 A toy manufacturer is considering the installation of a new process machine for its toy manufacturing facility. The machine costs $350,000 installed, will generate additional revenues of $120,000 per year, and will save $50,000 per year in labor and material costs. The machine will be financed by a $250,000 bank loan repayable in three equal annual principal installments plus 9% interest on the outstanding balance. The machine will be depreciated by seven-year MACRS. The useful life of this process machine is 10 years at which time it will be sold for $20,000. The combined marginal tax rate is 40%.

(a) Find the year-by-year after-tax cash flow for the project.

(b) Compute the IRR for this investment.

(c) At MARR = 18%, is this project economically justifiable?

10.33 Consider the following financial information about a retooling project at a computer manufacturing company:

- The project costs $2 million and has a five-year service life.
- The project can be classified as a seven-year property under the MACRS rule.
- At the end of the fifth year, any assets held for the project will be sold. The expected salvage value will be about 10% of the initial project cost.
- The firm will finance 40% of the project money from an outside financial institution at an interest rate of 10%. The firm is required to repay the loan with five equal annual payments.
- The firm's incremental (marginal) tax rate on this investment is 35%.
- The firm's MARR is 18%.

Use this financial information to complete the following tasks:

(a) Determine the after-tax cash flows.

(b) Compute the annual equivalent cost for this project.

10.34 A manufacturing company is considering the acquisition of a new injection-molding machine at a cost of $110,000. Because of a rapid change in product mix, the need for this particular machine is expected to last only eight years after which time the machine is expected to have a salvage value of $10,000. The annual operating cost is estimated to be $8,000. The addition of this machine to the current production facility is expected to generate annual revenue of $60,000. The firm has only $70,000 available from its equity funds, so it must borrow the additional $40,000 required at an interest rate of 10% per year with repayment of principal and interest in eight equal annual amounts. The applicable marginal income tax rate for the firm is 40%. Assume that the asset qualifies for a seven-year MACRS property classification.

(a) Determine the after-tax cash flows.

(b) Determine the NPW of this project at MARR = 14%.

10.35 Suppose an asset has a purchase cost of $15,000, a life of five years, a salvage value of $3,000 at the end of five years, and a net annual before-tax revenue of $7,500. The firm's marginal tax rate is 35%. The asset will be depreciated by five-year MACRS.

(a) Determine the cash flow after taxes, assuming that the purchase cost will be entirely financed by the equity funds.

(b) Rework part (a), assuming that the entire investment would be financed by a bank loan at an interest rate of 9%.

(c) Given a choice between paying the purchase cost up front from the firm's equity and using the financing method of part (b), show calculations to justify which is the better choice at an interest rate of 9%.

10.36 A construction company is considering the proposed acquisition of a new earthmover. The purchase price is $100,000, and an additional $25,000 is required to modify the equipment for special use by the company. The equipment falls into the MACRS five-year classification (tax life), and it will be sold after five years (project life) for $50,000. Purchase of the earthmover will have no effect on revenues, but it is expected to save the firm $60,000 per year in before-tax operating costs—mainly labor. The firm's marginal tax rate is 40%. Assume that the initial investment is to be financed by a bank loan at an interest rate of 10% payable annually. Determine the after-tax cash flows and the worth of investment for this project if the firm's MARR is known to be 12%.

10.37 A leading regional airline that is now carrying 54% of all the passengers that pass through the Southeast is considering the possibility of adding a new long-range aircraft to its fleet. The aircraft being considered for purchase is the Boeing 717-200, which is quoted at $35 million per unit. Boeing requires a 10% down payment at the time of delivery, and the balance is to be paid over a 10-year period at an interest rate of 9% compounded annually. The actual payment schedule calls for making only interest payments over the 10-year period, with the original principal amount to be paid off at the end of the 10th year. The airline expects to generate $40 million per year by adding this aircraft to its current fleet but also estimates an operating and maintenance cost of $30 million per year. The aircraft is expected to have a 15-year service life with a salvage value of 15% of the original purchase price. If the airline purchases the aircraft, it will be depreciated by the seven-year MACRS property classification. The firm's combined federal and state marginal tax rate is 38%, and its MARR is 18%.

(a) Determine the cash flow associated with the debt financing.

(b) Is this project acceptable?

Comparing Mutually Exclusive Alternatives

10.38 The headquarters building, Building A, owned by a rapidly growing company, is not large enough for current needs. A search for enlarged quarters revealed two new alternatives that would provide sufficient room, enough parking, and the desired appearance and location; or the company could remodel its existing building to create more usable space. The company's three options are as follows:

- ■ Option 1: Lease Building B for $144,000 per year.
- ■ Option 2: Purchase Building C for $800,000, including a $150,000 cost for land.
- ■ Option 3: Remodel Building A.

It is believed that land values will not decrease over the ownership period, but the value of all structures will decline to 10% of the purchase price in 30 years. Annual property tax payments are expected to be 5% of the purchase price. The present headquarters building is already paid for and is now valued at $300,000. The land it is on is appraised at $60,000. The structure can be remodeled at a cost of $300,000 to make it comparable with the other alternatives. However, the remodeled Building A will occupy part of the existing parking lot. An adjacent, privately owned parking lot can be leased for 30 years under an agreement that the first year's rental of $9,000 will increase by $500 each year. The annual property taxes on the remodeled property will again be 5% of the present valuation plus the cost to remodel. The study period for the comparison is 30 years, and the desired rate of return on investments is 12%. Assume that the firm's marginal tax rate is 40% and the new building (C) and remodeled structure will be depreciated under MACRS at a real-property recovery period of 39 years. If the annual upkeep costs are the same for all three alternatives, which one is preferable?

10.39 An international manufacturer of prepared food items needs 50,000,000 kWh of electrical energy a year with a maximum demand of 10,000 kW. The local utility presently charges $0.085 per kWh, a rate considered high throughout the industry. Because the firm's power consumption is so large, its engineers are considering installing a 10,000-kW steam-turbine plant. Three types of plant have been proposed as shown in the following table ($ units in thousands):

	Plant A	Plant B	Plant C
Average station heat rate (BTU/kWh)	16,500	14,500	13,000
Total investment (boiler, turbine, electrical, and structures)	$8,530	$9,498	$10,546
Annual operating cost:			
Fuel	$1,128	$930	$828
Operating labor	$616	$616	$616
Maintenance	$150	$126	$114
Supplies	$60	$60	$60
Insurance and property taxes	$10	$12	$14

The service life of each plant is expected to be 20 years. The plant investment will be subject to a 20-year MACRS property classification. The expected salvage value of the plant at the end of its useful life is about 10% of the original investment. The firm's MARR is known to be 12%. The firm's marginal income-tax rate is 39%.

(a) Determine the unit power cost ($/kWh) for each plant.

(b) Which plant would provide the most economical power?

10.40 H&H Machine Systems Inc. needs to acquire a new lift truck for transporting final products to their warehouse. One alternative is to purchase the lift truck for $40,000, which will be financed by a bank loan at an interest rate of 12%. The loan must be repaid in four equal installments payable at the end of each year. Under the borrow-to-purchase arrangement, H&H would have to maintain the truck at an annual cost of $1,200, payable at year-end. Alternatively, H&H could lease the truck on a four-year contract for a lease payment of $11,000 per year. Each annual lease payment must be made at the beginning of each year. The truck would be maintained by the lessor. The truck falls into the five-year MACRS classification, and it has a salvage value of $10,000, which is the expected market value after four years, at which time H&H plans to replace the truck, regardless of whether the company leases or buys. H&H has a marginal tax rate of 40% and an MARR of 15%.

(a) What is H&H's cost of leasing in present worth?

(b) What is H&H's cost of owning in present worth?

(c) Should the truck be leased or purchased?

10.41 Janet Wigandt, an electrical engineer for Instrument Control, Inc. (ICI), has been asked to perform a lease–buy analysis on a new pin-inserting machine for

ICI's PC-board manufacturing operation. The details of the two options are as follows:

- **Buy option:** The equipment costs $120,000. To purchase it, ICI could obtain a term loan for the full amount at 10% interest with four equal annual installments (end-of-year payments). The machine falls into a five-year MACRS property classification. Annual revenues of $200,000 and annual operating costs of $40,000 are anticipated. The machine requires annual maintenance at a cost of $10,000. Because technology is changing rapidly in pin-inserting machinery, the salvage value of the machine is expected to be only $20,000.

- **Lease option:** BLI is willing to write a four-year operating lease on the equipment for payments of $44,000 at the beginning of each year. Under this operating-lease arrangement, BLI will maintain the asset, so the annual maintenance cost of $10,000 will be saved. ICI's marginal tax rate is 40%, and its MARR is 15% during the analysis period.

(a) What is ICI's present-worth (incremental) cost of owning the equipment?

(b) What is ICI's present-worth (incremental) cost of leasing the equipment?

(c) Should ICI buy or lease the equipment?

10.42 Oregon Machinery Company (OMC) has decided to acquire a screw machine. One alternative is to lease the machine on a three-year contract for a lease payment of $22,000 per year with payments to be made at the beginning of each year. The lease would include maintenance. The second alternative is to purchase the machine outright for $97,000, financing the investment with a bank loan for the net purchase price and amortizing the loan over a three-year period at an interest rate of 12% per year (annual payment $= \$40,386$).

Under the borrow-to-purchase arrangement, the company would have to maintain the machine at an annual cost of $6,000, payable at year-end. The machine falls into the seven-year MACRS classification, and it has a salvage value of $45,000, which is the expected market value at the end of year 3. After three years, the company plans to replace the machine regardless of whether it leases or buys. The tax rate is 40%, and the MARR is 15%.

(a) What is OMC's PW cost of leasing?

(b) What is OMC's PW cost of owning?

(c) From the financing analyses in parts (a) and (b), what are the advantages and disadvantages of leasing and owning?

Effects of Inflation on Project Cash Flows

10.43 Gentry Machines, Inc., has just received a special job order from one of its clients.

The following financial data on the order have been collected:

- This two-year project requires the purchase of a special-purpose piece of equipment for $55,000. The equipment falls into the MACRS five-year class.

- The machine will be sold at the end of two years for $27,000 (today's dollars).

- The project will bring in an additional annual revenue of $114,000 (actual dollars), but it is expected to incur an additional annual operating cost of $53,800 (today's dollars).

■ To purchase the equipment, the firm expects to borrow $50,000 at 10% over a two-year period (equal annual payments of $28,810 in actual dollars). The remaining $5,000 will be taken from the firm's retained earnings.

■ The firm expects a general inflation of 5% per year during the project period. The firm's marginal tax rate is 40%, and its market interest rate is 18%.

(a) Compute the after-tax cash flows in actual dollars.

(b) What is the equivalent present worth of this amount at time 0?

10.44 Hugh Health Product Corporation is considering the purchase of a computer to control plant packaging for a spectrum of health products. The following data have been collected:

■ First cost = $130,000 to be borrowed at 9% interest, where only interest is paid each year and the principal is due in a lump sum at the end of year 2.

■ Economic service life = six years.

■ Estimated selling price in year-0 dollars = $20,000.

■ Depreciation method = five-year MACRS property.

■ Marginal income-tax rate = 40% (remains constant).

■ Annual revenue = $155,000 (today's dollars).

■ Annual expense (not including depreciation and interest) = $88,000 (today's dollars).

■ Market interest rate = 18%.

(a) An average general inflation rate of 5%, affecting all revenues, expenses, and the salvage value, is expected during the project period. Determine the cash flows in actual dollars.

(b) Compute the net present worth of the project under inflation.

(c) Compute the net-present-worth loss (or gain) due to inflation.

(d) Compute the present-worth loss (or gain) due to borrowing.

10.45 J. F. Manning Metal Company is considering the purchase of a new milling machine during year 0. The machine's base price is $135,000, and it will cost another $15,000 to modify the machine for special use by the firm, resulting in a $150,000 cost base for depreciation. The machine falls into the MACRS seven-year property class. The machine will be sold after three years for $80,000 (actual dollars). Use of the machine will require an increase in net working capital (inventory) of $10,000 at the beginning of the project year. The machine will have no effect on revenues, but it is expected to save the firm $80,000 (today's dollars) per year in before-tax operating costs—mainly labor. The firm's marginal tax rate is 40%, and this rate is expected to remain unchanged over the project's duration. However, the company expects that the labor cost will increase at an annual rate of 5% and that the working-capital requirement will grow at an annual rate of 8% caused by inflation. The selling price of the milling machine is not affected by inflation. The general inflation rate is estimated to be 6% per year over the project period. The firm's market interest rate is 20%.

(a) Determine the project cash flows in actual dollars.

(b) Determine the project cash flows in constant (time-zero) dollars.

(c) Is this project acceptable?

10.46 Suppose a business is considering the purchase of a $40,000 machine whose operation will result in increased sales of $30,000 per year and increased operating costs of $10,000; additional profits will be taxed at a rate of 50%. Depreciation is assumed to be taken on a straight-line basis over four years with no expected salvage value. What will happen to this project's real rate of return if inflation during the next four years is expected to be 10% compounded annually?

10.47 Fuller Ford Company is considering the purchase of a vertical drill machine. The machine will cost $50,000 and will have an eight-year service life. The selling price of the machine at the end of eight years is expected to be $5,000 in today's dollars. The machine will generate annual revenues of $20,000 (today's dollars) but is expected to have an annual expense (excluding depreciation) of $8,000 (today's dollars). The asset is classified as a seven-year MACRS property. The project requires a working-capital investment of $10,000 at year 0. The marginal income-tax rate for the firm is averaging 35%. The firm's market interest rate is 18%.

(a) Determine the internal rate of return of this investment.

(b) Assume that the firm expects a general inflation rate of 5%, but that it also expects an 8% annual increase in revenue and working capital and a 6% annual increase in expenses, caused by inflation. Compute the real (inflation-free) internal rate of return. Is this project acceptable?

10.48 You have $10,000 cash, which you want to invest. Normally, you would deposit the money in a savings account that pays an annual interest rate of 6%. However, you are now considering the possibility of investing in a bond. Your marginal tax rate is 30% for both ordinary income and capital gains. You expect the general inflation rate to be 3% during the investment period. You can buy a high-grade municipal bond costing $10,000 that pays interest of 9% ($900) per year. This interest is not taxable. A comparable high-grade corporate bond is also available that is just as safe as the municipal bond but pays an interest rate of 12% ($1,200) per year. This interest is taxable as ordinary income. Both bonds mature at the end of year 5.

(a) Determine the real (inflation-free) rate of return for each bond.

(b) Without knowing your MARR, can you make a choice between these two bonds?

10.49 Air Florida is considering two types of engines for use in its planes, each of which has the same life, same maintenance costs, and same repair record:

- Engine *A* costs $100,000 and uses 50,000 gallons of fuel per 1,000 hours of operation at the average service load encountered in passenger service.

- Engine *B* costs $200,000 and uses 32,000 gallons of fuel per 1,000 hours of operation at the same service load.

Both engines are estimated to operate for 10,000 service hours before any major overhaul of the engines is required. If fuel currently costs $1.25 per gallon and its price is expected to increase at a rate of 8% because of inflation, which engine should the firm install for an expected 2,000 hours of operation per year? The firm's marginal income-tax rate is 40%, and the engine will be depreciated by the units-of-production method. Assume that the firm's market interest rate is 20%. It is estimated that both engines will retain a market value of 40% of their initial cost (actual dollars) if they are sold on the market after 10,000 hours of operation.

(a) Using the present-worth criterion, which project would you select?

(b) Using the annual-equivalence criterion, which project would you select?

(c) Using the future-worth criterion, which project would you select?

10.50 K&G Chemical Company has just received a special subcontracting job from one of its clients. This two-year project requires the purchase of a special-purpose painting sprayer for $60,000. This equipment falls into the MACRS five-year class. After the subcontracting work is completed at the end of two years, the painting sprayer will be sold for $40,000 (actual dollars). The painting system will require an increase in the company's net working capital (for spare-parts inventory, such as spray nozzles) of $5,000. This investment in working capital will be fully recovered at the project termination. The project will bring in an additional annual revenue of $120,000 (today's dollars), but it is expected to incur an additional annual operating cost of $60,000 (today's dollars). It is projected that, because of inflation, there will be sales-price increases at an annual rate of 5%, which implies that annual revenues will also increase at an annual rate of 5%. An annual increase of 4% for expenses and working-capital requirements is expected. The company has a marginal tax rate of 30%, and it uses a market interest rate of 15% for project evaluation during the inflationary period. The firm expects a general inflation of 8% during the project period.

(a) Compute the after-tax cash flows in actual dollars.

(b) What is the rate of return on this investment (real earnings)?

(c) Is this special order profitable?

10.51 Land Development Corporation is considering the purchase of a bulldozer. The bulldozer will cost $100,000 and will have an estimated salvage value of $30,000 at the end of six years. The asset will generate annual before-tax revenues of $80,000 over the next six years. The asset is classified as a five-year MACRS property. The marginal tax rate is 40%, and the firm's market interest rate is known to be 18%. All dollar figures represent constant dollars at time zero and are responsive to the general inflation rate $\bar{f}$.

(a) With $\bar{f} = 6\%$ compute the after-tax cash flows in actual dollars.

(b) Determine the real rate of return of this project on an after-tax basis.

(c) Suppose that the initial cost of the project will be financed through a local bank at an interest rate of 12% and with an annual payment of $24,323 over six years. With this additional condition, rework part (a).

(d) From your answer to part (a), determine the PW loss due to inflation.

(e) From your answer to part (c), determine how much the project has to generate in additional before-tax annual revenues in actual dollars (equal amount) in order to make up the inflation loss.

Short Case Studies with Excel

10.52 USA Aluminum Company is considering making a major investment of $150 million ($5 million for land, $45 million for buildings, and $100 million for manufacturing equipment and facilities) to produce a stronger, lighter material, called aluminum lithium, that will make aircraft sturdier and more fuel efficient. Aluminum lithium has been sold commercially as an alternative to composite materials for only a few years. It will likely be the material of choice for the next generation of commercial and military aircraft because it is so much lighter than conventional aluminum alloys. Another advantage of aluminum lithium is that it is cheaper than composites. The firm predicts that aluminum lithium will account for about 5% of the structural weight of the average commercial aircraft within 5 years and 10% within 10 years. The proposed plant, which has an estimated service life of 12 years, would have a production capacity of about 10 million pounds of aluminum lithium, although domestic consumption of the material is expected to be only 3 million pounds during the first four years, five million for the next three years, and eight million for the remaining plant life. Aluminum lithium costs $15 a pound to produce, and the firm would expect to sell it at $28 a pound. The building, which will be placed in service on July 1 of the first year, will be depreciated according to the 39-year MACRS real-property class. All manufacturing equipment and facilities will be classified as seven-year MACRS property. At the end of project life, the land will be worth $8 million, the building $30 million, and the equipment $10 million. The firm's marginal tax rate is 40%, and its capital gains tax rate is 35%.

(a) Determine the net after-tax cash flows.

(b) Determine the IRR for this investment.

(c) Determine whether the project is acceptable if the firm's MARR is 15%.

10.53 The Pittsburgh division of Vermont Machinery, Inc., manufactures drill bits. One of the production processes for a drill bit requires tipping, whereby carbide tips are inserted into the bit to make it stronger and more durable. This tipping process usually requires four or five operators, depending on the weekly work load. The same operators are also assigned to the stamping operation, where the size of the drill bit and the company's logo are imprinted on the bit. Vermont is considering acquiring three automatic tipping machines to replace the manual tipping and stamping operations. If the tipping process is automated, the division's engineers will have to redesign the shapes of the carbide tips to be used in the machine. The new design requires less carbide, resulting in savings on materials. The following financial data have been compiled:

- Project life: six years.
- Expected annual savings: reduced labor, $56,000; reduced material, $75,000; other benefits (reduced carpal tunnel syndrome and related problems), $28,000; reduced overhead, $15,000.
- Expected annual O&M costs: $22,000.
- Tipping machines and site preparation: equipment costs (for three machines), including delivery, $180,000; site preparation, $20,000.
- Salvage value: $30,000 (total for the three machines) at the end of six years.
- Depreciation method: seven-year MACRS.
- Investment in working capital: $25,000 at the beginning of the project year, which will be fully recovered at the end of the project year.
- Other accounting data: marginal tax rate of 39%; MARR of 18%.

To raise $200,000, Vermont is considering the following financing options:

- Option 1: Finance the tipping machines by using retained earnings.
- Option 2: Secure a 12% term loan over six years (with six equal annual installments).
- Option 3: Lease the tipping machines. Vermont can obtain a six-year financial lease on the equipment (maintenance costs are taken care of by the lessor) for payments of $55,000 at the beginning of each year.

(a) Determine the net after-tax cash flows for each financing option.

(b) What is Vermont's PW cost of owning the equipment by borrowing?

(c) What is Vermont's PW cost of leasing the equipment?

(d) Recommend the best course of action for Vermont.

10.54 H-Robot Incorporated (HRI), a world leader in the robotics industry, produces a line of industrial robots and peripheral equipment, which perform many routine assembly-line tasks. The company enjoyed much success in the past when automobile manufacturers and other durable goods producers sought to cut costs by automating the production process. However, increased competition, particularly from Japanese firms, had caused HRI's management to be concerned about the company's growth potential. Therefore, HRI's research and development department has been applying industrial-robot technology to develop a line of household robots. The household robot is designed to function as a maid, mainly performing such tasks as vacuuming floors and carpets. This R&D effort has now reached the stage where a decision must be made on whether to go forward with production.

HRI's marketing department has plans to target sales of the robots to households with working mothers in the United States, and if it is successful there, then the robots could be marketed even to college students or households in other countries. Additional data follow.

- The marketing vice president believes that annual sales would be somewhere between 150,000 and 300,000 units (most likely, 200,000 units) if the robots were priced at $400 each.

- The engineering department has estimated that the firm would need a new manufacturing plant; this plant could be built and made ready for production in two years once the "go" decision is made. The plant would require a 35-acre site, and HRI currently has an option to purchase a suitable tract of land for $2.5 million. Building construction would begin in early 2013 and continue through 2014. The building, which would fall into the MACRS 39-year class, would cost an estimated $10.5 million. A $3.5-million payment would be due to the contractor on December 31, 2012, and another $7 million payable on December 31, 2014.

- The necessary manufacturing equipment would be installed late in 2014 and would be paid for on December 31, 2014. The equipment, which would fall into the MACRS seven-year class, would have a cost of $18.5 million, including transportation, plus another $500,000 for installation.

- To date, the company has spent $12 million on research and development associated with the household robot. The company has expenses of $4 million for the R&D costs; the remaining $8 million already has been capitalized and will be amortized over the life of the project. However, if HRI decides not to go forward with the project, the capitalized R&D expenditures could be written off on December 31, 2012.

- The project would also require an initial investment in net working capital equal to 12% of the estimated sales in the first year. The initial working capital investment would be made on December 31, 2014. On December 31 of each following year, net working capital would be increased by an amount equal to 12% of any sales increase expected during the coming year.

- The project's estimated economic life is eight years (not counting the construction period). At the end of that time, the land is expected to have a market value of $4.5 million, the building a value of $3 million, and the equipment a value of $3.5 million.

■ The production department has estimated that variable manufacturing costs would total 65% of dollar sales, and that fixed overhead costs, excluding depreciation, would be $8.5 million for the first year of operations. Sales prices and fixed overhead costs, other than depreciation and amortization, are projected to increase with inflation, which is estimated to average 5% per year over the eight-year life of the project. (Note that the first year's sales would be $400 × 200,000 units = $80 million. The second year's sales would be 5% higher than $80 million, and so forth.)

■ HRI's marginal combined tax rate is 38%; its weighted average cost of capital is 15% (meaning that its minimum attractive rate of return is 15%); and the company's policy, for capital budgeting purposes, is to assume that cash flows occur at the end of each year.

■ Since the plant would begin operations on January 1, 2015, the first operating cash flows would thus occur on December 31, 2015. Assume that the current decision point is December 31, 2012.

(a) Develop the project cash flows, after taxes, over the life of the project. Use Excel to prepare the project cash flow worksheet.

(b) Determine the equivalent net worth of the project at the time of commercialization.

(c) Determine the equivalent annual worth of the project and the unit profit per production.

(d) Determine the internal rate of return of the project.

(e) Determine the break-even annual unit sales to justify the investment.

(f) Suppose that the unit sale price could decline 3% annually over the previous year's price due to market competition. (But all other costs, other than depreciation and amortization, would increase at an annual rate of 5%.) What is your course of action?

10.55 A&H Chemical Corporation is a multinational manufacturer of industrial chemical products. A&H has made great progress in energy-cost reduction and has implemented several cogeneration projects in the United States and Puerto Rico, including the completion of a 35-megawatt (MW) unit in Chicago and a 29-MW unit in Baton Rouge. The division of A&H being considered for one of its more recent cogeneration projects is at a chemical plant located in Texas. The plant has a power usage of 80 million kilowatt-hours (kWh) annually. However, on average, it uses 85% of its 10-MW capacity, which would bring the average power usage to 68 million kWh annually. Texas Electric presently charges $0.09 per kWh of electric consumption for the A&H plant, a rate that is considered high throughout the industry. Because A&H's power consumption is so large, the purchase of a cogeneration unit is considered to be desirable. Installation of the cogeneration unit would allow A&H to generate its own power and to avoid the annual $6,120,000 expense to Texas Electric. The total initial investment cost would be $10,500,000. This would cover $10,000,000 for the purchase of the power unit itself—a gas-fired 10-MW Allison 571—and engineering, design, and site preparation. The remaining $500,000 would include the purchase of interconnection equipment, such as poles and distribution lines, that would be used to interface the cogenerator with the existing utility facilities.

As A&H's management has decided to raise the $10.5 million by selling bonds, the company's engineers have estimated the operating costs of the cogeneration project. The annual cash flow is composed of many factors: maintenance costs, overhaul costs, expenses for standby power, and other miscellaneous expenses. Maintenance costs are projected to be approximately $500,000 per year. The unit must be overhauled every three years, at a cost of $1.5 million per overhaul. Standby power is the service provided by the utility in the event of a cogeneration-unit trip or scheduled maintenance outage. Unscheduled outages are expected to occur four times annually with each outage averaging 2 hours in duration at an annual expense of $6,400. In addition, overhauling the unit takes approximately 100 hours and occurs every three years, requiring another triennial standby-power cost of $100,000. Miscellaneous expenses, such as additional personnel and insurance, are expected to total $1 million. Fuel (spot gas) will be consumed at a rate of 8,000 BTU per kWh, including the heat-recovery cycle. At $2.00 per million BTU, the annual fuel cost will reach $1,280,000. Due to obsolescence, the expected life of the cogeneration project will be 12 years, after which Allison will pay A&H $1 million for the salvage of all equipment.

Revenues will be incurred from the sale of excess electricity to the utility company at a negotiated rate. Since the chemical plant will consume, on average, 85% of the unit's 10-MW output, 15% of the output will be sold at $0.04 per kWh, bringing in an annual revenue of $480,000. A&H's marginal tax rate (combined federal and state) is 36%, and its minimum required rate of return for any cogeneration project is 27%. The anticipated costs and revenues are summarized as follows:

Initial Investment	
Cogeneration unit and engineering, design, and site preparation (15-year MACRS class)	$10,000,000
Interconnection equipment (five-year MACRS class)	$500,000
Salvage value after 12 years of use	$1,000,000
Annual Expenses	
Maintenance	$500,000
Miscellaneous (additional personnel and insurance)	$1,000,000
Standby power	$6,400
Fuel	$1,280,000
Other Operating Expenses	
Overhaul every three years	$1,500,000
Standby power during overhaul	$100,000
Revenues	
Sale of excess power to Texas Electric	$480,000

(a) If the cogeneration unit and other connecting equipment could be financed by issuing corporate bonds at an interest rate of 9%, compounded annually, determine the net cash flow from the cogeneration project.

(b) If the cogeneration unit can be leased, what would be the maximum annual lease amount that A&H should be willing to pay?

10.56 Wilson Machine Tools, Inc., a manufacturer of fabricated metal products, is considering the purchase of a high-tech computer-controlled milling machine at a cost of $95,000. The cost of installing the machine, preparing the site, wiring, and rearranging other equipment is expected to be $15,000. This installation cost will be added to the cost of the machine in order to determine the total cost basis for depreciation. Special jigs and tool dies for the particular product will also be required at a cost of $10,000. The milling machine is expected to last 10 years, but the jigs and dies for only five years. Therefore, another set of jigs and dies has to be purchased at the end of five years. The milling machine will have a $10,000 salvage value at the end of its life, and the special jigs and dies are worth only $300 as scrap metal at any time in their lives. The machine is classified as a seven-year MACRS property, and the special jigs and dies are classified as a three-year MACRS property. With the new milling machine, Wilson expects additional annual revenue of $80,000 from increased production. The additional annual production costs are estimated as follows: materials, $9,000; labor, $15,000; energy, $4,500; and miscellaneous O&M costs, $3,000. Wilson's marginal income-tax rate is expected to remain at 35% over the project life of 10 years. All dollar figures are in today's dollars. The firm's market interest rate is 18%, and the expected general inflation rate during the project period is estimated at 6%.

(a) Determine the project cash flows in the absence of inflation.

(b) Determine the internal rate of return for the project based on your answer to part (a).

(c) Suppose that Wilson expects the following price increases during the project period: materials at 4% per year, labor at 5% per year, and energy and other O&M costs at 3% per year. To compensate for these increases in prices, Wilson is planning to increase annual revenue at the rate of 7% per year by charging its customers a higher price. No changes in salvage value are expected for the machine, the jigs, and the dies. Determine the project cash flows in actual dollars.

(d) From your answer to part (c), determine the real (inflation-free) rate of return of the project.

(e) Determine the economic loss (or gain) in present worth caused by inflation.

CHAPTER ELEVEN

Handling Project Uncertainty

Solar Energy—Is It Worth the Risk? The Obama Administration has pushed federal subsidies to stimulate economic growth through green jobs. Like many other countries, the United States places green energy high on its political agenda. Amid the push to find domestic energy sources that are less polluting than fossil fuels, getting energy from the sun could be very appealing. This is especially true when government air-quality standards are becoming more rigorous, and consumer interest in the environmental is strong.

In the United States, solar power accounts for less than 1 percent of electricity use. Annually, this amounts to only 2,500 megawatts of photovoltaic (PV) cell production. One of the administration's goals is to transform American companies from a minor player in the solar power industry into the main producer of an increasingly competitive source of electricity.

U.S. Solar Companies at a Loss For many decades, scientists and engineers have tried to come up with economical ways to harness the power of the sun. Despite the impressive technological advances made in converting solar energy into electricity, it is still expensive to produce. Although the cost of PV has fallen substantially over the decades, generating power from photovoltaic panels costs more than four times as much as coal, and more than twice what wind power costs. Therefore, without government subsidies, U.S. companies are not willing to invest in electricity generated from the sun's rays; it requires the purchase of new equipment and heavy expenditures in evolving technologies.

Moreover, even with government support, American companies have a hard time competing with foreign producers. While most U.S., Japanese, and European companies still have a technological edge, China has a definite cost advantage. Solar panel prices plunged by 42 percent per kilowatt-hour since December 2010 as Chinese manufacturers have sharply increased capacity.

Meanwhile, demand has been somewhat weak in the main markets in the United States and Europe, so in August 2011 three major U.S. solar power companies all filed for bankruptcy. In comparison, China has emerged as the dominant player in green energy—especially in solar power. It accounted for at least half the world's production in 2010, with close to 11,000 megawatts of PV capacity and its market share continues to grow rapidly. China has achieved this market dominance through generous government subsidies in its solar industry.

Solar Frontier KK's Bold Move in Japan Japan installed close to 1,000 megawatts of new PV capacity in 2010. In terms of installed PV capacity, Japan is ranked third, with a total of 3,600 megawatts. As solar adoption accelerates in Japan, the Japanese solar industry is little more optimistic than their U.S. counterparts.

While American companies are putting the manufacturing of new solar panels on hold, one Japanese company is blazing the trail forward. The opening of Solar Frontier KK's $1.25 billion factory in southern Japan marks the company's foray into unchartered territory—and an uncertain future.

With a declining demand on oil, and an increasing demand on hybrid cars in southern Japan, Solar Frontier KK's parent company, Showa Shell, saw an opportunity to capitalize. And although heading in the solar panel direction seems promising, it's still a gamble. Solar Frontier KK's new plant will be producing technologically advanced, highly efficient solar cells, but will be competing in a semi-saturated market filled with companies offering less efficient and less expensive panels.

But the products Solar Frontier KK produces are expected to grow at a faster rate, as mass production will work to lower costs in the long run. It is a gamble—but one that may prove to be worth it.

What appears to be the greatest risk of undertaking this solar project by Solar Frontier? Even though Solar Frontier has rosy revenue projections for years to come, there are two issues of great concern. First issue is the demand – if the demand is not there, what is the degree of the financial risk associated with this $1.25 billion investment? The second issue is related to the technical problem of bringing the efficiency of converting sunlight into energy to higher than 11% for Solar Frontier's current thin-film panels. In what way did Solar Frontier weigh the risks and costs associated with the technology?

In previous chapters, cash flows from projects were assumed to be known with complete certainty; our analysis was concerned with measuring the economic worth of projects and selecting the best investment projects. Although these types of analyses can provide a reasonable decision basis in many investment situations, we should admit that most projects involve uncertainty. In this type of situation, management rarely has precise expectations about the future cash flows to be derived from a particular project. In fact, the best that a firm can reasonably expect is to estimate the range of possible future costs and benefits and the relative chances of achieving a reasonable return on the investment.

We use the term **risk** to describe an investment project where cash flows are not known in advance with certainty but for which an array of outcomes and their probabilities (odds) can be considered. We will also use the term **project risk** to refer to variability in a project's net present worth. Higher project risk reflects a higher anticipated variability in a project's NPW. In essence, we can see *risk as the potential for loss.* This chapter begins by exploring the origins of project risk.

11.1 Origins of Project Risk

When deciding whether to make a major capital investment, an entity must consider and estimate a number of issues. The factors to be estimated include the total market size for the product, the market share that the firm can attain, the growth of the market, the cost of production, the selling price of the product, the life span of the product, the cost and life span of the equipment needed, and the effective tax rates. Many of these factors are subject to substantial uncertainty. A common approach is to generate single-number "best estimates" for each of the uncertain factors and then to calculate measures of profitability, such as NPW or rate of return for the project. This approach has two drawbacks:

1. No guarantee can ensure that the best estimates will ever match the actual values.
2. No provision is made to measure the risk associated with the investment or the project risk. In particular, managers have no way of determining either the probability that a project will lose money or the probability that it will generate large profits.

Because cash flows can be so difficult to estimate accurately, project managers frequently consider a range of possible values for cash flow elements. If a range of values for individual cash flows is possible to make, then logically determining a range of values for the NPW of a given project is also possible. Clearly, the analyst will want to try to gauge the probability and reliability of individual cash flows occurring and, consequently, the level of certainty about overall project worth.

Quantitative statements about risk are given as numerical probabilities or as values for the likelihood (odds) of occurrence. Probabilities are given as decimal fractions in the interval 0.0 to 1.0. An event or outcome that is certain to occur has a probability of 1.0. As the probability of an event approaches 0, the event becomes increasingly less likely to occur. The assignment of probabilities to the various outcomes of an investment project is generally called **risk analysis**.

11.2 Methods of Describing Project Risk

We may begin analyzing project risk by first determining the uncertainty inherent in a project's cash flows. We can do this analysis in a number of ways, which range from making informal judgments to performing complex economic and statistical analyses. In this section, we will introduce three methods of determining project risk: (1) sensitivity analysis, (2) break-even analysis, and (3) scenario analysis. Each method will be explained with reference to a single example. We also introduce the method for conducting sensitivity analysis for mutually exclusive alternatives.

11.2.1 Sensitivity Analysis

One way to glean a sense of all possible outcomes of an investment is to perform a **sensitivity analysis**, a technique whereby different values of certain key variables are tested to see how sensitive investment results are to possible change in assumptions. It is a method of evaluating the riskiness of an investment. In calculating cash flows, some items have more influence on the final result (NPW) than others. In some problems, the most significant item is easily identified. For example, the estimate of sales volume can have a major impact in a project's NPW, especially in new product introductions.

We may want to identify the items that have an important influence on the final results so that they can be subjected to special scrutiny. Sensitivity analysis is sometimes called "**what-if analysis**" because it answers questions such as, **if** incremental sales are only 1,000 units, rather than 2,000 units, **what** will the NPW be?

- Sensitivity analysis begins with a base-case situation, which we develop by using the most likely value for each input. We then change the specific variable of interest by several specified percentages above and below the most likely value while holding other variables constant.
- Next, we calculate a new NPW for each of these values. A convenient and useful way to present the results of a sensitivity analysis is to plot **sensitivity graphs**. The slopes of the lines show how sensitive the NPW will be to changes in each of the inputs: the steeper the slope, the more sensitive the NPW will be to a change in a particular variable. Sensitivity graphs identify the crucial variables that affect the final outcome the most.

We will use Example 11.1 to illustrate the concept of sensitivity analysis.

EXAMPLE 11.1 Sensitivity Analysis—Know Which Variable Is Most Critical to Your Bottom Line

Capstone Turbine Corporation is the world's leading provider of micro-turbine-based MicroCHP (combined heat and power) systems for clean, continuous, distributed-generation electricity. The MicroCHP unit is a compact turbine generator that delivers electricity on-site or close to the point where it is needed. Designed to operate on a variety of gaseous and liquid fuels, this form of distributed-generation technology first debuted in 1998 for commercial use.

Capstone is considering marketing a modified but downsized version of the system unit for residential use, primarily for vacation properties in remote places. The project requires an initial investment of $55 million, but Capstone managers are uneasy about this project because too many uncertain elements have not been considered in the analysis. Two primary factors that are difficult to estimate are the initial market size and how the market size will grow over the life of the project. The company has prepared the following financial data related to the project:

Key Cash Flow Variables	Low	Most Likely	High
Initial market size (units), year 1	1,000	1,500	2,000
Market growth rate (annual)	3%	5%	8%
Unit price	$72,000	$80,000	$86,000
Unit variable cost	$56,000	$60,000	$65,000
Fixed cost (annual) excluding depreciation	$6,500,000	$8,000,000	$9,000,000
Salvage value	$4,000,000	$7,000,000	$8,000,000

The initial investment can be depreciated on a seven-year MACRS, and the project is expected to have an economic service life of five years. The product life is relatively short, as the technology changes in the energy sector are evolving rapidly. The firm's marginal tax rate is 40%, and its MARR is known to be 15%.

(a) Develop the cash flow series over the project life based on the assumption of most likely estimates.

(b) Conduct a sensitivity analysis for each variable and develop a sensitivity graph.

DISSECTING THE PROBLEM

Table 11.1 shows Capstone's expected but ultimately uncertain cash flows based on the most likely estimates. The annual revenues and expenses are estimated with the following relationship:

- Revenues = market size × unit price × $(1 + \text{growth rate})^{(n-1)}$.

- Costs = market size × variable unit cost
  × $(1 + \text{growth rate})^{(n-1)}$ + Fixed cost (excluding depreciation).

If everything goes well as expected, it appears that the project is worth undertaking with NPW = \$11,107 (or \$11,107,000).

Suppose that Capstone is not confident in its revenue forecasts in particular. The managers think that if the product is not well accepted in the U.S. marketplace, Capstone will need to sell the units outside the United States, primarily in the European market. However, the company is not guaranteed success in that market either. Before undertaking the project described, the company needs to identify the key variables that will determine whether the project will succeed or fail.

After defining the market size, growth rate, unit price, unit variable cost, fixed cost, and salvage value, we conduct a sensitivity analysis with respect to these key input variables. We do this by varying each of the estimates by a given percentage and determining what effect the variation in that item will have on the final results. If the effect is large, the result is sensitive to that item. Our objective is to locate the most sensitive item(s).

Given: Range of estimates of key input variables and the cash flow estimates based on most likely estimates given in Table 11.1.

Find: (a) Which input variable is the most critical? (b) Plot a sensitivity graph.

METHODOLOGY

Develop a cash flow series in Excel and plot the sensitivity graph.

SOLUTION

(a) **Sensitivity analysis:** We begin the sensitivity analysis with a consideration of the base-case situation, which reflects the most likely estimate (expected value) for each input variable. In developing Table 11.2, we changed a given variable by 20% in 5% increments above and below the base-case value and calculated new NPWs while other variables were held constant. Now we ask a series of what-if questions: What if sales are 20% below the expected level? What if operating costs rise? What if the unit price drops from \$80,000 to \$64,000 (20% drop)? Table 11.2 summarizes the results of our varying the values of the key input variables.

TABLE 11.1 Cash Flows for Capstone's MicroCHP Project, Based on Most Likely Estimates (unit: $000, except demand)

	A	B	C	D	E	F	G
1							
2							
3							
4	**Input Data (Base):**			**Sensitivity Analysis:**			
5							
6	Unit Price ($)	80.00		Category		% Change	
7	Demand	1500		Unit price		0%	
8	Growth rate	5%		Growth rate		0%	
9	Var. cost ($/unit)	60.00		Demand		0%	
10	Fixed cost ($)	8000		Var. cost (unit)		0%	
11	Salvage ($)	7000		Fixed cost		0%	
12	Tax rate (%)	40%		Salvage		0%	
13	MARR (%)	15%					
14				Output (PW)		$11,107	
15							
16							
17			0	1	2	3	4	5
18	**Income Statement**				=C22*(1+$B$8*(1+$F$8))		
19							
20	Revenues:						
21	Unit Price		$ 80	$ 80	$ 80	$ 80	$ 80
22	Demand (units)		1500	1575	1654	1736	1823
23	Sales Revenue		$ 120,000	$ 126,000	$ 132,300	$ 138,915	$ 145,861
24	Expenses:						
25	Unit Variable Cost		$ 60	$ 60	$ 60	$ 60	$ 60
26	Variable Cost		90,000	94,500	99,225	104,186	109,396
27	Fixed Cost		8,000	8,000	8,000	8,000	8,000
28	Depreciation		7,860	13,470	9,620	6,870	2,453
30	Taxable Income		$ 14,141	$ 10,031	$ 15,456	$ 19,859	$ 26,012
31	Income Taxes (40%)		5,656	4,012	6,182	7,944	10,405
33	Net Income		$ 8,484	$ 6,018	$ 9,273	$ 11,916	$ 15,607
34							
35	**Cash Flow Statement**	=-$B$41*0.1429					
36							
37	Operating Activities:						
38	Net Income		$ 8,484	$ 6,018	$ 9,273	$ 11,916	$ 15,607
39	Depreciation		$ 7,860	$ 13,470	$ 9,620	$ 6,870	$ 2,453
40	Investment Activities:						
41	Investment	$ (55,000)					
42	Salvage			=-0.4*(G42-(-B41-SUM(C28:G28)))			$ 7,000
43	Gains Tax						$ 3,092
45	Net Cash Flow	$ (55,000)	$ 16,344	$ 19,488	$ 18,893	$ 18,785	$ 28,152
46							
47	IRR=	23%	=IRR(B45:G45,10%)				
48	PW(15%) =	$ 11,107					
49							
50			=NPV(15%,C45:G45)+B45				
51							

(b) **Sensitivity graph:** Figure 11.1 shows the Capstone project's sensitivity graphs for six of the key input variables. The base-case NPW is plotted on the ordinate of the graph at the value 1.0 on the abscissa (or 0% deviation). Next, the value of product demand is reduced to 95% of its base-case value, and the

TABLE 11.2 Sensitivity Analysis for Six Key Input Variables (Example 11.1)

Key Input Variables	NPW as a Function of Percent Deviation from the Most Likely Estimates				Base				
	−20%	−15%	−10%	−5%	0%	5%	10%	15%	20%
Unit price	($41,520)	($28,363)	($15,207)	($2,050)	$11,107	$24,263	$37,420	$50,577	$63,733
Demand	($2,050)	$1,239	$4,528	$7,818	$11,107	$14,396	$17,685	$20,974	$24,263
Growth rate	$9,978	$10,258	$10,540	$10,823	$11,107	$11,392	$11,679	$11,967	$12,257
Variable cost	$50,577	$40,709	$30,842	$20,974	$11,107	$1,239	($8,628)	($18,496)	($28,363)
Fixed cost	$14,325	$13,520	$12,716	$11,911	$11,107	$10,302	$9,498	$8,693	$7,889
Salvage value	$10,689	$10,794	$10,898	$11,002	$11,107	$11,211	$11,316	$11,420	$11,524

NPW is recomputed with all other variables held at their base-case value. We repeat the process by either decreasing or increasing the relative deviation from the base case. The lines for the variable unit price, variable unit cost, fixed cost, and salvage value are obtained in the same manner.

COMMENTS: In Figure 11.1, we see that the project's NPW is (1) very sensitive to changes in the unit price and variable cost, (2) fairly sensitive to changes in demand, and (3) relatively insensitive to changes in growth rate, fixed cost, and salvage value. Graphic displays such as the one in Figure 11.1 provide a useful means to communicate the relative sensitivities of the different variables on the

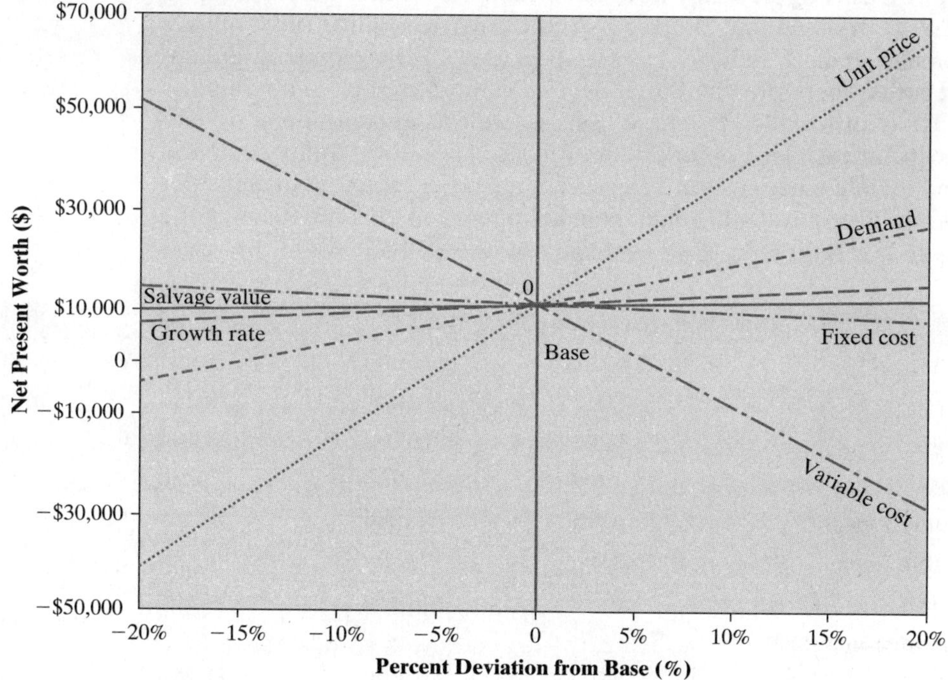

Figure 11.1 Sensitivity graph for Capstone's MicroCHP project

corresponding NPW value. However, sensitivity graphs do not explain any interactions among the variables or the likelihood of realizing any specific deviation from the base case. Certainly, it is conceivable that a project might not be very sensitive to changes in either of two items but might be very sensitive to combined changes in them.

11.2.2 Sensitivity Analysis for Mutually Exclusive Alternatives

In Figure 11.1, each variable is uniformly adjusted by $\pm 20\%$ and all variables are plotted on the same chart. This uniform adjustment can be too simplistic an assumption; in many situations, each variable can have a different range of uncertainty. Also, plotting all variables on the same chart could be confusing if there are too many variables to consider. When we perform sensitivity analysis for mutually exclusive alternatives, it may be more effective to plot the NPWs (or any other measures, such as AEs) of all alternatives over the range of each input; in other words, create one plot for each input, with units of the input on the horizontal axis. Example 11.2 illustrates this approach.

EXAMPLE 11.2 Sensitivity Analysis for Mutually Exclusive Alternatives

A local U.S. Postal Service office is considering purchasing a 4,000 lb forklift truck, which will be used primarily for processing incoming as well as outgoing postal packages. Forklift trucks traditionally have been fueled by either gasoline, liquid propane gas (LPG), or diesel fuel. Battery-powered electric forklifts, however, are increasingly popular in many industrial sectors because of their economic and environmental benefits. Therefore, the Postal Service is interested in comparing the four different types of forklifts. Purchase costs as well as annual operating and maintenance costs for each type of forklift are provided by a local utility company. Annual fuel and maintenance costs are measured in terms of number of shifts per year, where one shift is equivalent to eight hours of operation. A comparison of the variables of the four forklift types is given in the following table:

	Electrical Power	LPG	Gasoline	Diesel Fuel
Life expectancy	7 years	7 years	7 years	7 years
Initial cost	$30,000	$21,000	$20,000	$25,000
Salvage value	$3,000	$2,000	$2,000	$2,200
Maximum shifts per year	260	260	260	260
Fuel consumption/shift	32 kWh	12 gal	11 gal	7 gal
Fuel cost/unit	$0.20/kWh	$3.15/gal	$3.60/gal	$3.95/gal
Fuel cost/shift	$6.40	$37.80	$39.60	$27.65
Annual maintenance cost:				
Fixed cost	$500	$1,000	$1,200	$1,500
Variable cost/shift	$5	$6	$7	$9

The Postal Service is unsure of the number of shifts per year, but it expects them to be somewhere between 200 and 260 shifts. Since the U.S. Postal Service does not pay income taxes, no depreciation or tax information is required. The U.S. government uses 10% as the discount rate for any project evaluation of this nature. Develop a sensitivity graph that shows how the best choice from the alternatives changes as a function of the number of shifts per year.

DISSECTING THE PROBLEM

Two annual cost components are pertinent to this problem: (1) ownership cost (capital cost) and (2) operating cost (fuel and maintenance cost). Since the operating cost is already given on an annual basis, we need only determine the equivalent annual ownership cost for each alternative.

Given: Financial data as given in the table, interest rate $= 10\%$, and range of operating shifts.

Find: Which alternative is the best as a function of the number of shifts?

METHODOLOGY

Calculate ownership (capital) cost, annual operating cost, and equivalent annual cost.

SOLUTION

(a) **Ownership cost (capital cost):** Using the capital-recovery-with-return formula developed in Eq. (6.2), we compute the following:

Electrical power:
$$\begin{aligned}
\text{CR } (10\%) &= (\$30,000 - \$3,000)(A/P, 10\%, 7) \\
&\quad + (0.10)\$3,000 \\
&= \$5,845;
\end{aligned}$$

$$\begin{aligned}
\text{LPG: CR}(10\%) &= (\$21,000 - \$2,000)(A/P, 10\%, 7) \\
&\quad + (0.10)\$2,000 \\
&= \$4,103;
\end{aligned}$$

$$\begin{aligned}
\text{Gasoline: CR}(10\%) &= (\$20,000 - \$2,000)(A/P, 10\%, 7) \\
&\quad + (0.10)\$2,000 \\
&= \$3,897;
\end{aligned}$$

$$\begin{aligned}
\text{Diesel fuel: CR}(10\%) &= (\$25,000 - \$2,200)(A/P, 10\%, 7) \\
&\quad + (0.10)\$2,200 \\
&= \$4,903.
\end{aligned}$$

(b) **Annual operating cost:** We can express the annual operating cost as a function of the number of shifts per year (M) by combining the variable- and fixed-cost portions of the fuel and maintenance expenditures:

$$\text{Electrical power: } \$500 + (6.40 + 5)M = \$500 + 11.40M;$$
$$\text{LPG: } \$1,000 + (37.80 + 6)M = \$1,000 + 43.80M;$$
$$\text{Gasoline: } \$1,200 + (39.60 + 7)M = \$1,200 + 46.60M;$$
$$\text{Diesel fuel: } \$1,500 + (27.65 + 9)M = \$1,500 + 36.65M.$$

(c) **Total equivalent annual cost:** This value is the sum of the ownership cost and operating cost:

$$\text{Electrical power: AEC(10\%)} = \$6,345 + 11.40\,M;$$
$$\text{LPG: AEC(10\%)} = \$5,103 + 43.80M;$$
$$\text{Gasoline: AEC(10\%)} = \$5,097 + 46.60M;$$
$$\text{Diesel fuel: AEC(10\%)} = \$6,403 + 36.65M.$$

In Figure 11.2, these four annual-equivalence costs are plotted as a function of the number of shifts, M. It appears that the economics of the electric forklift truck can be justified as long as the number of annual shifts exceeds approximately 39. If the number of shifts is fewer than 39, the LPG truck becomes the most economically viable option. In terms of a pairwise comparison with the electric lift truck, the diesel option is not a viable alternative for any range of M.

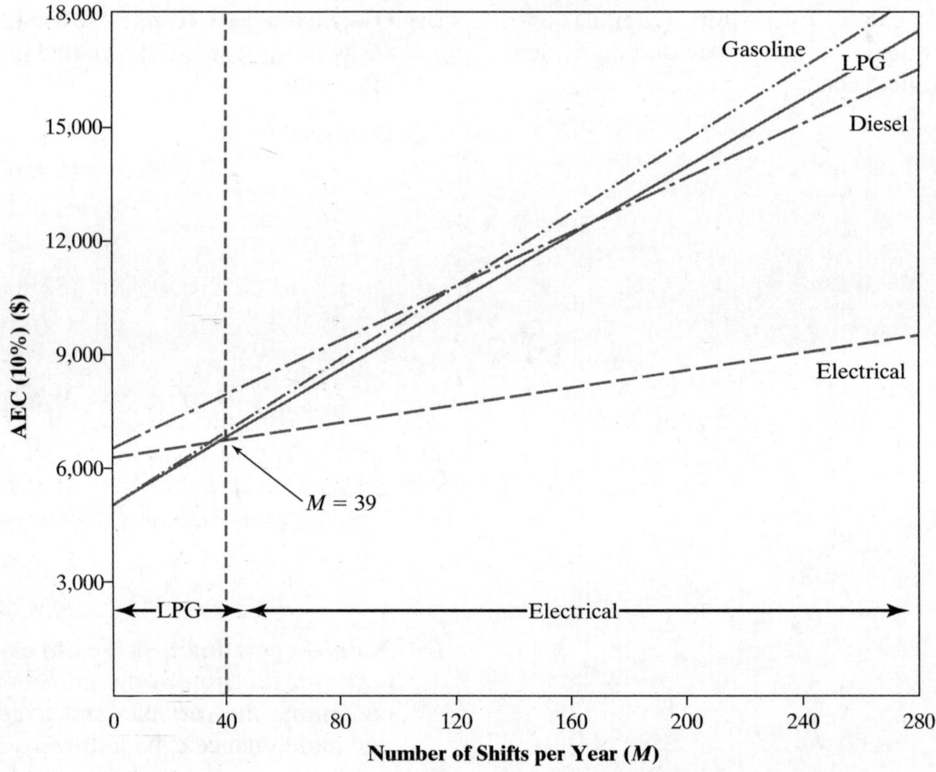

Figure 11.2 Sensitivity analyses for mutually exclusive alternatives. With $2 < M < 39$, select LPG lift truck; otherwise, select electrical power lift truck

11.2.3 Break-Even Analysis

When we perform a sensitivity analysis for a project, we are asking how serious the effect of lower revenues or higher costs will be on the project's profitability. Managers sometimes prefer to ask how much sales can decrease below forecasts before the project begins to lose money. This type of analysis is known as **break-even analysis**. To illustrate the procedure of break-even analysis based on NPW, we use the Goal Seek function from Excel. Note that this break-even value calculation is similar to the calculation we use for the internal rate of return when we want to find the interest rate that makes the NPW equal zero as well as when we want to find many other "cutoff values" when a choice changes.

EXAMPLE 11.3 Break-Even Analysis with Excel

From the sensitivity analysis discussed in Example 11.1, Capstone's managers are convinced that the NPW is most sensitive to changes in unit price. Determine the unit price to break even.

DISSECTING THE PROBLEM

The after-tax cash flows shown in Table 11.3 are basically the same as those in Table 11.1. The table is simply an Excel spreadsheet in which the cash flow entries are a function of the input variables. Here, what we are looking for is the minimum amount of unit price that makes the NPW zero.

Given: Cash flow statement given in Table 11.1.
Find: Break-even unit price.

METHODOLOGY

Use Excel's Goal Seek function to find the break-even unit price.

SOLUTION

Using the Goal Seek function, we want to set the NPW (cell $F$7) to zero by changing the unit price value (cell $B$6). Pressing the OK button will produce the results shown in Table 11.3, indicating that the project will break even when the unit price reaches exactly $76.62 ($76,620), or a mere 4.23% lower than the most likely estimate of $80.

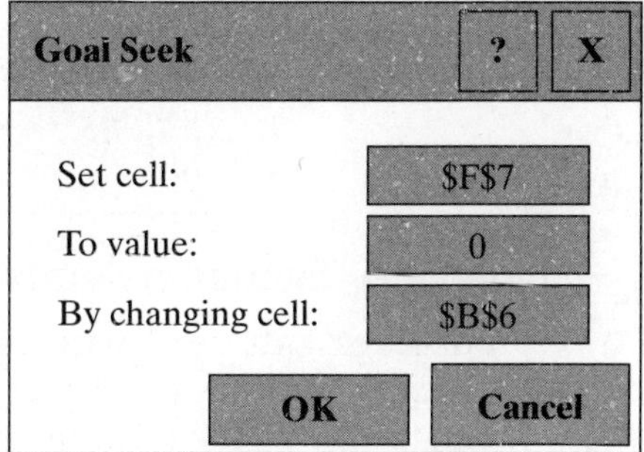

TABLE 11.3 Break-Even Analysis Using Excel's Goal Seek Function (unit: $000)

	A	B	C	D	E	F	G
2							
3							
4	**Input Data (Base):**			**Output Analysis**			
5							
6	Unit Price ($)	76.62			IRR=	15%	
7	Demand	1500			PW(15%) =	$ -	
8	Growth rate	5%					
9	Var. cost ($/unit)	60.00					
10	Fixed cost ($)	8000		By changing cell		Set cell	
11	Salvage ($)	7000					
12	Tax rate (%)	40%					
13	MARR (%)	15%			=NPV(15%,C45:G45)+B45		
14							
15							
16							
17			0	1	2	3	4	5
18	**Income Statement**						
19							
20	Revenues:						
21	Unit Price		$ 76.62	$ 76.62	$ 76.62	$ 76.62	$ 76.62
22	Demand (units)		1500	1575	1654	1736	1823
23	Sales Revenue		$ 114,935	$ 120,682	$ 126,716	$ 133,051	$ 139,704
24	Expenses:						
25	Unit Variable Cost		$ 60	$ 60	$ 60	$ 60	$ 60
26	Variable Cost		90,000	94,500	99,225	104,186	109,396
27	Fixed Cost		8,000	8,000	8,000	8,000	8,000
28	Depreciation		7,860	13,470	9,620	6,870	2,453
30	Taxable Income		$ 9,075	$ 4,712	$ 9,871	$ 13,996	$ 19,855
31	Income Taxes (40%)		3,630	1,885	3,948	5,598	7,942
33	Net Income		$ 5,445	$ 2,827	$ 5,923	$ 8,397	$ 11,913
34							
35	**Cash Flow Statement**						
36							
37	Operating Activities:						
38	Net Income		$ 5,445	$ 2,827	$ 5,923	$ 8,397	$ 11,913
39	Depreciation		$ 7,860	$ 13,470	$ 9,620	$ 6,870	$ 2,453
40	Investment Activities:						
41	Investment	$ (55,000)					
42	Salvage						$ 7,000
43	Gains Tax						$ 3,092
45	Net Cash Flow	$ (55,000)	$ 13,305	$ 16,297	$ 15,542	$ 15,267	$ 24,458
46							
47							
48							

11.2.4 Scenario Analysis

Although both sensitivity and break-even analyses are useful, they have limitations. Often, it is difficult to specify precisely the relationship between a particular variable and the NPW. The relationship is further complicated by interdependencies among the variables. Holding operating costs constant while varying unit sales may ease the analysis, but in reality, operating costs do not behave in this manner. Yet, it may complicate the analysis too much to permit movement in more than one variable at a time.

Scenario analysis is a technique that considers the sensitivity of the NPW to changes in both key variables and the range of likely variable values. For example, the decision maker may consider two extreme cases: a worst-case scenario (low unit sales, low unit price, high variable cost per unit, high fixed cost, and so on) and a best-case scenario. The NPWs under the worst and the best conditions are then calculated and compared with the expected, or base-case, NPW. Example 11.4 illustrates a plausible scenario analysis for Capstone's MicroCHP project.

EXAMPLE 11.4 Scenario Analysis

Consider again Capstone's MicroCHP project from Example 11.1. Given the three-point estimates for six key input variables (market size, market growth rate, unit price, unit variable cost, fixed cost, and salvage value), the marketing and engineering staffs come up with the scenarios shown in the following table.

Assume that the company's managers are fairly confident of other estimates such as project life, tax rate, and MARR. Furthermore, assume that they regard a decline in unit sales to below 1,000 or an increase above 2,000 as extremely unlikely. Thus, decremental annual sales of 500 units define the lower bound, or the worst-case scenario, whereas incremental annual sales of 500 units define the upper bound, or the best-case scenario. The same logic applies to other input estimates. Discuss the worst- and best-case scenarios.

Variable Considered	Worst-Case Scenario	Most Likely Scenario	Best-Case Scenario
Market size	1,000	1,500	2,000
Market growth rate	3%	5%	8%
Unit price	$72,000	$80,000	$86,000
Unit variable cost	$65,000	$60,000	$56,000
Fixed cost	$9,000,000	$8,000,000	$6,500,000
Salvage value	$4,000,000	$7,000,000	$8,000,000

DISSECTING THE PROBLEM

Given: Three-point estimates for the six key input variables in Example 11.1.

Find: NPW of the project under each scenario.

METHODOLOGY

To carry out the scenario analysis, we use the worst-case variable values to obtain the worst-case NPW and the best-case variable values to obtain the best-case NPW.

SOLUTION

The results of our analysis are summarized as follows:

(a) Worst-case scenario: With the input parameters under the worst-case scenario, the project cash flow statement would look like the results in Table 11.4. If this were to happen, Capstone would lose the entire investment made in the project to the extent of suffering a negative rate of return on its investment (−24%).

TABLE 11.4 Capstone's MicrCHP Project Cash Flows under the Worst-Case Scenario (unit: $000)

	A	B	C	D	E	F	G
15							
16							
17			0	1	2	3	4	5
18	**Income Statement**						
19							
20	Revenues:						
21	Unit Price		$ 72.00	$ 72.00	$ 72.00	$ 72.00	$ 72.00
22	Demand (units)		1000	1030	1061	1093	1126
23	Sales Revenue		$ 72,000	$ 74,160	$ 76,385	$ 78,676	$ 81,037
24	Expenses:						
25	Unit Variable Cost		$ 65	$ 65	$ 65	$ 65	$ 65
26	Variable Cost		65,000	66,950	68,959	71,027	73,158
27	Fixed Cost		9,000	9,000	9,000	9,000	9,000
28	Depreciation		7,860	13,470	9,620	6,870	2,453
30	Taxable Income		$ (9,860)	$ (15,260)	$ (11,193)	$ (8,220)	$ (3,574)
31	Income Taxes (40%)		(3,944)	(6,104)	(4,477)	(3,288)	(1,430)
33	Net Income		$ (5,916)	$ (9,156)	$ (6,716)	$ (4,932)	$ (2,145)
34							
35	**Cash Flow Statement**						
36							
37	Operating Activities:						
38	Net Income		$ (5,916)	$ (9,156)	$ (6,716)	$ (4,932)	$ (2,145)
39	Depreciation		$ 7,860	$ 13,470	$ 9,620	$ 6,870	$ 2,453
40	Investment Activities:						
41	Investment	$ (55,000)					
42	Salvage			=-0.4*(G42-(-B41-SUM(C28:G28)))			$ 4,000
43	Gains Tax						$ 4,292
45	Net Cash Flow	$ (55,000)	$ 1,944	$ 4,314	$ 2,904	$ 1,937	$ 8,600
46							
47							
48							
49		IRR =	-24%				
50		PW(15%) =	$ (42,755)	=NPV(15%,C45:G45)+B45			
51							
52							

(b) Best-case scenario: With the best-case scenario, Capstone would make a significant profit from the project, earning more than $87 million surplus after recovering all the investment made in the project. (See Table 11.5.) This is equivalent to realizing a 67% rate of return on the investment.

COMMENTS: We see that the base case produces a positive NPW ($11,107; see Table 11.1), the worst case produces a negative NPW (−$42,755), and the best case produces a large positive NPW ($87,231). Still, just by looking at the results in the table, it is not easy to interpret the scenario analysis or to make a decision. For example, we could say that there is a chance of losing money on the project, but we do not yet have a specific probability for that possibility. Clearly, we need estimates of the probabilities of occurrence of the worst case, the best case, the base (most likely) case, and all other possibilities.

TABLE 11.5 Capstone's MicroCHP Cash Flows under the Best-Case Scenario (unit: $000)

	A	B	C	D	E	F	G
15							
16							
17		0	1	2	3	4	5
18	**Income Statement**						
19							
20	Revenues:						
21	Unit Price		$ 86.00	$ 86.00	$ 86.00	$ 86.00	$ 86.00
22	Demand (units)		2000	2160	2333	2519	2721
23	Sales Revenue		$ 172,000	$ 185,760	$ 200,621	$ 216,670	$ 234,004
24	Expenses:						
25	Unit Variable Cost		$ 56	$ 56	$ 56	$ 56	$ 56
26	Variable Cost		112,000	120,960	130,637	141,088	152,375
27	Fixed Cost		6,500	6,500	6,500	6,500	6,500
28	Depreciation		7,860	13,470	9,620	6,870	2,453
30	Taxable Income		$ 45,641	$ 44,831	$ 53,865	$ 62,213	$ 72,676
31	Income Taxes (40%)		18,256	17,932	21,546	24,885	29,071
33	Net Income		$ 27,384	$ 26,898	$ 32,319	$ 37,328	$ 43,606
34							
35	**Cash Flow Statement**						
36							
37	Operating Activities:						
38	Net Income		$ 27,384	$ 26,898	$ 32,319	$ 37,328	$ 43,606
39	Depreciation		$ 7,860	$ 13,470	$ 9,620	$ 6,870	$ 2,453
40	Investment Activities:						
41	Investment	$ (55,000)					
42	Salvage				=-0.4*(G42-(-B41-SUM(C28:G28)))		$ 8,000
43	Gains Tax						$ 2,692
45	Net Cash Flow	$ (55,000)	$ 35,244	$ 40,368	$ 41,938	$ 44,197	$ 56,750
46							
47							
48							
49		IRR =	67%				
50		PW(15%) =	$ 87,231	=NPV(15%,C45:G45)+B45			
51							
52							

The need to estimate probabilities leads us directly to our next step: developing a probability distribution (or, put another way, the probability that the variable in question takes on a certain value). We will consider this issue in the next section.

11.3 Probabilistic Cash Flow Analysis

Once you have an idea of the degree of risk inherent in an investment, the next step is to incorporate this information into your evaluation of the proposed project. There are two fundamental approaches: (1) consider the risk elements directly through probabilistic assessments and (2) adjust the discount rate to reflect any perceived risk in the project's cash flows. We will consider both approaches briefly. However, the risk-adjusted discount-rate approach is more commonly practiced in the real world, as the method is mathematically much simpler than the probabilistic approach.

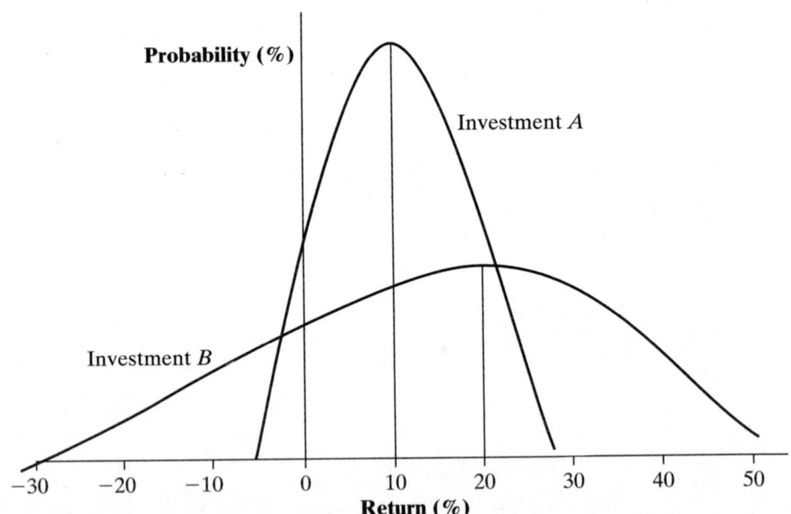

Figure 11.3 Illustration of investment risk: Investment A has a lower expected return but a lower risk than investment B

11.3.1 Including Risk in Investment Evaluation

In principle, investment risk is concerned with the range of possible outcomes from an investment: the wider this range, the higher is the risk. Figure 11.3 illustrates this intuitive notion. It shows, in the form of bell-shaped curves, the possible rates of return that might be earned on two investments. According to the figure, the expected return on investment A is about 10%, and the corresponding figure for investment B is about 20%.

Because we would define **expected return** as the probability-weighted average of possible returns, this expected figure represents the central tendency of the random outcome (in our case, the return). To take a simple example, if three returns are possible—6%, 9%, and 18%—and if the chance of each occurring is 0.40, 0.30, and 0.30, respectively, the investment's expected return is calculated as follows:

$$\text{Expected return } (\mu) = (0.40 \times 6\%) + (0.30 \times 9\%) + (0.30 \times 18\%)$$
$$= 10.5\%.$$

Basically, **risk** refers to the bunching of possible returns around an investment's expected return. If there is considerable bunching, as with investment A, the investment risk is low. With investment B, there is considerably less clustering of returns around the expected return, so it has a higher risk. The way to measure this clustering tendency is to calculate a probability-weighted average of the deviations of possible returns from the expected return. One such average is the **standard deviation** (σ) of returns.

To illustrate the calculation of the standard deviation of returns, we calculate the differences between the possible returns and the expected return, in the foregoing example, as $(6\% - 10.5\%), (9\% - 10.5\%)$, and $(18\% - 10.5\%)$. Because some of these deviations are positive and others are negative, they would tend to cancel one another out if we added them directly. So, we square them to ensure the same sign, calculate the probability-weighted average of the squared deviations [a value known as the variance (σ^2)], and then find the square root:

$$\text{Standard deviation } (\sigma) = (25.65)^{1/2} = 5.065\%.$$

Event	Deviations	Weighted Deviations
1	$(6\% - 10.5\%)^2$	$0.40 \times (6\% - 10.5\%)^2$
2	$(9\% - 10.5\%)^2$	$0.30 \times (9\% - 10.5\%)^2$
3	$(18\% - 10.5\%)^2$	$0.30 \times (18\% - 10.5\%)^2$
		$(\sigma^2) = 25.65$

What we can tell here is that risk corresponds to the *dispersion*, or *uncertainty*, in possible outcomes. We also know that statistical techniques exist to measure this dispersion. In our example, the smaller standard deviation means a considerable bunching, or less risk. When comparing investments with the same expected returns, conservative, or risk-averse, investors would prefer the investment with the smaller standard deviation of return.

11.3.2 Aggregating Risk over Time

Having defined risk and risk aversion in at least a general sense, we might be interested in estimating the amount of risk present in a particular investment opportunity. For an investment project, if we can determine the expected cash flow, as well as the variability of the cash flow, in each period over the project life, we may be able to aggregate the risk over the project life in terms of net present value $PW(r)$, as

$$E[\text{PW}(r)] = \sum_{n=0}^{N} \frac{E(A_n)}{(1 + r)^n} \tag{11.1}$$

and

$$V[\text{PW}(r)] = \sum_{n=0}^{N} \frac{V(A_n)}{(1 + r)^{2n}}, \tag{11.2}$$

where

$$
\begin{aligned}
r &= \text{risk-free discount rate,} \\
A_n &= \text{cash flow in period } n, \\
E(A_n) &= \text{expected cash flow in period } n, \\
V(A_n) &= \text{variance of the cash flow in period } n, \\
E[\text{PW}(r)] &= \text{expected net present value of the project, and} \\
V[\text{PW}(r)] &= \text{variance of the net present value of the project.}
\end{aligned}
$$

It is important to observe that we use a risk-free interest rate to discount the project cash flows, as the riskiness of project cash flows is reflected in the probability distributions.

In defining Eq. (11.2), we are also assuming the independence of cash flows, meaning that knowledge of what will happen to one particular period's cash flow will not allow us to predict what will happen to cash flows in other periods. Borrowing again from statistics, we are assuming mutually independent project cash flows. In the event

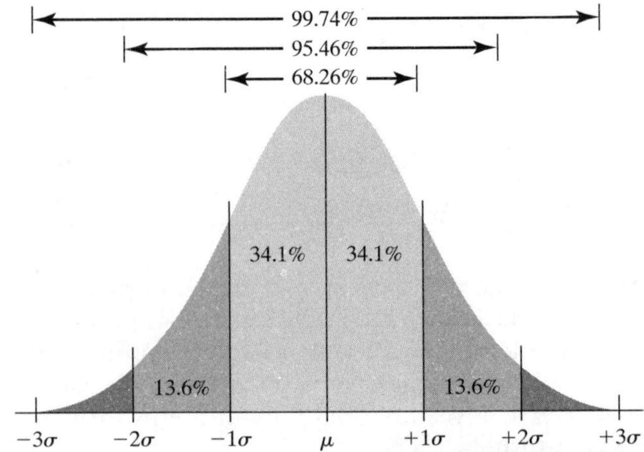

- The area under the normal curve equals 1.0, or 100%.
- Of the area under the curve, 99.74% is within $\pm 3\sigma$ of the mean (μ), indicating that the probability is 99.74% that actual outcome will be within the range $\mu - 3\sigma$ to $\mu + 3\sigma$.
- The larger the value of σ, the higher the probability will be the actual outcome will vary widely from the expected or most-likely estimate.
- Tables exist for finding the probability of other ranges, as shown in Appendix C.

Figure 11.4 Probability ranges for a normal distribution

that we cannot assume such a statistical independence among cash flows, we need to consider the degree of dependence among the cash flows.[2]

The normal distribution has the very important property that, under certain conditions, the distribution of a sum of a large number of *independent variables* is approximately normal. This is the central limit theorem. Since PW(r) is the sum of discounted random cash flows (A_n's), it follows that, under certain conditions, PW(r) is also closely approximated by a normal distribution with the mean and variance as calculated in Eqs. (11.1) and (11.2). A normal distribution is a bell-shaped probability distribution with many practical applications found in the real world. If a probability distribution is normal, the actual cash flow will be within ± 1 standard deviation (σ) of the expected cash flow 68.26% of the time. Figure 11.4 illustrates this point, and it also shows the situation for $\pm 2\sigma$ and $\pm 3\sigma$.

EXAMPLE 11.5 Computing the Mean and Variance of an Investment Opportunity

Assume that a project is expected to produce the following cash flows in each year, each periodic cash flow is independent of every other, and the risk-free rate is 6%:

Period	Expected Cash Flow	Estimated Standard Deviation
0	−$2,000	$100
1	$1,000	$200
2	$2,000	$500

Find the expected NPW as well as the variance of the NPW.

---

[2] As we seek further refinement in our decision under risk, we may consider dependent random variables or the degree of dependence through correlation coefficients, which is beyond the scope of this text. See C. S. Park, *Contemporary Engineering Economics*, Prentice Hall, 2011 (Chapter 12).

DISSECTING THE PROBLEM

Given: Periodic estimated project cash flows (means and variances); risk-free interest rate.

Find: $E[PW(r)]$ and $V[PW(r)]$.

METHODOLOGY

Calculate the expected NPW and the variance of the NPW.

SOLUTION

Using Eqs. (11.1) and (11.2), we find that the expected NPW and the variance of the NPW are

$$E[PW(6\%)] = -\$2{,}000 + \frac{\$1{,}000}{1.06} + \frac{\$2{,}000}{1.06^2} = \$723$$

and

$$Var[PW(6\%)] = 100^2 + \frac{200^2}{1.06^2} + \frac{500^2}{1.06^4} = 243{,}623,$$

respectively. Thus, the standard deviation is $494.

COMMENTS: How is this information used in decision making? It is assumed that most probability distributions are characterized by six standard deviations—three standard deviations above and three standard deviations below the mean. Therefore, the actual NPW of this project would almost certainly fall between $-\$759$ and $\$2{,}205$, as shown in Figure 11.5. If the NPW below 3σ from the mean is still positive, we may say that the project is quite safe. If that figure is negative, then it is up to the decision maker to determine whether the project is worth investing in given the expected mean and standard deviation of the project. If we assume a normal probability distribution, we could find the probability that the project's NPW will be negative, which is only 7.17%.

$$Pr(X \le x) = Pr(PW(6\%) \le 0)$$

$$= \Phi\left(\frac{X - \mu}{\sigma}\right) = \Phi\left(\frac{0 - 723}{494}\right) = \Phi\left(-1.4636\right)$$

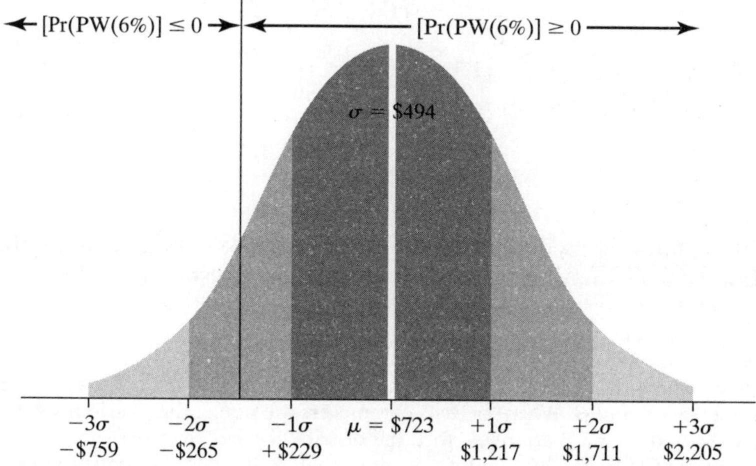

Figure 11.5 NPW distribution. With a normal probability assumption, the probability that the NPW will be negative is found to be 7.17%

$$= 1 - \Phi(1.4636)$$
$$= 1 - 0.9283$$
$$= 7.17\%.$$

See Appendix C for procedures on how to use the normal probability distribution.

11.3.3 Estimating Risky Cash Flows

In the previous section, we derived the expression of mean and variance of the net present worth distribution. These calculations, however, involve the mean and variance of the various individual cash flows and the statistical relationships among them. Knowledge of this information is a prerequisite to our analysis. The estimating procedure that is common in practice is to make an "optimistic" estimate, a "pessimistic" estimate, and a "most likely" estimate for each cash flow. Here, the meaning of these three estimates is as follows:

- Optimistic estimate: Everything will go as well as is reasonably possible.
- Pessimistic estimate: Everything will go as poorly as is reasonably possible.
- Most-likely estimate: Everything will go as most likely as is initially projected.

Then, these three estimates are used as the upper bound, the lower bound, and the mode of the corresponding cash flow probability distribution. The probability distribution itself is assumed to be a beta distribution[3] with a standard deviation of one-sixth of the spread between the upper and lower bounds (the optimistic and pessimistic estimates). With these assumptions, the mean and variance become explicit functions of the bounds and mode. Given the estimates

$$\text{Est}_o(A_n) = H(\text{optimistic estimate}),$$
$$\text{Est}_o(A_n) = L(\text{pessimistic estimate}), \text{ and}$$
$$\text{Est}_o(A_n) = M_o(\text{most likely estimate}),$$

of the bounds and mode of cash flow distribution of A_n at the end of period n, we find that

$$E[A_n] = \frac{H + 4M_o + L}{6} \tag{11.3}$$

and

$$\text{Var}[A_n] = \left(\frac{H - L}{6}\right)^2. \tag{11.4}$$

The model of an underlying beta distribution has been assumed primarily for convenience here, but these estimating formulas are based on a system developed for Program

---

[3] The beta distribution models events that are constrained to take place within an interval defined by a minimum and maximum value, and it is often used in the absence of data. The beta distribution has two shape parameters, α and β. When the two parameters are equal, the distribution is symmetrical. For example, when both α and β are equal to 1, the distribution becomes uniform. If α is less than β, the distribution is skewed to the left. And if α is more than β, the distribution is skewed to the right. Because of this modeling flexibility, the beta distribution is used extensively in estimating project cash flows.

Evaluation and Review Technique (PERT) for network planning and scheduling. It is important to note that the difference between the approximate expected values as just calculated and those resulting from the exact formula is relatively small for a wide range of beta-distribution conditions.

EXAMPLE 11.6 Developing a Present Worth Distribution for Capstone's Investment Project

Let's recall Example 11.4, where Capstone engineers have created three different scenarios based on the key input variables expressed in terms of three-point estimates in Example 11.1. If we examine the annual cash flows under each scenario, we find the following values:

Annual Cash Flow Estimates (unit: $000)

n	Worst-Case Scenario (Table 11.4) L	Most Likely Scenario (Table 11.1) M_o	Best-Case Scenario (Table 11.5) H
0	($55,000)	($55,000)	($55,000)
1	$1,944	$16,344	$35,244
2	$4,314	$19,488	$40,368
3	$2,904	$18,893	$41,938
4	$1,937	$18,785	$44,197
5	$8,600	$28,152	$56,750

Using these annual cash flow estimates as three-point estimates for each period, compute the mean and variance of the NPW distribution.

DISSECTING THE PROBLEM

Given: Three-point cash flow estimates for each period, interest rate = 15% per year.

Find: Mean and variance of the project, probability that the NPW will be negative.

METHODOLOGY

Calculate the mean and variance.

SOLUTION

$n = 0$: Since there is no variability in the initial investment amount, the variance is zero.

$n = 1$: Using Eqs. (11.3) and (11.4), we find that

$$E[A_1] = \frac{\$1,944 + 4(\$16,344) + \$35,244}{6} = \$17,094,$$

$$Var[A_1] = \left(\frac{35,244 - 1,944}{6}\right)^2 = 30,802,500.$$

Similarly, we can calculate the means and variances for other periods as follows:

n	L	M_0	H	$E[A_n]$	$Var[A_n]$
0	($55,000)	($55,000)	($55,000)	($55,000)	–
1	$1,944	$16,344	$35,244	$17,094	30,802,500
2	$4,314	$19,488	$40,368	$20,439	36,108,081
3	$2,904	$18,893	$41,938	$20,069	42,323,699
4	$1,937	$18,785	$44,197	$20,212	49,608,544
5	$8,600	$28,152	$56,750	$29,660	64,400,625

Now we are ready to find the mean and variance of the NPW by using Eqs. (11.1) and (11.2). We have

$$E[PW(15\%)] = -\$55,000 + \frac{\$17,094}{(1 + 0.15)} + \frac{\$20,439}{(1 + 0.15)^2} + \cdots$$

$$+ \frac{\$29,660}{(1 + 0.15)^5}$$

$$= \$14,817$$

$$Var[PW(15\%)] = \frac{30,802,500}{(1 + 0.15)^2} + \frac{36,108,081}{(1 + 0.15)^4} + \frac{42,323,699}{(1 + 0.15)^6}$$

$$+ \frac{49,608,544}{(1 + 0.15)^8} + \frac{64,400,625}{(1 + 0.15)^{10}}$$

$$= 94,369,701$$

$$\sigma[PW(15\%)] = \sqrt{94,369,701}$$

$$= \$9,714.$$

Once again, if we assume that the PW(15%) is normally distributed with the mean and variance as just calculated, we can determine the probability that the NPW will be negative:

$$Pr(X \le x) = Pr(PW(15\%) \le 0)$$

$$= \Phi\left(\frac{X - \mu}{\sigma}\right) = \Phi\left(\frac{0 - 14,817}{9,714}\right) = \Phi(-1.5253)$$

$$= 1 - \Phi(1.5253)$$

$$= 1 - 0.9364$$

$$= 6.36\%.$$

With the scenario approach in Example 11.4, the worst-case scenario resulted in PW(15%) = −$42,755. However, this possibility is truly remote with independent cash flow assumptions because this value is equivalent to 5.26σ below the mean, which is virtually nonexistent. We can say the same thing for the best-case scenario with PW(15%) = $87,231, which is equivalent to

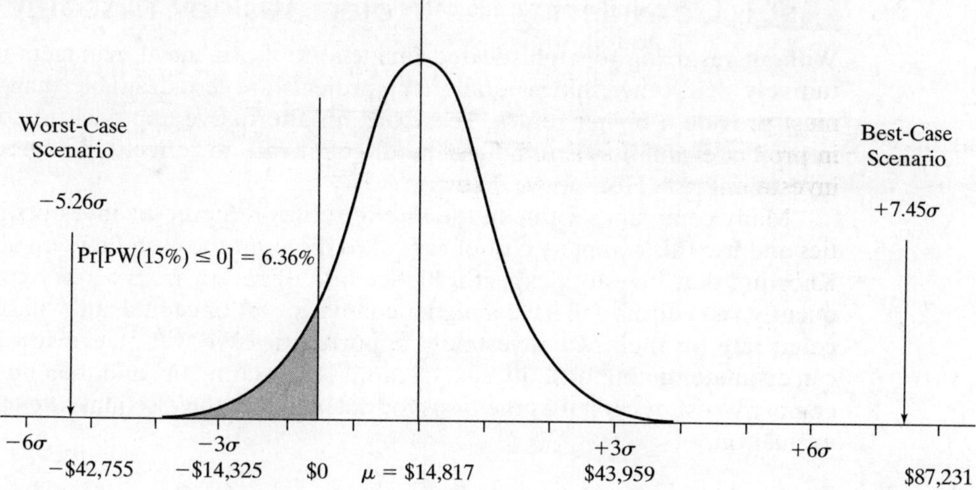

Figure 11.6 The NPW probability distribution for Capstone's MicroCHP project

7.45σ above the mean. (See Figure 11.6.) Clearly, the probabilistic approach outlined in this section provides much more meaningful information regarding the assessment of financial risk in investment evaluation.

COMMENTS: Recall that in deriving the mean and variance of the NPW, we assumed that the cash flows in each period are mutually independent.[4] In fact, these cash flows are not independent. They are perfectly positively correlated as these cash flow estimates are taken from the scenario analysis. In other words, if you assume a worst-case scenario, the cash flow in each period presents a worst case as well, indicating a perfect correlation. Similarly, if we assume a best-case scenario, the cash flow in each period reflects a best case as well. Then, we may easily determine the mean and variance of the NPW on the basis of the three NPW estimates as follows:

$$E[PW(15\%)] = \frac{\$87,231 + 4(\$11,107) + (-\$42,755)}{6}$$

$$= \$14,817$$

$$Var[PW(15\%)] = \left(\frac{87,231 - (-42,755)}{6}\right)^2$$

$$= (21,664)^2.$$

With this mean and this variance, the range of possible NPWs extends from $-\$50,175(-3\sigma)$ to $\$79,809(+3\sigma)$. What it implies is that the worst-case scenario $(-\$42,755$, or -2.66σ below the mean) cannot be ruled out completely, but the best-case scenario $(\$87,231$, or $+3.34\sigma$ above the mean) may be.

---

[4]Again, the analytical treatment of this type of dependent relationship is beyond the scope of this introductory text but can be found in Chan S. Park, *Contemporary Engineering Economics*, Prentice Hall, 2011 (Chapter 12).

$\boxed{11.4}$ Considering the Project Risk by Discount Rate

Without resorting to sophisticated financial tools, financial managers understand intuitively that, other things equal, risky projects are less desirable than safe ones and must provide a higher return. Therefore, an alternative approach to considering risk in project evaluation is to adjust the discount rate to reflect the degree of perceived investment risk. How do we do this?

Many companies estimate the rate of return required by investors in their securities and use this company cost of capital to discount the cash flows on all new projects. Knowing that investors expect a higher rate of return from a risky company, consequently, risky firms will have a higher company cost of capital and will set a higher discount rate for their new investment opportunities. We will first review how managers can estimate the opportunity cost of capital for a company and then how they use this company cost of capital as the basis for determining the discount rate to use in project evaluation.

11.4.1 Determining the Company Cost of Capital

When you invest money in a company, you incur an opportunity equal to the return you could have earned on an alternative, similar risky investment. The opportunity cost is the firm's **cost of capital**—it is the required rate of return the company must earn from existing assets and still meet the expectations of its capital providers. In most of the investment examples in the earlier chapters, we assumed that the projects under consideration were financed entirely with equity funds. In those cases, the **cost of capital** may have represented only the firm's required return on equity. However, most firms finance a substantial portion of their capital budget with long-term debt (bonds), and many also use common stock as a source of capital. In these cases, a firm's cost of capital must reflect the average cost of the various sources of long-term funds that the firm uses, not only the cost of equity. Therefore, we will examine cost of capital from two sources.

Cost of Equity Capital

Although debt and preferred stocks are contractual obligations that have easily determined costs, it is not easy to measure the cost of equity. In principle, the cost of equity capital involves an **opportunity cost**. In fact, the firm's after-tax cash flows belong to the stockholders. Management may either pay out these earnings in the form of dividends or retain the earnings and reinvest them in the business. If management decides to retain earnings, an opportunity cost is involved; stockholders could have received the earnings as dividends and invested this money in other financial assets. Therefore, the firm should earn on its retained earnings at least as much as the stockholders themselves could earn in alternative, but comparable, investments.

What rate of return can stockholders expect to receive on retained earnings? This question is difficult to answer, but the value sought is often regarded as the rate of return stockholders require on a firm's common stock. If a firm cannot invest retained earnings so as to earn at least the rate of return on equity, it should pay these funds to these stockholders and let them invest directly in other assets that do provide this return. In general, the expected return on any risky asset is composed of three factors:[5]

$$\begin{pmatrix} \text{Expected return} \\ \text{on risky asset} \end{pmatrix} = \begin{pmatrix} \text{Risk-free} \\ \text{interest rate} \end{pmatrix} + \begin{pmatrix} \text{Inflation} \\ \text{premium} \end{pmatrix} + \begin{pmatrix} \text{Risk} \\ \text{premium} \end{pmatrix}.$$

This equation says that the owner of a risky asset should expect to earn a return from three sources:

1. Compensation from the opportunity cost incurred in holding the asset. This is the risk-free interest rate.
2. Compensation for the declining purchasing power of the investment over time, known as the inflation premium.
3. Compensation for bearing risk, known as the risk premium.

Fortunately, we do not need to treat the first two terms as separate factors because together they equal the expected return on a default-free bond such as a government bond. In other words, owners of government bonds expect a return from the first two sources but not the third. So, we can simplify the previous equation as

$$\begin{pmatrix} \text{Expected return} \\ \text{on risky asset} \end{pmatrix} = \begin{pmatrix} \text{Interest rate on a} \\ \text{government bond} \end{pmatrix} + \begin{pmatrix} \text{Risk} \\ \text{premium} \end{pmatrix}.$$

When investors are contemplating buying a firm's stock, they have two primary things in mind: (1) cash dividends and (2) gains (share appreciation) at the time of sale. From a conceptual standpoint, investors determine market values of stocks by discounting expected future dividends at a rate that takes into account any future growth. Since investors seek growing and profitable companies, a desired growth factor for future dividends is usually included in the calculation.

The cost of equity is the risk-free interest rate (for example, a 20-year U.S. Treasury bond that returns around 6%) plus a premium for taking a risk as to whether a return will be received. The risk premium is the average return on the market—typically, the return for Standard & Poor's 500 largest U.S. stocks, or the S&P 500 (say, 12.5%), less the risk-free interest rate. This premium is multiplied by *beta*, an approximate measure of stock price volatility. **Beta** (β) quantifies risk by measuring one firm's stock price relative to all of the market's stock prices as a whole.

- If $\beta > 1$, it means that, on average, the stock is more volatile than the market.
- If $\beta < 1$, it means that, on average, the stock is less volatile than the market.

The values for beta are commonly found for most publicly traded stocks in various sources such as Value Line.[6] The cost of equity (i_e) is quantified by

$$i_e = r_f + \beta[r_M - r_f], \tag{11.5}$$

where

r_f = risk-free interest rate (commonly referenced to U.S. Treasury bond yield, inflation adjusted) and

---

[5] Robert C. Higgins, *Analysis for Financial Management*, 5th ed., New York: Irwin/McGraw-Hill, 1998.

[6] Value Line reports are presently available for more than 5,000 public companies, and that number is growing. The Value Line reports contain the following information: (1) total assets, (2) total liabilities, (3) total equity, (4) long-term debt as a percent of capital, (5) equity as a percent of capital, (6) financial strength (which is used to determine interest rates), (7) beta, and (8) return on invested capital.

r_M = market rate of return (commonly referenced to average return on S&P 500 stock index funds, inflation adjusted).

Note that this amount is almost always higher than the cost of debt. This is so because the U.S. Tax Code allows the deduction of interest expense but does not allow the deduction of the cost of equity, which could be considered more subjective and complex. Example 11.7 illustrates how we may determine the cost of equity.

EXAMPLE 11.7 Determining the Cost of Equity

Capstone Corporation needs to raise $55 million for the MicroCHP project described in Example 11.1. Capstone's target capital structure calls for a debt ratio of 0.4, indicating that $33 million has to be financed from equity. The pertinent information is as follows:

- Capstone is planning to raise $33 million from the financial markets.
- Capstone's beta is known to be 2.0, which is higher than 1, indicating that the firm is perceived to be riskier than the market average.
- The risk-free interest rate is 5.47%, and the average market return is 13%. (These interest rates are adjusted to reflect inflation in the economy.)
- The MicroCHP project is a normal risky project comparable to the firm's market risk.

Determine the cost of equity to finance the plant modernization.

DISSECTING THE PROBLEM	
	Given: $r_M = 13\%, r_f = 5.47\%$, and $\beta = 2.0$. **Find:** i_e.
METHODOLOGY	**SOLUTION**
Compute i_e.	We calculate i_e as follows: $$i_e = 0.0547 + 2.0(0.13 - 0.0547) = 20.53\%.$$

COMMENTS: What does this 20.53% represent? If Capstone finances the project entirely from its equity funds, the project must earn at least a 20.53% return on investment to be worthwhile, assuming that the project's risk is about the same as the average risk of the company's assets and operations.

Cost of Debt Capital

Now let us consider the calculation of the specific cost that is to be assigned to the debt financing. The calculation is relatively straightforward and simple. Two types of debt financing are term loans and bonds. Because the interest payments on both are tax deductible, they reduce the effective cost of debt. To determine the after-tax cost of debt (i_d), we can evaluate the expression

$$\text{After-tax cost of debt} = \text{pretax cost} \times (1 - \text{tax rate})$$

or,

$$i_d = \left(\frac{c_s}{c_d}\right)k_s(1 - t_m) + \left(\frac{c_b}{c_d}\right)k_b(1 - t_m), \qquad (11.6)$$

where

c_s = the amount of the term loan,
k_s = the before-tax interest rate on the term loan,
t_m = the firm's marginal tax rate,
k_b = the before-tax interest rate on the bond, and
c_b = the amount of bond financing and $c_s + c_b = c_d$.

Example 11.8 illustrates the process of computing the cost of debt for the Capstone Corporation scenario introduced in Example 11.7.

EXAMPLE 11.8 Determining the Cost of Debt

For the case in Example 11.7, suppose that Capstone decided to finance the remaining $22 million by securing a term loan and issuing 20-year $1,000 par bonds under the following conditions:

Source	Amount	Interest Fraction	Rate
Term loan	$6.6 million	0.30	12.16% per year
Bonds	$15.4 million	0.70	10.74% per year

Capstone's marginal tax rate is 40%, which is expected to remain constant in the future. Determine the after-tax cost of debt.

DISSECTING THE PROBLEM	
	Given: $k_s = 12.16\%, k_b = 10.74\%, c_s/c_d = 0.30, c_b/c_d = 0.70, t_m = 40\%$. **Find:** i_d.
METHODOLOGY Solve for i_d.	**SOLUTION** The after-tax cost of debt is the interest rate on debt multiplied by $(1 - t_m)$. In effect, the government pays part of the cost of debt because interest is tax deductible. Now we are ready to compute the after-tax cost of debt as follows: $i_d = (0.30)(0.1216)(1 - 0.40) + (0.70)(0.1074)(1 - 0.40)$ $\qquad = 6.70\%$.

COMMENTS: What does this 6.70% interest really mean? Even though you are borrowing the money at 12% and 10.74% from two different sources, your net cost of composite borrowing will be just 6.70%, as debt interest payments are tax deductible expenses.

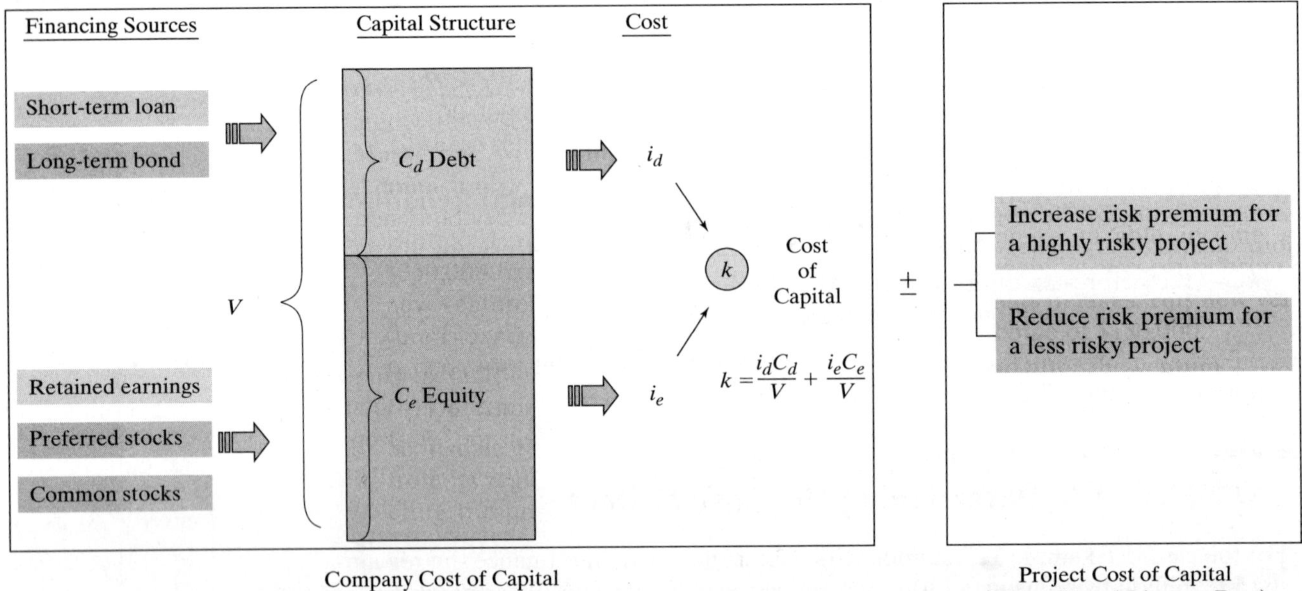

Figure 11.7 Company cost of capital versus project cost of capital. In project evaluation, we use the project cost of capital

Calculating the Company Cost of Capital

With the specific cost of each financing component determined, we are now ready to calculate the weighted-average cost of capital on the basis of total capital. Assuming that a firm raises capital on the basis of the target capital structure and that the target capital structure remains unchanged in the future, we can determine a **company cost of capital**, which is a **weighted-average cost of capital** (or, simply stated, the **cost of capital, k**). As illustrated in Figure 11.7, this cost of capital represents a composite index reflecting the cost of raising funds from different sources. The cost of capital is defined as

$$k = i_d\left(\frac{c_d}{V}\right) + i_e\left(\frac{c_e}{V}\right), \tag{11.7}$$

where

c_d = total debt capital (such as bonds) in dollars,
c_e = total equity capital in dollars,
$V = c_d + c_e$,
i_e = average equity interest rate per period, considering all equity sources,
i_d = after-tax average borrowing interest rate per period, considering all debt sources, and
k = weighted-average cost of capital.

Note that the cost of equity is already expressed in terms of after-tax cost because any return to holders of either common stock or preferred stock is made after the payment of income taxes.

In evaluating an investment project, the costs of debt and equity in Eq. (11.7) are the interest rates on *new debt* and *equity*,[7] not existing debt or equity, respectively. Our

---

[7] This is known as the **marginal cost of capital**, the cost of obtaining another dollar of new capital, and this value rises as more and more capital is raised during a given period.

primary concern with the cost of capital is to use it in evaluating a new investment project. The rate at which the firm has borrowed in the past is less important for this purpose. Example 11.9 works through the computations for finding the cost of capital (k).

EXAMPLE 11.9 Calculating the Company Cost of Capital

Reconsider Examples 11.7 and 11.8. The marginal income-tax rate (t_m) for Capstone is expected to remain at 40% in the future. Assuming that Capstone's capital structure (debt ratio) also remains unchanged in the future, determine the cost of capital (k) of raising $55 million in addition to Capstone's existing capital.

DISSECTING THE PROBLEM	
	Given: With c_d = \$22 million, c_e = \$33 million, V = \$55 million, i_d = 6.70%, i_e = 20.53%, and Eq. (11.7). **Find:** Marginal cost of capital (k).
METHODOLOGY Solve for cost of capital (k).	**SOLUTION** We calculate the marginal cost of capital as follows: $$k = \frac{(0.0692)(4)}{10} + \frac{(0.2053)(6)}{10} = 15\%.$$ This 15% would be the marginal cost of capital that a company with this capital structure would expect to pay to raise \$55 million, and this is the discount rate to be used in evaluating the Capstone's new investment project. In other words, the project must return more than 15% in order to be justified.

11.4.2 Project Cost of Capital: Risk-Adjusted Discount Rate Approach

It is important to distinguish between the *risk of the project* and the *risk of the company*. The risk of the company is reflected in the β value. So even if a risky company invests in a low-risk project, it should discount the cash flows at a correspondingly low cost of capital. If it invests in a high-risk project, those cash flows should be discounted at a high cost of capital. The most common way to do this is to add an increment to the discount rate — that is, discount the expected value of the risky cash flows at a rate that includes a premium for risk. The size of the risk premium naturally increases with the perceived risk of the investment. This discussion implies a simple rule — the discount rate of a project should be the expected return on a financial asset of comparable risk known as the **project cost of capital**.

What makes the risk-adjusted discount rate approach appealing in practical application is its simplicity. Most chief financial officers (CFOs) have at least a rough idea of how an investment's required rate of return should vary with perceived risk. For example, they know from the historical data that, over many years, common stocks have yielded an average annual return about 7% higher than the return on government bonds (risk-free return). If the present return on government bonds is 8%, it is plausible to expect an investment that is about as risky as common stocks to yield a return of about 15%. Similarly, CFOs know that an investment promising a return of 40% is attractive unless its risk is extraordinarily high. Granted, such reasoning is imprecise; nonetheless, it does lend some objectivity to risk assessment. To illustrate the use of such risk-adjusted discount rates, consider Example 11.10.

EXAMPLE 11.10 Risk-Adjusted Discount Rate Approach

Reconsider Example 11.6, where the expected cash flows for the Capstone project are

Period	0	1	2	3	4	5
Cash Flow	−$55,000	$17,094	$20,439	$20,069	$20,212	$29,660

Suppose that Capstone consider the MicroCHP project to be just one of their normal risky projects. Then the appropriate discount rate to use is 15%, as calculated in Example 11.9. However, Capstone considers the MicroCHP project to be much riskier than normal projects, so it believes an additional risk premium of 6.93% should be added. If management has decided to use a risk-adjusted discount rate of 21.93% to compensate for the uncertainty of the cash flows, is this project acceptable?

DISSECTING THE PROBLEM

You need to determine whether the project under consideration is of normal risk. If not, you need to come up with a desired risk premium to add.

Given: Annual cash flows given in most likely values, $N = 5$ years, $k = 15\%$, and additional risk premium $= 6.93\%$.

Find: PW.

METHODOLOGY

Use the risk-adjusted discount rate to calculate the net present value.

SOLUTION

First find the project cost of capital (risk-adjusted discount rate):

$$15\% + 6.93\% = 21.93\%.$$

Then calculate the net present value, using this project cost of capital:

$$PW(21.93\%) = -\$55,000 + \frac{\$17,094}{1.2193} + \frac{\$20,439}{1.2193^2} + \cdots + \frac{\$29,660}{1.2193^5}$$
$$= \$3,989 > 0.$$

Because the PW is still positive, the investment is attractive even after we adjust for further risk.

COMMENTS: Note that the risk-adjusted discount rate reduces the investment's appeal. If the investment were normal risk, its NPW at a 15% discount rate would be $14,817; but because a higher risk-adjusted rate is deemed appropriate, the NPW falls by $10,828. Certainly, as the perceived project risk increases beyond the 6.93% risk premium, management would require an inducement higher than this amount before it would be willing to make the investment.

SUMMARY

- Often, cash flow amounts and other aspects of investment project analysis are uncertain. Whenever such uncertainty exists, we are faced with the difficulty of **project risk**—the possibility that an investment project will not meet our minimum requirements for acceptability and success.

- Three of the most basic tools for assessing project risk are as follows:
  1. **Sensitivity analysis**—identifying the project variables that, when varied, have the greatest effect on project acceptability.
  2. **Break-even analysis**—identifying the value of a particular project variable that causes the project to exactly break even.
  3. **Scenario analysis**—comparing a base-case, or expected, project measurement (such as PW) with the measurement(s) for one or more additional scenarios, such as best and worst case, to identify the extreme and most likely project outcomes.

- In considering the risk elements in project evaluation, there are two common approaches.
  1. The first approach is to describe the riskiness of the project cash flows in terms of probability distributions and then to use the risk-free interest rate to determine the net-present-value distribution. Once you obtain the PW distribution (mean and variance), you need to determine whether the expected value of the PW distribution is large enough to undertake the risk perceived in the project, which is revealed by the variance of the PW distribution.
  2. The second approach is to adjust the discount rate to reflect your perceived risk in terms of the risk premium and then use this adjusted rate to discount the expected cash flows. In practice, the risk-adjusted discount-rate approach is much more popular, as the risk-assessment process is much simpler than the probabilistic approach.

- The company cost of capital (or **weighted-average cost of capital**, or simply **cost of capital, k**) is the rate of return that the firm must expect to earn on its average-risk investments in order to provide a fair expected return to all its stockholders. Therefore, if the firm uses the weighted-average cost of capital as a discount rate for project evaluation, it assumes that the project risk is about the same as the risk of the firm's existing business.

- The **project cost of capital** can be different from the company cost of capital if the firm uses the capital raised from all sources put in a project whose risk is different from the risk of existing business operation. The risk-adjusted discount rate refers to this project cost of capital.

SELF-TEST QUESTIONS

11s.1 For a certain investment project, the net present worth can be expressed as functions of sales price (X) and variable production cost Y of $PW = 12,550 (2X - Y) - 8000$. The base values for X and Y are $25 and $15, respectively. If the sales price is increased 15% over the base price, how much change in NPW can be expected?

(a) 10%   (b) 20%   (c) 13.68%   (d) 21.82%

11s.2 An investor bought 100 shares of stock at a cost of $10 per share. He held the stock for 15 years and wants to sell it now. For the first three years, he received no dividends. For each of the next seven years, he received total dividends of $100 per year. For each of the remaining five years, no dividends were paid. In the last 15 years, the investor's marginal tax rate and capital gain tax rate were averaging about 30% and 20%, respectively. What would be the break-even selling price to earn a 15% return on investment after tax?

(a) $6,579   (b) $7,977   (c) $8,224   (d) $9,398

11s.3 A company is currently paying a sales representative $0.50 per mile to drive her car for company business. The company is considering supplying the representative with a car, which would involve the following:

- Option 1: Continue to pay at the rate of 50 cents per mile.

- Option 2: Provide a company vehicle to the sales representative. A car costs $24,000 and has a service life of five years and a market value of $7,000 at the end of that time. The cost of keeping the car in the garage during the off-hours amounts to $2,500 a year, and the cost of fuel, tires, and maintenance is 30 cents per mile. The car will be depreciated by MACRS using a recovery period of five years (20%, 32%, 19.20%, 11.52%, 11.52%).

The firm's marginal tax rate is 40%. What annual mileage must the sales representative travel by car for the cost of the two options of providing transportation to be equal if the interest rate is 15%?

(a) 36,345 miles   (b) 41,235 miles   (c) 45,233 miles   (d) 47,518 miles

11s.4 A manufacturing company is considering a capacity expansion investment at the cost of $250,000. The expansion would enable the company to produce up to 100,000 more parts and the useful life of the additional capacity is seven years. Each part would generate $2 net profit and annual operating and maintenance costs are estimated at $25,000 per year. If the MARR of the firm is 10%, what is the minimum yearly production rate to make this investment justifiable? Assume a salvage value of 0.

(a) Less than 37,000   (b) Between 37,000 and 39,000
(c) Between 39,000 and 42,000   (d) More than 42,000

11s.5 Project A has the following probability distribution of expected future returns:

Probability	Net Future Worth
0.1	−$16,000
0.2	4,000
0.4	16,000
0.2	25,000
0.1	35,000

What is the expected future worth for Project A?
(a) $9,450   (b) $10,800   (c) $14,100   (d) $12,300

11s.6 In Problem 11s.5, what is the standard deviation of expected future worth for Project A?
(a) $10,735   (b) $3,686   (c) $13,289   (d) $12,280

11s.7 The Arizona Mining Company contemplates investing $4 million in new sets of ripping equipment to expand its copper mining operation. The management of the company forecasts that the new investment will generate incremental net cash inflows of A_n ($n = 1, 2, …, 5$), where each of the A_i is a random variable with a mean of $2 million and a standard deviation of $400,000. The salvage value of the mining equipment at the end of year 5 will be also a random variable with a mean of $1 million and a standard deviation of $300,000. Compute the *mean* of the present value of this investment. Assume that the cash inflows of A_n are mutually independent random variables and the risk-free interest rate is 10%.
(a) $2.9607   (b) $3.235   (c) $4.239   (d) −$3.276

11s.8 In Problem 11s.7, compute the variance of the present value of the investment.
(a) −0.2220   (b) 0.2220   (c) 0.4711   (d) 0.5029

11s.9 In Problem 11s.7, the degree of project cash flow uncertainty is instead captured by adjusting the discount rate from 10% to 15%. Determine the certainty equivalent present value of the project at this risk-adjusted discount rate.
(a) $2.5684   (b) $2.980   (c) $3.2015   (d) $3.674

11s.10 Harry Wilson, a mechanical engineer at Lehigh manufacturing, has found that the anticipated profitability of a newly developed motion detector for its popular home security device product line can be estimated as follows:

$$PW = 40.28W\,(2X - 11) - 77{,}860$$

where W is the number of units produced and sold and X is the sales price per unit. Harry also found that W parameter value could occur anywhere over a range of 1,000 to 6,000 units and the X parameter value anywhere between $20 and $40 per unit.

Suppose both W and X are statistically independent continuous random variables with the following means and variances:

$$E[W] = 3{,}500,\ V[W] = 2{,}083{,}333$$
$$E[X] = 30,\ V[X] = 33.$$

What is the variance of PW?
(a) 2.2309×10^{11} (b) 4.4618×10^{11}
(c) 2.769×10^{9} (d) 1.118549×10^{13}

11s.11 In 11s.10, W and X are mutually independent discrete random variables with the following probabilities:

W		X	
Event	Probability	Event	Probability
1,000	0.4	$20	0.7
6,000	0.6	$40	0.3

What is the probability that the PW would exceed $6,000,000?
(a) 0.28   (b) 0.40   (c) 0.60   (d) 0.82

PROBLEMS

Sensitivity Analysis

11.1 A machine, costing $30,000 to buy and $2,500 per year to operate, will save mainly labor expenses in packaging over seven years. The anticipated salvage value of the machine at the end of seven years is $4,500.

(a) If a 12% return on investment (rate of return) is desired, what is the minimum required annual savings in labor from this machine?

(b) If the service life is just five years, instead of seven years, what is the minimum required annual savings in labor for the firm to realize a 12% return on investment?

(c) If the annual operating cost increases 10%, say, from $2,500 to $2,750, what will happen to the answer to (a)?

11.2 Lane Construction Ltd. is considering the acquisition of a new dump truck. The truck's base price is $75,000, and it will cost another $15,000 to modify it for special use by the company. This truck falls into the MACRS five-year class. It will be sold after five years for $20,000. The truck purchase will have no effect on revenues, but it is expected to save the firm $35,000 per year in before-tax operating costs mainly in leasing expenses. The firm's marginal tax rate (federal plus state) is 40%, and its MARR is 15%.

(a) Is this project acceptable based on the most likely estimates given in the problem?

(b) If the firm's MARR is increased to 20%, what would be the required savings in leasing so that the project would remain profitable?

(c) If the projected savings figure is only $25,000, would you still recommend the project?

11.3 Autonumerics, Inc. has just invested $600,000 in a manufacturing process that is estimated to generate an after-tax annual cash flow of $250,000 in each of the next five years. At the end of year 5, no further market for the product and no salvage value for the manufacturing process are expected. If a manufacturing problem delays plant start-up for one year (leaving only four years of process life), what additional after-tax cash flow will be needed to maintain the same internal rate of return as if no delay had occurred?

11.4 You are considering an investment project with the following financial information:

(a) Required investment = $500,000

(b) Project life = 5 years

(c) Salvage value = $50,000

(d) Depreciation method = straight-line depreciation (no half-year convention)

(e) Unit price = $40

(f) Unit variable cost = $18

(g) Fixed annual cost = $230,000

(h) Annual sales volume = 100,000 units

(i) Tax rate = 35%

(j) MARR = 15%

Suppose the company is most concerned about the impact of its price estimate on the project's rate of return. How would you address this concern?

11.5 A real-estate developer seeks to determine the most economical height for a new office building. The building will be sold after five years. The relevant net annual revenues and salvage values are as follows:

	Height			
	2 Floors	**3 Floors**	**4 Floors**	**5 Floors**
First cost (net after tax)	$500,000	$750,000	$1,250,000	$2,000,000
Lease revenue	$199,100	$169,200	$149,200	$378,150
Net resale value (after tax)	$600,000	$900,000	$2,000,000	$3,000,000

(a) The developer is uncertain about the interest rate (i) to use but is certain that it is in the range of 5% to 20%. For each building height, find the range of values of i for which that building height is the most economical.

(b) Suppose that the developer's interest rate is known to be 15%. In terms of PW, what would be the cost of an error in overestimation of resale value such that the true value is 10% lower than the original estimate?

11.6 Jane Livingston, an industrial engineer at Energy Conservation Service, has found that the anticipated profitability of a newly developed water-heater temperature-control device can be measured by net present worth as $PW = 5.63V(4.3X - \$15) - 33{,}580$ where V is the number of units produced and sold and X is the sales price per unit. She also found that the V parameter value could occur anywhere in the range of 1,500 to 5,000 units and the X parameter value anywhere between $10 and $35 per unit. Develop a sensitivity graph as a function of number of units produced and sales price per unit.

11.7 Burlington Motor Carriers, a trucking company, is considering the installation of a two-way mobile satellite messaging service on its 2,000 trucks. From tests done last year on 120 trucks, the company found that satellite messaging could cut 60% of its $5 million bill for long-distance communications with truck drivers. More importantly, the drivers who used this system reduced the number of "deadhead" miles—those driven without paying loads—by 0.5%. Applying that improvement to all 230 million miles covered by the Burlington fleet each year would produce an extra $1.25 million in savings.

Equipping all 2,000 trucks with the satellite hookup will require an investment of $8 million and the construction of a message-relaying system costing $2 million. The equipment and onboard devices will have a service life of eight years and negligible salvage value; they will be depreciated under the five-year MACRS class. Burlington's marginal tax rate is about 38%, and its required minimum attractive rate of return is 18%.

(a) Determine the annual net cash flows from the project.

(b) Perform a sensitivity analysis on the project's data, varying savings on the telephone bill and savings in deadhead miles. Assume that each of these variables can deviate from its base-case expected value by ±10%, ±20%, and ±30%.

(c) Prepare sensitivity diagrams and interpret the results.

Break-Even Analysis

11.8 Matt Mona is in the process of purchasing a motel near a college town. The motel costs $3,500,000. The lot costs $500,000. Furniture and furnishings cost $700,000 and should be recovered in seven years (seven-year MACRS property), while the cost of the motel building should be recovered in 39 years (39-year MACRS real property placed in service on January 1). The land will appreciate at an annual rate of 5% over the project period, but the building will have zero salvage value after 25 years. When the motel is full (100% capacity), it takes in (receipts) $6,000 per day for 365 days per year. The motel has fixed operating expenses, exclusive of depreciation, of $430,000 per year. The variable operating expenses are $220,000 at 100% capacity and vary directly with percent capacity down to $0 at 0% capacity. If the interest rate is 10% compounded annually, at what percentage capacity must this motel operate in order to break even? (Assume that Matt's tax rate is 30% and the project life is 25 years.)

11.9 D&D Machinery has been making a part for its industrial rotary gear shaving machine. D&D engineers are asked to investigate alternative ways of obtaining the part, as the unit cost for the part currently is not competitive in the marketplace. D&D needs 25,000 parts per year for the next three years. At that point, any capital equipment could be sold. D&D's tax rate is 40%, and its MARR is 12%.

- Option A: Continue to produce the part with the old machine. The machine has been fully depreciated. The current machine could be sold for $6,000 in three years. Making the part with the old machine involves the following: Variable costs for the part are $4 for direct materials, $3 for direct labor, and $2 for variable manufacturing overhead.

- Option B: Purchase the part from outside for $13 per part, including shipping.

- Option C: Replace the old machine with the new model. The newer model would cost $55,000 and would depreciate according to a seven-year MACRS method. The new machine, if purchased, could be sold for $15,000 in three years. It would cut direct labor costs to $1.50 per unit and variable costs to $0.75 per part. If the new model is acquired, the old machine would be sold for $25,000.

    (a) When Option B is compared with Option A, determine the break-even outsourcing unit cost.

    (b) When Option B is compared with Option C, determine the break-even outsourcing cost per unit.

    (c) Which alternative is the most economical?

11.10 A plant engineer wishes to know which of two types of lightbulbs should be used to light a warehouse. The bulbs currently used cost $45.90 per bulb and last 14,600 hours before burning out. The new bulb ($60 per bulb) provides the same amount of light and consumes the same amount of energy but lasts twice as long. The labor cost to change a bulb is $16.00. The lights are on 19 hours a day, 365 days a year. If the firm's MARR is 15%, what is the maximum price (per bulb) the engineer should be willing to pay to switch to the new bulb? (Assume that the firm's marginal tax rate is 40%.)

11.11 Barbara Thompson is considering the purchase of a piece of business rental property containing stores and offices at a cost of $350,000. Barbara estimates that annual receipts from rentals will be $55,000 and that annual disbursements, other than income taxes, will be about $18,000. The property is expected to appreciate at the annual rate of 5%. Barbara expects to retain the property for 20 years once it is acquired. Then it will be depreciated on the basis of the 39-year real-property class (MACRS), assuming that the property would be placed in service on January 1. Barbara's marginal tax rate is 30%, and her MARR is 10%. What would be the minimum annual total of rental receipts that would make the investment break even?

11.12 A firm is considering two different methods of solving a production problem. Both methods are expected to be obsolete in six years. Method *A* would cost $80,000 initially and have annual operating costs of $22,000. Method *B* would cost $52,000 initially and have annual operating costs of $17,000. The salvage value realized with Method *A* would be $20,000 and with Method *B* would be $15,000. Method *A* would generate $16,000 of revenue a year more than Method *B*. Investments in both methods depreciate as a five-year MACRS property class. The firm's marginal income-tax rate is 40%. The firm's MARR is 20%. What would be the required additional annual revenue for Method *A* so the firm would be indifferent in its choice of method?

11.13 A national newspaper publishing group is considering introducing a new morning newspaper in Denver. Its direct competitor charges $0.75 per copy at retail, with $0.15 going to the retailer. For the level of news coverage the company desires, the fixed cost of editors, reporters, rent, press-room expenses, and wire-service charges are determined to be $300,000 per month. The variable cost of ink and paper is $0.20 per copy, but advertising revenues of $0.10 per paper will be generated. To print the morning paper, the publisher has to purchase a new printing press, which will cost $600,000. The press machine will be depreciated according to the method for the seven-year MACRS class. The press machine will be used for 10 years, at which time its salvage value will be about $100,000. Assume 25 weekdays of printing in a month, a 40% tax rate, and a 12% MARR. How many copies per day must be sold at a selling price of $0.50 per copy at retail in order for the publishing group to break even?

11.14 Weldon Cutting Tools Company is considering the purchase of a new broaching machine to produce finished parts. Two types of broaching machines are available on the market. The lives of Machine *A* and Machine *B* are 8 years and 10 years, respectively. The machines have the following receipts and disbursements:

Item	Machine *A*	Machine *B*
First cost	$65,000	$83,500
Service life	8 years	10 years
Salvage value	$5,000	$8,000
Annual O&M costs	$7,500	$5,800
Depreciation (MACRS)	7 year	7 year

Assume an after-tax MARR of 10% and a marginal tax rate of 30%.

(a) Which machine would be most economical to purchase under an infinite planning horizon? Explain any assumption that you need to make about future alternatives.

(b) Determine the break-even annual O&M costs for Machine *A* so that the present worths of Machines *A* and *B* are the same.

(c) Suppose that the required service life of the machine is only five years. The estimated salvage values at the end of the required service period are estimated to be $13,000 for Machine *A* and $18,500 for Machine *B*. Which machine is more economical?

Scenario Analysis

11.15 Peabody Corporation has the following base-case estimates for its new small engine assembly project:

- Price per unit = $500
- Variable costs = $120 per unit
- Fixed costs = $2.5 million
- Demand = 20,000 units per year
- Capital investment = $8 million at year 0
- Product life = 8 years
- Salvage value = $500,000
- Depreciation method = seven-year MACRS
- Tax rate = 35%
- MARR = 12%

Suppose the company believes that all of its estimates (except the product life, depreciation method, tax rate, and MARR) are accurate only to within ±20%.

(a) What is the NPW of the project based on its base-case scenario?

(b) What is the NPW of the project based on its best-case scenario?

(c) What is the worst-case scenario?

(d) What conclusion would you make about the project after seeing the scenario analyses?

11.16 Suppose you are considering an investment project that requires $800,000, has a six-year life, and has a salvage value of $100,000. Sales volume is projected to be 65,000 units per year. Price per unit is $63, variable cost per unit is $42, and fixed costs are $532,000 per year. The depreciation method is a five-year MACRS. The tax rate is 35% and you expect a 20% return on this investment.

(a) Determine the break-even sales volume.

(b) Calculate the cash flows of the base case over six years and its NPW.

(c) If the sales price per unit increases to $400, what is the required break-even volume?

(d) Suppose the projections given for price, sales volume, variable costs, and fixed costs are all accurate to within ±15%. What would be the NPW figures of the best-case and worst-case scenarios?

Probabilistic Analysis

11.17 The following information is available about Henson Manufacturing Co.:

Probability	Return on Investment
0.15	5%
0.25	15%
0.35	22%
0.15	30%
0.10	40%

Compute Henson's expected return and standard deviation.

11.18 Suppose that you are considering an investment project with a two-year life. If the annual cash flows are given in terms of three-point estimates and these cash flows are statistically independent of each other, compute the mean and variance of the NPW distribution. Use a risk-free discount rate of 10%.

Period (n)	Pessimistic	Most Likely	Optimistic
0	−$10,000	−$8,000	−$7,000
1	$5,000	$12,000	$15,000
2	$4,000	$10,000	$13,000

11.19 A corporation is trying to decide whether to buy the patent for a product designed by another company. The decision to buy will require an investment of $8 million, and the demand for the product is not known. If demand is light, the company expects a return of $1.3 million each year for three years. If the demand is moderate, the return will be $2.5 million each year for four years, and a high demand will mean a return of $4 million each year for four years. It is estimated that the probability of a high demand is 0.4 and the probability of a light demand is 0.2. The firm's interest rate (risk free) is 12%. Calculate the expected present worth of the investment. On this basis, should the company make the investment? (All figures represent after-tax values.)

11.20 Consider the following investment cash flows over a three-year life:

n	$E(A_n)$	$Var(A_n)$
0	−$1,000	0
1	$500	200^2
2	$1,500	300^2
3	$800	100^2

(a) If all cash flows are mutually independent, compute $E(\text{NPW})$ and $Var(\text{NPW})$ at $i = 10\%$.

(b) If all annual cash flows are normally distributed with the means and variances as previously specified, compute the probability that the project will make a profit higher than its expected NPW.

11.21 Assume that we can estimate a project's cash flows as follows:

n	Expected Flow $E(A_n)$	Estimate of Standard Deviation σ_n
0	−$300	$20
1	$120	$10
2	$150	$15
3	$150	$20
4	$110	$25
5	$100	$30

In this case, each annual flow can be represented by a random variable with known mean and variance. Further assume complete independence among the cash flows.

(a) Find the expected NPW and the variance of this project at $i = 10\%$.

(b) If all cash flows are normally distributed with the given means and variances, what is the probability that the NPW will exceed $200?

11.22 A consumer electronics firm is trying to decide whether to invest $18M in a new plant for expanding its output of cell phones. Management forecasts that the new expansion will generate incremental net cash flows over the next five years as follows:

n	Expected Flow $E(A_n)$	Estimate of Standard Deviation σ_n
0	−$18M	0
1	$5M	$8M
2	$8M	$9M
3	$12M	$10M
4	$10M	$5M
5	$5M	$3M

(a) If the firm's discount rate is 12%, determine the mean and variance of the NPW.

(b) If all annual cash flows are normally distributed with the means and variances as previously specified, compute the probability that the project will lose money.

11.23 Consider an investment with the following projected cash flows:

n	$E(A_n)$	$Var(A_n)$
0	−$2,500	100^2
1	$2,200	200^2
2	$1,800	300^2

The distributions are assumed to be independent of each other.

(a) Compute the mean of the NPW at $i = 10\%$. Using just the mean value, would the investment be accepted?

(b) Compute the standard deviation of the NPW distribution.

(c) Compute the two standard deviations below the mean. If these cash flows are normally distributed with the means and variances as previously specified, what is the probability that the actual NPW will fall 2σ below the mean?

Comparing Risky Projects

11.24 You are considering investing in one of two projects, which have the following returns and probabilities of occurrence:

	Return on Investment	
Probability	**Project *A***	**Project *B***
0.10	−20%	−35%
0.20	0	−10%
0.25	10%	15%
0.30	15%	25%
0.10	20%	40%
0.05	40%	50%

(a) Compute the mean return for each project.

(b) Compute the variance of return for each project.

(c) Which project would you prefer, and why?

11.25 You are considering two mutually exclusive projects with the following cash flows:

		Projected Cash Flows	
	Probabilities	**Project *A***	**Project *B***
Investment required	1.0	$150,000	$180,000
Annual cash flows and	0.3	$35,000	$45,000
probabilities of occurrence	0.5	$40,000	$55,000
for each of five years	0.2	$50,000	$67,000

(a) Compute the mean and variance of NPW distribution for each project using $i = 12\%$. Assume that project cash flows are mutually independent.

(b) Which project has a higher probability of losing money?

11.26 Juan Carols is considering two investment projects whose PWs are described as follows:

- Project 1: $PW(10\%) = 2X(X - Y)$, where X and Y are statistically independent discrete random variables with the following distributions:

X		Y	
Event	**Probability**	**Event**	**Probability**
$20	0.30	$10	0.60
$40	0.70	$20	0.40

- Project 2:

PW(10%)	**Probability**
0	0.24
$400	0.20
$1,600	0.36
$2,400	0.20

The cash flows between the two projects are assumed to be statistically independent.

(a) Develop the NPW distribution for Project 1.

(b) Compute the mean and variance of the NPW for Project 1.

(c) Compute the mean and variance of the NPW for Project 2.

(d) Suppose that Projects 1 and 2 are mutually exclusive. Which project would you select?

11.27 A financial investor has an investment portfolio. A bond in her investment portfolio will mature next month and provide her $25,000 to reinvest. The choices for reinvestment have been narrowed to the following two options:

■ Option 1: Reinvest in a foreign bond that will mature in one year. This transaction will entail a brokerage fee of $150. For simplicity, assume that the bond will provide interest over the one-year period of $2,450, $2,000, or $1,675 and that the probabilities of these occurrences are assessed to be 0.25, 0.45, and 0.30, respectively.

■ Option 2: Reinvest in a $25,000 certificate with a savings and loan association. Assume that this certificate has an effective annual rate of 7.5%.

Which form of reinvestment should the investor choose in order to maximize her expected financial gain?

11.28 A manufacturing firm is considering two mutually exclusive projects. Both projects have an economic service life of one year with no salvage value. The first cost of Project 1 is $1,000, and the first cost of Project 2 is $800. The net year-end revenue for each project is given as follows:

Project 1

	Probability	Revenue
Net revenue given in PW	0.2	$2,000
	0.6	$3,000
	0.2	$3,500

Project 2

	Probability	Revenue
Net revenue given in PW	0.3	$1,000
	0.4	$2,500
	0.3	$4,500

Assume that both projects are statistically independent of each other.

(a) If you make decisions by maximizing the expected NPW, which project would you select?

(b) If you also consider the variance of the projects, which project would you select?

11.29 A business executive is trying to decide whether to undertake one of two contracts or neither one. He has simplified the situation somewhat and feels that it is sufficient to estimate that the contracts can be compared as follows:

Contract *A*		Contract *B*	
PW	Probability	PW	Probability
$100,000	0.2	$40,000	0.3
$50,000	0.4	$10,000	0.4
$0	0.4	−$10,000	0.3

(a) Should the executive undertake either one of the contracts? If so, which one? What would he choose if he were to make decisions by maximizing his expected PW?

(b) What would be the probability that Contract *A* would result in a larger profit than that of Contract *B*?

11.30 Two machines are being considered for a cost-reduction project:

- Machine *A* has a first cost of $60,000 and a salvage value (after tax) of $22,000 at the end of six years of service life. Probabilities of annual after-tax operating costs of this machine are estimated as follows:

Annual O&M Costs	Probability
$5,000	0.20
$8,000	0.30
$10,000	0.30
$12,000	0.20

- Machine *B* has a first cost of $35,000, and its estimated salvage value (after tax) at the end of four years of service is negligible. Probabilities of its annual after-tax operating costs are estimated as follows:

Annual O&M Costs	Probability
$8,000	0.10
$10,000	0.30
$12,000	0.40
$14,000	0.20

The MARR on this project is 10%. The required service period of these machines is estimated to be 12 years, and no technological advance in either machine is expected.

(a) Assuming statistical independence of the two projects' cash flows, calculate the mean and variance for the equivalent annual cost of operating each machine.

(b) From the results of part (a), calculate the probability that the annual cost of operating Machine *A* will exceed the annual cost of operating Machine *B*.

11.31 Two mutually exclusive investment projects are under consideration. It is assumed that the cash flows are statistically independent random variables with means and variances estimated as follows:

	Project A	
End of Year	**Mean**	**Variance**
0	−$5,000	$1,000^2$
1	$4,000	$1,000^2$
2	$4,000	$1,500^2$

	Project B	
End of year	**Mean**	**Variance**
0	−$10,000	$2,000^2$
1	$6,000	$1,500^2$
2	$8,000	$2,000^2$

(a) For each project, determine the mean and standard deviation for the PW using an interest rate of 15%.

(b) From the results of part (a), which project would you recommend?

Cost of Capital

11.32 Calculate the after-tax cost of debt under each of the following conditions:

(a) Interest rate, 12%; tax rate, 25%.

(b) Interest rate, 14%; tax rate, 34%.

(c) Interest rate, 15%; tax rate, 40%.

11.33 The estimated beta (β) of a firm is 1.7. The market return (r_m) is 14%, and the risk-free rate (r_f) is 7%. Estimate the cost of equity (i_e).

11.34 A firm's cost of equity (i_e) is 25%. Its before-tax cost of debt is 12%, and its marginal tax rate is 40%. The firm's capital structure calls for a debt-to-equity ratio of 40%. Calculate the firm's cost of capital (k).

11.35 Consider the estimated beta values as of June 30, 2011, for the following companies:

Coca Cola	0.60
Microsoft	0.80
General Electric	1.20
Alcoa Inc.	1.45

If the risk-free rate is 4.35% and the average market return is 11.5%, estimate each company's cost of equity capital.

11.36 An automobile company is contemplating issuing stock to finance an investment in producing a new sport-utility vehicle. The annual return to the market portfolio is expected to be 15% and the current risk-free interest rate is 5%. The company's analysts further believe that the expected return to the project will be 20% annually. What is the maximum beta value that would induce the auto maker to issue the stock?

Risk-Adjusted Discount Rate Approach

11.37 Consider Problem 11.20. If you use a 25% risk-adjusted discount rate approach, would this project be justified?

11.38 Consider Problem 11.21. If your risk-adjusted discount rate is 18%, is this project justifiable?

11.39 Consider Problem 11.22. Determine the risk-adjusted discount rate at which the project breaks even.

Short Case Studies with Excel

11.40 Boston Metal Company (BMC), a small manufacturer of fabricated metal parts, must decide whether to compete to become the supplier of transmission housings for Gulf Electric. Gulf Electric produces transmission housings in its own in-house manufacturing facility, but it has almost reached its maximum production capacity. Therefore, Gulf is looking for an outside supplier. To compete, BMC must design a new fixture for the production process and purchase a new forge. The available details for this purchase are as follows:

- The new forge would cost $125,000. This total includes retooling costs for the transmission housings.

- If BMC gets the order, it may be able to sell as many as 2,000 units per year to Gulf Electric for $50 each, and variable production costs (such as direct-labor and direct-material costs) will be $15 per unit. The increase in fixed costs, other than depreciation, will amount to $10,000 per year.

- The firm expects that the proposed transmission-housings project will have about a five-year project life. The firm also estimates that the amount ordered by Gulf Electric for the first year will also be ordered in each of the subsequent four years. (Due to the nature of contracted production, the annual demand and unit price would remain the same over the project after the contract is signed.)

- The initial investment can be depreciated on a MACRS basis over a seven-year period, and the marginal income-tax rate is expected to remain at 40%. At the end of five years, the forge is expected to retain a market value of about 32% of the original investment. BMC's MARR is known to be 15%.

What Makes BMC Managers Worry: BMC's managers are uneasy about this project because too many uncertain elements have not been considered in the analysis:

- If it decides to compete for the project, BMC must invest in the forging machine in order to provide Gulf Electric with samples as a part of the bidding process. If Gulf Electric does not like BMC's samples, BMC stands to lose its entire investment in the forging machine.

- If Gulf likes BMC's samples, but feels that they are overpriced, BMC would be under pressure to bring the price in line with those of competing firms. Even the possibility that BMC would get a smaller order must be considered, as Gulf may use its overtime capacity to produce some units in-house instead of purchasing the entire number of units it needs. BMC is also not certain about the variable- and fixed-cost projections.

Recognizing these uncertainties, the managers want to assess a variety of possible scenarios before making a final decision. Put yourself in BMC's management's position mentally, and describe how you might address the uncertainty associated with the project. In doing so, perform a sensitivity analysis for each variable and develop a sensitivity graph.

Annual Revenue (X)	Probability	General Inflation Rate (Y)	Probability
$15,000	0.20	3%	0.25
$25,000	0.50	5%	0.50
$35,000	0.30	7%	0.25

11.41 MG Cutting Systems is considering an investment project with the following parameters, where all cost and revenue figures are estimated in constant dollars:

- The project requires the purchase of a $23,000 asset, which will be used for only two years (project life). The project also requires an investment of $3,000 in working capital, and this amount will be fully recovered at the end of year 2.
- The salvage value of this asset at the end of two years is expected to be $6,000.
- The annual revenue and the general inflation rate are discrete random variables but can be described by the following probability distributions:

Both random variables are statistically independent.

- The investment will be classified as a three-year MACRS property (tax life).
- It is assumed that the revenues, salvage value, and working capital are responsive to the general inflation rate.
- The revenue and inflation rate dictated during the first year will prevail over the remaining project period.
- The marginal income-tax rate for the firm is 40%. The firm's inflation-free interest rate (i') is 10%.

   (a) Determine the PW as a function of X.
   (b) Compute the expected NPW of this investment.
   (c) Compute the variance of the PW of this investment.

11.42 Mount Manufacturing Company produces industrial and public-safety shirts. As is done in most apparel manufacturing, the cloth must be cut into shirt parts in accordance with patterns marked on sheets of paper, which indicate the way that the particular cloth is to be cut. At present, these patterns are marked manually, and the annual labor cost of the process is running around $103,718. Mount has the option of purchasing one of two automated marking systems. The two systems are the Lectra System 305 and the Tex Corporation Marking System. The comparative characteristics of the two systems are as follows:

	Most Likely Estimates	
	Lectra System	Tex System
Annual labor cost	$51,609	$51,609
Annual material savings	$230,000	$274,000
Investment cost	$136,150	$195,500
Estimated life	6 years	6 years
Salvage value	$20,000	$15,000
Depreciation method (MACRS)	5 year	5 year

The firm's marginal tax rate is 40%, and the interest rate used for project evaluation is 12% after taxes.

(a) Based on the most likely estimates, which alternative is better?

(b) Suppose that the company estimates the material savings during the first year for each system on the basis of the following probability distributions:

Lectra System

Material Savings	Probability
$150,000	0.25
$230,000	0.40
$270,000	0.35

Tex System

Material Savings	Probability
$200,000	0.30
$274,000	0.50
$312,000	0.20

Further assume that the annual material savings for both Lectra and Tex are statistically independent. Compute the mean and variance for the equivalent annual value of operating each system.

11.43 The following is a comparison of the cost structure of a conventional manufacturing technology (CMT) system with that of a flexible manufacturing system (FMS) at one U.S. firm:

	Most Likely Estimates	
	CMT	FMS
Number of part types	3,000	3,000
Number of pieces produced/year	544,000	544,000
Variable labor cost/part	$2.15	$1.30
Variable material cost/part	$1.53	$1.10
Total variable cost/part	$3.68	$2.40
Annual overhead costs	$3.15M	$1.95M
Annual tooling costs	$470,000	$300,000
Annual inventory costs	$141,000	$31,500
Total annual fixed operating costs	$3.76M	$2.28M
Investment	$3.5M	$10M
Salvage value	$0.5M	$1M
Service life	10 years	10 years
Depreciation method (MACRS)	7 year	7 year

(a) The firm's marginal tax rate and MARR are 40% and 15%, respectively. Determine the incremental cash flow (FMS − CMT) based on the most likely estimates.

(b) Management feels confident about all input estimates for the CMT. However, the firm does not have any previous experience in operating an FMS. Therefore, many of the input estimates for that system, except the investment and salvage value, are subject to variation. Perform a sensitivity analysis on the project's data, varying the elements of the operating costs. Assume that each of these variables can deviate from its base-case expected value by ±10%, ±20%, and ±30%.

(c) Prepare sensitivity diagrams and interpret the results.

(d) Suppose that probabilities of the variable material cost and the annual inventory cost for the FMS are estimated as follows:

Material Cost

Cost per Part	Probability
$1.00	0.25
$1.10	0.30
$1.20	0.20
$1.30	0.20
$1.40	0.05

Inventory Cost

Annual Inventory Cost	Probability
$25,000	0.10
$31,000	0.30
$50,000	0.20
$80,000	0.20
$100,000	0.20

What are the best and the worst cases of incremental PW?

(e) In part (d), assuming that the random variables of the cost per part and the annual inventory cost are statistically independent, find the mean and variance of the PW for the incremental cash flows.

(f) In parts (d) and (e), what is the probability that the FMS would be a more expensive investment option?

4

Special Topics in Engineering Economics

CHAPTER TWELVE

Replacement Decisions

The Cost to Bridge the Gap The three-mile Tappan Zee Bridge, located about 13 miles north of New York City, carries the New York State Thruway over the Hudson River, between Rockland and Westchester Counties. The structure serves as a lifeline between New York City and Upstate New York. The bridge carries about 140,000 vehicles every day, with volumes as high as 170,000 vehicles daily. When the bridge opened in 1955, it carried an average of 18,000 vehicles daily in the first year of its opening.

This bridge is one of the many conduits to New York City, bringing bus- and carloads of commuters to work each day. And while the bridge's necessity is clearly evident, the New York State Thruway Authority—which is currently facing serious deficits in budgets and funding—was faced with a tough decision: dump a fortune into repairs (approximately $148 million a year) or spend billions of dollars on building an entirely new bridge.

Recommendations concerning bridge replacement and transit modes were made at the end of 2008 in conjunction with public information meetings. The results of these screenings are documented in two reports:

- Rehabilitation and replacement of the Tappan Zee Bridge as documented in the *Alternatives Analysis for Rehabilitation and Replacement of the Tappan Zee Bridge* report, March 2009. Replacement of the bridge is recommended.

- Selection of a transit mode (as documented in the *Transit Mode Selection Report*, May 2009). A cross-corridor bus rapid transit (BRT)

system is recommended from Suffern, NY to Port Chester, NY and a commuter rail transit (CRT) system is recommended across Rockland County (from Suffern, NY), across the replacement Tappan Zee Bridge, with a direct connection to the Hudson line in Tarrytown for the service to Grand Central Terminal.

But knowing the best way to improve this one bridge wasn't necessarily the entire problem. The bridge is one of approximately 3000 bridges in the state that are classified as a "deficient," meaning that they are functionally safe but in need of repair, whether general maintenance or emergency repair. The state rejected a $26 billion repair proposal that would span five years. In the midst of an ever-growing economic crunch, plans were scaled back to cover only two years.

The difficult part was determining who would pay the price tag for these repairs and for a potentially new bridge in the case of the Tappan Zee. Estimated costs for a new bridge ran from $9 billion to $16 billion: with $16 billion accounting for the full BRT system. The costs were argued by vehemently by both advocates and detractors of the BRT system.

Faced with the prospect of absorbing such costs while potentially building a new bridge, the New York State Thruway Authority and the state began to pursue private financial options and investors.

In October 2011, the Federal Highway Administration and the Federal Transit Administration rescinded all environmental studies regarding the BRT option and quickly greenlighted the bridge's replacement for cars and trucks only. The cost is now estimated at $5.2 billion. Construction is set to begin in 2013 with the bridge opening for traffic in 2017.

In Chapters 5 through 7, we presented methods to help us choose the best investment alternative. The problems we examined in those chapters primarily concern profit-adding projects. However, economic analysis is also frequently performed on projects with existing facilities or profit-maintaining projects. Profit-maintaining projects are projects whose primary purpose is not to increase sales but rather simply to maintain ongoing operations. In practice, profit-maintaining projects less frequently involve the comparison of new machines; instead, the problem—which we can classify as a **replacement problem**—often facing management is whether to buy new and more efficient equipment or to continue to use existing equipment. In this chapter, we examine the basic concepts and techniques related to replacement analysis.

12.1 Replacement-Analysis Fundamentals

In this section and the following two sections, we examine three aspects of the replacement problem: (1) approaches for comparing defender and challenger; (2) determination of economic service life; and (3) replacement analysis when the required service period is long. The impact of income-tax regulations will be ignored in these sections. In Section 12.4, we revisit these replacement problems and consider the effects of income taxes on them.

12.1.1 Basic Concepts and Terminology

Replacement projects are decision problems involving the replacement of existing obsolete or worn-out assets. The continuation of operations is dependent on these assets. Failure to make an appropriate decision results in a slowdown or shutdown of the operations. The question is when the existing equipment should be replaced with more efficient equipment. This situation has given rise to the use of the terms **defender** and **challenger**, terms commonly used in the boxing world. In every boxing class, the current defending champion is constantly faced with a new challenger. In replacement analysis, the defender is the existing machine (or system), and the challenger is the best available replacement equipment.

The question is not whether an existing piece of equipment will be removed but when it will be removed. An existing piece of equipment will be removed at some future time either when the task it performs is no longer necessary or when the task can be performed more efficiently by newer and better equipment. The question, then, is why we should replace existing equipment at this time rather than postponing replacement of the equipment by repairing or overhauling it. Another aspect of the defender–challenger comparison concerns deciding exactly which equipment is the best challenger. If the defender is to be replaced by the challenger, we would generally want to install the very best of the possible alternatives.

Current Market Value

The most common problem encountered in considering the replacement of existing equipment is the determination of what financial information is actually relevant to the analysis. Often, the inclusion of irrelevant information in the analysis is apparent. To illustrate this type of decision problem, let us consider Example 12.1.

EXAMPLE 12.1 Relevant Information for Replacement Analysis

Steve Hausmann, a production engineer at Euro Fashion-USA, a European-style furniture company, was considering replacing a 1,000 lb capacity industrial forklift truck, which was purchased three years ago for $18,000. The truck was being used to move assembled furniture from the finishing department to the warehouse. Recently, the truck had not been dependable and had been frequently out of service while awaiting repairs, a situation that eventually cost the company $3,000. Maintenance expenses were rising steadily. When the truck was not available, the company had to rent one. In addition, the forklift truck was diesel operated, and workers in the plant were complaining about the air pollution. If retained, the truck would have required an immediate engine overhaul to keep it in operable condition. The overhaul would have neither extended the originally estimated service life nor increased the value of the truck. Steve has found that the current truck has a book value of $0 (fully depreciated) and a market value of $7,500 today.

Steve is considering an electric forklift truck as a replacement, which would eliminate the air-pollution problem entirely. The new electric lift truck is quoted at $20,000. The equipment dealer will allow Steve $8,000 as trade-in on a new truck. What value(s) for the defender is (are) relevant in our analysis?

DISSECTING THE PROBLEM	
	Given: Financial data and history of the defender.
	Find: Identify all cost information relevant to making the best replacement decision.

METHODOLOGY	**SOLUTION**
Use the process of elimination.	In this example, four different dollar figures relating to the defender are presented:

1. Original cost: $18,000.
2. Market value: $7,500.
3. Book value: $0.
4. Trade-in allowance: $8,000.

In all replacement analyses, the relevant cost is the **current market value** of the equipment. The original cost, repair cost, and trade-in value are irrelevant.[2] A common misconception is that the trade-in value is always the same as the current market value of the equipment and thus could be used to assign a suitable current value to the equipment. This is not always the case. For example, a car dealer typically offers a trade-in value on a customer's old car to reduce the price of a new car. Would the dealer offer the same value on the old car if he or she were not also selling the new one to the customer? Not usually. In many instances, the trade-in allowance is inflated in order to make the deal look good, and the price of the new car is also inflated to compensate for the dealer's trade-in cost. In this type of situation, the trade-in value does not represent the true value of the item, so we should not use it in economic analysis.[3]

Sunk Costs

A **sunk cost** is any past cost unaffected by any future investment decision. In Example 12.1, the company recently spent $3,000 to repair the truck. However, if the truck were sold today, the company could get only $7,500 back. It is tempting to think that the company could count the $3,000 repair cost, in addition to the cost of the new truck, if the old truck were to be sold and replaced with a new one, but this interpretation is incorrect. In a proper engineering economic analysis, only future costs should be considered; past, or sunk, costs should be ignored. Thus, the value of the defender that should be used in a replacement analysis should be the *current market* value, not the cost when defender was originally purchased and not the cost of repairs that have already been made on it.

Sunk cost refers to money that has already been spent; no present action can recover it. These costs are the results of decisions made in the past. In making economic

---

[2] The original cost and current book value are relevant when you calculate any gains or losses associated with the disposal of the equipment.

[3] If we do make the trade, however, the actual net cash flow at this time, properly used, is certainly relevant.

decisions, we must consider options with only future results in mind—hopefully with the best possible future results. Incorporating sunk costs into the decision-making process would lead only to more bad decisions.

Operating Costs

The driving force in the decision to replace existing equipment is that equipment becomes more and more expensive to operate over time. The total cost of operating a piece of equipment may include repair and maintenance costs, wages for operators, energy consumption costs, and costs of materials. Increases in any one or a combination of these cost items over time may lead us to want a replacement for the existing asset. Since the challenger is usually newer than the defender and often incorporates design improvements and more advanced technology, it likely will be cheaper to operate than the defender.

Whether these savings in operating costs offset the initial investment of buying the challenger thus becomes the focus of our analysis. It is important to focus on those operating costs that differ between the defender and challenger. In many cases, projected labor, energy, and material costs may be identical for each asset—whereas repair and maintenance costs will differ because older assets require more maintenance. Regardless of which cost items we choose to include in the operating costs for our analysis, it is essential that the same items are included for both the defender and the challenger. For example, if energy costs are included in the operating costs of the defender, they should also be included in the operating costs of the challenger.

12.1.2 Approaches for Comparing Defender and Challenger

Although replacement projects are a subcategory of the mutually exclusive projects we studied in Chapter 5, they do possess unique characteristics that allow us to use specialized concepts and analysis techniques in their evaluation. We consider two basic approaches to analyzing replacement problems: the cash flow approach and the opportunity-cost approach. We start with a replacement problem where both the defender and the challenger have the same useful life.

Cash-Flow Approach

This approach can be used as long as *the analysis period is the same* for all replacement alternatives. In particular, with the actual cash flow approach, the salvage value of the defender is credited against the purchase price of the challenger. In other words, we explicitly consider the actual cash-flow consequences for each replacement alternative and compare them, using either PW or AE values.

EXAMPLE 12.2 Replacement Analysis Using the Cash-Flow Approach[4]

Adams Corporation is considering the purchase of equipment employing advanced technology to lower production costs in a product line. At the end of the third year, management will close down the line and liquidate the remaining assets.

---

[4] This problem statement is adapted from "Replacement Decision: Getting It Right," *Business Horizon*, 50 (2007): 231–237.

The project will require an investment of $500,000 in plant upgrade and equipment and an additional $30,000 in working capital, which will be recovered in full at the end of year 3.

Over its three-year useful life, the new equipment will reduce labor and raw materials usage sufficiently to cut operating costs from $9,000,000 to $8,850,000. It is estimated that the new equipment can be sold for $150,000 at the end of year 3. If the new equipment were purchased, the old machine would be sold to another company for $170,000 rather than be traded in for the new equipment. If the old equipment is kept for three more years, the salvage value would be reduced to $70,000. Adams management uses 10% to discount the cash flows. Decide whether replacement is justified now, ignoring any tax consideration.

DISSECTING THE PROBLEM

Given: Financial data for both defender and challenger, $N = 3$ years, $i = 10\%$ per year.

Find: Whether to replace the defender now.

METHODOLOGY

Use cash flow values to find the present worth of each option and then the annual-equivalent value for each.

SOLUTION

- **Option 1: Keep the old equipment.** If the old equipment is kept, there is no additional cash expenditure today. The machine is in good operational condition. The annual operating cost for the next three years will be $9,000,000 per year, and the equipment's salvage value three years from today will be $70,000. The cash-flow diagram for the defender is shown in Figure 12.1(a).

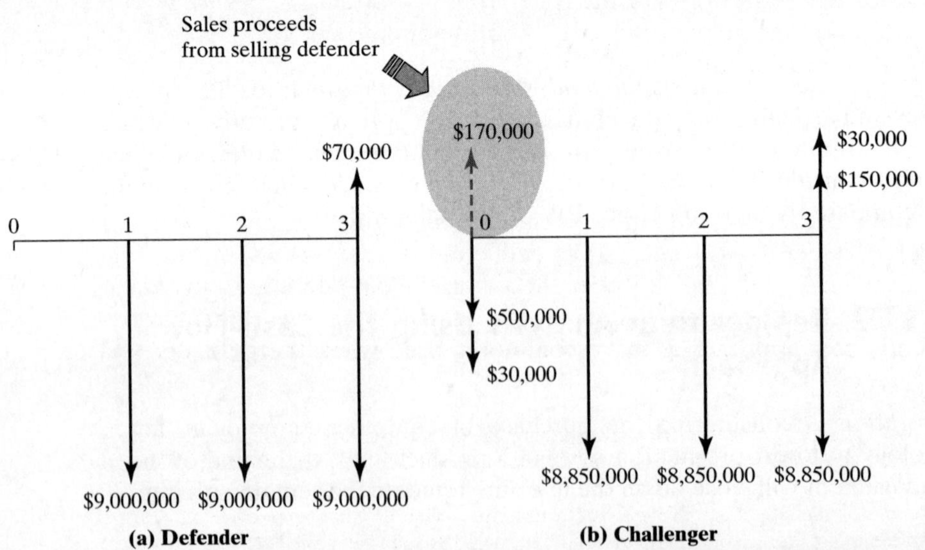

Figure 12.1 Comparison of defender and challenger based on the cash-flow approach

- **Option 2: Sell the old equipment and buy new.** If this option is taken, the defender (designated as D) can be sold for \$170,000. The cost of the challenger (designated as C) is \$530,000. Thus, the initial combined cash flow for this option is $-\$530,000 + \$170,000 = -\$360,000$. The annual operating cost of the challenger is \$8,850,000. The salvage value of the challenger after three years will be \$150,000, and the \$30,000 working capital will be fully recovered as well. The cash-flow diagram for this option is shown in Figure 12.1(b).

We now use these cash flow values to find the present worth of each option and then use this value to find the annual-equivalent value for the option. For the defender, we have

$$\text{PW}(10\%)_D = -\$9,000,000(P/A,\ 10\%,\ 3) + \$70,000(P/F,\ 10\%,\ 3)$$
$$= -\$22,329,076.$$
$$\text{AEC}(10\%)_D = \$22,329,076(A/P,\ 10\%,\ 3)$$
$$= \$8,978,852.$$

For the challenger, we have

$$\text{PW}(10\%)_C = -\$360,000 - \$8,850,000(P/A, 10\%, 3)$$
$$+ \$180,000(P/F,\ 10\%,\ 3)$$
$$= -\$22,233,402.$$
$$\text{AEC}(10\%)_C = \$22,233,402(A/P, 10\%,\ 3)$$
$$= \$8,940,380.$$

Because of the annual difference of \$38,472 in favor of the challenger, the replacement should be made now.

COMMENTS: Once again, the cash-flow approach works when both the defender and challenger have the same service lives. If not, we must make some adjustment to our analysis in calculating the AEC for the challenger. Suppose the challenger's life is six years, instead of three years, then the \$170,000 current salvage value of the defender should be spread over the three-year life of the challenger (not over the six-year life) as the remaining life of the defender is only three years. Otherwise, there is a distortion of the AEC figures.

Opportunity-Cost Approach

Another way to analyze such a problem is to charge the \$170,000 as an **opportunity cost** of keeping the asset.[5] That is, instead of deducting the salvage value from the purchase cost of the challenger, we consider the salvage value as a cash outflow for the defender (or investment required in keeping the defender). In replacement analysis, the opportunity-cost approach is more commonly used when the defender and challenger have unequal lifetimes.

[5] The opportunity-cost concept should not be confused with the outsider-viewpoint approach, which is commonly described in traditional engineering economics texts. The outsider-viewpoint method approaches a typical replacement problem from the standpoint of a person (an outsider) who has a need for the service that the defender or challenger can provide but owns neither. This view has some conceptual flaws, however. For example, the outsider purchases the defender at the seller's market price (or seller's tax rate) and assumes the seller's depreciation schedule. In practice, however, if you place a used asset in service, you will be able to depreciate it even though the asset may have been fully depreciated by the previous owner.

EXAMPLE 12.3 Replacement Analysis Using the Opportunity-Cost Approach

Rework Example 12.2 using the opportunity-cost approach.

DISSECTING THE PROBLEM

Recall that the cash-flow approach in Example 12.2 credited proceeds in the amount of $170,000 from the sale of the defender toward the $500,000 purchase price of the challenger, and no initial outlay would have been required had the decision been to keep the defender.

Given: Financial data for both defender and challenger, $N = 3$ years, $i = 10\%$ per year.

Find: Whether to replace the defender now.

METHODOLOGY

Use PW or AE analysis to determine the better option.

SOLUTION

If the decision to keep the defender had been made under the opportunity-cost approach, however, the $170,000 current salvage value of the defender would have been treated as an incurred cost. Figure 12.2 illustrates the cash flows related to these decision options.

Since the lifetimes are the same, we can use either PW or AE analysis to find the better option. For the defender, we have

$$PW(10\%)_D = -\$170,000 - \$9,000,000(P/A, \ 10\%, \ 3)$$
$$+ \ \$70,000(P/F, \ 10\%, \ 3)$$
$$= -\$22,499,076.$$

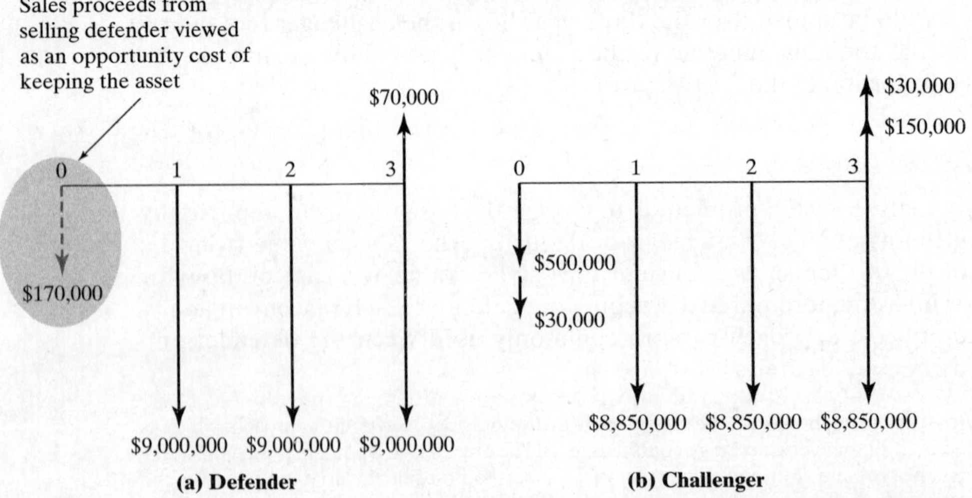

Figure 12.2 Comparison of defender and challenger based on the opportunity-cost approach

$$\begin{aligned}
\text{AEC}(10\%)_D &= \$22{,}499{,}076(A/P, 10\%, 3) \\
&= \$9{,}047{,}212.
\end{aligned}$$

For the challenger, we have

$$\begin{aligned}
\text{PW}(10\%)_C &= -\$530{,}000 - \$8{,}850{,}000(P/A, 10\%, 3) \\
&\quad + \$180{,}000(P/F, 10\%, 3) \\
&= -\$22{,}403{,}402. \\
\text{AEC}(10\%)_C &= \$22{,}403{,}402(A/P, 10\%, 3) \\
&= \$9{,}008{,}740.
\end{aligned}$$

The decision outcome is the same as in Example 12.2; that is, the replacement should be made. Since both the challenger and defender cash flows were adjusted by the same amount ($-\$170{,}000$) at time zero, this outcome should not be a surprise.

COMMENTS: Recall that we assumed the same service life for both the defender and the challenger in Examples 12.2 and 12.3. In general, however, old equipment has a relatively short remaining life compared with new equipment, so this assumption is overly simplistic. In Section 12.3.3, we will consider handling unequal service life problems in replacement analysis. In the next section, we discuss how to find the economic service life of equipment.

12.2 Economic Service Life

You have probably seen a 50-year-old automobile still in service—provided that it receives the proper repair and maintenance, almost anything can be kept operating for an extended period. If it is possible to keep a car operating for an almost indefinite period, why aren't there more old cars on the streets? There are several reasons. For example, some people get tired of driving the same old car. Others want to keep a car as long as it will last but realize that repair and maintenance costs will become excessive.

We need to consider explicitly how long an asset should be held once it is placed in service. For instance, a truck rental firm that frequently purchases fleets of identical trucks may wish to make a policy decision on how long to keep a vehicle before replacing it. If an appropriate life span is computed, the firm could stagger the schedule of truck purchases and replacements to smooth out annual capital expenditures for overall truck purchases. Recall that in Section 6.1.2, the costs of owning and operating an asset can be divided into two categories: **capital costs** and **operating costs**. The economic service life is found simply by examining the sum of these two costs as a function of holding period.

Capital (Ownership) Costs

Capital costs have two components: the initial investment and the salvage value at the time of disposal. The initial investment for the challenger is simply its purchase price. For the defender, we should treat the opportunity cost (current market value) as its initial investment. We will use N to represent the length of time in years that the asset will be kept, I to represent the initial investment, and S_N to represent the salvage value at the end of the ownership period of N years.

The annual equivalent of capital cost, which is called the capital-recovery (CR) cost (refer to Section 6.1.2), over the period of N years can be calculated with the following equation:

$$CR(i) = I(A/P, i, N) - S_N(A/F, i, N) \tag{12.1}$$
$$= (I - S_N)(A/P, i, N) + iS_N.$$

Generally speaking, as an asset becomes older, its salvage value becomes smaller. As long as the salvage value is less than the initial cost, the capital-recovery cost is a decreasing function of N. In other words, the longer we keep an asset, the lower the capital-recovery cost becomes. If the salvage value is equal to the initial cost, then no matter how long the asset is kept, the capital-recovery cost is also constant.

Operating Costs

As described earlier, operating and maintenance (O&M) costs tend to increase as a function of the age of the asset. Because of the increasing trend of the O&M costs, the total operating costs (OC) of an asset usually increase as the asset ages. We use OC_n to represent the total operating costs in year n of the ownership period and $OC(i)$ to represent the annual equivalent of the operating costs over a life span of N years. $OC(i)$ can be expressed as

$$OC(i) = \left(\sum_{n=1}^{N} OC_n(P/F, i, n) \right)(A/P, i, N). \tag{12.2}$$

Economic Service Life

The total annual equivalent costs (AECs) of owning and operating an asset are a summation of the capital-recovery costs and the annual equivalent of the operating costs of the asset:

$$AEC(i) = CR(i) + OC(i). \tag{12.3}$$

The economic service life of an asset is the period of useful life that minimizes the annual-equivalent costs, in constant dollars, of owning and operating that asset. From the foregoing discussions, we need to find the value of N that minimizes AEC as expressed in Eq. (12.3). If $CR(i)$ is a decreasing function of N and $OC(i)$ is an increasing function of N, as is often the case, then AEC will be a convex function of N with a unique minimum point as shown in Figure 12.3. In this book, we assume that AEC has a unique minimum point. Here are some special cases that the economic service life can be determined easily.

- If the salvage value is constant and equal to the initial cost, and the annual operating cost increases with time, AEC is an increasing function of N and attains its minimum at $N = 1$. In this case, we should try to replace the asset as soon as possible.
- If the annual operating cost is constant and the salvage value is less than the initial cost and decreases with time, AEC is a decreasing function of N. In this case, we would try to delay replacement of the asset as long as possible.
- If the salvage value is constant and equal to the initial cost and the annual operating costs are constant, AEC will also be constant. In this case, the time at which the asset is replaced does not make any economic difference.

If a new asset is purchased and operated for the length of its economic life, the annual-equivalent cost is minimized. If we further assume that a new asset of identical price and features can be purchased repeatedly over an indefinite period, we would always replace this kind of asset at the end of its economic life. By replacing perpetually according to an asset's economic life, we obtain the minimum AEC stream in *constant dollars* over an indefinite

- Capital Cost:
  $$CR(i) = I(A/P, i, N) - S_N(A/F, i, N)$$

- Operating Cost:
  $$OC(i) = \sum_{n=1}^{N} OC_n(P/F, i, n)\,(A/P, i, N)$$

- Total Cost:
  $$AEC(i) = CR(i) + OC(i)$$

- Objective: Find n^*
  that minimizes $AEC(i)$

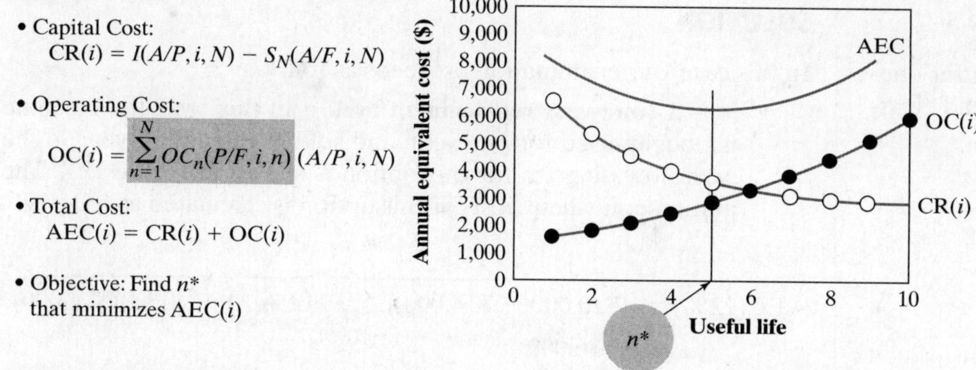

Figure 12.3 A schematic illustrating the trends of capital-recovery cost (ownership cost), annual operating cost, and total annual-equivalent cost, as a function of asset age

period. However, if the identical-replacement assumption cannot be made, we will have to use the methods to be covered in Section 12.3 to perform replacement analysis. The next example explains the computational procedure for determining economic service life.[6]

EXAMPLE 12.4 Economic Service Life for a Forklift Truck

As a challenger to the forklift truck described in Example 12.1, consider a new electric forklift truck that would cost $20,000, have operating costs of $6,000 in the first year, and have a salvage value of $14,000 at the end of the first year. For the remaining years, operating costs (including any loss of productivity due to maintenance) increase each year by 25% over the previous year's operating costs. Similarly, the salvage value declines each year by 30% from the previous year's salvage value. The truck has a maximum life of eight years without any major engine overhaul. The firm's required rate of return is 12%. Find the economic service life of this new machine without considering any income taxes.

DISSECTING THE PROBLEM

For an asset whose revenues are either unknown or irrelevant, we compute its economic life from the costs of the asset and its year-by-year market (salvage) values. To determine an asset's economic service life, we need to compare the options of keeping the asset for one year, two years, three years, and so forth. The option that results in the lowest AEC gives the economic service life of the asset.

Given: Changes in market values and O&M costs, physical eight years, $i = 12\%$ per year.

Find: Economic service life.

---

[6] Unless otherwise mentioned, or in the absence of income taxes, we are assuming that all cash flows are estimated in constant dollars. Therefore, the interest rate used in finding the economic service life represents the inflation-free (or real) interest rate.

METHODOLOGY

Create a cash-flow diagram for one-year, two-year, three-year, and eight-year replacement cycles.

SOLUTION

In this case, our examination proceeds as follows:

- **$N = 1$ (one-year replacement cycle):** In this case, the machine is bought, used for one year, and sold at the end of year 1. The cash-flow diagram for this option is shown in Figure 12.4. The annual-equivalent cost for this option is calculated as follows:

$$\text{AEC}(12\%) = \overbrace{(\$20{,}000 - \$14{,}000)(A/P, 12\%, 1) + (0.12)(\$14{,}000)}^{\text{CR}(12\%)}$$

$$+ \underbrace{\$6.000}_{\text{OC}(12\%)}$$

$$= \$14{,}400.$$

Note that $(A/P, 12\%, 1) = (F/P, 12\%, 1)$ and that the annual-equivalent cost is the equivalent cost at the end of year 1, since $N = 1$. Because we are calculating the annual-equivalent costs, we have treated cost items with a positive sign and the salvage value with a negative sign.

- **$N = 2$ (two-year replacement cycle):** In this case, the truck will be used for two years and disposed of at the end of year 2. The operating cost in year 2 is 25% higher than in year 1, and the salvage value at the end of year 2 is 30% lower than

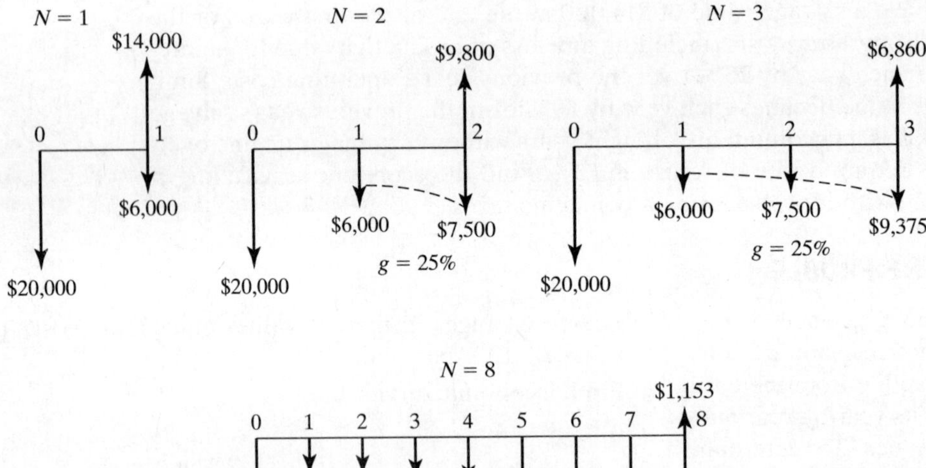

Figure 12.4 Cash-flow diagrams for the options of keeping the asset for one year, two years, three years, and eight years, where g represents a geometric gradient

at the end of year 1. The cash-flow diagram for this option is also shown in Figure 12.4. The annual-equivalent cost over the two-year period is calculated as follows:

$$\text{AEC}(12\%) = \overbrace{(\$20,000 - \$9,800)(A/P, 12\%, 2) + (0.12)(\$9,800)}^{\text{CR}(12\%)}$$
$$\underbrace{+ \ \$6,000(P/A_1, 25\%, 12\%, 2)(A/P, 12\%, 2)}_{\text{OC}(12\%)}$$
$$= \$13,919.$$

- $N = 3$ **(three-year replacement cycle):** In this case, the truck will be used for three years and sold at the end of year 3. The salvage value at the end of year 3 is 30% lower than at the end of year 2—that is, \$6,860. The operating cost per year increases at a rate of 25%. The cash-flow diagram for this option is also shown in Figure 12.4. For this case, the annual-equivalent cost is calculated as follows:

$$\text{AEC}(12\%) = \overbrace{(\$20,000 - \$6,860)(A/P, 12\%, 3) + (0.12)(\$6,860)}^{\text{CR}(12\%)}$$
$$\underbrace{+ \ \$6,000(P/A_1, 25\%, 12\%, 3)(A/P, 12\%, 3)}_{\text{OC}(12\%)}$$
$$= \$13,792.$$

- Similarly, we can find the annual-equivalent cost for the option of keeping the asset for each remaining year. The cash-flow diagram for $N = 8$ years is shown in Figure 12.4. The computed annual-equivalent costs over eight years are shown in Table 12.1.

From Table 12.1, we find that AEC (12%) is the smallest when $N = 3$. If the truck were to be replaced every three years, it would have an annual cost of \$13,792 per year. If it were to be used for a period other than three years, the annual-equivalent costs would be higher than \$13,792. Thus, a life span of three years for this truck results in the lowest annual cost. We conclude that the economic service life of the truck is three years. By replacing the assets perpetually, according to an economic life of three years, we obtain the minimum annual-equivalent cost stream. Figure 12.5 illustrates the concept of perpetual replacement for one- and two-year replacement cycles. Of course, we should envision a long period of required service for this kind of asset.

TABLE 12.1 Economic Service Life Calculation for Electric Fork Lift Truck (Example 12.4)

	A	B	C	D	E	F	G
1							
2		Annual changes in MV		-30%			
3		Annual increases in O&M		25%			
4		Interest rate		12%			
5							
6	*n*	Market Value	O&M Costs	CR(12%)	OC(12%)	AEC(12%)	
7							
8	0	$20,000					
9	1	$14,000	$6,000	$8,400	$6,000	$14,400	
10	2	$9,800	$7,500	$7,211	$6,708	$13,919	
11	3	$6,860	$9,375	$6,294	$7,498	$13,792	
12	4	$4,802	$11,719	$5,580	$8,381	$13,961	
13	5	$3,361	$14,648	$5,019	$9,368	$14,387	=D16+E16
14	6	$2,353	$18,311	$4,575	$10,470	$15,044	
15	7	$1,647	$22,888	$4,219	$11,701	$15,920	
16	8	$1,153	$28,610	$3,932	$13,075	$17,008	
17							
18							
19						=-PMT($D$4,A16,NPV($D$4,$C$9:C16),0)	
20		=B15*(1+$D$2)	=C15*(1+$D$3)				
21							
22			=-PMT($D$4,A16,$B$8,-B16)				
23							
24							

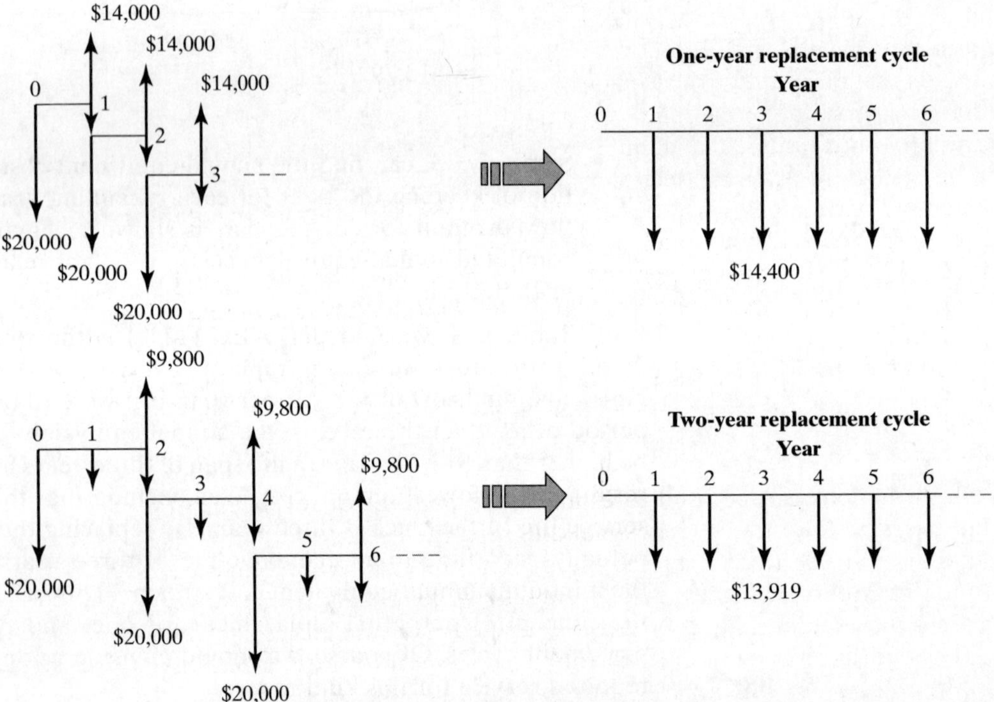

Figure 12.5 Conversion of an infinite number of replacement cycles to infinite AE cost streams

12.3 Replacement Analysis When the Required Service Period Is Long

Now that we understand how the economic service life of an asset is determined, the next question is how we can use this information to decide whether now is the time to replace the defender? If now is not the right time, when is the optimal time to replace the defender. Before presenting an analytical approach to answer this question, we consider several important assumptions.

12.3.1 Required Assumptions and Decision Frameworks

In deciding the replacement time for the defender, we need to consider the following three factors:

- Planning horizon (study period)
- Technology
- Relevant cash-flow information

Planning Horizon (Study Period)

By "planning horizon," we simply mean the service period required by the defender and a sequence of future challengers. The infinite planning horizon is used when we are unable to predict when the activity under consideration will be terminated. In other situations, it may be clear that the project will have a definite and predictable duration. In these cases, a replacement policy should be formulated more realistically on the basis of a finite planning horizon.

Technology

Predictions of technological patterns over the planning horizon refer to the development of types of challengers that may replace those under study. A number of possibilities exist in predicting purchase cost, salvage value, and operating cost as dictated by the efficiency of the asset over its life. If we assume that all future assets will be the same as those now in service, we are implicitly saying that no technological progress in the area will occur. In other cases, we may explicitly recognize the possibility of future technologies that will make new machines significantly more efficient, reliable, or productive than those currently on the market. (Personal computers are a good example.) This situation leads to the recognition of technological change, or obsolescence, via alternatives (such as smartphones eliminate GPS devices). Clearly, if the best available machine gets better and better over time, we should certainly investigate the possibility of delaying replacement for several years; this scenario contrasts with situations where technological change is unlikely.

Relevant Cash-Flow Information

Many varieties of predictions can be used to estimate the patterns of revenue, cost, and salvage value over the life of an asset. Sometimes revenue is constant, but costs increase and salvage value decreases over the life of a machine. In other situations, a decline in revenue over equipment life can be expected. The specific situation will determine whether replacement analysis is directed toward cost minimization (with constant revenue) or profit maximization (with varying revenue). We formulate a replacement policy for an asset for which the salvage value does not increase with age.

Decision Criterion

Although the economic life of the defender is defined as the number of years of service that minimizes the annual-equivalent cost (or maximizes the annual-equivalent revenue), the end of the economic life is not necessarily the *optimal time* to replace the defender. The correct replacement time depends on certain data for the challenger as well as on certain data for the defender.

As a decision criterion, the AEC method provides a more direct solution when the planning horizon is infinite. When the planning horizon is finite, the PW method is more convenient to use. We will develop the replacement-decision procedure for the infinite planning horizon. In case of a finite planning horizon, decision making requires some additional analysis techniques that are beyond the scope of this textbook; so we will not address them here. We begin by analyzing an infinite planning horizon without technological change. Even though a simplified situation such as this is not likely to occur in real life, the analysis of this replacement situation introduces methods useful for analyzing actual infinite-horizon replacement problems with technological change.

12.3.2 Handling Unequal Service Life Problems in Replacement Analysis

One important consideration in comparing defender and challenger is the question of how we can perform replacement analysis on assets with unequal lives. Recall from Chapter 6 that the use of AE with unequal lives is justified in some special circumstances. We have here another special situation in which AE with unequal lives gives valid results but only when using the opportunity-cost approach.

The implicit assumption made in using AE when the defender's remaining life is shorter than the challenger's life is that, after the initial decision, we make perpetual replacements with assets similar to those of the challenger. For example, let us consider a situation where you are comparing a defender (D) with an economic service life of three years and a challenger (C) with an economic service life of six years. This means that if we decide to keep the old machine (D) for three years, we will replace it at time 3 by an asset similar to the new machine. This asset will in turn be replaced six years later, at time 9, by another asset C. There are two implied infinite sequences in this scenario:

- Keep defender (D), buy a challenger (C) at time 3, buy another challenger (C) at time 9, buy another challenger (C) at time 15, and so on.
- Buy challenger (C) at time 0, buy a challenger (C) at time 6, buy a challenger (C) at time 12, and so on.

As shown in Figure 12.6, it is clear that the AE cost approach for either sequence of assets is the same after the remaining life of the defender. Therefore, we can directly compare the AEC for the remaining life of the defender with the AEC for the challenger over its economic service life.

12.3.3 Replacement Strategies under the Infinite Planning Horizon

Consider the situation where a firm has a machine in use in a process. The process is expected to continue for an indefinite period. Presently, a new machine is on the market that is, in some ways, more effective for the application than the defender. The question is, when, if at all, should the defender be replaced with the challenger?

Under the infinite planning horizon, the service is required for a very long time. Either we continue to use the defender to provide the service or we replace the defender with the best available challenger for the same service requirement. In such cases, the following procedure may be implemented in replacement analysis:

1. Compute the economic lives of both defender and challenger. Let us use N_D^* and N_C^* to indicate the economic lives of the defender and the challenger, respectively.

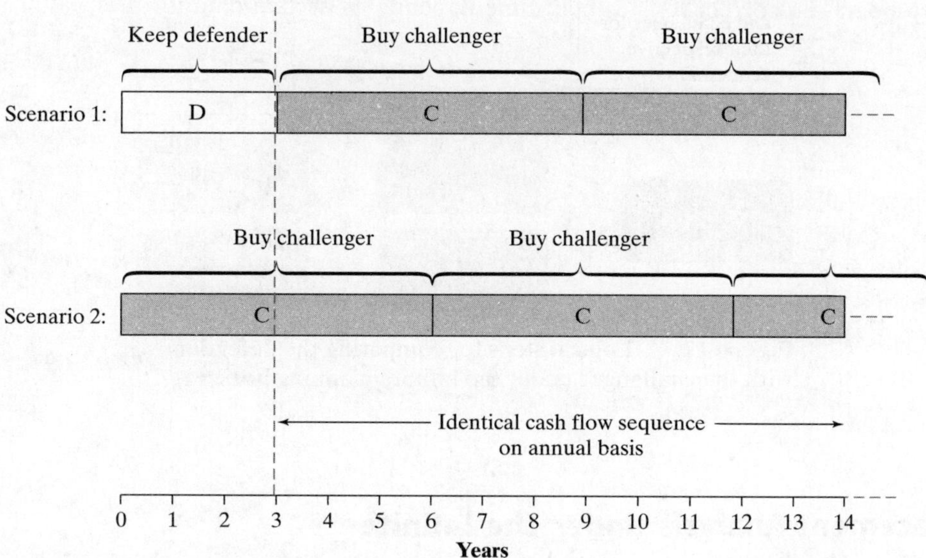

Figure 12.6 Implicit assumption made in AE method when the defender's remaining life is shorter than the challenger's life

The annual-equivalent costs for the defender and the challenger for their respective economic lives are indicated by AEC_D^* and AEC_C^*, respectively.

2. Compare AEC_D^* and AEC_C^*.

   - If AEC_D^* is more than AEC_C^*, we know that it is more costly to keep the defender than to replace it with the challenger. Thus, the challenger should replace the defender now.
   - If AEC_D^* is less than AEC_C^*, it costs less to keep the defender than to replace it with the challenger. Thus, the defender should not be replaced *now*. The defender should continue to be used at least for the duration of its economic life as long as there are no technological changes over the economic life of the defender.

3. If the defender should not be replaced now, when should it be replaced? First, we need to continue to use it until its economic life is over. Then we should calculate the cost of using the defender for one more year beyond its economic life. If this cost is higher than AEC_C^*, the defender should be replaced at the end of its economic life. Otherwise, we should calculate the cost of running the defender for the second year after its economic life. If this cost is more than AEC_C^*, the defender should be replaced one year after its economic life. This process should be continued until we find the optimal replacement time. This approach is called **marginal analysis**; that is, we calculate the incremental cost of operating the defender for just one more year. In other words, we want to see whether the cost of extending the use of the defender for an additional year exceeds the savings resulting from delaying the purchase of the challenger. Here, we have assumed that the best available challenger does not change. The sequential steps for replacement decision are summarized in Figure 12.7.

It should be noted that this procedure might be applied dynamically. For example, it may be performed annually for replacement analysis. Whenever there are updated data on the costs of the defender or data on new challengers available on the market, these new data should be used in the procedure. Example 12.5 illustrates this.

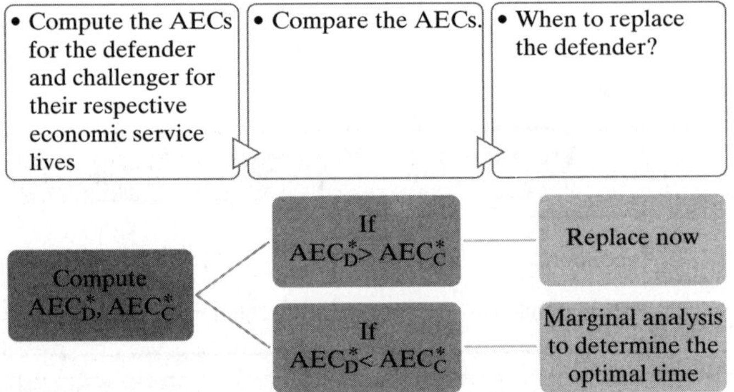

Figure 12.7 Logical steps for comparing the defender with the challenger under the infinite planning horizon

EXAMPLE 12.5 Replacement Analysis under the Infinite Planning Horizon

General Engineering Company is considering replacing an old vertical cylinder honing machine that had been used for honing automobile and tractor cylinders after the boring process. GEC is considering two options:

- **Option 1:** Retain the old honing machine. If kept, the old machine can be used for another six years with proper maintenance. The firm does not expect to realize any salvage value from scrapping it in six years. The market value of the machine is expected to decline 25% annually over the previous year's market value. The operating costs are estimated at $3,500 during the first year and are expected to increase by $1,000 per year thereafter.

- **Option 2:** Alternatively, the firm can sell the machine to another firm in the industry now for $4,000 and buy a new honing machine. The new machine costs $12,000 and will have operating costs of $2,300 in the first year, increasing by 20% per year thereafter. The expected salvage value is $8,000 after one year and will decline 30% each year thereafter.

The company requires a rate of return of 12% before tax. Find the economic life for each option, and determine when the defender should be replaced. Do not consider any income-tax effects.

DISSECTING THE PROBLEM	
	Given: Financial data for both defender and challenger.
	Find: (a) Economic service life for both defender and challenger and (b) the best time to replace the defender.

METHODOLOGY	SOLUTION
Use Excel work sheets to determine the economic service life for each option and compare the options.	**(a) Economic service life:**
	• **Defender:** If the company retains the honing machine, it is, in effect, forgoing the opportunity to cash in on the machine's current market

value, which is the opportunity cost of the machine, at $4,000. Other data for the defender are summarized as follows:

n	Forecasted Operating Cost	Market Value if Disposed of
0		$4,000
1	$3,500	$3,000
2	$4,500	$2,250
3	$5,500	$1,688
4	$6,500	$1,266
5	$7,500	$949
6	$8,500	$712

We can calculate the annual-equivalent costs if the defender is to be kept for one year, two years, three years, and so forth, respectively. In doing so, we may use the following expressions:

$$\text{AEC}(12\%)_N$$

$$= \overbrace{\$4,000\,(A/P,\,12\%,\,N) - \$4,000\,(1 - 0.25)^N\,(A/F,\,12\%,\,N)}^{\text{CR}\,(12\%)}$$

$$\underbrace{+\ \$3,500 + \$1,000\,(A/G,\,12\%,\,N).}_{\text{OC}\,(12\%)}$$

For example, the cash flow diagram for $N = 4$ years is shown in Figure 12.8.

For $N = 4$ years, we also calculate that

$$\text{AEC}(12\%) = \$4,000\,(A/P,\,12\%,\,4) - \$1,266\,(A/F,\,12\%,\,4)$$
$$+\ \$3,500 + \$1,000\,(A/G,\,12\%,\,4)$$
$$= \$5,911,$$

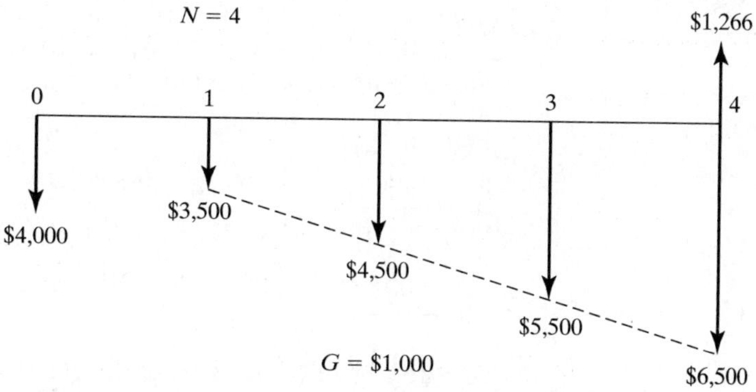

Figure 12.8 Cash flow transactions associated with keeping the defender for four years

TABLE 12.2 Economic Service Life Calculation for Defender

	A	B	C	D	E	F	G
1							
2		Annual changes in MV		-25%			
3		Annual increases in O&M		$1,000			
4		Interest rate		12%			
5							
6	n	Market Value	O&M Costs	CR(12%)	OC(12%)	AEC(12%)	
7							
8	0	$4,000					
9	1	$3,000	$3,500	$1,480	$3,500	$4,980	
10	2	$2,250	$4,500	$1,305	$3,972	$5,277	
11	3	$1,688	$5,500	$1,165	$4,425	$5,590	
12	4	$1,266	$6,500	$1,052	$4,859	$5,911	
13	5	$949	$7,500	$960	$5,275	$6,235	
14	6	$712	$8,500	$885	$5,672	$6,557	
15							
16							
17							
18						=D14+E14	
19	=B13*(1+$D$2)						
20			=C13+$D$3				
21				=-PMT($D$4,A14,NPV($D$4,$C$9:C14)+$C$8,0)			
22							
23			=-PMT($D$4,A14,$B$8,-B14)				
24							

where G represents the gradient amount. When $N = 1$ year, we get the lowest AEC value. Thus, the defender's economic life is one year. Using the notation we have defined in the procedure, we have

$$N_D^* = 1 \text{ year}$$

and

$$\text{AEC}^*_D = \$4,980.$$

For $N = 1$ to 6, the results are shown in Table 12.2.

- **Challenger:** The economic life of the challenger can be determined by using the same procedure shown in this example for the defender and in Example 12.4. A summary of the general equation for AEC calculation for the challenger is as follows:

$$\text{AEC}(12\%)_N$$

$$= \overbrace{\$12,000\,(A/P, 12\%, N) - \$8,000\,(1 - 0.30)^{N-1}(A/F, 12\%, N)}^{\text{CR (12\%)}}$$

$$+ \underbrace{\$2,300\,(P/A_1, 20\%, 12\%, N)(A/P, 12\%, N)}_{\text{OC (12\%)}}.$$

You do not have to express the AEC equation in this format. What you need to do is just calculate two different cost components—ownership cost (capital cost), CR(12%), and the operating cost, OC(12%) year by year. The obtained results are as shown in Table 12.3.

TABLE 12.3 Economic Service Life Calculation for Challenger

	A	B	C	D	E	F	G
1							
2		Annual changes in MV		-30%			
3		Annual increases in O&M		20%			
4		Interest rate		12%			
5							
6	n	Market Value	O&M Costs	CR(12%)	OC(12%)	AEC(12%)	
7							
8	0	$12,000					
9	1	$8,000	$2,300	$5,440	$2,300	$7,740	
10	2	$5,600	$2,760	$4,459	$2,517	$6,976	
11	3	$3,920	$3,312	$3,834	$2,753	$6,587	
12	4	$2,744	$3,974	$3,377	$3,008	$6,385	
13	5	$1,921	$4,769	$3,027	$3,285	$6,312	
14	6	$1,345	$5,723	$2,753	$3,586	$6,339	=D16+E16
15	7	$941	$6,868	$2,536	$3,911	$6,447	
16	8	$659	$8,241	$2,362	$4,263	$6,625	
17							
18							
19			=C15*(1+$D$3)				
20		=B15*(1+$D$2)			=-PMT($D$4,A16,NPV($D$4,$C$9:C16),0)		
21							
22			=-PMT($D$4,A16,$B$8,-B16)				
23							
24							

The economic life of the challenger is thus five years; that is,

$$N_C^* = 5 \text{ years}$$

and

$$\text{AEC}_C^* = \$6,312.$$

(b) Should the defender be replaced now?

Since $\text{AEC}_D^* = \$4,980 < \text{AEC}_C^* = \$6,312$, the answer is not to replace the defender now. If there are no technological advances in the next few years, the defender should be used for at least *one* more year.

- **When should the defender be replaced?**

  Our question is, then whether we should replace the defender at the end of its economic service life. As we will see shortly, it is not necessarily best to replace the defender right at the end of its economic life.

  If we need to find the answer to this question today, we have to calculate the cost of keeping and using the defender for the second year from today. That is, what is the cost of not selling the defender at the end of year 1, using it for the second year, and replacing it at the end of year 2? The following cash flows are related to this question:

  (1) Opportunity cost at the end of year 1, which is equal to the market value then: $3,000

  (2) Operating cost for the second year: $4,500

  (3) Market value of the defender at the end of year 2: $2,250

The diagram in Figure 12.9 represents these cash flows.

As shown in Figure 12.9, the cost of using the defender for one year beyond its economic life is

$$\$3,000 \times 1.12 + \$4,500 - \$2,250 = \$5,610.$$

Now compare this cost with $\text{AEC}^*_C = \$6,312$. It is less than AEC^*_C. So, it is less expensive to keep the defender for the second year than to replace it with the challenger. Thus, the conclusion is to keep the defender beyond its economic service life.

Since this second-year cost is still less than AEC^*_C, we need to calculate the cost of using the defender for the third year and then compare it with AEC^*_C.

$$\$2,250 \times 1.12 + \$5,500 - \$1,688 = \$6,332.$$

For year 3, keeping the defender is more expensive than replacing the defender with the challenger. This means that we should replace the defender at the end of year 2.

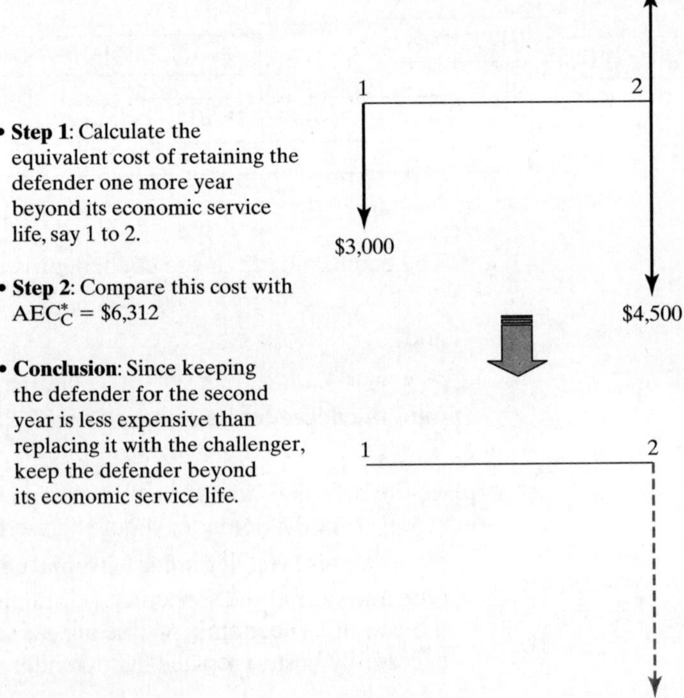

Figure 12.9   Illustration of marginal analysis to determine the optimal time for replacing the defender with the challenger

12.4 Replacement Analysis with Tax Considerations

Up to this point, we have covered various concepts and techniques that are useful in replacement analysis. In this section, we illustrate how to use those concepts and techniques to conduct replacement analysis on an after-tax basis.

To apply the concepts and methods covered in Sections 12.1 through 12.3 to after-tax comparisons of the defender with the challenger, we have to incorporate the tax effects of gains (or losses) whenever an asset is disposed of. Whether the defender is kept or the challenger is purchased, we also need to incorporate the tax effects of depreciation allowances and operating costs in our analysis.

Performing replacement studies requires knowledge of the depreciation schedule and of taxable gains or losses at disposal. Note that the depreciation schedule is determined at the time of asset acquisition whereas the current tax law determines the tax effects of gains at the time of disposal. In this section, we will use Example 12.6 to illustrate how to do replacement analyses on an after-tax basis.

EXAMPLE 12.6 Replacement Analysis under an Infinite Planning Horizon

Recall Example 12.5, where General Engineering Company was considering replacing an old honing machine. Let us assume the following additional data:

- The old machine has been fully depreciated, so it has zero book value. The machine could be used for another six years, but the firm does not expect to realize any salvage value from scrapping it in six years.
- The new machine falls into a seven-year MACRS property class and will be depreciated accordingly.

The marginal income-tax rate is 40%, and the after-tax MARR is 10%. Find the useful life for each option, and decide whether the defender should be replaced now or later.

DISSECTING THE PROBLEM

Given: Financial data as given in Example 12.5, tax rate $= 40\%$, and MARR $= 10\%$ after tax.

Find: (a) Economic service life for both defender and challenger and (b) optimal time to replace the defender.

METHODOLOGY

Use Excel to calculate the economic service lives for the defender and the challenger, and compare the results.

SOLUTION

(a) Economic service life:

- **Defender:** The defender is *fully depreciated*, so all salvage values can be treated as ordinary gains and taxed at 40%. The after-tax salvage values are thus as follows:

n	Current Market Value	After-Tax Salvage Value
0	$4,000	$4,000(1 − 0.40) = $2,400
1	$3,000	$3,000(1 − 0.40) = $1,800
2	$2,250	$2,250(1 − 0.40) = $1,350
3	$1,688	$1,688(1 − 0.40) = $1,013
4	$1,266	$1,266(1 − 0.40) = $760
5	$949	$949(1 − 0.40) = $569
6	$712	$712(1 − 0.40) = $427

If the company retains the old honing machine, it is, in effect, deciding to invest the machine's current market value (after taxes) in that alternative. Although there is no actual cash flow, the firm is withholding from the investment the market value of the honing machine (opportunity cost). The after-tax O&M costs are as follows:

n	Forecasted O&M Cost	After-Tax O&M Cost
0		
1	$3,500	$3,500(1 − 0.40) = $2,100
2	$4,500	$4,500(1 − 0.40) = $2,700
3	$5,500	$5,500(1 − 0.40) = $3,300
4	$6,500	$6,500(1 − 0.40) = $3,900
5	$7,500	$7,500(1 − 0.40) = $4,500
6	$8,500	$8,500(1 − 0.40) = $5,100

Using the current year's market value as the investment required to retain the defender, we obtain the data in Table 12.4, which indicate that the remaining useful life of the defender is still one year *in the absence of future challengers*. Note that we

TABLE 12.4 **Economic Service Life Calculation for Defender with Income-Tax Consideration**

	A	B	C	D	E	F	G
1							
2		Annual changes in MV		-25%			
3		Annual increases in A/T O&M		$600			=C10+$D$3
4		Interest rate (After tax)		10%			
5							
6		After-Tax	After-Tax				
7	n	Market Value	O&M Costs	CR(10%)	OC(10%)	AEC(10%)	
8							
9	0	$2,400					
10	1	$1,800	$2,100	$840	$2,100	$2,940	
11	2	$1,350	$2,700	$740	$2,386	$3,126	=D10+E10
12	3	$1,013	$3,300	$659	$2,662	$3,321	
13	4	$759	$3,900	$594	$2,929	$3,522	
14	5	$570	$4,500	$540	$3,186	$3,726	
15	6	$427	$5,100	$496	$3,434	$3,930	
16							
17							
18							
19		=B9*(1+$D$2)					
20				=-PMT($D$4,A10,NPV($D$4,$C$10:C10)+$C$9,0)			
21							
22			=-PMT($D$4,A10,$B$8,-B10)				
23							
24							

also use a 10% discount rate (instead of 12%) to reflect the return desired after-tax.

- **Challenger:** The economic service life with tax consideration can be calculated in several steps.

  - **Step 1:** Because the challenger will be depreciated over its tax life, we must determine the book value of the asset at the end of each holding period in order to compute the after-tax market value. This process is shown in rows 4 through 15 in Table 12.5. For example, if you keep the challenger for four years, the allowed MACRS depreciation amounts are as follows:

$$\text{Total depreciation} = \$1,715 + \$2,939 + \$2,099$$
$$+ (1/2)(\$1,499)$$
$$= \$7,503.$$
$$\text{Book value} = \$12,000 - \$7,503 = \$4,497.$$

  - **Step 2:** To determine the equivalent annual operating cost for each holding period, we need to consider two cash flow elements: (1) O&M cost and (2) depreciation tax shield. The process is illustrated in rows 17 through 28 in Table 12.5. For example, if you keep the challenger for four more years, the O&M cost each year will be as follows:

n	1	2	3	4
O&M Costs	$2,300	$2,760	$3,312	$3,974
A/T O&M	$1,380	$1,656	$1,987	$2,384
PW of A/T O&M	$1,255	$1,369	$1,493	$1,628

$$\text{Total PW of A/T O\&M Costs} = \$1,255 + \$1,369$$
$$+ \$1,493 + \$1,628$$
$$= \$5,745.$$

This figure is shown in cell K24 in Table 12.5.

  - **Step 3:** With the book value as calculated in Step 1, we can determine the after-tax market values. With $N = 4$,

$$\text{Taxable gains (losses)} = \$2,744 - \$4,497 = -\$1,753,$$
$$\text{Gains taxes (loss credit)} = (\$1,753)(0.40) = -\$701, \text{ and}$$
$$\text{Net A/T market value} = \$2,744 - (-\$701) = \$3,445.$$

  - **Step 4:** We are now ready to find the economic service life of the challenger by generating AEC entries. These calculations are summarized in rows 30 through 41 in Table 12.5.

  - **Step 5:** The economic life of the challenger is six years with an AEC(10%) of $4,018.

TABLE 12.5 Economics of Owning and Operating the Challenger for *N* More Years

	A	B	C	D	E	F	G	H	I	J	K
1											
2	Tax Rate	40%									
3	MARR	10%									
4		Permitted Annual Depreciation Amounts over the								Total	Book
5	Holding	Holding Period								Total	Book
6	Period	1	2	3	4	5	6	7	8	Depreciation	Value
7	0										$12,000
8	1	$1,715								$1,715	$10,285
9	2	$1,715	$1,470							$3,185	$8,815
10	3	$1,715	$2,939	$1,050						$5,704	$6,296
11	4	$1,715	$2,939	$2,099	$750					$7,503	$4,497
12	5	$1,715	$2,939	$2,099	$1,499	$536				$8,788	$3,212
13	6	$1,715	$2,939	$2,099	$1,499	$1,072	$535			$9,859	$2,141
14	7	$1,715	$2,939	$2,099	$1,499	$1,072	$1,070	$536		$10,930	$1,070
15	8	$1,715	$2,939	$2,099	$1,499	$1,072	$1,070	$1,072	$534	$12,000	$0
16											
17		Annual O&M Costs over the Holding Period									Total PW
18	Holding									Total PW of	of A/T
19	Period	1	2	3	4	5	6	7	8	O&M Costs	O&M Costs
20	0										
21	1	$2,300								$2,091	$1,255
22	2	$2,300	$2,760							$4,372	$2,623
23	3	$2,300	$2,760	$3,312						$6,860	$4,116
24	4	$2,300	$2,760	$3,312	$3,974					$9,575	$5,745
25	5	$2,300	$2,760	$3,312	$3,974	$4,769				$12,536	$7,522
26	6	$2,300	$2,760	$3,312	$3,974	$4,769	$5,723			$15,767	$9,460
27	7	$2,300	$2,760	$3,312	$3,974	$4,769	$5,723	$6,868		$19,291	$11,575
28	8	$2,300	$2,760	$3,312	$3,974	$4,769	$5,723	$6,868	$8,241	$23,136	$13,881
29											
30		Expected			Net A/T	A/T Operating Costs (in PW)					Total
31	Holding	Market	Taxable	Gains	Market	over the Holding Period			OC(10%)	CR(10%)	AEC(10%)
32	Period	Value	Gains	Tax	Value	O&M Costs	Tax Shield	Total OC			
33	0										
34	1	$8,000	($2,285)	($914)	$8,914	$1,255	$624	$631	$694	$4,286	$4,980
35	2	$5,600	($3,215)	($1,286)	$6,886	$2,623	$1,110	$1,514	$872	$3,635	$4,507
36	3	$3,920	($2,376)	($950)	$4,870	$4,116	$1,911	$2,205	$887	$3,354	$4,241
37	4	$2,744	($1,753)	($701)	$3,445	$5,745	$2,431	$3,314	$1,045	$3,043	$4,089
38	5	$1,921	($1,291)	($516)	$2,437	$7,522	$2,769	$4,753	$1,254	$2,766	$4,020
39	6	$1,345	($796)	($318)	$1,663	$9,460	$3,023	$6,437	$1,478	$2,540	$4,018
40	7	$941	($129)	($52)	$993	$11,575	$3,253	$8,321	$1,709	$2,360	$4,069
41	8	$659	$659	$264	$395	$13,881	$3,463	$10,418	$1,953	$2,215	$4,168
42											
43	Sample cell fomulas:										
44											
45	cell K13:=$K$7-J13				cell D39:=C39*$B$2			cell G39:=NPV($B$3,B13:I13)*$B$2			
46	cell K26:==J26*(1-$B$2)				cell E39:=B39-D39			cell I39:=-PMT($B$3,A26,H39,0,0)			
47	cell C39:=B39-K13				cell F39:=K26			cell J39:=-PMT($B$3,A26,12000,-E39)			

(b) Optimal time to replace the defender:

Since the AEC for the defender's remaining useful life (one year) is $2,940, which is less than $4,018, the best decision will be to keep the defender for now. Note, however, that the defender's remaining useful life of one year does not necessarily imply that the defender should be kept for only one year before it is switched for the challenger. The reason for this is that the defender's remaining useful life was calculated without considering for what type of challenger would be available in the future. When a challenger's financial data are available, we need to enumerate all timing possibilities for replacement. Since the defender can be used for another six years, seven replacement strategies exist:

- Replace now with the challenger.
- Replace in year 1 with the challenger.
- Replace in year 2 with the challenger.
- Replace in year 3 with the challenger.
- Replace in year 4 with the challenger.
- Replace in year 5 with the challenger.
- Replace in year 6 with the challenger.

If the costs and efficiency of the current challenger remain unchanged in the future years, the possible replacement cash patterns associated with each alternative are as shown in Figure 12.10. From

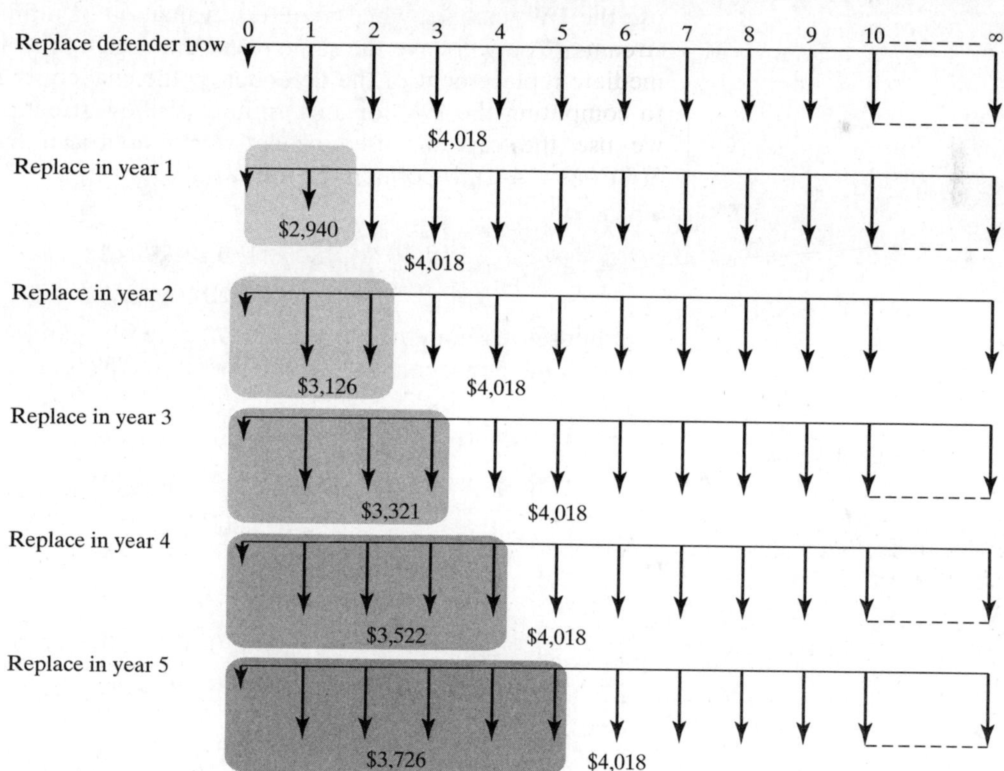

Figure 12.10 Equivalent annual cash flow streams when the defender is kept for n years followed by infinitely repeated purchases of the similar challenger every six years

the figure, we observe that, on an annual basis, the cash flows after six years are the same, regardless of how long the defender is kept.

Before we evaluate the economics of various replacement-decision options, recall the AEC figures for the defender and the challenger under the assumed service lives as shown in the accompanying chart. (A figure in box denotes the minimum AEC at $N_D^* = 1$ and $N_C^* = 6$, respectively.)

Annual-Equivalent Cost ($)

n	Defender	Challenger
1	$\boxed{\$2,940}$	$4,980
2	$3,126	$4,507
3	$3,321	$4,241
4	$3,522	$4,089
5	$3,726	$4,020
6	$3,930	$\boxed{\$4,018}$
7		$4,069
8		$4,168

Instead of using the marginal analysis in Example 12.5, we will use the PW analysis, which requires evaluation of infinite cash-flow streams. (You will have the same result under marginal analysis.) Immediate replacement of the defender by the challenger is equivalent to computing the PW for an infinite cash flow stream of $4,018. If we use the capitalized-equivalent-worth approach from Chapter 5($CE(i) = A/i$), we obtain the following:

- $n = 0$:

$$PW(10\%)_{n=0} = (1/0.10)(\$4,018)$$
$$= \$40,180.$$

Suppose we retain the old machine n more years and then replace it with the new one. Now we will compute $PW(i)_n$.

- $n = 1$:

$$PW(10\%)_{n=1} = \$2,940(P/A, 10\%, 1)$$
$$+ (1/0.10)(\$4,018)(P/F, 10\%, 1)$$
$$= \$39,200.$$

- $n = 2$:

$$PW(10\%)_{n=2} = \$3,126(P/A, 10\%, 2)$$
$$+ (1/0.10)(\$4,018)(P/F, 10\%, 2)$$
$$= \$38,631.$$

- $n = 3$:

$$PW(10\%)_{n=3} = \$3,321(P/A, 10\%, 3)$$
$$+ (1/0.10)(\$4,018)(P/F, 10\%, 3)$$
$$= \boxed{\$38,447}.$$

- $n = 4$:

$$PW(10\%)_{n=4} = \$3{,}522(P/A, 10\%, 4)$$
$$+ (1/0.10)(\$4{,}018)(P/F, 10\%, 4)$$
$$= \$38{,}608.$$

- $n = 5$:

$$PW(10\%)_{n=5} = \$3{,}726(P/A, 10\%, 5)$$
$$+ (1/0.10)(\$4{,}018)(P/F, 10\%, 5)$$
$$= \$39{,}073.$$

COMMENTS: This result leads us to conclude that the defender should be kept for three more years. The NPW of \$38,447 represents the net PW cost associated with retaining the defender for three years, replacing it with the challenger, and then replacing the challenger every six years for an indefinite period.

SUMMARY

- In replacement analysis, the **defender** is an existing asset; the **challenger** is the best available replacement candidate.

- The **current market value** is the value to use in preparing a defender's economic analysis. **Sunk costs**—past costs that cannot be changed by any future investment decision—should not be considered in any economic analysis.

- Two basic approaches to analyzing replacement problems are the **cash-flow approach** and the **opportunity-cost approach**. The cash flow approach explicitly considers the actual cash-flow consequences for each replacement alternative as it occurs. Typically, the net proceeds from the sale of the defender are subtracted from the purchase price of the challenger. The opportunity-cost approach views the net proceeds from the sale of the defender as an opportunity cost of keeping the defender. That is, instead of deducting the salvage value from the purchase cost of the challenger, we consider the salvage value an investment required in order to keep the asset.

- **Economic service life** is the remaining useful life of a defender (or a challenger) that results in the minimum equivalent annual cost or maximum annual-equivalent revenue. We should use the respective economic service lives of the defender and the challenger when conducting a replacement analysis.

- Ultimately, in replacement analysis, the question is not *whether* to replace the defender but *when* to do so. The AE method provides a marginal basis on which to make the year-by-year decision about the best time to replace the defender. As a general decision criterion, the PW method provides a more direct solution to a variety of replacement problems with either an infinite or a finite planning horizon or a technological change in a future challenger.

- The role of **technological change** in asset improvement should be weighed in making long-term replacement plans: If a particular item is undergoing rapid, substantial technological improvements, it may be prudent to shorten or delay replacement (to the extent where the loss in production does not exceed any savings from improvements in future challengers) until a desired future model is available.

SELF-TEST QUESTIONS

Problem Statement for Questions (12s.1–12s.5)

Consider the following replacement decision problem:

- **Option 1:** Continue to use the old machine: A machine now in use, which was bought five years ago for $5,000, has been fully depreciated. It can be sold for $3,000, but could be used for three more years (remaining useful life), at the end of which time it would have no salvage value. The annual operating and maintenance costs for the old machine amount to $12,00.

- **Option 2:** Replace the old machine: A new machine can be purchased at an invoice price of $15,000 to replace the present equipment. Because of the nature of the manufactured product, the new machine has an expected economic life of three years, and it will have no salvage value at the end of that time. The new machine's expected operating and maintenance costs amount to $2,500 for the first year and $3,500 for each of the next two years. The income tax rate is 35%. Any gains will also be taxed at 35%. The allowed depreciation amounts for the new machine are $1,500 during the first year, and $2,600 per year for the next two years. The firm's interest rate is 12%.

12s.1 If the old machine is to be sold now, what will be the gains tax?
    (a) $800   (b) $850   (c) $950   (d) $1,050

12s.2 If you decide to retain the old machine for now, what will be the opportunity cost?
    (a) $2,500   (b) $3,000   (c) $1,650   (d) $1,500

12s.3 If the old asset is to be sold now, its sunk cost is
    (a) $2,500   (b) $5,000   (c) $1,650   (d) $1,500

12s.4 For depreciation purposes, the first cost of the new machine under the opportunity cost approach will be
    (a) $14,000   (b) $11,500   (c) $12,000   (d) $16,500

12s.5 What is the incremental annual after-tax flow of replacing the old machine?
    (a) $8,091   (b) $9,199   (c) $9,670   (d) $2,298

12s.6 A local delivery company has purchased a delivery truck for $15,000. The truck will be depreciated under MACRS as a five-year property. The truck's market value (or selling price) is expected to be $2,500 less each year. The O&M costs are expected to be $3,000 per year. The firm is in a 40% tax bracket, and its MARR is 15%. Compute the annual-equivalent cost for retaining the truck for a two-year period, which will be
    (a) $5,527   (b) $5,175   (c) $5,362   (d) $5,014

12s.7 The following table summarizes the financial data for a proposed new asset. The issue is how long the asset should be kept. Assume an interest rate of 12% and determine the economic service life of the asset before taxes.

End of Year (n)	Investment Cost	O&M Cost	Salvage Value
0	$14,000		
1		$3,400	$8,000
2		4,600	6,000
3		5,800	4,000
4		7,200	2,000
5		8,300	0

    (a) 2 years   (b) 3 years   (c) 4 years   (d) 5 years

12s.8 The annual-equivalent after-tax costs of retaining a defender over its three-year remaining life and the annual equivalent operating costs for its challenger over its four-year physical life are as follows:

	Annual-Equivalent Cost	
Holding Period	Defender	Challenger
1	$3,000	$5,000
2	$2,500	$4,000
3	$3,200	$3,100
4		$4,500

Assume an MARR of 12% and determine the optimal replacement time for the defender. Assume an infinite planning horizon and no technological change (cost) in the challenger. What would be your decision?

(a) Replace now

(b) Replace one year later

(c) Replace two years later

(d) Replace three years later

PROBLEMS

Replacement Basics without Considering Income-Tax Effects

12.1 Newnan Furniture owns and operates an industrial lift truck in its warehousing operation. The record indicates that the lift truck was purchased four years ago at $15,000. The estimated salvage value is $4,000 after four years of operation. First-year O&M expenses were $2,000, but the O&M expenses have increased by $400 each year for the first four years of operation. Using $i = 10\%$, compute the annual equivalent costs of the lift truck for four years on a before-tax basis.

12.2 Macintosh Printing Inc. purchased a $20,000 printing machine two years ago. The company expected this machine to have a five-year life and a salvage value of $5,000. Unfortunately, the company spent $5,000 last year on repairs, and current operating costs are now running at the rate of $8,000 per year. Furthermore, the anticipated salvage value has now been reduced to $2,500 at the end of the printer's remaining useful life. In addition, the company has found that the current machine has a book value of $14,693 and a market value of $10,000 today. The equipment vendor will allow the company the full amount of the market value as a trade-in on a new machine. What value(s) for the defender is (are) relevant in our analysis?

12.3 Consider again the scenario in Problem 12.2. Suppose that the company has been offered the opportunity to purchase another printing machine for $15,000. Over its three-year useful life, the machine will reduce labor and raw-materials usage sufficiently to cut operating costs from $8,000 to $6,000. This reduction in costs will allow after-tax profits to rise by $2,000 per year. It is estimated that the new machine can be sold for $5,500 at the end of year 3. If the new machine were purchased, the old machine would be sold to another company rather than be traded in for the new machine. Suppose that the firm will need either machine (old or new) for only three years and that it does not expect a new, superior machine to become available on the market during the required service period. Assuming that the firm's interest rate is 12%, decide whether replacement is justified now.

12.4 Razorback Manufacturing is considering replacing a broken metal cutting machine. Several options have been proposed.

- Option 1: The broken machine can be sold today for $3,000.
- Option 2: It can be overhauled completely for $7,000, after which it will produce $2,500 in annual cash flows over the next five years. The resale value of the asset at the end of five years is zero.
- Option 3: It can be replaced for $18,000. The life of the replacement machine is five years, and it has an estimated salvage value of $2,000 at the end of five years. The anticipated operating cash inflows for each year will be $5,000.

If the firm's required rate of return of 12%, what should Razorback do?

12.5 A firm is considering the replacement of a 2,000 lb capacity pressing machine purchased five years ago at a cost of $22,000. The machine was originally expected to have a useful life of 10 years and a $2,000 estimated salvage value at the end of that period. However, the machine has not been dependable and is frequently out of service while awaiting repairs. The maintenance expenses of the pressing machine have been rising steadily and currently amount to about $5,000 per year. The machine could be sold now for $6,000. If retained, the machine will require an immediate $2,500 overhaul to keep it in operable condition. This overhaul will neither extend the originally estimated service life nor increase the value of the machine. The updated annual operating costs, engine overhaul cost, and market values over the next five years are estimated as follows:

N	O&M	Depreciation	Engine Overhaul	Market Value
−5				
−4		$2,858		
−3		$4,898		
−2		$3,498		
−1		$2,500		
0		$1,784	$2,500	$6,000
1	$5,000	$1,786		$4,500
2	$5,500	$1,840		$3,500
3	$6,000	$892		$3,000
4	$6,500	$0	$3,000	$2,500
5	$7,500	$0		$2,000

A drastic increase in operating costs during the fourth year is expected as a result of another overhaul, which will be required to keep the machine in operating condition. The firm's MARR is 15%.

(a) If the machine is to be sold now, what will be its sunk cost?

(b) What is the opportunity cost of not replacing the machine now?

(c) What is the equivalent annual cost of owning and operating the machine for two more years?

(d) What is the equivalent annual cost of owning and operating the machine for five more years?

12.6   A manufacturing firm is considering replacing one of its CNC machines with a machine that is newer and more efficient. The company has an MARR of 12%.

■ **Old Machine:** The firm purchased the current CNC machine 10 years ago at a cost of $155,000. It had an expected economic life of 12 years at the time of purchase and an expected salvage value of $10,000 at the end of the 12 years. The original salvage estimate is still good, and the machine has a remaining useful life of two years. The firm can sell this old machine now to another firm in the industry for $30,000.

■ **New Machine:** The new machine can be purchased for $175,000, including installation costs. It has an estimated useful (economic) life of eight years. The new machine is expected to reduce cash operating expenses by $35,000 per year over its eight-year life. At the end of its useful life, the machine is estimated to be worth only $8,000.

(a) What is the opportunity cost of retaining the old asset?

(b) Compute the cash flows associated with retaining the old machine for the next two years (years 1 to 2).

(c) Compute the cash flows associated with purchasing the new machine for use over the next eight years (years 1 to 8). (Use the opportunity-cost concept.)

(d) If the firm needs the service of this type of machine for an indefinite period and no technology improvement is expected in future machines, what would be your decision?

12.7   A manufacturer is considering the replacement of one of its boring machines with a newer and more efficient one. The relevant details for both defender and challenger are as follows:

■ **Defender:** The current book value of the old boring machine is $50,000, and it has a remaining useful life of five years. The salvage value expected from scrapping the old machine at the end of five years is zero, but the company can sell the machine now to another firm in the industry for $10,000.

■ **Challenger:** The new boring machine can be purchased at a price of $150,000 and has an estimated useful life of seven years. It has an estimated salvage value of $50,000 and is expected to realize economic savings on electric power usage, labor, and repair costs and to reduce the amount of reworks. In total, annual savings of $80,000 will be realized if the new machine is installed.

The firm uses an MARR of 12%. Using the opportunity-cost approach, address the following questions:

(a) What is the initial cash outlay required for the new machine?

(b) What are the cash flows for the defender in years zero to five?

(c) Should the firm purchase the new machine?

12.8   A local hospital has the following replacement decision problem:

■ **Old machine:** The hospital purchased a digital image-processing machine three years ago at a cost of $50,000. The machine had an expected life of eight years at the time of purchase and an expected salvage value of $8,000 at the end of the eight years. However, the old machine has been slow at handling the increased business volume, so management is considering replacing it. The old machine can be sold today for $12,000.

■ **New machine:** A new machine can be purchased for $80,000, including installation costs. Over its five-year life, the new machine will reduce cash operating expenses by $30,000 per year. Sales are not expected to change. At the end of its useful life, the new machine is estimated to be worthless.

The hospital's interest rate for project justification is known to be 12%. The hospital does not expect a better machine (other than the current challenger) to be available for the next five years. Assume that the economic service life for the new machine and the remaining useful life for the old machine are both five years.

(a) Determine the cash flows associated with each option (keeping the defender versus purchasing the challenger).

(b) Should the hospital replace the defender now?

12.9 Higgins Machine Tools, Inc. is currently manufacturing one of its products on a hydraulic stamping press machine. The unit cost of the product is $16, and in the past year 4,000 units were produced and sold for $24 each. It is expected that the future demand of the product and the unit price will remain steady at 4,000 units per year and $24 per unit, respectively.

■ **Defender:** The machine has a remaining useful life of three years and could be sold on the open market now for $8,000. Three years from now, the machine is expected to have a salvage value of $1,800.

■ **Challenger:** A new machine would cost $40,000, and the unit manufacturing cost on the new machine is projected to be $14. The new machine has an expected economic life of five years and an expected salvage of $8,000.

The appropriate MARR is 10%. The firm does not expect a significant improvement in the machine's technology to occur, and it needs the service of either machine for an indefinite period of time.

(a) Compute the cash flows over the remaining useful life if the firm decides to retain the old machine.

(b) Compute the cash flows over the useful service life if the firm decides to purchase the machine.

(c) Should the new machine be acquired now?

Economic Service Life

12.10 You purchased an industrial oven five years ago for $70,000. O&M costs are $20,000 this year but are expected to increase by $1,500 each year for the next five years. The current salvage value of the machine is $20,000; salvage value after one year is estimated to be $10,000; after two years, $9,000; after three years, $8,000; after four years, $7,000; and so on. At $i = 12\%$, find the remaining economic life of the asset.

12.11 A special-purpose machine is to be purchased at a cost of $30,000. The following table shows the expected annual operating and maintenance cost and the salvage value for each year of service:

Year of Service	O&M Cost	Market Value
1	$5,000	$25,800
2	$6,500	$16,000
3	$10,000	$10,000
4	$12,500	$5,000
5	$14,800	$0

If the interest rate is 12%, what is the economic service life for this machine?

12.12 Consider a new electric forklift truck that would cost $18,000, have operating costs of $1,000 in the first year, and have a salvage value of $10,000 at the end of the first year. For the remaining years, operating costs increase each year by 15% over the previous year's operating costs. Similarly, the salvage value declines each year by 25% from the previous year's salvage value. The truck has a maximum life of seven years. Overhauls costing $3,000 and $4,500 will be required during the fifth and seventh years of service, respectively. The firm's required rate of return is 15%. Find the economic service life of this new machine.

12.13 A firm is considering replacing a machine that has been used for making a certain kind of packaging material. The new machine will cost $31,000 and will have an estimated economic life of 10 years with a salvage value of $2,500. Operating costs are expected to be $1,000 per year throughout its service life. The machine currently in use had an original cost of $25,000 four years ago, and its service life (physical life) at the time of purchase was estimated to be seven years with a salvage value of $5,000. This machine has a current market value of $7,700. If the firm retains the old machine, its updated market values and operating costs for the next four years will be as follows:

Year End	Market Value	Book Value	Operating Costs
0	$7,700	$7,809	
1	$4,300	$5,578	$3,200
2	$3,300	$3,347	$3,700
3	$1,100	$1,116	$4,800
4	$0	$0	$5,850

The firm's minimum attractive rate of return is 12%.

(a) Working with the updated estimates of market values and operating costs over the next four years, determine the remaining useful life of the old machine.

(b) Determine whether it is economical to make the replacement now.

(c) If the firm's decision in part (b) is to replace the old machine, when should the replacement occur?

Replacement Decisions When Required Service Life Is Long

12.14 Eight years ago, a firm purchased a lathe for $45,000. The operating expenses for the lathe are $8,700 per year. An equipment vendor offers the firm a new machine for $53,500 with operating costs of $5,700 per year. An allowance of $8,500 would be made for the old machine on the purchase of the new one. The old machine was expected to be scrapped at the end of five years. The new machine's economic service life is five years with a salvage value of $12,000. The new machine's O&M cost is estimated to be $4,200 for the first year, increasing at an annual rate of $500 thereafter. The firm's MARR is 12%. Which option would you recommend?

12.15 Advanced Electrical Insulator Company is considering replacing a broken inspection machine, which has been used to test the mechanical strength of electrical insulators with a newer and more efficient one. If repaired, the old machine can be used for another five years although the firm does not expect to realize any salvage value from scrapping it in five years. Alternatively, the firm can sell the machine to another firm in the industry now for $5,000. If the machine is kept, it will require an immediate $1,200 overhaul to restore it to operable condition. The overhaul will neither extend the service life originally estimated nor increase the value of the inspection machine. The operating costs are estimated at $2,000 during the first year and are expected to increase by $1,500 per year thereafter. Future market values are expected to decline by $1,000 per year.

The new machine costs $10,000 and will have operating costs of $2,000 in the first year, increasing by $800 per year thereafter. The expected salvage value is $6,000 after one year and will decline 15% each following year. The company requires a rate of return of 15%. Find the economic life for each option and determine when the defender should be replaced.

12.16 CTI Corporation purchased a special-purpose turnkey stamping machine four years ago for $18,000. It was estimated at that time that this machine would have a life of 10 years and a salvage value of $4,000 with a removal cost of $1,500. These estimates are still good. This machine has annual operating costs of $3,000. A new machine, which is more efficient, will reduce the annual operating costs to $1,500 but will require an investment of $22,000, plus $2,000 for installation. The life of the new machine is estimated to be 12 years with a salvage value of $4,000 and a removal cost of $2,000. An offer of $7,000 has been made for the old machine, and the purchaser is willing to pay for its removal. Find the economic advantage of replacement or of continuing with the present machine. State any assumptions that you make. (Assume $i = 12\%$.)

12.17 Cushman Manufacturing Company has a five-year-old vertical numerical chucker (VNC) that has a current market value of $5,000 and expected O&M costs of $3,000 this year, which increase by $1,500 per year. Future market values are expected to decline by $1,000 per year. The VNC machine can be used for another three years. The challenger costs $10,000 and has O&M costs of $2,000 per year, which increase by $1,000 per year. The machine will be needed for only three years, and the salvage value at the end of the three years is expected to be $4,000. The MARR is 15%.

(a) Determine the annual cash flows for retaining the old VNC machine for three years.

(b) Determine whether now is the best time to replace the old machine.

12.18 Greenleaf Company is considering the purchase of a new set of air-electric quill units to replace an obsolete machine. The current machine has a market value of zero; however, it is in good working order, and it will last physically for at least an additional five years. The new quill units will perform the operation with so much more efficiency that the firm's engineers estimate that labor, material, and other direct costs will be reduced by $3,000 a year if the units are installed. The new set of quill units costs $10,000 delivered and installed, and its economic life is estimated to be five years with zero salvage value. The firm's MARR is 10%.

(a) What is the investment required to keep the old machine?

(b) Compute the cash flow to use in the analysis of each option.

(c) If the firm uses the internal-rate-of-return criterion, would the analysis indicate that the firm should buy the new machine?

12.19 Acme-Denver Corporation is considering the replacement of an old, relatively inefficient surface-grinder machine that was purchased seven years ago at a cost of $12,000. The machine had an original expected life of 10 years and a zero estimated salvage value at the end of that period. The current market value of the machine is $2,000. The divisional manager reports that a new machine can be bought and installed for $14,000. Over its five-year life, this machine will expand sales from $10,000 to $12,500 a year and, furthermore, will reduce labor and raw-materials usage sufficiently to cut annual operating costs from $7,000 to $5,000. The new machine has an estimated salvage value of $4,000 at the end of its five-year life. The firm's MARR is 12%.

(a) Should the new machine be purchased now?

(b) What current market value of the new machine would make the two options equal?

12.20 An auto-part manufacturer is faced with the prospect of replacing its old robot, which has been used in stamping operation for 10 years. This particular robot was installed at a cost of $100,000 and was assumed to have a 15-year life with no appreciable salvage value. The current annual operating costs are $20,000 for this old robot, and these costs are presumed to be the same for the rest of its life. A sales representative from Advanced Robotic Systems is trying to sell this company a new-highly efficient robot. The new system would require an investment of $200,000 for installation. The economic life of this new robot is estimated to be 10 years with a salvage value of $18,000, and the robot will reduce annual operating costs to $5,000. No detailed agreement has been made with the sales representative about the disposal of the old robot. Determine the range of resale values associated with the old system that would justify installation of the new system at a MARR of 14%.

12.21 A company is currently producing chemical compounds by a process installed 10 years ago at a cost of $100,000. It was assumed that the process would have a 20-year life with a zero salvage value. The current market value of the equipment, however, is $60,000, and the initial estimate of its economic life is still good. The annual operating costs associated with this process are $18,000. A sales representative from U.S. Instrument Company is trying to sell a new chemical-compound-making process to the company. This new process will cost $200,000 have a service life of 10 years with a salvage value of $20,000, and reduce annual operating costs to $4,000. Assuming the company desires a return of 12% on all investments, should it invest in the new process?

12.22 Four years ago, a firm purchased an industrial batch oven for $23,000. The oven had an estimated life of 10 years with $1,000 salvage value. These original estimates are still good. If sold now, the machine will bring in $2,000. If sold at the end of the year, it will bring in $1,500. The market value after the first year has decreased at annual rate of 25%. Annual operating costs for subsequent years are $3,800. A new machine will cost $50,000 and have a 12-year life with a $3,000 salvage value. The operating cost for the new machine will be $3,000 as of the end of each year, where the $6,000-per-year savings are due to better quality control. If the firm's MARR is 10%, should the new machine be purchased now?

12.23 Georgia Ceramic Company has an automatic glaze sprayer that has been used for the past 10 years. The sprayer can be used for another 10 years and will have a zero salvage value at that time. The annual operating and maintenance costs for the sprayer amount to $15,000 per year. Due to an increase in business, a new sprayer must be purchased, either in addition to or as a replacement for the old sprayer.

- Option 1: If the old sprayer is retained, a new, smaller capacity sprayer will be purchased at a cost of $48,000; this new sprayer will have a $5,000 salvage value in 10 years and annual operating and maintenance costs of $12,000. The old sprayer has a current market value of $6,000.

- Option 2: If the old sprayer is sold, a new sprayer of larger capacity will be purchased for $84,000. This sprayer will have a $9,000 salvage value in 10 years and annual operating and maintenance costs of $24,000.

Which option should be selected at MARR $= 12\%$?

Replacement Analysis with Tax Considerations

12.24 Rework Problem 12.1, assuming the following additional information: The asset is classified as a five-year MACRS property. The firm's marginal tax rate is 40%, and its after-tax MARR is 8%.

12.25 Rework Problem 12.7, assuming the following additional information:
- The current book value of the old machine is $0 (fully depreciated).
- The new machine will be depreciated under a seven-year MACRS class.
- The company's marginal tax rate is 40%, and the firm uses an after-tax MARR of 12%.

12.26 Rework Problem 12.8, assuming the following additional information:
- The old machine will be depreciated according to the straight-line method for the remaining useful life.
- The new machine will be depreciated according to seven-year MACRS. The income tax rate is 35%, and the after-tax MARR is 12%.

Economic Service Life with Tax Considerations

12.27 Rework Problem 12.11, assuming the following additional information:
- The machine is classified as a seven-year MACRS recovery period. The tax rate is 40%, and the after-tax MARR is 10%.

12.28 Rework Problem 12.13 with the following additional information:
- The current book value of the old machine is $7,809. The anticipated book values for the next four years are as follows: year 1, $5,578; year 2, $3,347; year 3, $1,116; and year 4, $0.
- The new machine will be depreciated under a seven-year MACRS class.
- The company's marginal tax rate is 35%, and the firm uses an after-tax MARR of 10%.

12.29 A machine has a purchase cost of $10,000. End-of-year book values, salvage values, and annual O&M costs are provided over its useful life as follows:

Year-End	Book Value	Salvage Value	Operating Costs
1	$8,000	$5,300	$1,500
2	$4,800	$3,900	$2,100
3	$2,880	$2,800	$2,700
4	$1,728	$1,800	$3,400
5	$576	$1,400	$4,200
6	$0	$600	$4,900

(a) Determine the economic life of the machine if the MARR is 15% and the marginal tax rate is 40%.

(b) Determine the economic life of the machine if the MARR is changed to 10% and the marginal tax rate remains at 40%.

12.30 Assume, for a particular asset, that

$$I = \$30,000,$$
$$S_n = 22,000 - 2,000n,$$
$$B_n = 30,000 - 3,000n,$$
$$O\&M_n = 3,000(1 + 0.15)^{n-1},$$

and

$$t_m = 0.40,$$

where

$$I = \text{asset purchase price},$$
$$S_n = \text{market value at the end of year } n,$$
$$B_n = \text{book value at the end of year } n,$$
$$O\&M_n = \text{O\&M cost during year } n, \text{ and}$$
$$t_m = \text{marginal tax rate}.$$

(a) Determine the economic service life of the asset if $i = 10\%$.

(b) Determine the economic service life of the asset if $i = 25\%$.

(c) Assuming that $i = 0$, determine the economic service life mathematically.

12.31 Rework Problem 12.11, assuming the following additional information:

- For tax purposes, the entire cost of $30,000 can be depreciated according to a five-year MACRS property class.
- The firm's marginal tax rate is 40%.

Replacement Decisions When the Required Service Period Is Long (with tax considerations)

12.32 Rework Problem 12.16, assuming the following additional information:

- The current book value of the old machine is $5,623, and the asset has been depreciated according to a seven-year MACRS property class.
- The new asset is also classified as a seven-year MACRS property.
- The company's marginal tax rate is 30%, and the firm uses an after-tax MARR of 8%.

12.33 Rework Problem 12.18, assuming the following additional information:

- The current book value of the old machine is $4,000, and the annual depreciation charge is $800 if the firm decides to keep the old machine for the additional five years.
- The new asset is classified as a seven-year MACRS property.
- The company's marginal tax rate is 40%, and the firm uses an after-tax MARR of 10%.

12.34 Rework Problem 12.20, assuming the following additional information:

- The old switching system has been fully depreciated.
- The new system falls into the five-year MACRS property class.
- The company's marginal tax rate is 40%, and the firm uses an after-tax MARR of 14%.

12.35 Five years ago, a conveyor system was installed in a manufacturing plant at a cost of $35,000. It was estimated that the system, which is still in operating condition, would have a useful life of eight years with a salvage value of $3,000. If the firm continues to operate the system, it's estimated market values and operating costs for the next three years are as follows:

Year-End	Market Value	Book Value	Operating Costs
0	$11,500	$15,000	
1	$5,200	$11,000	$4,500
2	$3,500	$7,000	$5,300
3	$1,200	$3,000	$6,100

A new system can be installed for $43,500. This system would have an estimated economic life of 10 years with a salvage value of $3,500. The operating costs for the new system are expected to be $1,500 per year throughout its service life. The firm's MARR is 18%. The system belongs to the seven-year MACRS property class. The firm's marginal tax rate is 35%.

(a) Should the existing system be replaced?

(b) If the decision in (a) is to replace the existing system, when should replacement occur?

12.36 Rework Problem 12.14, assuming the following additional information:

- The old machine has been fully depreciated.
- The new machine will be depreciated under the seven-year MACRS class.
- The marginal tax rate is 35%, and the firm's after-tax MARR is 12%.

12.37 Rework Problem 12.23, assuming the following additional information:

- Option 1: The old sprayer has been fully depreciated. The new sprayer is classified as a seven-year MACRS property.
- Option 2: The larger capacity sprayer is classified as a seven-year MACRS property.
- Tax Information: The company's marginal tax rate is 40%, and the firm uses an after-tax MARR of 12%.

12.38 A six-year old CNC machine that originally cost $8,000 has been fully depreciated, and its current market value is $1,500. If the machine is kept in service for the next five years, its O&M costs and salvage values are estimated as follows:

	O & M Costs		
End of Year	**Operation and Repairs**	**Delays due to Repairs**	**Salvage Value**
1	$1,300	$600	$1,200
2	$1,500	$800	$1,000
3	$1,700	$1,000	$500
4	$1,900	$1,200	$0
5	$2,000	$1,400	$0

It is suggested that the machine be replaced by a new CNC machine of improved design at a cost of $6,000. It is believed that this purchase will completely eliminate breakdowns, and the resulting combined savings in delays, operation, and repairs will be a reduction of $200 more a year at each age than is the case with the old machine. Assume a five-year life and a $1,000 terminal salvage value for the challenger. The new machine falls into the five-year MACRS property class. The firm's MARR is 12%, and its marginal tax rate is 30%. Should the old machine be replaced now?

Short Case Studies with Excel

12.39 Quintana Electronic Company is considering the purchase of new robot-welding equipment to perform operations currently being performed by less efficient equipment.

- The new machine's purchase price is $150,000 delivered and installed. A Quintana industrial engineer estimates that the new equipment will produce savings of $30,000 in labor and other direct costs annually as compared with the present equipment. He estimates the proposed equipment's economic life at 10 years, with a zero salvage value. Depreciation of the new equipment for tax purposes is computed on the basis of the seven-year MACRS property class.

- The present equipment is in good working order and will last, physically, for at least 10 more years.

Quintana Company expects to pay income taxes of 40%, and any gains will also be taxed at 40%. Quintana uses a 10% discount rate for analysis performed on an after-tax basis.

(a) Assuming that the present equipment has zero book value and zero salvage value, should the company buy the proposed equipment?

(b) Assuming that the present equipment is being depreciated at a straight-line rate of 10%, has a book value of $72,000 (a cost of $120,000 and accumulated depreciation of $48,000) and zero net salvage value today, should the company buy the proposed equipment?

(c) Assuming that the present equipment has a book value of $72,000 and a salvage value today of $45,000 and that, if the equipment is retained for 10 more years, its salvage value will be zero, should the company buy the proposed equipment?

(d) Assume that the new equipment will save only $15,000 a year, but that its economic life is expected to be 12 years. If all other conditions are as described in (a), should the company buy the proposed equipment?

(e) Assume that Quintana Company decided to purchase the new equipment (hereafter called "Model A"). Two years later, even better equipment (called "Model B") comes onto the market. This equipment makes Model A completely obsolete with no resale value. The Model B equipment costs $300,000 delivered and installed, but it is expected to result in annual savings of $75,000 over the cost of operating the Model A equipment. The economic life of Model B is estimated to be 10 years with a zero salvage value. (Model B also is classified as a seven-year MACRS property.) What action should the company take with respect to the potential replacement of Model A with Model B?

(f) In (e), If the company decides to purchase the Model B equipment, a mistake must have been made because good equipment bought only two years previously is being scrapped. How did this mistake come about?

12.40 Rivera Industries, a manufacturer of home-heating appliances, is considering the purchase of a used Amada turret punch press to replace its less advanced present system, which uses four old, small presses. Currently, the four smaller presses are used (in varying sequences, depending on the product) to produce one component of a product until a scheduled time when all machines must retool in order to set up for a different component. Because setup cost is high, production runs of individual components are long. This factor results in large inventory buildups of one component, which are necessary to prevent extended backlogging while other products are being manufactured.

The four presses in use now were purchased six years ago at a price of $100,000. The manufacturing engineer expects that these machines can be used for eight more years, but they will have no market value after that. These presses have been depreciated by the MACRS method (seven-year property). The current book value is $13,387, and the present market value is estimated to be $40,000. The average setup cost, which is determined by the number of required labor hours times the labor rate for the old presses, is $80 per hour, and the number of setups per year expected by the production control department is 200. These conditions yield a yearly setup cost of $16,000. The expected operating and maintenance costs for each year in the remaining life of this system are estimated as follows:

Year	Setup Costs	O&M Costs
1	$16,000	$15,986
2	$16,000	$16,785
3	$16,000	$17,663
4	$16,000	$18,630
5	$16,000	$19,692
6	$16,000	$20,861
7	$16,000	$22,147
8	$16,000	$23,562

These costs, which were estimated by the manufacturing engineer with the aid of data provided by the vendor, represent a reduction in efficiency and an increase in needed service and repair over time.

The price of the two-year-old Amada turret punch press is $135,000 and would be paid for with cash from the company's capital fund. In addition, the company would incur installation costs totaling $1,200. Also, an expenditure of $12,000 would be required in order to recondition the press to its original condition. The reconditioning would extend the Amada's economic service life to eight years. It would have no salvage value at the end of that time. The Amada would be depreciated under the MACRS with the half-year convention as a seven-year property. The average setup cost of the Amada is $15, and it would require 1,000 setups per year, yielding a yearly setup cost of $15,000. Rivera's accounting department has estimated that at least $26,000, and probably $36,000, per year could be saved by shortening production runs and thus, carrying costs. The operating and maintenance costs of the Amada as estimated by the manufacturing engineer are similar to, but somewhat less than, the O&M costs for the present system:

Year	Setup Costs	O&M Costs
1	$15,000	$11,500
2	$15,000	$11,950
3	$15,000	$12,445
4	$15,000	$12,990
5	$15,000	$13,590
6	$15,000	$14,245
7	$15,000	$14,950
8	$15,000	$15,745

The reduction in the O&M costs is caused by the age difference of the machines and the reduced power requirements of the Amada.

If Rivera Industries delays the replacement of the current four presses for another year, the secondhand Amada machine will no longer be available, and the company will have to buy a brand-new machine at an installed price of $200,450. Its expected setup costs would be the same as those for the secondhand machine, but the annual O&M costs of the new one would be about 10% lower than the estimated O&M costs for the secondhand machine. The expected economic service life of the brand-new press would be eight years with no salvage value at the end of that period. The brand-new press also falls into a seven-year MACRS property class.

Rivera's MARR is 12% after taxes, and the marginal income-tax rate is expected to be 40% over the life of the project.

(a) Assuming that the company would need the service of either the Amada press or the current presses for an indefinite period, which option would you recommend?

(b) Assuming that the company would need the press system for only five more years, which option would you recommend?

CHAPTER THIRTEEN

Understanding Financial Statements

Warren Edward Buffett[1] He is an American investor, businessman, and philanthropist. He has amassed an enormous fortune from astute investments, particularly through the company Berkshire Hathaway of which he is the largest shareholder and CEO. With an estimated current net worth of around US $50 billion, he is ranked by *Forbes*[2] as the third-richest person in the world behind Microsoft cofounder Bill Gates.

[1] "Warren Buffet," Wikipedia (June 21, 2011).
[2] "The World's Billionaires 2011," *Forbes*, March 2011 (www.forbes.com/wealth/billionaires/list).

Buffett's philosophy on business investing is a modification of the value investing approach of his mentor Benjamin Graham.[3] Graham bought companies because they were cheap compared to their intrinsic value. He was of the belief that as long as the market undervalued them relative to their intrinsic value, he was making a solid investment. He reasoned that the market will eventually realize it has undervalued the company and will correct its course regardless of what type of business the company was in. In addition, he believed that the business has to have solid economics behind it.

In order to determine whether an investment is visible, he considered the following factors:

- Does the company have a consumer monopoly or a strong brand name?
- Does the company have high operational costs, low capital expenditure, or investment cash outflow?
- Does the company have flat earnings or are they on a consistent upward trend with good margins?
- Does the company have high and consistent returns on investments?
- Does the company reinvest earnings and profit from these investments?
- Does the company have a low debt-to-equity ratio? A high earnings-to-debt ratio? When earnings are low, can the company repay its debt?
- Does the company have the ability to adjust prices for inflation?
- Does the company have enough earnings to grow?

Where would Mr. Buffett collect all these pieces of information for a company to purchase? And what all these pieces of information have to do with the topic of engineering economics?

---

[3] Benjamin Graham, Jason Zweig, and Warren E. Buffett, *The Intelligent Investor: The Definitive Book on Value Investing* (Harper Business Essentials, 2003).

While knowledge of PW criterion, AE analysis, and the other topics we have covered are essential, understanding how a project impacts the firm's bottom line is also important. In this chapter, we begin by discussing the characteristics of these financial statements and the factors that each comprises. Our purpose is not to present bookkeeping aspects of accounting but to acquaint you with financial statements and to give you the basic information you need to make sound engineering economic decisions. Good economic decisions will in turn improve the market value of the corporation, as investors like Warren Buffett will bid on the company's stock.

13.1 Accounting: The Basis of Decision Making

We need financial information to make business decisions. Virtually all businesses and most individuals keep accounting records to aid them in making decisions. As illustrated in Figure 13.1, accounting is the information system that measures business activities, processes that information into reports, and communicates the results to decision makers. For this reason, we call accounting "the language of business." The better you understand this language, the better you can manage your financial well-being and make financial decisions.

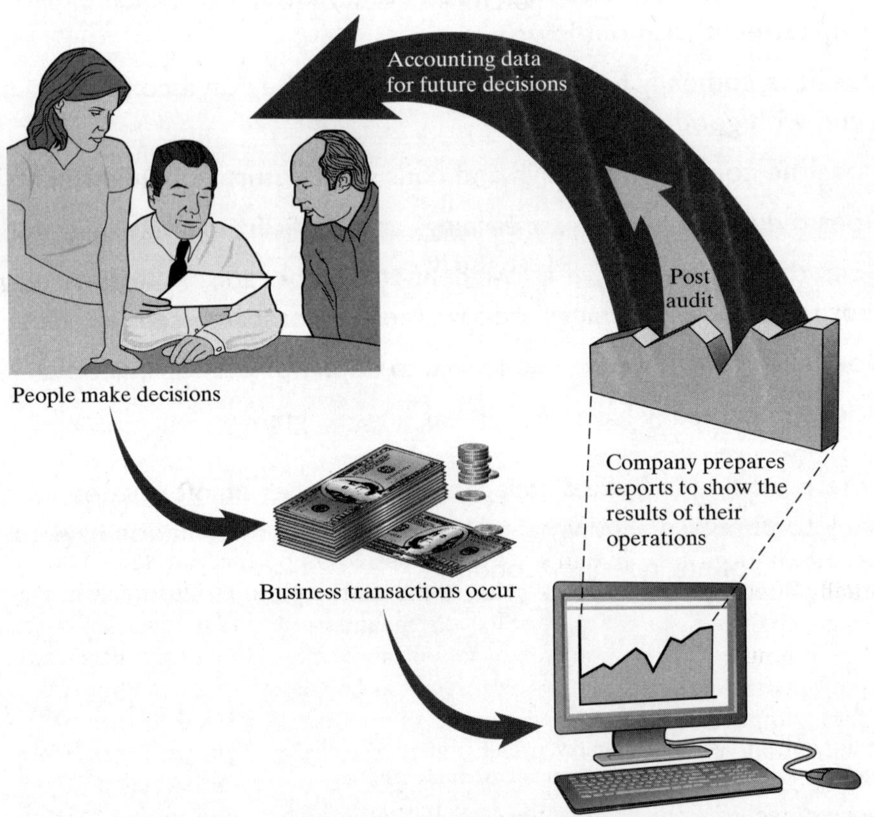

Figure 13.1 An illustration of the flow of information in the accounting system

Personal financial planning, education expenses, loans, car payments, income taxes, and investments are all determined on the basis of the information system we call accounting. The use of accounting information is diverse and varied:

- Business managers use accounting information to set goals for their organizations, to evaluate progress toward those goals, and to take corrective actions if necessary. Decisions based on accounting information may include which building or equipment to purchase, how much merchandise inventory to keep on hand, and how much cash to borrow.
- Investors and creditors provide the money a business needs to begin operations. To decide whether to help start a new venture, potential investors evaluate what income they can expect on their investment. This means analyzing the financial statements of the business. Before making a loan, banks determine the borrower's ability to meet scheduled payments. This evaluation includes a projection of future operations and revenue, which is based on accounting information.

An essential product of accounting is a series of financial statements that allow people to make informed decisions. For business use, these statements are the documents that report financial information about a business entity to decision makers. They tell us how a business is performing and where it stands financially. These financial statements include the balance sheet, income statement, and statement of cash flows.

13.2 Financial Status for Businesses

All businesses must record and report on their financial status. Of the various reports corporations issue to their stockholders, the annual report is by far the most important. The annual report contains basic financial statements as well as management's opinion of the past year's operations and the firm's future prospects. What would managers and investors want to know about a company at the end of the fiscal year (or another fiscal period, such as a quarter)? Managers or investors are likely to ask the following four basic questions:

- What is the company's financial position at the end of the fiscal period?
- How much profit did the company make during the fiscal period?
- How did the company decide to use its profits?
- How much cash did the company generate and spend during the period?

As illustrated in Figure 13.2, the answer to each question is provided by one of the financial statements. The fiscal year (or operating cycle) can be any 12-month term but is usually January 1 through December 31 of a calendar year.

As mentioned in Section 1.2.1, one of the primary business responsibilities for engineers is to plan for the acquisition of equipment (capital expenditure) that will enable the firm to design and produce products economically. This task requires estimation of savings and costs associated with the equipment acquisition and the degree of risk associated with project execution. These amounts affect the business's bottom line (profitability), which eventually affects the firm's stock price in the marketplace as illustrated in Figure 13.3. Therefore, engineers should understand the meanings of various financial statements in order to communicate with upper management about the nature of a project's profitability.

For illustration purposes, we use data taken from Lam Research Corporation, a leading supplier of wafer fabrication equipment and services to the world's semiconductor industry. In particular, Lam is a technology and market leader in etch products. Founded in 1980, Lam is headquartered in Fremont, California, and maintains a network of facilities throughout the United States, Japan, Europe, and Asia in order to meet the needs of its global customer base.

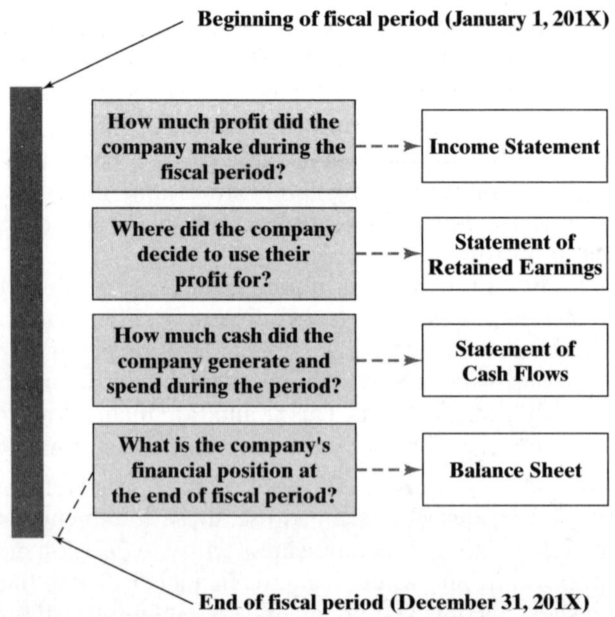

Figure 13.2   Information reported on a company's financial statements

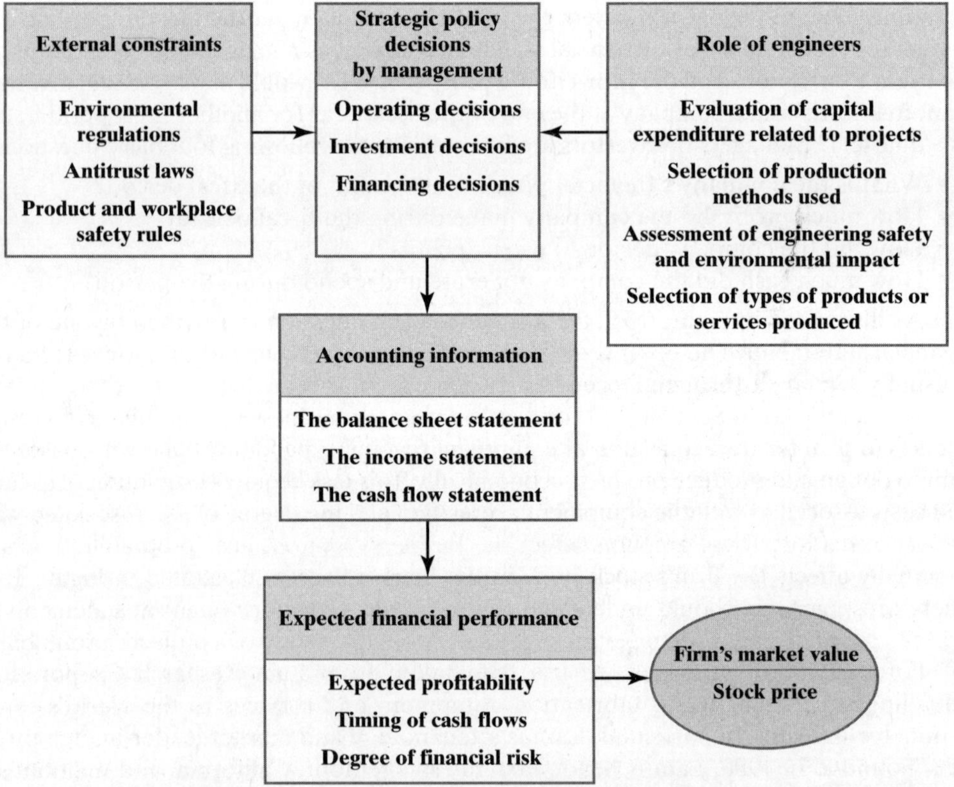

Figure 13.3   Summary of major factors affecting stock price

The company's revenue for the last four quarters of 2011 totaled $3.24 billion. The increase in net revenues for both fiscal year 2011 and fiscal year 2010 was principally driven by an increase in export sales in Korea, Japan, and the Asia Pacific region. In its 2011 annual report, management painted an optimistic picture for the future, stating that Lam Research will continue to invest in research, development, and engineering activities to support its growth and to provide for new competitive products. Lam Research's 2011 Annual Report starts like this:

To Our Stockholders:

Lam Research delivered strong fiscal 2011 results as the semiconductor equipment industry quickly recovered from the recent global recession. Our fiscal year ending June 26, 2011, was a year of records for the Company, including shipments of $3.3 billion, revenues of $3.2 billion, and diluted earnings per share of $5.79. We also generated strong cash flows from operations of more than $880 million, or 27% of revenues, and ended the fiscal year with approximately $2.1 billion cash, cash equivalents, and short-term investments.

The shipment performance reinforces the significant gains in market share Lam Research achieved in calendar year of 2010. We remain the market share leader in etch, with an estimated shipped share greater than 50% at the end of fiscal 2011. We are also building a solid position in single-wafer clean, with market share of approximately 30% at fiscal year-end... Our ability to consistently deliver leading-edge technology and cost-effective production performance positions us well for the critical new application wins that ultimately drive future share gains.

Over the next several years, we see the potential for strong semiconductor demand and healthy levels of WFE spending. The rapid growth and penetration of content-rich devices such as smartphones, tablets, and notebook computers should rive unit growth of integrated circuits in the low double digits over the next several years, reaching as many as 275 billion units by 2014....

To summarize several of the key financial highlights:

- Revenue topped $3.2 billion (or precisely $3,237,693,000), an increase of 52% year-over-year

- Our closing total net cash balance reached $1.492 billion

- Gross margins exceeded 46.24% of revenues

- Operating margins were 24.84%

- Net income swing to a profit in the amount of $724 million

What can individual investors make of all this? Actually, they can make quite a bit. As you will see, investors use the information contained in an annual report to form expectations about future earnings and dividends. Therefore, the annual report is certainly of great interest to investors.

13.2.1 The Balance Sheet

What is a company's financial position at the end of a reporting period? A company's **balance sheet statement** will provide the answer. A balance sheet, sometimes called a **statement of financial position**, reports three main categories of items: assets, liabilities, and stockholders' equity. Figure 13.4 illustrates the relationship between assets and liabilities, including equity, and how these items appear in the balance sheet. The financial statements are based on the most basic tool of accounting, the **accounting**

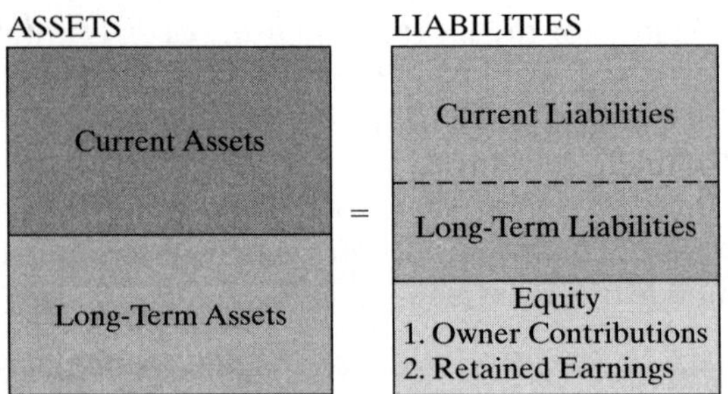

Figure 13.4   The four quadrants of the balance sheet

equation. The accounting equation shows the relationship among assets, liabilities, and owners' equity:

$$\text{Assets} = \text{Liabilities} + \text{Stockholder's Equity}.$$

Every business transaction, no matter how simple or complex, can be expressed in terms of its effect on the accounting equation. Regardless of whether a business grows or contracts, this equality between its assets and the claims against those assets is always maintained. In other words, any change in the amount of total assets is necessarily accompanied by an equal change on the other side of the equation—that is, by an increase or decrease in either the liabilities or the owners' equity.

As shown in Table 13.1, the first half of Lam Research's year-end 2011 and 2010 balance sheets lists the firm's assets while the remaining portion shows the liabilities and equity, or claims against these assets.

Assets

The dollar amounts shown under the Assets column in Table 13.1 represent how much the company owns at the time of reporting. We list the asset items in the order of their "liquidity," or the length of time it takes to convert them to cash, according to the following three categories:

- **Current assets** can be converted to cash or its equivalent in less than one year. This type of asset generally includes four major accounts:

  1. The first account is *cash and cash equivalents*. A firm typically has a cash account at a bank to provide for the funds needed to conduct day-to-day business. Although we state all the assets in terms of dollars, only items labeled as cash represent actual money. Cash-equivalent items include marketable securities such as stocks and bonds.

  2. The second account includes *short-term investments* such as savings accounts, money market funds, certificates of deposit, and U.S. Treasury securities.

  3. The third account is *accounts receivable*, which is money that is owed to the firm but has not yet been received. For example, when Lam Research receives an order from a manufacturer, it will send an invoice along with the shipment to the manufacturer. Then the unpaid bill immediately falls into the accounts-receivable category. When this bill is paid, it is deducted from the accounts-receivable category and placed into the cash category. Normally, a typical firm will have 30- to 45-day accounts receivable, depending on the frequency of its bills and the payment terms for customers. We can treat sales on credit cards in a similar category.

TABLE 13.1 Consolidated Statement of Financial Position

LAM RESEARCH CORPORATION
CONSOLIDATED BALANCE SHEETS
(in thousands, except per share data)

PERIOD ENDING	26-Jun-11	27-Jun-10
ASSETS		
Current Assets:		
Cash and Cash Equivalents	$1,492,132	$545,767
Short Term Investments	630,115	280,690
Accounts Receivables	590,568	499,890
Inventories	396,607	318,479
Other Current Assets	167,370	111,835
Total Current Assets	**$3,276,792**	**$1,756,661**
Property Plant and Equipment, Net	270,458	200,336
Goodwill	169,182	169,182
Other Intangible Assets	47,434	67,724
Other Long Term Assets	293,528	293,489
Total Assets	**$4,057,394**	**$2,487,392**
LIABILITIES AND STOCKHOLDERS' EQUITY		
Current Liabilities		
Accounts Payable	163,541	$121,099
Accrued Expenses	358,756	309,397
Other Current	161,989	128,161
Total Current Liabilities	**684,286**	**558,657**
Long-Term Debt	738,488	17,645
Income Taxes Payable	113,582	110,462
Other Long-Term Liabilities	51,193	32,493
Total Liabilities	**1,587,549**	**719,257**
Stockholders' Equity:		
Preferred Stock		–
Common Stock	124	126
Treasury Stock	(1,761,591)	(1,581,417)
Paid-in Capital (Capital Surplus)	1,531,465	1,452,939
Accumulated Other Comprehensive Loss	9,761	(69,849)
Retained Earnings	2,690,086	1,966,336
Total Stockholder Equity	**2,469,845**	**1,768,135**
Total Liabilities and Stockholder's Equity	**$4,057,394**	**$2,487,392**

4. The fourth account is *inventories*, which show the dollars the company has invested in raw materials, work-in-process, and finished goods available for sale.

- **Fixed assets** are relatively permanent and take time to convert into cash. Fixed assets reflect the amount of money a company has paid for its plant and equipment acquired at some time in the past. The most common fixed assets include the physical investment in the business, such as land, buildings, factory machinery, office equipment, and automobiles. With the exception of land, most fixed assets have a limited useful life. For example, buildings and equipment are expended over a period of years. Each year, a portion of the usefulness of these assets expires, and a portion of their total cost should thus be recognized as a depreciation expense. As stated previously in this book, the term *depreciation* refers to the accounting process for this gradual conversion of fixed assets into expenses. The item "property, plant, and equipment, net" thus represents the current book value of these assets after such depreciation expenses have been deducted.
- **Other assets** are listed at the end of this category. Typical assets in this category include investments made in other companies and intangible assets such as goodwill, copyrights, franchises, and so forth. Goodwill appears on the balance sheet only when an operating business is purchased in its entirety. This item indicates any additional amount paid for the business above the fair market value of the business. (Here, the fair market value is defined as the price that a buyer is willing to pay when the business is offered for sale.)

Liabilities and Stockholders' Equity (Owners' Net Worth)

The claims against assets are of two types: liabilities and stockholders' equity. Liabilities refer to money the company owes. Stockholders' equity indicates the portion of the assets of a company that is provided by the investors (owners). Therefore, stockholders' equity is also the liability of a company to its owners. (Recall Figure 13.4, which illustrates the relationship between assets and liabilities, including equity.) The different categories of liabilities and stockholders' equity are described as follows:

- **Current liabilities** are what a company currently owes to its suppliers and creditors. Major current liabilities include accounts and notes payable within a year as well as accrued expenses (wages, salaries, interest, rent, taxes, etc., owed but not yet due for payment) and advance payments and deposits from customers. Accrued expenses are bills that the company has incurred that it has not yet paid. In other words, accrued expenses are the opposite of prepaid expenses.
- **Other liabilities** include *long-term liabilities* such as bonds, mortgages, and long-term notes, which are due and payable more than one year in the future. Another example is *Income Tax Payable*, which is the income tax a company accrues over the years that it does not have to pay yet according to various federal, state, and local tax schedules.
- **Stockholders' equity** represents the amount that is available to the stockholders (owners) after all other debts have been paid. It generally consists of preferred and common stock, treasury stock, capital surplus, and retained earnings.
  1. **Preferred stock** is a hybrid between common stock and debt. Such stock promises a fixed dividend (much like a bond's interest payment) but often limited voting rights. In the case of bankruptcy, preferred stockholders receive money after debt holders and before common stockholders are paid. Many firms do

not use any preferred stock. The common stockholders' equity, or **net worth**, is a residual and is calculated as follows:

Assets − Liabilities − Preferred stock = Common stockholders' equity.

2. **Common stock** is the aggregate par value of the company's issued stock. Companies rarely issue stocks at a discount (i.e., at an amount below the stated par). Corporations normally set the par value low enough so that, in practice, stock is usually sold at a premium.

3. **Treasury stock:** If the corporation buys back part of its own issued stock, the value of the repurchase is listed as *treasury stock* on the balance sheet. Companies buy back their shares for a variety of reasons. In most cases, it is a sign that management believes the stock is undervalued. Depending upon its objectives, a company can either retire the shares it purchases or hold them with the intention of reselling them to raise cash when the stock price rises.

4. **Paid-in capital** (capital surplus) is the amount of money received from the sale of stock over the par value. Outstanding stock is the number of shares issued that actually is held by the public.

5. **Retained earnings** represent the cumulative net income of the firm since its beginning, less the total dividends that have been paid to stockholders. In other words, retained earnings indicate the amount of assets that the company has financed by plowing profits back into the business. Therefore, these retained earnings belong to the stockholders.

What to Read from Lam Research's Balance Sheet

Recall that all financial data related to the annual report is shown in thousands of dollars, except share value. Lam Research generated revenue of $3,237,693 (this number means $3.238 billion) for fiscal year 2011. The $4,057,394 of total assets shown in Table 13.1 were necessary to support the sales of $3,237,693.

- **Acquisition of Fixed Assets:** One way we can determine the amount of new fixed assets added during FY 2011 is to observe the change in the Property Plant and Equipment account, which shows a net increase in the amount of $70,122 (=$270,458 − $200,336). By adding back the depreciation taken during year 2011 ($45,322 = $322,274 − $276,952), we find that Lam Research acquired $115,444 (= $70,122 + $45,322) in new fixed assets in FY 2011.

	26-Jun-11	27-Jun-10
Property Plant and Equipment, Net	(in thousands)	(in thousands)
Manufacturing, engineering, and office equipment	$345,684	$252,771
Computer equipment and software	95,770	77,249
Land	14,758	15,788
Buildings	65,429	62,085
Leasehold improvements	55,833	55,300
Furniture and fixtures	15,258	14,095
	592,732	477,288
Less: accumulated depreciation and amortization	(322,274)	(276,952)
	$270,458	**$200,336**

- **Debt:** Lam Research had a total long-term debt of $738,488 that consisted of the several bonds issued in previous years. The interest payments associated with these long-term debts were about $5,380.
- **Equity:** Lam Research had 123,529 shares of common stock outstanding. Investors initially provided the company with a total capital of $124 + $1,531,465. However, Lam Research has retained the current as well as previous earnings of $2,690,086 since it was incorporated. These earnings belong to Lam Research's common stockholders. At the end of 2011, the combined net stockholder's equity was $2,469,845. (This net equity figure includes $1,761,591 worth of treasury stock.)
- **Share value:** Stockholders on average have a total investment of $20 per share ($2,469,845/123,529 shares) in the company; this investment is known as the stock's book value. In June 2011, the stock was traded in the general range of $43 to $48 per share. Note that this market price is quite different from the stock's book value. Many factors affect the market price—most importantly, how investors expect the company to do in the future. Certainly, the company's unique etch products have had a major influence on the market value of its stock.

13.2.2 The Income Statement

The second financial report is the **income statement**, which indicates whether the company is making or losing money during a stated *period*. Most businesses prepare quarterly and monthly income statements in addition to annual ones. For Lam Research's income statement, the accounting period begins on June 27 and ends on June 26 of the following year. Table 13.2 gives the 2011 and 2010 income statements for Lam Research.

Net Income

Typical elements that are itemized in the income statement are as follows:

- The **total revenue** (or **net sales**) figure represents the gross sales less any sales return and allowances.
- The expenses and costs of doing business are listed on the next several lines as deductions from the revenues. The largest expense for a typical manufacturing firm is its production expense for making a product (such as labor, materials, and overhead) called the **cost of goods sold** (or **cost of revenue**).
- Total revenue less the cost of goods sold indicates the **gross profit (margin)**.
- Next, we subtract any other **operating expenses** from operating income. These other operating expenses are items such as interest, lease, selling, research and development (R&D), and administration expenses. This operation results in the operating income period.
- If the company generated **other income** from investments or any nonoperating activities, this item will be a part of income subject to income taxes as well.
- Finally, we determine the **net income** (or net profit) by subtracting the income taxes from the taxable income. This net income is also commonly known as the *accounting income.*

Earnings per Share

Another important piece of financial information provided in the income statement is the **earnings per share** (EPS) figure. In simple situations, we compute this amount by dividing the available earnings to common stockholders by the number of shares of common stock outstanding. Stockholders and potential investors want to know what

TABLE 13.2 The Income Statement for Lam Research Corporation

LAM RESEARCH CORPORATION
INCOME STATEMENT
(in thousands, except per share data)

PERIOD ENDING	26-Jun-11	27-Jun-10
Total Revenue	$3,237,693	$2,133,776
Cost of Goods Sold	1,740,461	1,163,841
Gross Profit (Margin)	1,497,232	969,935
Research Development	373,293	320,859
Selling General and Administrative	308,075	240,942
Nonrecurring-Restructuring Charges	11,579	(17,276)
Operating Income or Loss	804,285	425,410
Interest Income	15,572	8,598
Earnings before Interest and Taxes	819,857	434,008
Interest Expense	5,380	994
Other	13,601	2,873
Income before Tax	800,876	430,141
Income Tax Expense	77,128	83,472
Net Income	**$723,748**	**$346,669**
Net Income per Share		
Basic	$5.86	$2.73
Diluted	$5.79	$2.71
Number of Shares Used in Per Share		
Basic	123,529	126,933
Diluted	125,019	128,126

their relative share of profits is, not just the total dollar amount. Presentation of profits on a per-share basis allows stockholders to relate earnings to what they paid for a share of stock. Naturally, companies want to report a higher EPS to their investors as a means of summarizing how well they managed their businesses for the benefit of their owners.

Dividends and Retained Earnings

As a supplement to the income statement, corporations also report their retained earnings during the accounting period. When a corporation makes some profits, it has to decide what to do with these profits. The corporation may decide to pay out some of the profits as dividends to its stockholders. Alternatively, it may retain the remaining profits in the business in order to finance expansion or support other business activities.

When the corporation declares dividends, preferred stock has priority over common stock in regard to the receipt of dividends. Preferred stock pays a stated dividend much like the interest payment on bonds. The dividend is not a legal liability until the board of directors has declared it. However, many corporations view the dividend payments to preferred stockholders as a liability. Therefore, the term "available earnings for common stockholders" reflects the net earnings of the corporation less the preferred-stock dividends. When preferred- and common-stock dividends are subtracted from net income, the remainder is retained earnings (profits) for the year. As mentioned previously, these retained earnings are reinvested in the business.

What to Read from Lam's Income Statement

(All numbers in thousands except per share.) Net sales were $3,237,693 in 2011, compared with $2,133,776 in 2010, a whopping gain of 52%. Profits from operations (operating income) rose to $804,285, and net income was up to a profit of $723,748 from $346,669 a year ago. We can infer the following:

1. **Dividends:** Lam Research issued no preferred stock, so there is no required cash dividend. In fact, Lam Research did not even pay any cash dividends to its common stockholders either.

2. **EPS:** Earnings per common share climbed at a faster pace to $5.86 from $2.73 in 2010. We can see that Lam Research had earnings available to common stockholders of $723,748. The beginning balance of the retained earnings was $1,966,336. See Table 13.1 for the retained earning entry in 2010, so if the entire earnings were retained, the ending balance should be $2,690,084. However, the ending balance of the retained earnings in 2011 was $2,690,086, implying that Lam Research had an extra $2 from other business activities including reissuance of treasury stock.

3. **Profit margins:** Table 13.3 illustrates the calculation of the gross margin, operating margin, and net margin, which are expressed as percentages of total sales. Lam Research's net margin is about 22.35%, meaning that for every dollar of sales, Lam Research is making 22.35 cents of net profit.

13.2.3 The Cash-Flow Statement

The income statement explained in the previous section indicates only whether the company was making or losing money during the reporting period. Therefore, the emphasis was on determining the net income (profits) of the firm, mainly for the operating activities. However, the income statement ignores two other important business activities for the period: financing and investing activities. Therefore, we need another financial statement—the **cash-flow statement**—that details how the company generated cash and how the company used its cash during the reporting period. This statement is concerned with how the company actually used its cash in its period, thus explaining how the firm went from the level of cash in its accounts reported at the start of the year to the level of cash it had at the end of the year.

TABLE 13.3 Understanding Operating Margin and Net Margin

LAM RESEARCH CORPORATION
Operating and Profit Margins
(in thousands, except percentage data)

PERIOD ENDING	26-Jun-11	% of Total Revenue
Total Revenue	$3,237,693	100.00%
Cost of Goods Sold	1,740,461	53.76%
Gross Profit (Gross Margin)	1,497,232	**46.24%**
Research Development	373,293	11.53%
Selling General and Administrative	308,075	9.52%
Nonrecurring-Restructuring Charges	11,579	0.36%
Operating Profit (Operating Margin)	804,285	**24.84%**
Interest Income/Other Expenses, Net	1,971	0.06%
Earnings before Interest and Taxes	806,256	24.90%
Interest Expense	5,380	0.17%
Income before Tax	800,876	24.74%
Income Tax Expense	77,128	2.38%
Net Income (Net Margin)	**$723,748**	**22.35%**

Sources and Uses of Cash

The difference between the sources (inflows) and uses (outflows) of cash represents the net cash flow during the reporting period. This is a very important piece of information because investors determine the value of an asset (or a whole firm) by the cash flows it generates. Figure 13.5 illustrates how a firm generates cash flows and summarizes the sources and uses of cash during its business cycle. We may also summarize the sources and uses of funds according to the changes in account activities (see Figure 13.6).

Certainly, a firm's net income is important, but cash flows are even more important because we need cash to pay dividends and to purchase the assets required for continuing operations. As we mentioned previously, the goal of the firm should be to maximize the price of its stock. Since the value of any asset depends on the cash flows produced by the asset, managers want to maximize cash flows available to its investors over the long run. Therefore, managers should make investment decisions on the basis of cash flows rather than profits. For such investment decisions, it is necessary to convert profits (as determined in the income statement) to cash flows. Table 13.4 is Lam Research's statement of cash flows as it would appear in the company's annual report.

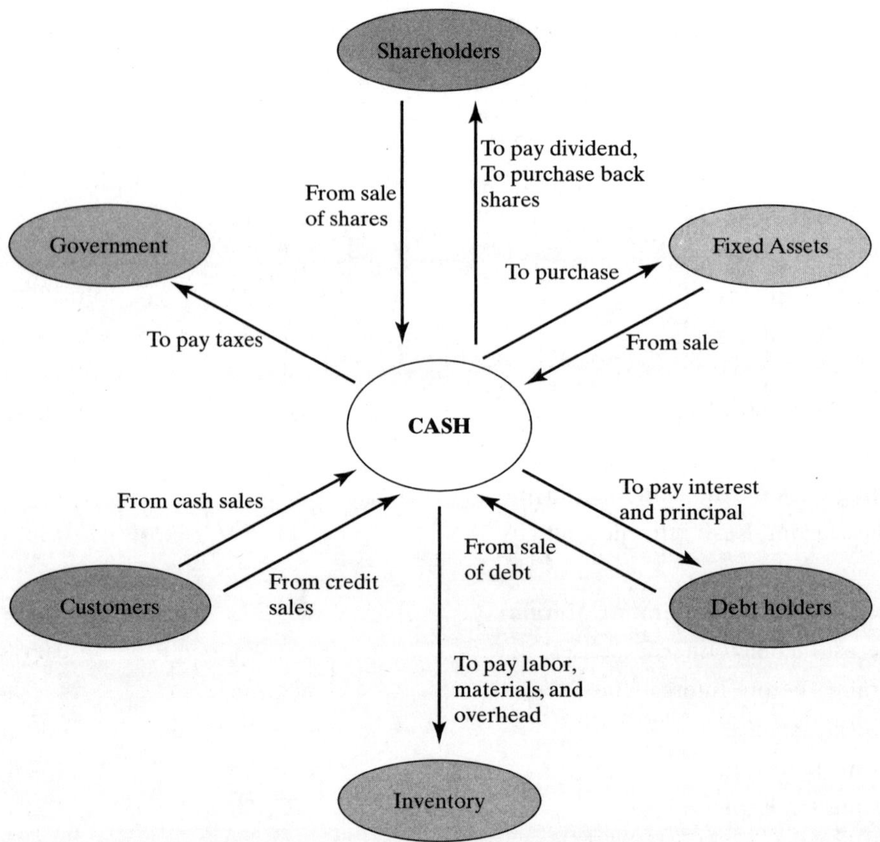

Figure 13.5   The cash flow cycle in a typical manufacturing firm

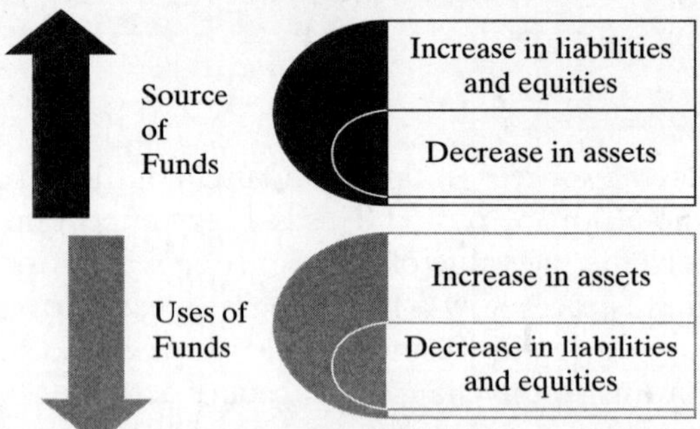

Figure 13.6   Summary of sources and uses
of funds according to changes in account
activities

Reporting Format

In preparing a cash-flow statement such as the one in Table 13.4, many companies identify the sources and uses of cash according to the types of business activities. There are three types of activities:

- **Operating activities:** We start with the net change in operating cash flows from the income statement. Here, operating cash flows represent those cash flows related

TABLE 13.4 The Cash-Flow Statement for Lam Research Corporation

LAM RESEARCH CORPORATION
CASH FLOW STATEMENT
(in thousands, except per share data)

PERIOD ENDING	26-Jun-11	27-Jun-10
Net Income	**$723,748**	**$346,669**
Cash Flows from Operating Activities		
Depreciation	78,313	71,401
Other Noncash Items	57,014	92,524
Change in Accounts Receivables	(89,716)	(246,653)
Changes in Liabilities	214,412	190,120
Changes in Inventories	(77,461)	(79,701)
Changes in Other Operating Activities	(25,282)	(23,647)
Total Cash Flow from Operating Activities	**881,028**	**350,713**
Cash Flows from Investing Activities		
Capital Expenditures	(127,495)	(35,590)
Investments	(352,418)	(67,766)
Total Cash Flows from Investing Activities	**(479,913)**	**(103,356)**
Cash Flows from Financing Activities		
Financing Cash Flow Items	23,290	10,234
Dividends Paid	–	–
Issuance (Retirement) of Stock, Net	(225,016)	(62,194)
Issuance (Retirement) of Debt, Net	878,301	(20,704)
Other Cash Flows from Financing Activities	(149,589)	–
Total Cash Flows from Financing Activities	**526,986**	**(72,664)**
Effect of Exchange Rate Changes	18,264	(3,093)
Change in Cash and Cash Equivalents	**$946,365**	**$171,600**

to the production and sales of goods or services. All noncash expenses are added back to net income (or after-tax profits). For example, an expense such as depreciation is only an accounting expense (bookkeeping entry). While we may charge such an item against current income as an expense, it does not involve an actual cash outflow. The actual cash flow may have occurred when the asset was purchased. Any adjustments in working-capital terms will also be listed here. Once again, **working capital** is defined as the difference between current assets and current liabilities. Furthermore, we can determine the net change in **working capital requirement** by the difference between "change in current assets" and "change in

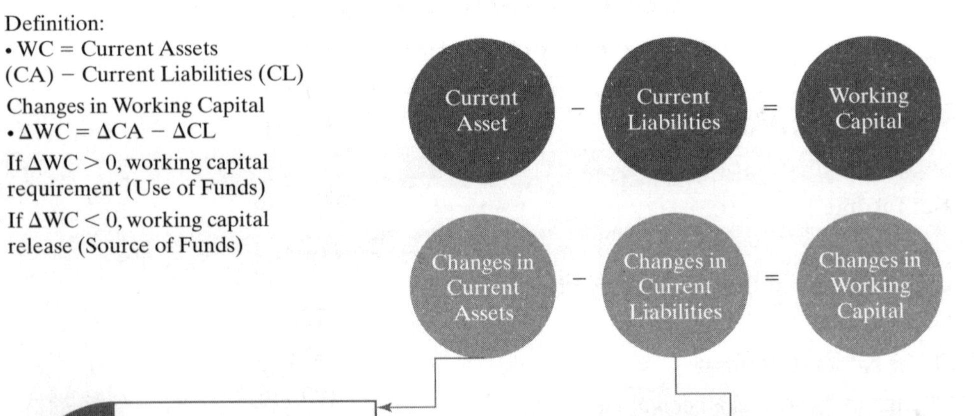

Figure 13.7 Working capital and its impact on cash flow statement

current liabilities." If this net change is positive, the working capital requirement appears as *uses* of cash in the cash flow statement. This concept is illustrated in Figure 13.7.

- **Investing activities:** After determining the operating cash flows, we consider any cash flow transactions related to investment activities. Investment activities include transactions such as purchasing new fixed assets (cash outflow), reselling old equipment (cash inflow), and buying and selling financial assets.

- **Financing activities:** Finally, we detail cash transactions related to financing any capital used in business. For example, the company could borrow or sell more stock, resulting in cash inflows. Paying off existing debt would result in cash outflows.

By summarizing cash inflows and outflows from these three types of activities for a given accounting period, we obtain the net changes in cash flow position of the company.

What to Read from Lam Research's Cash Flow Statement

As shown in Table 13.4, Lam Research's cash flow from operations in fiscal year 2011 amounted to $946,365. Note that this amount is much different from the net income of $723,748 earned during the reporting period. Where did the rest of the money come from? Basically, we are trying to explain the sources and uses of funds during the business cycle, as depicted in Figure 13.8, a graphical presentation similar to Figure 13.5, with emphasis on cash flow from operational activities.

1. **Cash flow from operations:** The main reason for the difference (net income versus cash flow from operations) is the accrual-basis accounting principle used by

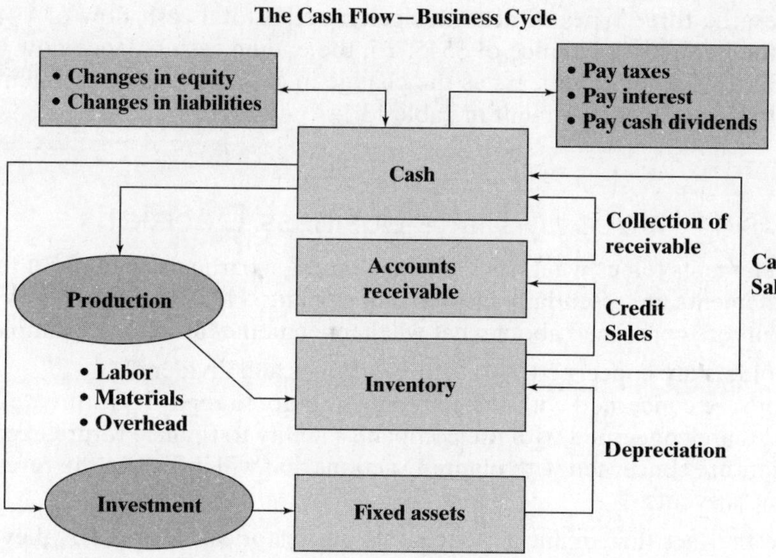

The Cash Flow—Business Cycle

Figure 13.8 Explaining the cash flow activities by the business cycle, showing where the cash is generated and where the cash is spent

Lam Research Corporation. In **accrual-basis accounting**, an accountant recognizes the impact of a business event as it occurs. When the business performs a service, makes a sale, or incurs an expense, the accountant enters the transaction into the books, no matter whether cash has been received or paid. For example, the increase in accounts receivable during 2011 from \$499,890 to \$590,568 (in Table 13.1) represents the increased amount of total sales on credit. Since this figure was included in the total sales in determining the net income, we need to subtract this figure in order to determine the true cash position. In general,

- Sources of funds are indicated by increase in equities and decrease in assets.
- Uses of funds are indicated by increases in assets and decreases in equities.

After making similar adjustments in other operating cash flows, the net cash provided from operating activities is \$881,028.

2. **Cash flow from investing activities:** From the investment activities, Lam Research purchased capital assets worth \$127,495. It made \$352,418 worth of investments during the period. The net cash flow used from these investing activities amounted to \$479,913, which means that there was an outflow.

3. **Cash flow from financing activities:** Financing decision making generated financing activities that produced a net inflow of \$526,986, including a repurchase of Lam Research's own shares worth \$225,016, and an issuance of debt worth \$878,301. (This repurchase of its own stock is equivalent to investing its idle cash from operations in the stock market. Lam Research could have bought another company's stock, such as that of Apple or Microsoft, with the money. However, it viewed its own stock undervalued, so it ended up buying it instead.)

Finally, there was the effect of exchange-rate changes on cash for foreign sales. This amounts to a net increase of \$18,264.

Together, the three types of activities generated a total cash flow of $946,365 in 2011. With the initial cash balance of $545,767, the ending cash balance now increases to $1,492,132. This amount appears as the change in cash and cash equivalent in Lam Research's balance-sheet statement in Table 13.1.

▍13.3▐ Using Ratios to Make Business Decisions

Financial statements tell us what has happened during a particular period. In that sense, financial statements are essentially historical documents. However, most users of financial statements are concerned about what will happen in the future. For example,

- Stockholders are concerned with future earnings and dividends.
- Creditors are concerned with the company's ability to repay its future debts.
- Managers are concerned with the company's ability to finance future expansion.
- Engineers are concerned with planning actions that will influence the future course of business events.

Despite the fact that financial statements are historical documents, they can still provide valuable information that addresses all of these concerns. An important part of financial analysis is the calculation and interpretation of various financial ratios,[4] which provide insight into a firm's future status. In this section, we consider some of the widely used ratios that analysts use in attempting to predict the future course of events in business organizations. We may group these ratios in five categories (debt management, liquidity, asset management, profitability, and market trend) as outlined in Figure 13.9. In all of the upcoming financial-ratio calculations, we will use the 2011 financial statements for Lam Research Corporation as summarized in Tables 13.1, 13.2, and 13.4.

We often compare a company's financial ratios with industry average figures; however, we should note at this point that an industry average is not an absolute number that all firms should strive to maintain. In fact, some very well-managed firms will be above the average while other good firms will be below it. However, if a firm's ratios are quite different from the average for its industry, we should examine the reason that this variance occurs.

13.3.1 Debt Management Analysis

All businesses need assets in order to operate. To acquire assets, a firm must raise capital. When the firm finances its long-term needs externally, it may obtain funds from the capital markets. Capital comes in two forms, **debt** and **equity**. Debt capital refers to borrowed capital from financial institutions and bond markets. Equity capital refers to capital obtained from the owners of the company. Use of debt increases returns to shareholders in good times (if money is put to use in creating profits) and reduces them in bad times. Therefore, the degree to which a business is utilizing borrowed money is known as **financial leverage**.

The basic methods of debt financing include bank loans and bond sales. For example, say that a firm needs $10,000 to purchase a computer. In this situation, the firm could borrow the money from a bank and repay the loan and the specified interest

---

[4] Financial ratios can be calculated in several different ways. Therefore, financial ratios that we calculate for Lam Research might be different from some other published figures. So be warned: You should not accept a ratio at face value without knowing how it has been calculated.

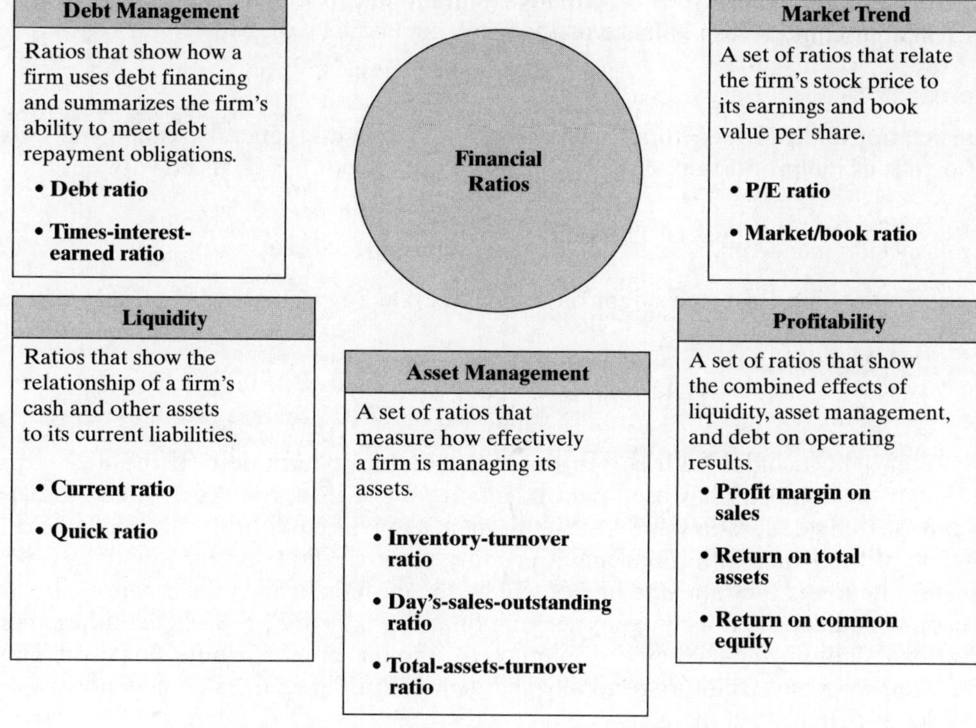

Figure 13.9 Types of financial ratios used in evaluating a firm's financial health

in a few years, an approach known as a *short-term debt financing*. Now suppose that the firm needs $100 million for a construction project. It would normally be very expensive (or require a substantial amount of mortgage) to borrow the money directly from a bank. In this situation, the firm would go public in order to borrow money on a long-term basis. When investors lend capital to a company and the company agrees to repay the loan at an agreed interest rate, the investor is a creditor of the corporation. The document that records the nature of the arrangement between the issuing company and the investor is called a **bond**. Raising capital through issuing bonds is called *long-term debt financing*.

Similarly, there are different types of equity capital. For example, the equity of a proprietorship represents the money provided by the owner. For a corporation, equity capital comes in two forms: *preferred* and *common stock*. Investors provide capital to a corporation, and the company agrees to provide the investor with fractional ownership in the corporation.

Since a company must pay its creditors on time and in full to remain solvent and out of bankruptcy, one primary concern of financial analysis is to determine how able a firm is to cover its required debt payments. To do so, we first examine the extent to which a company uses debt financing (or financial leverage) in business operations, as follows:

- Check the balance sheet to determine the extent to which borrowed funds have been used to finance assets, and
- Review the income statement to see the extent to which fixed charges (interests) are covered by operating profits.

Two essential indicators of a business' ability to pay its long-term liabilities are the *debt ratio* and the *times-interest-earned ratio*.

Debt Ratio

The relationship between total liabilities and total assets, generally called the **debt ratio**, tells us the proportion of the company's assets that it has financed with debt:

$$\text{Debt ratio} = \frac{\text{total debt}}{\text{total assets}}. \tag{13.1a}$$

For example, Lam Research's debt ratio for 2011 can be calculated from Table 13.1 as follows:

$$\text{Debt ratio} = \frac{\$1,587,549}{\$4,057,394} = 39.13\%.$$

Total debt includes both current liabilities and long-term debt. If the debt ratio is 1, then the company has used debt to finance all of its assets. As of June 26, 2011 Lam Research's debt ratio was 39.13%; this means that its creditors have supplied close to 40% of the firm's total financing. Certainly, most creditors prefer low debt ratios because the lower the ratio, the higher will be the cushion against the creditor's losses in case of liquidation. If a company seeking financing already has large liabilities, then additional debt payments may be too much for the business to handle. For this highly leveraged company, creditors generally charge higher interest rates on new borrowing in order to help protect them.

Another way to express leverage is in terms of company's debt-to-equity ratio:

$$\text{Debt-equity ratio} = \frac{\text{long-term debt}}{\text{equity}}. \tag{13.1b}$$

If this ratio is more than 1, the majority of assets are financed through debt. If it is less than 1, assets are primarily financed through equity. For Lam Research, the debt-equity ratio in 2011 was

$$\text{Debt-equity ratio} = \frac{\$738,488}{\$2,469,845} = 0.2990.$$

This indicates that almost 70% of Lam Research's assets were financed through equity.

Times-Interest-Earned Ratio

The most common measure of the ability of a company's operations to provide protection to the long-term creditor is the **times-interest-earned ratio**. We find this ratio by dividing earnings before interest and income taxes (EBIT) by the yearly interest charges that must be met. For example, Lam Research issued $738,488 worth of senior notes and long-term bonds. This results in $5,380 in interest expenses in the year 2011, so we calculate the following:

$$\text{Times-interest-earned ratio} = \frac{\text{EBIT}}{\text{Interest expense}} \tag{13.2}$$

$$= \frac{\$806,256}{\$5,380}$$

$$= 149.86 \text{ times}.$$

The ratio measures the extent to which operating income can decline before the firm is unable to meet its annual interest costs. Failure to meet this obligation can lead to legal action by the firm's creditors, possibly resulting in bankruptcy. Note that we use the earnings before interest and income taxes, rather than net income in the numerator. Because Lam Research must pay interest with pretax dollars, Lam Research's ability to pay current interest is not affected by income taxes. Only those earnings remaining after all interest charges have been incurred are subject to income taxes. For Lam Research, the times-interest-earned ratio for 2011 is almost 150 times.

13.3.2 Liquidity Analysis

Lam Research's short-term suppliers and creditors are also concerned with the level of liabilities. Short-term creditors want to be repaid on time. Therefore, they focus on Lam Research's cash flows and on its working capital, as these quantities are Lam Research's primary sources of cash in the near future. The excess of current assets over current liabilities is known as **working capital**. This figure indicates the extent to which current assets can be converted to cash in order to meet current obligations. Therefore, we view a firm's net working capital as a measure of its *liquidity position*. In general, the larger the working capital, the better able the business will be to pay its debts.

Current Ratio

We calculate the current ratio by dividing current assets by current liabilities:

$$\text{Current ratio} = \frac{\text{current assets}}{\text{current liabilities}}. \tag{13.3}$$

For example, Lam Research's current ratio in 2011 can be calculated as follows:

$$\text{Current ratio} = \frac{\$3,276,792}{\$684,286} = 4.79 \text{ times.}$$

If a company is getting into financial difficulty, it begins paying its bills (accounts payable) more slowly, borrowing from its bank, and so on. If current liabilities are rising faster than current assets, the current ratio will fall, and this could spell trouble. What is an acceptable current ratio? The answer depends on the nature of the industry. The general rule calls for a current ratio of 2 to 1. This rule, of course, is subject to many exceptions, depending heavily on the composition of the assets involved.

Quick (Acid Test) Ratio

The quick ratio tells us whether the company could pay all its current liabilities if they came due immediately. We calculate the quick ratio by deducting inventories from current assets and then dividing the remainder by current liabilities:

$$\text{Quick ratio} = \frac{\text{current assets} - \text{inventories}}{\text{current liabilities}}. \tag{13.4}$$

For example, Lam Research's quick ratio in 2011 can be calculated as follows:

$$\text{Quick ratio} = \frac{\$3,276,792 - \$396,607}{\$684,286} = 4.21 \text{ times.}$$

The quick ratio measures how well a company can meet its obligations without having to liquidate or depend too heavily on selling its inventory. Inventories are typically the least liquid of a firm's current assets; hence, they are the assets on which losses are most likely to occur in case of liquidation. Since Lam Research's current ratio for 2011 is 4.79, its liquidity position is relatively strong, as it carried a small amount of inventory in its current assets (only $396,607 out of $3,276,792 of current assets).

13.3.3 Asset Management Analysis

The ability to sell inventory and collect accounts receivable is fundamental to business success. Therefore, the third group of ratios measures how effectively the firm is managing its assets. We will review three ratios related to a firm's asset management: (1) inventory-turnover ratio, (2) days-sale-outstanding ratio, and (3) total-assets-turnover ratio. The purpose of these ratios is to answer the following question: Does the total amount of each type of asset as reported on the balance sheet seem reasonable in view of current and projected sales levels? Any asset acquisition requires the use of funds. If a firm has an excess of assets, its cost of capital will be too high; as a result, its profits will be depressed. On the other hand, if assets are too low, the firm is likely to lose profitable sales.

Inventory-Turnover Ratio

We find this by measuring how many times a company has sold and replaced its inventory during the year. We compute the ratio by dividing sales by the average level of inventories on hand. We compute the average inventory figure by taking the average of the beginning and ending inventory figures. Since Lam Research has a beginning inventory amount of $318,479 and an ending inventory amount of $396,607, its average inventory for the year would be $357,543. Then we compute Lam Research's inventory-turnover ratio for 2011 as follows:

$$\text{Inventory-turnover ratio} = \frac{\text{sales}}{\text{average inventory balance}} \tag{13.5}$$

$$= \frac{\$3,237,693}{\$357,543} = 9.06 \text{ times}.$$

As a rough approximation, Lam Research was able to sell and restock its inventory 9.06 times in 2011. Its turnover of 9.06 times is a little faster than that of its industry average, 7.2 times, during the same operating period. This result suggests that Lam Research's competitors are holding excessive stocks of inventory; excess stocks are, of course, unproductive, and they represent an investment with a low or zero rate of return. A relatively high ratio compared with those of competitors in the same industry may indicate that the firm is working close to capacity, signaling that it would need additional investment to generate additional business.

Days-Sales-Outstanding (Accounts Receivable Turnover) Ratio

The days-sales-outstanding (DSO) ratio is a rough measure of how many times a company's accounts receivable have been turned into cash during the year. We determine the ratio, also called the **average collection period**, by dividing accounts receivable by average sales per day. In other words, this ratio indicates the average length of time the firm must wait after making a sale before receiving cash. For Lam Research in 2011, we have

$$\text{DSO} = \frac{\text{accounts receivables}}{\text{average sales per day}} = \frac{\text{accounts receivables}}{\text{annual sales}/365} \qquad (13.6)$$

$$= \frac{\$590{,}568}{\$3{,}237{,}693/365} = \frac{\$590{,}568}{\$8{,}870}$$

$$= 66.58 \text{ days}.$$

Thus, for Lam Research, on average, it takes about 66.58 days to collect on a credit sale. Whether its average of 66.58 days taken to collect on an account is good or bad depends on the credit terms Lam Research is offering its customers. If credit terms are 90 days, we can say that Lam Research's customers, on average, are paying their bills on time. In order to improve their working-capital position, most customers tend to withhold payment for as long as the credit terms will allow and may even go over by a few days. The long collection period may signal that customers are in financial trouble or the company has poor credit management.

Total-Assets-Turnover Ratio

The total-assets-turnover ratio measures how effectively a firm uses its total assets in generating its revenues. It is the ratio of sales to all of the firm's assets. For Lam Research in 2011,

$$\text{Total-assets-turn over ratio} = \frac{\text{sales}}{\text{total assets}} \qquad (13.7)$$

$$= \frac{\$3{,}237{,}693}{\$4{,}057{,}394}$$

$$= 0.80 \text{ times}.$$

Lam Research's ratio of 0.80 times, when compared with the industry average ratio of 0.9 times, is almost 11.11% slower, indicating that Lam Research is using its total assets about 11.11% less intensively than its peers. If this ratio does not improve, we can say that Lam Research has relatively high investment in inventory, plant, and equipment compared with the size of sales.

13.3.4 Profitability Analysis

One of the most important goals for any business is to earn a profit. The ratios examined thus far provide useful clues as to the effectiveness of a firm's operations, but profitability ratios show the combined effects of liquidity, asset management, and debt on operating results. Therefore, ratios that measure profitability play a large role in decision making.

Profit Margin on Sales

We calculate the profit margin on sales by dividing net income by sales. This ratio indicates the profit per dollar of sales. For Lam Research in 2011,

$$\text{Profit margin on sales} = \frac{\text{net income available to common stockholders}}{\text{sales}} \qquad (13.8)$$

$$= \frac{\$723{,}748}{\$3{,}237{,}693} = 22.35\%.$$

Thus, Lam Research's profit margin is equivalent to 22.35 cents for each sales dollar generated. Lam Research's net profit margin is higher than the industry average of 16.8%. This difference indicates that Lam Research's operation is more efficient than its competitors. Recall that net income is income after taxes. Thus, if two firms have identical operations in the sense that their sales, operating costs, and earnings before income tax are the same but one company uses more debt than the other, then the company with more debt will have higher interest charges. Those interest charges will pull net income down, and because sales are the same, the result will be a relatively low profit margin for the indebted company.

Return on Total Assets

The return on total assets (ROA), or simply return on assets, measures a company's success in using its assets to earn a profit. The ratio of net income to total assets measures the return on total assets after interest and taxes. For Lam Research in 2011,

$$\text{Return on total assets} = \frac{\text{net income} + \text{interest expense} (1 - \text{tax rate})}{\text{average total assets}} \quad (13.9)$$

$$= \frac{\$723,748 + \$5,380(1 - 0.096)}{(\$2,487,392 + \$4,057,394)/2} = 22.27\%.$$

Adding a portion of interest expenses back to net income results in an adjusted earnings figure that shows what earnings would have been if the assets had been acquired solely through equity. (Note that Lam Research's effective tax rate is 9.6% in 2011.) With this adjustment, we may be able to compare the return on total assets among companies with differing amounts of debt. Again, Lam Research's 22.27% return on assets is well above the industry average of 14.7%. This high return results from (1) the company's high basic earning power and (2) its low use of debt, both of which cause its net income to be relatively high.

Return on Common Equity

Another popular measure of profitability is the rate of return on common equity (ROE). This ratio shows the relationship between net income and the common stockholders' investment in the company. That is, it answers the following question: How much income is earned for every $1 invested by common shareholders? To compute this ratio, we first subtract preferred dividends from net income; the result is known as "net income available to common stockholders." We then divide this net income available to common stockholders by the average common (stockholders) equity during the year. We compute average common equity by using the beginning and ending balances. At the beginning of fiscal year 2011, Lam Research's common equity balance was $1,768,135, and its ending balance was $2,469,845. The average balance is, then, simply $2,118,990. So, we find the following:

$$\text{Return on common equity} = \frac{\text{net income available to common stockholders}}{\text{average common equity}} \quad (13.10)$$

$$= \frac{\$723,748}{(\$1,768,135 + \$2,469,845)/2}$$

$$= \frac{\$723,748}{\$2,118,990} = 34.16\%.$$

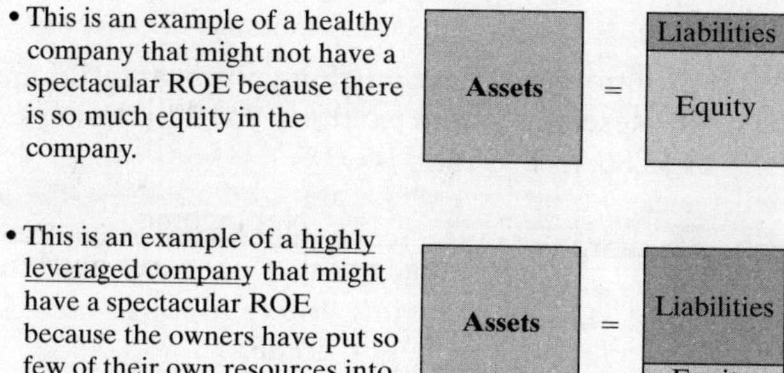

Figure 13.10 How the debt-to-equity ratio affects the return on equity

The rate of return on common equity for Lam Research was 34.16% during 2011.

To learn more about what management can do to increase ROE, we may rewrite ROE in terms of the following three components:

$$\text{ROE} = \frac{\text{Net income}}{\text{Average shareholders' equity}}$$

$$= \frac{\text{Net income}}{\text{Sales}} \times \frac{\text{Sales}}{\text{Assets}} \times \frac{\text{Assets}}{\text{Average shareholders' equity}}. \qquad (13.11)$$

The three principal components can be described as the profit margin, asset turnover, and financial leverage, respectively.

$$\text{ROE} = (\text{Profit margin}) \times (\text{Asset turnover}) \times (\text{Financial leverage})$$

$$= (22.35\%) \times (0.80) \times \left(\frac{\$4,057,394}{\$2,118,990}\right)$$

$$= 34.24\%.$$

The slight difference is due to rounding errors. This expression tells us that management has only three key ratios for controlling the ROE: (1) the earnings from sales (profit margin), (2) the revenue generated from each dollar of assets employed (asset turnover), and (3) the amount of equity used to finance the assets in business operation (financial leverage).

Figure 13.10 illustrates how the debt-to-equity ratio (total debt over total equity) (distinct from the debt ratio) impacts the return on equity.

13.3.5 Market-Value Analysis

When purchasing a company's stock, what would be your primary factors in valuing that stock? In general, investors purchase stock to earn a return on their investment. This return consists of two parts: (1) gains (or losses) from selling the stock at a price that is higher (or lower) than the purchase price and (2) dividends, the periodic distributions of profits to stockholders. The market-value ratios, such as price–earnings ratio and market–book ratio, relate the firm's stock price to its earnings and book value per share. These ratios give management an indication of what investors think of the company's past performance and future prospects. If a firm's asset management and debt management are sound and its profit is rising, then its market-value ratios and stock price will be high.

Price/Earnings Ratio

The price/earnings (P/E) ratio shows how much investors are willing to pay per dollar of reported profits. Lam Research's stock sold for \$43.22 (closing price) on June 24, 2011, so with an EPS of \$5.86, its P/E ratio is:

$$\text{Earnings per share} = \frac{\text{Net income}}{\text{Average number of shares outstanding}} \quad (13.12)$$

$$= \frac{\$723,748}{123,529} = \$5.86$$

$$\text{P/E ratio} = \frac{\text{price per share}}{\text{earnings per share}} \quad (13.13)$$

$$= \frac{\$43.22}{\$5.86} = 7.38.$$

That is, the stock was selling for about 7.38 times its current earnings per share. In general, P/E ratios are higher for firms with high growth prospects with all other things held constant but lower for firms with lower expected earnings. Lam Research's expected annual increase in operating earnings is 16% over the next three to five years. Since Lam Research's expected growth is more than 4.17%, the average for the semiconductor industry, we may infer that investors value Lam Research's stock more highly than most other stocks in the industry. However, all stocks with high P/E ratios will also carry high risk whenever the expected growth does not materialize. Any slight earnings disappointment tends to punish the market price significantly.

Book Value per Share

Another ratio frequently used in assessing the well-being of common stockholders is book value per share. The book value per share measures the amount that would be distributed to holders of each share of common stock if all assets were sold at their balance-sheet carrying amounts and if all creditors were paid off. We compute the book value per share for Lam Research's common stock in 2011 as follows:

$$\text{Book value per share} = \frac{\text{total stockholders' equity} - \text{preferred stock}}{\text{shares outstanding}} \quad (13.14)$$

$$= \frac{\$2,469,845 - \$0}{123,529} = \$20.$$

If we compare this book value with the market price of \$43.22 at the time of publication, then we may say that the stock appears to be overpriced. Once again, market prices reflect expectations about future earnings and dividends whereas book value largely reflects the results of events that occurred in the past. Therefore, the market value of a stock tends to exceed its book value.

There are many sources of financial ratio information in addition to those we have examined here. For example, www.reuters.com shows a variety of financial ratios for publically traded companies. Table 13.5 summarizes the financial ratios for Lam Research Corporation in reference to industry and the S&P averages. In looking at numbers such as these, you may find the figures that we have calculated could be different

TABLE 13.5 **Comparisons of Key Financial Ratios for Lam Research Corporation with the Industry Average and the S&P 500 (as of May 18, 2011)**

Category	Financial ratios	LRCX	Industry	S&P 500
Debt Management	Debt/Equity Ratio	0.299	0.14	1.2
	Time-interest-earned ratio	149.86	38.6	83.4
Liquidity Analysis	Current ratio	4.79	3.9	1.4
	Quick ratio	4.21	3.2	0.9
Asset Management	Inventory-turnover ratio	9.06	7.2	14.2
	Days-sales-outstanding ratio	66.58	50.69	8.33
	Total-assets turnover ratio	0.80	0.9	2
Profitability	Profit margin	22.35%	16.8	12.6
	Return on total assets	22.27%	14.7	14.2
	Return on common equity	34.16%	21.60%	38.60%
Market Trend	P/E ratio	7.38	19	19.6
	Book value/share	$20	9.52	25.23

Source: MSN Finance – http://money.msn.com

from the published numbers. The reason is that different sources frequently do their calculations somewhat differently even if the ratio names are the same. Table 13.6 summarizes the financial ratios introduced in this section.

13.3.6 Limitations of Financial Ratios in Business Decisions

Business decisions are made in an uncertain world. As useful as ratios are, they have limitations. We can draw an analogy between the use of financial ratios in decision making and a physician's use of a thermometer. A reading of 102°F indicates that something is wrong with the patient, but the temperature alone does not indicate what the problem is or how to cure it. In other words, ratio analysis is useful, but analysts should be aware of ever-changing market conditions and make adjustments as necessary. It is also difficult to generalize about whether a particular ratio is "good" or "bad." For example, a high current ratio may indicate a strong liquidity position, which is good, but holding too much cash in a bank account (which will increase the current ratio) may not be the best use of funds. In addition, ratio analysis based on any one year may not represent the true business condition. It is important to analyze trends in various financial ratios as well as their absolute levels, for trends give clues as to whether the financial situation is likely to improve or to deteriorate. To do a **trend analysis**, we simply

TABLE 13.6 Summary of Key Financial Ratios

Category	Formula	Comments
Debt Management	• Debt ratio $= \dfrac{\text{total debt}}{\text{total assets}}$. • Debt-equity ratio $= \dfrac{\text{long-term debt}}{\text{equity}}$	Debt ratio may be measured in many different forms.
	• Times-interest-earned ratio $= \dfrac{\text{EBIT}}{\text{Interest expense}}$	EBIT: Earnings before interest and taxes. This ratio is also known as the *interest coverage ratio*.
Liquidity Analysis	• Current ratio $= \dfrac{\text{current assets}}{\text{current liabilities}}$.	
	• Quick ratio $= \dfrac{\text{current assets} - \text{inventories}}{\text{current liabilities}}$.	
Asset Management	• Inventory-turnover ratio $= \dfrac{\text{sales}}{\text{average inventory balance}}$	As a variation, "*sales*" may be replaced by "*cost of goods sold*" in ratio calculation.
	• DSO $= \dfrac{\text{receivables}}{\text{average sales per day}} = \dfrac{\text{receivables}}{\text{annual sales}/365}$	
	• Total-assets-turnover ratio $= \dfrac{\text{sales}}{\text{total assets}}$	As a variation, the "*total assets*" may be replaced by the "*average of the assets*."
Profitability Analysis	• Profit margin on sales $= \dfrac{\text{net income available to common stockholders}}{\text{sales}}$	
	• Return on total assets $= \dfrac{\text{net income} + \text{interest expense}(1 - \text{tax rate})}{\text{average total assets}}$	
	• Return on common equity $= \dfrac{\text{net income available to common stockholders}}{\text{average common equity}}$ $= \dfrac{\text{Net income}}{\text{Sales}} \times \dfrac{\text{Sales}}{\text{Assets}} \times \dfrac{\text{Assets}}{\text{Average common equity}}$.	
Market Trend Analysis	• P/E ratio $= \dfrac{\text{price per share}}{\text{earnings per share}}$	
	• Book value per share $= \dfrac{\text{total stockholders' equity} - \text{preferred stock}}{\text{shares outstanding}}$	

plot a ratio over time. As a typical engineering student, your judgment in interpreting a set of financial ratios is understandably weak at this point, but it will improve as you encounter many facets of business decision making in the real world. Again, accounting is a language of business, and as you speak it more often, it will provide useful insights into a firm's operations.

13.3.7 Where We Get the Most Up-to-Date Financial Information

Recall that all the financial ratio analyses given in the previous section were based the Lam Research's 2011 Annual Report, as of June 26, 2011. This is a historical document that allows us to examine the past performance of the corporation as well as some business outlooks portrayed by the management. To get the most up-to-date financial information, you may visit many online financial information sources such as Yahoo Finance or the company's website under the heading "Investor Relations." Certainly, you need to find out how other competitors did during the same period before making a financial decision.

13.4 Principle of Investing in Financial Assets

When you want to invest in an individual company, the financial analysis such as we have done for Lam Research Corporation in the previous sections would be a starting point. Once you understand the implications of financial risk associated with the company, you need to come up with an investment strategy that tells you what to do as far as putting together an appropriate investment portfolio. The next question involves how do you go about actually implementing the decisions you have made. Because investing is an inexact science, *it is better to be approximately right than precisely wrong*. This is the approach taken in this section. The technique that is commonly practiced in financial investment is the concept of project diversification. The same concept also applies to the creation of an investment project portfolio.

13.4.1 Trade-Off between Risk and Reward

When it comes to investing, trying to weigh risk and reward can be a challenging task. Investors do not know the actual returns that project assets will deliver or the difficulties that will occur along the way. Risk and reward are the two key words that will form the foundation for much of this section. This is what investing is all about: the trade-off between the opportunity to earn higher returns and the consequences of trying to do so and failing. The greater the risk, the more you stand to gain or lose. There is no such thing as a truly risk-free investment. So, the real task is not to try to find "risk-free" investments; strictly speaking, there are not any. The challenge is to decide what level of risk you are willing to assume and then, having decided on your risk tolerance, to understand the implications of that choice. Your range of investment choices—and their relative risk factors—may be classified into three types of investment groups: cash, debt, and equities.

13.4.2 Broader Diversification Reduces Risk

Even if you find risk exciting sometimes, you will probably sleep better if you have your money spread among different assets; do not put all your eggs in one basket. Your best protection against risk is diversification—spreading your investments around instead of investing in only one thing. For example, you can balance cash investments such as certificates of deposit (CDs) and money-market funds with stocks, bonds, and mutual funds. Even within equity investments, you can buy stocks of small, growing companies while also investing in large and well-established companies. What would you gain from this diversification practice? Well, you would hope to reduce the effect of market volatility on your holdings.

Usually, when returns are low in one area, you would like to see returns go up in another area. We may explain the concept of diversification graphically as shown in Figure 13.11. This figure shows three different investment scenarios explained as follows:

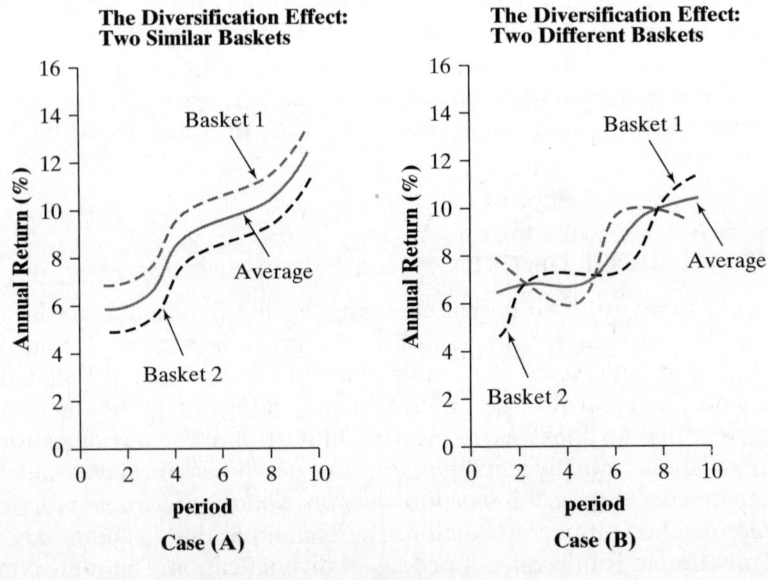

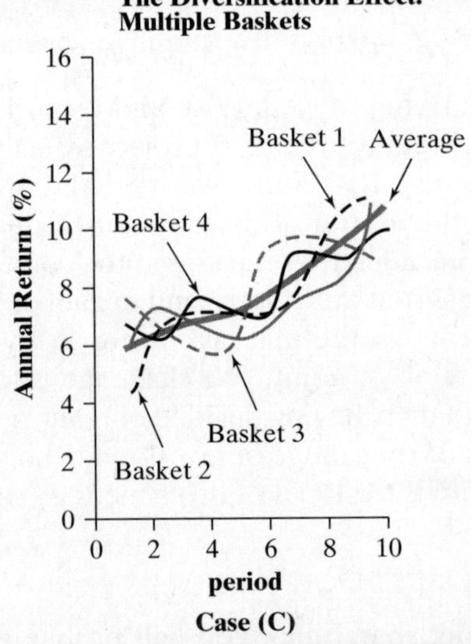

Figure 13.11　Reducing investment risks by asset diversification

- **Case (A)—Invest in two assets with similar return characteristics:** Suppose you have the two types of investments shown in Figure 13.11(a). These two investments are similar in their pattern of return; that is, they fluctuate to the same degree such that as one goes up or down, so does the other.[5] In other words, you will experience a great deal of volatility while you are in the market. If you keep both investments, your expected rate of return is simply the weighted average of their returns.

- **Case (B)—Invest in two assets with dissimilar return characteristics:** Suppose you find the set of investments shown in Figure 13.11(b). The investments both have the same potential return, but the returns come at opposite times. That is, as one goes down, the other goes up.[6] Again, the return would be the weighted average of the returns of the two investments, but we may control the risk (fluctuation) considerably. All the negative returns of one investment would be offset by the positive returns of the other.

- **Case (C)—Invest in multiple assets with dissimilar return characteristics:** Of course, in the real world, we are not likely to find either of the foregoing scenarios. The more likely situation is that larger portfolios will have a number of assets in them with differing, but not necessarily opposite, patterns of return. Then the results could be as shown in Figure 13.11(c). The overall yield of the portfolio is the weighted average of the individual assets, but the fluctuation—the risk—is dampened. It is therefore possible to achieve a higher rate of return without considerably increasing the risk by building a multiple-asset portfolio. This is exactly what we achieve in asset investment through diversification.

13.4.3 Broader Diversification Increases Expected Return

As we observe in Figure 13.11, diversification reduces risk. However, there is far more to the power of diversification than simply spreading your assets over a number of investments. Well-diversified portfolios contain various mixes of stocks, bonds, mutual funds, and cash equivalents such as treasury bills. With such portfolios, over lengthy periods, you do not have to sacrifice much in the way of returns in order to get that reduced volatility. Finding the right mix depends on your assets, your age, and your risk tolerance. Diversification also requires regularly evaluating your assets and realigning the investment mix. For example, if your stocks increase in value, they will make up a larger percentage of your portfolio. To maintain a certain level of risk tolerance, you may want to decrease your stock holdings and increase your cash or bond holdings. Example 13.1 illustrates the difference an asset allocation makes for a long-term investor.

EXAMPLE 13.1 Broader Diversification Increases Return

Suppose you have $10,000 in cash and are considering the following two options for investing money:

- Option 1: You put the entire $10,000 into a secure-investment mutual fund consisting of a long-term U.S. Treasury bond with a yield of 7%.

---

[5] Mathematicians refer to such a relationship as a *perfect positive* cross correlation.

[6] This relationship is technically called a *perfect negative* cross correlation.

- Option 2: You split the $10,000 into equal amounts of $2,000 and diversify among five investment opportunities with varying degrees of risk from, say, extremely risky to very conservative and with potential returns ranging from −100% to 15%.

Amount	Investment	Expected Return
$2,000	Buying lottery tickets	−100% (?)
$2,000	Under the mattress	0%
$2,000	Term deposit (CD)	5%
$2,000	Corporate bond	10%
$2,000	Mutual fund (stocks)	15%

Given these two options, which would you choose?

DISSECTING THE PROBLEM

The $10,000 bond investment, which earns 7%, poses virtually no risk. With the diversified approach, you are going to lose the first $2,000 with practical certainty, make nothing on the next $2,000, make only 5% on the third $2,000, make 10% on the fourth $2,000, and make 15% on the last $2,000. At first glance, you might think Option 1 is a more rational strategy because of the very limited risk potential. Indeed, that might well be the best alternative for many short-term investors. However, say that we add one more element to our scenario: Our time horizon is 25 years. Would that make a difference?

Given: Rate of return for each investment option.

Find: Value of the investments at the end of 25 years.

METHODOLOGY

Create a table of expected returns and values in 25 years for both options.

SOLUTION

As you will see, the longer the time horizon, the better choice certain investments, such as stocks (represented by the mutual fund in this example), become. First, we can find the value of the government bond in 25 years as follows:

$$F = \$10,000(F/P, 7\%, 25) = \$54,274.$$

Similarly, we can find the value for each investment class in Option 2:

Option	Amount	Investment	Expected Return	Value in 25 Years
1	$10,000	Bond	7%	$54,274
	$2,000	Lottery tickets	−100%	$0
	$2,000	Under mattress	0%	$2,000
2	$2,000	Term deposit (CD)	5%	$6,773
	$2,000	Corporate bond	10%	$21,669
	$2,000	Mutual fund (stocks)	15%	$65,838
				$96,280

At the outset, Option 2 appears to be a losing proposition, but you would end up with about 77% more money despite the fact that the first two choices you made were, at best, unproductive. Of course, you can come up with a counterexample where Option 1 would be a better choice. However, the message is clear: Diversification among properly chosen assets can increase your return without unnecessary risks as long as you keep the assets invested in the market over a long period.

COMMENTS: In an extreme case, if you invested the entire $10,000 in the stock, the expected return over 25 years would be $10,000(1 + 0.15)^{25} = $329,190, which is much more than the return expected from the diversification. Therefore, it is commonly suggested that if you are a long-term investor, you can increase your exposure to riskier assets, such as stocks.

SUMMARY

■ The primary purposes of this chapter were (1) to describe basic financial statements, (2) to present some background information on cash flows and corporate profitability, and (3) to discuss techniques used by investors and managers to analyze financial statements.

■ Before making any major business decisions, it is important to understand the impact of the decisions on the firm's financial statements.

■ The three basic financial statements contained in a company's annual report are the balance sheet, the income statement, and the statement of cash flows. Investors use the information provided in these statements to form expectations about future levels of earnings and dividends and about the firm's riskiness.

■ A firm's balance sheet shows a snapshot of the firm's financial position at a particular point in time.

■ A firm's income statement reports the results of operations over a certain period, and it shows earnings per share as its "bottom line."

- A firm's statement of cash flows reports the impact of operating, investing, and financing activities on cash flows over an accounting period.

- The purpose of calculating a set of financial ratios is twofold: (1) to examine the relative strengths and weaknesses of a company compared with other companies in the same industry and (2) to show whether the company's financial position has been improving or deteriorating over time.

- Liquidity ratios show the relationship of a firm's current assets to its current liabilities, and thus its ability to meet maturing debts. Two commonly used liquidity ratios are the current ratio and the quick (acid test) ratio.

- Asset management ratios measure how effectively a firm is managing its assets. Some of the major ratios include the inventory-turnover ratio, the collection period, and the total-assets-turnover ratio.

- Debt management ratios reveal (1) the extent to which a firm is financed with debt and (2) the firm's likelihood of defaulting on its debt obligations. In this category, we may include the debt ratio and the times-interest-earned ratio.

- Profitability ratios show the combined effects of liquidity, asset management, and debt management policies on operating results. Profitability ratios include the profit margin on sales, the return on total assets, and the return on common equity.

- Market-value ratios relate a firm's stock price to its earnings and book value per share and give management an indication of what investors think of the company's past performance and future prospects. Market value ratios include the price/earnings ratio and the market/book ratio.

- Trend analysis, where a ratio over time is plotted, is important because it reveals whether a firm's ratios are improving or deteriorating over time.

- Once you set your risk tolerance, you are establishing an upper-bound limit on the portfolio's long-term expected rate of return.

- There is no such thing as a risk-free investment. The challenge is to decide what level of risk you are willing to assume and then, having decided on your risk tolerance, to understand the implications of that choice.

- There is far more to the power of **diversification** than simply spreading your assets over a number of investments to reduce risk. By combining assets with different patterns of return, it is possible to achieve a higher rate of return without significantly increasing risk.

SELF-TEST QUESTIONS

13s.1 Which of the following statements is most correct?

(a) The balance sheet statement summarizes how much the firm owns as well as owes for a typical operating period.

(b) The income statement summarizes the net income produced by the corporation at a specified reporting date.

(c) The cash flow statement summarizes how the corporation generated cash during the operating period.

(d) None of the above.

13s.2 Which of the following statements is most correct?

    (a) Working capital measures the company's ability to repay current liabilities using only current assets.

    (b) The days sales outstanding (DSO) represents the average length of time that the firm must wait after making a sale before receiving cash.

    (c) The lower debt ratio, the more the protection afforded creditors in the event of liquidation.

    (d) All of the above.

13s.3 Which of the following statements is most correct?

    (a) P/E ratios are higher for firms with high growth prospects, other things held constant, but they are lower for riskier firms.

    (b) Higher market/book (MB) ratios are generally associated with firms that have a high rate of return on common equity.

    (c) A high quick ratio is not always a good indication of a well-managed liquidity position.

    (d) All of the above.

13s.4 Which of the following statements is most correct?

    (a) A decline in inventory turnover ratio suggests that the firm's liquidity position is improving.

    (b) The profit margin on sales is calculated by dividing net operating income by sales

    (c) When a corporation buys back its own stock, this is called Treasury Stock. The firm's cash and equity are both reduced.

    (d) None of the above.

13s.5 Which of the following statements is most correct?

    (a) Generally, firms with high profit margins have high asset turnover ratios.

    (b) Having a high current ratio and a high quick ratio is always a good indication a firm is managing its liquidity position well.

    (c) Knowing that return on assets (ROA) measures the firm's effective utilization of assets without considering how these assets are financed, two firms with the same EBIT must have the same ROA.

    (d) One way to improve the current ratio is to use cash to pay off current liabilities.

The following data apply to the next six problems. Consider Fisher & Company's financial data as follows (unit: millions of dollars except ratio figures):

Cash and marketable securities	$100
Fixed assets	$280
Sales	$1,200
Net income	$358
Inventory	$180
Current ratio	3.2
Average collection period	45 days
Average common equity	$500

13s.6 Find Fisher's accounts receivable.
  (a) $147.95   (b) $127.65
  (c) $225.78   (d) $290.45

13s.7 Calculate the amount of current assets.
  (a) $223   (b) $248
  (c) $280   (d) $428

13s.8 Determine the amount of current liabilities.
  (a) $156   (b) $134
  (c) $244   (d) $334

13s.9 Determine the amount of total assets.
  (a) $528   (b) $428
  (c) $328   (d) $708

13s.10 Calculate the amount of the long-term debt.
  (a) $134   (b) $500
  (c) $74   (d) $208

13s.11 Calculate the profit margin.
  (a) 20%   (b) 30%
  (c) 35%   (d) 40%

The following financial statements apply to the next six problems, 13s.12–13s.18.

Inland Manufacturing Balance Sheet
(Dollars in millions)

	December 31, 2011	December 31, 2010
Cash	$400	$300
Account receivables	560	450
Inventory	790	550
Total current assets	$1,750	$1,300
Total fixed assets	1,200	1,210
Total assets	$2,950	$2,510
Account payable	$350	$250
Note payable	470	330
Other current liabilities	220	130
Total current liabilities	$1,040	$710
Long-term debt	580	580
Common equity	$1,330	$1,220
Total liabilities and equity	$2,950	$2,510

Inland Manufacturing Income Statement December 31, 2011
(Dollars in Millions)

Gross sales		$2,450
Cost of goods sold:		
Materials	$230	

Inland Manufacturing Income Statement December 31, 2011 *(continued)*		
(Dollars in Millions)		
Labor	850	
Overhead	230	
Depreciation	400	$1,710
Gross profit		$740
Selling expenses		40
General and administrative expenses		60
Earnings before interest and taxes (EBIT)		$640
Interest expenses		25
Earnings before income taxes		$615
Provision for income taxes (40%)		246
Net income		$369

13s.12 Calculate the liquidity ratios, that is, the current and quick ratios.

(a) (1.68, 0.92) (b) (1.56, 0.92)

(c) (1.68, 0.82) (d) None of the above

13s.13 Calculate the debt management ratios, that is, the debt and times-interest-earned ratios.

(a) (1.22, 12.56) (b) (0.55, 26.60)

(c) (0.75, 26.60 (d) (1.22, 22.55)

13s.14 Calculate the inventory-turnover ratio.

(a) 3.66 (b) 7.33

(c) 2.88 (d) 4.21

13s.15 Calculate the return on equity.

(a) 14% (b) 29%

(c) 15% (d) None of the above

13s.16 Calculate the price/earnings ratio. Inland had an average of 100 million shares outstanding during 2005, and the stock price on December 31, 2005, was $35.

(a) 2.63 (b) 13.3

(c) 9.49 (d) 5.23

13s.17 If Inland uses $350 of cash to pay off $350 of its accounts payable, what is the new current ratio after this action?

(a) 1.68 (b) 2.03

(c) 3.12 (d) 1.45

13s.18 If Inland uses its $400 cash balance to pay off $400 of its long-term debt, what will be its new current ratio?

(a) 1.68 (b) 2.03

(c) 1.35 (d) 3.12

PROBLEMS

Financial Statements

13.1   Definitional problems: Listed are eight terms that relate to financial statements:
   1. Balance-sheet statement
   2. Income statement
   3. Cash-flow statement
   4. Operating activities
   5. Investment activities
   6. Financing activities
   7. Treasury account
   8. Capital account

Choose the term from the list that most appropriately completes each of the following statements:

■ As an outside investor, you would view a firm's __________ as the most important financial report for gauging the quality of earnings.

■ Retained earnings as reported in the __________ represent income earned by the firm in past years that has not been paid out as dividends.

■ The __________ is designed to show how a firm's operations have affected its cash position by providing actual net cash flows into or out of the firm during some specified period.

■ Typically, a firm's cash flow statement is categorized into three activities: __________, __________, and __________.

■ When you issue stock, the money raised beyond the par value is shown in the __________ in the balance-sheet statement.

13.2   Definitional problems: Listed are 11 terms that relate to ratio analysis:
   1. Book value per share
   2. Inventory turnover
   3. Debt-to-equity ratio
   4. Average collection period
   5. Average sales period
   6. Return on common equity
   7. Earnings per share
   8. Price/earnings ratio
   9. Return on total assets
   10. Current ratio
   11. Accounts-receivable turnover

Choose the financial ratio or term from the list that most appropriately completes each of the following statements:

■ The __________ tends to have an effect on the market price per share as reflected in the price/earnings ratio.

■ The __________ indicates whether a stock is relatively cheap or relatively expensive in relation to current earnings.

- The _________ measures the amount that would be distributed to holders of common stock if all assets were sold at their balance-sheet carrying amount and if all creditors were paid off.
- The _________ is a rough measure of how many times a company's accounts receivable have been turned into cash during the year.
- The _________ is a measure of the amount of assets being provided by creditors for each dollar of assets being provided by the stockholders.
- The _________ measures how well management has employed its assets.

13.3　Consider the following balance-sheet entries for Delta Corporation:

Balance Sheet Statement as of December 31, 201X	
Assets	
Cash	$150,000
Marketable securities	$200,000
Accounts receivable	$150,000
Inventories	$50,000
Prepaid taxes and insurance	$30,000
Manufacturing plant at cost	$600,000
Less accumulated depreciation	$100,000
Net fixed assets	$500,000
Goodwill	$20,000
Liabilities and Shareholders' Equity	
Notes payable	$50,000
Accounts payable	$100,000
Income taxes payable	$80,000
Long-term mortgage bonds	$400,000
Preferred stock, 6%, $100 par value (1,000 shares)	$100,000
Common stock, $15 par value (10,000 shares)	$150,000
Capital surplus	$150,000
Retained earnings	$70,000

(a) Compute the following for the firm:
　　Current assets: $ _________
　　Current liabilities: $ _________
　　Working capital: $ _________
　　Shareholders' equity: $ _________

(b) If the firm had a net income after taxes of $500,000, what are the earnings per share?

(c) When the firm issued its common stock, what was the market price of the stock per share?

13.4　Birmingham Steels has the following (incomplete) balance sheet and income statement.

Balance Sheet

Assets	2012	2011
Current assets	200	100
Fixed assets	700	600

Liabilities and Shareholders' Equity		
Current liabilities	90	60
Long-term debt	550	450

Income Statement, 2012	
Revenue	2,350
Cost of revenue	1130
Depreciation	420
Interest expense	210

All figures in million dollars

(a) Determine the shareholders' equity in 2011 and 2012.

(b) Determine the net working capital in 2011 and 2012.

(c) Assuming that Birmingham Steels has a 35% tax rate, determine the income taxes paid in year 2012.

(d) What is cash generated from operation in year 2012?

Financial-Ratio Analysis

13.5 The following data are available for two companies, Apple and Oracle, all stated in thousands of dollars.

Description	Apple	Oracle
Total revenue	$42,905,000	$23,253,000
Earnings before interest and taxes	12,066,000	8,464,000
Interest expenses	0	630,000
Earnings before tax	12,066,000	7,834,000
Taxes at 40%	3,831,000	2,241,000
Earnings after tax (net income)	8,235,000	5,593,000
Debt	$15,861,000	$22,326,000
Equity	31,640,000	$25,090,000

(a) Calculate each company's return on equity (ROE) and return on assets (ROA).

(b) Which company has performed better in terms of profitability?

(c) If the two companies were combined (merged), what would be the impact on the results on ROE? Under what conditions would such a combination make sense?

13.6 The following data were taken from the income statements of Metronix Corporation.

	2012	2011
Total revenue	$4,658,125	$3,776,395
Beginning inventory	$231,313	$202,794
Purchases	$510,711	$566,145
Ending inventory	$366,106	$231,313

Compute the inventory-turnover ratio for each year. What conclusions concerning the management of the inventory can be drawn from the data?

13.7 If Company A uses more debt than Company B and both companies have identical operations in terms of sales, operating costs, etc., which of the following statements is true?

(a) Company B will definitely have a higher current ratio.

(b) Company B has a higher profit margin on sales than Company A.

(c) The two companies have the identical profit margin on sales.

(d) Company B's return on total assets would be higher.

13.8 You are looking to buy stock in a high-growth company. Which of the following ratios best indicates the company's growth potential?

(a) Debt ratio

(b) Price/earnings ratio

(c) Profit margin

(d) Total-assets-turnover ratio

13.9 Which of the following statements is false?

(a) The quickest way to determine whether a firm has too much debt is to calculate the debt-to-equity ratio.

(b) The best guideline to determine the firm's liquidity is to calculate the current ratio.

(c) From the investor's point of view, the rate of return on common equity is a good indicator of whether the firm is generating an acceptable return to the investor.

(d) We can determine the operating margin by expressing net income as a percentage of total sales.

13.10 The table that follows summarizes the financial performances of four companies in the year 2012. From the given information, which company generated the highest return on equity?

Company	Profit Margin (%)	Asset Turnover (times)	Total Assets (millions)	Total Equity (millions)
A	12%	0.5	$12,510	$4,500
B	5.6%	1.6	$6,890	$3,250
C	7%	1.3	$7,791	$4,900
D	10%	0.8	$10,368	$7,200

(a) Company A
(b) Company B
(c) Company C
(d) Company D

13.11 J. C. Olson & Co. had earnings per share of $8 in 2012, and it paid a $4 dividend. Book value per share at year-end was $80. During the same period, the total retained earnings increased by $24 million. Olson has no preferred stock, and no new common stock was issued during the year. If Olson's year-end debt (which equals its total liabilities) was $240 million, what was the company's year-end debt ratio?

13.12 Consider the following financial statements for Dell Corporation:

Income Statement (All numbers in thousands)

Period Ending	Jan 28, 2011	Jan 29, 2010
Total Revenue	61,494,000	52,902,000
Cost of Revenue	50,098,000	52,902,000
Gross Profit	11,396,000	43,641,000
Operating Expenses		
Research and Development	661,000	44,745
Selling General and Administrative	7,302,000	743,142
Operating Income or Loss	3,433,000	2,172,000
Earnings before Interest and Taxes	3,350,000	2,024,000
Interest Expense	0	0
Income before Tax	3,350,000	2,024,000
Income Tax Expense	715,000	2,024,000
Net Income	2,635,000	1,433,000
Net Income Applicable to Common Shares	2,635,000	**1,433,000**
Outstanding Shares		

Balance Sheet Statement (All numbers in thousands)

Period Ending	Jan 28, 2011	Jan 29, 2010
Assets		
Current Assets		
Cash and Cash Equivalents	13,913,000	10,635,000
Short-Term Investments	452,000	373,000

Period Ending	Jan 28, 2011	Jan 29, 2010
Net Receivables	10,136,000	8,543,000
Inventory	1,301,000	1,051,000
Other Current Assets	3,219,000	3,643,000
Total Current Assets	**29,021,000**	**24,245,000**
Long-Term Investments	1,503,000	1,113,000
Property Plant and Equipment	1,953,000	2,181,000
Goodwill	4,365,000	4,074,000
Intangible Assets	1,495,000	1,694,000
Other Assets	262,000	345,000
Total Assets	**38,599,000**	**33,652,000**
Liabilities		
Current Liabilities		
Accounts Payable	15,474,000	15,257,000
Short/Current Long-Term Debt	851,000	663,000
Other Current Liabilities	3,158,000	3,040,000
Total Current Liabilities	**19,483,000**	**18,960,000**
Long-Term Debt	5,146,000	3,417,000
Other Liabilities	2,686,000	2,605,000
Deferred Long-Term Liability Charges	3,518,000	3,029,000
Total Liabilities	**30,833,000**	**28,011,000**
Stockholders' Equity		
Preferred Stock	-	-
Common Stock	11,797,000	11,472,000
Retained Earnings	24,744,000	22,110,000
Treasury Stock Capital Surplus	(28,704,000)	(27,904,000)
Other Stockholder Equity	(71,000)	(37,000)
Total Stockholder Equity	**7,766,000**	**5,641,000**

The closing stock price for Dell was $13.47 on January 28, 2011. The numbers of outstanding shares were 1,944 million in 2011 and 1,944 million in 2010, respectively. The income tax rates were 21.3% in 2011 and 29.2% in 2010. From the financial data presented, compute the following financial ratios for 2011, and make an informed analysis of Dell's financial health:

(a) Debt ratio
(b) Times-interest-earned ratio
(c) Current ratio
(d) Quick (acid test) ratio
(e) Inventory-turnover ratio
(f) Days-sales-outstanding ratio
(g) Total-assets-turnover ratio
(h) Profit margin on sales

    (i) Return on total assets
    (j) Return on common equity
    (k) Price/earnings ratio
    (l) Book value per share

13.13 Incomplete financial statements for ABC Company are as follows:

Income Statement

For the Year Ended December 31, 2012

Sales	$1,800,000
Less cost of goods sold	A
Gross margin	$900,000
Less operating expenses	B
Net operating income	C
Less interest expense	$45,000
Net income before taxes	D
Less income taxes (40%)	E
Net income	F

Balance Sheet

	December 31, 2012	January 1, 2012
Current assets:		
Cash	0	
Accounts receivable, net	1	$160,000
Inventory	2	$280,000
Total current assets	3	
Plant and equipment, net	4	
Total assets	5	$1,200,000
Current liabilities	$250,000	
Bonds payable, 10%	6	
Total liabilities	7	
Stockholder's equity:		
Common stock, $2.50 par value	8	
Retained earnings	9	
Total stockholders' equity	10	
Total liabilities and stockholders' equity	5	

The following additional information is available about the company:

(a) Selected financial ratios computed from the preceding statements are given as follows:

- Current ratio   2.40 to 1
- Quick (acid-test) ratio   1.12 to 1
- Average collection period   24.3333 days
- Inventory turnover   6.0 times

- Debt-to-equity ratio   0.875 to 1
- Earnings per share $4.05
- Return on total assets   14%

(b) All sales during the year were on account.

(c) The interest expense on the income statement relates to the bonds payable; the amount of bonds outstanding did not change throughout the year.

(d) There were no issues or retirements of common stock during the year.

Required: Compute the missing amounts on the company's financial statements.

Income Statement:

A	B	C	D	E	F

Balance Sheet:

0	1	2	3	4	5	6	7	8	9	10

Investment Strategies

13.14 Which of the following statements is incorrect?

(a) Holding on to cash is the most risk-free investment option.

(b) To maximize your return on total assets (ignoring financial risk), you must put all your money into the same type of investment category.

(c) Diversification among well-chosen investments can reduce market volatility.

(d) Broader diversification among well-chosen assets always leads to a higher return without increasing additional risk.

Short Case Study with Excel

13.15 Consider the Coca-Cola Company and Pepsi-Cola Company. Both companies compete with each other in the soft-drink sector. Get the most recent annual report for each company, and answer the following questions. (*Note*: You can visit the firms' websites to download their annual reports. Look for "Investor' Relations.")

(a) Review the most recent financial statements and comment on each company's financial performance in the following areas:
- Asset management
- Liquidity
- Debt management
- Profitability
- Market value

(b) Check the current stock prices for both companies. The stock ticker symbols are KO for Coca-Cola and PEP for Pepsi. Based on your analysis in part (a), in which company would you invest your money and why?

13.16 A chemical-processing firm is planning on adding a second polyethylene plant at another location. The financial information for the first project year is provided as follows:

Sales	$1,500,000
Manufacturing costs:	
Direct materials	$150,000
Direct labor	$200,000
Overhead	$100,000
Depreciation	$200,000
Operating expenses	$150,000
Equipment purchase	$400,000
Borrowing to finance equipment	$200,000
Increase in inventories	$100,000
Decrease in accounts receivable	$20,000
Increase in wages payable	$30,000
Decrease in notes payable	$40,000
Income taxes	$272,000
Interest payment on financing	$20,000

(a) Compute the working-capital requirement during this project period.
(b) What is the taxable income during this project period?
(c) What is the net income during this project period?
(d) Compute the net cash flow from this project during the first year.

13.17 Compare Google and Baidu, a Chinese search engine, using a thorough financial ratios analysis.

Part A: For each company, compute all the ratios listed in Figure 13.7 for the current year (or the most recent financial statements available) (i.e., debt management, liquidity, asset management, market trend, and profitability).

Part B: Compare and contrast these companies using the ratios you calculated from part A.

Part C: Carefully read and summarize the "Risk Management" or "hedging" practices described in the financial statements for each company.

Parts D: If you were a mutual fund manager and could invest in only one of these companies, which one would you select and why? Be sure to justify your answer using your results from parts A, B, and C.

I would recommend using the companies' websites to acquire the financial statements. This assignment should be typed, single spaced, with between two and five pages of discussion (not counting any tables or calculations). Include a table that summarizes all comparative ratio calculations.

Answers to the Self-Test Questions

Chapter 1

1s.1　(a)
1s.2　(d)
1s.3　(c)
1s.4　(d)

Chapter 2

2s.1　(d)

$$P = \$20,000\,(P/F,\ 12\%,\ 8)$$
$$= \$8,078$$

2s.2　(b)

$$F = P\{(F/P,\ 8\%,\ 9) + (F/P,\ 8\%,\ 7) + (F/P, 8\%, 5)$$
$$+ (F/P,\ 8\%,\ 3) + (F/P,\ 8\%,\ 1)\}$$
$$= 1,000\,\{1.9990 + 1.7138 + 1.4693$$
$$+ 1.2597 + 1.08) = \$7521.8$$
$$= \$7,521.8$$

2s.3　(a)

$$600\,(F/A,\ 10\%,\ 10) = P\,(F/P,\ 10\%,\ 7)$$
$$P = \frac{600 \times 15.9374}{1.9487}$$
$$= \$4,907$$

2s.4　(b)

$$[\{100\,(F/P, 4\%, 1) + X\}\,(F/P, 6\%, 1)\,(F/P, 8\%, 1)$$
$$+ 200]\,(F/P, 10\%, 1) = 800$$
$$[\{100 \times 1.04 + X\}\,(1.06 \times 1.08 + 200] \times 1.1 = 800$$
$$X = -\$100.71$$

2s.5   (d)

$$A = P(A/P, 12\%, 5) \implies$$
$$P = \frac{8,000}{0.2774} = \$28,839.2$$

2s.6   (b)

$$50(F/A, 12\%, 4) + 50(F/A, 12\%, 2) = C(F/A, 12\%, 4)$$
$$+ 2C(F/A, 12\%, 3) - 2C$$
$$50 \times 4.7793 + 50 \times 2.12 = C\{4.7793 + 2 \times 3.3744 - 2\}$$
$$C = \$33.598$$

2s.7   (c)

$$F = 3,000(F/A, 8\%, 20)(1.08)$$
$$= \$148,268.8$$

2s.8   (d)

$$A = P(A/P, i\%, N) = 28,000(A/P, 12\%, 4)$$
$$= 28,000 \times 0.3292 = \$9,217.6$$
$$\text{First year's interest} = 28,000 \times 0.12 = \$3,360$$
$$\text{Principal paid in first year} = 9,217.6 - 3,360 = \$5,857.6$$
$$\text{Interest paid in second year} = (28,000 - 5,857.6) \times 0.12 = \$2,657.08$$

2s.9   (b)

$$600(F/A, 8\%, 6) = X\{(F/P, 8\%, 5) + 1.08\}$$
$$X = \$1,726.56$$

2s.10   (b)

$$F = A(F/A, i\%, N) = P = \frac{A_1[1 - (1 + i)^{-N_1}(1 + g)^{N_1}]}{i - g}$$
$$A(F/A, 7\%, 10) = \frac{2,000[1 - (1 + 0.07)^{-5}(1 + 0.05)^5]}{0.07 - 0.05}$$
$$A = \frac{2,000[1 - (1 + 0.07)^{-5}(1 + 0.05)^5]}{(0.07 - 0.05) \times 13.8164}$$
$$= \$652.6$$

2s.11   (c)

$$5,000 \times 1.1 = C(P/A, 10\%, 5) \implies$$
$$C = \$1,407.44$$

2s.12   (c)

$$[\{1,200(P/F, 6\%, 1) + 1,200\}(P/F, 8\%, 1)$$
$$+ 1,800](P/F, 6\%, 1) + 1,200 = 4,935.178$$
$$4,935.178(P/F, 4\%, 1) = \$4,745.136$$

2s.13   (c)

$$2,500 = 1,200(1 + i \times N)$$
$$= 1,200(1 + i \times 12)$$
$$\Rightarrow i = 9.02\%$$

2s.14   (a)

$$A\{(P/A, 6\%, 9) - (P/F, 6\%, 5)\} = 25,000$$
$$A = \$4,129.22$$

2s.15   (d)

$$1,200(F/A, 6\%, 15) + 400(A/G, 6\%, 15)(F/A, 6\%, 15) = \$83,104.63$$

2s.16   (d)

$$N = \frac{\log 3}{\log 1.06} = 18.85 \text{ years}$$

2s.17   (a)

$$20,000(F/P, 8\%, 2) = A(P/A, 8\%, 13) \Rightarrow A = \$2,951.49$$

2s.18   (d)

$$1,500(F/A, 8\%, 20)(1.08) = \$74,144.44$$

Chapter 3

3s.1   (c)

$$F = A(F/A, 0.5\%, 180) = 5,000\left(\frac{(1 + 0.005)^{180} - 1}{0.005}\right)$$
$$= \$1,454,053.62$$

3s.2   (d)

Bank A: APR $= 8\%$

$$\text{APY} = i_a = \left(1 + \frac{0.08}{4}\right)^4 - 1 = 8.24\%$$

Bank B: APR $= 7.9\%$

$$\text{APY} = i_a = e^{0.079} - 1 = 8.22\%$$

3s.3 (b)

$$i = e^{0.08/2} - 1 = 4.081\%$$

3s.4 (b)

$$i_a = \left(1 + \frac{r}{M}\right)^M - 1 = \left(1 + \frac{0.08}{12}\right)^{12} - 1 = 0.0825$$

$$F = 4,000\left(\frac{(1 + 0.0825)^{20} - 1}{0.0825}\right) = \$188,196.55$$

3s.5 (d)

$$\text{Monthly interest rate} = 15/12 = 1.25\%$$

$$15,000(1 + 0.0125)^{36} = A\left(\frac{(1 + 0.0125)^{36} - 1}{0.0125}\right)$$

$$A = \$519.97$$

$$\text{Payoff balance at the end of 14th payment} = 519.97 \times \left\{\frac{(1 + 0.0125)^{22} - 1}{0.0125(1 + 0.0125)^{22}}\right\}$$

$$= \$9,947.31$$

$$\text{Interest paid in 15th payment} = 9,947.31 \times 0.0125 = \$124.34$$

3s.6 (d)

$$\text{Monthly interest rate} = 12/12 = 1\%$$

$$A = 25,000\left(\frac{0.01(1 + 0.01)^{48}}{(1 + 0.01)^{48} - 1}\right) = \$658.58$$

$$\text{Payoff balance after 20th payment} = 658.58\left(\frac{(1 + 0.01)^{28} - 1}{0.01(1 + 0.01)^{28}}\right)$$

$$= \$16,017.65$$

3s.7 (a)

$$A = P(A/P, 9\%, 12) = 120,000 \times 0.1397 = \$16,764$$

$$\text{Payoff balance after 5th payment} = A(P/A, 9\%, 7) = 16,764 \times 5.033$$

$$= \$84,373.21$$

3s.8 (c)

$$C\{(1 + 0.08)^3 + (1 + 0.08)^2\} = 300 + 300(1 + 0.08)^2$$

$$+ 400(1 + 0.08)^1$$

$$C = \frac{300 + 300(1 + 0.08)^2 + 400(1 + 0.08)^1}{\{(1 + 0.08)^3 + (1 + 0.08)^2\}} = \$455.94$$

3s.9 (a)

$$P = \$1{,}000(P/F,\ 8\%,\ 2)$$
$$+\ \$1{,}000\,(P/F,\ 2.25\%,\ 8)(P/F,\ 8\%,\ 2)$$
$$+\ \$1{,}000\,(P/F,\ 1\%,\ 24)\,(P/F,\ 2.25\%,\ 8)(P/F,\ 8\%,\ 2)$$
$$=\ \$2{,}140$$

3s.10 (d)

$$P = \$45(P/A,\ 3\%,\ 10)\ +\ \$1{,}000(P/F,\ 3\%,\ 10)$$
$$=\ \$1{,}127.95$$

3s.11 (a)

$$\text{Monthly interest rate} = 8/12 = 0.667\%$$
$$A = P(A/P,\ 0.667\%,\ 18)$$

$$=\ 180{,}000\left(\frac{0.0066\,(1\ +\ 0.0066)^{18}}{(1\ +\ 0.0066)^{18}\ -\ 1}\right)$$
$$=\ \$10{,}532.78$$

$$\text{Payoff balance after 12th payment} = A\,(P/A,\ 0.66\%,\ 8)$$
$$=\ 10{,}532.78\ \times\ \frac{(1\ +\ 0.0066)^{8}\ -\ 1}{0.0066\,(1\ +\ 0.0066)^{8}}$$
$$=\ \$81{,}816.512$$

3s.12 (c)

Cost of buying:

$$P_{\text{Buy}} = -\$2{,}000\ -\ \$608\!\left(P/A,\ \frac{6\%}{12},\ 36\right)\ +\ S\!\left(P/F,\ \frac{6\%}{12},\ 36\right)$$
$$=\ -\$21{,}985.58\ +\ 0.8356S$$

Cost of leasing:

$$P_{\text{Lease}} = -\$400\ -\ \$420\ -\ \$420\!\left(P/A,\ \frac{6\%}{12},\ 35\right)$$
$$=\ -\$14{,}274.86$$

Let $P_{\text{Buy}} = P_{\text{Lease}}$ and solve for S:

$$-\$21{,}985.58\ +\ 0.8356S\ =\ -\$14{,}274.86$$
$$S\ =\ \$9{,}227.76$$

Chapter 4

4s.1 (d)

Using the rule of 72:

$$N = \frac{\log 3}{\log 1.07} = 16.23$$

4s.2 (c)

$$\$80{,}000 = \$50{,}000(F/P, f, 5)$$
$$= \$50{,}000(1 + f)^5$$
$$f = 5.42\%$$

4s.3 (a)

$$i' = \frac{i - \overline{f}}{1 + \overline{f}} = \frac{0.0075 - 0.0025}{1.0025} = 0.00498 = 6.86\%$$

$$A = \frac{60{,}000 \times 0.00498 \times 1.00498^{60}}{1.00498^{60} - 1} = \$1{,}159.29$$

4s.4 (c)

$$A = \{50{,}000 + 51{,}000 \times 1.07 + 52{,}000 \times 1.07^2$$
$$+ 53{,}000 \times 1.07^3\}\left\{\frac{0.07}{1.07^8 - 1}\right\}$$
$$= \$22{,}323.2$$

4s.5 (b)

$$i = i' + \overline{f} + i'\overline{f}$$
$$= 0.03 + 0.05 + 0.03 \times 0.05 = 0.0815 = 8.15\%$$

$$\text{PW of fifth payment} = 80{,}000\left(\frac{1}{1 + 0.0815}\right)^5 = \$54{,}070.12$$

4s.6 (a)

$$i = i' + \overline{f} + i'\overline{f}$$
$$= 0.07 + 0.04 + 0.07 \times 0.04 = 0.1128 = 11.28\%$$

$$\text{PW of fuel cost} = A(P/A, 11.28\%, 5) = 1.8\left\{\frac{(1 + 0.1128)^5 - 1}{0.1128(1 + 0.1128)^5}\right\}$$
$$= \$6.606 \text{ million.}$$

4s.7 (c)

$$i' = \frac{i - \overline{f}}{1 + \overline{f}} = \frac{10.12 - 0.05}{1 + 0.05} = 0.0666$$

$$P = A\left\{\frac{1 - (1 + g)^n(1 + i')^{-n}}{i' - g}\right\}$$

$$= 8{,}000\left\{\frac{1 - (1 + 0.05)^5(1 + 0.066)^{-5}}{0.066 - 0.05}\right\}$$

$$= \$36{,}413.62$$

4s.8 (b)

$$i' = \frac{0.07 - 0.05}{1 + 0.05} = 1.9048\%$$

$$\$100\,(P/A, 1.9048\%, 3) = \$288.92$$

$$\$108\,(P/A, 7\%, 3) = \$283.42$$

4s.9 (d)

$$20{,}000(1 + 0.05)^{10} - 500(F/A, 2\%, 40)$$
$$= \$32{,}578 - \$30{,}201$$
$$= \$2{,}377$$

Chapter 5

5s.1 (b)

Period	Cash Flow	Cumulative Cash Flow
0	−$90,000	−$90,000
1	$30,000	−$60,000
2	$30,000	−$30,000
3	$30,000	0
4	$30,000	$30,000
5	$30,000	$30,000

5s.2 (c)

$$\begin{aligned} PW &= -1{,}000 - 2{,}000(P/F, 8\%, 1) + 3{,}000(P/F, 8\%, 2) \\ &\quad + 4{,}500(P/F, 8\%, 3) + 1{,}500(P/F, 8\%, 4) \\ &= -1{,}000 - 2{,}000 \times 0.9259 + 3{,}000 \times 0.8573 \\ &\quad + 4{,}500 \times 0.7938 + 1{,}500 \times 0.7350 \\ &= \$4{,}394.70 \end{aligned}$$

5s.3 (b)

$$\begin{aligned} P &= 40{,}000(P/A, 15\%, 10) + 0.05P(P/F, 15\%, 10) \\ &= 40{,}000 \times 5.0188 + 0.05P \times 0.2472 \\ 0.9876P &= 200{,}720 \Rightarrow \\ P &= \$203{,}240.17 \end{aligned}$$

5s.4 (b)

$$\begin{aligned} FW(12\%) &= 5{,}000(F/P, 12\%, 10) + 10{,}000(F/P, 12\%, 7) \\ &\quad + 8{,}000(F/P, 12\%, 5) \\ &= \$51{,}734.79 \end{aligned}$$

5s.5 (c)

$$\begin{aligned} FW(10\%) &= -100{,}000(F/P, 10\%, 3) + 40{,}000(F/P, 10\%, 2) \\ &\quad + 40{,}000(F/P, 10\%, 1) + 30{,}000 \\ &= -\$10{,}700 \end{aligned}$$

5s.6 (c)

$$\text{AE}(10\%)_{\text{First Cycle}} = \$500 - \$100(A/G, 10\%, 4) = \$361.88$$

$$\text{CE}(10\%) = \frac{\$361.88}{0.10} = \$3,618.80$$

5s.7 (a)

Statement 1: $-\$1,000(1 + 0.1) + A_1 = -\$1,500 \Rightarrow$

$$A_1 = -\$400, \text{ not true}$$

5s.8 (d)

It will take 6–7 years before this machine becomes profitable.

Period	Cash Flow	Cost of Funds (15%)	Cumulative Cash Flow
0	−$20,000	0	−$20,000
1	$5,000	−$3,000	−$18,000
2	$5,000	−$2,700	−$15,700
3	$5,000	−$2,355	−$13,055
4	$5,000	−$1,958	−10,013
5	$5,000	−$1,502	−$6,514
6	$5,000	−$977	−$2,491
7	$5,000	−$374	$2,135

5s.9 (c)

$$\text{PW}(8\%) = -\$550,000 + \$720,000(P/A, 8\%, 10)$$
$$+ \$2,225,000\,(P/F, 8\%, 10)$$
$$= \$5,311,865$$

5s.10 (a)

- Revenues from years 1 to 9:

$$10,000(P/A, 10\%, 9) + 5,000(P/G, 10\%, 9) = \$154,697.73$$

- Revenues after year 10:

$$\frac{\$52,000}{0.1}(P/F, 10\%, 9) = \$220,532$$

- Machine overhaul fee:

$$\frac{\$40,000(P/F, 10\%, 10)(A/P, 10\%, 10)}{0.1} = \$25,088.34$$

- Find the maximum investment (I):

$$\$100,000 = -I + \$154,697.73 + \$220,532 - \$25,088.34$$
$$I = \$250,141.39$$

5s.11 (b)

$$PW(10\%)_A = -\$2,000 - \$600(P/F, 10\%, 1) + (S - \$700)(P/F, 10\%, 2)$$
$$= -\$3,123.96 + 0.8264S$$
$$PW(10\%)_B = -\$1,000 - \$900(P/F, 10\%, 1) - \$800(P/F, 10\%, 2)$$
$$= -\$2,479.33$$

Let $PW(10\%)_A = PW(10\%)_B$ and solve for S.

$$-\$3,123.96 + 0.8264S = -\$2,479.33$$
$$S = \$780$$

Chapter 6

6s.1 (d)

- Capital cost:

$$CR(12\%) = \$80,000(A/P, 12\%, 5)$$
$$= \$22,192.78$$

- Equivalent annual revenue:

$$AE(12\%)_{Revenue} = \$50,000 + \$30,000(A/G, 12\%, 5)$$
$$= \$103,237.83$$

- Equivalent annual O&M cost:

$$AE(12\%)_{O\&M} = \$20,000 + \$10,000(A/G, 12\%, 5)$$
$$= \$37,745.94$$

- Equivalent annual worth:

$$AE(12\%) = \$103,237.83 - \$22,192.78 - \$37,745.94$$
$$= \$43,299.11$$

6s.2 (a)

- Capital cost:

$$CR(12\%) = (\$10,000 - \$1,000)(A/P, 12\%, 10) + 0.12(\$1,000)$$
$$= \$1,712.86$$

- Energy cost:

$$O\&M(12\%) = \left(\frac{30HP \times 0.7457\,kW/HP}{0.89}\right)(2,000\,hrs/yr)(0.09/kWh)$$
$$= \$4,524.47/yr$$

- Total equivalent cost in present worth:

$$AEC(12\%) = \$1,712.86 + \$4,524.47$$
$$= \$6,237.33$$
$$PW(12\%) = \$6,237.33(P/A, 12\%, 10)$$
$$= \$35,242.30$$

6s.3 (b)

$$9,740 = (I - S)(A/P, i\%, N) + i.S$$
$$= (50,000 - X)(A/P, 12\%, 8) + 0.12 \times 4,000$$
$$X = 4,000$$

6s.4 (a)

$$\$50M = (X - 15M)(P/A, 20\%, 10) + (0.15)(50M)(P/F, 20\%, 10)$$
$$= 4.1925X - 62.89M + 1.21M$$
$$4.1925X = \$111.68M$$
$$X = \$26.64M$$

6s.5 (b)

Capital cost:

$$CR(10\%) = (\$120,000 - \$20,000)(A/P, 10\%, 10) + 0.1(\$20,000)$$
$$= \$18,274.53$$

- Equivalent annual energy savings:

$$AE(10\%)_{\text{Energy Savings}} = \$45,000 \overbrace{(P/A_1, 5\%, 10\%, 10)}^{\$334,791.40} \overbrace{(A/P, 10\%, 10)}^{0.16275}$$
$$= \$54,485.75$$

- Net annual savings:

$$\$54,485.75 - \$18,274.53 = \$36,211.22$$

- Savings per operating hour:

$$\frac{\$36,211.22}{5,000} = \$7.24/\text{hr}$$

6s.6 (d)

- Capital cost:

$$CR(5\%) = (\$8,000,000 - \$750,000)(A/P, 5\%, 10) + 0.05(\$750,000)$$
$$= \$976,409$$

- Equivalent annual O&M cost: $2,000,000
- Total annual equivalent cost:

$$AEC(5\%) = \$976,409 + \$2,000,000 = \$2,976,409$$

- Cost per trip:

$$\frac{\$2,976,409}{600,000} = \$4.96/\text{trip}$$

6s.7 (c)

$$CR(15\%) = (\$12,500,000 - \$14,000,000)(A/P, 15\%, 5)$$
$$+ (0.15)(\$14,000,000)$$
$$= \$1,652,526$$
$$AEC(15\%)_{\text{O\&M}} = \$250,000 + \$50,000(A/G, 15\%, 5) + \$80,000$$
$$= \$416,141$$

$$AEC(15\%) = \$1,652,526 + \$416,141$$
$$= \$2,068,667$$
$$\frac{\$2,068,667}{50} = \$41,373 \text{ per unit}$$

6s.8   (b)

- Option 1:

$$\$5,000\,(A/P, 10\%, 10) = \$813.72$$

- Option 2:

$$[\$3,000 + \$3,000(P/F, 10\%, 5)](A/P, 10\%, 10) = \$791.39$$
$$\$791.39 - \$813.72 = -\$22.33, \text{select}\,(b)$$

6s.9   (b)

Let c be the price of a DELTA-4 shaving system

$$0 = -\$500 - \$175(P/A, 25\%, 10) + \$75(c)(P/A, 25\%, 10)$$
$$+ \$120(P/F, 25\%, 10)$$
$$c = \$4.15$$

Chapter 7

7s.1   (c)

$$\$490.92 = \$108\,(1+i)^8 \Rightarrow i = 20.84\%$$

7s.2   (b)

$$PW(i) = -1,600,000 + \frac{1,500,000}{1+i} + \frac{1,500,000}{(1+i)^2} - \frac{700,000}{(1+i)^3} = 0$$

By using Excel, $i = 38\%$

7s.3   (c)

$$\$16,205 = \frac{[\$2,000 + (X - \$2,000)(F/A, 20\%, 2)(A/F, 20\%, 4)]}{0.2}$$
$$X = \$5,027.76$$

7s.4   (d)

$$0 = -\$12,000 + \$2,500(P/F, 23\%, 1) + \$5,500(P/F, 23\%, 2)$$
$$+ X(P/F, 23\%, 3) + X(P/F, 23\%, 4)$$
$$= -\$6,332.07 + 0.9742X$$
$$X = \$6,499.76$$

7s.5   (b)

$$0 = -\$100,000 + (12X - \$30,000)(P/A, 15\%, 5) + \$20,000\,(P/F, 15\%, 5)$$
$$= -\$100,000 + 40.22586X - \$100,564.65 + \$9,943.53$$
$$= -\$190,621.12 + 40.22586X$$
$$X = \$4,738.77$$

7s.6 (c)

$$0 = -\$308{,}758 + \$60{,}000\,(P/A, i, 10) + \$30{,}875.8\,(P/F, i, 10)$$
$$i = 15\%$$

7s.7 (c)

Project C is a borrowing project whose rate of return is positive and unique.

7s.8 (a)

7s.9 (d)

- Statement 1: $\$200\,(1 + 0.15) + A_1 = \$300 \Rightarrow A_1 = \$70$, not true
- Statement 2: $\mathrm{FW}(i) = \mathrm{PB}(i)_2 = \$150$, true
- Statement 3: $\$650\,(1 + i)^{-2} = \$416 \Rightarrow i = 25\%$, true
- Statement 4: Since $\mathrm{PB}(15\%)_2 = 300 \to \mathrm{PW}(15\%) > 0, i^* > 15\%$, true

7s.10 (a)

n	Project 2-1
0	−$800
1	$900
2	0

$$0 = -800 + \frac{900}{1+i} + 0$$
$$i_{2-1} = 12.5\%$$

7s.11 (c)

Chapter 8

8s.1 (b)

$$I = \$2{,}000{,}000$$
$$C' = \$200{,}000(P/A, 10\%, 8) = \$1{,}066{,}985$$
$$B = \$500{,}000(P/A, 10\%, 8) = \$2{,}667{,}463$$
$$\mathrm{BC}(6\%) = \frac{B}{I + C'} = \frac{\$2{,}667{,}463}{\$2{,}000{,}000 + \$1{,}066{,}985}$$
$$= 0.87 < 1\,(\text{not profitable yet})$$

8s.2 (c)

$$I = \$1{,}200{,}000 - \$50{,}000(P/F, 6\%, 25) = \$1{,}188{,}350$$
$$C' = \$100{,}000(P/A, 6\%, 25) = \$1{,}278{,}336$$
$$B = \$250{,}000(P/A, 6\%, 25) = \$3{,}195{,}839$$
$$\mathrm{BC}(6\%) = \frac{B}{I + C'} = \frac{\$3{,}195{,}839}{\$1{,}188{,}350 + \$1{,}278{,}336}$$
$$= 1.30$$

8s.3   (a)

Alternative	I	C'	B	B/C Ratio	PW(8%)
A1	$800,000	$985,056	$2,184,010	1.22	$398,954
A2	1,000,000	1,182,067	2,521,744	1.16	339,677
A2 – A1	$200,000	197,011	337,734	0.85	–$59,277

Clearly, A1 is a better choice. Even the B/C ratio for A1 happens to exceed that of A2; we should not select the project based on the magnitude of B/C ratio alone. We should apply the incremental analysis to select the correct alternative. Since $BC(8\%)_{A2-A1} = 0.85 < 1$, A1 is a better alternative. The answer is (a) because A1 is selected with a wrong reason.

8s.4   (b)

Both options are acceptable as their B/C ratios exceed 1. To find the correct alternative, apply the incremental analysis.

Alternative	$I + C'$	B	B/C Ratio	$PW = B - (I + C')$
Option 1	$9.3 million	$28.1 million	3.02	$18.8 million
Option 2	$14.7 million	$38.9 million	2.65	$24.2 million
2 – 1	$5.4 million	$10.80 million	2.00	$5.40 million

With $BC_{2-1} > 1$, Option 2 becomes the better choice.

8s.5   (b)

If there were no budget constraint, all projects would be selected. However, with the budget constraint, we may eliminate any dominated projects from the list. For example, when we compare I-A with II-B, both projects cost the same, but I-A brings in a larger benefit, so I-A dominates II-B. So, we can drop II-B from the list. When we compare I-B with III-B, both projects generate the same amount of benefit, but I-B costs more than III-B. So, we also drop I-B from the list. The nondominated set is (I-A, II-A, III-A, and III-B).

Location	Alternative	Benefit $(B - C')$	Cost (I)	B/C Ratio
I	I-A	$45	12	3.75
II	II-A	35	6	5.83
III	III-A	25	2	12.5
	III-B	30	7	4.29

The best combination is (I-A, II-A, III-B). It gives the total benefit in the amount of $110 million and costs just $25 million.

8s.6   (c)

Need to perform an incremental analysis – (A1-A2)

n	Project 1-2
0	–$36,500
1	$23,000
2	$23,000
ΔPI	1.09 > 1

Select A1.

8s.7 (a)

If $\text{IRR}_{B-A} > \text{MARR}$, select B. In this case, $\text{IRR}_{B-A} = 15.73\%$ Thus, if the airport's interest rate (MARR) is less than 15.73%, Vender B is preferred.

Chapter 9

9s.1 (c)

$$D_1 = D_2 = \frac{(\$50,000 - \$4,500)}{5} = \$9,100$$

$$B_2 = B_0 - D_1 - D_2 = \$50,000 - 2(\$9,100)$$
$$= \$50,000 - \$18,200 = \$31,800$$

9s.2 (b)

Step 1: Find the declining balance rate (α) to be used.

$$\alpha = 2\left(\frac{1}{5}\right) = 40\%$$

Step 2: Find the depreciation amount each year as follows.

$$D_1 = 0.4(\$50,000) = \$20,000$$
$$D_2 = 0.4(\$50,000 - D_1) = \$12,000$$

9s.3 (a)

$$\alpha = 2\left(\frac{1}{4}\right) = 50\%$$

$$D_1 = 0.5(\$45,000) = \$22,500$$
$$D_2 = 0.5(\$45,000 - D_1) = \$11,250$$
$$D_3 = 0.5(\$45,000 - D_1 - D_2) = \$5,625$$
$$B_3 = B_2 - D_3 = \$11,250 - \$5,625 = \$5,652 < S$$

Recalculated D_3 and B_3:

$$D_3 = \$1,250$$
$$B_3 = \$10,000$$

9s.4 (b)

$$\text{Depreciation rate} = \frac{\$20,000 - \$2,000}{200,000 \text{ miles}} = \$0.09 \text{ per mile}$$

9s.5 (a)

Depreciation base $= \$170,000 + \$30,000$
$$= \$200,000$$
$$B_4 = \$200,000 - (D_1 + D_2 + D_3 + D_4)$$
$$= \$200,000 - \$200,000(0.1429 + 0.2449 + 0.1749$$
$$+ 0.1249)$$
$$= \$62,480$$

9s.6 (d)

$$D_1 = \frac{\$200,000}{39}\left(\frac{11.5}{12}\right) = \$4,915$$

9s.7   (b)

$$\text{Book value for the traded-in asset} = \$144,000$$
$$\text{Implied salvage value} = \$180,000 - \$144,000 = \$36,000$$
$$\text{Unrecognized loss} = \$36,000 - \$21,000 = \$15,000$$
$$\text{New cost basis for the new asset} = \$200,000 + \$15,000 = \$215,000$$

9s.8   (c)

Tugboat Project	Tax Year 1
Operating revenue	$200,000
Operating expenses	84,000
Depreciation	4,000
Taxable income	112,000
Income taxes (30%)	33,600
Net income	$78,400

9s.9   (a)

$$\text{Net cash flow from operation} = \text{Net income} + \text{Depreciation}$$
$$= \$78,400 + \$4,000$$
$$= \$82,400$$

9s.10   (c)

The depreciation expense for year 5 will be zero because the asset would be fully depreciated by then. Therefore, the book value at year 5 will be zero as well. The entire $20,000 is treated as an ordinary income.

	Net Income
Revenue	$110,000
Salvage value	20,000
Expenses:	
O&M	X
Depreciation	0
Taxable income	$\$130,000 - X$
Income taxes	$\$52,000 - 0.4X$
Net income	$\$78,000 - 0.6X$
Net cash flow	$30,000

Note that the net cash flow is obtained by adding the noncash expenses (depreciation) to net income,

$$\$30,000 = \$78,000 - 0.6X + \text{Depreciation}\,(\$0)$$
$$X = \$80,000$$

9s.11 (a)

$$\text{Total depreciation} = \$80,000\underbrace{\left(0.20 + 0.32 + \frac{0.192}{2}\right)}_{0.616} = \$49,280$$

$$\text{Book value} = \$80,000 - \$49,280 = \$30,720$$
$$\text{Taxable gains} = \$42,000 - \$30,720 = \$11,280$$

Chapter 10

10s.1 (c)

Revenue	$100,000
Expenses	40,000
Depreciation	6,000
Taxable income	$ 54,000

	Before Project	After Project	Due to Project
Taxable income	$320,000	$374,000	$54,000
Income taxes	108,050	127,160	19,110
Tax rate	33.77%	34%	35.39%

10s.2 (a)

	Year 10
Income Statement	
Revenue	$150,000
Expenses:	
O&M cost	$50,000
Depreciation	0
Taxable income	$100,000
Income taxes (40%)	$40,000
Net income	$60,000
Cash Flow Statement	
Cash flow from operation:	
Net income	$60,0000
Depreciation	0
Cash flow from investing:	
Investment	
Salvage value	$15,000
Gains taxes	(6,000)
Net cash flow	$69,000

10s.3   (d)

	Year 10
Income Statement	
Revenue	$150,000
Expenses:	
O&M cost	$50,000
Depreciation	0
Debt interest	1,480
Taxable income	$98,520
Income taxes (40%)	$39,408
Net income	$59,112
Cash Flow Statement	
Cash flow from operation:	
Net income	$59,112
Depreciation	0
Cash flow from investing:	
Investment	
Salvage value	$15,000
Gains taxes	(6,000)
Cash flow from financing:	
Principal repayment	($14.795)
Net cash flow	$53,317

10s.4   (b)

MACRS-7	14.29%	24.49%	17.49%	12.49%	8.93%	8.92%		
	0	**1**	**2**	**3**	**4**	**5**	**6**	**...11**	**12**
Income Statement								
Revenue		$52,500	$52,500	$52,500	$52,500	$52,500	$52,500	$52,500	$52,500
Depreciation		$51,444	$88,164	$62,964	$44,964	$32,148	$32,112	$0	$0
Taxable Income		$1,056	($35,664)	($10,464)	$7,536	$20,352	$20,388	$52,500	$52,500
Income Taxes (40%)		$422	($14,266)	($4,186)	$3,014	$8,141	$8,155	$21,000	$21,000
Net Income		$634	($21,398)	($6,278)	$4,522	$12,211	$12,233	$31,500	$31,500
Cash Flow Statement								
Operating Activities:								
Net Income		$634	($21,398)	($6,278)	$4,522	$12,211	$12,233	$31,500	$31,500
Depreciation		$51,444	$88,164	$62,964	$44,964	$32,148	$32,112	$0	$0

(*continued*)

(Continued)	0	1	2	3	4	5	6	...11	12
Investment	($360,000)								$20,000
Gain Tax									($8,000)
Net Cash Flow	($360,000)	$52,078	$66,766	$56,686	$49,486	$44,359	$44,345	$31,500	$43,500
PW(15%)	($63,739)								

10s.5 (b)

$$PW(14\%) = -\$120,000 + (X - 20,000)(P/A, 14\%, 4)$$
$$= -\$120,000 + 2.9137X - \$58,274 = 0$$
$$2.9137X = \$178,274$$
$$X = \$61,184$$

10s.6 (a)

	0	1	2	3	4	5
Income Statement						
Savings		$200,000	$200,000	$200,000	$200,000	$200,000
Depreciation		$25,000	$25,000	$25,000	$25,000	$25,000
O&M		$80,000	$80,000	$80,000	$80,000	$80,000
Taxable Income		$95,000	$95,000	$95,000	$95,000	$95,000
Income Taxes (40%)		$38,000	$38,000	$38,000	$38,000	$38,000
Net Income		$57,000	$57,000	$57,000	$57,000	$57,000
Cash Flow Statement						
Net Income		$57,000	$57,000	$57,000	$57,000	$57,000
Depreciation		$25,000	$25,000	$25,000	$25,000	$25,000
Investment/Salvage	($150,000)					$25,000
Gains Tax						$0
Net Cash Flow	($150,000)	$82,000	$82,000	$82,000	$82,000	$107,000
PW (15%)=		$137,306				

10s.7 (a)

The correct answer is (a). Under the inflationary economy, lenders will normally charge a higher interest rate to protect them from loss in purchasing power.

10s.8 (c)

	0	1	2	3	4	5	6
Income Statement							
Operating Revenues		$15,000	$15,000	$15,000	$15,000	$15,000	$15,000
Depreciation		$4,000	$6,400	$3,840	$2,304	$2,304	$1,152
Operating Expenses		$4,000	$4,000	$4,000	$4,000	$4,000	$4,000

	0	1	2	3	4	5	6
Taxable Income		$7,000	$4,600	$7,160	$8,696	$8,696	$9,848
Income Taxes (40%)		$2,800	$1,840	$2,864	$3,478	$3,478	$3,939
Net Income		$4,200	$2,760	$4,296	$5,218	$5,218	$5,909
Cash Flow Statement							
Net Income		$4,200	$2,760	$4,296	$5,218	$5,218	$5,909
Depreciation		$4,000	$6,400	$3,840	$2,304	$2,304	$1,152
Investment/Salvage	($20,000)						$5,000
Gains Tax							($2,000)
Net Cash Flow	($20,000)	$8,200	$9,160	$8,136	$7,522	$7,522	$10,061
PW (15%)=		$11,796					
IRR=		35%					

10s.9   (a)

Income Statement		20%	32%	9.60%			
	0	1	2	3	4	5	6
Income Statement							
Saving		$12,500	$12,500	$12,500	$12,500	$12,500	$12,500
Depreciation		$2,400	$3,840	$1,152	$2,400	$3,840	$1,152
O&M		$2,500	$2,500	$2,500	$2,500	$2,500	$2,500
Taxable Income		$7,600	$6,160	$8,848	$7,600	$6,160	$8,848
Income Taxes (40%)		$3,040	$2,464	$3,539	$3,040	$2,464	$3,539
Net Income		$4,560	$3,696	$5,309	$4,560	$3,696	$5,309
Cash Flow Statement							
Net Income		$4,560	$3,696	$5,309	$4,560	$3,696	$5,309
Depreciation		$2,400	$3,840	$1,152	$2,400	$3,840	$1,152
Investment/Salvage	($12,000)			$3,000			$3,000
Gains Tax				$643			$643
		First Cycle		($12,000)		Second Cycle	
Net Cash Flow	($12,000)	$6,960	$7,536	($1,896)	$6,960	$7,536	$10,104
PW (15%)=		$10,598 for two cycles					
PW (15%)=		$6,394 for the first cycle					

10s.10 (b)

10s.11 (d)

	0	1	2	3
Income Statement				
Savings		$45,000	$45,000	$45,000
Depreciation		20,000	32,000	9,600
Taxable Income		$25,000	$13,000	$35,400
Income Taxes (40%)		$10,000	$5,200	$14,160
Net Income		$15,000	$7,800	$21,240
Cash Flow Statement				
Net Income		$15,000	$7,800	$21,240
Depreciation		$20,000	$32,000	$9,600
Investment/Salvage	($100,000)			$30,000
Gains Tax				$3,360
Net Cash Flow	($100,000)	$35,000	$39,800	$64,200
PW (15%)=		$2,742		

10s.12 (a)

$$\text{Total depreciation: } \$6,666 + \$4,445 = \$11,111$$
$$BV = \$20,000 - \$11,111 = \$8,889$$
$$\text{Taxable gains (Gains)} = \$8,989 - \$8,889 = \$100$$
$$\text{Gain credit} = \$100 \times 0.40 = (\$40)$$
$$\text{Loan repayment schedule: } A = \$10,000\,(A/P, 10\%, 2) = \$5,761.90$$

	Inflation Rate	0	1	2
Income Statement				
Saving	6%		$31,800	$33,708
O&M	6%		$5,300	$5,618
Depreciation			6,666	4,445
Debt Interest			1,000	524
Taxable Income			$18,834	$23,121
Income Taxes (40%)			$7,534	$9,248
Net Income			$11,300	$13,873

Cash Flow Statement	Inflation Rate	0	1	2
Net Income			$11,300	$13,873
Depreciation			$6,666	$4,445
Investment/Salvage	6%	($20,000)		$8,989
Gains Tax				($40)
Borrowed Fund/Principal Payment		$10,000	($4,762)	($5,238)
Net Cash Flow		($10,000)	$13,204	$22,028
		PW (20%)=	$16,301	

Chapter 11

11s.1   (d)

$$X = \$20 \quad X \rightarrow \$22\,(\text{or } \Delta = \$2)$$
$$Y = \$10$$
$$\text{PW}_{\text{base}} = 10{,}450\,(2 \times 20 - 10) - 7890 = \$305{,}610$$
$$\text{PW}_{\Delta=10\%} = 10{,}450\,(2 \times 22 - 10) - 7890 = \$347{,}410$$
$$\Delta = \frac{347{,}410 - 305{,}610}{305{,}610} = 13.68\%$$

11s.2   (b)

$$\begin{aligned}
\text{PW}(15\%) &= -\$1{,}000 + \$100\,(1 - 0.30)(P/A,\, 15\%,\, 7)(P/F,\, 15\%,\, 3) \\
&\quad + \big[X - (X - 1{,}000)0.2\big](P/F,\, 15\%,\, 5) \\
&= -\$1{,}000 + \$191.49 + 0.0983X + \$24.58 \\
&= 0 \\
0.0983X &= \$784.12 \\
X &= \$7{,}977
\end{aligned}$$

11s.3   (d)

- Option 1: Reimbursement plan

$$\text{PW}(15\%)_{\text{Option 1}} = 0.25X(1 - 0.40)(P/A,\, 15\%,\, 5) = 0.5028X$$

- Option 2: Plan for owning and operating a vehicle

$$\begin{aligned}
\text{PW}(15\%)_{\text{Option 2}} &= \$12{,}000 + (960 + 0.15X)(1 - 0.4)(P/A,\, 15\%,\, 5) \\
&\quad - 0.4(\$12{,}000)\big[0.20(P/F,\, 15\%,\, 1) + 0.32(P/F,\, 15\%,\, 2) \\
&\quad + 0.1920(P/F,\, 15\%,\, 3) + 0.1152(P/F,\, 15\%,\, 4) \\
&\quad + (0.5)(0.1152)(P/F,\, 15\%,\, 5)\big] \\
&\quad - \big[\$3{,}500 - (\$3{,}500 - \$1{,}382)(0.4)\big](P/F,\, 15\%,\, 5) \\
&= \$9{,}556 + 0.3017X
\end{aligned}$$

- Break-even value (X)

$$0.5028X = \$9{,}556 + 0.3017X$$
$$X = 47{,}518 \text{ miles}$$

11s.4 (b)

$$\text{PW}(10\%) = -\$250{,}000 + (2X - 25{,}000)(P/A, 10\%, 7)$$
$$\Rightarrow (2X - 25{,}000)(4.8648) = 0$$
$$\therefore X = 38{,}194.8 \text{ parts}$$

11s.5 (d)

$$E(X) = \sum_{i=1}^{N} x_i \cdot p_i$$

11s.6 (c)

$$V(X) = E[X - E(X)]^2$$

11s.7 (c)

$$E[\text{PW}(10\%)] = -\$4 + \$2(P/A, 10\%, 5) + \$1(P/F, 10\%, 5)$$
$$= \$4.20$$

11s.8 (d)

$$\text{Var}[\text{PW}(10\%)] = \frac{0.4^2}{(1+0.10)^2} + \frac{0.4^2}{(1+0.10)^4} + \frac{0.4^2}{(1+0.10)^6} + \frac{0.4^2}{(1+0.10)^8}$$
$$+ \frac{0.4^2 + 0.3^2}{(1 + 0.10)^{10}}$$
$$= 0.502856$$
$$\sigma = \sqrt{0.502856}$$
$$= \$0.7091$$

Note: Mean and variance calculation. For a random variable Y, which can be expressed as a linear function of another random variable X (say, $Y = aX$, where a is a constant), the variance of Y can be calculated as a function of variance of X, $\text{Var}[Y] = a^2\text{Var}[X]$.

11s.9 (c)

$$\text{PW}(15\%) = -\$4 + \$2(P/A, 15\%, 5) + \$1(P/F, 15\%, 5)$$
$$= \$3.2015$$

11s.10 (d)

- Mean of PW

$$\text{Var}[Y] = \text{Var}[2X - 11] = 2^2\text{Var}[X] = 4(33) = 132$$
$$E[\text{PW}] = E[40.28WY - 77{,}860]$$
$$= 40.28E[W]E[Y] - 77{,}860$$
$$= \$6{,}830{,}160$$

- Variance of PW

$$\mathrm{Var}[PW] = \mathrm{Var}[40.28WY - 77{,}860]$$
$$= 40.28^2\mathrm{Var}[WY]$$
$$= 40.28^2 E\{[WY - E(WY)]^2\}$$
$$= 40.28^2 E[(WY)^2] - [E(WY)]^2$$
$$= 40.28^2\{E(W^2)E(Y^2) - [E(W)E(Y)]^2\}$$

Knowing that $E(W^2) = \mathrm{Var}[W] + \{E[W]\}^2$ and $E(Y^2)$
$$= \mathrm{Var}[Y] + \{E[Y]\}^2$$

$$\mathrm{Var}[PW] = 40.28^2\{[E(W)]^2\mathrm{Var}[Y] + [E(Y)]^2\mathrm{Var}[W]$$
$$+ \mathrm{Var}[W]\mathrm{Var}[Y]\}$$
$$= 40.28^2\{(3500)^2(132) + (49)^2(2{,}083{,}333)$$
$$+ (2{,}083{,}333)(132)\}$$
$$= 40.28^2(6{,}894{,}082{,}489)$$
$$= 1.118549 \times 10^{13}$$
$$\sigma[PW] = \$3{,}344{,}473$$

11s.11   (c)

Event	(W,X)	Joint Probabilities	PW = 40.28W(2X − 11) − 77,860
1	(1000,20)	(0.4)(0.7) = 0.28	$1,090,260
2	(1000,40)	(0.4)(0.3) = 0.12	$2,701,460
3	(6000,20)	(0.6)(0.7) = 0.42	$6,930,860
4	(6000,40)	(0.6)(0.3) = 0.18	$16,598,060
		Σ = 1.00	E[PW] = $6,528,060

The probability that PW will exceed $6,000,000 is 0.60 (=0.42 + 0.18). In other words, only Events 3 and 4 will satisfy the statement.

Chapter 12

12s.1   (d)

$$\text{Gains tax} = (\text{Salvage value} - \text{Book value})(\text{Tax rate})$$
$$= (\$3{,}000 - \$0)(35\%) = \$1{,}050$$

12s.2   (b)

12s.3   (b)

$$\text{Sunk cost} = (\text{Initial cost} - \text{Current market value})$$
$$= (\$4{,}000 - \$2{,}500)$$
$$= \$1{,}500$$

12s.4 (c)

First cost for challenger $=$ Depreciation base $=$ \$12,000

12s.5 (d)

EOY	Incremental cash flow	Depreciation	Taxable income	ATCF
0	$-15,000 + 3,000$			
1	$-2,500 + 1,200$	1,500	$-2,800$	980
2	$-3,500 + 1,200$	2,600	$-4,900$	1,715
3	$-3,500 + 1,200$	2,600	$-4,900$	1,715

$$\text{AW of ATCF} = 980\,(A/F, 12\%, 1) + 1,715\,(A/F, 12\%, 2)$$
$$+ \ 1,715\,(A/F, 12\%, 3) = \$2,297.12$$

12s.6 (c)

n	Market Value (S_n)	Depreciation	O&M
0	\$15,000		
1	12,500	\$3,000	\$3,000
2	10,000	4,800	3,000
3	7,500	2,880	3,000
4	2,500	1,728	3,000
5	0	1,728	3,000
6	0	864	3,000

$$
\begin{aligned}
\text{PW}(15\%)_{N=2\,\text{years}} = {} & \$15,000 \\
& + (1 - 0.40)(\$3,000)(P/A, 15\%, 2) \\
& - 0.40[\$3,000\,(P/F, 15\%, 1) \\
& + (0.5)(\$4,800)(P/F, 15\%, 2)] \\
& - [\$10,000 - (\$10,000 - \$9,600)(0.40)](P/F, 15\%, 2) \\
= {} & \$8,717 \\
\text{AEC}(15\%)_{N=2\,\text{years}} = {} & \$8,717(A/P, 15\%, 2) \\
= {} & \$5,362
\end{aligned}
$$

Note that the book value of the asset at the end of year 2 is \$9,600. There will be taxable gains in the amount of \$400.

12s.7 (b)

Sample calculation: $n = 3$

$$\text{AEC}(12\%)_{n=3} = (\$14{,}000 - \$4{,}000)(A/P, 12\%, 3) + 0.12(\$4{,}000)$$
$$+ \left[\$3{,}400(P/F, 12\%, 1) + \$4{,}600(P/F, 12\%, 2)\right.$$
$$\left.+ \$5{,}800(P/F, 12\%, 3)\right](A/P, 12\%, 3)$$
$$= \$9{,}153$$

n	Market Value	O&M Costs	CR(12%)	OC(12%)	AEC(12%)
0	$14,000				
1	$8,000	$3,400	$7,680	$3,400	$11,080
2	$6,000	$4,600	$5,454	$3,966	$9,420
3	$4,000	$5,800	$4,643	$4,510	$9,153
4	$2,000	$7,200	$4,191	$5,072	$9,263
5	$0	$8,300	$3,884	$5,581	$9,464

12s.8 (c)

$$\text{PW}(12\%)_{n=0} = \frac{\$3{,}100}{0.12} = \$25{,}833$$
$$\text{PW}(12\%)_{n=1} = \left[\$3{,}000 + \$25{,}833\right](P/F, 12\%, 1)$$
$$= \$25{,}744$$
$$\text{PW}(12\%)_{n=2} = \$2{,}500(P/A, 12\%, 2) + \$25{,}833(P/F, 12\%, 2)$$
$$= \$24{,}819$$
$$\text{PW}(12\%)_{n=3} = \$3{,}200(P/A, 12\%, 3) + \$25{,}833(P/F, 12\%, 3)$$
$$= \$26{,}073$$

Keep the defender for two years and then replace it with the challenger.

Chapter 13

13s.1 (d)

[F] (a) The balance sheet statement summarizes how much the firm owns as well as owes for a *typical operating period*. (Note: a specified reporting period)

[F] (b) The income statement summarizes the net income produced by the corporation at a *specified reporting date*. (Note: a typical operating period)

[F] (c) The cash flow statement summarizes how the corporation generated cash during the operating period. *Note: It summarizes how the company generates its cash and where it spent during the reporting period.*

13s.2 (d)

13s.3 (c)

[T] (c) A high quick ratio is NOT always a good indication of a well-managed liquidity position. *Note: Excess cash resulting from poor management could produce a high quick ratio. Similarly, if accounts receivable are not collected promptly, this could also lead to a high quick ratio.*

13s.4 (c)

[F] (a) A decline in inventory turnover ratio suggests that the firm's liquidity position is improving. *Note: A decline in inventory turnover ratio indicates that it takes longer to liquidate inventory.*
[F] (b) The profit margin on sales is calculated by dividing net *operating income* by sales
(Note: Net income rather than operating income)

13s.5 (d)

Statement (a) is just the reverse of what actually occurs. Firms with high profit margins have low turnover ratios and vice versa. Statement (b) is false, as excess cash resulting from poor management could produce a high quick ratio. Statement (c) is also false, as two firms with the same EBIT do not necessarily have the same total assets. Statement (d) is correct—whenever the same amount of reduction in the numerator and denominator, the ratio is increasing.

13s.6 (a)

$$\text{Average collection period} = \frac{A/R}{\text{Annual sales}/365}$$

$$= \frac{A/R}{\$1,200/365}$$

$$= 45 \text{ days}$$

$$A/R = 45(1200/365) = \$147.95$$

13s.7 (d)

$$\text{Current assets} = \text{Cash and marketable securities} + A/R + \text{Inventory}$$

$$= \$100 + 148 + \$180 = \$428$$

13s.8 (b)

$$\text{Current ratio} = \frac{\text{Current assets}}{\text{Current liabilities}} = \frac{\$428}{\text{Current liabilities}} = 3.2$$

$$\text{Current liabilities} = \$428/3.2 = \$134$$

13s.9 (d)

$$\text{Total assets} = \text{Current assets} + \text{Fixed assets} = \$428 + \$280$$

$$= \$708$$

13s.10   (c)

$$\text{Total assets} = \text{Current assets} + \text{Fixed assets} = \$428 + \$280$$
$$= \$708$$
$$\text{Total assets} = \text{Common equity} + \text{Current liabilities} + \text{Long-term debt}$$
$$\$708 = \$500 + \$134 + \text{Long-term liabilities}$$
$$\text{Long-term liabilities} = \$74$$

13s.11   (b)

$$\text{Profit margin} = \frac{\text{Net income}}{\text{Net sales}} = \frac{\$358}{\$1,200} = 30\%$$

13s.12   (a)

$$\text{Current ratio} = \frac{\text{Current assets}}{\text{Current liabilities}} = \frac{\$1,750}{\$1,040} = 1.68$$

$$\text{Quick ratio} = \frac{\text{Current assets} - \text{Inventory}}{\text{Current liabilities}} = \frac{\$1,750 - \$790}{\$1,040} = 0.92$$

13s.13   (b)

$$\text{Debt ratio} = \frac{\text{Total debt}}{\text{Total assets}} = \frac{\$\$1,620}{\$2,950} = 0.55$$

$$\text{Times-interest-earned ratio} = \frac{\text{EBIT}}{\text{Interest expense}} = \frac{\$640 + \$25}{\$25} = 26.60$$

13s.14   (a)

$$\text{Inventory-turnover ratio} = \frac{\text{Sales}}{\text{Average inventory}} = \frac{\$2,450}{(\$790 + \$550)/2}$$
$$= 3.66 \text{ times}$$

$$\text{Total-assets-turnover ratio} = \frac{\text{Sales}}{\text{Total assets}} = \frac{\$2,450}{\$\$2,950} = 0.83 \text{ times}$$

$$\text{Days sales outstanding} = \frac{\text{Accounts receivable}}{\text{Average sales per day}} = \frac{\$560}{\$2,450/365}$$
$$= 83.43 \text{days}$$

13s.15   (b)

$$\text{Profit margin on sales} = \frac{\text{Net income}}{\text{Sales}} = \frac{\$369}{\$2,450} = 15\%$$

$$\text{Return on total assets} = \frac{\text{Net income} + \text{Interest expense}\,(1 - \text{Tax rate})}{\text{Average total assets}}$$
$$= \frac{\$369 + \$25(1 - 0.40)}{(\$2,510 + \$2,950)/2} = 14\%$$

$$\text{Return on equity} = \frac{\text{Net income}}{\text{Average common equity}}$$

$$= \frac{\$369}{(\$1,330 + \$1,220)/2} = 29\%$$

13s.16 (c)

$$\text{P/E ratio} = \frac{\text{Market price per share}}{\text{Earning per share}} = \frac{\$35}{\$369/100} = 9.49$$

$$\text{Book value} = \frac{\text{Total stockholders' equity} - \text{Preferred stock}}{\text{Shares outstanding}}$$

$$= \frac{\$1,330 - 0}{100} = \$13.30$$

$$\text{Market/BV} = \frac{\$35 \text{ per share}}{\$13.30 \text{ per share}} = 2.63$$

13s.17 (b)

$$\text{Current ratio before action} = 1.68$$

$$\text{Current ratio after action} = \frac{\$1,750 - \$350}{\$1,040 - \$350} = 2.03$$

13s.18 (c)

$$\text{Current ratio before action} = 1.68$$

$$\text{Current ratio after action} = \frac{\$1,750 - \$350}{\$1,040} = 1.35$$

Interest Factors for Discrete Compounding

0.25%

	Single Payment		Equal Payment Series				Gradient Series		
	Compound Amount Factor	Present Worth Factor	Compound Amount Factor	Sinking Fund Factor	Present Worth Factor	Capital Recovery Factor	Gradient Uniform Series	Gradient Present Worth	
N	(F/P,i,N)	(P/F,i,N)	(F/A,i,N)	(A/F,i,N)	(P/A,i,N)	(A/P,i,N)	(A/G,i,N)	(P/G,i,N)	N
1	1.0025	0.9975	1.0000	1.0000	0.9975	1.0025	0.0000	0.0000	1
2	1.0050	0.9950	2.0025	0.4994	1.9925	0.5019	0.4994	0.9950	2
3	1.0075	0.9925	3.0075	0.3325	2.9851	0.3350	0.9983	2.9801	3
4	1.0100	0.9901	4.0150	0.2491	3.9751	0.2516	1.4969	5.9503	4
5	1.0126	0.9876	5.0251	0.1990	4.9627	0.2015	1.9950	9.9007	5
6	1.0151	0.9851	6.0376	0.1656	5.9478	0.1681	2.4927	14.8263	6
7	1.0176	0.9827	7.0527	0.1418	6.9305	0.1443	2.9900	20.7223	7
8	1.0202	0.9802	8.0704	0.1239	7.9107	0.1264	3.4869	27.5839	8
9	1.0227	0.9778	9.0905	0.1100	8.8885	0.1125	3.9834	35.4061	9
10	1.0253	0.9753	10.1133	0.0989	9.8639	0.1014	4.4794	44.1842	10
11	1.0278	0.9729	11.1385	0.0898	10.8368	0.0923	4.9750	53.9133	11
12	1.0304	0.9705	12.1664	0.0822	11.8073	0.0847	5.4702	64.5886	12
13	1.0330	0.9681	13.1968	0.0758	12.7753	0.0783	5.9650	76.2053	13
14	1.0356	0.9656	14.2298	0.0703	13.7410	0.0728	6.4594	88.7587	14
15	1.0382	0.9632	15.2654	0.0655	14.7042	0.0680	6.9534	102.2441	15
16	1.0408	0.9608	16.3035	0.0613	15.6650	0.0638	7.4469	116.6567	16
17	1.0434	0.9584	17.3443	0.0577	16.6235	0.0602	7.9401	131.9917	17
18	1.0460	0.9561	18.3876	0.0544	17.5795	0.0569	8.4328	148.2446	18
19	1.0486	0.9537	19.4336	0.0515	18.5332	0.0540	8.9251	165.4106	19
20	1.0512	0.9513	20.4822	0.0488	19.4845	0.0513	9.4170	183.4851	20
21	1.0538	0.9489	21.5334	0.0464	20.4334	0.0489	9.9085	202.4634	21
22	1.0565	0.9466	22.5872	0.0443	21.3800	0.0468	10.3995	222.3410	22
23	1.0591	0.9442	23.6437	0.0423	22.3241	0.0448	10.8901	243.1131	23
24	1.0618	0.9418	24.7028	0.0405	23.2660	0.0430	11.3804	264.7753	24
25	1.0644	0.9395	25.7646	0.0388	24.2055	0.0413	11.8702	287.3230	25
26	1.0671	0.9371	26.8290	0.0373	25.1426	0.0398	12.3596	310.7516	26
27	1.0697	0.9348	27.8961	0.0358	26.0774	0.0383	12.8485	335.0566	27
28	1.0724	0.9325	28.9658	0.0345	27.0099	0.0370	13.3371	360.2334	28
29	1.0751	0.9301	30.0382	0.0333	27.9400	0.0358	13.8252	386.2776	29
30	1.0778	0.9278	31.1133	0.0321	28.8679	0.0346	14.3130	413.1847	30
31	1.0805	0.9255	32.1911	0.0311	29.7934	0.0336	14.8003	440.9502	31
32	1.0832	0.9232	33.2716	0.0301	30.7166	0.0326	15.2872	469.5696	32
33	1.0859	0.9209	34.3547	0.0291	31.6375	0.0316	15.7736	499.0386	33
34	1.0886	0.9186	35.4406	0.0282	32.5561	0.0307	16.2597	529.3528	34
35	1.0913	0.9163	36.5292	0.0274	33.4724	0.0299	16.7454	560.5076	35
36	1.0941	0.9140	37.6206	0.0266	34.3865	0.0291	17.2306	592.4988	36
40	1.1050	0.9050	42.0132	0.0238	38.0199	0.0263	19.1673	728.7399	40
48	1.1273	0.8871	50.9312	0.0196	45.1787	0.0221	23.0209	1040.0552	48
50	1.1330	0.8826	53.1887	0.0188	46.9462	0.0213	23.9802	1125.7767	50
60	1.1616	0.8609	64.6467	0.0155	55.6524	0.0180	28.7514	1600.0845	60
72	1.1969	0.8355	78.7794	0.0127	65.8169	0.0152	34.4221	2265.5569	72
80	1.2211	0.8189	88.4392	0.0113	72.4260	0.0138	38.1694	2764.4568	80
84	1.2334	0.8108	93.3419	0.0107	75.6813	0.0132	40.0331	3029.7592	84
90	1.2520	0.7987	100.7885	0.0099	80.5038	0.0124	42.8162	3446.8700	90
96	1.2709	0.7869	108.3474	0.0092	85.2546	0.0117	45.5844	3886.2832	96
100	1.2836	0.7790	113.4500	0.0088	88.3825	0.0113	47.4216	4191.2417	100
108	1.3095	0.7636	123.8093	0.0081	94.5453	0.0106	51.0762	4829.0125	108
120	1.3494	0.7411	139.7414	0.0072	103.5618	0.0097	56.5084	5852.1116	120
240	1.8208	0.5492	328.3020	0.0030	180.3109	0.0055	107.5863	19398.9852	240
360	2.4568	0.4070	582.7369	0.0017	237.1894	0.0042	152.8902	36263.9299	360

0.50%

| | Single Payment | | Equal Payment Series | | | | Gradient Series | | |
| | Compound Amount Factor | Present Worth Factor | Compound Amount Factor | Sinking Fund Factor | Present Worth Factor | Capital Recovery Factor | Gradient Uniform Series | Gradient Present Worth | |
N	(F/P,i,N)	(P/F,i,N)	(F/A,i,N)	(A/F,i,N)	(P/A,i,N)	(A/P,i,N)	(A/G,i,N)	(P/G,i,N)	N
1	1.0050	0.9950	1.0000	1.0000	0.9950	1.0050	0.0000	0.0000	1
2	1.0100	0.9901	2.0050	0.4988	1.9851	0.5038	0.4988	0.9901	2
3	1.0151	0.9851	3.0150	0.3317	2.9702	0.3367	0.9967	2.9604	3
4	1.0202	0.9802	4.0301	0.2481	3.9505	0.2531	1.4938	5.9011	4
5	1.0253	0.9754	5.0503	0.1980	4.9259	0.2030	1.9900	9.8026	5
6	1.0304	0.9705	6.0755	0.1646	5.8964	0.1696	2.4855	14.6552	6
7	1.0355	0.9657	7.1059	0.1407	6.8621	0.1457	2.9801	20.4493	7
8	1.0407	0.9609	8.1414	0.1228	7.8230	0.1278	3.4738	27.1755	8
9	1.0459	0.9561	9.1821	0.1089	8.7791	0.1139	3.9668	34.8244	9
10	1.0511	0.9513	10.2280	0.0978	9.7304	0.1028	4.4589	43.3865	10
11	1.0564	0.9466	11.2792	0.0887	10.6770	0.0937	4.9501	52.8526	11
12	1.0617	0.9419	12.3356	0.0811	11.6189	0.0861	5.4406	63.2136	12
13	1.0670	0.9372	13.3972	0.0746	12.5562	0.0796	5.9302	74.4602	13
14	1.0723	0.9326	14.4642	0.0691	13.4887	0.0741	6.4190	86.5835	14
15	1.0777	0.9279	15.5365	0.0644	14.4166	0.0694	6.9069	99.5743	15
16	1.0831	0.9233	16.6142	0.0602	15.3399	0.0652	7.3940	113.4238	16
17	1.0885	0.9187	17.6973	0.0565	16.2586	0.0615	7.8803	128.1231	17
18	1.0939	0.9141	18.7858	0.0532	17.1728	0.0582	8.3658	143.6634	18
19	1.0994	0.9096	19.8797	0.0503	18.0824	0.0553	8.8504	160.0360	19
20	1.1049	0.9051	20.9791	0.0477	18.9874	0.0527	9.3342	177.2322	20
21	1.1104	0.9006	22.0840	0.0453	19.8880	0.0503	9.8172	195.2434	21
22	1.1160	0.8961	23.1944	0.0431	20.7841	0.0481	10.2993	214.0611	22
23	1.1216	0.8916	24.3104	0.0411	21.6757	0.0461	10.7806	233.6768	23
24	1.1272	0.8872	25.4320	0.0393	22.5629	0.0443	11.2611	254.0820	24
25	1.1328	0.8828	26.5591	0.0377	23.4456	0.0427	11.7407	275.2686	25
26	1.1385	0.8784	27.6919	0.0361	24.3240	0.0411	12.2195	297.2281	26
27	1.1442	0.8740	28.8304	0.0347	25.1980	0.0397	12.6975	319.9523	27
28	1.1499	0.8697	29.9745	0.0334	26.0677	0.0384	13.1747	343.4332	28
29	1.1556	0.8653	31.1244	0.0321	26.9330	0.0371	13.6510	367.6625	29
30	1.1614	0.8610	32.2800	0.0310	27.7941	0.0360	14.1265	392.6324	30
31	1.1672	0.8567	33.4414	0.0299	28.6508	0.0349	14.6012	418.3348	31
32	1.1730	0.8525	34.6086	0.0289	29.5033	0.0339	15.0750	444.7618	32
33	1.1789	0.8482	35.7817	0.0279	30.3515	0.0329	15.5480	471.9055	33
34	1.1848	0.8440	36.9606	0.0271	31.1955	0.0321	16.0202	499.7583	34
35	1.1907	0.8398	38.1454	0.0262	32.0354	0.0312	16.4915	528.3123	35
36	1.1967	0.8356	39.3361	0.0254	32.8710	0.0304	16.9621	557.5598	36
40	1.2208	0.8191	44.1588	0.0226	36.1722	0.0276	18.8359	681.3347	40
48	1.2705	0.7871	54.0978	0.0185	42.5803	0.0235	22.5437	959.9188	48
50	1.2832	0.7793	56.6452	0.0177	44.1428	0.0227	23.4624	1035.6966	50
60	1.3489	0.7414	69.7700	0.0143	51.7256	0.0193	28.0064	1448.6458	60
72	1.4320	0.6983	86.4089	0.0116	60.3395	0.0166	33.3504	2012.3478	72
80	1.4903	0.6710	98.0677	0.0102	65.8023	0.0152	36.8474	2424.6455	80
84	1.5204	0.6577	104.0739	0.0096	68.4530	0.0146	38.5763	2640.6641	84
90	1.5666	0.6383	113.3109	0.0088	72.3313	0.0138	41.1451	2976.0769	90
96	1.6141	0.6195	122.8285	0.0081	76.0952	0.0131	43.6845	3324.1846	96
100	1.6467	0.6073	129.3337	0.0077	78.5426	0.0127	45.3613	3562.7934	100
108	1.7137	0.5835	142.7399	0.0070	83.2934	0.0120	48.6758	4054.3747	108
120	1.8194	0.5496	163.8793	0.0061	90.0735	0.0111	53.5508	4823.5051	120
240	3.3102	0.3021	462.0409	0.0022	139.5808	0.0072	96.1131	13415.5395	240
360	6.0226	0.1660	1004.5150	0.0010	166.7916	0.0060	128.3236	21403.3041	360

0.75%

	Single Payment		Equal Payment Series				Gradient Series		
	Compound Amount Factor	Present Worth Factor	Compound Amount Factor	Sinking Fund Factor	Present Worth Factor	Capital Recovery Factor	Gradient Uniform Series	Gradient Present Worth	
N	$(F/P,i,N)$	$(P/F,i,N)$	$(F/A,i,N)$	$(A/F,i,N)$	$(P/A,i,N)$	$(A/P,i,N)$	$(A/G,i,N)$	$(P/G,i,N)$	N
1	1.0075	0.9926	1.0000	1.0000	0.9926	1.0075	0.0000	0.0000	1
2	1.0151	0.9852	2.0075	0.4981	1.9777	0.5056	0.4981	0.9852	2
3	1.0227	0.9778	3.0226	0.3308	2.9556	0.3383	0.9950	2.9408	3
4	1.0303	0.9706	4.0452	0.2472	3.9261	0.2547	1.4907	5.8525	4
5	1.0381	0.9633	5.0756	0.1970	4.8894	0.2045	1.9851	9.7058	5
6	1.0459	0.9562	6.1136	0.1636	5.8456	0.1711	2.4782	14.4866	6
7	1.0537	0.9490	7.1595	0.1397	6.7946	0.1472	2.9701	20.1808	7
8	1.0616	0.9420	8.2132	0.1218	7.7366	0.1293	3.4608	26.7747	8
9	1.0696	0.9350	9.2748	0.1078	8.6716	0.1153	3.9502	34.2544	9
10	1.0776	0.9280	10.3443	0.0967	9.5996	0.1042	4.4384	42.6064	10
11	1.0857	0.9211	11.4219	0.0876	10.5207	0.0951	4.9253	51.8174	11
12	1.0938	0.9142	12.5076	0.0800	11.4349	0.0875	5.4110	61.8740	12
13	1.1020	0.9074	13.6014	0.0735	12.3423	0.0810	5.8954	72.7632	13
14	1.1103	0.9007	14.7034	0.0680	13.2430	0.0755	6.3786	84.4720	14
15	1.1186	0.8940	15.8137	0.0632	14.1370	0.0707	6.8606	96.9876	15
16	1.1270	0.8873	16.9323	0.0591	15.0243	0.0666	7.3413	110.2973	16
17	1.1354	0.8807	18.0593	0.0554	15.9050	0.0629	7.8207	124.3887	17
18	1.1440	0.8742	19.1947	0.0521	16.7792	0.0596	8.2989	139.2494	18
19	1.1525	0.8676	20.3387	0.0492	17.6468	0.0567	8.7759	154.8671	19
20	1.1612	0.8612	21.4912	0.0465	18.5080	0.0540	9.2516	171.2297	20
21	1.1699	0.8548	22.6524	0.0441	19.3628	0.0516	9.7261	188.3253	21
22	1.1787	0.8484	23.8223	0.0420	20.2112	0.0495	10.1994	206.1420	22
23	1.1875	0.8421	25.0010	0.0400	21.0533	0.0475	10.6714	224.6682	23
24	1.1964	0.8358	26.1885	0.0382	21.8891	0.0457	11.1422	243.8923	24
25	1.2054	0.8296	27.3849	0.0365	22.7188	0.0440	11.6117	263.8029	25
26	1.2144	0.8234	28.5903	0.0350	23.5422	0.0425	12.0800	284.3888	26
27	1.2235	0.8173	29.8047	0.0336	24.3595	0.0411	12.5470	305.6387	27
28	1.2327	0.8112	31.0282	0.0322	25.1707	0.0397	13.0128	327.5416	28
29	1.2420	0.8052	32.2609	0.0310	25.9759	0.0385	13.4774	350.0867	29
30	1.2513	0.7992	33.5029	0.0298	26.7751	0.0373	13.9407	373.2631	30
31	1.2607	0.7932	34.7542	0.0288	27.5683	0.0363	14.4028	397.0602	31
32	1.2701	0.7873	36.0148	0.0278	28.3557	0.0353	14.8636	421.4675	32
33	1.2796	0.7815	37.2849	0.0268	29.1371	0.0343	15.3232	446.4746	33
34	1.2892	0.7757	38.5646	0.0259	29.9128	0.0334	15.7816	472.0712	34
35	1.2989	0.7699	39.8538	0.0251	30.6827	0.0326	16.2387	498.2471	35
36	1.3086	0.7641	41.1527	0.0243	31.4468	0.0318	16.6946	524.9924	36
40	1.3483	0.7416	46.4465	0.0215	34.4469	0.0290	18.5058	637.4693	40
48	1.4314	0.6986	57.5207	0.0174	40.1848	0.0249	22.0691	886.8404	48
50	1.4530	0.6883	60.3943	0.0166	41.5664	0.0241	22.9476	953.8486	50
60	1.5657	0.6387	75.4241	0.0133	48.1734	0.0208	27.2665	1313.5189	60
72	1.7126	0.5839	95.0070	0.0105	55.4768	0.0180	32.2882	1791.2463	72
80	1.8180	0.5500	109.0725	0.0092	59.9944	0.0167	35.5391	2132.1472	80
84	1.8732	0.5338	116.4269	0.0086	62.1540	0.0161	37.1357	2308.1283	84
90	1.9591	0.5104	127.8790	0.0078	65.2746	0.0153	39.4946	2577.9961	90
96	2.0489	0.4881	139.8562	0.0072	68.2584	0.0147	41.8107	2853.9352	96
100	2.1111	0.4737	148.1445	0.0068	70.1746	0.0143	43.3311	3040.7453	100
108	2.2411	0.4462	165.4832	0.0060	73.8394	0.0135	46.3154	3419.9041	108
120	2.4514	0.4079	193.5143	0.0052	78.9417	0.0127	50.6521	3998.5621	120
240	6.0092	0.1664	667.8869	0.0015	111.1450	0.0090	85.4210	9494.1162	240
360	14.7306	0.0679	1830.7435	0.0005	124.2819	0.0080	107.1145	13312.3871	360

1.0%

	Single Payment		Equal Payment Series				Gradient Series		
	Compound Amount Factor	Present Worth Factor	Compound Amount Factor	Sinking Fund Factor	Present Worth Factor	Capital Recovery Factor	Gradient Uniform Series	Gradient Present Worth	
N	(F/P,i,N)	(P/F,i,N)	(F/A,i,N)	(A/F,i,N)	(P/A,i,N)	(A/P,i,N)	(A/G,i,N)	(P/G,i,N)	N
1	1.0100	0.9901	1.0000	1.0000	0.9901	1.0100	0.0000	0.0000	1
2	1.0201	0.9803	2.0100	0.4975	1.9704	0.5075	0.4975	0.9803	2
3	1.0303	0.9706	3.0301	0.3300	2.9410	0.3400	0.9934	2.9215	3
4	1.0406	0.9610	4.0604	0.2463	3.9020	0.2563	1.4876	5.8044	4
5	1.0510	0.9515	5.1010	0.1960	4.8534	0.2060	1.9801	9.6103	5
6	1.0615	0.9420	6.1520	0.1625	5.7955	0.1725	2.4710	14.3205	6
7	1.0721	0.9327	7.2135	0.1386	6.7282	0.1486	2.9602	19.9168	7
8	1.0829	0.9235	8.2857	0.1207	7.6517	0.1307	3.4478	26.3812	8
9	1.0937	0.9143	9.3685	0.1067	8.5660	0.1167	3.9337	33.6959	9
10	1.1046	0.9053	10.4622	0.0956	9.4713	0.1056	4.4179	41.8435	10
11	1.1157	0.8963	11.5668	0.0865	10.3676	0.0965	4.9005	50.8067	11
12	1.1268	0.8874	12.6825	0.0788	11.2551	0.0888	5.3815	60.5687	12
13	1.1381	0.8787	13.8093	0.0724	12.1337	0.0824	5.8607	71.1126	13
14	1.1495	0.8700	14.9474	0.0669	13.0037	0.0769	6.3384	82.4221	14
15	1.1610	0.8613	16.0969	0.0621	13.8651	0.0721	6.8143	94.4810	15
16	1.1726	0.8528	17.2579	0.0579	14.7179	0.0679	7.2886	107.2734	16
17	1.1843	0.8444	18.4304	0.0543	15.5623	0.0643	7.7613	120.7834	17
18	1.1961	0.8360	19.6147	0.0510	16.3983	0.0610	8.2323	134.9957	18
19	1.2081	0.8277	20.8109	0.0481	17.2260	0.0581	8.7017	149.8950	19
20	1.2202	0.8195	22.0190	0.0454	18.0456	0.0554	9.1694	165.4664	20
21	1.2324	0.8114	23.2392	0.0430	18.8570	0.0530	9.6354	181.6950	21
22	1.2447	0.8034	24.4716	0.0409	19.6604	0.0509	10.0998	198.5663	22
23	1.2572	0.7954	25.7163	0.0389	20.4558	0.0489	10.5626	216.0660	23
24	1.2697	0.7876	26.9735	0.0371	21.2434	0.0471	11.0237	234.1800	24
25	1.2824	0.7798	28.2432	0.0354	22.0232	0.0454	11.4831	252.8945	25
26	1.2953	0.7720	29.5256	0.0339	22.7952	0.0439	11.9409	272.1957	26
27	1.3082	0.7644	30.8209	0.0324	23.5596	0.0424	12.3971	292.0702	27
28	1.3213	0.7568	32.1291	0.0311	24.3164	0.0411	12.8516	312.5047	28
29	1.3345	0.7493	33.4504	0.0299	25.0658	0.0399	13.3044	333.4863	29
30	1.3478	0.7419	34.7849	0.0287	25.8077	0.0387	13.7557	355.0021	30
31	1.3613	0.7346	36.1327	0.0277	26.5423	0.0377	14.2052	377.0394	31
32	1.3749	0.7273	37.4941	0.0267	27.2696	0.0367	14.6532	399.5858	32
33	1.3887	0.7201	38.8690	0.0257	27.9897	0.0357	15.0995	422.6291	33
34	1.4026	0.7130	40.2577	0.0248	28.7027	0.0348	15.5441	446.1572	34
35	1.4166	0.7059	41.6603	0.0240	29.4086	0.0340	15.9871	470.1583	35
36	1.4308	0.6989	43.0769	0.0232	30.1075	0.0332	16.4285	494.6207	36
40	1.4889	0.6717	48.8864	0.0205	32.8347	0.0305	18.1776	596.8561	40
48	1.6122	0.6203	61.2226	0.0163	37.9740	0.0263	21.5976	820.1460	48
50	1.6446	0.6080	64.4632	0.0155	39.1961	0.0255	22.4363	879.4176	50
60	1.8167	0.5504	81.6697	0.0122	44.9550	0.0222	26.5333	1192.8061	60
72	2.0471	0.4885	104.7099	0.0096	51.1504	0.0196	31.2386	1597.8673	72
80	2.2167	0.4511	121.6715	0.0082	54.8882	0.0182	34.2492	1879.8771	80
84	2.3067	0.4335	130.6723	0.0077	56.6485	0.0177	35.7170	2023.3153	84
90	2.4486	0.4084	144.8633	0.0069	59.1609	0.0169	37.8724	2240.5675	90
96	2.5993	0.3847	159.9273	0.0063	61.5277	0.0163	39.9727	2459.4298	96
100	2.7048	0.3697	170.4814	0.0059	63.0289	0.0159	41.3426	2605.7758	100
108	2.9289	0.3414	192.8926	0.0052	65.8578	0.0152	44.0103	2898.4203	108
120	3.3004	0.3030	230.0387	0.0043	69.7005	0.0143	47.8349	3334.1148	120
240	10.8926	0.0918	989.2554	0.0010	90.8194	0.0110	75.7393	6878.6016	240
360	35.9496	0.0278	3494.9641	0.0003	97.2183	0.0103	89.6995	8720.4323	360

1.25%

	Single Payment		Equal Payment Series				Gradient Series		
	Compound Amount Factor	Present Worth Factor	Compound Amount Factor	Sinking Fund Factor	Present Worth Factor	Capital Recovery Factor	Gradient Uniform Series	Gradient Present Worth	
N	$(F/P,i,N)$	$(P/F,i,N)$	$(F/A,i,N)$	$(A/F,i,N)$	$(P/A,i,N)$	$(A/P,i,N)$	$(A/G,i,N)$	$(P/G,i,N)$	N
1	1.0125	0.9877	1.0000	1.0000	0.9877	1.0125	0.0000	0.0000	1
2	1.0252	0.9755	2.0125	0.4969	1.9631	0.5094	0.4969	0.9755	2
3	1.0380	0.9634	3.0377	0.3292	2.9265	0.3417	0.9917	2.9023	3
4	1.0509	0.9515	4.0756	0.2454	3.8781	0.2579	1.4845	5.7569	4
5	1.0641	0.9398	5.1266	0.1951	4.8178	0.2076	1.9752	9.5160	5
6	1.0774	0.9282	6.1907	0.1615	5.7460	0.1740	2.4638	14.1569	6
7	1.0909	0.9167	7.2680	0.1376	6.6627	0.1501	2.9503	19.6571	7
8	1.1045	0.9054	8.3589	0.1196	7.5681	0.1321	3.4348	25.9949	8
9	1.1183	0.8942	9.4634	0.1057	8.4623	0.1182	3.9172	33.1487	9
10	1.1323	0.8832	10.5817	0.0945	9.3455	0.1070	4.3975	41.0973	10
11	1.1464	0.8723	11.7139	0.0854	10.2178	0.0979	4.8758	49.8201	11
12	1.1608	0.8615	12.8604	0.0778	11.0793	0.0903	5.3520	59.2967	12
13	1.1753	0.8509	14.0211	0.0713	11.9302	0.0838	5.8262	69.5072	13
14	1.1900	0.8404	15.1964	0.0658	12.7706	0.0783	6.2982	80.4320	14
15	1.2048	0.8300	16.3863	0.0610	13.6005	0.0735	6.7682	92.0519	15
16	1.2199	0.8197	17.5912	0.0568	14.4203	0.0693	7.2362	104.3481	16
17	1.2351	0.8096	18.8111	0.0532	15.2299	0.0657	7.7021	117.3021	17
18	1.2506	0.7996	20.0462	0.0499	16.0295	0.0624	8.1659	130.8958	18
19	1.2662	0.7898	21.2968	0.0470	16.8193	0.0595	8.6277	145.1115	19
20	1.2820	0.7800	22.5630	0.0443	17.5993	0.0568	9.0874	159.9316	20
21	1.2981	0.7704	23.8450	0.0419	18.3697	0.0544	9.5450	175.3392	21
22	1.3143	0.7609	25.1431	0.0398	19.1306	0.0523	10.0006	191.3174	22
23	1.3307	0.7515	26.4574	0.0378	19.8820	0.0503	10.4542	207.8499	23
24	1.3474	0.7422	27.7881	0.0360	20.6242	0.0485	10.9056	224.9204	24
25	1.3642	0.7330	29.1354	0.0343	21.3573	0.0468	11.3551	242.5132	25
26	1.3812	0.7240	30.4996	0.0328	22.0813	0.0453	11.8024	260.6128	26
27	1.3985	0.7150	31.8809	0.0314	22.7963	0.0439	12.2478	279.2040	27
28	1.4160	0.7062	33.2794	0.0300	23.5025	0.0425	12.6911	298.2719	28
29	1.4337	0.6975	34.6954	0.0288	24.2000	0.0413	13.1323	317.8019	29
30	1.4516	0.6889	36.1291	0.0277	24.8889	0.0402	13.5715	337.7797	30
31	1.4698	0.6804	37.5807	0.0266	25.5693	0.0391	14.0086	358.1912	31
32	1.4881	0.6720	39.0504	0.0256	26.2413	0.0381	14.4438	379.0227	32
33	1.5067	0.6637	40.5386	0.0247	26.9050	0.0372	14.8768	400.2607	33
34	1.5256	0.6555	42.0453	0.0238	27.5605	0.0363	15.3079	421.8920	34
35	1.5446	0.6474	43.5709	0.0230	28.2079	0.0355	15.7369	443.9037	35
36	1.5639	0.6394	45.1155	0.0222	28.8473	0.0347	16.1639	466.2830	36
40	1.6436	0.6084	51.4896	0.0194	31.3269	0.0319	17.8515	559.2320	40
48	1.8154	0.5509	65.2284	0.0153	35.9315	0.0278	21.1299	759.2296	48
50	1.8610	0.5373	68.8818	0.0145	37.0129	0.0270	21.9295	811.6738	50
60	2.1072	0.4746	88.5745	0.0113	42.0346	0.0238	25.8083	1084.8429	60
72	2.4459	0.4088	115.6736	0.0086	47.2925	0.0211	30.2047	1428.4561	72
80	2.7015	0.3702	136.1188	0.0073	50.3867	0.0198	32.9822	1661.8651	80
84	2.8391	0.3522	147.1290	0.0068	51.8222	0.0193	34.3258	1778.8384	84
90	3.0588	0.3269	164.7050	0.0061	53.8461	0.0186	36.2855	1953.8303	90
96	3.2955	0.3034	183.6411	0.0054	55.7246	0.0179	38.1793	2127.5244	96
100	3.4634	0.2887	197.0723	0.0051	56.9013	0.0176	39.4058	2242.2411	100
108	3.8253	0.2614	226.0226	0.0044	59.0865	0.0169	41.7737	2468.2636	108
120	4.4402	0.2252	275.2171	0.0036	61.9828	0.0161	45.1184	2796.5694	120
240	19.7155	0.0507	1497.2395	0.0007	75.9423	0.0132	67.1764	5101.5288	240
360	87.5410	0.0114	6923.2796	0.0001	79.0861	0.0126	75.8401	5997.9027	360

1.5%

	Single Payment		Equal Payment Series				Gradient Series		
N	Compound Amount Factor (F/P,i,N)	Present Worth Factor (P/F,i,N)	Compound Amount Factor (F/A,i,N)	Sinking Fund Factor (A/F,i,N)	Present Worth Factor (P/A,i,N)	Capital Recovery Factor (A/P,i,N)	Gradient Uniform Series (A/G,i,N)	Gradient Present Worth (P/G,i,N)	N
1	1.0150	0.9852	1.0000	1.0000	0.9852	1.0150	0.0000	0.0000	1
2	1.0302	0.9707	2.0150	0.4963	1.9559	0.5113	0.4963	0.9707	2
3	1.0457	0.9563	3.0452	0.3284	2.9122	0.3434	0.9901	2.8833	3
4	1.0614	0.9422	4.0909	0.2444	3.8544	0.2594	1.4814	5.7098	4
5	1.0773	0.9283	5.1523	0.1941	4.7826	0.2091	1.9702	9.4229	5
6	1.0934	0.9145	6.2296	0.1605	5.6972	0.1755	2.4566	13.9956	6
7	1.1098	0.9010	7.3230	0.1366	6.5982	0.1516	2.9405	19.4018	7
8	1.1265	0.8877	8.4328	0.1186	7.4859	0.1336	3.4219	25.6157	8
9	1.1434	0.8746	9.5593	0.1046	8.3605	0.1196	3.9008	32.6125	9
10	1.1605	0.8617	10.7027	0.0934	9.2222	0.1084	4.3772	40.3675	10
11	1.1779	0.8489	11.8633	0.0843	10.0711	0.0993	4.8512	48.8568	11
12	1.1956	0.8364	13.0412	0.0767	10.9075	0.0917	5.3227	58.0571	12
13	1.2136	0.8240	14.2368	0.0702	11.7315	0.0852	5.7917	67.9454	13
14	1.2318	0.8118	15.4504	0.0647	12.5434	0.0797	6.2582	78.4994	14
15	1.2502	0.7999	16.6821	0.0599	13.3432	0.0749	6.7223	89.6974	15
16	1.2690	0.7880	17.9324	0.0558	14.1313	0.0708	7.1839	101.5178	16
17	1.2880	0.7764	19.2014	0.0521	14.9076	0.0671	7.6431	113.9400	17
18	1.3073	0.7649	20.4894	0.0488	15.6726	0.0638	8.0997	126.9435	18
19	1.3270	0.7536	21.7967	0.0459	16.4262	0.0609	8.5539	140.5084	19
20	1.3469	0.7425	23.1237	0.0432	17.1686	0.0582	9.0057	154.6154	20
21	1.3671	0.7315	24.4705	0.0409	17.9001	0.0559	9.4550	169.2453	21
22	1.3876	0.7207	25.8376	0.0387	18.6208	0.0537	9.9018	184.3798	22
23	1.4084	0.7100	27.2251	0.0367	19.3309	0.0517	10.3462	200.0006	23
24	1.4295	0.6995	28.6335	0.0349	20.0304	0.0499	10.7881	216.0901	24
25	1.4509	0.6892	30.0630	0.0333	20.7196	0.0483	11.2276	232.6310	25
26	1.4727	0.6790	31.5140	0.0317	21.3986	0.0467	11.6646	249.6065	26
27	1.4948	0.6690	32.9867	0.0303	22.0676	0.0453	12.0992	267.0002	27
28	1.5172	0.6591	34.4815	0.0290	22.7267	0.0440	12.5313	284.7958	28
29	1.5400	0.6494	35.9987	0.0278	23.3761	0.0428	12.9610	302.9779	29
30	1.5631	0.6398	37.5387	0.0266	24.0158	0.0416	13.3883	321.5310	30
31	1.5865	0.6303	39.1018	0.0256	24.6461	0.0406	13.8131	340.4402	31
32	1.6103	0.6210	40.6883	0.0246	25.2671	0.0396	14.2355	359.6910	32
33	1.6345	0.6118	42.2986	0.0236	25.8790	0.0386	14.6555	379.2691	33
34	1.6590	0.6028	43.9331	0.0228	26.4817	0.0378	15.0731	399.1607	34
35	1.6839	0.5939	45.5921	0.0219	27.0756	0.0369	15.4882	419.3521	35
36	1.7091	0.5851	47.2760	0.0212	27.6607	0.0362	15.9009	439.8303	36
40	1.8140	0.5513	54.2679	0.0184	29.9158	0.0334	17.5277	524.3568	40
48	2.0435	0.4894	69.5652	0.0144	34.0426	0.0294	20.6667	703.5462	48
50	2.1052	0.4750	73.6828	0.0136	34.9997	0.0286	21.4277	749.9636	50
60	2.4432	0.4093	96.2147	0.0104	39.3803	0.0254	25.0930	988.1674	60
72	2.9212	0.3423	128.0772	0.0078	43.8447	0.0228	29.1893	1279.7938	72
80	3.2907	0.3039	152.7109	0.0065	46.4073	0.0215	31.7423	1473.0741	80
84	3.4926	0.2863	166.1726	0.0060	47.5786	0.0210	32.9668	1568.5140	84
90	3.8189	0.2619	187.9299	0.0053	49.2099	0.0203	34.7399	1709.5439	90
96	4.1758	0.2395	211.7202	0.0047	50.7017	0.0197	36.4381	1847.4725	96
100	4.4320	0.2256	228.8030	0.0044	51.6247	0.0194	37.5295	1937.4506	100
108	4.9927	0.2003	266.1778	0.0038	53.3137	0.0188	39.6171	2112.1348	108
120	5.9693	0.1675	331.2882	0.0030	55.4985	0.0180	42.5185	2359.7114	120
240	35.6328	0.0281	2308.8544	0.0004	64.7957	0.0154	59.7368	3870.6912	240
360	212.7038	0.0047	14113.5854	0.0001	66.3532	0.0151	64.9662	4310.7165	360

1.75%

	Single Payment		Equal Payment Series				Gradient Series		
	Compound Amount Factor	Present Worth Factor	Compound Amount Factor	Sinking Fund Factor	Present Worth Factor	Capital Recovery Factor	Gradient Uniform Series	Gradient Present Worth	
N	$(F/P,i,N)$	$(P/F,i,N)$	$(F/A,i,N)$	$(A/F,i,N)$	$(P/A,i,N)$	$(A/P,i,N)$	$(A/G,i,N)$	$(P/G,i,N)$	N
1	1.0175	0.9828	1.0000	1.0000	0.9828	1.0175	0.0000	0.0000	1
2	1.0353	0.9659	2.0175	0.4957	1.9487	0.5132	0.4957	0.9659	2
3	1.0534	0.9493	3.0528	0.3276	2.8980	0.3451	0.9884	2.8645	3
4	1.0719	0.9330	4.1062	0.2435	3.8309	0.2610	1.4783	5.6633	4
5	1.0906	0.9169	5.1781	0.1931	4.7479	0.2106	1.9653	9.3310	5
6	1.1097	0.9011	6.2687	0.1595	5.6490	0.1770	2.4494	13.8367	6
7	1.1291	0.8856	7.3784	0.1355	6.5346	0.1530	2.9306	19.1506	7
8	1.1489	0.8704	8.5075	0.1175	7.4051	0.1350	3.4089	25.2435	8
9	1.1690	0.8554	9.6564	0.1036	8.2605	0.1211	3.8844	32.0870	9
10	1.1894	0.8407	10.8254	0.0924	9.1012	0.1099	4.3569	39.6535	10
11	1.2103	0.8263	12.0148	0.0832	9.9275	0.1007	4.8266	47.9162	11
12	1.2314	0.8121	13.2251	0.0756	10.7395	0.0931	5.2934	56.8489	12
13	1.2530	0.7981	14.4565	0.0692	11.5376	0.0867	5.7573	66.4260	13
14	1.2749	0.7844	15.7095	0.0637	12.3220	0.0812	6.2184	76.6227	14
15	1.2972	0.7709	16.9844	0.0589	13.0929	0.0764	6.6765	87.4149	15
16	1.3199	0.7576	18.2817	0.0547	13.8505	0.0722	7.1318	98.7792	16
17	1.3430	0.7446	19.6016	0.0510	14.5951	0.0685	7.5842	110.6926	17
18	1.3665	0.7318	20.9446	0.0477	15.3269	0.0652	8.0338	123.1328	18
19	1.3904	0.7192	22.3112	0.0448	16.0461	0.0623	8.4805	136.0783	19
20	1.4148	0.7068	23.7016	0.0422	16.7529	0.0597	8.9243	149.5080	20
21	1.4395	0.6947	25.1164	0.0398	17.4475	0.0573	9.3653	163.4013	21
22	1.4647	0.6827	26.5559	0.0377	18.1303	0.0552	9.8034	177.7385	22
23	1.4904	0.6710	28.0207	0.0357	18.8012	0.0532	10.2387	192.5000	23
24	1.5164	0.6594	29.5110	0.0339	19.4607	0.0514	10.6711	207.6671	24
25	1.5430	0.6481	31.0275	0.0322	20.1088	0.0497	11.1007	223.2214	25
26	1.5700	0.6369	32.5704	0.0307	20.7457	0.0482	11.5274	239.1451	26
27	1.5975	0.6260	34.1404	0.0293	21.3717	0.0468	11.9513	255.4210	27
28	1.6254	0.6152	35.7379	0.0280	21.9870	0.0455	12.3724	272.0321	28
29	1.6539	0.6046	37.3633	0.0268	22.5916	0.0443	12.7907	288.9623	29
30	1.6828	0.5942	39.0172	0.0256	23.1858	0.0431	13.2061	306.1954	30
31	1.7122	0.5840	40.7000	0.0246	23.7699	0.0421	13.6188	323.7163	31
32	1.7422	0.5740	42.4122	0.0236	24.3439	0.0411	14.0286	341.5097	32
33	1.7727	0.5641	44.1544	0.0226	24.9080	0.0401	14.4356	359.5613	33
34	1.8037	0.5544	45.9271	0.0218	25.4624	0.0393	14.8398	377.8567	34
35	1.8353	0.5449	47.7308	0.0210	26.0073	0.0385	15.2412	396.3824	35
36	1.8674	0.5355	49.5661	0.0202	26.5428	0.0377	15.6399	415.1250	36
40	2.0016	0.4996	57.2341	0.0175	28.5942	0.0350	17.2066	492.0109	40
48	2.2996	0.4349	74.2628	0.0135	32.2938	0.0310	20.2084	652.6054	48
50	2.3808	0.4200	78.9022	0.0127	33.1412	0.0302	20.9317	693.7010	50
60	2.8318	0.3531	104.6752	0.0096	36.9640	0.0271	24.3885	901.4954	60
72	3.4872	0.2868	142.1263	0.0070	40.7564	0.0245	28.1948	1149.1181	72
80	4.0064	0.2496	171.7938	0.0058	42.8799	0.0233	30.5329	1309.2482	80
84	4.2943	0.2329	188.2450	0.0053	43.8361	0.0228	31.6442	1387.1584	84
90	4.7654	0.2098	215.1646	0.0046	45.1516	0.0221	33.2409	1500.8798	90
96	5.2882	0.1891	245.0374	0.0041	46.3370	0.0216	34.7556	1610.4716	96
100	5.6682	0.1764	266.7518	0.0037	47.0615	0.0212	35.7211	1681.0886	100
108	6.5120	0.1536	314.9738	0.0032	48.3679	0.0207	37.5494	1816.1852	108
120	8.0192	0.1247	401.0962	0.0025	50.0171	0.0200	40.0469	2003.0269	120
240	64.3073	0.0156	3617.5602	0.0003	56.2543	0.0178	53.3518	3001.2678	240
360	515.6921	0.0019	29410.9747	0.0000	57.0320	0.0175	56.4434	3219.0833	360

2.0%

	Single Payment		Equal Payment Series				Gradient Series		
	Compound Amount Factor	Present Worth Factor	Compound Amount Factor	Sinking Fund Factor	Present Worth Factor	Capital Recovery Factor	Gradient Uniform Series	Gradient Present Worth	
N	(F/P,i,N)	(P/F,i,N)	(F/A,i,N)	(A/F,i,N)	(P/A,i,N)	(A/P,i,N)	(A/G,i,N)	(P/G,i,N)	N
1	1.0200	0.9804	1.0000	1.0000	0.9804	1.0200	0.0000	0.0000	1
2	1.0404	0.9612	2.0200	0.4950	1.9416	0.5150	0.4950	0.9612	2
3	1.0612	0.9423	3.0604	0.3268	2.8839	0.3468	0.9868	2.8458	3
4	1.0824	0.9238	4.1216	0.2426	3.8077	0.2626	1.4752	5.6173	4
5	1.1041	0.9057	5.2040	0.1922	4.7135	0.2122	1.9604	9.2403	5
6	1.1262	0.8880	6.3081	0.1585	5.6014	0.1785	2.4423	13.6801	6
7	1.1487	0.8706	7.4343	0.1345	6.4720	0.1545	2.9208	18.9035	7
8	1.1717	0.8535	8.5830	0.1165	7.3255	0.1365	3.3961	24.8779	8
9	1.1951	0.8368	9.7546	0.1025	8.1622	0.1225	3.8681	31.5720	9
10	1.2190	0.8203	10.9497	0.0913	8.9826	0.1113	4.3367	38.9551	10
11	1.2434	0.8043	12.1687	0.0822	9.7868	0.1022	4.8021	46.9977	11
12	1.2682	0.7885	13.4121	0.0746	10.5753	0.0946	5.2642	55.6712	12
13	1.2936	0.7730	14.6803	0.0681	11.3484	0.0881	5.7231	64.9475	13
14	1.3195	0.7579	15.9739	0.0626	12.1062	0.0826	6.1786	74.7999	14
15	1.3459	0.7430	17.2934	0.0578	12.8493	0.0778	6.6309	85.2021	15
16	1.3728	0.7284	18.6393	0.0537	13.5777	0.0737	7.0799	96.1288	16
17	1.4002	0.7142	20.0121	0.0500	14.2919	0.0700	7.5256	107.5554	17
18	1.4282	0.7002	21.4123	0.0467	14.9920	0.0667	7.9681	119.4581	18
19	1.4568	0.6864	22.8406	0.0438	15.6785	0.0638	8.4073	131.8139	19
20	1.4859	0.6730	24.2974	0.0412	16.3514	0.0612	8.8433	144.6003	20
21	1.5157	0.6598	25.7833	0.0388	17.0112	0.0588	9.2760	157.7959	21
22	1.5460	0.6468	27.2990	0.0366	17.6580	0.0566	9.7055	171.3795	22
23	1.5769	0.6342	28.8450	0.0347	18.2922	0.0547	10.1317	185.3309	23
24	1.6084	0.6217	30.4219	0.0329	18.9139	0.0529	10.5547	199.6305	24
25	1.6406	0.6095	32.0303	0.0312	19.5235	0.0512	10.9745	214.2592	25
26	1.6734	0.5976	33.6709	0.0297	20.1210	0.0497	11.3910	229.1987	26
27	1.7069	0.5859	35.3443	0.0283	20.7069	0.0483	11.8043	244.4311	27
28	1.7410	0.5744	37.0512	0.0270	21.2813	0.0470	12.2145	259.9392	28
29	1.7758	0.5631	38.7922	0.0258	21.8444	0.0458	12.6214	275.7064	29
30	1.8114	0.5521	40.5681	0.0246	22.3965	0.0446	13.0251	291.7164	30
31	1.8476	0.5412	42.3794	0.0236	22.9377	0.0436	13.4257	307.9538	31
32	1.8845	0.5306	44.2270	0.0226	23.4683	0.0426	13.8230	324.4035	32
33	1.9222	0.5202	46.1116	0.0217	23.9886	0.0417	14.2172	341.0508	33
34	1.9607	0.5100	48.0338	0.0208	24.4986	0.0408	14.6083	357.8817	34
35	1.9999	0.5000	49.9945	0.0200	24.9986	0.0400	14.9961	374.8826	35
36	2.0399	0.4902	51.9944	0.0192	25.4888	0.0392	15.3809	392.0405	36
40	2.2080	0.4529	60.4020	0.0166	27.3555	0.0366	16.8885	461.9931	40
48	2.5871	0.3865	79.3535	0.0126	30.6731	0.0326	19.7556	605.9657	48
50	2.6916	0.3715	84.5794	0.0118	31.4236	0.0318	20.4420	642.3606	50
60	3.2810	0.3048	114.0515	0.0088	34.7609	0.0288	23.6961	823.6975	60
72	4.1611	0.2403	158.0570	0.0063	37.9841	0.0263	27.2234	1034.0557	72
80	4.8754	0.2051	193.7720	0.0052	39.7445	0.0252	29.3572	1166.7868	80
84	5.2773	0.1895	213.8666	0.0047	40.5255	0.0247	30.3616	1230.4191	84
90	5.9431	0.1683	247.1567	0.0040	41.5869	0.0240	31.7929	1322.1701	90
96	6.6929	0.1494	284.6467	0.0035	42.5294	0.0235	33.1370	1409.2973	96
100	7.2446	0.1380	312.2323	0.0032	43.0984	0.0232	33.9863	1464.7527	100
108	8.4883	0.1178	374.4129	0.0027	44.1095	0.0227	35.5774	1569.3025	108
120	10.7652	0.0929	488.2582	0.0020	45.3554	0.0220	37.7114	1710.4160	120
240	115.8887	0.0086	5744.4368	0.0002	49.5686	0.0202	47.9110	2374.8800	240
360	1247.5611	0.0008	62328.0564	0.0000	49.9599	0.0200	49.7112	2483.5679	360

3.0%

	Single Payment		Equal Payment Series				Gradient Series		
	Compound Amount Factor	Present Worth Factor	Compound Amount Factor	Sinking Fund Factor	Present Worth Factor	Capital Recovery Factor	Gradient Uniform Series	Gradient Present Worth	
N	$(F/P,i,N)$	$(P/F,i,N)$	$(F/A,i,N)$	$(A/F,i,N)$	$(P/A,i,N)$	$(A/P,i,N)$	$(A/G,i,N)$	$(P/G,i,N)$	N
1	1.0300	0.9709	1.0000	1.0000	0.9709	1.0300	0.0000	0.0000	1
2	1.0609	0.9426	2.0300	0.4926	1.9135	0.5226	0.4926	0.9426	2
3	1.0927	0.9151	3.0909	0.3235	2.8286	0.3535	0.9803	2.7729	3
4	1.1255	0.8885	4.1836	0.2390	3.7171	0.2690	1.4631	5.4383	4
5	1.1593	0.8626	5.3091	0.1884	4.5797	0.2184	1.9409	8.8888	5
6	1.1941	0.8375	6.4684	0.1546	5.4172	0.1846	2.4138	13.0762	6
7	1.2299	0.8131	7.6625	0.1305	6.2303	0.1605	2.8819	17.9547	7
8	1.2668	0.7894	8.8923	0.1125	7.0197	0.1425	3.3450	23.4806	8
9	1.3048	0.7664	10.1591	0.0984	7.7861	0.1284	3.8032	29.6119	9
10	1.3439	0.7441	11.4639	0.0872	8.5302	0.1172	4.2565	36.3088	110
11	1.3842	0.7224	12.8078	0.0781	9.2526	0.1081	4.7049	43.5330	11
12	1.4258	0.7014	14.1920	0.0705	9.9540	0.1005	5.1485	51.2482	12
13	1.4685	0.6810	15.6178	0.0640	10.6350	0.0940	5.5872	59.4196	13
14	1.5126	0.6611	17.0863	0.0585	11.2961	0.0885	6.0210	68.0141	14
15	1.5580	0.6419	18.5989	0.0538	11.9379	0.0838	6.4500	77.0002	15
16	1.6047	0.6232	20.1569	0.0496	12.5611	0.0796	6.8742	86.3477	16
17	1.6528	0.6050	21.7616	0.0460	13.1661	0.0760	7.2936	96.0280	17
18	1.7024	0.5874	23.4144	0.0427	13.7535	0.0727	7.7081	106.0137	18
19	1.7535	0.5703	25.1169	0.0398	14.3238	0.0698	8.1179	116.2788	19
20	1.8061	0.5537	26.8704	0.0372	14.8775	0.0672	8.5229	126.7987	20
21	1.8603	0.5375	28.6765	0.0349	15.4150	0.0649	8.9231	137.5496	21
22	1.9161	0.5219	30.5368	0.0327	15.9396	0.0627	9.3186	148.5094	22
23	1.9736	0.5067	32.4529	0.0308	16.4436	0.0608	9.7093	159.6566	23
24	2.0328	0.4919	34.4265	0.0290	16.9355	0.0590	10.0954	170.9711	24
25	2.0938	0.4776	36.4593	0.0274	17.4131	0.0574	10.4768	182.4336	25
26	2.1566	0.4637	38.5530	0.0259	17.8768	0.0559	10.8535	194.0260	26
27	2.2213	0.4502	40.7096	0.0246	18.3270	0.0546	11.2255	205.7309	27
28	2.2879	0.4371	42.9309	0.0233	18.7641	0.0533	11.5930	217.5320	28
29	2.3566	0.4243	45.2189	0.0221	19.1885	0.0521	11.9558	229.4137	29
30	2.4273	0.4120	47.5754	0.0210	19.6004	0.0510	12.3141	241.3613	30
31	2.5001	0.4000	50.0027	0.0200	20.0004	0.0500	12.6678	253.3609	31
32	2.5751	0.3883	52.5028	0.0190	20.3888	0.0490	13.0169	265.3993	32
33	2.6523	0.3770	55.0778	0.0182	20.7658	0.0482	13.3616	277.4642	33
34	2.7319	0.3660	57.7302	0.0173	21.1318	0.0473	13.7018	289.5437	34
35	2.8139	0.3554	60.4621	0.0165	21.4872	0.0465	14.0375	301.6267	35
40	3.2620	0.3066	75.4013	0.0133	23.1148	0.0433	15.6502	361.7499	40
45	3.7816	0.2644	92.7199	0.0108	24.5187	0.0408	17.1556	420.6325	45
50	4.3839	0.2281	112.7969	0.0089	25.7298	0.0389	18.5575	477.4803	50
55	5.0821	0.1968	136.0716	0.0073	26.7744	0.0373	19.8600	531.7411	55
60	5.8916	0.1697	163.0534	0.0061	27.6756	0.0361	21.0674	583.0526	60
65	6.8300	0.1464	194.3328	0.0051	28.4529	0.0351	22.1841	631.2010	65
70	7.9178	0.1263	230.5941	0.0043	29.1234	0.0343	23.2145	676.0869	70
75	9.1789	0.1089	272.6309	0.0037	29.7018	0.0337	24.1634	717.6978	75
80	10.6409	0.0940	321.3630	0.0031	30.2008	0.0331	25.0353	756.0865	80
85	12.3357	0.0811	377.8570	0.0026	30.6312	0.0326	25.8349	791.3529	85
90	14.3005	0.0699	443.3489	0.0023	31.0024	0.0323	26.5667	823.6302	90
95	16.5782	0.0603	519.2720	0.0019	31.3227	0.0319	27.2351	853.0742	95
100	19.2186	0.0520	607.2877	0.0016	31.5989	0.0316	27.8444	879.8540	100

4.0%

	Single Payment		Equal Payment Series				Gradient Series		
N	Compound Amount Factor $(F/P,i,N)$	Present Worth Factor $(P/F,i,N)$	Compound Amount Factor $(F/A,i,N)$	Sinking Fund Factor $(A/F,i,N)$	Present Worth Factor $(P/A,i,N)$	Capital Recovery Factor $(A/P,i,N)$	Gradient Uniform Series $(A/G,i,N)$	Gradient Present Worth $(P/G,i,N)$	N
1	1.0400	0.9615	1.0000	1.0000	0.9615	1.0400	0.0000	0.0000	1
2	1.0816	0.9246	2.0400	0.4902	1.8861	0.5302	0.4902	0.9246	2
3	1.1249	0.8890	3.1216	0.3203	2.7751	0.3603	0.9739	2.7025	3
4	1.1699	0.8548	4.2465	0.2355	3.6299	0.2755	1.4510	5.2670	4
5	1.2167	0.8219	5.4163	0.1846	4.4518	0.2246	1.9216	8.5547	5
6	1.2653	0.7903	6.6330	0.1508	5.2421	0.1908	2.3857	12.5062	6
7	1.3159	0.7599	7.8983	0.1266	6.0021	0.1666	2.8433	17.0657	7
8	1.3686	0.7307	9.2142	0.1085	6.7327	0.1485	3.2944	22.1806	8
9	1.4233	0.7026	10.5828	0.0945	7.4353	0.1345	3.7391	27.8013	9
10	1.4802	0.6756	12.0061	0.0833	8.1109	0.1233	4.1773	33.8814	10
11	1.5395	0.6496	13.4864	0.0741	8.7605	0.1141	4.6090	40.3772	11
12	1.6010	0.6246	15.0258	0.0666	9.3851	0.1066	5.0343	47.2477	12
13	1.6651	0.6006	16.6268	0.0601	9.9856	0.1001	5.4533	54.4546	13
14	1.7317	0.5775	18.2919	0.0547	10.5631	0.0947	5.8659	61.9618	14
15	1.8009	0.5553	20.0236	0.0499	11.1184	0.0899	6.2721	69.7355	15
16	1.8730	0.5339	21.8245	0.0458	11.6523	0.0858	6.6720	77.7441	16
17	1.9479	0.5134	23.6975	0.0422	12.1657	0.0822	7.0656	85.9581	17
18	2.0258	0.4936	25.6454	0.0390	12.6593	0.0790	7.4530	94.3498	18
19	2.1068	0.4746	27.6712	0.0361	13.1339	0.0761	7.8342	102.8933	19
20	2.1911	0.4564	29.7781	0.0336	13.5903	0.0736	8.2091	111.5647	20
21	2.2788	0.4388	31.9692	0.0313	14.0292	0.0713	8.5779	120.3414	21
22	2.3699	0.4220	34.2480	0.0292	14.4511	0.0692	8.9407	129.2024	22
23	2.4647	0.4057	36.6179	0.0273	14.8568	0.0673	9.2973	138.1284	23
24	2.5633	0.3901	39.0826	0.0256	15.2470	0.0656	9.6479	147.1012	24
25	2.6658	0.3751	41.6459	0.0240	15.6221	0.0640	9.9925	156.1040	25
26	2.7725	0.3607	44.3117	0.0226	15.9828	0.0626	10.3312	165.1212	26
27	2.8834	0.3468	47.0842	0.0212	16.3296	0.0612	10.6640	174.1385	27
28	2.9987	0.3335	49.9676	0.0200	16.6631	0.0600	10.9909	183.1424	28
29	3.1187	0.3207	52.9663	0.0189	16.9837	0.0589	11.3120	192.1206	29
30	3.2434	0.3083	56.0849	0.0178	17.2920	0.0578	11.6274	201.0618	30
31	3.3731	0.2965	59.3283	0.0169	17.5885	0.0569	11.9371	209.9556	31
32	3.5081	0.2851	62.7015	0.0159	17.8736	0.0559	12.2411	218.7924	32
33	3.6484	0.2741	66.2095	0.0151	18.1476	0.0551	12.5396	227.5634	33
34	3.7943	0.2636	69.8579	0.0143	18.4112	0.0543	12.8324	236.2607	34
35	3.9461	0.2534	73.6522	0.0136	18.6646	0.0536	13.1198	244.8768	35
40	4.8010	0.2083	95.0255	0.0105	19.7928	0.0505	14.4765	286.5303	40
45	5.8412	0.1712	121.0294	0.0083	20.7200	0.0483	15.7047	325.4028	45
50	7.1067	0.1407	152.6671	0.0066	21.4822	0.0466	16.8122	361.1638	50
55	8.6464	0.1157	191.1592	0.0052	22.1086	0.0452	17.8070	393.6890	55
60	10.5196	0.0951	237.9907	0.0042	22.6235	0.0442	18.6972	422.9966	60
65	12.7987	0.0781	294.9684	0.0034	23.0467	0.0434	19.4909	449.2014	65
70	15.5716	0.0642	364.2905	0.0027	23.3945	0.0427	20.1961	472.4789	70
75	18.9453	0.0528	448.6314	0.0022	23.6804	0.0422	20.8206	493.0408	75
80	23.0498	0.0434	551.2450	0.0018	23.9154	0.0418	21.3718	511.1161	80
85	28.0436	0.0357	676.0901	0.0015	24.1085	0.0415	21.8569	526.9384	85
90	34.1193	0.0293	827.9833	0.0012	24.2673	0.0412	22.2826	540.7369	90
95	41.5114	0.0241	1012.7846	0.0010	24.3978	0.0410	22.6550	552.7307	95
100	50.5049	0.0198	1237.6237	0.0008	24.5050	0.0408	22.9800	563.1249	100

5.0%

	Single Payment		Equal Payment Series				Gradient Series		
	Compound Amount Factor	Present Worth Factor	Compound Amount Factor	Sinking Fund Factor	Present Worth Factor	Capital Recovery Factor	Gradient Uniform Series	Gradient Present Worth	
N	(F/P,i,N)	(P/F,i,N)	(F/A,i,N)	(A/F,i,N)	(P/A,i,N)	(A/P,i,N)	(A/G,i,N)	(P/G,i,N)	N
1	1.0500	0.9524	1.0000	1.0000	0.9524	1.0500	0.0000	0.0000	1
2	1.1025	0.9070	2.0500	0.4878	1.8594	0.5378	0.4878	0.9070	2
3	1.1576	0.8638	3.1525	0.3172	2.7232	0.3672	0.9675	2.6347	3
4	1.2155	0.8227	4.3101	0.2320	3.5460	0.2820	1.4391	5.1028	4
5	1.2763	0.7835	5.5256	0.1810	4.3295	0.2310	1.9025	8.2369	5
6	1.3401	0.7462	6.8019	0.1470	5.0757	0.1970	2.3579	11.9680	6
7	1.4071	0.7107	8.1420	0.1228	5.7864	0.1728	2.8052	16.2321	7
8	1.4775	0.6768	9.5491	0.1047	6.4632	0.1547	3.2445	20.9700	8
9	1.5513	0.6446	11.0266	0.0907	7.1078	0.1407	3.6758	26.1268	9
10	1.6289	0.6139	12.5779	0.0795	7.7217	0.1295	4.0991	31.6520	10
11	1.7103	0.5847	14.2068	0.0704	8.3064	0.1204	4.5144	37.4988	11
12	1.7959	0.5568	15.9171	0.0628	8.8633	0.1128	4.9219	43.6241	12
13	1.8856	0.5303	17.7130	0.0565	9.3936	0.1065	5.3215	49.9879	13
14	1.9799	0.5051	19.5986	0.0510	9.8986	0.1010	5.7133	56.5538	14
15	2.0789	0.4810	21.5786	0.0463	10.3797	0.0963	6.0973	63.2880	15
16	2.1829	0.4581	23.6575	0.0423	10.8378	0.0923	6.4736	70.1597	16
17	2.2920	0.4363	25.8404	0.0387	11.2741	0.0887	6.8423	77.1405	17
18	2.4066	0.4155	28.1324	0.0355	11.6896	0.0855	7.2034	84.2043	18
19	2.5270	0.3957	30.5390	0.0327	12.0853	0.0827	7.5569	91.3275	19
20	2.6533	0.3769	33.0660	0.0302	12.4622	0.0802	7.9030	98.4884	20
21	2.7860	0.3589	35.7193	0.0280	12.8212	0.0780	8.2416	105.6673	21
22	2.9253	0.3418	38.5052	0.0260	13.1630	0.0760	8.5730	112.8461	22
23	3.0715	0.3256	41.4305	0.0241	13.4886	0.0741	8.8971	120.0087	23
24	3.2251	0.3101	44.5020	0.0225	13.7986	0.0725	9.2140	127.1402	24
25	3.3864	0.2953	47.7271	0.0210	14.0939	0.0710	9.5238	134.2275	25
26	3.5557	0.2812	51.1135	0.0196	14.3752	0.0696	9.8266	141.2585	26
27	3.7335	0.2678	54.6691	0.0183	14.6430	0.0683	10.1224	148.2226	27
28	3.9201	0.2551	58.4026	0.0171	14.8981	0.0671	10.4114	155.1101	28
29	4.1161	0.2429	62.3227	0.0160	15.1411	0.0660	10.6936	161.9126	29
30	4.3219	0.2314	66.4388	0.0151	15.3725	0.0651	10.9691	168.6226	30
31	4.5380	0.2204	70.7608	0.0141	15.5928	0.0641	11.2381	175.2333	31
32	4.7649	0.2099	75.2988	0.0133	15.8027	0.0633	11.5005	181.7392	32
33	5.0032	0.1999	80.0638	0.0125	16.0025	0.0625	11.7566	188.1351	33
34	5.2533	0.1904	85.0670	0.0118	16.1929	0.0618	12.0063	194.4168	34
35	5.5160	0.1813	90.3203	0.0111	16.3742	0.0611	12.2498	200.5807	35
40	7.0400	0.1420	120.7998	0.0083	17.1591	0.0583	13.3775	229.5452	40
45	8.9850	0.1113	159.7002	0.0063	17.7741	0.0563	14.3644	255.3145	45
50	11.4674	0.0872	209.3480	0.0048	18.2559	0.0548	15.2233	277.9148	50
55	14.6356	0.0683	272.7126	0.0037	18.6335	0.0537	15.9664	297.5104	55
60	18.6792	0.0535	353.5837	0.0028	18.9293	0.0528	16.6062	314.3432	60
65	23.8399	0.0419	456.7980	0.0022	19.1611	0.0522	17.1541	328.6910	65
70	30.4264	0.0329	588.5285	0.0017	19.3427	0.0517	17.6212	340.8409	70
75	38.8327	0.0258	756.6537	0.0013	19.4850	0.0513	18.0176	351.0721	75
80	49.5614	0.0202	971.2288	0.0010	19.5965	0.0510	18.3526	359.6460	80
85	63.2544	0.0158	1245.0871	0.0008	19.6838	0.0508	18.6346	366.8007	85
90	80.7304	0.0124	1594.6073	0.0006	19.7523	0.0506	18.8712	372.7488	90
95	103.0347	0.0097	2040.6935	0.0005	19.8059	0.0505	19.0689	377.6774	95
100	131.5013	0.0076	2610.0252	0.0004	19.8479	0.0504	19.2337	381.7492	100

6.0%

| | Single Payment | | Equal Payment Series | | | | Gradient Series | | |
| | Compound Amount Factor | Present Worth Factor | Compound Amount Factor | Sinking Fund Factor | Present Worth Factor | Capital Recovery Factor | Gradient Uniform Series | Gradient Present Worth | |
N	$(F/P,i,N)$	$(P/F,i,N)$	$(F/A,i,N)$	$(A/F,i,N)$	$(P/A,i,N)$	$(A/P,i,N)$	$(A/G,i,N)$	$(P/G,i,N)$	N
1	1.0600	0.9434	1.0000	1.0000	0.9434	1.0600	0.0000	0.0000	1
2	1.1236	0.8900	2.0600	0.4854	1.8334	0.5454	0.4854	0.8900	2
3	1.1910	0.8396	3.1836	0.3141	2.6730	0.3741	0.9612	2.5692	3
4	1.2625	0.7921	4.3746	0.2286	3.4651	0.2886	1.4272	4.9455	4
5	1.3382	0.7473	5.6371	0.1774	4.2124	0.2374	1.8836	7.9345	5
6	1.4185	0.7050	6.9753	0.1434	4.9173	0.2034	2.3304	11.4594	6
7	1.5036	0.6651	8.3938	0.1191	5.5824	0.1791	2.7676	15.4497	7
8	1.5938	0.6274	9.8975	0.1010	6.2098	0.1610	3.1952	19.8416	8
9	1.6895	0.5919	11.4913	0.0870	6.8017	0.1470	3.6133	24.5768	9
10	1.7908	0.5584	13.1808	0.0759	7.3601	0.1359	4.0220	29.6023	10
11	1.8983	0.5268	14.9716	0.0668	7.8869	0.1268	4.4213	34.8702	11
12	2.0122	0.4970	16.8699	0.0593	8.3838	0.1193	4.8113	40.3369	12
13	2.1329	0.4688	18.8821	0.0530	8.8527	0.1130	5.1920	45.9629	13
14	2.2609	0.4423	21.0151	0.0476	9.2950	0.1076	5.5635	51.7128	14
15	2.3966	0.4173	23.2760	0.0430	9.7122	0.1030	5.9260	57.5546	15
16	2.5404	0.3936	25.6725	0.0390	10.1059	0.0990	6.2794	63.4592	16
17	2.6928	0.3714	28.2129	0.0354	10.4773	0.0954	6.6240	69.4011	17
18	2.8543	0.3503	30.9057	0.0324	10.8276	0.0924	6.9597	75.3569	18
19	3.0256	0.3305	33.7600	0.0296	11.1581	0.0896	7.2867	81.3062	19
20	3.2071	0.3118	36.7856	0.0272	11.4699	0.0872	7.6051	87.2304	20
21	3.3996	0.2942	39.9927	0.0250	11.7641	0.0850	7.9151	93.1136	21
22	3.6035	0.2775	43.3923	0.0230	12.0416	0.0830	8.2166	98.9412	22
23	3.8197	0.2618	46.9958	0.0213	12.3034	0.0813	8.5099	104.7007	23
24	4.0489	0.2470	50.8156	0.0197	12.5504	0.0797	8.7951	110.3812	24
25	4.2919	0.2330	54.8645	0.0182	12.7834	0.0782	9.0722	115.9732	25
26	4.5494	0.2198	59.1564	0.0169	13.0032	0.0769	9.3414	121.4684	26
27	4.8223	0.2074	63.7058	0.0157	13.2105	0.0757	9.6029	126.8600	27
28	5.1117	0.1956	68.5281	0.0146	13.4062	0.0746	9.8568	132.1420	28
29	5.4184	0.1846	73.6398	0.0136	13.5907	0.0736	10.1032	137.3096	29
30	5.7435	0.1741	79.0582	0.0126	13.7648	0.0726	10.3422	142.3588	30
31	6.0881	0.1643	84.8017	0.0118	13.9291	0.0718	10.5740	147.2864	31
32	6.4534	0.1550	90.8898	0.0110	14.0840	0.0710	10.7988	152.0901	32
33	6.8406	0.1462	97.3432	0.0103	14.2302	0.0703	11.0166	156.7681	33
34	7.2510	0.1379	104.1838	0.0096	14.3681	0.0696	11.2276	161.3192	34
35	7.6861	0.1301	111.4348	0.0090	14.4982	0.0690	11.4319	165.7427	35
40	10.2857	0.0972	154.7620	0.0065	15.0463	0.0665	12.3590	185.9568	40
45	13.7646	0.0727	212.7435	0.0047	15.4558	0.0647	13.1413	203.1096	45
50	18.4202	0.0543	290.3359	0.0034	15.7619	0.0634	13.7964	217.4574	50
55	24.6503	0.0406	394.1720	0.0025	15.9905	0.0625	14.3411	229.3222	55
60	32.9877	0.0303	533.1282	0.0019	16.1614	0.0619	14.7909	239.0428	60
65	44.1450	0.0227	719.0829	0.0014	16.2891	0.0614	15.1601	246.9450	65
70	59.0759	0.0169	967.9322	0.0010	16.3845	0.0610	15.4613	253.3271	70
75	79.0569	0.0126	1300.9487	0.0008	16.4558	0.0608	15.7058	258.4527	75
80	105.7960	0.0095	1746.5999	0.0006	16.5091	0.0606	15.9033	262.5493	80
85	141.5789	0.0071	2342.9817	0.0004	16.5489	0.0604	16.0620	265.8096	85
90	189.4645	0.0053	3141.0752	0.0003	16.5787	0.0603	16.1891	268.3946	90
95	253.5463	0.0039	4209.1042	0.0002	16.6009	0.0602	16.2905	270.4375	95
100	339.3021	0.0029	5638.3681	0.0002	16.6175	0.0602	16.3711	272.0471	100

7.0%

	Single Payment		Equal Payment Series				Gradient Series		
N	Compound Amount Factor (F/P,i,N)	Present Worth Factor (P/F,i,N)	Compound Amount Factor (F/A,i,N)	Sinking Fund Factor (A/F,i,N)	Present Worth Factor (P/A,i,N)	Capital Recovery Factor (A/P,i,N)	Gradient Uniform Series (A/G,i,N)	Gradient Present Worth (P/G,i,N)	N
1	1.0700	0.9346	1.0000	1.0000	0.9346	1.0700	0.0000	0.0000	1
2	1.1449	0.8734	2.0700	0.4831	1.8080	0.5531	0.4831	0.8734	2
3	1.2250	0.8163	3.2149	0.3111	2.6243	0.3811	0.9549	2.5060	3
4	1.3108	0.7629	4.4399	0.2252	3.3872	0.2952	1.4155	4.7947	4
5	1.4026	0.7130	5.7507	0.1739	4.1002	0.2439	1.8650	7.6467	5
6	1.5007	0.6663	7.1533	0.1398	4.7665	0.2098	2.3032	10.9784	6
7	1.6058	0.6227	8.6540	0.1156	5.3893	0.1856	2.7304	14.7149	7
8	1.7182	0.5820	10.2598	0.0975	5.9713	0.1675	3.1465	18.7889	8
9	1.8385	0.5439	11.9780	0.0835	6.5152	0.1535	3.5517	23.1404	9
10	1.9672	0.5083	13.8164	0.0724	7.0236	0.1424	3.9461	27.7156	10
11	2.1049	0.4751	15.7836	0.0634	7.4987	0.1334	4.3296	32.4665	11
12	2.2522	0.4440	17.8885	0.0559	7.9427	0.1259	4.7025	37.3506	12
13	2.4098	0.4150	20.1406	0.0497	8.3577	0.1197	5.0648	42.3302	13
14	2.5785	0.3878	22.5505	0.0443	8.7455	0.1143	5.4167	47.3718	14
15	2.7590	0.3624	25.1290	0.0398	9.1079	0.1098	5.7583	52.4461	15
16	2.9522	0.3387	27.8881	0.0359	9.4466	0.1059	6.0897	57.5271	16
17	3.1588	0.3166	30.8402	0.0324	9.7632	0.1024	6.4110	62.5923	17
18	3.3799	0.2959	33.9990	0.0294	10.0591	0.0994	6.7225	67.6219	18
19	3.6165	0.2765	37.3790	0.0268	10.3356	0.0968	7.0242	72.5991	19
20	3.8697	0.2584	40.9955	0.0244	10.5940	0.0944	7.3163	77.5091	20
21	4.1406	0.2415	44.8652	0.0223	10.8355	0.0923	7.5990	82.3393	21
22	4.4304	0.2257	49.0057	0.0204	11.0612	0.0904	7.8725	87.0793	22
23	4.7405	0.2109	53.4361	0.0187	11.2722	0.0887	8.1369	91.7201	23
24	5.0724	0.1971	58.1767	0.0172	11.4693	0.0872	8.3923	96.2545	24
25	5.4274	0.1842	63.2490	0.0158	11.6536	0.0858	8.6391	100.6765	25
26	5.8074	0.1722	68.6765	0.0146	11.8258	0.0846	8.8773	104.9814	26
27	6.2139	0.1609	74.4838	0.0134	11.9867	0.0834	9.1072	109.1656	27
28	6.6488	0.1504	80.6977	0.0124	12.1371	0.9824	9.3289	113.2264	28
29	7.1143	0.1406	87.3465	0.0114	12.2777	0.0814	9.5427	117.1622	29
30	7.6123	0.1314	94.4608	0.0106	12.4090	0.0806	9.7487	120.9718	30
31	8.1451	0.1228	102.0730	0.0098	12.5318	0.0798	9.9471	124.6550	31
32	8.7153	0.1147	110.2182	0.0091	12.6466	0.0791	10.1381	128.2120	32
33	9.3253	0.1072	118.9334	0.0084	12.7538	0.0784	10.3219	131.6435	33
34	9.9781	0.1002	128.2588	0.0078	12.8540	0.0778	10.4987	134.9507	34
35	10.6766	0.0937	138.2369	0.0072	12.9477	0.0772	10.6687	138.1353	35
40	14.9745	0.0668	199.6351	0.0050	13.3317	0.0750	11.4233	152.2928	40
45	21.0025	0.0476	285.7493	0.0035	13.6055	0.0735	12.0360	163.7559	45
50	29.4570	0.0339	406.5289	0.0025	13.8007	0.0725	12.5287	172.9051	50
55	41.3150	0.0242	575.9286	0.0017	13.9399	0.0717	12.9215	180.1243	55
60	57.9464	0.0173	813.5204	0.0012	14.0392	0.0712	13.2321	185.7677	60
65	81.2729	0.0123	1146.7552	0.0009	14.1099	0.0709	13.4760	190.1452	65
70	113.9894	0.0088	1614.1342	0.0006	14.1604	0.0706	13.6662	193.5185	70
75	159.8760	0.0063	2269.6574	0.0004	14.1964	0.0704	13.8136	196.1035	75
80	224.2344	0.0045	3189.0627	0.0003	14.2220	0.0703	13.9273	198.0748	80
85	314.5003	0.0032	4478.5761	0.0002	14.2403	0.0702	14.0146	199.5717	85
90	441.1030	0.0023	6287.1854	0.0002	14.2533	0.0702	14.0812	200.7042	90
95	618.6697	0.0016	8823.8535	0.0001	14.2626	0.0701	14.1319	201.5581	95
100	867.7163	0.0012	12381.6618	0.0001	14.2693	0.0701	14.1703	202.2001	100

8.0%

| | Single Payment | | Equal Payment Series | | | | Gradient Series | | |
| | Compound Amount Factor | Present Worth Factor | Compound Amount Factor | Sinking Fund Factor | Present Worth Factor | Capital Recovery Factor | Gradient Uniform Series | Gradient Present Worth | |
N	(F/P,i,N)	(P/F,i,N)	(F/A,i,N)	(A/F,i,N)	(P/A,i,N)	(A/P,i,N)	(A/G,i,N)	(P/G,i,N)	N
1	1.0800	0.9259	1.0000	1.0000	0.9259	1.0800	0.0000	0.0000	1
2	1.1664	0.8573	2.0800	0.4808	1.7833	0.5608	0.4808	0.8573	2
3	1.2597	0.7938	3.2464	0.3080	2.5771	0.3880	0.9487	2.4450	3
4	1.3605	0.7350	4.5061	0.2219	3.3121	0.3019	1.4040	4.6501	4
5	1.4693	0.6806	5.8666	0.1705	3.9927	0.2505	1.8465	7.3724	5
6	1.5869	0.6302	7.3359	0.1363	4.6229	0.2163	2.2763	10.5233	6
7	1.7138	0.5835	8.9228	0.1121	5.2064	0.1921	2.6937	14.0242	7
8	1.8509	0.5403	10.6366	0.0940	5.7466	0.1740	3.0985	17.8061	8
9	1.9990	0.5002	12.4876	0.0801	6.2469	0.1601	3.4910	21.8081	9
10	2.1589	0.4632	14.4866	0.0690	6.7101	0.1490	3.8713	25.9768	10
11	2.3316	0.4289	16.6455	0.0601	7.1390	0.1401	4.2395	30.2657	11
12	2.5182	0.3971	18.9771	0.0527	7.5361	0.1327	4.5957	34.6339	12
13	2.7196	0.3677	21.4953	0.0465	7.9038	0.1265	4.9402	39.0463	13
14	2.9372	0.3405	24.2149	0.0413	8.2442	0.1213	5.2731	43.4723	14
15	3.1722	0.3152	27.1521	0.0368	8.5595	0.1168	5.5945	47.8857	15
16	3.4259	0.2919	30.3243	0.0330	8.8514	0.1130	5.9046	52.2640	16
17	3.7000	0.2703	33.7502	0.0296	9.1216	0.1096	6.2037	56.5883	17
18	3.9960	0.2502	37.4502	0.0267	9.3719	0.1067	6.4920	60.8426	18
19	4.3157	0.2317	41.4463	0.0241	9.6036	0.1041	6.7697	65.0134	19
20	4.6610	0.2145	45.7620	0.0219	9.8181	0.1019	7.0369	69.0898	20
21	5.0338	0.1987	50.4229	0.0198	10.0168	0.0998	7.2940	73.0629	21
22	5.4365	0.1839	55.4568	0.0180	10.2007	0.0980	7.5412	76.9257	22
23	5.8715	0.1703	60.8933	0.0164	10.3711	0.0964	7.7786	80.6726	23
24	6.3412	0.1577	66.7648	0.0150	10.5288	0.0950	8.0066	84.2997	24
25	6.8485	0.1460	73.1059	0.0137	10.6748	0.0937	8.2254	87.8041	25
26	7.3964	0.1352	79.9544	0.0125	10.8100	0.0925	8.4352	91.1842	26
27	7.9881	0.1252	87.3508	0.0114	10.9352	0.0914	8.6363	94.4390	27
78	8.6271	0.1159	95.3388	0.0105	11.0511	0.0905	8.8289	97.5687	28
29	9.3173	0.1073	103.9659	0.0096	11.1584	0.0896	9.0133	100.5738	29
30	10.0627	0.0994	113.2832	0.0088	11.2578	0.0888	9.1897	103.4558	30
31	10.8677	0.0920	123.3459	0.0081	11.3498	0.0881	9.3584	106.2163	31
32	11.7371	0.0852	134.2135	0.0075	11.4350	0.0875	9.5197	108.8575	32
33	12.6760	0.0789	145.9506	0.0069	11.5139	0.0869	9.6737	111.3819	33
34	13.6901	0.0730	158.6267	0.0063	11.5869	0.0863	9.8208	113.7924	34
35	14.7853	0.0676	172.3168	0.0058	11.6546	0.0858	9.9611	116.0920	35
40	21.7245	0.0460	259.0565	0.0039	11.9246	0.0839	10.5699	126.0422	40
45	31.9204	0.0313	386.5056	0.0026	12.1084	0.0826	11.0447	133.7331	45
50	46.9016	0.0213	573.7702	0.0017	12.2335	0.0817	11.4107	139.5928	50
55	68.9139	0.0145	848.9232	0.0012	12.3186	0.0812	11.6902	144.0065	55
60	101.2571	0.0099	1253.2133	0.0008	12.3766	0.0808	11.9015	147.3000	60
65	148.7798	0.0067	1847.2481	0.0005	12.4160	0.0805	12.0602	149.7387	65
70	218.6064	0.0046	2720.0801	0.0004	12.4428	0.0804	12.1783	151.5326	70
75	321.2045	0.0031	4002.5566	0.0002	12.4611	0.0802	12.2658	152.8448	75
80	471.9548	0.0021	5886.9354	0.0002	12.4735	0.0802	12.3301	153.8001	80
85	693.4565	0.0014	8655.7061	0.0001	12.4820	0.0801	12.3772	154.4925	85
90	1018.9151	0.0010	12723.9386	0.0001	12.4877	0.0801	12.4116	154.9925	90
95	1497.1205	0.0007	18701.5069	0.0001	12.4917	0.0801	12.4365	155.3524	95
100	2199.7613	0.0005	27484.5157	0.0000	12.4943	0.0800	12.4545	155.6107	100

9.0%

	Single Payment		Equal Payment Series				Gradient Series		
N	Compound Amount Factor (F/P,i,N)	Present Worth Factor (P/F,i,N)	Compound Amount Factor (F/A,i,N)	Sinking Fund Factor (A/F,i,N)	Present Worth Factor (P/A,i,N)	Capital Recovery Factor (A/P,i,N)	Gradient Uniform Series (A/G,i,N)	Gradient Present Worth (P/G,i,N)	N
1	1.0900	0.9174	1.0000	1.0000	0.9174	1.0900	0.0000	0.0000	1
2	1.1881	0.8417	2.0900	0.4785	1.7591	0.5685	0.4785	0.8417	2
3	1.2950	0.7722	3.2781	0.3051	2.5313	0.3951	0.9426	2.3860	3
4	1.4116	0.7084	4.5731	0.2187	3.2397	0.3087	1.3925	4.5113	4
5	1.5386	0.6499	5.9847	0.1671	3.8897	0.2571	1.8282	7.1110	5
6	1.6771	0.5963	7.5233	0.1329	4.4859	0.2229	2.2498	10.0924	6
7	1.8280	0.5470	9.2004	0.1087	5.0330	0.1987	2.6574	13.3746	7
8	1.9926	0.5019	11.0285	0.0907	5.5348	0.1807	3.0512	16.8877	8
9	2.1719	0.4604	13.0210	0.0768	5.9952	0.1668	3.4312	20.5711	9
10	2.3674	0.4224	15.1929	0.0658	6.4177	0.1558	3.7978	24.3728	10
11	2.5804	0.3875	17.5603	0.0569	6.8052	0.1469	4.1510	28.2481	11
12	2.8127	0.3555	20.1407	0.0497	7.1607	0.1397	4.4910	32.1590	12
13	3.0658	0.3262	22.9534	0.0436	7.4869	0.1336	4.8182	36.0731	13
14	3.3417	0.2992	26.0192	0.0384	7.7862	0.1284	5.1326	39.9633	14
15	3.6425	0.2745	29.3609	0.0341	8.0607	0.1241	5.4346	43.8069	15
16	3.9703	0.2519	33.0034	0.0303	8.3126	0.1203	5.7245	47.5849	16
17	4.3276	0.2311	36.9737	0.0270	8.5436	0.1170	6.0024	51.2821	17
18	4.7171	0.2120	41.3013	0.0242	8.7556	0.1142	6.2687	54.8860	18
19	5.1417	0.1945	46.0185	0.0217	8.9501	0.1117	6.5236	58.3868	19
20	5.6044	0.1784	51.1601	0.0195	9.1285	0.1095	6.7674	61.7770	20
21	6.1088	0.1637	56.7645	0.0176	9.2922	0.1076	7.0006	65.0509	21
22	6.6586	0.1502	62.8733	0.0159	9.4424	0.1059	7.2232	68.2048	22
23	7.2579	0.1378	69.5319	0.0144	9.5802	0.1044	7.4357	71.2359	23
24	7.9111	0.1264	76.7898	0.0130	9.7066	0.1030	7.6384	74.1433	24
25	8.6231	0.1160	84.7009	0.0118	9.8226	0.1018	7.8316	76.9265	25
26	9.3992	0.1064	93.3240	0.0107	9.9290	0.1007	8.0156	79.5863	26
27	10.2451	0.0976	102.7231	0.0097	10.0266	0.0997	8.1906	82.1241	27
28	11.1671	0.0895	112.9682	0.0089	10.1161	0.0989	8.3571	84.5419	28
29	12.1722	0.0822	124.1354	0.0081	10.1983	0.0981	8.5154	86.8422	29
30	13.2677	0.0754	136.3075	0.0073	10.2737	0.0973	8.6657	89.0280	30
31	14.4618	0.0691	149.5752	0.0067	10.3428	0.0967	8.8083	91.1024	31
32	15.7633	0.0634	164.0370	0.0061	10.4062	0.0961	8.9436	93.0690	32
33	17.1820	0.0582	179.8003	0.0056	10.4644	0.0956	9.0718	94.9314	33
34	18.7284	0.0534	196.9823	0.0051	10.5178	0.0951	9.1933	96.6935	34
35	20.4140	0.0490	215.7108	0.0046	10.5668	0.0946	9.3083	98.3590	35
40	31.4094	0.0318	337.8824	0.0030	10.7574	0.0930	9.7957	105.3762	40
45	48.3273	0.0207	525.8587	0.0019	10.8812	0.0919	10.1603	110.5561	45
50	74.3575	0.0134	815.0836	0.0012	10.9617	0.0912	10.4295	114.3251	50
55	114.4083	0.0087	1260.0918	0.0008	11.0140	0.0908	10.6261	117.0362	55
60	176.0313	0.0057	1944.7921	0.0005	11.0480	0.0905	10.7683	118.9683	60
65	270.8460	0.0037	2998.2885	0.0003	11.0701	0.0903	10.8702	120.3344	65
70	416.7301	0.0024	4619.2232	0.0002	11.0844	0.0902	10.9427	121.2942	70
75	641.1909	0.0016	7113.2321	0.0001	11.0938	0.0901	10.9940	121.9646	75
80	986.5517	0.0010	10950.5741	0.0001	11.0998	0.0901	11.0299	122.4306	80
85	1517.9320	0.0007	16854.8003	0.0001	11.1038	0.0901	11.0551	122.7533	85
90	2335.5266	0.0004	25939.1842	0.0000	11.1064	0.0900	11.0726	122.9758	90
95	3593.4971	0.0003	39916.6350	0.0000	11.1080	0.0900	11.0847	123.1287	95
100	5529.0408	0.0002	61422.6755	0.0000	11.1091	0.0900	11.0930	123.2335	100

10.0%

	Single Payment		Equal Payment Series				Gradient Series		
N	Compound Amount Factor $(F/P,i,N)$	Present Worth Factor $(P/F,i,N)$	Compound Amount Factor $(F/A,i,N)$	Sinking Fund Factor $(A/F,i,N)$	Present Worth Factor $(P/A,i,N)$	Capital Recovery Factor $(A/P,i,N)$	Gradient Uniform Series $(A/G,i,N)$	Gradient Present Worth $(P/G,i,N)$	N
1	1.1000	0.9091	1.0000	1.0000	0.9091	1.1000	0.0000	0.0000	1
2	1.2100	0.8264	2.1000	0.4762	1.7355	0.5762	0.4762	0.8264	2
3	1.3310	0.7513	3.3100	0.3021	2.4869	0.4021	0.9366	2.3291	3
4	1.4641	0.6830	4.6410	0.2155	3.1699	0.3155	1.3812	4.3781	4
5	1.6105	0.6209	6.1051	0.1638	3.7908	0.2638	1.8101	6.8618	5
6	1.7716	0.5645	7.7156	0.1296	4.3553	0.2296	2.2236	9.6842	6
7	1.9487	0.5132	9.4872	0.1054	4.8684	0.2054	2.6216	12.7631	7
8	2.1436	0.4665	11.4359	0.0874	5.3349	0.1874	3.0045	16.0287	8
9	2.3579	0.4241	13.5795	0.0736	5.7590	0.1736	3.3724	19.4215	9
10	2.5937	0.3855	15.9374	0.0627	6.1446	0.1627	3.7255	22.8913	10
11	2.8531	0.3505	18.5312	0.0540	6.4951	0.1540	4.0641	26.3963	11
12	3.1384	0.3186	21.3843	0.0468	6.8137	0.1468	4.3884	29.9012	12
13	3.4523	0.2897	24.5227	0.0408	7.1034	0.1408	4.6988	33.3772	13
14	3.7975	0.2633	27.9750	0.0357	7.3667	0.1357	4.9955	36.8005	14
15	4.1772	0.2394	31.7725	0.0315	7.6061	0.1315	5.2789	40.1520	15
16	4.5950	0.2176	35.9497	0.0278	7.8237	0.1278	5.5493	43.4164	16
17	5.0545	0.1978	40.5447	0.0247	8.0216	0.1247	5.8071	46.5819	17
18	5.5599	0.1799	45.5992	0.0219	8.2014	0.1219	6.0526	49.6395	18
19	6.1159	0.1635	51.1591	0.0195	8.3649	0.1195	6.2861	52.5827	19
20	6.7275	0.1486	57.2750	0.0175	8.5136	0.1175	6.5081	55.4069	20
21	7.4002	0.1351	64.0025	0.0156	8.6487	0.1156	6.7189	58.1095	21
22	8.1403	0.1228	71.4027	0.0140	8.7715	0.1140	6.9189	60.6893	22
23	8.9543	0.1117	79.5430	0.0126	8.8832	0.1126	7.1085	63.1462	23
24	9.8497	0.1015	88.4973	0.0113	8.9847	0.1113	7.2881	65.4813	24
25	10.8347	0.0923	98.3471	0.0102	9.0770	0.1102	7.4580	67.6964	25
26	11.9182	0.0839	109.1818	0.0092	9.1609	0.1092	7.6186	69.7940	26
27	13.1100	0.0763	121.0999	0.0083	9.2372	0.1083	7.7704	71.7773	27
28	14.4210	0.0693	134.2099	0.0075	9.3066	0.1075	7.9137	73.6495	28
29	15.8631	0.0630	148.6309	0.0067	9.3696	0.1067	8.0489	75.4146	29
30	17.4494	0.0573	164.4940	0.0061	9.4269	0.1061	8.1762	77.0766	30
31	19.1943	0.0521	181.9434	0.0055	9.4790	0.1055	8.2962	78.6395	31
32	21.1138	0.0474	201.1378	0.0050	9.5264	0.1050	8.4091	80.1078	32
33	23.2252	0.0431	222.2515	0.0045	9.5694	0.1045	8.5152	81.4856	33
34	25.5477	0.0391	245.4767	0.0041	9.6086	0.1041	8.6149	82.7773	34
35	28.1024	0.0356	271.0244	0.0037	9.6442	0.1037	8.7086	83.9872	35
40	45.2593	0.0221	442.5926	0.0023	9.7791	0.1023	9.0962	88.9525	40
45	72.8905	0.0137	718.9048	0.0014	9.8628	0.1014	9.3740	92.4544	45
50	117.3909	0.0085	1163.9085	0.0009	9.9148	0.1009	9.5704	94.8889	50
55	189.0591	0.0053	1880.5914	0.0005	9.9471	0.1005	9.7075	96.5619	55
60	304.4816	0.0033	3034.8164	0.0003	9.9672	0.1003	9.8023	97.7010	60
65	490.3707	0.0020	4893.7073	0.0002	9.9796	0.1002	9.8672	98.4705	65
70	789.7470	0.0013	7887.4696	0.0001	9.9873	0.1001	9.9113	98.9870	70
75	1271.8954	0.0008	12708.9537	0.0001	9.9921	0.1001	9.9410	99.3317	75
80	2048.4002	0.0005	20474.0021	0.0000	9.9951	0.1000	9.9609	99.5606	80
85	3298.9690	0.0003	32979.6903	0.0000	9.9970	0.1000	9.9742	99.7120	85
90	5313.0226	0.0002	53120.2261	0.0000	9.9981	0.1000	9.9831	99.8118	90
95	8556.6760	0.0001	85556.7605	0.0000	9.9988	0.1000	9.9889	99.8773	95
100	13780.6123	0.0001	137796.1234	0.0000	9.9993	0.1000	9.9927	99.9202	100

11.0%

	Single Payment		Equal Payment Series				Gradient Series		
N	Compound Amount Factor $(F/P,i,N)$	Present Worth Factor $(P/F,i,N)$	Compound Amount Factor $(F/A,i,N)$	Sinking Fund Factor $(A/F,i,N)$	Present Worth Factor $(P/A,i,N)$	Capital Recovery Factor $(A/P,i,N)$	Gradient Uniform Series $(A/G,i,N)$	Gradient Present Worth $(P/G,i,N)$	**N**
1	1.1100	0.9009	1.0000	1.0000	0.9009	1.1100	0.0000	0.0000	1
2	1.2321	0.8116	2.1100	0.4739	1.7125	0.5839	0.4739	0.8116	2
3	1.3676	0.7312	3.3421	0.2992	2.4437	0.4092	0.9306	2.2740	3
4	1.5181	0.6587	4.7097	0.2123	3.1024	0.3223	1.3700	4.2502	4
5	1.6851	0.5935	6.2278	0.1606	3.6959	0.2706	1.7923	6.6240	5
6	1.8704	0.5346	7.9129	0.1264	4.2305	0.2364	2.1976	9.2972	6
7	2.0762	0.4817	9.7833	0.1022	4.7122	0.2122	2.5863	12.1872	7
8	2.3045	0.4339	11.8594	0.0843	5.1461	0.1943	2.9585	15.2246	8
9	2.5580	0.3909	14.1640	0.0706	5.5370	0.1806	3.3144	18.3520	9
10	2.8394	0.3522	16.7220	0.0598	5.8892	0.1698	3.6544	21.5217	10
11	3.1518	0.3173	19.5614	0.0511	6.2065	0.1611	3.9788	24.6945	11
12	3.4985	0.2858	22.7132	0.0440	6.4924	0.1540	4.2879	27.8388	12
13	3.8833	0.2575	26.2116	0.0382	6.7499	0.1482	4.5822	30.9290	13
14	4.3104	0.2320	30.0949	0.0332	6.9819	0.1432	4.8619	33.9449	14
15	4.7846	0.2090	34.4054	0.0291	7.1909	0.1391	5.1275	36.8709	15
16	5.3109	0.1883	39.1899	0.0255	7.3792	0.1355	5.3794	39.6953	16
17	5.8951	0.1696	44.5008	0.0225	7.5488	0.1325	5.6180	42.4095	17
18	6.5436	0.1528	50.3959	0.0198	7.7016	0.1298	5.8439	45.0074	18
19	7.2633	0.1377	56.9395	0.0176	7.8393	0.1276	6.0574	47.4856	19
20	8.0623	0.1240	64.2028	0.0156	7.9633	0.1256	6.2590	49.8423	20
21	8.9492	0.1117	72.2651	0.0138	8.0751	0.1238	6.4491	52.0771	21
22	9.9336	0.1007	81.2143	0.0123	8.1757	0.1223	6.6283	54.1912	22
23	11.0263	0.0907	91.1479	0.0110	8.2664	0.1210	6.7969	56.1864	23
24	12.2392	0.0817	102.1742	0.0098	8.3481	0.1198	6.9555	58.0656	24
25	13.5855	0.0736	114.4133	0.0087	8.4217	0.1187	7.1045	59.8322	25
26	15.0799	0.0663	127.9988	0.0078	8.4881	0.1178	7.2443	61.4900	26
27	16.7386	0.0597	143.0786	0.0070	8.5478	0.1170	7.3754	63.0433	27
28	18.5799	0.0538	159.8173	0.0063	8.6016	0.1163	7.4982	64.4965	28
29	20.6237	0.0485	178.3972	0.0056	8.6501	0.1156	7.6131	65.8542	29
30	22.8923	0.0437	199.0209	0.0050	8.6938	0.1150	7.7206	67.1210	30
31	25.4104	0.0394	221.9132	0.0045	8.7331	0.1145	7.8210	68.3016	31
32	28.2056	0.0355	247.3236	0.0040	8.7686	0.1140	7.9147	69.4007	32
33	31.3082	0.0319	275.5292	0.0036	8.8005	0.1136	8.0021	70.4228	33
34	34.7521	0.0288	306.8374	0.0033	8.8293	0.1133	8.0836	71.3724	34
35	38.5749	0.0259	341.5896	0.0029	8.8552	0.1129	8.1594	72.2538	35
40	65.0009	0.0154	581.8261	0.0017	8.9511	0.1117	8.4659	75.7789	40
45	109.5302	0.0091	986.6386	0.0010	9.0079	0.1110	8.6763	78.1551	45
50	184.5648	0.0054	1668.7712	0.0006	9.0417	0.1106	8.8185	79.7341	50
55	311.0025	0.0032	2818.2042	0.0004	9.0617	0.1104	8.9135	80.7712	55
60	524.0572	0.0019	4755.0658	0.0002	9.0736	0.1102	8.9762	81.4461	60

12.0%

	Single Payment		Equal Payment Series				Gradient Series		
	Compound Amount Factor	Present Worth Factor	Compound Amount Factor	Sinking Fund Factor	Present Worth Factor	Capital Recovery Factor	Gradient Uniform Series	Gradient Present Worth	
N	$(F/P,i,N)$	$(P/F,i,N)$	$(F/A,i,N)$	$(A/F,i,N)$	$(P/A,i,N)$	$(A/P,i,N)$	$(A/G,i,N)$	$(P/G,i,N)$	N
1	1.1200	0.8929	1.0000	1.0000	0.8929	1.1200	0.0000	0.0000	1
2	1.2544	0.7972	2.1200	0.4717	1.6901	0.5917	0.4717	0.7972	2
3	1.4049	0.7118	3.3744	0.2963	2.4018	0.4163	0.9246	2.2208	3
4	1.5735	0.6355	4.7793	0.2092	3.0373	0.3292	1.3589	4.1273	4
5	1.7623	0.5674	6.3528	0.1574	3.6048	0.2774	1.7746	6.3970	5
6	1.9738	0.5066	8.1152	0.1232	4.1114	0.2432	2.1720	8.9302	6
7	2.2107	0.4523	10.0890	0.0991	4.5638	0.2191	2.5515	11.6443	7
8	2.4760	0.4039	12.2997	0.0813	4.9676	0.2013	2.9131	14.4714	8
9	2.7731	0.3606	14.7757	0.0677	5.3282	0.1877	3.2574	17.3563	9
10	3.1058	0.3220	17.5487	0.0570	5.6502	0.1770	3.5847	20.2541	10
11	3.4785	0.2875	20.6546	0.0484	5.9377	0.1684	3.8953	23.1288	11
12	3.8960	0.2567	24.1331	0.0414	6.1944	0.1614	4.1897	25.9523	12
13	4.3635	0.2292	28.0291	0.0357	6.4235	0.1557	4.4683	28.7024	13
14	4.8871	0.2046	32.3926	0.0309	6.6282	0.1509	4.7317	31.3624	14
15	5.4736	0.1827	37.2797	0.0268	6.8109	0.1468	4.9803	33.9202	15
16	6.1304	0.1631	42.7533	0.0234	6.9740	0.1434	5.2147	36.3670	16
17	6.8660	0.1456	48.8837	0.0205	7.1196	0.1405	5.4353	38.6973	17
18	7.6900	0.1300	55.7497	0.0179	7.2497	0.1379	5.6427	40.9080	81
19	8.6128	0.1161	63.4397	0.0158	7.3658	0.1358	5.8375	42.9979	19
20	9.6463	0.1037	72.0524	0.0139	7.4694	0.1339	6.0202	44.9676	20
21	10.8038	0.0926	81.6987	0.0122	7.5620	0.1322	6.1913	46.8188	21
22	12.1003	0.0826	92.5026	0.0108	7.6446	0.1308	6.3514	48.5543	22
23	13.5523	0.0738	104.6029	0.0096	7.7184	0.1296	6.5010	50.1776	23
24	15.1786	0.0659	118.1552	0.0085	7.7843	0.1285	6.6406	51.6929	24
25	17.0001	0.0588	133.3339	0.0075	7.8431	0.1275	6.7708	53.1046	25
26	19.0401	0.0525	150.3339	0.0067	7.8957	0.1267	6.8921	54.4177	26
27	21.3249	0.0469	169.3740	0.0059	7.9426	0.1259	7.0049	55.6369	27
28	23.8839	0.0419	190.6989	0.0052	7.9844	0.1252	7.1098	56.7674	28
29	26.7499	0.0374	214.5828	0.0047	8.0218	0.1247	7.2071	57.8141	29
30	29.9599	0.0334	241.3327	0.0041	8.0552	0.1241	7.2974	58.7821	30
31	33.5551	0.0298	271.2926	0.0037	8.0850	0.1237	7.3811	59.6761	31
32	37.5817	0.0266	304.8477	0.0033	8.1116	0.1233	7.4586	60.5010	32
33	42.0915	0.0238	342.4294	0.0029	8.1354	0.1229	7.5302	61.2612	33
34	47.1425	0.0212	384.5210	0.0026	8.1566	0.1226	7.5965	61.9612	34
35	52.7996	0.0189	431.6635	0.0023	8.1755	0.1223	7.6577	62.6052	35
40	93.0510	0.0107	767.0914	0.0013	8.2438	0.1213	7.8988	65.1159	40
45	163.9876	0.0061	1358.2300	0.0007	8.2825	0.1207	8.0572	66.7342	45
50	289.0022	0.0035	2400.0182	0.0004	8.3045	0.1204	8.1597	67.7624	50
55	509.3206	0.0020	4236.0050	0.0002	8.3170	0.1202	8.2251	68.4082	55
60	897.5969	0.0011	7471.6411	0.0001	8.3240	0.1201	8.2664	68.8100	60

13.0%

	Single Payment		Equal Payment Series				Gradient Series		
	Compound Amount Factor	Present Worth Factor	Compound Amount Factor	Sinking Fund Factor	Present Worth Factor	Capital Recovery Factor	Gradient Uniform Series	Gradient Present Worth	
N	(F/P,i,N)	(P/F,i,N)	(F/A,i,N)	(A/F,i,N)	(P/A,i,N)	(A/P,i,N)	(A/G,i,N)	(P/G,i,N)	N
1	1.1300	0.8850	1.0000	1.0000	0.8850	1.1300	0.0000	0.0000	1
2	1.2769	0.7831	2.1300	0.4695	1.6681	0.5995	0.4695	0.7831	2
3	1.4429	0.6931	3.4069	0.2935	2.3612	0.4235	0.9187	2.1692	3
4	1.6305	0.6133	4.8498	0.2062	2.9745	0.3362	1.3479	4.0092	4
5	1.8424	0.5428	6.4803	0.1543	3.5172	0.2843	1.7571	6.1802	5
6	2.0820	0.4803	8.3227	0.1202	3.9975	0.2502	2.1468	8.5818	6
7	2.3526	0.4251	10.4047	0.0961	4.4226	0.2261	2.5171	11.1322	7
8	2.6584	0.3762	12.7573	0.0784	4.7988	0.2084	2.8685	13.7653	8
9	3.0040	0.3329	15.4157	0.0649	5.1317	0.1949	3.2014	16.4284	9
10	3.3946	0.2946	18.4197	0.0543	5.4262	0.1843	3.5162	19.0797	10
11	3.8359	0.2607	21.8143	0.0458	5.6869	0.1758	3.8134	21.6867	11
12	4.3345	0.2307	25.6502	0.0390	5.9176	0.1690	4.0936	24.2244	12
13	4.8980	0.2042	29.9847	0.0334	6.1218	0.1634	4.3573	26.6744	13
14	5.5348	0.1807	34.8827	0.0287	6.3025	0.1587	4.6050	29.0232	14
15	6.2543	0.1599	40.4175	0.0247	6.4624	0.1547	4.8375	31.2617	15
16	7.0673	0.1415	46.6717	0.0214	6.6039	0.1514	5.0552	33.3841	16
17	7.9861	0.1252	53.7391	0.0186	6.7291	0.1486	5.2589	35.3876	17
18	9.0243	0.1108	61.7251	0.0162	6.8399	0.1462	5.4491	37.2714	18
19	10.1974	0.0981	70.7494	0.0141	6.9380	0.1441	5.6265	39.0366	19
20	11.5231	0.0868	80.9468	0.0124	7.0248	0.1424	5.7917	40.6854	20
21	13.0211	0.0768	92.4699	0.0108	7.1016	0.1408	5.9454	42.2214	21
22	14.7138	0.0680	105.4910	0.0095	7.1695	0.1395	6.0881	43.6486	22
23	16.6266	0.0601	120.2048	0.0083	7.2297	0.1383	6.2205	44.9718	23
24	18.7881	0.0532	136.8315	0.0073	7.2829	0.1373	6.3431	46.1960	24
25	21.2305	0.0471	155.6196	0.0064	7.3300	0.1364	6.4566	47.3264	25
26	23.9905	0.0417	176.8501	0.0057	7.3717	0.1357	6.5614	48.3685	26
27	27.1093	0.0369	200.8406	0.0050	7.4086	0.1350	6.6582	49.3276	27
28	30.6335	0.0326	227.9499	0.0044	7.4412	0.1344	6.7474	50.2090	28
29	34.6158	0.0289	258.5834	0.0039	7.4701	0.1339	6.8296	51.0179	29
30	39.1159	0.0256	293.1992	0.0034	7.4957	0.1334	6.9052	51.7592	30
31	44.2010	0.0226	332.3151	0.0030	7.5183	0.1330	6.9747	52.4380	31
32	49.9471	0.0200	376.5161	0.0027	7.5383	0.1327	7.0385	53.0586	32
33	56.4402	0.0177	426.4632	0.0023	7.5560	0.1323	7.0971	53.6256	33
34	63.7774	0.0157	482.9034	0.0021	7.5717	0.1321	7.1507	54.1430	34
35	72.0685	0.0139	546.6808	0.0018	7.5856	0.1318	7.1998	54.6148	35
40	132.7816	0.0075	1013.7042	0.0010	7.6344	0.1310	7.3888	56.4087	40
45	244.6414	0.0041	1874.1646	0.0005	7.6609	0.1305	7.5076	57.5148	45
50	450.7359	0.0022	3459.5071	0.0003	7.6752	0.1303	7.5811	58.1870	50
55	830.4517	0.0012	6380.3979	0.0002	7.6830	0.1302	7.6260	58.5909	55
60	1530.0535	0.0007	11761.9498	0.0001	7.6873	0.1301	7.6531	58.8313	60

14.0%

| | Single Payment | | Equal Payment Series | | | | Gradient Series | | |
| | Compound Amount Factor $(F/P,i,N)$ | Present Worth Factor $(P/F,i,N)$ | Compound Amount Factor $(F/A,i,N)$ | Sinking Fund Factor $(A/F,i,N)$ | Present Worth Factor $(P/A,i,N)$ | Capital Recovery Factor $(A/P,i,N)$ | Gradient Uniform Series $(A/G,i,N)$ | Gradient Present Worth $(P/G,i,N)$ | |
N									N
1	1.1400	0.8772	1.0000	1.0000	0.8772	1.1400	0.0000	0.0000	1
2	1.2996	0.7695	2.1400	0.4673	1.6467	0.6073	0.4673	0.7695	2
3	1.4815	0.6750	3.4396	0.2907	2.3216	0.4307	0.9129	2.1194	3
4	1.6890	0.5921	4.9211	0.2032	2.9137	0.3432	1.3370	3.8957	4
5	1.9254	0.5194	6.6101	0.1513	3.4331	0.2913	1.7399	5.9731	5
6	2.1950	0.4556	8.5355	0.1172	3.8887	0.2572	2.1218	8.2511	6
7	2.5023	0.3996	10.7305	0.0932	4.2883	0.2332	2.4832	10.6489	7
8	2.8526	0.3506	13.2328	0.0756	4.6389	0.2156	2.8246	13.1028	8
9	3.2519	0.3075	16.0853	0.0622	4.9464	0.2022	3.1463	15.5629	9
10	3.7072	0.2697	19.3373	0.0517	5.2161	0.1917	3.4490	17.9906	10
11	4.2262	0.2366	23.0445	0.0434	5.4527	0.1834	3.7333	20.3567	11
12	4.8179	0.2076	27.2707	0.0367	5.6603	0.1767	3.9998	22.6399	12
13	5.4924	0.1821	32.0887	0.0312	5.8424	0.1712	4.2491	24.8247	13
14	6.2613	0.1597	37.5811	0.0266	6.0021	0.1666	4.4819	26.9009	14
15	7.1379	0.1401	43.8424	0.0228	6.1422	0.1628	4.6990	28.8623	15
16	8.1372	0.1229	50.9804	0.0196	6.2651	0.1596	4.9011	30.7057	16
17	9.2765	0.1078	59.1176	0.0169	6.3729	0.1569	5.0888	32.4305	17
18	10.5752	0.0946	68.3941	0.0146	6.4674	0.1546	5.2630	34.0380	18
19	12.0557	0.0829	78.9692	0.0127	6.5504	0.1527	5.4243	35.5311	19
20	13.7435	0.0728	91.0249	0.0110	6.6231	0.1510	5.5734	36.9135	20
21	15.6676	0.0638	104.7684	0.0095	6.6870	0.1495	5.7111	38.1901	21
22	17.8610	0.0560	120.4360	0.0083	6.7429	0.1483	5.8381	39.3658	22
23	20.3616	0.0491	138.2970	0.0072	6.7921	0.1472	5.9549	40.4463	23
24	23.2122	0.0431	158.6586	0.0063	6.8351	0.1463	6.0624	41.4371	24
25	26.4619	0.0378	181.8708	0.0055	6.8729	0.1455	6.1610	42.3441	25
26	30.1666	0.0331	208.3327	0.0048	6.9061	0.1448	6.2514	43.1728	26
27	34.3899	0.0291	238.4993	0.0042	6.9352	0.1442	6.3342	43.9289	27
28	39.2045	0.0255	272.8892	0.0037	6.9607	0.1437	6.4100	44.6176	28
29	44.6931	0.0224	312.0937	0.0032	6.9830	0.1432	6.4791	45.2441	29
30	50.9502	0.0196	356.7868	0.0028	7.0027	0.1428	6.5423	45.8132	30
31	58.0832	0.0172	407.7370	0.0025	7.0199	0.1425	6.5998	46.3297	31
32	66.2148	0.0151	465.8202	0.0021	7.0350	0.1421	6.6522	46.7979	32
33	75.4849	0.0132	532.0350	0.0019	7.0482	0.1419	6.6998	47.2218	33
34	86.0528	0.0116	607.5199	0.0016	7.0599	0.1416	6.7431	47.6053	34
35	98.1002	0.0102	693.5727	0.0014	7.0700	0.1414	6.7824	47.9519	35
40	188.8835	0.0053	1342.0251	0.0007	7.1050	0.1407	6.9300	49.2376	40
45	363.6791	0.0027	2590.5648	0.0004	7.1232	0.1404	7.0188	49.9963	45
50	700.2330	0.0014	4994.5213	0.0002	7.1327	0.1402	7.0714	50.4375	50

15.0%

	Single Payment		Equal Payment Series				Gradient Series		
N	Compound Amount Factor (F/P,i,N)	Present Worth Factor (P/F,i,N)	Compound Amount Factor (F/A,i,N)	Sinking Fund Factor (A/F,i,N)	Present Worth Factor (P/A,i,N)	Capital Recovery Factor (A/P,i,N)	Gradient Uniform Series (A/G,i,N)	Gradient Present Worth (P/G,i,N)	N
1	1.1500	0.8696	1.0000	1.0000	0.8696	1.1500	0.0000	0.0000	1
2	1.3225	0.7561	2.1500	0.4651	1.6257	0.6151	0.4651	0.7561	2
3	1.5209	0.6575	3.4725	0.2880	2.2832	0.4380	0.9071	2.0712	3
4	1.7490	0.5718	4.9934	0.2003	2.8550	0.3503	1.3263	3.7864	4
5	2.0114	0.4972	6.7424	0.1483	3.3522	0.2983	1.7228	5.7751	5
6	2.3131	0.4323	8.7537	0.1142	3.7845	0.2642	2.0972	7.9368	6
7	2.6600	0.3759	11.0668	0.0904	4.1604	0.2404	2.4498	10.1924	7
8	3.0590	0.3269	13.7268	0.0729	4.4873	0.2229	2.7813	12.4807	8
9	3.5179	0.2843	16.7858	0.0596	4.7716	0.2096	3.0922	14.7548	9
10	4.0456	0.2472	20.3037	0.0493	5.0188	0.1993	3.3832	16.9795	10
11	4.6524	0.2149	24.3493	0.0411	5.2337	0.1911	3.6549	19.1289	11
12	5.3503	0.1869	29.0017	0.0345	5.4206	0.1845	3.9082	21.1849	12
13	6.1528	0.1625	34.3519	0.0291	5.5831	0.1791	4.1438	23.1352	13
14	7.0757	0.1413	40.5047	0.0247	5.7245	0.1747	4.3624	24.9725	14
15	8.1371	0.1229	47.5804	0.0210	5.8474	0.1710	4.5650	26.6930	15
16	9.3576	0.1069	55.7175	0.0179	5.9542	0.1679	4.7522	28.2960	16
17	10.7613	0.0929	65.0751	0.0154	6.0472	0.1654	4.9251	29.7828	17
18	12.3755	0.0808	75.8364	0.0132	6.1280	0.1632	5.0843	31.1565	18
19	14.2318	0.0703	88.2118	0.0113	6.1982	0.1613	5.2307	32.4213	19
20	16.3665	0.0611	102.4436	0.0098	6.2593	0.1598	5.3651	33.5822	20
21	18.8215	0.0531	118.8101	0.0084	6.3125	0.1584	5.4883	34.6448	21
22	21.6447	0.0462	137.6316	0.0073	6.3587	0.1573	5.6010	35.6150	22
23	24.8915	0.0402	159.2764	0.0063	6.3988	0.1563	5.7040	36.4988	23
24	28.6252	0.0349	184.1678	0.0054	6.4338	0.1554	5.7979	37.3023	24
25	32.9190	0.0304	212.7930	0.0047	6.4641	0.1547	5.8834	38.0314	25
26	37.8568	0.0264	245.7120	0.0041	6.4906	0.1541	5.9612	38.6918	26
27	43.5353	0.0230	283.5688	0.0035	6.5135	0.1535	6.0319	39.2890	27
28	50.0656	0.0200	327.1041	0.0031	6.5335	0.1531	6.0960	39.8283	28
29	57.5755	0.0174	377.1697	0.0027	6.5509	0.1527	6.1541	40.3146	29
30	66.2118	0.0151	434.7451	0.0023	6.5660	0.1523	6.2066	40.7526	30
31	76.1435	0.0131	500.9569	0.0020	6.5791	0.1520	6.2541	41.1466	31
32	87.5651	0.0114	577.1005	0.0017	6.5905	0.1517	6.2970	41.5006	32
33	100.6998	0.0099	664.6655	0.0015	6.6005	0.1515	6.3357	41.8184	33
34	115.8048	0.0086	765.3654	0.0013	6.6091	0.1513	6.3705	42.1033	34
35	133.1755	0.0075	881.1702	0.0011	6.6166	0.1511	6.4019	42.3586	35
40	267.8635	0.0037	1779.0903	0.0006	6.6418	0.1506	6.5168	43.2830	40
45	538.7693	0.0019	3585.1285	0.0003	6.6543	0.1503	6.5830	43.8051	45
50	1083.6574	0.0009	7217.7163	0.0001	6.6605	0.1501	6.6205	44.0958	50

16.0%

| | Single Payment | | Equal Payment Series | | | | Gradient Series | | |
| | Compound Amount Factor | Present Worth Factor | Compound Amount Factor | Sinking Fund Factor | Present Worth Factor | Capital Recovery Factor | Gradient Uniform Series | Gradient Present Worth | |
N	$(F/P,i,N)$	$(P/F,i,N)$	$(F/A,i,N)$	$(A/F,i,N)$	$(P/A,i,N)$	$(A/P,i,N)$	$(A/G,i,N)$	$(P/G,i,N)$	N
1	1.1600	0.8621	1.0000	1.0000	0.8621	1.1600	0.0000	0.0000	1
2	1.3456	0.7432	2.1600	0.4630	1.6052	0.6230	0.4630	0.7432	2
3	1.5609	0.6407	3.5056	0.2853	2.2459	0.4453	0.9014	2.0245	3
4	1.8106	0.5523	5.0665	0.1974	2.7982	0.3574	1.3156	3.6814	4
5	2.1003	0.4761	6.8771	0.1454	3.2743	0.3054	1.7060	5.5858	5
6	2.4364	0.4104	8.9775	0.1114	3.6847	0.2714	2.0729	7.6380	6
7	2.8262	0.3538	11.4139	0.0876	4.0386	0.2476	2.4169	9.7610	7
8	3.2784	0.3050	14.2401	0.0702	4.3436	0.2302	2.7388	11.8962	8
9	3.8030	0.2630	17.5185	0.0571	4.6065	0.2171	3.0391	13.9998	9
10	4.4114	0.2267	21.3215	0.0469	4.8332	0.2069	3.3187	16.0399	10
11	5.1173	0.1954	25.7329	0.0389	5.0286	0.1989	3.5783	17.9941	11
12	5.9360	0.1685	30.8502	0.0324	5.1971	0.1924	3.8189	19.8472	12
13	6.8858	0.1452	36.7862	0.0272	5.3423	0.1872	4.0413	21.5899	13
14	7.9875	0.1252	43.6720	0.0229	5.4675	0.1829	4.2464	23.2175	14
15	9.2655	0.1079	51.6595	0.0194	5.5755	0.1794	4.4352	24.7284	15
16	10.7480	0.0930	60.9650	0.0164	5.6685	0.1764	4.6086	26.1241	16
17	12.4677	0.0802	71.6730	0.0140	5.7487	0.1740	4.7676	27.4074	17
18	14.4625	0.0691	84.1407	0.0119	5.8178	0.1719	4.9130	28.5828	18
19	16.7765	0.0596	98.6032	0.0101	5.8775	0.1701	5.0457	29.6557	19
20	19.4608	0.0514	115.3797	0.0087	5.9288	0.1687	5.1666	30.6321	20
21	22.5745	0.0443	134.8405	0.0074	5.9731	0.1674	5.2766	31.5180	21
22	26.1864	0.0382	157.4150	0.0064	6.0113	0.1664	5.3765	32.3200	22
23	30.3762	0.0329	183.6014	0.0054	6.0442	0.1654	5.4671	33.0442	23
24	35.2364	0.0284	213.9776	0.0047	6.0726	0.1647	5.5490	33.6970	24
25	40.8742	0.0245	249.2140	0.0040	6.0971	0.1640	5.6230	34.2841	25
26	47.4141	0.0211	290.0883	0.0034	6.1182	0.1634	5.6898	34.8114	26
27	55.0004	0.0182	337.5024	0.0030	6.1364	0.1630	5.7500	35.2841	27
28	63.8004	0.0157	392.5028	0.0025	6.1520	0.1625	5.8041	35.7073	28
29	74.0085	0.0135	456.3032	0.0022	6.1656	0.1622	5.8528	36.0856	29
30	85.8499	0.0116	530.3117	0.0019	6.1772	0.1619	5.8964	36.4234	30
31	99.5859	0.0100	616.1616	0.0016	6.1872	0.1616	5.9356	36.7247	31
32	115.5196	0.0087	715.7475	0.0014	6.1959	0.1614	5.9706	36.9930	32
33	134.0027	0.0075	831.2671	0.0012	6.2034	0.1612	6.0019	27.2318	33
34	155.4432	0.0064	965.2698	0.0010	6.2098	0.1610	6.0299	37.4441	34
35	180.3141	0.0055	1120.7130	0.0009	6.2153	0.1609	6.0548	37.6327	35
40	378.7212	0.0026	2360.7572	0.0004	6.2335	0.1604	6.1441	38.2992	40
45	795.4438	0.0013	4965.2739	0.0002	6.2421	0.1602	6.1934	38.6598	45
50	1670.7038	0.0006	10435.6488	0.0001	6.2463	0.1601	6.2201	38.8521	50

18.0%

	Single Payment		Equal Payment Series				Gradient Series		
N	Compound Amount Factor (F/P,i,N)	Present Worth Factor (P/F,i,N)	Compound Amount Factor (F/A,i,N)	Sinking Fund Factor (A/F,i,N)	Present Worth Factor (P/A,i,N)	Capital Recovery Factor (A/P,i,N)	Gradient Uniform Series (A/G,i,N)	Gradient Present Worth (P/G,i,N)	N
1	1.1800	0.8475	1.0000	1.0000	0.8475	1.1800	0.0000	0.0000	1
2	1.3924	0.7182	2.1800	0.4587	1.5656	0.6387	0.4587	0.7182	2
3	1.6430	0.6086	3.5724	0.2799	2.1743	0.4599	0.8902	1.9354	3
4	1.9388	0.5158	5.2154	0.1917	2.6901	0.3717	1.2947	3.4828	4
5	2.2878	0.4371	7.1542	0.1398	3.1272	0.3198	1.6728	5.2312	5
6	2.6996	0.3704	9.4420	0.1059	3.4976	0.2859	2.0252	7.0834	6
7	3.1855	0.3139	12.1415	0.0824	3.8115	0.2624	2.3526	8.9670	7
8	3.7589	0.2660	15.3270	0.0652	4.0776	0.2452	2.6558	10.8292	8
9	4.4355	0.2255	19.0859	0.0524	4.3030	0.2324	2.9358	12.6329	9
10	5.2338	0.1911	23.5213	0.0425	4.4941	0.2225	3.1936	14.3525	10
11	6.1759	0.1619	28.7551	0.0348	4.6560	0.2148	3.4303	15.9716	11
12	7.2876	0.1372	34.9311	0.0286	4.7932	0.2086	3.6470	17.4811	12
13	8.5994	0.1163	42.2187	0.0237	4.9095	0.2037	3.8449	18.8765	13
14	10.1472	0.0985	50.8180	0.0197	5.0081	0.1997	4.0250	20.1576	14
15	11.9737	0.0835	60.9653	0.0164	5.0916	0.1964	4.1887	21.3269	15
16	14.1290	0.0708	72.9390	0.0137	5.1624	0.1937	4.3369	22.3885	16
17	16.6722	0.0600	87.0680	0.0115	5.2223	0.1915	4.4708	23.3482	17
18	19.6733	0.0508	103.7403	0.0096	5.2732	0.1896	4.5916	24.2123	18
19	23.2144	0.0431	123.4135	0.0081	5.3162	0.1881	4.7003	24.9877	19
20	27.3930	0.0365	146.6280	0.0068	5.3527	0.1868	4.7978	25.6813	20
21	32.3238	0.0309	174.0210	0.0057	5.3837	0.1857	4.8851	26.3000	21
22	38.1421	0.0262	206.3448	0.0048	5.4099	0.1848	4.9632	26.8506	22
23	45.0076	0.0222	244.4868	0.0041	5.4321	0.1841	5.0329	27.3394	23
24	53.1090	0.0188	289.4945	0.0035	5.4509	0.1835	5.0950	27.7725	24
25	62.6686	0.0160	342.6035	0.0029	5.4669	0.1829	5.1502	28.1555	25
26	73.9490	0.0135	405.2721	0.0025	5.4804	0.1825	5.1991	28.4935	26
27	87.2598	0.0115	479.2211	0.0021	5.4919	0.1821	5.2425	28.7915	27
28	102.9666	0.0097	566.4809	0.0018	5.5016	0.1818	5.2810	29.0537	28
29	121.5005	0.0082	669.4475	0.0015	5.5098	0.1815	5.3149	29.2842	29
30	143.3706	0.0070	790.9480	0.0013	5.5168	0.1813	5.3448	29.4864	30
31	169.1774	0.0059	934.3186	0.0011	5.5227	0.1811	5.3712	29.6638	31
32	199.6293	0.0050	1103.4960	0.0009	5.5277	0.1809	5.3945	29.8191	32
33	235.5625	0.0042	1303.1253	0.0008	5.5320	0.1808	5.4149	29.9549	33
34	277.9638	0.0036	1538.6878	0.0006	5.5356	0.1806	5.4328	30.0736	34
35	327.9973	0.0030	1816.6516	0.0006	5.5386	0.1806	5.4485	30.1773	35
40	750.3783	0.0013	4163.2130	0.0002	5.5482	0.1802	5.5022	30.5269	40
45	1716.6839	0.0006	9531.5771	0.0001	5.5523	0.1801	5.5293	30.7006	45
50	3927.3569	0.0003	21813.0937	0.0000	5.5541	0.1800	5.5428	30.7856	50

20.0%

	Single Payment		Equal Payment Series				Gradient Series		
	Compound Amount Factor	Present Worth Factor	Compound Amount Factor	Sinking Fund Factor	Present Worth Factor	Capital Recovery Factor	Gradient Uniform Series	Gradient Present Worth	
N	$(F/P,i,N)$	$(P/F,i,N)$	$(F/A,i,N)$	$(A/F,i,N)$	$(P/A,i,N)$	$(A/P,i,N)$	$(A/G,i,N)$	$(P/G,i,N)$	N
1	1.2000	0.8333	1.0000	1.0000	0.8333	1.2000	0.0000	0.0000	1
2	1.4400	0.6944	2.2000	0.4545	1.5278	0.6545	0.4545	0.6944	2
3	1.7280	0.5787	3.6400	0.2747	2.1065	0.4747	0.8791	1.8519	3
4	2.0736	0.4823	5.3680	0.1863	2.5887	0.3863	1.2742	3.2986	4
5	2.4883	0.4019	7.4416	0.1344	2.9906	0.3344	1.6405	4.9061	5
6	2.9860	0.3349	9.9299	0.1007	3.3255	0.3007	1.9788	6.5806	6
7	3.5832	0.2791	12.9159	0.0774	3.6046	0.2774	2.2902	8.2551	7
8	4.2998	0.2326	16.4991	0.0606	3.8372	0.2606	2.5756	9.8831	8
9	5.1598	0.1938	20.7989	0.0481	4.0310	0.2481	2.8364	11.4335	9
10	6.1917	0.1615	25.9587	0.0385	4.1925	0.2385	3.0739	12.8871	10
11	7.4301	0.1346	32.1504	0.0311	4.3271	0.2311	3.2893	14.2330	11
12	8.9161	0.1122	39.5805	0.0253	4.4392	0.2253	3.4841	15.4667	12
13	10.6993	0.0935	48.4966	0.0206	4.5327	0.2206	3.6597	16.5883	13
14	12.8392	0.0779	59.1959	0.0169	4.6106	0.2169	3.8175	17.6008	14
15	15.4070	0.0649	72.0351	0.0139	4.6755	0.2139	3.9588	18.5095	15
16	18.4884	0.0541	87.4421	0.0114	4.7296	0.2114	4.0851	19.3208	16
17	22.1861	0.0451	105.9306	0.0094	4.7746	0.2094	4.1976	20.0419	17
18	26.6233	0.0376	128.1167	0.0078	4.8122	0.2078	4.2975	20.6805	18
19	31.9480	0.0313	154.7400	0.0065	4.8435	0.2065	4.3861	21.2439	19
20	38.3376	0.0261	186.6880	0.0054	4.8696	0.2054	4.4643	21.7395	20
21	46.0051	0.0217	225.0256	0.0044	4.8913	0.2044	4.5334	22.1742	21
22	55.2061	0.0181	271.0307	0.0037	4.9094	0.2037	4.5941	22.5546	22
23	66.2474	0.0151	326.2369	0.0031	4.9245	0.2031	4.6475	22.8867	23
24	79.4968	0.0126	392.4842	0.0025	4.9371	0.2025	4.6943	23.1760	24
25	95.3962	0.0105	471.9811	0.0021	4.9476	0.2021	4.7352	23.4276	25
26	114.4755	0.0087	567.3773	0.0018	4.9563	0.2018	4.7709	23.6460	26
27	137.3706	0.0073	681.8528	0.0015	4.9636	0.2015	4.8020	23.8353	27
28	164.8447	0.0061	819.2233	0.0012	4.9697	0.2012	4.8291	23.9991	28
29	197.8136	0.0051	984.0680	0.0010	4.9747	0.2010	4.8527	24.1406	29
30	237.3763	0.0042	1181.8816	0.0008	4.9789	0.2008	4.8731	24.2628	30
31	284.8516	0.0035	1419.2579	0.0007	4.9824	0.2007	4.8908	24.3681	31
32	341.8219	0.0029	1704.1095	0.0006	4.9854	0.2006	4.9061	24.4588	32
33	410.1863	0.0024	2045.9314	0.0005	4.9878	0.2005	4.9194	24.5368	33
34	492.2235	0.0020	2456.1176	0.0004	4.9898	0.2004	4.9308	24.6038	34
35	590.6682	0.0017	2948.3411	0.0003	4.9915	0.2003	4.9406	24.6614	35
40	1469.7716	0.0007	7343.8578	0.0001	4.9966	0.2001	4.9728	24.8469	40
45	3657.2620	0.0003	18281.3099	0.0001	4.9986	0.2001	4.9877	24.9316	45

25.0%

	Single Payment		Equal Payment Series				Gradient Series		
	Compound Amount Factor	Present Worth Factor	Compound Amount Factor	Sinking Fund Factor	Present Worth Factor	Capital Recovery Factor	Gradient Uniform Series	Gradient Present Worth	
N	(F/P,i,N)	(P/F,i,N)	(F/A,i,N)	(A/F,i,N)	(P/A,i,N)	(A/P,i,N)	(A/G,i,N)	(P/G,i,N)	N
1	1.2500	0.8000	1.0000	1.0000	0.8000	1.2500	0.0000	0.0000	1
2	1.5625	0.6400	2.2500	0.4444	1.4400	0.6944	0.4444	0.6400	2
3	1.9531	0.5120	3.8125	0.2623	1.9520	0.5123	0.8525	1.6640	3
4	2.4414	0.4096	5.7656	0.1734	2.3616	0.4234	1.2249	2.8928	4
5	3.0518	0.3277	8.2070	0.1218	2.6893	0.3718	1.5631	4.2035	5
6	3.8147	0.2621	11.2588	0.0888	2.9514	0.3388	1.8683	5.5142	6
7	4.7684	0.2097	15.0735	0.0663	3.1611	0.3163	2.1424	6.7725	7
8	5.9605	0.1678	19.8419	0.0504	3.3289	0.3004	2.3872	7.9469	8
9	7.4506	0.1342	25.8023	0.0388	3.4631	0.2888	2.6048	9.0207	9
10	9.3132	0.1074	33.2529	0.0301	3.5705	0.2801	2.7971	9.9870	10
11	11.6415	0.0859	42.5661	0.0235	3.6564	0.2735	2.9663	10.8460	11
12	14.5519	0.0687	54.2077	0.0184	3.7251	0.2684	3.1145	11.6020	12
13	18.1899	0.0550	68.7596	0.0145	3.7801	0.2645	3.2437	12.2617	13
14	22.7374	0.0440	86.9495	0.0115	3.8241	0.2615	3.3559	12.8334	14
15	28.4217	0.0352	109.6868	0.0091	3.8593	0.2591	3.4530	13.3260	15
16	35.5271	0.0281	138.1085	0.0072	3.8874	0.2572	3.5366	13.7482	16
17	44.4089	0.0225	173.6357	0.0058	3.9099	0.2558	3.6084	14.1085	17
18	55.5112	0.0180	218.0446	0.0046	3.9279	0.2546	3.6698	14.4147	18
19	69.3889	0.0144	273.5558	0.0037	3.9424	0.2537	3.7222	14.6741	19
20	86.7362	0.0115	342.9447	0.0029	3.9539	0.2529	3.7667	14.8932	20
21	108.4202	0.0092	429.6809	0.0023	3.9631	0.2523	3.8045	15.0777	21
22	135.5253	0.0074	538.1011	0.0019	3.9705	0.2519	3.8365	15.2326	22
23	169.4066	0.0059	673.6264	0.0015	3.9764	0.2515	3.8634	15.3625	23
24	211.7582	0.0047	843.0329	0.0012	3.9811	0.2512	3.8861	15.4711	24
25	264.6978	0.0038	1054.7912	0.0009	3.9849	0.2509	3.9052	15.5618	25
26	330.8722	0.0030	1319.4890	0.0008	3.9879	0.2508	3.9212	15.6373	26
27	413.5903	0.0024	1650.3612	0.0006	3.9903	0.2506	3.9346	15.7002	27
28	516.9879	0.0019	2063.9515	0.0005	3.9923	0.2505	3.9457	15.7524	28
29	646.2349	0.0015	2580.9394	0.0004	3.9938	0.2504	3.9551	15.7957	29
30	807.7936	0.0012	3227.1743	0.0003	3.9950	0.2503	3.9628	15.8316	30
31	1009.7420	0.0010	4034.9678	0.0002	3.9960	0.2502	3.9693	15.8614	31
32	1262.1774	0.0008	5044.7098	0.0002	3.9968	0.2502	3.9746	15.8859	32
33	1577.7218	0.0006	6306.8872	0.0002	3.9975	0.2502	3.9791	15.9062	33
34	1972.1523	0.0005	7884.6091	0.0001	3.9980	0.2501	3.9828	15.9229	34
35	2465.1903	0.0004	9856.7613	0.0001	3.9984	0.2501	3.9858	15.9367	35
40	7523.1638	0.0001	30088.6554	0.0000	3.9995	0.2500	3.9947	15.9766	40

30.0%

	Single Payment		Equal Payment Series				Gradient Series		
N	Compound Amount Factor $(F/P,i,N)$	Present Worth Factor $(P/F,i,N)$	Compound Amount Factor $(F/A,i,N)$	Sinking Fund Factor $(A/F,i,N)$	Present Worth Factor $(P/A,i,N)$	Capital Recovery Factor $(A/P,i,N)$	Gradient Uniform Series $(A/G,i,N)$	Gradient Present Worth $(P/G,i,N)$	N
1	1.3000	0.7692	1.0000	1.0000	0.7692	1.3000	0.0000	0.0000	1
2	1.6900	0.5917	2.3000	0.4348	1.3609	0.7348	0.4348	0.5917	2
3	2.1970	0.4552	3.9900	0.2506	1.8161	0.5506	0.8271	1.5020	3
4	2.8561	0.3501	6.1870	0.1616	2.1662	0.4616	1.1783	2.5524	4
5	3.7129	0.2693	9.0431	0.1106	2.4356	0.4106	1.4903	3.6297	5
6	4.8268	0.2072	12.7560	0.0784	2.6427	0.3784	1.7654	4.6656	6
7	6.2749	0.1594	17.5828	0.0569	2.8021	0.3569	2.0063	5.6218	7
8	8.1573	0.1226	23.8577	0.0419	2.9247	0.3419	2.2156	6.4800	8
9	10.6045	0.0943	32.0150	0.0312	3.0190	0.3312	2.3963	7.2343	9
10	13.7858	0.0725	42.6195	0.0235	3.0915	0.3235	2.5512	7.8872	10
11	17.9216	0.0558	56.4053	0.0177	3.1473	0.3177	2.6833	8.4452	11
12	23.2981	0.0429	74.3270	0.0135	3.1903	0.3135	2.7952	8.9173	12
13	30.2875	0.0330	97.6250	0.0102	3.2233	0.3102	2.8895	9.3135	13
14	39.3738	0.0254	127.9125	0.0078	3.2487	0.3078	2.9685	9.6437	14
15	51.1859	0.0195	167.2863	0.0060	3.2682	0.3060	3.0344	9.9172	15
16	66.5417	0.0150	218.4722	0.0046	3.2832	0.3046	3.0892	10.1426	16
17	86.5042	0.0116	285.0139	0.0035	3.2948	0.3035	3.1345	10.3276	17
18	112.4554	0.0089	371.5180	0.0027	3.3037	0.3027	3.1718	10.4788	18
19	146.1920	0.0068	483.9734	0.0021	3.3105	0.3021	3.2025	10.6019	19
20	190.0496	0.0053	630.1655	0.0016	3.3158	0.3016	3.2275	10.7019	20
21	247.0645	0.0040	820.2151	0.0012	3.3198	0.3012	3.2480	10.7828	21
22	321.1839	0.0031	1067.2796	0.0009	3.3230	0.3009	3.2646	10.8482	22
23	417.5391	0.0024	1388.4635	0.0007	3.3254	0.3007	3.2781	10.9009	23
24	542.8008	0.0018	1806.0026	0.0006	3.3272	0.3006	3.2890	10.9433	24
25	705.6410	0.0014	2348.8033	0.0004	3.3286	0.3004	3.2979	10.9773	25
26	917.3333	0.0011	3054.4443	0.0003	3.3297	0.3003	3.3050	11.0045	26
27	1192.5333	0.0008	3971.7776	0.0003	3.3305	0.3003	3.3107	11.0263	27
28	1550.2933	0.0006	5164.3109	0.0002	3.3312	0.3002	3.3153	11.0437	28
29	2015.3813	0.0005	6714.6042	0.0001	3.3317	0.3001	3.3189	11.0576	29
30	2619.9956	0.0004	8729.9855	0.0001	3.3321	0.3001	3.3219	11.0687	30
31	3405.9943	0.0003	11349.9811	0.0001	3.3324	0.3001	3.3242	11.0775	31
32	4427.7926	0.0002	14755.9755	0.0001	3.3326	0.3001	3.3261	11.0845	32
33	5756.1304	0.0002	19183.7681	0.0001	3.3328	0.3001	3.3276	11.0901	33
34	7482.9696	0.0001	24939.8985	0.0000	3.3329	0.3000	3.3288	11.0945	34
35	9727.8604	0.0001	32422.8681	0.0000	3.3330	0.3000	3.3297	11.0980	35

35.0%

	Single Payment		Equal Payment Series				Gradient Series		
N	Compound Amount Factor (F/P,i,N)	Present Worth Factor (P/F,i,N)	Compound Amount Factor (F/A,i,N)	Sinking Fund Factor (A/F,i,N)	Present Worth Factor (P/A,i,N)	Capital Recovery Factor (A/P,i,N)	Gradient Uniform Series (A/G,i,N)	Gradient Present Worth (P/G,i,N)	N
1	1.3500	0.7407	1.0000	1.0000	0.7407	1.3500	0.0000	0.0000	1
2	1.8225	0.5487	2.3500	0.4255	1.2894	0.7755	0.4255	0.5487	2
3	2.4604	0.4064	4.1725	0.2397	1.6959	0.5897	0.8029	1.3616	3
4	3.3215	0.3011	6.6329	0.1508	1.9969	0.5008	1.1341	2.2648	4
5	4.4840	0.2230	9.9544	0.1005	2.2200	0.4505	1.4220	3.1568	5
6	6.0534	0.1652	14.4384	0.0693	2.3852	0.4193	1.6698	3.9828	6
7	8.1722	0.1224	20.4919	0.0488	2.5075	0.3988	1.8811	4.7170	7
8	11.0324	0.0906	28.6640	0.0349	2.5982	0.3849	2.0597	5.3515	8
9	14.8937	0.0671	39.6964	0.0252	2.6653	0.3752	2.2094	5.8886	9
10	20.1066	0.0497	54.5902	0.0183	2.7150	0.3683	2.3338	6.3363	10
11	27.1439	0.0368	74.6967	0.0134	2.7519	0.3634	2.4364	6.7047	11
12	36.6442	0.0273	101.8406	0.0098	2.7792	0.3598	2.5205	7.0049	12
13	49.4697	0.0202	138.4848	0.0072	2.7994	0.3572	2.5889	7.2474	13
14	66.7841	0.0150	187.9544	0.0053	2.8144	0.3553	2.6443	7.4421	14
15	90.1585	0.0111	254.7385	0.0039	2.8255	0.3539	2.6889	7.5974	15
16	121.7139	0.0082	344.8970	0.0029	2.8337	0.3529	2.7246	7.7206	16
17	164.3138	0.0061	466.6109	0.0021	2.8398	0.3521	2.7530	7.8180	17
18	221.8236	0.0045	630.9247	0.0016	2.8443	0.3516	2.7756	7.8946	18
19	299.4619	0.0033	852.7483	0.0012	2.8476	0.3512	2.7935	2.9547	19
20	404.2736	0.0025	1152.2103	0.0009	2.8501	0.3509	2.8075	8.0017	20
21	545.7693	0.0018	1556.4838	0.0006	2.8519	0.3506	2.8186	8.0384	21
22	736.7886	0.0014	2102.2532	0.0005	2.8533	0.3505	2.8272	8.0669	22
23	994.6646	0.0010	2839.0418	0.0004	2.8543	0.3504	2.8340	8.0890	23
24	1342.7973	0.0007	3833.7064	0.0003	2.8550	0.3503	2.8393	8.1061	24
25	1812.7763	0.0006	5176.5037	0.0002	2.8556	0.3502	2.8433	8.1194	25
26	2447.2480	0.0004	6989.2800	0.0001	2.8560	0.3501	2.8465	8.1296	26
27	3303.7848	0.0003	9436.5280	0.0001	2.8563	0.3501	2.8490	8.1374	27
28	4460.1095	0.0002	12740.3128	0.0001	2.8565	0.3501	2.8509	8.1435	28
29	6021.1478	0.0002	17200.4222	0.0001	2.8567	0.3501	2.8523	8.1481	29
30	8128.5495	0.0001	23221.5700	0.0000	2.8568	0.3500	2.8535	8.1517	30

40.0%

	Single Payment		Equal Payment Series				Gradient Series		
N	Compound Amount Factor (F/P,i,N)	Present Worth Factor (P/F,i,N)	Compound Amount Factor (F/A,i,N)	Sinking Fund Factor (A/F,i,N)	Present Worth Factor (P/A,i,N)	Capital Recovery Factor (A/P,i,N)	Gradient Uniform Series (A/G,i,N)	Gradient Present Worth (P/G,i,N)	N
1	1.4000	0.7143	1.0000	1.0000	0.7143	1.4000	0.0000	0.0000	1
2	1.9600	0.5102	2.4000	0.4167	1.2245	0.8167	0.4167	0.5102	2
3	2.7440	0.3644	4.3600	0.2294	1.5889	0.6294	0.7798	1.2391	3
4	3.8416	0.2603	7.1040	0.1408	1.8492	0.5408	1.0923	2.0200	4
5	5.3782	0.1859	10.9456	0.0914	2.0352	0.4914	1.3580	2.7637	5
6	7.5295	0.1328	16.3238	0.0613	2.1680	0.4613	1.5811	3.4278	6
7	10.5414	0.0949	23.8534	0.0419	2.2628	0.4419	1.7664	3.9970	7
8	14.7579	0.0678	34.3947	0.0291	2.3306	0.4291	1.9185	4.4713	8
9	20.6610	0.0484	49.1526	0.0203	2.3790	0.4203	2.0422	4.8585	9
10	28.9255	0.0346	69.8137	0.0143	2.4136	0.4143	2.1419	5.1696	10
11	40.4957	0.0247	98.7391	0.0101	2.4383	0.4101	2.2215	5.4166	11
12	56.6939	0.0176	139.2348	0.0072	2.4559	0.4072	2.2845	5.6106	12
13	79.3715	0.0126	195.9287	0.0051	2.4685	0.4051	2.3341	5.7618	13
14	111.1201	0.0090	275.3002	0.0036	2.4775	0.4036	2.3729	5.8788	14
15	155.5681	0.0064	386.4202	0.0026	2.4839	0.4026	2.4030	5.9688	15
16	217.7953	0.0046	541.9883	0.0018	2.4885	0.4018	2.4262	6.0376	16
17	304.9135	0.0033	759.7837	0.0013	2.4918	0.4013	2.4441	6.0901	17
18	426.8789	0.0023	1064.6971	0.0009	2.4941	0.4009	2.4577	6.1299	18
19	597.6304	0.0017	1491.5760	0.0007	2.4958	0.4007	2.4682	6.1601	19
20	836.6826	0.0012	2089.2064	0.0005	2.4970	0.4005	2.4761	6.1828	20
21	1171.3556	0.0009	2925.8889	0.0003	2.4979	0.4003	2.4821	6.1998	21
22	1639.8978	0.0006	4097.2445	0.0002	2.4985	0.4002	2.4866	6.2127	22
23	2295.8569	0.0004	5737.1423	0.0002	2.4989	0.4002	2.4900	6.2222	23
24	3214.1997	0.0003	8032.9993	0.0001	2.4992	0.4001	2.4925	6.2294	24
25	4499.8796	0.0002	11247.1990	0.0001	2.4994	0.4001	2.4944	6.2347	25
26	6299.8314	0.0002	15747.0785	0.0001	2.4996	0.4001	2.4959	6.2387	26
27	8819.7640	0.0001	22046.9099	0.0000	2.4997	0.4000	2.4969	6.2416	27
28	12347.6696	0.0001	30866.6739	0.0000	2.4998	0.4000	2.4977	6.2438	28
29	17286.7374	0.0001	43214.3435	0.0000	2.4999	0.4000	2.4983	6.2454	29
30	24201.4324	0.0000	60501.0809	0.0000	2.4999	0.4000	2.4988	6.2466	30

50.0%

	Single Payment		Equal Payment Series				Gradient Series		
	Compound Amount Factor	Present Worth Factor	Compound Amount Factor	Sinking Fund Factor	Present Worth Factor	Capital Recovery Factor	Gradient Uniform Series	Gradient Present Worth	
N	$(F/P,i,N)$	$(P/F,i,N)$	$(F/A,i,N)$	$(A/F,i,N)$	$(P/A,i,N)$	$(A/P,i,N)$	$(A/G,i,N)$	$(P/G,i,N)$	N
1	1.5000	0.6667	1.0000	1.0000	0.6667	1.5000	0.0000	0.0000	1
2	2.2500	0.4444	2.5000	0.4000	1.1111	0.9000	0.4000	0.4444	2
3	3.3750	0.2963	4.7500	0.2105	1.4074	0.7105	0.7368	1.0370	3
4	5.0625	0.1975	8.1250	0.1231	1.6049	0.6231	1.0154	1.6296	4
5	7.5938	0.1317	13.1875	0.0758	1.7366	0.5758	1.2417	2.1564	5
6	11.3906	0.0878	20.7813	0.0481	1.8244	0.5481	1.4226	2.5953	6
7	17.0859	0.0585	32.1719	0.0311	1.8829	0.5311	1.5648	2.9465	7
8	25.6289	0.0390	49.2578	0.0203	1.9220	0.5203	1.6752	3.2196	8
9	38.4434	0.0260	74.8867	0.0134	1.9480	0.5134	1.7596	3.4277	9
10	57.6650	0.0173	113.3301	0.0088	1.9653	0.5088	1.8235	3.5838	10
11	86.4976	0.0116	170.9951	0.0058	1.9769	0.5058	1.8713	3.6994	11
12	129.7463	0.0077	257.4927	0.0039	1.9846	0.5039	1.9068	3.7842	12
13	194.6195	0.0051	387.2390	0.0026	1.9897	0.5026	1.9329	3.8459	13
14	291.9293	0.0034	581.8585	0.0017	1.9931	0.5017	1.9519	3.8904	14
15	437.8939	0.0023	873.7878	0.0011	1.9954	0.5011	1.9657	3.9224	15
16	656.8408	0.0015	1311.6817	0.0008	1.9970	0.5008	1.9756	3.9452	16
17	985.2613	0.0010	1968.5225	0.0005	1.9980	0.5005	1.9827	3.9614	17
18	1477.8919	0.0007	2953.7838	0.0003	1.9986	0.5003	1.9878	3.9729	18
19	2216.8378	0.0005	4431.6756	0.0002	1.9991	0.5002	1.9914	3.9811	19
20	3325.2567	0.0003	6648.5135	0.0002	1.9994	0.5002	1.9940	3.9868	20

How to Read the Cumulative Standardized Normal Distribution Function

Note 1: The standard normal distribution is the function of $f(z) = \dfrac{1}{\sigma\sqrt{2\pi}} e^{\frac{-z^2}{2}}$. Its graph is a bell curve above a region of area 1 with inflection points at $z = -1$ and $z = +1$.

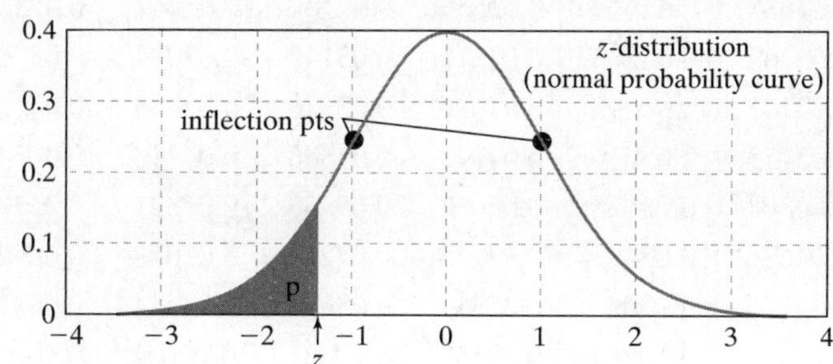

Note 2: If a normal variable X is not standard, its value must be standardized: $z = \dfrac{x - \mu}{\sigma}$.

To find the area **P** under the normal probability curve, $P(X \le x) = \Phi\left(z = \dfrac{x - \mu}{\sigma}\right)$

and $\Phi(-z) = 1 - \Phi(z)$. For example, to find probability that the NPW would be negative where the NPW distribution is normally distributed with mean of \$20 and variance of 400, we evaluate the following:

$$P(\text{NPW} \le 0) = \Phi\left(z = \frac{0 - 20}{\sqrt{400}} = -1\right) = 0.15866.$$

Or if we want to find the probability that the NPW exceeds \$50, we calculate

$$P(\text{NPW} \ge 50) = 1 - P(\text{NPW} \le 50) = 1 - \Phi\left(z = \frac{50 - 20}{\sqrt{400}} = 1.5\right)$$

$$= 1 - 0.93319 = 0.0668.$$

Part A: The Cumulative Standardized Normal Distribution Function

z	0.00	0.01	0.02	0.03	0.04	0.05	0.06	0.07	0.08	0.09
−3	0.00135	0.00131	0.00126	0.00122	0.00118	0.00114	0.00111	0.00107	0.00104	0.00100
−2.9	0.00187	0.00181	0.00175	0.00169	0.00164	0.00159	0.00154	0.00149	0.00144	0.00139
−2.8	0.00256	0.00248	0.00240	0.00233	0.00226	0.00219	0.00212	0.00205	0.00199	0.00193
−2.7	0.00347	0.00336	0.00326	0.00317	0.00307	0.00298	0.00289	0.00280	0.00272	0.00264
−2.6	0.00466	0.00453	0.00440	0.00427	0.00415	0.00402	0.00391	0.00379	0.00368	0.00357
−2.5	0.00621	0.00604	0.00587	0.00570	0.00554	0.00539	0.00523	0.00508	0.00494	0.00480
−2.4	0.00820	0.00798	0.00776	0.00755	0.00734	0.00714	0.00695	0.00676	0.00657	0.00639
−2.3	0.01072	0.01044	0.01017	0.00990	0.00964	0.00939	0.00914	0.00889	0.00866	0.00842
−2.2	0.01390	0.01355	0.01321	0.01287	0.01255	0.01222	0.01191	0.01160	0.01130	0.01101
−2.1	0.01786	0.01743	0.01700	0.01659	0.01618	0.01578	0.01539	0.01500	0.01463	0.01426
−2	0.02275	0.02222	0.02169	0.02118	0.02068	0.02018	0.01970	0.01923	0.01876	0.01831
−1.9	0.02872	0.02807	0.02743	0.02680	0.02619	0.02559	0.02500	0.02442	0.02385	0.02330
−1.8	0.03593	0.03515	0.03438	0.03362	0.03288	0.03216	0.03144	0.03074	0.03005	0.02938
−1.7	0.04457	0.04363	0.04272	0.04182	0.04093	0.04006	0.03920	0.03836	0.03754	0.03673
−1.6	0.05480	0.05370	0.05262	0.05155	0.05050	0.04947	0.04846	0.04746	0.04648	0.04551
−1.5	0.06681	0.06552	0.06426	0.06301	0.06178	0.06057	0.05938	0.05821	0.05705	0.05592
−1.4	0.08076	0.07927	0.07780	0.07636	0.07493	0.07353	0.07215	0.07078	0.06944	0.06811
−1.3	0.09680	0.09510	0.09342	0.09176	0.09012	0.08851	0.08691	0.08534	0.08379	0.08226
−1.2	0.11507	0.11314	0.11123	0.10935	0.10749	0.10565	0.10383	0.10204	0.10027	0.09853
−1.1	0.13567	0.13350	0.13136	0.12924	0.12714	0.12507	0.12302	0.12100	0.11900	0.11702
−1	0.15866	0.15625	0.15386	0.15151	0.14917	0.14686	0.14457	0.14231	0.14007	0.13786
−0.9	0.18406	0.18141	0.17879	0.17619	0.17361	0.17106	0.16853	0.16602	0.16354	0.16109
−0.8	0.21186	0.20897	0.20611	0.20327	0.20045	0.19766	0.19489	0.19215	0.18943	0.18673
−0.7	0.24196	0.23885	0.23576	0.23270	0.22965	0.22663	0.22363	0.22065	0.21770	0.21476
−0.6	0.27425	0.27093	0.26763	0.26435	0.26109	0.25785	0.25463	0.25143	0.24825	0.24510
−0.5	0.30854	0.30503	0.30153	0.29806	0.29460	0.29116	0.28774	0.28434	0.28096	0.27760
−0.4	0.34458	0.34090	0.33724	0.33360	0.32997	0.32636	0.32276	0.31918	0.31561	0.31207
−0.3	0.38209	0.37828	0.37448	0.37070	0.36693	0.36317	0.35942	0.35569	0.35197	0.34827
−0.2	0.42074	0.41683	0.41294	0.40905	0.40517	0.40129	0.39743	0.39358	0.38974	0.38591
−0.1	0.46017	0.45620	0.45224	0.44828	0.44433	0.44038	0.43644	0.43251	0.42858	0.42465
0	0.50000	0.50399	0.50798	0.51197	0.51595	0.51994	0.52392	0.52790	0.53188	0.53586

Part B: The Cumulative Standardized Normal Distribution Function

z	0.00	0.01	0.02	0.03	0.04	0.05	0.06	0.07	0.08	0.09
0	0.50000	0.50399	0.50798	0.51197	0.51595	0.51994	0.52392	0.52790	0.53188	0.53586
0.1	0.53983	0.54380	0.54776	0.55172	0.55567	0.55962	0.56356	0.56749	0.57142	0.57535
0.2	0.57926	0.58317	0.58706	0.59095	0.59483	0.59871	0.60257	0.60642	0.61026	0.61409
0.3	0.61791	0.62172	0.62552	0.62930	0.63307	0.63683	0.64058	0.64431	0.64803	0.65173
0.4	0.65542	0.65910	0.66276	0.66640	0.67003	0.67364	0.67724	0.68082	0.68439	0.68793
0.5	0.69146	0.69497	0.69847	0.70194	0.70540	0.70884	0.71226	0.71566	0.71904	0.72240
0.6	0.72575	0.72907	0.73237	0.73565	0.73891	0.74215	0.74537	0.74857	0.75175	0.75490
0.7	0.75804	0.76115	0.76424	0.76730	0.77035	0.77337	0.77637	0.77935	0.78230	0.78524
0.8	0.78814	0.79103	0.79389	0.79673	0.79955	0.80234	0.80511	0.80785	0.81057	0.81327
0.9	0.81594	0.81859	0.82121	0.82381	0.82639	0.82894	0.83147	0.83398	0.83646	0.83891
1	0.84134	0.84375	0.84614	0.84849	0.85083	0.85314	0.85543	0.85769	0.85993	0.86214
1.1	0.86433	0.86650	0.86864	0.87076	0.87286	0.87493	0.87698	0.87900	0.88100	0.88298
1.2	0.88493	0.88686	0.88877	0.89065	0.89251	0.89435	0.89617	0.89796	0.89973	0.90147
1.3	0.90320	0.90490	0.90658	0.90824	0.90988	0.91149	0.91309	0.91466	0.91621	0.91774
1.4	0.91924	0.92073	0.92220	0.92364	0.92507	0.92647	0.92785	0.92922	0.93056	0.93189
1.5	0.93319	0.93448	0.93574	0.93699	0.93822	0.93943	0.94062	0.94179	0.94295	0.94408
1.6	0.94520	0.94630	0.94738	0.94845	0.94950	0.95053	0.95154	0.95254	0.95352	0.95449
1.7	0.95543	0.95637	0.95728	0.95818	0.95907	0.95994	0.96080	0.96164	0.96246	0.96327
1.8	0.96407	0.96485	0.96562	0.96638	0.96712	0.96784	0.96856	0.96926	0.96995	0.97062
1.9	0.97128	0.97193	0.97257	0.97320	0.97381	0.97441	0.97500	0.97558	0.97615	0.97670
2	0.97725	0.97778	0.97831	0.97882	0.97932	0.97982	0.98030	0.98077	0.98124	0.98169
2.1	0.98214	0.98257	0.98300	0.98341	0.98382	0.98422	0.98461	0.98500	0.98537	0.98574
2.2	0.98610	0.98645	0.98679	0.98713	0.98745	0.98778	0.98809	0.98840	0.98870	0.98899
2.3	0.98928	0.98956	0.98983	0.99010	0.99036	0.99061	0.99086	0.99111	0.99134	0.99158
2.4	0.99180	0.99202	0.99224	0.99245	0.99266	0.99286	0.99305	0.99324	0.99343	0.99361
2.5	0.99379	0.99396	0.99413	0.99430	0.99446	0.99461	0.99477	0.99492	0.99506	0.99520
2.6	0.99534	0.99547	0.99560	0.99573	0.99585	0.99598	0.99609	0.99621	0.99632	0.99643
2.7	0.99653	0.99664	0.99674	0.99683	0.99693	0.99702	0.99711	0.99720	0.99728	0.99736
2.8	0.99744	0.99752	0.99760	0.99767	0.99774	0.99781	0.99788	0.99795	0.99801	0.99807
2.9	0.99813	0.99819	0.99825	0.99831	0.99836	0.99841	0.99846	0.99851	0.99856	0.99861
3	0.99865	0.99869	0.99874	0.99878	0.99882	0.99886	0.99889	0.99893	0.99896	0.99900

INDEX

A

Abandonment decision, 210
Absolute (dollar) measures of investment, 313
Accelerated cost recovery system (ACRS), 397
Accept–reject decision rule
  benchmark rate, 308
  for a single revenue projects, 250
Accounting depreciation, 386
  asset depreciation ranges (ADRs), 388–389
  book depreciation method, 388–396
  cost basis of an asset, 387
  depreciable property, 386–387
  salvage value, 388
  useful life, 388
Accounting equation, 580
Accounting information, use of, 577
Accounting profit, 403
Accrual-basis accounting, 591
Acquisition of fixed assets, 583
Actual dollars, 42
  analysis under inflation, 166, 168–169
Administrative costs, 430
Allan Company, 219–220
Alternatives, evaluation of for decision making, 25–26
Amortized loan, 131
Analysis period, 213, 266, 366
Annual basis, 359, 364
Annual effective yield, 115–116
Annual equivalent cost method, 254
Annual-equivalent worth (AE) criterion, 250–251
  benefits of, 254
Annual percentage rate (APR), 114–115
  effective interest rates at various compounding intervals for 22%–30% APRs, 116
  under inflation, 174
Annual percentage yield (APY), 115
Annual-worth analysis techniques, 259, 271
Annuity factor, 66–67
Ansell, Inc., 215
Asset depreciation ranges (ADRs), 386, 388–389

Asset management analysis, 596–597, 602
Assets, 580–582
Average collection period, 596
Average inflation rate, 163
Average tax rate, 405–406

B

Balance sheet statement, 579
  assets, 580–582
  of Lam Research Corporation, 580, 583–584
  liabilities and stockholders' equity (owners' net worth), 582–583
  use, 579
Base case, 366
Base-case analysis, 354–355
Benchmark interest rate, 308
Benefit–cost analysis, 350–351
  B/C-ratio, 355–357
  difference between profitability index and, 363
  general framework for, 352
  goals, 352
  highway, 366–371
  incremental B/C-ratio, 358–359
  secondary effects, 353
  social discount rate, 354–355
  sponsor's costs, 353
  steps for a typical public project, 355
  users' benefits, 353
  valuation of, 353
Beta (β), 505
Bonds, 55, 593
Book depreciation method, 388–396
  units-of-production method, 396
Book value per share, 600–601
Break-even analysis, 491
Break-even interest rate, 204
Break-even point, 433–434
Break-even sales volume, 433–434
B&S Company, 264
Buffett, Warren Edward, 574–575
Buffettology, 575
Bureau of Labor and Statistics (BLS), 160–161

C

Capacity costs, 432
Capital costs, 254, 367
Capital-expenditure decisions, 28, 403
Capitalized asset, 386
Capitalized cost, 212
Capitalized-equivalent (CE) method, 211–212
Capital (ownership) costs, 254–255, 539–540
Capital-recovery cost, 255, 257
Capital-recovery factor, 66, 297
Cash-flow approach, 535
Cash flows
  actual-dollar expression for, 167
  constant-dollar expression for, 167
  diagram, 43–44
  diagram of a strict gradient series, 76–77
  in economic analysis, 435–436
  equal-payment series, 70–75
  estimating risky, 500–503
  future worth, 50, 56
  incremental/differential, 439–443
  interest formulas for single, 51–60
  loan *vs* project, 194–195
  net, 43
  present worth, 50, 53–56
  uneven stream of payments, 58
  vs net income, 436
Cash-flow statement, 586
  after-tax, 443
  borrowing (financing) activities, 443
  Excel worksheet, 448–449, 452, 454
  financing activities, 590
  investing activities, 442, 590
  for Lam Research Corporation, 589–592
  operating activities, 588–590
  project, 443–447
  reporting format, 588–590
  sources (inflows) and uses (outflows) of cash, 587
  in a typical manufacturing firm, 588
  working capital and its impact on, 590
Challenger, 533
  annual equivalent costs, 547
  comparison of defender with, 535–537, 548
Chena Hot Springs Resort, 175
Coca-Cola Company, 426–428
Commercial loans, 131
  calculating installments over time, 131
  loan repayment schedule, 130, 133

Common stock, 583, 593
Company cost of capital, 508–509
Composite series, 76
Compound-amount factor, 51
  equal-payment-series, 60–62
  uniform-series, 62
Compounding process, 51
Compound growth, 82
Compound interest, 45
Constant dollar analysis
  under inflation, 166–167
Constant-dollar benefit–cost analyses, 354–355
Consumer price index (CPI), 160
  between 2002 and 2011, 162
  original measure, 160
  revised measure, 160
Contribution margin, 433
Conventional-payback method, 195
Corning Greater China, 192–193
Corporate taxes
  average tax rate, 405–406
  book value calculation, 407–408
  determining accounting profit, 403–405
  determining ordinary gains and capital gains, 409
  gain taxes on asset disposals, 407–409
  marginal tax rate, 405
  net income, 403–404
  salvage value calculation, 408–409
  taxable gains (or losses), 408–409
  treatment of depreciation expenses, 403
  U.S. corporate-tax-rate structure, 405–406
Cost basis, 387
Cost behavior, 432
Cost-of-living index, 160
Cost (s), 386
  administrative, 430
  of capital, 504
  capital (ownership), 539–540
  classification, for predicting cost behavior, 431–434
  of debt capital, 506–507
  direct labor, 428
  direct raw materials, 428
  of equity capital, 504–506
  fixed, 432
  flow in a manufacturing company, 430–431
  of goods sold (or cost of revenue), 430, 584
  inventory, 430

manufacturing, 428–429
manufacturing overhead, 429
marketing, 430
mixed, 433
of money, 40
nonmanufacturing, 429–430
operating, 535, 540
overheads, 430
period, 430
product, 430
sunk, 534–535
unit contribution margin, 433
variable, 432–433
Cost-volume-profit graph, 435
Coupon of bond, 55
Credit cards, management of, 112–113, 128
Current assets, 580, 582
Current liabilities, 582
Current market value, 533–534
Current ratio, 595

D

Days-sales-outstanding (DSO) ratio,
   596–597
Dealer's (bank's) interest rate, 135
Debt, 584
Debt-equity ratio, 594
Debt management
   analysis for firms, 592–595, 602
   borrowing with credit cards, 128
   commercial loans, 131
   dealer's (bank's) interest rate, 135
   debt-equity ratio, 594
   debt ratio, 594
   financing options, comparison of,
      134–135
   long-term debt financing, 593
   methods of calculating interests on
      credit cards, 128
   methods of debt financing, 592–593
   short-term debt financing, 593
   times-interest-earned ratio, 594–595
Debt ratio, 447, 594
Decision making
   alternatives, evaluation of, 25–26
   basis of, 576–577
   capital expenditure, 28
   economic decisions, 27–28
   engineering design problem,
      decision-making in, 25–27
   engineering economic decisions,
      28–36

impact of engineering projects on
     financial statements, 30–31
   personal, 22–24
Declining balance method, 392
Declining-balance (DB) method, of
     calculating depreciation, 392–394
Defender, 533
   annual equivalent costs, 547
   comparison of challenger with, 535–537,
     548
Deflation, 159–160
Dell®, 21
Depreciable asset, 386
   and gain taxes, 407–409
Depreciated value, 384
Depreciation, 386, 433, 582
   and allowance under inflation, 449
   cost basis of an asset, 387
   declining-balance (DB) method,
     392–394
   depreciable property, 386–387
   salvage value, 388
   straight-line (SL) method, 390
   switching policy, from DB depreciation
     to SL depreciation, 393–394, 398–399
   tax methods, 397–401
   units-of-production method, 396
   useful life, 388
Depreciation accounting, 386
Depreciation allowance, 385
Depreciation rate (19/ N), 392
Differential/incremental, cash flows, 439
Direct labor, 428
Direct raw materials, 428
Discounted cash flow techniques (DCFs),
   200
Discounted-payback method, 195, 198
Discounting factor, 54
Discounting process, 53
Discount rate, 47–48, 54, 355
Discrete compounding, 118
   Interest factors for, 649–678
Dividends, 586
Diversification of investment, 603–609
"Do-nothing alternative" approach, 214,
   315, 366

E

Earning power, 41
Earning power of money, 172
Earnings before interest and income taxes
   (EBIT), 594

Earnings per share (EPS), 584–586, 600
E-commerce, 34
Economic decisions, 27–28. *See also* engineering economic decisions
Economic equivalence
  basis for comparison, 50
  calculations, 47–48
  definition, 47
  mixed-payment series at an interest rate of 33%, 86–90
Economic Service Life, 539–544
Education, investment point of view, 294–295
Effective annual interest rate, *see* annual effective yield
Effective annual yield, 307
Effective interest rates
  compounding at different rates from payments, 124
  compounding period equal to payment period, 121–122
  continuous compounding, 119–120
  discrete compounding, 118
  equivalence calculations with, 121–122, 124
  relationship with nominal interest rates, 115
End-of-period convention, 44
Engineering design problem, decision-making in
  benefit–cost analyses, 26–27
  environmental concerns, 27
  establishing goals or objectives, 25
  evaluating design alternatives, 25–26
  getting an idea, 25
  investment decisions, 27
Engineering economic decisions, 28, 82
  fundamental principles, 35–36
  impact of engineering projects on financial statements, 30–31
  large-scale, 28–30
  strategic, 31–35
Environmental reuse concerns, 34
Equal-payment-series
  capital-recovery factor (annuity factor), 66
  compound-amount factor, 60–62
  present value of perpetuities, 74–75
  present-worth factor, 69
  sinking-fund factor, 64
Equipment replacement, 530–559
Equity, 584
Equivalence calculations
  with effective interest rates, 121–122, 124

football tickets, price of, 158–159
under inflation, 172–174, 178
Equivalent annual operating costs, 255–256
Equivalent cash flow, *see* economic equivalence
Excel worksheet
  break-even analysis, 492
  to calculate equivalent cash value, 81
  to calculate tax depreciation amounts by MACRS, 401
  to calculate the annual equivalent worth, 253
  to calculate the depreciation amounts by the declining-balance method, 394
  to calculate the depreciation amounts with DB switching to SL, 395
  calculation of break-even number of operating hours, 270
  Capstone's MicrCHP Project cash flows under best-case scenario, 495
  Capstone's MicrCHP Project cash flows under worst-case scenario, 494
  cash-flow statement, 447–448, 452, 454, 486
  to compare two mutually exclusive alternatives, 224
  to computation of present worth, 89
  constant-dollar analysis, 177
  creating loan repayment schedule, 130, 133
  to determine a loan's principal and interest payments between two payment periods, 134
  to determine the size of the gradient amount, 79
  economic service life calculation for defender, 550, 554
  economic service life calculation for electric fork lift truck, 544
  economics of owning and operating the challenger, 551, 556
  example of a total highway user benefit tallying spreadsheet, 369
  for finding the required quarterly deposits, 180
  finding unknown *i* by a linear interpolation, 71
  to find the break-even interest rate to make two options equivalent, 74
  to generate a depreciation schedule for a real property, 402
  to illustrate how cash balance changes over time, 54, 63, 66

to illustrate how to determine the IRR, 310
to illustrate the process of accumulating the future worth, 126
to illustrate the process of calculating the savings required for retirement, 85
to illustrate the process of computing the NPW, 203
to illustrate the process of deleting $122 million initial cash balance over time, 72
rate-of-return analysis (ROR), 304
Expected return, 496
Expected return on risky asset, 505
Expenses, 403
External interest rate, 311

F

Facebook, 20–21
Face value of bond, 55
Ferguson Company, 257
Financial leverage, 592
Financial ratios, 592–601
Financial statements
accounting information, use of, 577
asset management analysis, 596–597, 602
balance sheet, 579–584
basis of decision making, 576–577
comparisons of key financial ratios for Lam Research Corporation with industry average, 601
current ratio, 595
debt management analysis, 592–595, 602
and engineering economic decisions, 30–31, 576
factors affecting stock price, 578
financial status, 577–579
income statement, 584–592
Lam Research's 2010 Annual Report, 579
limitations of financial ratios in business decisions, 601–603
liquidity analysis, 595–596, 602
market-value analysis, 599–602
methods of debt financing, 592–593
and principle of investing in financial assets, 603–605
profitability analysis, 597–599, 602
ratios for business decisions, 592–603
trend analysis, 601–603
Financing activities, 590
Finished-goods inventory, 431

Fixed assets, 582
Fixed costs, 432
Future amount of money, 42
Future worth of cash flows, 50, 56

G

Gain taxes on asset disposal, 407–409
General inflation rate, 164–165, 167
Geometric-gradient-series present worth factor, 83
Globalization, 34
Goal Seek function, Excel, 73, 78, 139, 179, 348, 491–492
Google™, 20–21
Gradient series (G)
geometric series, 82–83
linear as a composite series, 76
present-worth factor of linear gradient, 76–77
Green engineering considerations, 27
Gross domestic product (GDP), 34
Gross profit, 584
Gross revenues, 403

H

Half-year convention, 398–399
Harrison Company, 259
Highway benefit–cost analysis
base case, 366
benefits, 367
capital costs, 367
case example, 368–371
proposed alternatives, 366
rehabilitation costs, 367
remaining capital value (RCV), 368
routine annual maintenance costs, 368
safety benefits, 367
sponsors' costs, 367–368
travel-time savings, 367
vehicle operating cost savings, 367

I

Income statement, 584
dividends and retained earnings, 585–586
earnings per share (EPS), 584–585
gross margin, operating margin, and net margin, 587
for Lam Research Corporation, 585–587
net income, 584

Income taxes, 404
Incremental analysis, 308, 314–315
Incremental-investment analysis, 314–315
Industrial-product price index, 161
Inflation, 42, 159–160
    actual (current) dollars analysis, 166, 168–169, 174
    average inflation rate, 163
    BLS method of assessing, 160
    complexity of multiple inflation rates, 453
    constant dollar analysis, 166–167, 173
    consumer price index (CPI), 160
    conversion from actual to constant dollars, 168–169
    conversion from constant to actual dollars, 167
    depreciation allowance under, 449
    effect on project cash flows, 449, 453
    equivalence calculations under, 172–174, 178
    general inflation rate, 164–165, 167
    inflation-free interest rate, 173
    market interest rate, 173
    mixed-dollar analysis, 178
    producer price index, 161–162
    specific inflation rate, 165
Inflation-adjusted required rate of return, 173
Inflation-free interest rate, 173
Interest, 40
    factor notation, 52
    methods of calculating, 44–45
    period, 42
    rate, 40, 42
    tables, 51–52
    and time value, 41
    transactions involving, 42–44
Internal-rate-of-return criterion
    decision rule for nonsimple investments, 311
    decision rule for simple investments, 307–308
    and present-worth (PW), 307
Internal rate of return (IRR), 204, 296, 298
    on incremental investment, 315
    for unequal-service-life problems, 320
Inventory costs, 430
Inventory-turnover ratio, 596
Investing activities, 590
Investment evaluation
    break-even analysis, 491

    company cost of capital, 508–509
    cost of debt capital, 506–507
    cost of equity capital, 504–505
    determining amount of risk in a particular investment opportunity, 497–498
    diversifications, 603–605
    probabilistic approach, 495–501
    risk-adjusted discount rate approach, 509–510
    scenario analysis, 492–493
    sensitivity analysis, 483–484, 487–488
    standard deviation (σ) of returns, 496–497
    trade-off between risk and reward, 603
Investment pool, 200, 206–208
Investment project, 298

K

Key financial ratios, 602

L

Lambert Manufacturing Corporation, 248
Liabilities, 582–583
Life-cycle-cost analysis, 266
Linear interpolation, 302
Liquidity analysis, 595–596, 602
Loan cash flow, 194
Lowest common multiple, 221, 272

M

MACRS, 397
Make-or-buy (or outsourcing) decision, 33–34, 263
Manufacturing overhead costs, 429
Marginal analysis, 547
Marginal cost of capital, 508
Marginal efficiency of capital, 296
Marginal tax rate, 405
Market basket of goods and services, 160
Marketing costs, 430
Market interest rate, 42, 173–174
    annual effective yield, 115–116
    definition, 114
    nominal interest rates, 114–115
    relationship between nominal and effective interest rates, 115
Market-value analysis, 599–602
Matching principle, 430, 435

Maturity of bond, 55
Microsoft®, 21
Midmonth convention, 401
Minimum attractive rate of return
     (MARR), 200
   decision rules, 308, 315
   guidelines for selecting, 205–206
   and IRR, 308
Mixed costs (or semivariable costs), 433
Mixed-dollar analysis, 178
Mixed investment, 342
Modified accelerated cost recovery system
     (MACRS), 397
   book value calculation, 407–408
   guidelines, 397–398
   half-year convention, 398–399
   midmonth convention, 401
   for personal property with half-year
     convention, 398–399
   property classifications (ADR = asset
     depreciation range), 398
   real property depreciation, 401
   recovery allowance percentage, 398
   recovery periods, 397–398
Monroe Manufacturing, 217
Musser, Eric, 192
Mutually exclusive alternatives, 213–222
   analysis period and project lives, 266,
     271
   decision rules, 308
   "do-nothing alternative" approach, 214,
     315
   incremental-investment analysis,
     314–315
   profitability index ratio analysis for, 364
   rate-of-return (ROR) analysis, 313–314
   revenue projects, 215
   sensitivity analysis for, 488
   service projects, 214
   unequal-service-life problems, IRR
     approach, 320

N

National Broadband Network (NBN) Co.,
     350–351
Net cash flows, 43
Net future worth, 210–211
   discounted payback period, 210
   exposure to financial risk, 210
   profit potential, 210
   surplus, 211
Net income, 403–404

Net investment, 342
Net-present-worth (NPW) method,
     200–205, 364. *See also* Present-worth
     (PW) analysis
   borrowed-fund concept, 208–209
   break-even interest rate, 204
   internal rate of return, 204
   investment pool, 200, 206–208
   of the loan transaction at rate of return
     (28%), 297
   minimum attractive rate of return
     (MARR), 200, 205–206
   sensitivity analysis, 483–484, 487
Net worth, 582–583
Nippon Oil Corp., 481
Nominal interest rates, 114–115, 173
   relationship with effective interest rates,
     115
Nonsimple (or nonconventional)
     investment, 299
NPW, *see* Net present worth
Number of interest periods, 42

O

Obama, proposal permitting businesses to
     write off full costs of capital, 384–385
Operating activities, 588–589
Operating costs, 254, 535, 540
   equivalent annual, 255–256
Operating expenses, 584
Opportunity cost, 504, 537
Opportunity-cost approach, 537
Outstanding principal, 297
Overheads, 430
Ownership (capital) costs, 254, 539

P

Paid-in capital, 583
Payback methods, 195
   benefits and flaws of, 197–198
   conventional, 195
   discounted, 195, 198
   screening, 195, 197–198
Period, 43
Period costs, 430
Perpetual service life, 211–212
Personal decisions, making
   establishing goals or objectives, 22
   evaluation of feasible alternatives, 22–24
   knowing other opportunities, 24
   logical steps involved in, 24

Personal financial planning, 577
Phoenix Manufacturing Company, 222
Plan for receipts/disbursements, 42–43
Planning horizon (study period), 545
Preferred stock, 582–583, 593
Present worth of cash flows, 50, 53–56
Present-worth (PW) analysis, 271.
    See also net-present-worth
      (NPW) method
  analysis period differs from project lives,
    219–222
  analysis period equals project lives, 215
  capitalized-equivalent (CE) method,
    211–212
  decision rules, 307–308, 311
  and internal-rate-of-return criterion, 307
  minimum attractive rate of return
    (MARR), 200, 205–206
  mutually exclusive alternatives,
    213–222
  net future worth, 210–211
  net-present-worth (NPW) method,
    200–205
  trial-and-error method, 302
Price/earnings (P/E) ratio, 600
Primary benefit, 353
Principal, 42
Probabilistic Cash Flow Analysis, 495–503
Producer price index, 161–162
Product costs, 430
Profitability analysis, 597–599, 602
Profitability index
  definition, 362
  difference between the benefit–cost
    ratio and, 363
  ratio analysis for mutually exclusive
    alternatives, 364
Profit margin on sales, 597–598
Program Evaluation and Review
    Technique (PERT), for network
    planning and scheduling, 500–501
Project balance, 209
  as a function of time, 211
  and internal rate of return, 298
  net future worth of the project and,
    210–211
Project cash-flow analysis, 194, 443–447
Project cost of capital, 509
Project risk, 482–483
  break-even analysis, 491
  company cost of capital, 508–509
  cost of debt capital, 506–507
  cost of equity capital, 504–505

  determining amount of risk in a
    particular investment opportunity,
    497–498
  and discount rate, 504–510
  expected return on risky asset, 505
  methods of describing, 483–484
  origins of, 483
  probabilistic approach, 495–501
  risk-adjusted discount rate approach,
    509–510
  scenario analysis, 492–493
  sensitivity analysis, 483–484, 487–488
  standard deviation (σ) of returns,
    496–497
Proposed alternatives, 366
Purchasing power, 41, 172
Pure borrowing, 342
Pure investment, 342

Q

Quick (acid test) ratio, 595–596

R

Rate-of-return analysis (ROR), 295–296
  decision rules, 307–308, 311, 315
  direct-solution method, 300
  Excel calculations for, 304
  internal rate of return, 298
  internal-rate-of-return criterion, 307
  methods for finding, 298–300,
    302, 304
  nonsimple investments, 298–299
  project selection rules under the IRR
    criterion, 308
  return on invested capital, 297–298
  return on investment, 296–297
  simple investments, 298–299
  trial-and-error method, 302
Rational decision making
  capital expenditure, 28
  economic decisions, 27–28
  in engineering, 25–27
  engineering economic decisions, 28–30
  impact of engineering projects on
    financial statements, 30–31
  personal, 22–24
Ratios, *see* Financial ratios
Raw-materials inventory, 431
Real interest rate, 173
Recovery allowance percentage, 398
Recovery periods, 397–398

Relative (percentage) measure of
investment, 313
Relevant range, 432
Replacement analysis
capital (ownership) costs, 539–540
cash-flow consequences, 535
challenger, 533
comparison of defender and challenger,
535–537, 548
decision criterion, 545–546
defender, 533
determination of current market value,
533
economic service life, calculation,
539–541
fundamentals, 533–537
management of unequal service life
problems in, 546
operating costs, 535, 540
opportunity cost, 537
planning horizon (study period), 545
predictions of technological patterns,
545
required assumptions and decision
frameworks, 545–548
with tax considerations, 552–553
Replacement chain approach, 271
Replacement problem, 532
Retained earnings, 583
Return on common equity (ROE),
598–599
Return on invested capital (RIC),
297–298, 345
Return on investment
as break-even interest rate, 297
definition, 296
indication of negative balance, 296
Return on total assets (ROA), 598
Revenue projects, 215
accept–reject decision rule for a single,
250
Risk-adjusted discount rate approach,
509–510
Risk analysis, 483
Risk-free interest rate, 505
Risk premium, 505

S

Salvage value, 219, 255, 388
corporate taxes, 408–409
Sanyo Electric Co., 481–482
Scenario analysis, 492–493

Secondary effects, 353
Sensitivity analysis, 483–484, 487
for mutually exclusive alternatives, 488
Sensitivity graphs, 483–484
Service life, *see* Economic service life
Service projects, 214
comparing of multiple alternatives,
250–251
Service sector of the U.S. economy, 34
Share value, 584
Showa Shell Sekiyu KK, 480–482
Simple-borrowing, 300
Simple interest, 45, 255
Simple-investment, 299
Simple (or conventional) investment, 299
Single-payment compound-amount factor,
52, 54
Single-payment present-worth factor, 82
Sinking-fund factor, 64
Social discount rate, 354
Office of Management and Budget
(OMB) from, 354–355
projects without private counterparts,
354
projects with private counterparts, 354
Solar Frontier KK, 480–482
Specific inflation rate, 165
Standard deviation, 496
Standard deviation (σ) of returns, 496–497
Statement of financial position, 579
Stockholders' equity (owners' net worth),
582–583
Stocks, 582–583
Straight line method (SL), 390
Strategic engineering economic decisions
cost-reduction project, 33–34
equipment and process selection, 32
equipment replacement, 34
news products/product expansion, 32
service or quality improvement, 34–35
Study period, *see* Analysis period
Sunk costs, 534–535
Survey of Current Business, 161
Switching policy, 393

T

Tappan Zee Bridge, 530–532
Taxable income, 404
Tax depreciation method, 388
Tax depreciation methods, 388, 397–401
Taxes, on the investment's projected
income, 436–437

Terminal project balance and terminal
project balance, 210–211
Times-interest-earned ratio, 594–595
Time value of money, 40–42
Total-assets-turnover ratio, 597
Total revenue (or net sales), 584
Treasury stock, 583
Trend analysis, 601
Trial-and-error method, 302
True IRR, 345
True rate of return, 345
Truth-in-lending laws, 116

U

Unequal service lives, alternatives
investment projects for, 320, 359, 364
mutually exclusive, 219–222, 266
Uniform-series compound-amount
factor, 62
Uniform-series present-worth factor, 212
Unit contribution margin, 433
Unit profit (or unit cost) of operating an
asset, 259
Unit-profit/unit-cost calculation, 259
Units-of-production method, of
calculating depreciation, 396
U.S. corporate-tax-rate structure, 405–406

Useful life, 298, 388
Users' benefits, 353

V

Variable costs, 432–433
Volume index, 432
Voyager Ethanol, 29–31

W

Weighted-average cost of capital, 508
"what-if analysis," 484
Working capital, 449, 589, 595
impact on cash-flow statement, 590
Working-capital investment, 442
Working capital requirement, 589
Work-in-process inventory, 431

Y

Yahoo!®, 21
Yield, 296, 298
Yield to maturity (or return on
investment), 305

Z

Zuckerberg, Mark, 20–21

Summary of Useful Excel's Financial Functions (Part A)

Description		Excel Function	Example	Solution
Single-Payment Cash Flows	Find: F Given: P	=FV($i\%, N, 0, P$)	Find the future worth of $500 in 5 years at 8%.	= FV(8%,5,0,–500) = $734.66
	Find: P Given: F	=PV($i\%, N, 0, F$)	Find the present worth of $1,300 due in 10 years at 16% interest rate.	= PV(16%,10,0,1300) = ($294.69)
Equal-Payment-Series	Find: F Given: A	=FV($i\%, N, A$)	Find the future worth of a payment series of $200 per year for 12 years at 6%	= FV(6%,12,–200) = $3,373.99
	Find: P Given: A	=PV($i\%, N, A$)	Find the present worth of a payment series of $900 per year for 5 years at 8% interest rate.	= PV(8%,5,900) = ($3,593,44)
	Find: A Given: P	=PMT($i\%, N, P$)	What equal-annual-payment series is required to repay $25,000 in 5 years at 9% interest rate?	= PMT(9%,5,–25000) = $6,427.31
	Find: A Given: F	=PMT($i\%, N, 0, F$)	What is the required annual savings to accumulate $50,000 in 3 years at 7% interest rate?	= PMT(7%,3,0,50000) = ($15,552.58)
Measures of Investment Worth	Find: NPW Given: Cash flow series	=NPV($i\%$, series)	Consider a project with the following cash flow series at 12% ($n = 0, -$200;\ n = 1, $150,\ n = 2, $300,\ n = 3, 250$).	= NPV(12%,B3:B5)+B2 = $351.03
	Find: IRR Given: Cash flow series	=IRR(values, guess)		=IRR(B2:B4,10%) =89%
	Find: AE Given: Cash flow series	=PMT($i\%, N$, NPW)		= PMT(12%,3,–351.03) = $146.15

	A	B
1	Period	Cash Flow
2	0	–200
3	1	150
4	2	300
5	3	250

Note: When specifying the cash flow input parameters in any Excel function, an outflow must be a negative number.

Summary of Useful Excel's Financial Functions (Part B)

Description		Excel Function	Example	Solution
Loan Analysis Functions	Loan payment size	=PMT($i\%, N, P$)	Suppose you borrow $10,000 at 9% interest over 48 months. Find the amount of the equal monthly payment.	= PMT(9%/12,48,10000) = ($248.45)
	Interest payment	=IPMT($i\%, n, N, P$)	Find the portion of interest payment for the 10th payment.	= IPMT(9%/12,10,48,10000) = ($62.91)
	Principal payment	=PPMT($i\%, n, N, P$)	Find the portion of principal payment for the 10th payment.	= PPMT(9%/12,10,48,10000) = ($185.94)
	Cumulative interest payment	=CUMIPMT(($i\%$, N, P, start_period, end_period, type)	Find the total interest payment over 48 months.	= CUMIPMT(9%/12,48,10000,1,48,0) = ($1,944.82) (type "0 $\rightarrow$ payment at the end of period)
	Interest rate	=RATE(N, A, P, F)	What nominal interest rate is being paid on the following financing arrangement? Loan amount: $10,000; loan period: 60 months; and monthly payment: $207.58.	= RATE(60,207.58,−10000) = 0.7499% APR = 0.7499% × 12 = 9%
	Number of payments	=NPER($i\%$, A, P, F)	Find the number of months required to pay off a loan of $10,000 with 12% APR where you can afford a monthly payment of $200.	= NPER(12%/12,200,−10000) = 69.66 months
Depreciation Functions	Straight-line	=SLN(cost, salvage, life)	Cost = $100,000, S = $20,000, life = 5 years	= SLN(100000,20000,5) = $16,000
	Declining balance	=DB(cost, salvage, life, period)	Find the depreciation amount in period 3.	= DB(100000,20000,5,3) = $14,455
	Double declining balance	=DDB(cost, salvage, life, period, factor)	Find the depreciation amount in period 3 with α = 150%.	= DDB(100000,20000,5,3,1.5) = $14,700
	Declining balance with switching to straight-line	=VDB(cost, salvage, life, start_period, end_period, factor)	Find the depreciation amount in period 3 with α = 150% with switching allowed.	= VDB(100000,20000,5,3,4,1.5) = $10,290